Teaching Discipline-Specific Literacies in Grades 6–12

Comprehensive, timely, and relevant, this text offers an approach to discipline-specific literacy instruction that is aligned with the Common Core State Standards and the needs of teachers, students, and secondary schools across the nation.

It is essential that teachers know how to provide instruction that both develops content and literacy knowledge and skills, and aims at reducing student achievement gaps. Building on the research-supported premise that discipline-specific reading instruction is key to achieving these goals, this text provides practical guidance and strategies for prospective and practicing content area teachers (and other educators) on how to prepare *all* students to succeed in college and the workforce.

Pedagogical features in each chapter engage readers in digging deeper and in applying the ideas and strategies presented in their own contexts:

- Classroom Life (real 6–12 classroom scenarios and interviews with content area teachers)
- Common Core State Standards Connections
- College, Career, and Workforce Connections
- Applying Discipline-Specific Literacies
- Think Like an Expert ("habits of thinking and learning" specific to each discipline)
- Digital Literacies
- Differentiating Instruction
- Reflect and Apply Questions
- Extending Learning Activities

The **Companion Website** includes

- Lesson plan resources
- Annotated links to video files
- Annotated links to additional resources and information
- Glossary/flashcards
- For Instructors: All images and figures used in the text provided in an easily downloadable format
- For Instructors: PowerPoint lecture slides

Vassiliki ("Vicky") I. Zygouris-Coe is Professor of Reading Education and Program Coordinator for the Ph.D. in Reading Education Track of the College of Education and Human Performance, University of Central Florida, USA.

Teaching Discipline-Specific Literacies in Grades 6–12

Preparing Students for College, Career, and Workforce Demands

Vassiliki ("Vicky") I. Zygouris-Coe

Routledge
Taylor & Francis Group

NEW YORK AND LONDON

First published 2015
by Routledge
711 Third Avenue, New York, NY 10017

Simultaneously published in the UK
by Routledge
2 Park Square, Milton Park, Abingdon, Oxon OX14 4RN

Routledge is an imprint of the Taylor & Francis Group, an informa business

Library of Congress Cataloging in Publication Data
Zygouris-Coe, Vassiliki I.
    Teaching discipline-specific literacies in grades 6–12 : preparing students
    for college, career, and workforce demands / Vassiliki I. Zygouris-Coe.
        pages cm
    ISBN 978-0-415-66178-2 (hbk) — ISBN 978-0-415-66179-9 (pbk) —
    ISBN 978-0-203-07316-2 (ebk)   1. Language arts (Secondary)
    2. Literacy.   3. Inquiry-based learning.   I. Title.
    LB1631.Z94 2014
    428.0071′2—dc23
                                                            2014012929

ISBN: 978-0-415-66178-2 (hbk)
ISBN: 978-0-415-66179-9 (pbk)
ISBN: 978-0-203-07316-2 (ebk)

Typeset in Minion Pro
by RefineCatch Limited, Bungay, Suffolk, UK

Printed and bound in the United States of America by Sheridan Books, Inc. (a Sheridan Group Company).

To my husband, Mike, and daughter,
Rebecca—thank you for your love, and endless
encouragement, support, and understanding.
You are my joy, and my strength.

Brief Contents

Preface xiii

Acknowledgements xix

About the Author.. xxi

CHAPTER 1 – Preparing Students for Today and Tomorrow..1

CHAPTER 2 – Literacy as a Discipline-Specific Process...30

CHAPTER 3 – Reading Complex Texts Beyond the Textbook...60

CHAPTER 4 – Rigorous Instruction in the Disciplines 91

CHAPTER 5 – Vocabulary Learning and Instruction in the Disciplines.............................132

CHAPTER 6 – Questioning and Comprehension in the Disciplines 174

CHAPTER 7 – Discipline-Specific Comprehension Instruction..221

CHAPTER 8 – Disciplinary Literacy Learning Environments 286

CHAPTER 9 – Writing in the Disciplines..330

CHAPTER 10 – Assessing Student Learning in the Disciplines...380

CHAPTER 11 – Teaching Discipline-Specific Literacies and Professional Development..................418

Index..453

Contents

Preface xiii

Acknowledgements xix

About the Author xxi

CHAPTER 1 – Preparing Students for Today and Tomorrow 1
    College and Career Readiness 2
    Workforce Readiness 3
    What is 21st Century Learning? 5
    Wanted: Highly Qualified Teachers for a New Era of Learning 5
    Reconceptualizing Literacy 6
    New Literacies 7
    Adolescent Literacy and New Educational Standards 11
    The Secondary Schools We Need 16

CHAPTER 2 – Literacy as a Discipline-Specific Process 30
    Content Area Literacy 31
    The Shift from Content Area Literacy to Disciplinary Literacy 33
    Disciplinary Literacy 35
    Academic Disciplines 37
    Why Position Literacy in the Disciplines? 47
    Disciplinary Literacy Learning Principles 50

CHAPTER 3 – Reading Complex Texts Beyond the Textbook...**60**
New Educational Standards and Text Complexity...61
What Is Text Complexity?...65
Qualitative Dimensions of Text Complexity 67
Quantitative Factors of Text Complexity 72
Reader Characteristics and Text Complexity...76
How Can Teachers Prepare Students to Read and Comprehend Complex Text? 77
Close Reading of Complex Text...78
Text-Dependent Questions 80
Accountable Talk 85
Text Complexity and a Disciplinary Literacy Learning Framework in Grades 6–12 86

CHAPTER 4 – Rigorous Instruction in the Disciplines **91**
Classroom Instruction and Student Achievement..92
What Is Rigorous Instruction?..94
Planning for Rigorous Instruction in the Disciplines......................................100
High and Clear Expectations for All..102
Classroom Norms and Procedures 103
Student Engagement and Motivation 107
Rigorous Materials 108
Learning Goals...111
Explicit Instruction 118
Rigorous Instruction and Informal Assessment 123
Teacher Reflection 126

CHAPTER 5 – Vocabulary Learning and Instruction in the Disciplines.............**132**
The Role of Vocabulary in the Context of New Educational Standards 133
Vocabulary and Learning 134
The Vocabulary of Core Disciplines...137
Vocabulary Instructional Decisions: Which Words to Teach? 141
Effective Vocabulary Instruction..145
Introducing and Teaching Vocabulary Strategies 147
Fostering Students' Independence 155
Reinforcing and Extending Vocabulary Knowledge.......................................162

CHAPTER 6 – Questioning and Comprehension in the Disciplines **174**
The Importance of Critical Thinking Skills and Processes in the 21st Century................175
The Role of Comprehension in College, Career, Workforce, and Life Readiness................176
What Does It Mean to Comprehend?..178
Questions, Questioning, and Comprehension 181
What Makes a "Good" Question, "Good"?..186
What Questions to Ask? 187
Discipline-Specific Habits of Mind and Questioning 209
How to Create a Disciplinary Inquiry Classroom Culture 213

CHAPTER 7 – Discipline-Specific Comprehension Instruction **221**
Teaching Comprehension...222
Fluency and Comprehension..225

Independent Reading 227
Building Comprehension through Text 227
Text Structure Instruction..229
Text Marking, Annotating, and Text Coding..234
Note-Taking...236
Summarizing 240
Strategies for Discipline-Specific Comprehension Instruction 242
Metacognition and Comprehension Monitoring..275
The Goal: Deep, Transferable Learning..277

CHAPTER 8 – Disciplinary Literacy Learning Environments **286**
The Role of Discourse and Collaboration in the Common Core State Standards (CCSS)......287
What Is Academic Language?...288
Disciplinary Literacy and Classroom Talk 293
Characteristics of Discipline-Specific Learning Environments 296
Accountable Talk in the Disciplines 300
Collaborative Inquiry...306
Motivation, Engagement, and Student Voice 317
The Classroom Environment and How Students Learn 321

CHAPTER 9 – Writing in the Disciplines **330**
Writing for Postsecondary and Life Success...331
Transitioning from High School to College Writing 333
Writing and Writing Instruction...334
Writing and the Common Core State Standards 341
Writing in the Disciplines 354
Writing to Learn 359
The Role of Collaboration in Writing...371
Digital Writing: Writing on the Screen 373
What Is the Best Approach to Improve Students' Writing?..374

CHAPTER 10 – Assessing Student Learning in the Disciplines........................**380**
Assessment and Instruction..381
Types of Assessment 382
Response to Intervention 396
Assessing Materials 401
Assessing Students' Understanding of Texts..403
Policy, High-Stakes Testing, and Accountability 405
Assessing Student Learning in the Era of New Educational Standards 407
Assessing Student Learning in the Disciplines: Now What?..409

CHAPTER 11 – Teaching Discipline-Specific Literacies and Professional Development **418**
Teacher Professional Development, and Student College, Career and Workforce Readiness 420
Andragogy: The Study of Adult Learning 422
What Is Professional Development?...423
Professional Development and Teacher Evaluation 425
Teacher Collaboration and Professional Development..434
The Need for Discipline-Specific Professional Development 440

A Not-So-Different Perspective on Change 441
Teacher Snapshots 445
Neither Standards, Nor Programs Teach; Teachers Do 446

Index...**453**

Preface

This book is designed to prepare new and to support master content area teachers as they develop effective curriculum and instruction that will prepare students to succeed in college, career, and the workforce. My approach draws from current research, educational policy, and classroom experience on effective models of teaching and learning in secondary content area classrooms, which content area teachers can consider as they can facilitate the success of all students. I also demonstrate how content area teachers in grades 6–12 can develop instruction that is aligned with discipline-specific structures and ways of knowing, the Common Core State Standards (CCSS), adolescent literacy, and college, career, and workforce readiness.

The book offers a different approach to the commonly used "reading in the content areas" approach to reading in grades 6–12. Discipline-specific (or disciplinary) literacy is neither a synonym nor a new concept for "content area" reading.

Discipline-specific literacies involve what we teach in each subject area—how to read, learn, use, and communicate knowledge like a scientist, a mathematician, a historian, or an author. Disciplinary literacy seeks answers to the following questions: What constitutes knowledge in each discipline? How is new knowledge created? What is the discourse of each discipline? How is knowledge communicated? What kinds of evidence are fitting for each discipline?

Content area reading focuses more on in-school textbook reading; it carries a widely used "every teacher is a teacher of reading" slogan that has resulted in content area teachers' resistance to content reading instruction. Many content area teachers have been trying to "add" reading to their content instruction; they have been spending time teaching students reading and study skills so they can study better and hopefully improve on, or pass, tests. The underlying assumption of this slogan is that if every content area teacher assumes responsibility for helping students learn through reading, the content and other educational curricular goals will also be met. If that has been the case, why have we had stagnation in adolescents' reading scores? Why are there so many students in grades 6–12 who have struggled with content and literacy learning? How come so many content area teachers puzzle over students' lack of critical thinking skills, comprehension, and engagement in discipline learning?

Disciplinary literacy aims at getting students to participate in knowledge generation, evaluation, dissemination, and discipline-specific reading, practices, and discourse. Disciplinary literacy does not take away from studying well; on the contrary, it promotes careful, close, and purposeful reading of discipline-specific texts; it focuses on deep and transferable learning instead of surface-type learning that will be forgotten even if students do pass the test. One advantage of disciplinary literacy is that it enables each content area teacher to focus on discipline-specific goals, allow content to determine process, and collaborate with other peers in communities of practice (e.g., science teachers working together to address science-specific curricular and instructional goals).

If teachers and schools are to meet the knowledge and literacy demands of the 21st century, they can no longer contain literacy learning in intensive, or corrective, reading classrooms, or make the English language arts teachers solely responsible for students' literacy knowledge and skills. Literacy has to be developed in each content area for the purpose of knowing and learning *within* each discipline. Content and literacy learning cannot be separated; they must develop together. As educators, we have an opportunity to continue to learn, grapple with core disciplinary and instructional issues, and seek effective ways to help all students learn and succeed. I agree with John Dewey that "if we teach today's students as we taught yesterday's, we rob them of tomorrow."

I hope to equip pre-service and in-service teachers with knowledge and tools that will help them decide how to address complex instructional challenges related to discipline-specific literacies in secondary grades. It is an outcome of years of passion for the topic, research, teaching in higher education, and collaborations with secondary school teachers, literacy coaches, and administrators. I am a learner, a teacher, a researcher, and someone who continues to puzzle about literacy in the secondary grades. I enjoy learning about discipline-specific literacies and treasure the collaborations I have had with educators and students. As a teacher, I am challenged by today's teaching demands, and at the same time excited by them. I believe that as educators we have amazing opportunities to prepare students for today and tomorrow.

Overview of the Book

This textbook contains information on a much-needed topic: discipline-specific literacies and student preparation for college, career, and the workforce. The information I present in the 11 chapters of this book has a unified message about developing students' discipline-specific literacies, knowledge and skills *within* each subject area, and about the role of content area teachers in providing quality instruction that will prepare students to succeed in school, college, and life. Each chapter builds on the previous one in a scaffolded way, but there are core ideas that are reflected throughout the textbook.

I use an informal and informed writing style for readability, relevance, and engagement. As the reader, you will hear a voice akin to a trusted colleague, a "knowledgeable mentor," who is providing relevant and adequate evidence from various sources and perspectives on each topic. I share my expertise with you and have created activities for you to reflect on your learning and instructional decisions.

The book positions literacy as an integral part of disciplinary teaching and learning, and attempts to shed some light on how this can be done in secondary classrooms. It aims to inform teacher instruction about the unique structure, content and literacy challenges and demands, and ways of knowing and learning in each discipline.

It is designed to help prepare pre-service teachers to provide quality instruction and effectively address their future students' content and subject-specific challenges. In addition, the book's content will expand in-service content area teachers' knowledge about discipline-specific instruction that supports students' content and literacy learning.

The book's purpose is to develop and support *all* readers' content and literacy knowledge and skills. In addition, it includes examples and instructional suggestions for differentiating instruction for struggling (or striving) students (including English language learners [ELLs]). The main message is that disciplinary literacy is not an "add-on." Although it is founded on general literacy strategies, it cannot be achieved through them. In order to effectively prepare students to succeed in school, college, career, or the workforce, educators need to move literacy from the periphery of each content area, and place it in the center. Discipline-specific literacies are inherently connected to the nature, discourse, texts, ways of knowing and learning, and complexity of each discipline. I also wrote this book to equip content area teachers with core instructional principles every teacher could implement in his or her classroom. Lastly, I also provide discipline-specific "how to" strategies in my effort to "tailor" these instructional principles to each subject area.

Chapter 1 provides the context for educational shifts in secondary education, and highlights the need for developing advanced literacy knowledge and skills in the secondary grades for the purpose of helping students to meet the ever-increasing demands of college, career, and workforce in the 21st century and beyond.

Chapter 2 positions disciplinary literacy as the core approach to college, career, and workforce readiness. I present a model for literacy as a discipline-specific process, I analyze the literacy demands of core content areas (i.e., English language arts, mathematics, science, social studies, and technical subjects), and I discuss the role of literacy in each discipline for student learning and success in school and beyond.

Chapter 3 addresses the importance of teaching students to read complex texts in the disciplines. I discuss complex texts and close reading of complex texts, elements of complexity, text-dependent questions, and share ideas about how to develop reader engagement with texts, and cognitive stamina.

Chapter 4 examines the concept of rigor and rigorous instruction. I present information on the characteristics of rigorous instruction, and suggest that rigor in the disciplines needs to exist in the learning environment, in the instruction teachers provide, in the materials students use, in their engagement with learning, and in the assessment of student learning

Chapter 5 examines the importance of vocabulary learning and instruction in the disciplines. I pay particular attention to developing students' academic vocabulary, share elements of effective vocabulary instruction, and offer examples of how to develop students' vocabulary in discipline-specific ways.

Chapter 6 investigates the role of questioning on students' comprehension, with a particular emphasis on higher-order questioning skills, essential questions, and evidence-based thinking. I present discipline-specific examples and discuss how to help students collect, read, and critically evaluate information from multiple sources to support their judgments.

Chapter 7 highlights the importance of discipline-specific comprehension instruction and how to support students' comprehension. I present a variety of discipline-specific strategies for developing students' comprehension of texts, and for promoting deep learning..

Chapter 8 places attention on the role of the learning environments in which students learn and interact with others. Discourse, accountable talk, and collaborative inquiry are important elements of rigorous classrooms.

Chapter 9 focuses on the importance of writing in the disciplines, and for preparation for college, career, and workforce readiness. I present examples on discipline-specific writing and digital writing, and place particular emphasis on writing to inform and persuade as it is necessary for college readiness and beyond.

Chapter 10 clarifies the role of formative and summative assessment in each content area classroom. I offer specific suggestions for collecting informal and formal data and using it to reflect on student progress and needs, and on your instruction. I also discuss the importance of collaborative teacher reflection on student data and planning for instruction.

Chapter 11 concludes with evidence on the importance of school-wide collaborative inquiry on discipline-specific literacy and student learning issues in the secondary grades. I offer suggestions based on research and on my experiences from collaborating with content area teachers, instructional coaches, and administrators on implementing a disciplinary literacy learning framework

Pedagogical Features

Each chapter has the following pedagogical features to help future or current content area teachers. All the activities and resources are designed to help teachers think critically about their future or current instruction and their students' needs.

- *Classroom Life* scenarios from various content areas help guide your attention to the unique content and literacy instructional demands of each discipline as experienced through various teachers. You will have an opportunity to reflect on these scenarios, make connections, and further discuss with your peers.
- Connections between the text and the *Common Core State Standards (CCSS)* provide you with the rationale for discipline-specific instruction.
- *College, Career, and Workforce Connections* offer "real-world" examples and will also highlight the need for discipline-specific instruction.
- *Applying Discipline-Specific Literacies* equip you with valuable tools for supporting content and literacy knowledge and skills.
- *Think Like an Expert* boxes reinforce disciplinary experts' habits of thinking and learning in each subject area.
- *Digital Literacies* include resources, tools, and ideas for incorporating technology across the disciplines.
- A *Summary* at the end of each chapter captures essential information about each topic.
- *Differentiating Instruction* for striving students and ELLs offer suggestions for meeting the needs of diverse learners.
- *Reflect and Apply* questions at the end of each chapter invite you to think critically about what you have learned, provide you with opportunities to further discuss the topic with peers or colleagues, and give you opportunities to transfer your insights to real classroom situations.
- *Extending Learning* activities at the end of each chapter focus on giving you more opportunities to expand or extend your learning about the topic through classroom observations, peer discussions and collaborations, and further investigations.
- A companion website (www.routledge.com/cw/zygouris-coe) provides resources to relevant instructional ideas per discipline, suggestions for further discussion in professional learning communities (PLCs), a glossary with flashcards, links to research articles and discipline-specific professional organizations, annotated links to video files, and images from the text in a downloadable format.

How to Use This Book

Studying a book will not make anyone an expert! This book will be helpful to you if you carefully process and reflect on its insights, discuss them with peers, and reflect on your role as a content area teacher. As you engage with this text, assess your own perceptions, attitudes, and beliefs about discipline-specific literacies, about content and processes, and about the role you, the teacher, and your students will play in the learning process. Test ideas from this text with peers, discuss them with colleagues or with your instructor, and field-test them through interactions with students. Learning is an active process—whether it takes place in a university classroom or a secondary school.

You are expected to play an active and reflective role in the learning process; the book will challenge you and inspire you to be accountable to yourself, to your future or current students, and to the learning community, in general. To become an effective teacher, you have to be willing to continue to learn and improve your knowledge and skills. Effective teachers have several traits, which include being knowledgeable, holding high expectations for all students, being engaging, and being professional. Effective teachers assess students' understanding on an ongoing basis and make instructional modifications and accommodations to ensure everyone's success. Effective teachers are also committed to continued professional development and learning. The book provides methods and practices for developing and strengthening students' discipline-specific content and literacy knowledge and skills.

The activities I have included in this book have been successful with "real" teachers and students in grades 6–12; they are a product of my own work and research in secondary schools. As you interact with the text, think about what you are learning and also think about the implications for future or current teaching. Throughout the book I provide opportunities and resources to reflect and extend on what you are learning. You can continue to use the book's resources (and its companion website) to engage in further discussions with your peers about instructional challenges in your content area, and effective ways to meet the needs of students in grades 6–12.

Vassiliki ("Vicky") I. Zygouris-Coe

Acknowledgements

I would like to express my heartfelt thanks to Naomi Silverman, Mary Altman, and Darcy Bullock, Routledge/Taylor and Francis editors, who helped me throughout the book's development, editing, and production. Thanks to all of the reviewers for their sincere and thoughtful feedback that helped shape this book. Finally, I wish to thank all of the educators who shared their expertise and feedback with me.

About the Author

Vassiliki ("Vicky") Zygouris-Coe is currently a professor of reading education at the University of Central Florida (UCF), where she has taught undergraduate and graduate level literacy courses for the past 13 years. Dr. Zygouris-Coe has taught in the US and abroad over the past 31 years. She has received over $9,000,000 in research and funded literacy projects. Her research has been published in *The Reading Teacher, Reading & Writing Quarterly, Reading Horizons, Childhood Education, Topics in Language Disorders, Early Childhood Education Journal, The International Journal of Qualitative Studies in Education, Focus in the Middle, Journal of Technology and Teacher Education, The International Journal of E-Learning, Florida Educational Leadership Journal*, and *Florida Reading Quarterly* among others. She is also an editorial review board member for the *Journal of Literacy Research, Reading Psychology*, the *International Journal for the Scholarship of Teaching & Learning* and the *Florida Association of Teacher Educators*. She is co-editor of the *Literacy Research and Instruction* journal, associate editor of the *Florida Educational Leadership*, and former associate editor of the *Florida Association of Teacher Educators* journals. In addition, Dr. Zygouris-Coe is the developer of Florida's first large-scale professional development in reading (Florida Online Reading Professional Development) for K–12 teachers that serviced 44,344 educators from 2003–2010 and continues to be offered through the Florida Department of Education (FLDOE) to all certified Florida K–12 teachers. Dr. Zygouris-Coe has been a leader in Florida statewide literacy initiatives and for years has been collaborating with the FLDOE in consulting, reviewing, and participating in core statewide literacy initiatives for K–12 and teacher education sectors.

one
Preparing Students for Today and Tomorrow

A world-class education is the single most important factor in determining not just whether our kids can compete for the best jobs but whether America can out-compete countries around the world. America's business leaders understand that when it comes to education, we need to up our game. That's why we're working together to put an outstanding education within reach for every child.
–President Barack Obama, July 18, 2011

Chapter Highlights

- The evolving definition of the concept of literacy in the 21st century.
- The state of US adolescent literacy.
- The Common Core State Standards and college, career, and workforce readiness.
- Characteristics of exemplary secondary schools.
- Preparing students for college, career, and workforce success.
- The importance of the teacher's role in an era of new educational standards.

Classroom Life

Ms. Morrison teaches Earth Science for 9th graders in a small urban-city school. The lesson for the day includes a lab about the use of the process of condensation to produce ethanol, an alternative fuel source. There are 24 students in the class but five students are missing. This means Ms. Morrison will have to figure out how those students will make this lab up. Students have been prepped for three days for the lab and have been working in groups to prepare for it. Students should have spent time researching on the Internet about the topic, identifying advantages, challenges, and cause and effect relationships, and collecting information from diverse sources on the topic. In addition, they should have reviewed pertinent vocabulary, studied up on the equipment that they will use, should have created a data chart, and have pre-read the procedure for understanding. And yet on lab day, students cannot set up the equipment correctly and do not understand the vocabulary when Ms. Morrison asks them questions in order to help. Some of the students do not have their data tables and some have not used rulers to make their tables neat as instructed. When solicited, students do not understand the purpose of the lab or for that matter, the purpose of the equipment they are using. Some students do not understand the concept of units. One student has his hands in the aquarium trying to catch the fish when Ms. Morrison is busy working with another group. The room is somewhat loud and many students are off task. Students do not seem to understand the purpose of the lab and are proceeding incorrectly. The 50 minutes goes by quickly and only two-thirds of the students finish and have data as they walk out the door. Ms. Morrison is exhausted but has four minutes to set up for the next group coming in. *(Dr. Carmen M. Woodhall, Teaching Assistant Professor in Science Education, East Carolina University, North Carolina).*

College and Career Readiness

College and career readiness in high school is not a recent focus. What makes it a new initiative is the idea that "all students should be capable of pursuing formal learning opportunities beyond high school" (Conley, 2010, p. 1). Reports have shown that postsecondary education readiness is not a focal goal of the typical high school (ACT, 2006, 2010, 2011, 2012; Baker, Clay, & Gratama, 2005; Strong American Schools, 2008; Texas Association of School Boards, 2009). College and career readiness can be defined as success—without remediation—in credit-bearing general education courses or a two-year certificate program. Success is defined as being able to progress successfully in a chosen program (ACT, 2011; Conley, 2010).

Being college ready means being prepared in the four dimensions of college readiness necessary to succeed in entry-level general education courses. The four dimensions are: (1) Key content knowledge (key foundational content and big ideas from core subjects); (2) Key cognitive strategies (problem formulation, analysis, research, interpretation, communication, precision, and accuracy, problem solving, and reasoning); (3) Academic behaviors (self-management, time management, and study skills, self-awareness, and persistence); and, (4) Contextual skills and awareness (admissions requirements, college) (Conley, 2009; National Research Council, 2013).

Key content knowledge refers to knowledge of actual information, key concepts and terminology, organizing concepts, and making connections among ideas. Key cognitive strategies are discipline-specific ways of thinking that allow students to apply what they know and are learning to achieve a goal. In addition, students need to know how to identify a problem, conduct independent research, interpret conflicting views of a phenomenon under study, and express themselves effectively in speech and in writing. To be college ready, students need to be able to set goals, work independently and collaboratively, manage their time, and persevere with complex tasks. Lastly, students need to be knowledgeable about the process of selecting a college, locating and applying for financial aid, and working with a diverse group of people (professors, peers, others) when they get there (Conley, 2010). In other words, college readiness implies college knowledge owned by a learner who is prepared well in content, tools, processes, and skills for college success.

Often in secondary schools, emphasis is on broad content coverage that results in shallow understanding of it. There is lots of emphasis on procedural learning and test-taking skills. Although the content changes, the learning strategies often remain the same. As a result, students arrive in college and the workplace not knowing how the experts in each subject area read, think, or problem-solve complex issues in their field. Students need learner-centered methods, and problem-based and authentic learning opportunities that will allow them to collaborate on complex ideas and world problems.

Students in secondary grades need to develop "expertise" over time—that is, become "expert" thinkers not only in having good (and transferable) understanding of the subject matter, but also in knowing how to develop and use their knowledge at inner-disciplinary and intra-disciplinary levels. How do novices versus experts think? Are there any distinct characteristics, skills, and processes teachers can teach students to use and develop in secondary grades? Experts have developed content knowledge that affects what they notice, how they understand their subject matter, and how they organize, interpret, represent, and use information in their environment. They chunk information, they make connections between new and prior knowledge, are able to retrieve information with little effort, and generalize knowledge to new settings.

Novice thinkers often identify problems in terms of surface elements, do not think strategically about how to solve problems, do not consider connections between concepts, and use memorization to solve problems. On the other hand, expert thinkers are self-efficacious about solving problems, first seek to develop an understanding of the problem and apply principles to solve it, notice meaningful patterns of information, persevere with problem solving, review their approach in relation to the question at hand, and memorize only a few select key principles.

A college ready student should possess "deep understanding of and facility applying key foundational ideas and concepts from the core academic subjects" (Conley, 2010, p. 49) and should be able to "read with understanding a range of nonfiction publications and materials, using appropriate decoding and comprehension strategies to identify key points, note areas of question or confusion, remember key terminology, and understand the basic conclusions reached and points of view expressed" (Conley, 2010, p. 51). Do college and career readiness today require the same foundational knowledge and skills in reading and mathematics? The answer is "yes" according to ACT (2011). College and career ready students are more likely to enroll in college, stay in college, and graduate from college (Conley, 2010).

Workforce Readiness

Thomas Friedman, a journalist who wrote the book, *The World is Flat: A Brief History of the Twenty-First Century* (2007), presents the flattening effects of globalization. People can communicate, collaborate, and compete from anywhere, to anywhere (Association for Career and Technical Education [ACTE], 2006). Industries and companies seek employees with higher levels of expertise. Several reports have identified a skills gap in employees; employers report that employees need more technical skills, reading, writing, communication, and employability skills

(National Association of Manufacturers, 2005). As a result, there are several national efforts to develop a workforce readiness credential that will equip students with skills for any type of occupation (skilled or professional) and any level of education.

Career and technical education (CTE) provides literacy and numeracy learning that is relevant to real world work contexts. The Southern Regional Education Board (SREB) defines "technical literacy" as the ability to (1) apply academic knowledge and skills to a broad field of technical studies; (2) read, understand, and communicate in the technical field; (3) understand technical concepts and principles; and (4) use technology to complete projects in technical fields (SREB, 2003). The ability to think critically, problem-solve, collaborate, and apply academic knowledge and situational judgment are important skills for the US workforce and economy (ACTE, 2008). The economy and future of the nation require a "knowledge- and innovation-centered workforce" (Alliance for Excellent Education, 2012, p. 2).

The reauthorization of the Carl D. Perkins Career and Technical Education (CTE) Improvement Act of 2006 is the US' largest investment in secondary and postsecondary, CTE. It aims to strengthen the academic achievement of CTE students and the link between secondary and postsecondary education.

> If the students who dropped out of the [high school] class of 2001 had graduated, the nation's economy would likely benefit from nearly $154 billion in additional income over the course of their lifetimes.
>
> (Alliance for Excellent Education, 2012)

According to the 2006 report, *The Silent Epidemic: Perspectives of High School Dropouts*, nearly half of the high school dropouts said they left high school because their classes were not engaging or relevant to them (Bridgeland, Dilulio, & Morrison, 2006). All students should have rigorous and relevant academic classes; CTE students will benefit from rigorous course work that is engaging and aligned with college expectations, career and technical education for in-demand occupations, applied learning, and support services (Alliance for Excellent Education, 2012).

In this book, I present you with a different perspective on literacy for the 21st century. This book will expand your knowledge about what literacy means for today's and tomorrow's learning and how you can best prepare your students for college, career, workforce, and lifelong learning. Throughout this book, I use the terms "discipline-specific literacy" and "disciplinary literacy" interchangeably. Disciplinary literacy involves the tasks and processes of reading, thinking, inquiring, speaking, writing, and communicating required for learning and developing discipline-appropriate content knowledge. Discipline-specific literacy, which I will examine in detail in Chapter 2, is literacy that reflects and addresses the structure, content and literacy demands, discourse, and habits of mind that are specific to each discipline.

College, Career, and Workforce Connections

- A variety of knowledge, skills, dispositions and behaviors, and educational, career, and civic engagement abilities are needed for all students to be ready for their endeavors beyond high school.
- Twenty-first century skills, such as critical thinking and problem solving, are best learned through rigorous academic programs that connect students' college and career goals and aspirations. Students need to develop robust knowledge in core subjects and they also need to be better equipped to apply that knowledge to problem solve about real work issues.

- Students need to become accountable for their own learning (i.e., take responsibility, be ethical, and manage their goals, time, and money).
- *Students need to take risks and be resilient in the face of failure. They need to learn how to get out of their comfort zones and collaborate with people from different disciplinary backgrounds as well as understand how to use real-time data to make decisions* (Paul Jarley, Dean, Business Administration, University of Central Florida).

What is 21st Century Learning?

Twenty-first century learning involves enabling today's students to be academically competent and competitive in global situations, productive citizens in society, effective in their workplace, and pursuers of learning and personal growth. It means that education must equip students with rigorous academic coursework, engage them in emerging technologies, and foster innovation and creativity. Twenty-first century learning is "learner-driven." Twenty-first century learning means that students master content while at the same time producing, synthesizing, and evaluating information from multiple texts and other sources, and demonstrate academic, civic, and cultural integrity and responsibility.

Twenty-first century students must be able to read, write, think, listen, view, do math, and communicate knowledge in print and non-print forms but they must also demonstrate creativity, communication, and collaboration in digital and non-digital contexts. Twenty-first century learning requires mastery of content and skills; success in 21st century means knowing how to learn. Without deep understanding of content and possession of learning skills, students will resort to memorization and surface-type learning that might result in passing the chapter test but will not result in transferable learning.

Technology today allows for 24/7 access to information, social interactions, production, and dissemination of digital content. Although 21st century learning is not just about technology and digital media, students need to have mastery of core academic subjects, and also need to know how to use essential learning, life, and work tools in the 21st century. Twenty-first century learners must possess strong critical thinking, interpersonal communication, and collaboration skills, in order to succeed and continue to learn in a highly networked and complex world.

Success in 21st century learning, college, career, and the workforce demands well prepared learners (in content, processes, and skills) who know how to read, analyze, evaluate, and communicate information critically, possess a learning attitude and complex communication skills, embrace change and lifelong learning, and persevere with problem solving independently and collaboratively.

Wanted: Highly Qualified Teachers for a New Era of Learning

Have you ever heard teachers say, "Students today don't value learning!" or "My students don't like to read; all they like to do is play with computers!" or "I am very concerned about the quality of students we are graduating; these kids are not ready for college!" Often teachers tend to "blame" students and their earlier educational experiences. Could it be that students today learn differently than the way you or I did when we were in school? In addition, this generation of students has a different relationship with information technologies, the Internet, and learning environments than previous generations did (Oblinger, 2004).

While national progress reports show that the percentage of elementary students who are proficient on state measures has increased, middle and high school students' performance has been pretty stagnant. In addition, many adolescents drop out of school. Last, many of those who do graduate and go on to college, take remedial courses in English and Mathematics. Twenty-first century learning requires teaching for meaning (McTighe, Seif, & Wiggins, 2004). For students to succeed in today's and tomorrow's world, they need well-prepared teachers who also embrace lifelong learning, are adaptive to, and create change, and problem-solve collaboratively with colleagues to solve complex problems of practice.

Adolescents need stellar teachers. Teachers need to deliver rigorous, relevant, research-based, integrated, interdisciplinary, multimedia, "learner-driven," and active instruction that will prepare students for college, career, and the workforce. Teachers need to not only help students read, think about, inquire, and respond to the texts and issues of each discipline, but they also need to help them develop the habits of mind of the experts in each discipline. In addition, teachers need to develop a culture of collaborative inquiry and respect, address student diversity, use formative and summative assessments, and promote student self-monitoring of learning.

The 21st century teacher's role is that of a facilitator of student learning, similar to that of an orchestra conductor. There's a shift, especially, in the secondary content area teacher's role from "sage on the stage" to "guide on the side." All content area teachers should help all students access, build, generate, analyze, evaluate, synthesize, create, and disseminate knowledge.

Digital Literacies

- Partnership for 21st Century Skills: http://www.p21.org. A framework for 21st century learning, innovation, and citizenship for the 21st century.
- Digital Literacy: http://www.digitalliteracy.gov/content/educator. Resources for integrating digital literacy in the classroom.
- What is Digital Citizenship?: http://blog.iste.org/what-is-digital-citizenship-and-why-should-educators-care/. Learn about digital literacy, citizenship, and learning.

Reconceptualizing Literacy

Prior to the 21st century, a person's ability to read and write separated him or her from the uneducated. Literacy and numeracy have never been optional for fully functioning members of a society. Literacy is not a static concept; rather, it is a complex and dynamic concept that can be defined in a variety of ways. The meaning of literacy has shifted over the past 50 years from viewing it as a process of acquiring basic cognitive skills to developing the capacity for critical reflection of concepts and ideas that brings about personal and social change. There are several perspectives on the definition of literacy; for you to understand the need for discipline-specific literacies in grades 6–12, you first have to become aware of the evolution of literacy. The most common understanding of literacy is the ability to read a language competently. Literacy is often viewed as a set of reading and writing skills that are independent of the content in which they develop and the characteristics of the person who acquires them.

The word "literacy" has been used in a broader sense to refer to the following skills and competencies such as:

- "information literacy," referring to the ability to articulate, identify, and access a variety of information sources to solve an information need, critically apply the information, and determine if the need has been met;
- "media literacy," the ability to access, analyze, evaluate, create, and participate with media in a variety of forms—from print, to video, to the Internet;

- "digital literacy," the ability to use information and communication technologies to locate, evaluate, use, and create information;
- "scientific literacy," the knowledge and understanding of scientific concepts and processes required for personal decision making, participation in civic life, and economic productivity;
- "numeracy," the ability to process, interpret, and communicate numerical, quantitative, spatial, statistical, and mathematical information in ways appropriate for a variety of contexts;
- "financial literacy," the skills and knowledge that enable a person to make informed decisions about financial matters; and
- "health literacy," an individual's ability to read, understand, and use healthcare information to make decisions and follow instructions for health treatment.

Literacy has come to represent a more complex and multidimensional concept. Some scholars propose the use of "multiple literacies" as a more useful representation of what literacy means today. That is, ways of "reading the world" in information, technological, digital, media, visual, health, and financial contexts (The New London Group, 2000; Lankshear & Knobel, 2003). Reading today involves decoding and understanding of words, but also reading and understanding of signs, images, symbols, pictures, and sounds (The New London Group, 2000). In addition, literacy is practiced differently depending on social and cultural contexts (Barton, 1994). The New Literacy Studies (Barton & Hamilton, 2000; Gee, 1996; Heath, 1983) presented literacy as a social practice that is socially situated.

New Literacies

I am reminded of a quote by Alvin Toffler, an American writer, futurist, and former editor of *Fortune* magazine, whose work has influenced governments, businesses, technology, and social science. "The illiterate of the 21st century will not be those who cannot read and write, but those who cannot learn, unlearn, and relearn." This quote resonates with me; just as change is non-linear, so are 21st century literacies—they can go back, forward, and sideways. Today's youth are still reading, writing, thinking, and collaborating, but their texts, collaborations and products are less likely to be printed on paper (Frey, Fisher, & Gonzalez, 2010). More and more, today's adolescents are reading, writing, collaborating, and learning in digital contexts. In today's technologically advanced world, a literate person is able to read a variety of print and digital texts in various mediums (computer, e-readers, tablets), interact, collaborate, and produce in various virtual social networking contexts that require knowledge of Web 2.0 and Web 3.0 tools, and critically analyze, evaluate, and synthesize multimodal texts (Albers, 2007; Doering, Beach, & O'Brien, 2007). Web 2.0 refers to technology that has made the Internet collaborative and allows for two-way communication, active involvement, and user-generated content and blogging. Web 3.0 refers to the next evolution of the Internet that will create a more intelligent web and computer-facilitated understanding of information.

It is difficult to harness the evolution of literacy when "the meaning of 'tomorrow' becomes 'today' every 24 hours" (Leu, Kinzer, Coiro, Castek, & Henry, 2013, p. 1). Literacy today is deictic; the forms and functions of literacy change as quickly as new technologies for Information Communication Technologies (ICT) emerge and as individuals develop new uses for them (Leu & Kinzer, 2000). Twenty-first century technological advancements, information and communication technologies, and the exploding potential of the Internet, warrant new literacies (Alvermann, 2008; Lankshear & Knobel, 2003, 2006a; Leu, 2000; Leu et al. 2007; McKenna, Labbo,

Kieffer, & Reinking, 2006). Literacy is no longer viewed as an individual transformation, but as a contextual and societal one. The concept of "new literacies" is representative of 21st century reading, writing, and communicating. New literacies refers to the knowledge, skills, strategies, and dispositions needed to use and adapt to the changing nature of information and communication technologies in the 21st century (Karchmer, Mallette, Kara-Soteriou, & Leu, 2005).

New literacies refers to both "technical stuff" and "ethos stuff." What is key to new literacies is not that people now read on an iPad, or access information online from anywhere, anytime. Rather, it is how the "technical stuff" enables people to participate in different literacy practices that involve different kinds of norms, procedures, and values from those of conventional literacies. These values are called the "new ethos stuff" (Lankshear & Knobel, 2006). New literacies are collaborative, participatory, and distributed; they create a new type of mindset. As society is becoming more technologically advanced, students will need to not only read print text and write on paper, but also read digital text and use graphics, signs, and sounds (IRA, 2012), and different mindsets about learning, collaborating, creating, and sharing in new learning spaces and through new mediums, norms, and systems.

The New Literacies Theory defines literacy within the frame of the skills and strategies necessary to be successful in ever-changing technological environments. The four key principles, as highlighted by Coiro, Knobel, Lankshear, and Leu (2008), that guide educators' understandings of New Literacies are as follows:

1. Internet and other Information Communication Technologies require us to bring new knowledge, skills, strategies, dispositions, and social practices to their effective use.
2. The acquired skills are central to full civic, economic, and personal participation in a global community.
3. New Literacies are deictic; they change regularly.
4. New Literacies are multiple, multimodal, and multifaceted and people's understanding of them affects teaching and learning.

These understandings present a frame from which educators recognize that as technology evolves, so does the nature of literacy and the skills needed for students to be successful in the future. As the research on New Literacies points to the new skills and strategies needed by the student, they also present new challenges for teachers; they require a change in teacher knowledge and instructional practices (Leu, McVerry, O'Bryne, Zawilinski, Castek, & Hartman, 2009; Leu, O'Byrne, Zawilinski, McVerry, & Everett-Cacopardo, 2009).

The Changing Nature of Texts

If literacy has evolved, what counts as "text" today? For centuries, it has been uni-dimensional—from beginning to end, scanning from left to right, right to left, up and down. Print text is stable; its narrative is inalterable by the reader. However, with the advent of electronic digital media, linear text is being replaced with hypertext, text that is non-linear, interactive, and dynamic. As a result of reading, working, and interacting in digital environments, the very nature of text is undergoing fundamental changes. Hypertext is fluid, dynamic, interactive, is connected with digital objects (such as the creation of webs), is multi-sequential, and it allows for simultaneous co-authoring. These features derive from hyperlinks, digital codes embedded by an author in a text to direct the reader elsewhere (i.e., another place in the document, a reference in a bibliography, or a definition in a glossary). Through hyperlinks, the reader experiences the text in a nonlinear form and proceeds to another level of reading. Hypertext requires the reader to (a) be familiar with computers and know how to access information in digital environments; (b) use navigational tools to guide the student through a text; (c) read text in a nonlinear fashion, link to other pieces of information outside the text and access topic related information.

Reading hypertext is a totally different experience than reading print text. It is experiencing text as part of a set of interactive, digital, text navigational actions (Hartman, Morsink, & Zheng, 2010). It also requires knowledge of technology, how search engines work, and how information is organized in websites (Coiro, 2005). Much research suggests that students need to have new comprehension skills and strategies to read and learn from text on the Internet (Biancarosa & Snow, 2004; Coiro, 2003b, 2003c). Reading hypertext requires the learner to have different types of knowledge, reading skills, and new literacies to search for, navigate, negotiate, critically evaluate, synthesize, create, and share meaning in digital contexts. In order for the 21st century mind to manage the complexity and diversity of a highly networked world, it will need to become more critical, metacognitive (the ability to reflect on one's own learning and make adjustments as needed), reflective, fluid, flexible, and more innovative (Cookson, 2009).

Teaching New Literacies

To best prepare students to learn and work in 21st century learning spaces, teachers will need to help students "learn how to learn" new technologies (International Reading Association [IRA], 2009; National Council of Teachers of English [NCTE], 2008). Just because today's generation is viewed as "tech savvy" that does not mean that today's youth are skilled or strategic in their use of ICT for academic learning purposes. Current research suggests that comprehension of print text is necessary when reading digital text, but not sufficient; digital text requires additional strategies (Coiro, 2009; Coiro & Dobler, 2007; Leu, Kinzer, Coiro, & Cammack, 2004). Comprehension of digital text requires critical thinking, problem solving skills, and metacognitive skills (Hartman, Morsink, & Zheng, 2010; Wilson, Zygouris-Coe, & Cardullo, 2014).

Students need to develop the multiliteracies of the 21st century but they cannot do it alone; teachers must make metacognitive strategies an essential part of teaching digital comprehension skills (Kramarski & Feldman, 2000). Students will benefit from knowledgeable and metacognitive teachers who will help them to determine their purpose for reading, locate information, and critically evaluate and synthesize information. Teachers should guide students through the metacognitive thinking process, provide deliberate and effective feedback, and teach them how to self-regulate their understanding (Kamil, Mosenthal, Pearson, & Barr, 2000). Leu and Kinzer (2000) suggest that because new literacies are fluid and variable, there will be a higher demand for critical thinking skills as technologies advance and transform literacy and learning (Leu & Kinzer, 2000; Leu, Kinzer, Coiro, & Cammack, 2004).

To become literate in today's world, students must become proficient with ICT, reading hypertext, and multimedia (Coiro, 2003a). Today's teachers must re-conceptualize their definitions of literacy, become knowledgeable about how students learn in 21st century environments, be culturally responsive to a diverse student population, create instruction that is aligned with standards and student needs, and create learning environments that value and allow for inquiry, exploration, and innovation.

Students need to be taught how to access, read and comprehend print and hypermedia texts, and embrace the process of developing knowledge and skills that will help them learn and succeed in various contexts. But before teachers help students do that, they first need to use their knowledge to adapt to changes around them. In the context of disciplinary literacy in grades 6–12, educators need to learn, unlearn, and relearn what it takes to help students learn and succeed in school and in life.

If you are struggling as a teacher candidate, or as a classroom teacher, about how to teach your content and help students became engaged with learning about your discipline, then, learn and unlearn. Learn about how to develop and support discipline-specific literacy knowledge, skills, practices, and dispositions in your classroom. What do I mean by unlearn? Identify your perceptions, beliefs, and attitudes about how students learn, where learning takes place, and how they can demonstrate learning. Do you have any misconceptions about the role of literacy in your discipline? What might those be? I believe that the best gifts educators can give to themselves and to their students, are the ability to embrace ambiguity, embrace learning, and finally, embrace unlearning and relearning.

What does all this have to do with 21st century literacies? Well, I think it has to do a lot with it; the forms and functions of literacy have been determined by social changes and the technologies such changes produce (Gee, 2007; Manguel, 1996). What are important social changes today that frame, and are framed by, the changing definition of literacy or literacies of today? Here are a few that are bringing about change in educational standards, curricula, classroom instruction, and assessment of student progress and teacher effectiveness: (1) global economic comparisons; (2) international comparisons of student attainment; (3) the role of the Internet and ICT in daily life; and, (4) national policies to integrate literacy and technology into daily instruction.

Critical Literacy

For students to become critical readers and thinkers, they also need to think about the author's identity, point of view, beliefs, values and attitudes, and the role of the historical, social, and cultural context in which the text was written. Critical literacy skills will help students understand the author's values and why they portray characters in a certain manner. Critical literacy refers to the ability to read (print and digital) texts and multi-media in a manner that promotes a deeper understanding of social practice, power, domination, representation, misrepresentation, access to goods and services, inequality, and injustice in human relationships.

Paulo Freire, in *Pedagogy of the Oppressed* (2007) proposed that students will become more socially aware and active if they are given opportunities to engage in conversations that question power relations and critique multiple forms of injustice. Critical literacy is essential for college, career, and workforce readiness, and citizenry. Critical literacy skills enable the student to discover hidden agendas within texts and multi-media. Although students use social media, their lack of critical literacy is significant; they need to develop critical media literacy skills. For example, who wrote the book, or designed certain software and hardware, and why? What is the effect of popular teen television programs, video games, movies, and contemporary music on pop culture? What does a text or the lyrics of a popular song communicate about the social, economic, and political issues faced by a certain culture or group? How do Facebook or Twitter shape the way students view technology, interactions, or relationships?

Applying Discipline-Specific Literacies

- Teachers need to help students recognize and understand each discipline's structure, discourse, and ways of knowing and learning.
- To promote discipline-specific (or disciplinary) literacy, teachers should promote reading, writing, listening, speaking and critical thinking using authentic materials that facilitate the development of content-specific knowledge.
- Students need to learn discipline-specific literacy strategies that strengthen students' content knowledge and promote deep, transferable learning to real world situations.

● Learning to read, think, speak, write, inquire, communicate like the experts of each discipline requires a paradigm shift in how teachers "do the business" of teaching and learning in content area classes in grades 6–12.

Adolescent Literacy and New Educational Standards

Nowadays, students are expected to learn more, process more, and produce more. The US education system is challenged by a complex and competitive technology-driven global economy that requires a skilled and literate workforce. Everything is calling for deeper learning. How can educators prepare all students to succeed in college, career, and life?

For the United States to stay economically competitive in a global economy, it needs to have an educated citizenry. According to the Organisation for Economic Co-operation and Development (OECD), the US ranks 15th out of 23 counties in high school completion (OECD, 2010). Results from the Programme for International Student Assessment (PISA) report US 15 year olds ranked 25th out of 30 countries in mathematical literacy, 21st out of 30 in science literacy, and 24th out of 29 in problem solving (OECD, 2010). Today, the US ranks 16th in the world in the percentage of population with college degrees, in a time when by 2018, nearly two-thirds of all American jobs will require a postsecondary degree. For many, no degree means no job. Industries and businesses are struggling to find qualified applicants.

National US assessments have "painted" a crisis in secondary schools—that is, low levels of literacy achievement among millions of middle and high school students. Many high school graduates do not have the advanced reading and writing skills they need to succeed in college and career (Graham & Hebert, 2010). According to the National Assessment for Educational Progress (NAEP), 70% of middle and high school students score below the proficient level in reading achievement, and more than 40% of minority students score at or below the basic level in reading achievement (National Center for Educational Statistics, 2010).

Many students who struggle with reading and writing make up a large proportion of the 1.2 million students who drop out of high school without a diploma each year. One in four students fails to graduate from high school on time and African American and Hispanic students drop out at twice the rate of their white peers (Editorial Projects in Education, 2011). Carnevale, Smith, and Strohl (2010) predict that in the next few years the US will be short nearly three million workers with the necessary knowledge and skills to fill these jobs.

A Snapshot of the Evolution of the Adolescent Literacy Crisis

The adolescent literacy crisis is not a new phenomenon. During the past decade, however, major federal investments (i.e., No Child Left Behind Act of 2001 [US Department of Education, 2001]) provided support for implementing recommendations from the National Reading Council's *Preventing Reading Difficulties in Young Children* (Snow, Burns, & Griffin, 1998) and the National Reading Panel's *Teaching Children to Read* (National Institute of Child Health and Human Development, 2000) to prevent reading difficulties in younger readers and develop effective reading programs for students in primary grades. In 1999, IRA issued a position statement (Moore, Bean, Birdshaw, & Rycik, 1999) that outlined several principles for promoting adolescent literacy.

In 2002, the RAND Corporation's *Reading for Understanding* (RAND, 2002) addressed the need for effective comprehension instruction. In 2004, the Alliance for Excellent Education issued a report, *Reading Next: A Vision for Action and Research in Middle and High School Literacy* (Biancarosa & Snow, 2004), which outlined the following 15 elements of effective adolescent literacy programs:

A. *Instructional Elements*
   1. Direct explicit comprehension instruction
   2. Effective instructional principles embedded in content
   3. Motivation and self-directed learning
   4. Text-based collaborative learning
   5. Strategic tutoring
   6. Diverse texts
   7. Intensive writing
   8. Technology component
   9. Ongoing formative assessment
B. *Infrastructural Improvements*
   1. Extended time for literacy
   2. Professional development
   3. Ongoing summative assessment of students and programs
   4. Teacher teams
   5. Leadership
   6. A comprehensive literacy program

The challenge is complex as reflected by several other reports from various national organizations (e.g., IRA, 2000a, 2000b, 2004a, 2006; NAEP, 2005; National Association of State Boards of Education [NASBE], 2006; National Endowment of the Arts, 2004; NCTE, 2004, 2006, 2007; McCombs, Kirby, Barney, Darilek & Magee, 2005) and the US Department of Education (e.g., Office of Elementary and Secondary Education—see Kamil et al., 2008) that have been calling for action in adolescent literacy.

Research Evidence about the Adolescent Crisis

Here are some related statistics about the state of US adolescent literacy and the need for discipline-specific literacy instruction.

- NAEP results show that more than 60% of students in secondary grades scored below the proficient level in reading achievement; millions of students who cannot comprehend or evaluate text, provide evidence-based responses, or support their understanding of text (National Center for Education Statistics, 2011).
- Twenty-five percent of eighth-grade students and 27% of twelfth-grade students lack basic mastery of the appropriate grade-level knowledge and skills (US Department of Education, 2009).
- Only 18% of eighth-grade students eligible for free and reduced-price lunch reached the proficient level in reading (compared with 44% of their more affluent peers) (US Department of Education, 2011).
- Only 14% of African American, 18% of Hispanic, and 22% of Native American eighth graders scored at or above the proficient level in reading (US Department of Education, 2011).
- Only 3% of eighth-grade English language learners (ELLs) scored at or above proficient on the NAEP reading assessment (US Department of Education, 2011).
- Only 52% of high school graduates tested on the 2011 ACT met the reading readiness benchmark, required for success in credit-bearing first-year college courses (ACT, 2011).
- High school students' ability to read complex texts is a strong predictor of their performance in college math and science courses. Only one in four of ACT-tested graduates met or

exceeded the college readiness benchmarks in English, reading, mathematics, and science (ACT, 2006).

- About 40% of employers indicated that they were dissatisfied with high school graduates' ability to read and understand work related materials, think analytically, and problem-solve (Bridgeland, Dilulio, & Morrison, 2006). Private industry spends an estimated $3.1 billion annually to strengthen entry-level workers' literacy skills (National Commission on Writing for America's Families, Schools, and Colleges, 2004).

Although the 2013 NAEP results show a slight improvement in 4th–8th grade students' performance in reading and mathematics, the improvement is not sufficient, and it is pretty stagnant in grade eight. According to the National Clearinghouse for English Language Acquisition (2011), the number of ELLs in US classrooms from 1997–98 to 2008–09 increased from 3.5 million to 5.3 million (a 51% increase). These growing numbers of ELLs pose unique challenges for educators who are trying to meet ELLs' needs and ensure success for every student.

In the *Reading Next: A Vision for Action and Research in Middle School and High School Literacy* report, Biancarosa and Snow (2006) call for a shift in the traditional secondary model of instruction by placing literacy in the core academic areas as a way to develop deep content knowledge, communication, and learning skills needed for a wide range of postsecondary environments. This does not mean that content area teachers should become reading and writing teachers, but rather that they should teach literacy practices that are specific to their subjects (Biancarosa & Snow, 2006).

In 2010, The Carnegie Foundation of New York, Carnegie Council for Advancing Adolescent Literacy, released a report titled, *Time to Act: An Agenda for Advancing Adolescent Literacy for College and Career Readiness* (Lee & Spratley, 2010). This report calls for restructuring secondary schools around literacy. It advocates for hiring teachers who have good preparation in literacy, know how to support the in and out of school literacies of youth, and provide instruction that will prepare students in grades 6–12 to read and comprehend the texts of each discipline. To do so, students will need to be immersed in the discourse, content, and thinking processes of each discipline.

CCSS Connections

- The common core English language arts, Literacy and Mathematics standards represent a set of expectations for student knowledge and skills that high school graduates need to master to succeed in college, career, and the workforce.
- By positioning literacy within each discipline, students can build content knowledge and mastery across academic literacies.
- New educational standards call for 21st century skills integration of media and technology use, critical analysis, and production, across the disciplines.

The Common Core State Standards

How are various states responding to these adolescent literacy challenges? The *Common Core State Standards Initiative* (CCSS) (2010) led by the Council of Chief State School Officials and the National Governors Association Center for Best Practices, is an effort to define fewer, clearer, and more rigorous standards in English language arts, literacy and mathematics. The CCSS are internationally benchmarked against those of high performing countries and are designed to prepare students for college, career, and the 21st century workforce. The standards call for new ways of teaching that are consistent with rigorous learning, competency on subject mastery, and advance students' learning skills and disciplinary understanding. The implementation of the CCSS in 2014 requires a coherent framework about curriculum, assessments, instruction, and teacher preparation and development (Carnegie Council for Advancing Adolescent Literacy, 2010).

The CCSS describe a literate student as one that demonstrates independence, has deep content knowledge, can respond to the demands of audience, task, purpose and discipline, comprehends as well as critiques and values evidence, uses technology and digital media strategically, and understands other perspectives and cultures (NGAC & CCSSO, 2010). The CCSS are designed to prepare students for postsecondary education; they promise rigor, consistency, clarity, and validity (Zygouris-Coe, 2012). They are separated into the two main domains: (1) English Language Arts and Literacy in History/Social Studies, Science, and Technical Subjects and, (2) Mathematics. The CCSS reposition literacy *within* each discipline.

In the areas of English language arts and literacy, many students have difficulty reading and understanding complex text. According to the CCSS (2010), only 31% of students are college and career ready, in relation to understanding complex text. Students need to develop discipline-specific reading; they need to know how to read the texts of each discipline, as well as write and communicate discipline-related concepts and ideas. Students across grade levels need to read more informational text. To help prepare all students for the challenges of college and career level reading, states should ensure that students are reading progressively more complex texts as they advance through the grades. In addition, students need to have developed language skills, know how language varies according to context, know how to use language for different purposes and audiences, and have robust vocabulary knowledge and skills for college and careers (ACT, 2010).

According to the ACT (2006) report on college readiness in reading, there is a core factor that distinguishes college-ready to college-unready students. "The clearest differentiator in reading between students who are college ready and students who are not is the ability to comprehend complex texts" (p. 2). Students in secondary grades lack experiences and practice with reading complex texts. "The type of text students are exposed to in high school has a significant impact on their readiness for college-ready reading" (p. 23). Complex texts require close, purposeful, slow, and strategic reading. Students need to know how to read and comprehend the complex texts of each discipline. They can benefit from tools that will help them track meaning while reading, make necessary connections with prior knowledge and new ideas, know what to do when meaning fails, persevere when understanding does not come easily or text is ambiguous, and develop deep understanding of texts.

In the area of mathematics, students are having difficulty with Number and Quantity. They need to learn how to make meaning of numbers, operations, and arithmetic expressions, and to use their understanding to solve problems, reason about mathematics, and explain their thinking. All students need to be working and solving challenging problems, explaining their methods for solving problems, justifying their conclusions, and evaluating the effectiveness of their methods, and looking for patterns and structure in places like diagrams, equations, number systems, proofs, problems, tables, graphs, and real-world objects (ACT, 2010).

Although the standards define expectations for what students should know and be able to do by the time they finish high school, not all students will be ready to meet these expectations in the same way or at the same time. Provisions need to be made to ensure the preparation of all students for postsecondary education and life. To do so, teachers will need to have a clear framework for what they teach, how they assess student learning, what curriculum they will use to achieve their goals, and what instructional methods are most effective to teach it (Conley, 2010).

The CCSS call for teaching that focuses more on what students are able to do and achieve and how teachers respond to student learning. Students need inquiry-based learning experiences that engage them in deep understanding of knowledge, critical examination of learning, and transfer of knowledge to new settings. Teachers will benefit from collaborative inquiry with peers where they can examine student data, work together to solve problems of practice, and support student learning. What can be done about the approximately 8.7 million students in grades 4–12 who struggle with advanced reading and writing tasks (Carnegie Council for Advancing Adolescent Literacy, 2010)? There needs to be a change in many areas of teaching—in assessing of student progress and learning, in teacher preparation and professional development, and in funding for support and interventions. Effective secondary school teachers should be knowledgeable about their discipline, the kinds of reading and writing that are important to their discipline, and effective ways to read the texts of the discipline, complex texts, and engage and excite students about learning.

Adoption of the CCSS and development of comprehensive assessment systems are first steps toward promoting student success. Improving education will never happen by just changing the standards; standards do not teach: teachers, do. Although the CCSS will bring a shift in what students learn and are able to do, they are not being field-tested. Whether they will result in improved student achievement, or in closing or widening the achievement gap, remains to be seen. Questions also remain on how the CCSS will be assessed and how the results will be used to evaluate teacher and school effectiveness and teacher preparation programs. The common core standards offer teachers much freedom in the "how" of the curriculum. For students to be prepared to learn, work, and live in today's and tomorrow's world, they will need content area teachers who teach their subject matter in a way that informs students about the structure of knowledge in each discipline; how one reads, writes, thinks, speaks, and learns in each discipline.

The message of the CCSS for making sure that students are college and career ready by the time they graduate high school is also paralleled by the messages of the revised standards, *National Curriculum Standards for Social Studies: A Framework for Teaching, Learning, and Assessment* (2010), published by the National Council for the Social Studies, and the Next Generation Science Standards (2010) Science Teachers' Association. The *National Curriculum Standards for Social Studies* (2010) place much emphasis on helping young people develop the ability to "make informed and reasoned decisions for the public good as citizens of a culturally diverse, democratic society in an interdependent world" (http://www.socialstudies.org/standards/execsummary). They emphasize the purpose for learning social studies, questions for exploration, and identify what learners need to understand (knowledge), what they need be capable of doing (processes), and how they need to demonstrate their learning (products).

The Next Generation Science Standards

The *Next Generation Science Standards* (NGSS) (2012) take into account the importance of having the scientific and educational research communities identify core ideas in science and articulate them across grade bands and describe what it means to be proficient in science. The standards also present and explain the interrelationships among practices, cross-disciplinary concepts and disciplinary core ideas. The NGSS (2012) identify eight core scientific and engineering practices: 1) asking questions (for science) and defining problems (for engineering); 2) developing and using models; 3) planning and carrying out investigations; 4) analyzing and interpreting data; 5) using mathematics and computational thinking; 6) constructing explanations (for science) and designing solutions (for engineering); 7) engaging in argument from evidence; and, 8) obtaining, evaluating, and communicating information.

Preparing students for the demands of learning, working, and living in the 21st century is the goal of each disciplinary educational organization and of society, in general. Developing critical thinkers, students who are curious about life and learning, and students who are active participants and producers in the knowledge-making process should be everyone's goal (i.e., policymakers, educators, parents, society). Helping students understand what it means to think like an expert in each discipline will prepare them to learn in school and in life; and, if teachers do it in a motivating and relevant way, they have a winning ticket. Teachers need to delve deep into each academic discipline. They need to help students develop a robust understanding of core academic content, think critically and solve problems, work collaboratively with others, incorporate feedback, communicate effectively, retain and transfer knowledge, and be self-directed. Last, they need to equip students with discipline-specific tools to access, process, organize, evaluate, and synthesize information for deeper learning.

Think Like An Expert

- Psychologists are skeptical, critical thinkers; they need to be convinced by evidence that something is true; they draw from research, evaluate which theory is best, and use evidence to make diagnoses of mental disorders and determine the most effective treatment. (Social Sciences)
- Mathematicians question everything. When presented with an A implies B type statement, a mathematician will ask "Is the converse true?" (Mathematics)
- Scientists use deduction (going from the general to the specific; making predictions based on theories) and induction (going from the specific to the general; gathering observations together to create a new theory). (Science)
- Historians attempt to explain the causes and effects of events and offer interpretations of them. (Social Studies)

The Secondary Schools We Need

Statistics show that although three-quarters of high school graduates enroll in postsecondary education within two years of graduation, slightly more than half of students entering four-year institutions complete a degree, with an even lower completion rate at two-year colleges (US Department of Education, National Center for Education Statistics, 2008). According to ACT (2012), inadequate student preparation for college accounts for the following results:

- Only 74% of ACT-tested 2011 high school graduates took a core curriculum in high school.
- Even among those taking core coursework within a given subject area, only 68% are ready for college English composition, 47% for college Algebra, 54% for introductory college Social Sciences courses, and 33% for Biology.

Many students in grades 6–12 and beyond have difficulty formulating and solving problems, evaluating material from multiple print and non-print sources, incorporating reference material appropriately, developing an evidence-based explanation, interpreting data or considering conflicting points of view, and completing their assignments with precision and accuracy (Conley, McGaughy, & Gray, 2008). Students need to learn how to read the informational texts of each discipline, they need to read texts from a variety of genres, they need to do close reading of texts, think critically about texts, express their ideas backed by evidence, and possess lifelong learning skills.

How will teachers prepare students for postsecondary education and life success if they still teach the same way they did 25 or 50 years ago? How are they going to foster the development of the knowledge, skills, and dispositions students need for college, work, and career success if they still use the same study guide or test they developed 10 years ago? Teachers need to implement what they know about effective teaching and learning in secondary grades and create supportive learner-centered environments.

Classrooms that are learning communities are rigorous, challenging, collaborative, authentic, and responsive to student needs. They foster the development of habits of knowing and learning according to the structure and demands of each discipline. They equip students with tools and methods to learn critically, they do not separate content from the literacy demands of that content and student characteristics, and they feel different than the average content area classroom.

So far, I have presented you with evidence on the need for focused and rigorous academic work, relevant learning, monitoring of student progress, and a classroom environment that promotes inquiry and collaboration. All of the national efforts I have shared call for a transformation in standards, instruction, assessment, and classroom learning environment. In the following section, I will examine what research has shown about exemplary middle and high schools.

Characteristics of Exemplary Middle Schools

Report guidelines from the following organizations (i.e., The National Forum to Accelerate Middle-Grades Reform's vision statement (2012); *Turning Points 2000: Educating Adolescents for the 21st Century* (Jackson & Davis, 2000); *Beating the Odds: Teaching Middle and High School Students to read and Write Well* (Langer, 2000); National Middle School Association's (NMSA) position statement, *This We Believe: Successful Schools for Young Adolescents* (2003); and, the National Association of Secondary School Principals' (NASSP) report, *Breaking Ranks in the Middle: Strategies for Leading Middle Level Reform* (2006)), call for the following core exemplary middle school elements:

- *Curriculum that is relevant, integrated, and exploratory.* Curriculum has to consider students' interests and address their needs, be based on the intersection between the interests and needs of young adolescents and larger social issues. Curriculum standards have to be based on core academic disciplines (e.g., language arts, mathematics, social studies, science) and be reflective of how students learn when their learning is grounded in big ideas or concepts instead of isolated facts and bits of information. Students need authentic and relevant learning experiences that allow them to connect school learning with the real world and provide them with avenues to explore and express themselves and their learning.
- *Educators who value adolescent learning and are well prepared to work with them.* The teacher factor makes a difference in student achievement. Teachers need to be well prepared for teaching in the middle grades and they also need to participate in continued professional development. They need to be knowledgeable about adolescent development, have a rigorous academic content preparation, pedagogical knowledge, and skills, and they also need to have extensive experiences in middle schools.
- *Instruction that connects student characteristics, curriculum, and assessment.* Instruction needs to be aligned with standards, build on what students know, focus on what students are learning, prepare them to demonstrate learning, and respond to how they learn best.
- *Assessment that allows students to demonstrate their knowledge and skills and enables teachers to make curricular and instructional adjustments to promote student learning.* Teachers need to use a variety of assessments to capture student progress and needs. Assessment should take place on an ongoing basis and it should inform instruction. Teachers should also encourage students to self-monitor their learning.

- *Relationships between and among adults and students and a supportive school environment.* Middle schools should be communities of learning that promote a positive school experience for every student. Schools that value collaborative leadership have a shared vision about student learning, hold high expectations for all students, and a school culture that values collaborative problem solving.
- *High levels of family and community involvement.* Students thrive in environments that promote positive relationships with home, school, and the community.

Characteristics of Exemplary High Schools

What works for high school reform? Results from the following reports (i.e., *Beating the Odds: Teaching Middle and High School Students to Read and Write Well* (Langer, 2000); *Redesigning High Schools: Effective High School Reform: Research and Policy That Works* (The National Conference of State Legislatures, 2005); *Ready for the Real World? Americans Speak on High School Reform* (Educational Testing Service, 2005); *Is Your Local High School Making the Grade? 10 Elements of a Successful High School, Rigorous Academic Coursework* (Alliance for Excellent Education, 2006); *Diploma to Nowhere* (Strong American Schools, 2008); *Barriers to Implementing College and Career Workforce Readiness Initiatives in Texas* (Texas Association of School Boards, 2009); *Meaningful Measurement: The Role of Assessments in Improving High School Education in the 21st Century* (Pinkus, 2009); *A First Look at the Common Core and College and Career Readiness* (ACT, 2010)), showed that the majority of high school reform efforts made by state legislatures have focused on reducing high school dropout rates and improving postsecondary preparation.

A study by the US Department of Education found that the rigor of high school course work is more important than parent education level, socioeconomic status or race/ethnicity in predicting whether a student will earn a postsecondary credential; it is the strongest predictor of success in college and career (Adelman, 1999). A rigorous high school curriculum includes (a) high expectations for all students; (b) interventions and support for low-performing students; and (c) a requirement that each student complete a curriculum that is aligned with college and workforce standards and expectations. For high schools to prepare students for 21st century college, career, and workforce success, they will need to reevaluate their structure and ways for doing learning, be proactive with meeting all students' needs, integrate technology into the regular curriculum, and provide ongoing professional development for teachers.

Elements of exemplary high schools include the following:

- *Rigorous curriculum, challenging courses.* Students need a rigorous, not a watered down, curriculum. Every student should have the necessary knowledge and skills for success in college, the workforce, and life. Each student should take rigorous courses in English, history, science, and math, develop their knowledge and skills with digital tools and new technologies, and should be given the opportunity to earn industry certification or some college credit while in high school through available programs. Students should develop solid academic knowledge, critical thinking skills, and be given opportunities to apply their knowledge and skills to problem-solve and work collaboratively with others.
- *Relevant learning opportunities.* Students need to have a variety of pathways to graduation; elements of relevant learning opportunities include (a) smaller learning communities; (b) personalized learning opportunities; (c) college-level learning opportunities; and (d) an understanding of what is involved in postsecondary admissions and placement. Small learning communities provide students with safe and positive experiences, valuable

support, extra help to low-performing students, monitoring of student progress and prevention of students dropping out of school, and richer, positive experiences with adults and peers. Personalized learning opportunities help match learning and postsecondary education plans to students' interests, needs, and the real world and also provide students with a sense of control over their future. Students need to have (and become aware of) dual enrollment options, online course options, meaningful external educational experiences and apprenticeships, and college-level learning opportunities. They also need to learn about the college and workforce demands and expectations and can benefit from support about applying for access and financial aid for postsecondary education. Meaningful relationships with adults, receiving personal attention, mentoring, and advising are all very important to high school students' success.

- *Qualified teachers.* Effective teachers are critical to helping all students meet rigorous high school coursework standards and prepare them for postsecondary education. Effective teachers have rigorous preparation, knowledge and skills in the subjects they teach, hold high expectations for all students, are equipped to help low-performing students succeed, are skilled in motivating all students to learn about the subject matter, use technology and multi-media for student learning and assessment, and are focused on equipping all students with the tools to learn subject matter at a deep level. Effective teachers participate in ongoing professional development.
- *Flexible scheduling.* High school students benefit from flexible scheduling that enables them to earn more credits and complete either an academic or a career/technical concentration.
- *Strong collaborative leadership.* Effective principals create a clear vision about student culture of high expectations for all students, high accountability, collaborative problem solving, clear goals for student achievement, attendance and truancy rates, graduation rates, and staff retention. They value, encourage, and support ongoing teacher professional development.
- *Monitoring of student progress.* Students need constant feedback on their learning and progress; ongoing assessment of student progress, formative and summative assessments, self-monitoring of goals, and conferencing are important to all students' success.
- *Family and community involvement.* Students succeed when their high schools encourage positive learning relationships among families, businesses, local organizations, and the greater community.

The purpose of secondary education today is to learn how to learn, which means understanding how one goes about gaining new knowledge and skills, creating knowledge, sharing it, collaborating with others, and developing habits for lifelong learning. Let's develop students' ability to learn, apply, and transfer knowledge to new contexts instead of just memorizing facts or learning for the test. Let's teach students how to read and think critically, evaluate information, and participate in the world of events inside and outside the classroom—make rigor, relevance, and relationships a staple in your classroom. Let's engage students in challenging tasks and provide scaffolded support and feedback. Let's create classroom environments that focus on inquiry, problem solving, experimentation, and collaboration. Let's make secondary schools centers of learning, excitement, and hope instead of places where young people come to watch "old" people stand up and deliver a monologue for 45 minutes at a time. And, let's all innovate in teacher preparation, collaborate with others, and continue to learn how to solve complex problems of practice.

In my view, there is a need for a new paradigm for grades 6–12 and postsecondary learning and success. There is also a need for a shift in educators' perspectives about teaching and learning in the 21st century, and a perspective shift about curriculum, standards and assessment systems, and teacher preparation and professional development. Teachers and students will also need commitment and support from policymakers and the community. In a recent report by the National Research Council of the National Academies, *Education for Life and Work: Developing Transferable Knowledge and Skills in the 21st Century* (2012), editors Pellegrino and Hilton identified three broad knowledge domains necessary for 21st century living and learning into three categories: (1) cognitive, (2) intrapersonal, and (3) interpersonal. The cognitive domain involves cognitive processes and strategies, knowledge, and creativity. Related competencies include critical thinking, information literacy, reasoning and argumentation, and innovation. The intrapersonal domain includes intellectual openness, work ethic and conscientiousness, and positive core self-evaluation. Competencies related to these clusters include flexibility, initiative, appreciation for diversity, and metacognition. The interpersonal domain includes teamwork and collaboration, and leadership. These clusters include competencies such as communication, collaboration, responsibility, and conflict resolution. The above competency domains are reflected in the CCSS and are also necessary for disciplinary learning in grades 6–12.

College, career, and workforce readiness warrant deep learning, critical thinking skills, non-routine problem solving, constructing and evaluating evidence-based arguments, and skills and knowledge that will transfer beyond the classroom walls. How can you promote deep learning in your content area classroom? Pellegrino and Hilton (2012) suggest, "Through teaching practices that create a positive learning community, in which students gain content knowledge and also develop intrapersonal and interpersonal competencies" (p. 19).

Effective Teaching and Student Learning

A highly qualified, effective teacher makes a difference in students' achievement (Darling-Hammond, 2000a; Darling-Hammond & Bransford, 2005; Rice, 2003). Teacher knowledge of subject matter, and teacher attitudes and beliefs about students guide instructional decisions and practices. As a beginning or a veteran content area teacher you are probably looking for the best way to teach students about your discipline and help them to learn and want to learn more about it. There are no golden formulas, or silver bullets for teachers who wish for their students to develop effective habits of mind and core academic knowledge in each discipline. To make things worse, there are no magic strategies that will get all of your students to read and comprehend the texts of your discipline.

Teachers need to have well-developed content and pedagogical content knowledge (Shulman, 1986, 1987). Pedagogical content knowledge refers to what teachers do to transform the subject matter and communicate it in a way that facilitates student learning. According to Shulman (1987), the following are elements of pedagogical content knowledge: (1) content knowledge; (2) understanding of students' conceptions of the subject and what makes specific subject matter difficult for them to learn; (3) specific subject-matter teaching strategies; (4) curriculum knowledge; (5) knowledge of educational contexts; and (6) knowledge of the purposes of education. Pedagogical content knowledge refers to knowing what to teach, why teach it, when to teach it, and how to teach it so students learn it.

What you do counts. Your teacher preparation counts. And, no matter how improved standards, materials, or programs are, they do not teach; you do. What are teachers supposed to know and be able to do to prepare all students for secondary and postsecondary success? The answer to this question is not simple; it is multi-faceted. Content knowledge separated from pedagogy and literacy is an incomplete formula for knowledge development. Effective teaching takes time, requires multiple layers of knowledge, data-based decision-making, and adaptive metacognition (Lin, Schwartz, & Hatano, 2005), the ability to "transform, adapt, merge, and synthesize, criticize and invent" (Shulman, 1998, p. 519), and thinking on one's feet (Carter, 1990); teaching is a science, and an art. Bransford, Darling-Hammond, & LePage (2005) describe it very well:

> Teaching looks simple from the perspective of students who see a person talking and listening, handing out papers, and giving assignments. Invisible . . . are the many kinds of knowledge, unseen plans, and backstage moves—the skunkworks, if you will—that allow a teacher to purposefully move a group of students from one set of understandings and skills to quite another over the space of many months.
>
> (p. 1)

Let's examine some core areas of knowledge and abilities all teachers need to have below:

- Deep knowledge of subject matter is a key element of knowing how to teach subject matter so that students understand it and want to learn more about it (Darling-Hammond, 1998, 2000; Wenglinski, 2000). Teacher expertise (what teachers know and are able to do) guides everything in teaching. What teachers know about content and how students learn, shapes how they present material, select texts, motivate students to learn, assess student talk, work, and learning. Do you have a solid understanding of the material at hand? Do you know your discipline—how it is structured, what its goals are, how texts are written, how knowledge is accessed, developed, communicated, and assessed, and the ways of knowing and learning in and about it?
- Pedagogical content knowledge is equally important to effective teaching and student learning (Shulman, 1987; Darling-Hammond, 1998, 2000; Wenglinski, 2000). Learning involves physical, cognitive, social, cultural, and emotional factors. Knowing how students learn is important for presenting material, using their background knowledge to make connections, tapping into their interests, addressing misconceptions, making connections, and continuing to learn (Allen, 2003; Darling-Hammond & Ball, 1998). Teachers need to know what material to select and how to present it for specific purposes and in different contexts. Being able to address "what," "why," and "how to" questions requires that the teacher has expertise in content and instructional skills to guide students to think meaningfully about the topic at hand (Bransford, Darling-Hammond & LePage, 2005; Duffy, Miller, Parsons, & Meloth, 2009; Scherer, 2008).
- Teaching in ways that connect with students is motivating. Teachers need to recognize students' interests, goals, and aspirations and provide encouragement, motivation, support, and mentoring. They also need to know how to organize and present material in relevant, meaningful, active, hands-on, and authentic ways to promote active student engagement and higher-order thinking skills (Darling-Hammond & Baratz-Snowden, 2005).
- Creating a positive learning environment, communicating clear expectations, and communicating clearly about objectives, course content, and assessment are necessary for student learning.
- Teachers need to know how to identify students' strengths and needs, monitor their progress, and use data to make necessary instructional accommodations.
- Teachers need to teach with and about new literacies and build students' experiences with technology and media.

- Effective teachers are metacognitive thinkers. Metacognition refers to thinking about one's thinking and regulation of that thinking (Flavell, 1976; 1979). Teacher metacognition is very complex; although teachers, just like students, need to monitor and regulate their thinking, teachers have the added tasks of motivating students, promoting content learning, selecting appropriate strategies, creating a learning environment, and adapting instruction to meet students' needs, to name a few (Duffy et al., 2009; Zohar, 2006). Metacognitive teachers produce metacognitive students.

- Teachers need to reflect on their practice, assess the impact of their teaching on student learning, use formative and summative assessment of student progress, use assessment data to improve their instruction, collaborate with other teachers on pedagogical content knowledge issues, and work with parents and others to ensure positive learning experiences for all students.

Secretary of Education, Arne Duncan, reemphasized that every student has the right to a highly qualified and effective classroom teacher (US Department of Education, 2009). High-need schools that serve predominantly low-income minority students have lack of access to highly qualified teachers (Darling-Hammond, 2010; National Commission on Teaching and America's Future [NCTAF], 1996). The US scenario looks very different from that of other countries—one-third of secondary math teachers did not major in math or related disciplines; on the other hand, Japan has almost no out-of-field teachers (Ingersoll et al., 2007).

As a middle or high school content area teacher, you are becoming an expert in your field, but first and foremost, you are a teacher of youth. Preparation for middle and high school teachers requires a solid foundation in subject matter, including the principles, theories, concepts, ways of thinking and learning, and literacy strategies specific to the discipline. In addition, it requires that teachers have a repertoire of engaging and motivating instructional strategies that provide students with intellectually challenging and relevant coursework. Lastly, it includes the ability to foster positive relationships with students. For students to develop competence in an area of study, they must have a deep foundation of factual knowledge, understand core facts and ideas, and organize information in ways that facilitate retrieval and transfer in new contexts. Student competence in any area of inquiry cannot be achieved without a metacognitive approach to instruction (Bransford, Brown, & Cocking, 2000).

Students will benefit from learner- and knowledge-centered classrooms where attention is given to learning the subject matter at a deep level, knowing how to learn, and also knowing what mastery in each discipline looks like. Teachers need to conduct formative assessments to monitor student progress and use results to provide instructional interventions for students who are not yet college and career ready. Teachers will benefit from professional development in CCSS, discipline-specific literacy instruction, assessment, and college and career readiness. High performing schools have consistently set high expectations for all students, developed challenging academic objectives, implemented rigorous, discipline-specific, responsive, relevant, and engaging instruction that helps progress all students to college and career readiness, and facilitated a school and classroom culture of collaborative inquiry (ACT, 2010).

Summary

- For all students to compete and succeed in the global economy, they need to become skilled readers, writers, and metacognitive thinkers.

- All educators are living in an era of "shifts": (a) a shift to higher educational standards; (b) a shift for deeper content and literacy knowledge; (c) a shift to New Literacies;

(d) a shift to 21st century teaching and learning; and (e) a shift toward literacy within the disciplines.

● New educational standards call for a discipline-specific approach to teaching and learning in grades 6–12.

Differentiating Instruction

● English language learners (ELLs) are students who were not born in the US or whose native language is not English; they cannot participate fully in the regular curriculum English-speaking classroom because of difficulties in speaking, reading, writing, and understanding English language. The US Department of Education defines struggling readers as students who read at least two grade years below grade level (Federal Register/Vol.70, No., 189/Friday, September 30, 2005/Notices, p. 57257).

● Gifted learners are skilled readers and writers, perform above their grade levels, have advanced language abilities, and enjoy inquiry, enrichment activities, and exploration.

● Value cultural diversity and have a working knowledge and understanding of the role of culture in language development and academic achievement, and of the linguistic and learning demands of subjects areas and academic tasks. Success is more likely when content is meaningful and relevant to the student, when support and intervention systems exist, and when students learn in supportive, collaborative, and challenging learning environments.

● Use media and technology to motivate and engage students. Use clear objectives, break down multi-step directions, present models of the expected outcome, make expectations explicit, and offer feedback.

Reflect and Apply

1. Reflect on the content area teachers you have had as a middle, or high school student. Do you remember the best and least effective teacher? What made each one memorable? How did each motivate you, or dissuade you to learn? Share your thoughts in small group discussions.

2. Think of yourself as a future or current content area teacher. What are your attitudes, beliefs, and perceptions about 21st century literacies in secondary content area classrooms? What will you do to develop and support the development of students' discipline-specific literacies in your classroom? Discuss your ideas with a small group of peers.

3. What insights from the chapter could you use to offer some suggestions to Ms. Morrison (see Classroom Life vignette)? Discuss your responses with a small group, and share your group's response with the class.

Extending Learning

1. Get together with a couple of your peers and discuss three of the pressing problems in discipline-specific literacies. As a group, provide an evidence-based "solution" to each problem.

2. Suppose that you are invited by a school principal to present at a faculty meeting what you are learning about preparing students for college, career, and the workforce. You

have 15 minutes to present, and 15 minutes for a discussion. What key information would you include in your presentation? How would you involve the faculty in a relevant and authentic conversation on the topic? Share your thoughts with others.

3. What are three specific ways you plan to have a dialogue with your peers about literacy and learning related issues for 21st century learning?

References

Adelman, C. (1999). *Answers in the tool box: Academic intensity, attendance patterns and bachelor's degree attainment.* Washington, DC: US Department of Education.

Albers, P. (2007). Visual discourse analysis: An introduction to the analysis of school-generated visual texts. In D. W. Rowe, R. T. Jiménez, D. L. Compton, D. K. Dickinson, Y. Kim, K. M. Leander, & V. J. Risko (Eds), *56th yearbook of the National Reading Conference* (pp. 81–95). Oak Creek, WI: National Reading Conference.

Allen, S. (2003). An analytic comparison of three models of reading strategy instruction. *International Review of Applied Linguistics in Language, 41*(4), 319–339.

Alliance for Excellent Education. (2006). 10 elements every high school should have in place. Retrieved from http://www.all4ed.org/what_you_can_do/successful_high_school

Alliance for Excellent Education. (2012). *A framework for advancing career and technical education: Recommendations for the reauthorization of the Carl D. Perkins Act: A Policy Brief.* Retrieved from www.all4ed.org/files/FrameworkCTE.pdf

Alvermann, D. E. (2008). Commentary: Why bother theorizing adolescents' online literacies for classroom practice and research? *Journal of Adolescent & Adult Literacy, 52*(1), 8–19.

American College Testing. (2006). *Reading between the lines: What the ACT reveals about college readiness in reading.* Iowa City, IA: Author.

American College Testing. (2010). *A first look at college at the common core and college and career readiness.* Iowa City, IA: Author.

American College Testing. (2011). *The condition of college and career readiness.* Iowa City, IA: Author.

American College Testing. (2012). *Staying on target: The importance of monitoring student progress towards college and career readiness: A research and policy brief.* Retrieved from http://www.act.org/research/policymakers/

Association for Career and Technical Education. (2006). *Career and technical education's role in American competitiveness: An issue brief.* Alexandria, VA: ACCTE. Retrieved from https://www.acteonline.org/uploadedFiles/. . ./Competitiveness.pdf

Association for Career and Technical Education. (2008). *Career and technical education's role in workforce readiness and credentials: An issue brief.* Alexandria, VA: ACCTE. Retrieved from https://www.acteonline.org/. . .and. . ./WorkReadinessCredentials.pdf

Baker, D. B., Clay, J. N., & Gratama, C. A. (2005). *The essence of college readiness: Implications for students, parents, schools, and researchers.* The BERC Group, LLC: Author.

Barton, D. (1994). *Literacy: An introduction to the ecology of written language.* Oxford: Blackwell.

Barton, D., & Hamilton, M. (2000). Literacy practices. In D. Barton, M. Hamilton, & R. Ivanic (Eds), *Situated literacies: Reading and writing in context* (pp. 7–15). New York: Routledge.

Biancarosa, G., & Snow, C. E. (2004). *Reading next: A vision for action and research in middle and high school literacy. A report to the Carnegie Corporation of New York.* Washington, DC: Alliance for Excellent Education.

Biancarosa, G., & Snow, C. E. (2006). *Reading next: A vision for action and research in middle and high school literacy. A report to Carnegie Corporation of New York* (2nd ed.). Washington, DC: Alliance for Excellent Education.

Bransford, J. D., Brown, A. L., and Cocking, R. R. (Eds). (2000). *How people learn.* Washington, DC: National Academy Press.

Bransford, J., Darling-Hammond, L., & LePage, P. (2005). Introduction. In L. Darling-Hammond & J. Bransford (Eds), *Preparing teachers for a changing world: What teachers should learn and be able to do* (pp. 1–39). San Francisco, CA: Jossey-Bass.

Bridgeland, J. M., Dilulio, J. J., & Morrison, K. (2006). *The silent epidemic: Perspectives of high school dropouts.* A report by Civic Enterprises in association with Peter D. Hart Research

Associates for the Bill & Melinda Gates Foundation. Retrieved from www.ignitelearning.com/pdf/ TheSilentEpidemic3–06FINAL.pdf

Carnegie Council for Advancing Adolescent Literacy. (2010). *Time to act: An agenda for advancing adolescent literacy for college and career success.* New York, NY: Carnegie Corporation of New York.

Carnevale, A. P., Smith, N., & Strohl, J. (2010). *Projections of employment and education demand 2008–2018.* Washington, DC: Georgetown Center on Education and the Workforce.

Carter, K. (1990). Teachers' knowledge and learning to teach. In W. Houston (Ed.), *Handbook of research on teacher education* (pp. 291–310). NY: MacMillan.

Coiro, J. (2003a). Reading comprehension on the Internet: Expanding our understanding of reading comprehension to encompass new literacies. *The Reading Teacher, 56,* 458–464.

Coiro, J. (2003b). Reading comprehension on the Internet. Reading Online. Retrieved from: www.readingonline.org/electronic/elec_index.asp?HREF=/electronic/rt/2-03_Column

Coiro, J. (2003c). Rethinking comprehension strategies to better prepare students for critically evaluating content on the Internet. *The NERA Journal, 39,* 29–34.

Coiro, J. (2005). Making sense of online text. *Educational Leadership, 63*(2), 30–35.

Coiro, J. (2009). Rethinking reading assessment in a digital age: How is reading comprehension different and where do we turn now? *Educational Leadership, 66*(6), 59–63.

Coiro, J., & Dobler, E. (2007). Exploring the online comprehension strategies used by sixth-grade skilled readers to search for and locate information on the Internet. *Reading Research Quarterly, 42,* 214–257.

Coiro, J., Knobel, M., Lankshear, C., & Leu, D. J. (2008). Central issues in new literacies and new literacies research. In J. Coiro, M. Knobel, C. Lankshear, & D. J. Leu. *The handbook of research on new literacies* (pp. 1–22). Mahwah, NJ: Erlbaum.

Conley, D. T. (2009). *College knowledge: What it really takes for students to succeed and what we can do to get them ready.* San Francisco, CA: Jossey-Bass.

Conley, D. T. (2010). *College and career ready: Helping all students succeed beyond high school.* San Francisco, CA: Jossey-Bass.

Conley, D. T., McGaughy, C., & Gray, E. (2008). *College readiness performance assessment system (C-PAS).* Eugene, OR: Educational Policy Improvement Center.

Cookson, P. (2009). Teaching for the 21st century: What would Socrates say? *Leadership, 67*(1), 8–14.

Darling-Hammond, L. (1998). Teachers and teaching: Testing policy hypotheses from a national commission report. *Educational Researcher, 27*(1), 5–15.

Darling-Hammond, L. (2000). Reforming teacher preparation and licensing: Debating the evidence. *Teachers College Record, 102*(1), 28–56.

Darling-Hammond, L. (2010). *The flat world and education: How America's commitment to equity will determine our future.* New York, NY: Teachers College Press.

Darling-Hammond, L., & Ball, L. (1998). *Teaching for high standards: What policy makers need to know and be able to do.* Philadelphia, PA: National Commission on Teaching and America's Future and Consortium for Policy Research in Education.

Darling-Hammond, L., & Baratz-Snowden, J. (Eds). (2005). *A good teacher in every classroom: Preparing the highly qualified teachers our children deserve.* San Francisco, CA: Jossey-Bass.

Darling-Hammond, L., & Bransford, J. (Eds). (2005). *Preparing teachers for a changing world.* National Academy of Education Committee on Teacher Education. San Francisco, CA: Jossey-Bass.

Doering, A., Beach, R., & O'Brien, D. (2007). Infusing multimodal tools and digital literacies into an English education program. *English Education, 40*(1), 41–60.

Duffy, G. G. (2005). Developing metacognitive teachers: Visioning and the expert's changing role in teacher education and professional development. In S. E. Israel, C. C. Block, K. L. Bauserman, & K. Kinnucan-Welsch (Eds), *Metacognition in literacy learning: Theory, assessment, instruction, and professional development* (pp. 299–314). Mahwah, NJ: Lawrence Erlbaum.

Duffy, G. G., Miller, S. D., Parsons, S. A., & Meloth, M. (2009). Teachers as metacognitive professionals. In D. J. Hacker, J. Dunlosky, & A. C. Graesser (Eds), *Handbook of metacognition in education* (pp. 240–256). Mahwah, NJ: Lawrence Erlbaum.

Editorial Projects in Education. (2011). Diplomas count 2010: Graduating by the number: Putting data to work for student success. Special issue, *Education Week, 29,* 34.

Educational Testing Service. (2005). *Ready for the real world? Americans speak on high school reform.* Retrieved from www.ets.org/Media/Education_Topics/. . ./2005highschoolreform.pdf

Flavell, J. H. (1976). Metacognitive aspects of problem solving. In L. B. Resnick (Ed.), *The nature of intelligence* (pp. 231–235). Hillsdale, NJ: Erlbaum.

Flavell, J. H. (1979). Metacognition and cognitive monitoring: A new area of cognitive developmental inquiry. *American Psychologist, 34*, 906–911.

Freire, P. (2007). *Pedagogy of the oppressed*. New York, NY: Continuum.

Frey, N., Fisher, D., & Gonzalez, A. (2010). *Literacy 2.0: Reading and writing in the 21st century*. Bloomington, IN: Solution Tree.

Friedman. T. (2007). *The world is flat: A brief history of the twenty-first century* (3rd ed.). New York, NY: Picador.

Gee, J. P. (1996). *Social linguistics and literacies: Ideology in discourses*. London, UK: Taylor & Francis.

Gee, J. P. (2007). *Good video games and good learning: Collected essays on video games, learning, and literacy*. New York: Peter Lang.

Graham, S., & Hebert, M. A. (2010). *Writing to read: Evidence for how writing can improve reading: A Carnegie Corporation Time to Act Report*. Washington, DC: Alliance for Excellent Education.

Hartman, D. K., Morsink, P. M., & Zheng, J. (2010). From print to pixels: The evolution of cognitive conceptions of reading comprehension. In E. A. Baker (Ed.), *Multiple perspectives on new literacies research and instruction* (pp. 131–164). New York, NY: Guilford.

Heath, S. B. (1983). *Ways with words: Language, life, and work in communities and classrooms*. New York: Cambridge University Press.

Ingersoll, R., Boonyananta, S., Fujita, H., Gang, D., Kim, E. G., Lai, K. C., Maynard, R., Siribanpitak, P., Tan, S., & Wong, A. F. L. (2007). *A comparative study of teacher preparation and qualifications in six nations*. Philadelphia, PA: Consortium for Policy Research in Education.

International Reading Association (IRA). (2000a). *Excellent reading teachers: A position statement of the International Reading Association*. Newark, DE: Author.

International Reading Association (IRA). (2000b). *Teaching all children to read: The roles of the reading specialist: A position statement of the International Reading Association*. Newark, DE: Author.

International Reading Association (IRA). (2004). Standards for reading professionals: Revised 2003. Newark, DE: Author.

International Reading Association (IRA). (2006). Standards for middle and high school literacy coaches. Newark, DE: Author.

International Reading Association (IRA). (2009). *New literacies and 21st century technologies: A position statement*. Newark, DE: Author.

International Reading Association. (2012). *Adolescent literacy* (Position statement, Rev. 2012). Newark, DE: Author.

Jackson, A. W., & Davis, G. A. (2000). *Turning points 2000: Educating adolescents in the 21st century*. NY: Teachers College Press.

Kamil, M. L. (2003). *Adolescents and literacy: Reading for the 21st century*. Washington, DC: Alliance for Excellent Education.

Kamil, M. L., Mosenthal, P. B., Pearson, P. D., & Barr, R. (Eds). (2000). *Handbook of reading research: Volume III*. Mahwah, NJ: Erlbaum.

Kamil, M. L., Borman, G. D., Dole, J., Kral, C. C., Salinger, T., & Torgesen, J. (2008). *Improving adolescent literacy: Effective classroom intervention practices: A practice guide* (NCEE#2008–4017). Washington, DC: National Center for Education Evaluation and Regional Assistance, Institute of Educational Sciences, US Department of Education. Retrieved from http://ies.ed.gov/ncee/wwc/pdf/practice_guides/adlit_pg_082608.pdf

Karchmer, R. A., Mallette, M., Kara-Soteriou, J., & Leu, D. J., Jr. (Eds). (2005). *New literacies for new times: Innovative models of literacy education using the Internet*. Newark, DE: International Reading Association.

Kramarski, B., & Feldman, Y. (2000). Internet in the classroom: Effects on reading comprehension, motivation and metacognitive awareness. *Educational Media International, 37*(3), 149–155.

Langer, J. (2000). *Beating the Odds: Teaching middle and high school students to read and write well*. (CELA Research Report Number 1201). Albany, NY: University at Albany, State University of New York, National Center on English Learning & Achievement.

Lankshear, C., & Knobel, M. (2003). *New literacies: Changing knowledge in the classroom*. Buckingham, UK: Open University Press.

Lankshear, C., & Knobel, M. (2006). *New literacies: Everyday practices and classroom learning* (2nd ed.). Maidenhead, UK: Open University Press.

Lee, C. D., & Spratley, A. (2010). *Reading in the disciplines: The challenges of adolescent literacy.* New York, NY: Carnegie Corporation of New York.

Leu, D. J., Jr. (2000). Literacy and technology: Deictic consequences for literacy education in an information age. In M. L. Kamil, P. Mosenthal, P. D. Pearson, & R. Barr (Eds). *Handbook of reading research, Volume III* (pp. 743–770). Mahwah, NJ: Erlbaum.

Leu, D. J., Jr., & Kinzer, C. K. (2000). The convergence of literacy instruction and networked technologies for information and communication. *Reading Research Quarterly, 35,* 108–127.

Leu, D. J., Jr., Kinzer, C. K., Coiro, J., & Cammack, D. (2004). Toward a theory of new literacies emerging from the Internet and other information and communication technologies. In R. B. Ruddell & N. Unrau (Eds), *Theoretical models and processes of reading* (5th ed., pp. 1568–1611). International Reading Association: Newark, DE.

Leu, D. J., Kinzer, C. K., Coiro, J., Castek, J., & Henry, L. A. (2013). *New literacies: A dual-level theory of the changing nature of literacy instruction and assessment.* In D.E. Alvermann, N.J. Unrau, & R.B. Ruddell (Eds), *Theoretical models and processes of reading* (6th ed., pp. 1550–1181). Newark, DE: International Reading Association.

Leu, D., McVerry, G., O'Byrne, I., Zawilinski, L., Castek, J., & Hartman, D. (2009). The new literacies of online reading comprehension and the irony of *No Child Left Behind*: Students who require our assistance the most, actually receive it the least. In M. Morrow, R. Rueda, & D. Lapp (Eds), *Handbook of research on literacy instruction: Issues of diversity, policy, and equity* (pp. 173–195). New York, NY: Guilford.

Leu, D., O'Byrne, W., Zawilinski, L., McVerry, G., & Everett-Cacopardo, H. (2009). Comments on Greenhow, Robelia, and Hughes: Expanding the new literacies conversation. *Educational Researcher, 38,* 264–269.

Leu, D. J., Zawilinski, L., Castek, J., Banerjee, M., Housand, B. C., Liu, Y., & O'Neil, M. (2007). What is new About the new literacies of online reading comprehension?. In *Secondary school literacy: What research reveals for classroom practice* (pp. 37–68). Urbanna, IL: National Council of Teachers of English. Retrieved from http://teachers.westport.k12.ct.us/ITL/wkspmaterials/NCTE%20chapter.pdf

Lin, X., Schwartz, D. L., & Hatano, G. (2005). Toward teachers' adaptive metacognition. *Educational Psychologist, 40*(4), 245–255.

Manguel, A. (1996). *A history of reading.* New York: Viking.

McCombs, J. S., Kirby, S. N., Barney, H., Darilek, H., & Magee, S. (2005). *Achieving state and national literacy goals: A long uphill road.* Santa Monica, CA: Rand Corporation. Retrieved from http://www.rand.org/pubs/technical_reports/2005/RAND_TR180-1.pdf

McKenna, M. C., Labbo, L. D., Kieffer, R. D., & Reinking, D. (Eds). (2006). *International handbook of literacy and technology* (Vol. 2). Mahwah, NJ: Erlbaum.

McTighe, J., Seif, E., & Wiggins, G. (2004, September). You can teach for meaning. *Educational Leadership, 62*(1), 26–31.

Moore, D. W., Bean T. W., Birdyshaw, D., & Rycik, J. A. (1999). Adolescent literacy: A position statement. *Journal of Adolescent & Adult Literacy, 43,* 97–112.

National Assessment of Educational Progress (NAEP). (2005). *The nation's report card: Reading 2005.* Washington, DC: Author. Retrieved from http://nces.ed.gov/nationsreportcard/pdf/main2005/2006451.pdf

National Association of Manufacturers. (2005). 2005 skills gap report: A survey of the American manufacturing workforce. Retrieved from www.nam.org/~/media/ Files/s_nam/docs/235800/235731.pdf.ashx

National Association of Secondary School Principals. (2006). *Breaking ranks in the middle: Strategies for leading middle level reform.* Retrieved from www.nassp.org/portals/0/content/53495.pdf

National Association of State Boards of Education. (2006). Reading at risk: The state response to the crisis in adolescent literacy. Alexandria, VA: NASBE.

National Center for Education Statistics. (2010). *Reading 2011: National assessment of educational progress at grades 4 and 8 (NCES 2012–457).* Washington, DC: Institute of Education Sciences, US Department of Education.

National Center for Education Statistics. (2013). *The nation's report card: A first look: 2013 mathematics and reading (NCES 2014–451).* Washington, DC: Institute of Education Sciences, US Department of Education.

National Clearinghouse for English Language Acquisition. (2011). *The growing number of English language learner students 1998/1999–2008/09.* Retrieved from http://www.ncela.us/files/uploads/9/growingLEP_0809.pdf

National Commission on Teaching and America's Future. (1996). *What matters most: teaching for America's future.* Woodridge, VA: The National Commission on Teaching & America's Future. Retrieved from http://nctaf.org/wp-content/uploads/2012/01/WhatMattersMost.pdf

National Commission on Writing for America's Families, Schools, and Colleges. (2004). *Writing: A ticket to work . . . Or a ticket out: A survey of business leaders.* New York: The College Board.

National Conference of State Legislatures. (2005). *Redesigning high schools: Effective high school reform: Research and policy that works.* Retrieved from http://www.ncsl.org/issues-research/educ/high-school-redesign-effective-high-school-reform.aspx

National Council for the Social Studies. (2010). *National curriculum standards for social studies: A framework for teaching, learning, and assessment.* Washington, DC: NCSS.

National Council of Teachers of English. (2004). *A call to action: What we know about adolescent literacy and ways to support teachers in meeting students' needs.* Urbana, IL: Author. Retrieved from http://www.ncte.org/positions/statements/adolescent literacy

National Council of Teachers of English. (2006). *NCTE principles of adolescent literacy reform: A policy brief.* Urbana, IL: Author.

National Council of Teachers of English. (2007). *Adolescent literacy: A policy research brief.* Urbana, IL: Author.

National Council of Teachers of English. (2008). *The NCTE definition of 21st century literacies.* Retrieved from: http://www.ncte.org/positions/statements/21stcentdefinition

National Endowment of the Arts. (2004). *Reading at risk: A survey of literacy reading in America.* Washington, DC: Author.

National Forum to Accelerate Middle Grades Reform. (2012). *Our vision statement.* Retrieved from http://www.middlegradesforum.org/index.php/about/vision-mission

National Governors Association Center (NGAC) for Best Practices, Council of Chief State School Officers. (2010). *Common Core State Standards.* Retrieved from http://corestandards.org

National Institute of Child Health and Human Development. (2000). *Report of the National Reading Panel: Teaching children to read: An evidence-based assessment of the scientific research literature on reading and its implications for reading instruction.* Washington, DC: US Government Printing Office.

National Middle School Association. (2003). *This we believe: Successful schools for young adolescents.* Ohio: NMSA.

National Research Council. (2002). *Learning and understanding: Improving advanced study of mathematics and science in US high schools.* Washington, DC: National Academy Press.

National Research Council. (2013). *Next generation science standards: For states, by states.* Washington, DC: The National Academies Press. Retrieved at http://www.nextgenscience.org/next-generation-science-standards

National Science Teachers' Association. (2012). *Next generation science standards for states, by states.* Arlington, VA. Retrieved from: http://www.nsta.org/about/standardsupdate/default.aspx

New London Group, The. (2000). A pedagogy of multiliteracies: Designing social futures. In B. Cope & M. Kalantzis (Eds), *Multiliteracies: Literacy learning and the design of social futures* (pp. 9–38). London: Routledge.

Oblinger, D. (2004, May). The next generation of educational engagement. *Journal of Interactive Media in Education*, 8.

Organization for Economic Cooperation and Development (OECD). (2010). *PISA 2009 results: What students know and can do: Student performance in reading, mathematics and science* (Vol. I). OECD Publishing.

Pellegrino, J. W., & Hilton, M. L. (Eds). (2012). *Education for life and work: Developing transferable knowledge and skills in the 21st century.* Committee on Defining Deeper Learning and 21st Century Skills; Center for Education; Division on Behavioral and Social Sciences and Education; National Research Council.

Pinkus, L. (2009). *Moving beyond AYP: High school performance indicators.* Washington, DC: Alliance for Excellent Education.

RAND Reading Study Group. (2002). *Reading for understanding: Toward a research and development program in reading comprehension.* Santa Monica, CA: Office of Education Research and Improvement.

Rice, J. K. (2003). *Teacher quality: Understanding the effectiveness of teacher attributes.* Washington, DC: Economic Policy Institute.

Scherer, M. (2008). The thinking teacher. *Educational Leadership Journal, 65*(5), 7.

Shulman, L. S. (1986). Paradigms and research programs for the study of teaching. In M. C. Wittrock (Ed.), *Handbook of research on teaching* (3rd ed.). New York: Macmillan.

Shulman, L. (1987). Knowledge and teaching: Foundations of the new reform. *Harvard Educational Review, 57*(1), 1–22.

Shulman, L. (1998). Theory, practice and the education of professionals. *Elementary School Journal, 98*, 511–526.

Snow, C. E., Burns, M. S., & Griffin, P. (Eds). (1998). *Preventing reading difficulties in young children.* Washington, DC: National Academy Press.

Southern Regional Educational Board. (2003). Literacy across the curriculum: Setting and implementing goals for grades six through 12. Retrieved from http://publications.sreb.org/2003/03V63_literacy_guide_chapter_1.pdf

Strong American Schools. (2008). *Diploma to nowhere.* Washington, DC: Strong American Schools (Rockefeller Philanthropy Advisors).

Texas Association of School Boards. (2009). *Barriers to implementing college and workforce readiness initiatives in Texas.* Retrieved from http://www.tasb.org/legislative/resources/college.aspx

United States Department of Education. (2001). The No Child Left Behind Act of 2001. Retrieved from http://www.state.nj.us/education/grants/nclb/

US Department of Education. (October 22, 2009). Teacher preparation: Reforming the uncertain profession—Remarks of Secretary Arne Duncan at Teachers College, Columbia University. Retrieved at http://www2.ed.gov/news/speeches/2009/10/10222009.html?exp=7

US Department of Education, National Center for Education Statistics. (2008). *The condition of education 2008* (NCES 2008–031). Retrieved from: nces.ed.gov/pubs2008/2008031.pdf

US Department of Education, National Center for Education Statistics. (2011a). *The condition of education 2011 (NCES 2011–033).* Retrieved from: http://nces.ed.gov/programs/coe/pdf/coe_lsm.pdf

US Department of Education, National Center for Education Statistics. (2011b). *The Nation's Report Card: Reading 2011 (NCES 2012–457).* Washington, DC: US Government Printing Office.

Wenglinsky, H. (2000). *How teaching matters: Bringing the classroom back into discussions of teacher quality.* Princeton, NJ: The Milken Family Foundation and Educational Testing Service.

Wilson, N., Zygouris-Coe, V., & Cardullo, V. (2014). Trying to make sense of reading with E-readers. *Journal of Reading Education, 39*(3), 36–42.

Zohar, A. (2006). The nature and development of teachers' metastrategic knowledge in the context of teaching higher order thinking. *The Journal of Learning Sciences, 15*(3), 331–377.

Zygouris-Coe, V. (2012). Disciplinary literacy and the common core state standards. *Topics in Language Disorders, 32*(1), 35–50.

Zygouris-Coe, V., Cardullo, V. M., & Wilson, N. (under revision). Fifth grade students reading fiction text with e-readers: An exploratory study.

two
Literacy as a Discipline-Specific Process

People are not recorders of information but builders of knowledge structures. To know something is not just to have received information but also to have interpreted it and related it to other knowledge.
–Lauren B. Resnick and Leopold E. Klopfer, "Toward the Thinking Curriculum"

Chapter Highlights

- Twenty-first century learning requires citizens who are thinkers, problem solvers, collaborators, and developers of new knowledge.
- Each discipline has a unique body of knowledge, discourse, habits of mind, tools, and processes through which it makes sense of the world.
- General content area literacy strategies cannot sufficiently prepare students to meet the complex content and literacy demands of each discipline.
- Disciplinary literacy is specific to each discipline's structure, goals, and ways of knowing and learning. It carries, also, Common Core State Standards (CCSS) and considerations and can prepare students to think, learn, and work like the professionals in each discipline.
- Disciplinary literacy learning principles facilitate content and literacy development within each discipline.
- Learning as apprenticeship allows students to experience, apply, and reflect on "learning and doing" in each discipline.

Classroom Life

I teach Geometry to Standard level students and to the lower quartile students. I teach two geometry blocks (2 periods) because these students did not pass the Algebra End of Course (EOC) exam last year. The biggest challenge that I face when working with these students in regards to literacy is their inability to pick out key words and understand what these words mean, and the inability to comprehend what they have read. If they see a word problem, they immediately get scared and think it's going to be too hard.

For example, they cannot understand that the word "less" is a clue for subtraction. I often times suggest to underline words or even use a highlighter, but most do not take the time to do so. Also, if a word problem says, "a motorcycle's tire has a 25 in. diameter. . . .", they are not able to draw a circle and the line going through showing the diameter of 25 inches. If I have this picture drawn for them, they understand the concept and what to do, but they have an extremely difficult time drawing this, which prohibits them from solving the problem correctly. It is very difficult to teach math when students do not have the reading, vocabulary, and content knowledge and skills they need to learn and do math. *(Ms. Candace Hilston, Mathematics Teacher, Winter Spring HS, Seminole County Public Schools, Florida).*

Content Area Literacy

Content area literacy refers to "the ability to use reading and writing for the acquisition of new content in a given discipline" (McKenna & Robinson, 1990, p. 184). Content knowledge is not the same as content area literacy; content knowledge is a must for content area literacy. The more content knowledge students have about a topic, the more that knowledge facilitates their reading and writing. Many adolescents struggle in secondary school because they have underdeveloped background knowledge, reading, vocabulary and comprehension skills. Content area teachers must develop students' content and literacy knowledge and skills, mindsets, processes, and encourage them to read and learn more out of school.

Much research has established the connections between literacy and content area learning (Alvermann, Fitzerald, & Simmons, 2006; Biancarosa & Snow, 2004; Kamil et al., 2008; RAND, 2002; Torgesen et al., 2007). Content area literacy instruction focuses on general reading and writing strategies for accessing text, organizing notes and ideas about text, interpreting the meanings of unfamiliar vocabulary, recording class or study notes, raising questions about text, and writing reflective responses. All of these (and other) general literacy strategies are useful for accessing ideas, organizing, and responding to information.

In Chapter 1, I presented research evidence on the status of adolescent literacy and the need for improving adolescents' knowledge, skills, and performance. All of the evidence called for improvement in adolescents' reading comprehension and critical thinking skills. The RAND Reading Study Group (RAND, 2002) found that comprehension scores decreased as the text complexity and technicality of content area texts increased. In addition, the same report highlighted the importance of teacher preparation—many secondary content area teachers are not adequately prepared to teach comprehension skills in the disciplines. They have expertise in, and passion about, their content area, but they many are not fully aware about the cognitive and literacy demands of their discipline on students. The complexity of each discipline and acquisition of knowledge in each discipline will not happen through mere lecture, memorization, or occasional writing and classroom talk.

Ness (2007) found that the content area teachers she observed devoted only 3% of their instructional time to explicit instruction, modeling, and providing scaffolded support to students' comprehension of text. Only 3%! How are teachers going to prepare students to comprehend the texts of each discipline, to think critically about what they are learning, and to transfer that knowledge to new settings if they only "sprinkle" explicit instruction and support? Comprehension should be taught explicitly, meaningfully, and strategically. What role should content area instruction play in developing deep understanding of academic subject matter and critical thinking skills?

In this chapter, I position disciplinary literacy as the core approach for ensuring adolescents' college and career readiness. I also present an analysis of the literacy demands of core content areas (i.e., arts, English language arts, mathematics, science, social studies, and technical subjects) and will discuss the role of reading in each discipline for preparing both the content and literacy knowledge and skills students will need to succeed in college and in the workforce. The message I communicate throughout this book is that although general content area reading strategies for reading and accessing informational texts are necessary for secondary and postsecondary student learning and success, they are not sufficient. Content area reading strategies provide the foundation for disciplinary literacy.

General content area strategies and disciplinary literacy can co-exist, but teachers also need to develop students' advanced literacy skills that are contextualized to serve the subject area. In this book, I present a discipline-specific approach to teaching and learning in grades 6–12, and I also demonstrate when and how to weave general and discipline-specific practices in your instruction. My goals are to inform you, provide you with evidence for my claims, invite you to rethink about your discipline and how to teach in ways that will help students develop deep learning, provide you with a discipline-specific teaching and learning framework, and offer you several examples on related topics and practices.

CCSS Connections

- Students must be able to read to be ready for the demands of college- and career-level reading no later than the end of high school. They also need to be able to write logical arguments based on substantive claims, sound reasoning, and relevant evidence.
- Students gain, evaluate, and present increasingly complex information, ideas, and evidence through listening and speaking as well as through media in one-on-one, small group, and whole-class settings.
- Students should be able to think and reason mathematically, practice, and apply mathematical ways of thinking to real world problems.

Misconceptions about Content Area Literacy

There are several assumptions many content area teachers have about students in grades 6–12. Here are some core content area teacher misconceptions: students know how to read and comprehend the texts they read; they have sufficient prior knowledge and comprehension skills; they have adequate vocabularies, and they know how to write and communicate; they have the motivation and interest to read and learn; and they can collaborate with others. Well, Herber (1978) referred to the above as "assumptive teaching" and advised content areas teachers to refrain from it. As I shared in Chapter 1, many US adolescents struggle with any or all of the above areas in secondary grades.

Content area learning is demanding and challenging for many students. To begin with, the content area texts (i.e., informational texts) are written very differently than narrative texts. Content area texts are dense and abstract, have different text structures and features, are loaded with technical and specialized vocabulary, and also include many images, captions, graphs, charts, etc. aside from text. For example, science textbooks require reading mathematical computations and data in addition to text.

Elementary students come to middle school with more narrative than informational text experiences. Some adolescents might comfortably read fictional works, but be at a loss when it comes to reading a chemistry or American Government textbook. This is one of the reasons the Common Core State Standards call for a shift in informational text reading. The CCSS suggest that students should read 45% literary and 55% informational texts in Grade 8 and 30% literary and 70% informational texts in grade 12. Why this shift? Because (a) students' success, or failure in school is tied to their ability to comprehend informational text (Kamil, 2003); (b) by 6th Grade, 80% of school-related reading tasks are informational (Kamil & Lane, 1998; Venezky, 2000); (c) there is a need to close the knowledge gap (Hirsch, 2006); (d) standardized tests are 85% informational; and, (e) the main factor for college and workforce success is the ability to read and comprehend informational text (ACT, 2006).

Many students have difficulty reading and comprehending academic texts because of the technical and specialized vocabulary. Many lack grade-appropriate academic vocabulary, have underdeveloped background knowledge, and do not know how to determine the meaning of unknown words. In addition, many students have underdeveloped general vocabularies and language skills—they do not know how language functions in different contexts, or how to express their thoughts, experiences, or feelings in a grade- or discipline-appropriate manner.

Applying Discipline-Specific Literacies

- Identify three key questions from the text, defend your choices with evidence, and connect them to the overall theme. (English Language Arts)
- Read the problem and identify essential versus non-essential information for solving this problem. (Mathematics)
- Identify facts versus opinions in this scientific article. (Science)
- Determine the significance of different kinds of historical change. (Social Studies)

The Shift from Content Area Literacy to Disciplinary Literacy

Content area material requires critical comprehension skills. When it comes to informational texts, students often quit reading because they struggle with purpose, relevance, background knowledge, or reading and vocabulary skills. Informational text requires different types of reading and thinking. Active, close, purposeful reading and re-reading of text is necessary in the disciplines where ideas are not often explicit, information is widespread, and students have to identify, build, track, and evaluate meaning and accuracy across multiple sources, and make inter-textual connections. Disciplinary texts require close reading instead of skimming, searching, or noting some isolated facts.

Content area literacy and learning require active engagement in subject matter through writing. Students are expected to write arguments using valid reasoning and sufficient evidence, use technology to produce, publish and collaborate in writing, and write routinely for research, expression, reflection, and revision purposes. College, workforce, and career readiness seek citizens who can express their ideas clearly and persuasively, listen to, analyze, and evaluate others' points of view, contribute to conversations, and collaborate to solve problems of practice. Shanahan & Shanahan (2008) remind us that basic or general literacy skills are insufficient for the literacy and learning demands of the 21st century. So many national results and international comparisons point to adolescents developing advanced literacy skills and to expanding literacy from intermediate through high school grades to better support the literacy development of older students.

Shanahan and Shanahan (2008) present a model of literacy progression and highlight the need for disciplinary literacy. See Figure 2.1 for the three phases of literacy across grade levels. According to this figure, the first phase involves the development of basic literacy skills such as decoding and knowledge of high frequency words and basic fluency routines that take place in primary grades. Intermediate literacy skills develop as students in intermediate grades are exposed to more complex text structures, and develop their fluency, vocabulary, and generic comprehension skills. The last phase, disciplinary literacy, is inherent to middle and high school reading and learning. In those grades students are expected to read, write, and think, in discipline-specific ways. They encounter much complex text and need to have knowledge and processes that are appropriate for each discipline (Heller & Greenleaf, 2007; Shanahan & Shanahan, 2008, 2012; Shanahan, Shanahan, & Misichia, 2011).

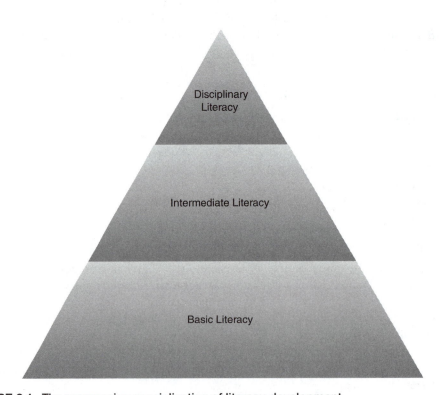

FIGURE 2.1. The progressive specialization of literacy development.

Source: Adapted from: Timothy Shanahan and Cynthia Shanahan, "Teaching Disciplinary Literacy to Adolescents Rethinking Content-Area Literacy," *Harvard Educational Review, 78*(1) (Spring 2008), p. 44. Copyright © by the President and Fellows of Harvard College. All rights reserved. For more information, please visit www.harvardeducationalreview.org

Although the federal emphasis on helping every student to read by Grade 3 was a needed and productive one, Grade 3 reading proficiency will not guarantee advanced reading mastery or success. As Shanahan and Shanahan (2008) stated, "Although most students manage to master basic and even intermediate literacy skills, many never gain proficiency with the more advanced skills that would enable them to read challenging texts in science, history, literature, mathematics, or technology" (p. 45). Disciplinary literacy is contextualized (Gee, 2000); it is "cemented" in each discipline (Zygouris-Coe, 2012); therefore, students in secondary grades are expected to become advanced and specialized readers and writers.

Disciplinary Literacy

Discipline-specific literacy or disciplinary literacy is aimed at learning how to read, think about, write, communicate, and use information like each discipline's experts; i.e., like an artist (arts), an author (ELA), a mathematician (math), a scientist (science), or a historian (social studies). Disciplinary literacy is not aimed at teaching to the test. It involves the tasks and processes of reading, thinking, inquiring, speaking, writing, and communicating required to learn and develop discipline-appropriate content knowledge. Discipline-specific literacy is literacy that reflects and addresses the structure, content and literacy demands, discourse (Fang & Schleppegrell, 2008, 2010), and habits of mind that are specific to each discipline (Shanahan & Shanahan, 2008, 2012; Zygouris-Coe, 2012). It is characterized by deep comprehension of text and related concepts, specialized mindsets, simultaneous development of content and literacy knowledge and skills, critical thinking skills, evidence-based argumentation, and effective means of communication and sharing of knowledge.

Disciplinary literacy is literacy that becomes an integral part of disciplinary practice rather than a set of general strategies, or tools transplanted into the disciplines to improve reading and writing of disciplinary texts (Moje, 2008). For example, a history teacher who implements disciplinary literacy principles in her classroom might focus on primary document analysis by teaching her students how to use sourcing, contextualization, and corroboration strategies whereas another history teacher who is using general literacy strategies might ask her students to just find similarities and differences between sources. The outcome in historical thinking, practice, and comprehension of content will be different from teacher to teacher.

Figure 2.2 reflects the elements of disciplinary literacy I espouse throughout the book. It highlights the important components of discipline-specific literacy and the dynamic interrelationships among them. I will continue to examine all of these elements throughout the book. Disciplinary literacy carries CCSS considerations as they both call for reading and understanding complex texts independently and proficiently, identifying and integrating key ideas, citing several pieces of textual evidence to support inferences, comparing and contrasting information, focusing on text-dependent questions, evaluating evidence, and writing focused on argument (Zygouris-Coe, 2012). The CCSS (2010) position literacy in the heart of each discipline and extend the responsibility of literacy development beyond the English language arts classroom. Another shift the CCSS is bringing about is the placement of 10 College and Career Readiness Anchor Standards for Reading and 10 Anchor Standards for Writing for Literacy in History/Social Studies, Science, and Technical Subjects for grades 6–12.

The Standards set requirements not only for English language arts (ELA) but also for literacy in history/social studies, science, and technical subjects. Just as students must learn to read, write, speak, listen, and use language effectively in a variety of content areas, so too must the Standards specify the literacy skills and understandings required for college and career readiness in multiple disciplines. Literacy standards for Grade 6 and above are predicated on teachers of ELA, history/ social studies, science, and technical subjects using their content area expertise to help students meet the particular challenges of reading, writing, speaking, listening, and language in their respective fields. It is important to note that the 6–12 literacy standards in history/social studies, science, and technical subjects are not meant to replace content standards in those areas but rather to supplement them. States may incorporate these standards into their standards for those subjects or adopt them as content area literacy standards.

(The Standards, English Language Arts, para. 5)

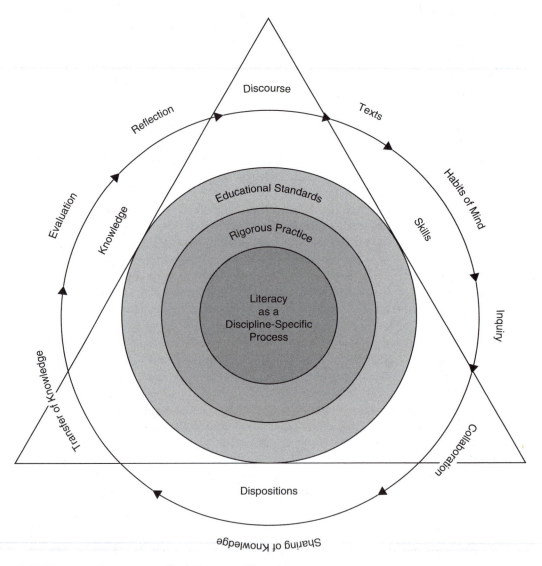

FIGURE 2.2. Literacy as a discipline-specific process.

Source: Model developed by Dr. Vicky Zygouris-Coe, 2014. Image created by UCF Center for Distributed Learning.

So, why develop students' discipline-specific literacy skills? General literacy skills although necessary, are not sufficient to help students master disciplinary content and prepare them for college and life. The CCSS (2010) call for deep reading and learning, content and literacy development in each discipline, and college, career, and workforce readiness. Disciplinary literacy is demanding, complex, and requires much teacher preparation and active student involvement; it requires a shift in how teachers think and practice teaching and learning in content area classrooms.

Think Like An Expert

- Identify multiple points of view on the topic and provide evidence that supports the existence of each point of view. (English Language Arts)
- What strategy, operation, or tools will I use to solve this problem? (Mathematics)
- What scientific problem, or dilemma does this text address? (Science)
- Provide evidence that this document relates to other documents (first-, second-, and third-order) through this theme and narrative. (Social Studies)

Academic Disciplines

The Oxford English Dictionary defines academic discipline as "a branch of learning or scholarly instruction." Each academic discipline has its own unique approach to making sense of the world; each discipline approaches an object or event from a different perspective. Each discipline has its own purpose, focus and unique object of research (e.g., society, human physiology). It also has a body of specialized knowledge related to that object of research, theories and concepts that can organize the specialized knowledge, and specific technical language or terminologies that are used and valued to convey ideas. Last, it has its own requirements to knowing and demonstrating how much one knows in that field, its own practices for studying related topics, standards for what counts as inquiry, evidence and accuracy, forms of communication, and places where they are taught and researched.

There are millions of students who can memorize facts but they cannot apply knowledge to new situations. Teachers need to guide students in developing habits of mind (Costa, 1991; Costa & Kallick, 2000) that are appropriate for each discipline. The term "habits of mind" refers to a combination of attitudes, dispositions, skills, past experiences, and tendencies for formal and informal learning. Habits of mind are essential problem solving skills, thought processes, and behaviors that shape inquiry and encourage independent learning—they are ways of knowing, thinking, and learning. I like to refer to habits of mind as discipline-specific mindsets that are vital to knowing and learning. Students' ways of thinking impact their understanding of disciplinary concepts.

Content area teachers should help students develop discipline-specific habits of mind to the point where they acquire and incorporate them in their thinking inside and outside the classroom. If these specific mindsets become part of students' thinking repertoire, students will internalize specific ways of thinking and understanding and will apply them to problem solving and learning. Instruction or curriculum that ignores sense making will produce students who ignore and lack sense making. Aristotle said, "We are what we repeatedly do. Excellence, then, is not an act but a habit." Within the context of this book, one of the biggest paradigm shifts for content areas teachers is that teaching content area courses in middle and high school grades does not mean focusing on content coverage, but emphasizing the development of students' mindsets, learning processes, ideas, and attitudes towards learning disciplinary content and developing one's own competence. How can teachers facilitate the development of discipline-specific mind-sets that will help students develop deep content and literacy knowledge and skills?

Each discipline has a unique way of thinking about the world and informs the contexts in which students live (Boix Mansilla & Gardner, 1999). Each discipline offers students both content knowledge and ways of knowing, learning, and reasoning specific to the discipline. Before teachers can expect students to embrace, read, learn, and apply academic knowledge, they first have to equip them with certain prerequisite types of knowledge. For example, why is it important that teachers and students understand the structure, focus, and goals of each academic discipline? Why should students learn from disciplinary experts? Why is it important to develop a strong knowledge base for each academic discipline? Why is it important that students learn to read the texts of each discipline like its experts do? Why is it important to learn about and use the inquiry methods of each discipline? Why should students learn the language and forms of communication in each discipline? What do the words deep learning, flexibility, collaboration, and reflection have to do with learning in the academic disciplines? What are core messages from disciplines about students' roles as learners? All of these questions encompass learning and literacy issues in the academic disciplines.

Keep in mind that thinking and learning like a historian will not equip students to think and learn in mathematics, science, literature, or art. Another important distinction is that learning about a discipline and doing the discipline are two different things; for example, learning about science and doing science involves different processes and skills. Adolescents need to be active co-constructors of knowledge instead of passive recipients of facts they don't know what to do with.

Disciplinary literacy will help students learn how complex texts, issues, knowledge and practices are approached and examined in different contexts and subject areas (Lee, 2004; Moje, 2007; Shanahan & Shanahan, 2008). It will guide students in conducting discipline-specific inquiry (i.e., using a range of cognitive, social, and physical practices required for doing discipline-specific thinking and learning, for developing knowledge, and understanding how discipline experts study the world). Inquiry is not something that only mathematicians or scientists do; historians conduct historical inquiry and authors conduct literary inquiry. Each discipline has its unique way of conducting inquiry, conducting investigations, collecting data from multiple sources, forming data-based explanations, and communicating and defending conclusions to peers and others.

Disciplinary literacy is not looking for generalization and "cross-pollination" of certain reading strategies across the disciplines. Instead, it aims to help students understand the role of expertise, inquiry, critical thinking skills, evidence, validation, and discipline-specific practices that promote knowledge development, communication, and evaluation. I like the use of the term discipline-specific practices instead of just discipline-specific skills because practices implies disciplinary investigation requires not only skills, but also knowledge that is specific to each practice.

There are a number of disciplines: for example, social sciences (sociology, psychology, anthropology, economics, social work, education), mathematics, natural and life sciences (biology, chemistry, physiology, physics, astronomy, earth science), arts (fine arts [art, drama, music], theater, foreign language, English language and rhetoric), humanities (history, philosophy, religion, literature), and applied fields (career fields, technology, business). Key types of thinking required to learn in social sciences involve evaluation of ideas and arguments and recognition of bias. Mathematical thinking involves sequential and methodical thinking, logical reasoning, and evaluation of solutions. Natural and life scientists ask a lot of questions, understand processes, identify relationships, and evaluate evidence. Thinking skills for learning in the arts are the ability to express one's ideas, evaluation of others' work, and critique of one's own work. Applied arts require following procedures and processes, making applications, and evaluating decisions. In the following section, I examine the structure of the arts, English language arts, mathematics, science, and social studies, and how disciplinary experts inquire or make sense of the world.

Arts

The arts include several sub-disciplines such as fine arts (art, drama, music, dance), theatre, foreign language, English language, and rhetoric. Art promotes high quality and lifelong learning experiences throughout the lifespan. It connects art to daily life and other disciplines. Artwork is a form of text and a communication medium. Because of the relationship between art and creative thinking, there is a renewed focus on the role of the arts in language arts, mathematics, and science. Nowadays, art and design coupled with Science, Technology, Engineering, and Mathematics (STEM) have resulted in Science, Technology, Engineering, Art, and Mathematics (STEAM). As a result, new programs have been developed to integrate art and design in K–20 education in innovative ways to prepare a new generation of artists and designers who will propel innovation.

Artists are knowledgeable about many subjects. They engage in deconstructing complex visual representation of ideas and use their knowledge of artistic elements to identify main and subordinate ideas and themes in the piece. Artists are keen observers, have good reasoning skills, raise a lot of art-specific questions, compare and contrast artistic element integration across multiple pieces of work, use evidence to support their critiques, and practice argument. Artists believe that art will enable every person to develop the critical thinking, problem solving, and creative and collaborative skills necessary to succeed in life.

Artists focus on the art of critical thinking, critical making, and performing. Deep learning that is transferable to new forms, images, products, performances, or compositions, is a main focus of artists. They engage in the study of the artistic process, the construction of knowledge, and reflection. Creativity and critique are core elements of artistic thinking and habits of mind. Artists create, reflect, analyze, interpret, and evaluate. They select different types of media, techniques, and processes to communicate their ideas, feeling and experiences. Artists strive to involve the audience in their interpretation of human life.

Artists consider a wide range of perspectives and ways to communicate their ideas, feelings and emotions. They study artwork carefully and look for details and facts. They consider the purpose of their work and incorporate style, and historical and cultural context. They describe, analyze, and demonstrate how principles of art and design dominate the work, and consider how factors of time, space, and context influence and give meaning and value to the work of art. They analyze the interplay of artistic, design, and performance elements in the work. Artists read widely and have rich and technical vocabulary knowledge that enables them to draw out of the audience the emotion created and experienced between the artist or performer and the audience. The arts help people understand and connect with the human experience, history, and culture.

Artists demonstrate their knowledge through creating, performing, and creatively and aesthetically challenging the audience to be involved in the artwork, performance, or production. What questions do artists ask? How do they develop and practice artistic inquiry? Sample questions include the following: What do I see? What do I think of the work (i.e., artwork, performance, or production)? What feelings do I have about the work? What is the name of the artist who created the work? What inspired this work? What is the art medium? What is the name of the work? When was it created? How is the work organized? If the art is a musical performance, how did the musician, performer, or composer use harmony, rhythm, texture, color, and form in the piece? If the work is a theater/play performance, what did I think about the play, its direction, the acting, and the use of design elements (i.e., scenery, costumes, lighting, music/sound)? What is the message or story of this work? What artistic elements did the artist use to convey the message? What elements of art are present in the work? What artistic elements stood out? What principles of design did the artist use and how? Does the work hold together visually? Does the work communicate with the viewer? Does the work reflect, imitate, or interpret what people see as real in the world? What mood does this art communicate?

Artists communicate the language of art through their work. They also write artistic critiques and statements that reflect their knowledge about art, interpretation, and judgment of the work. They write in ways that invite the audience to think about their interpretation of the world, history, culture, emotions, and relationships through their work. Their writing connects what their work expresses with the medium it expresses it in. Art, music, and drama teachers want students to be critical thinkers, to develop deep learning, and develop an appreciation of art. They also want the arts to be integrated in other disciplines to better prepare students for the careers of the present and the future.

Quality arts instruction is inquiry-based, makes art relevant and meaningful, fosters reflection, exploration, and problem solving, and helps students see connections between art and everyday life. The arts, design, media and technology, creativity and innovation are all important for postsecondary preparation and lifelong learning. The arts also provide life-changing connections to students who are not otherwise being reached through other curriculum, and valuable opportunities and artistic expression outlets for students with disabilities. Students need quality art education, sequential, standards-based arts curriculum, relevant and rigorous art experiences, and standards-based connections between the arts and other content areas. They also need access to in-school and community arts learning opportunities.

For example, what would students learn by joining a school orchestra, band, or chorus? Aside from learning more about music, instruments, musical and vocal performance, they will also learn more about themselves, about cooperation and collaboration, discipline, rigor, persistence, delivery and artistic elements, and ways to communicate with audiences. What would students learn from theatre classes? They will learn how to improve their verbal and non-verbal comprehension, their understanding of complex texts, including texts in science and mathematics, verbal skills, and their understanding of written material. In addition, they will learn about the importance of attendance, cooperation and collaboration, and personal reflection. Similarly, in a fine art class, students will learn about artistic and design elements, creativity and innovation, expression, argument and reflection, and collaboration. Last, in art classes students will learn about the importance of art for self-expression, communication, creativity, and bridging history, culture, and everyday life.

English Language Arts

English language arts (ELA) as a discipline focuses on developing English language skills and thought processes to construct meaning. English language arts involves reading, writing, spelling, listening, speaking, viewing and reading multimedia, visually representing and creating multimedia, literature study, and the study of the English language. The ELA comprise the vehicles of communication by which people live, work, learn, share, and develop ideas and understanding of the past, present, and future. In terms of content in ELA classes in middle and high schools, ELA includes the ideas, issues, problems, and conflicts found in classical and contemporary literature, and other texts (e.g., technical manuals, magazines, audio, video, media), and culture. In terms of process, ELA includes the skills of reading, writing, speaking, listening, viewing, expressing, and perspective taking. English language arts help people understand cultural, linguistic, and literary heritages, and participate in a democratic society. Through ELA, students learn about the world and each other. For example, through George Orwell's *Animal Farm*, a political satire, students will learn about totalitarianism, and how people deal with power. Through language, they learn how to interact with others, and how to appreciate knowledge and apply it in every facet of life. The goals of ELA are (a) to promote personal, social, occupational, and civic literacy; and (b) to understand and use ELA for personal enjoyment, understanding others' perspectives, communicating with others, accomplishing goals, shaping opinions and attitudes, and developing new knowledge.

English language arts experts seek insights about human experiences. They are curious, flexible, reflective, and persistent. They identify and solve problems, and think analytically and creatively about important concepts and the human experience. They appreciate the linguistic, social and cultural uniquenesses and differences across groups of people, the aesthetic elements of oral, visual, and written texts, and they communicate through printed and visual/auditory texts and media. They are skilled readers, writers, thinkers, and communicators. They have robust vocabularies, are knowledgeable about the structures and patterns of language, and they understand the role of language in fostering a democratic society. They ask critical questions, read between the lines, and interpret texts using evidence from multiple sources. They synthesize information and generate new knowledge.

English language arts experts conduct literary research on issues or interests by generating ideas, questions, and posing problems. They describe and analyze the message (or big idea) of text(s), the form, audience, imagery, tone, and conflict, they problematize interpretation, critically evaluate and appreciate literary works, and communicate their insights in ways that reflect their purpose and audience. Through literacy criticism they may examine an author's writings as a whole or compare various authors' writings on the same topic. They interpret and construct meaning from texts by carefully analyzing text elements and structures, including word meaning, sentence and paragraph structures, rhetorical and literary elements, and types of genres. They read a wide range of print and non-print texts (fiction, nonfiction, classic, and contemporary works) to develop an understanding of texts, of themselves, of cultures, and the world; they also read to acquire new information, respond to the demands of the workplace, and for personal fulfillment. They write to understand and demonstrate what they know, express themselves, inform, entertain, share experiences and emotions, persuade, and construct and share meaning. English language arts processes and strategies also play an important role in the learning of mathematics, science, social studies, and learning, in general. Reading, writing, speaking, listening, viewing and visually representing are essential forms of communication, are powerful life skills, and sources of pleasure, understanding, and fulfillment.

Authors and literacy critics construct meaning as they read, write, speak, listen, view, and visually represent; they analyze literal and figurative meanings. They reflect on, and make connections with, their own and others' life experiences, with other texts, and interactions with other readers and writers; they write and communicate with others about important cultural, social, and life issues. They use inquiry, reflection, creativity, and criticism for learning, enjoyment, persuasion, and exchange of information. The study of argument plays a fundamental role in English language arts. Argumentation is vital for the development of thinking and discussion of issues. Argumentation requires synthesizing data and viewpoints across diverse sources of information (written, visual, qualitative data). Literature affects us emotionally, intellectually, and esthetically.

Authors and literary critics ask questions like: Why do people respond the way they do to experiences, events, and circumstances? What is the relationship between works people have read and their view of the world and life? What symbols and patterns operate on a universal scale? What is the relationship between culture and the society from which a literary work came from? How do these influences affect the literature? How do authors and artists represent the effects of urbanization forces on family life and cultural traditions? What personal or political events influence the writer? What are the text's underlying assumptions and what biases and misconceptions does it include?

Many teachers complain about middle and high school students lacking (a) the motivation to read classical literature; (b) the vocabulary to read and comprehend narrative and informational texts; (c) the persistence to continue to read when meaning is implicit; and (d) the writing and communication skills necessary for them to learn and succeed in secondary grades and beyond. Several students view ELA as a boring and irrelevant subject. They do not see ELA as a means to understand past and present human experience, and they complain about the amount of material they have to read. Teaching ELA without engaging students in meaningful, authentic, and culturally relevant reading, writing, and communication activities will continue to result in negative attitudes toward it. Students need to be active participants in gathering information from various sources, asking appropriate questions, analyzing it, making connections with real-life situations, discussing it with others, using evidence to interpret it, and communicate it orally and in writing.

What does English language arts have to do with real life? What can students get out of reading *Their Eyes Were Watching God* by Zora Neal Hurston (1937)? Many may see it as a book about a woman who went through four marriages; so what does this have to do with adolescents in the 21st century? What connections could they make and what insights could they gain about themselves and the world? Teachers can guide students in discovering several big ideas in this classic: the power of the personal story to inspire us and connect us with others, the importance of discovering your passion and dreams, that leadership comes from within and not from a title, character counts, the importance of finding your own story, and identifying characteristics and qualities of leadership.

Students need to be asking critical questions about texts, ideas, and people; for example: What is the power of story? What is the power of people? Why are some types of people under-represented in literature? What are the effects of abuse of power on people? What would building an American Dream for the future look like? What causes civil disobedience? What is the role of leadership throughout history? How have various people made a difference in the world? Will the power of stories and poetry be lost if people do not listen?

Mathematics

Mathematics is one of the foundational areas of human knowledge. Mathematical thinking is not only important for developing mathematical knowledge in school; it also supports science, technology, economic life and overall development in an economy and society. Mathematics as a source of subject matter includes Algebra, Geometry and Topology, and Applied Mathematics (Probability and Statistics, Computational, and Physical Sciences). Mathematicians enjoy the challenge of a problem, find beauty in a pattern, and think about proof, knowledge, reality, elegance, truth, and ambiguity. They problem solve, make connections, question assumptions, consider extreme examples, argue and reason, represent, and communicate in the form of proof, create new examples, and question everything! Mathematicians try special cases and look at examples (specializing), look for patterns and relationships (generalizing), they predict relationships and results (conjecturing), and they find and communicate reasons for why something is true (convincing).

Mathematicians make it possible to buy things online and secure your privacy when you shop online; they contribute to animated film creation, space exploration, and robotics. They play a key role in analyzing data and designing models in biology, technology, and finance. Through emerging technologies, mathematicians continue to touch everyone in the world. Mathematicians are expert pattern makers—they explore the meaning of everyday problems by sorting out the pieces and making sense of how they are connected. They use the mathematical tools of systematic observation, study, experimentation, abstraction, symbolic representation, and symbolic manipulation (Shoenfeld, 1994). Mathematicians are flexible, curious, and fluent thinkers; they are keen observers of connections between mathematical problems and concepts, they gather information, and they seek patterns, logical explanations, and different ways to represent the problem. Mathematicians are reflective in their thinking, and are prepared to solve real problems even when the problems lack strategy or obvious solutions—they are persistent and systematic thinkers.

Today's technologically advanced culture uses mathematics as one of the main ways of making sense of the world around it. What is math for? Where do numbers come from? How big is infinity? Where do parallel lines meet? Is there a formula for everything? Can a butterfly's wings actually cause a hurricane? Can mathematicians create an unbreakable code? How are the digital calling centers in India affecting jobs in the US? How is urbanization affecting agricultural supply and demand? Can math predict the future? What shape is the universe? What is symmetry? How can math help people around the world who do not have access to clean water? What is the relationship between supply and demand for essential human goods (e.g., food, clothing) and the business they generate in an economy? What predictions can people make about life expectancy based on race, gender, lifestyle, and dietary choices of US adolescents? What does math have to do with the national debt?

Here is an example of how a mathematician problem-solves about real life problems. Let's take sports: Who was the better basketball player in the 2011–12 NBA season? Heat forward LeBron James or Knicks center Tyson Chandler? To answer this question most people would tally the points each player made during the season. But a mathematician would also gather information about the points they missed; he or she would compare the two players in many ways, from total points scored (equations) to percent of shots made (percents) to points per game/minute (unit rates and averages) to determine each player's efficiency rating. Mathematics is all about solving real life problems and applications. According to the CCSS (2010) (see Standards of Mathematical Practice, Mathematical Practice 4—http://www.corestandards.org/math/practice), "Mathematically proficient students can apply the mathematics they know to solve problems arising in everyday life, society, and the workplace."

When some students think of mathematics they feel lost, they think that math textbooks don't make any sense, that mathematics is an endless collection of definitions, formulas, and theorems that one should memorize. Many also think that math is irrelevant to everyday life. Learning mathematics with understanding is essential; students must learn mathematics with deep understanding and they must continue to build new knowledge from experience and prior knowledge (National Council of Teachers of Mathematics, 2009). In school, the mathematics curriculum entails (a) Number and Operations with Procedural Fluency, (b) Algebra, (c) Geometry and Measurement, (d) Data Analysis, Statistics, and Probability, and (e) Calculus. Mathematical thinking is not thinking about mathematics; school math typically involves learning procedures to solve standard math problems. Mathematical thinking is a function of particular operations, processes, and dynamics (Burton, 2004).

Mathematical thinking involves problem solving, metacognition, and sense making. Mathematicians do not just memorize procedures; they seek solutions. They don't memorize formulas; they explore patterns. They don't just do endless exercises; they formulate conjectures. Learning about and doing mathematics in grades 6–12 must take place in classrooms in which problem solving, reasoning, connections, communication, conceptual understanding, sense-making, and procedural fluency are all developed simultaneously, purposefully, and meaningfully. Teachers need to model making real connections and asking real problems and questions. If teachers' goals are to create independent thinkers and doers of mathematics, they should also encourage students to ask good questions about what they notice and wonder about.

Science

The word "science" comes from the Latin word "Scientia," meaning knowledge. Science as a discipline seeks to understand the physical world through systematic study, observation, experimentation, and scientific practice. The Next Generation Science Standards (NGSS) (2012) identify four major science domains: (a) physical sciences, (b) life sciences, (c) earth and space sciences, and (d) engineering, technology, and application of science. Scientists are not concerned with isolated bits of information; they use an objective, logical, and replicable approach to understanding the principles and forces that operate in the natural universe; they focus on contemplative observation, describing, explaining, and predicting natural phenomena. They employ an ongoing process of observation, hypothesis, data collection, experimentation, analysis and interpretation, and evaluation.

Scientists ask a lot of questions about how things happen in the world, they seek and use empirically based evidence, they develop and use models, they use mathematics, computational thinking, and technology, they engage in arguments from evidence, and they communicate information. They use logic and look at things from an empirical point of view where data can be verified. Scientific theories can be tested by experiment or by added observation. In the process of explaining the natural world, scientists conduct scientific investigations that are ongoing, resulting in new questions as old ones are answered.

Scientists ask questions like: What is the difference between scientific facts and other facts? What does science have the power to do? What makes certain ecosystems special? How do medical advancements improve human life? How can people best preserve life on the planet? What are the implications of embryonic stem cell research? What are ethical consequences of cloning? Why should scientists adhere to scientific ethics and safety? What are the effects of increased life expectancy on health care costs? How can people build more sustainable, innovative, and equitable communities in the 21st century? What are the liabilities of cities that are overburdened with skyscrapers in an energy scarce future? How does nanotechnology help produce better sunscreen protection, protect my sunglasses against unwanted scratches, and make it possible for me to store hundreds of songs on my MP3 player? How is nanotechnology mimicking nature's nanotechnology for the purpose of improving everyday life?

Science offers an understanding of human life, of the universe, and of people's place in it. Scientists think differently about what happens in the world. For example, how can deforestation effect world climate changes? Scientists not only examine the benefits of planned deforestation but also its harmful effects on everyday life. For example, scientists make connections between the rapid rate of deforestation and global warming—how? Trees are the most important aspect of the planet for the environment, humans, and animals; they act as filters of carbon dioxide. Deforestation causes soil erosion, disruption of the water cycle, loss of biodiversity, flooding and drought, and climate change. Why climate change? Global warming is largely caused by carbon dioxide emissions into the atmosphere. When 50% of the planet's tree cover has been removed due to human activity, larger quantities of carbon dioxide are released into the atmosphere. Scientists examine an issue such as this from various perspectives and help us to understand why educating the public about not starting fires, replacing what trees are missing, and monitoring legal logging, etc. are important steps toward protecting biodiversity and human existence on this planet.

Science, in school, is often viewed by students as a collection of boring and isolated facts one has to memorize; facts are never isolated—scientists find connections among facts through the process of discovery and present them into a coherent understanding of the natural world. Scientists are in the business of figuring things out—discovery is their "bread and butter." They look for connections between the past, present, and future, they develop new technologies that treat diseases, improve life on the planet, provide information about the human body, the foods people produce and eat, the air they breathe, and the places they live in. The job of a scientist is never finished; their contributions expand human knowledge of the universe and create new questions for future investigations.

Students need to experience science as a living, ongoing, exciting, and highly relevant body of knowledge and process of making sense of the world. Students need to learn about science and they also need to do science—they need to read, write, and think like scientists. If students do not experience the value and excitement of science, they will continue to view it as a set of isolated, meaningless facts they have to learn to pass the exam/course and move on.

Social Studies

Social studies as a term refers to the integrated study of social sciences and humanities to understand individuals, groups, and societies and promote civic competence (National Council for the Social Studies, 1993). Social sciences as sources of subject matter for the social studies include geography, history, economics, political science, anthropology, sociology, and psychology. For the purpose of this section, I will focus on history. "History is an *effort* to *reconstruct* the past to discover what people *thought* and *did* and how their beliefs and actions continue to *influence* human life" (McKay, Hill, & Buckler, 1992, p. 4). Historians are involved in an ongoing scientific process of collecting, interpreting facts and evidence from multiple sources (primary and secondary), and presenting large amounts of information in meaningful and organized formats. They often specialize in the study of a specific area, idea, person, place, trend, time in history, or a combination of the above. To think historically involves weighing much information from various sources and integrating it into a comprehensive explanation.

For historians, the past is their laboratory in which they collect, test, and interpret theories dealing with current issues and problems. Historians try to understand who humans are and how they came to be. Historians study human experience to meet the present and the future; they try to understand the difference between the past and conjecture and the complexity of historical cause; they distrust simple, unsupported answers, they question the stereotypes of others, they study character, ideas, and exploitation. History is an inquiry-based enterprise; historians often search for gaps, for what is missing in history. They read, research, question, and make connections across multiple sources of information. They study voluminous amounts of primary sources (e.g., journal articles, diaries, letters, and photographs) and secondary sources (e.g., textbooks), share their insights with other historians and write, publish, and disseminate their work.

When some students think of history, they think of loads of facts, dates, names, and events that often seem irrelevant and even unnecessary. Most of the time students cram a lot of information a few days before a history test; they make flash cards of dates, events, and people, and quiz each other on a series of facts. To many students, the words "history" and "exciting" do not go together; to them, history is an endless process of memorizing facts instead of an exciting inquiry or investigation. They believe that whichever aspect of history they are studying about, it tells a single, isolated story, that teachers and textbooks are neutral sources of accurate information, and that their own judgments about the past are pointless.

But historians think about history differently. They view themselves as detectives who do not know for sure what happened at a particular time in human history, what it means to different groups of people. They are involved in the process of searching, digging out information, weighing and analyzing conflicting information, and trying to figure out what really happened. Historians are involved in historical inquiry instead of endless and meaningless memorization. For example, what was the economic effect of the US–Afghanistan war on the US? If students are examining primary documents on the topic, they need to be evaluating information. For example: Is this information accurate? Who is the author and what do you know about him or her? What evidence can you use from the textbook and related primary sources you have examined on the topic that supports or contradicts this message?

Historians are masterful at asking essential questions; they ask many critical questions that are not only applicable to a particular time in history but also to all of humanity in any given place or time. Core types of questions involve: What happened? When did it happen? Who was involved? How and why did it happen? Sample specific questions include: How did civilizations rise? What causes the fall of empires? How did different political systems evolve? What economic systems did people create to sustain a complex civilization? How did civilizations like the Greeks produce magnificent cultures? Are there any similarities between the Holocaust and the Rwanda genocides? How will the rapidly escalating urbanization of the 21st century affect life as people know it? How is technological innovation promoting or inhibiting new forms of collaborations and partnerships? Why do nations go to war? What causes revolutions? How difficult is it to preserve civilizations? What can be done to better human life?

Historical thinking matters not only for understanding the past, but also for preparing people for the challenges they face as citizens in the present. Participation in everyday life means that people have to evaluate information critically. How many students do you know of who hold that view? How many teachers do you know of who reflect that view in their instruction? Historians do because it will help us to understand complex issues of today and tomorrow. Students should learn how to use the language and tools historians use to study the past, and extend this knowledge to make connections between the past and their own lives. How can history teachers develop lesson plans that do not stand alone as distinct pieces of a puzzle but over time help students identify and connect the dots, and develop historical understanding, thinking, and literacy? Thinking historically does not call for collection of large amounts of facts, but for critical inquiry, discrimination, and informed or evidence-based judgment (Spoehr & Spoehr, 1994; Wineburg, 2001).

Each academic discipline has unique goals, foci, discourse, texts, and specific inquiry tools and processes. Figure 2.3 opposite shows the unique differences between the four types of thinking and also the similar ingredient found in each discipline. Each discipline is a body of knowledge and a process; each one has a system of acquiring and developing knowledge.

Disciplinary thinking is thinking within, about, and for the structures of a given discipline; it is metacognitive and expert thinking that strives for conceptual understanding. Teaching students to think beyond the basic facts is a challenge for teachers across content areas.

College, Career, and Workforce Connections

- The ability to think systematically and logically is an important skill for college, career, and workforce success. Problem solving, analytical thinking, reading, writing, speaking, listening, and collaboration skills are part of work, learning, and life in any setting, career, and context.
- Support, mentoring, rigorous standards and instruction, and assessment are necessary for preparing students for professional careers and lifelong learning.

- Physical skills (e.g., wellness, appearance, legible writing, note-taking) are important for success.
- *Although accounting deals with applied mathematics and statistics, it is called the "language of business" and uses a distinct professional vocabulary. Learning accounting is like learning to master algebraic "story problems" that are written in a foreign language! For students to succeed in accounting, they must have a solid background in math and an aptitude for understanding technical language* (Robin Roberts, Chair, Accounting, University of Central Florida).

Why Position Literacy in the Disciplines?

Because each discipline is unique, it requires a different approach and set of learning strategies and practices. It is important to clarify that although general literacy strategies are necessary, they are insufficient for knowing and learning in the academic disciplines. Teachers need to understand the structure of each discipline, its content and literacy demands, and the way students learn how to learn and demonstrate mastery within and across disciplines.

For example, from the students who do develop disciplinary knowledge and skills, many are still unable to use that knowledge proficiently. What does it mean to know literature, mathematics, science, or history? When asked this question, most people think of certain topics or procedures. But in each discipline, what one does to understand and problem-solve related problems also matters. Knowing facts and concepts does not equip one to use disciplinary knowledge effectively; one would also need to use disciplinary practices and transfer that knowledge in new settings. Representing a problem or issue, problem solving, using the language, concepts, and ideas of the discipline, providing articulated and evidence-based reasoning and proof or evidence, communicating, arguing, generalizing, or recognizing patterns, are all examples of disciplinary practices.

Literary Thinking

Asking Questions, Paying Attention to Details
Examining Multiple Sources of Evidence
Determining Relationships
Comprehension of Complex Texts, Abstract Ideas, & Concepts
Analysis, Evaluation, & Interpretation
Criticism & Synthesis of Information
Drawing Logical & Accurate Inferences
Communicate Persuassively & Reflectively

Mathematical Thinking

Asking Questions & Identifying Problems
Problem Solving for Comprehension & Precision
Mathematical Tools & Problem Solving Methods
Analysis & Interpretations
Reasoning, Arguing, Justifying, & Proving
Creating Examples & Viable Arguments
Problem Solving for Communication
Express Thinking Systematically, Rationally, & Reflectively

Common Elements

Language
Texts
Inquiry & Metacognition
Critical Thinking Skills
Conceptual Understanding
Persistence
Collaboration
Communication
Evidence-Based Argumentation
Reflection

Scientific Thinking

Asking Questions & Defining Problems
Developing & Using Models
Planning and Carrying Out Problems
Analyzing and Interpreting Data
Using Mathematical, ICT, & Computational Thinking
onstructing Explanation & Designing Solutions
Evidence-Based Argumentation
Obtaining, Evaluating, & Communicating Information

Historical Thinking

Data-Gathering/Organizing/Processing Skills
Chronological Thinking
Historical Comprehension
Historical Heuristics
(sourcing, contextualization, corroborations, comparative thinking)
Historical Research Capbilities
Historical Analysis & Interpretantion
Evidence-Based Decision Making & Argumentation

FIGURE 2.3. Characteristics of disciplinary thinking and common elements.

Information matters, but disciplinary practices help develop knowledge—what teachers and students do with information and to what extent it creates knowledge matters more (Langer, 2012).

Students in secondary schools go from course to course each day without associating with any of them—they don't learn how to examine a document like a historian would or evaluate the accuracy of a solution to a problem like a mathematician; they do not think critically about text or synthesize concepts across texts. For many, their out-of-school literacies are more important than their in-school ones. Many view school learning as boring or irrelevant to their lives; just something they have to do to graduate and move on. Yet, the "writing on the wall" is clear: Teachers need to foster the development of adolescents who are competent readers, writers, and thinkers in all disciplines.

So, if teachers espouse the disciplinary literacy learning view, will students upon high school graduation go on to be experts in different content areas? No, they are not going to; an expert is someone who has extensive knowledge or ability that is based on education and research, intense experience through practice, or occupation in a particular field of study. What teachers aim to do though this approach is help adolescents become critical thinkers, not experts, and equip them with sufficient knowledge, experience, skills, and tools to continue to learn in college, work, and life.

I like Howard Gardner's (1999) perspective on the need for disciplinary focus in later grades. According to him, basic reading, writing, and mathematics skills are a prerequisite to entering the disciplinary fields. Facts are necessary for thinking about a topic but can only be used well if they are interconnected in meaningful ways. A student can know facts about a subject but have no disciplinary understanding. Understanding is formed to the extent one can transfer and apply knowledge to a new situation—how are teachers going to do it? Do they have to sacrifice content for process and skills and vice versa? How can they address the many complex challenges associated with teaching and learning for success in school and beyond? What does it mean to be literate in English language arts, mathematics, science, social studies, and other disciplines?

If you are going to teach students to think carefully and critically about what they are reading and learning in your discipline, you must be reflective about your own instruction (Noddings 2007, 2008). You might have heard the characterization of the US curriculum as "a mile high and an inch deep." Yes, there is a need to cover content in secondary classes, but there is a greater need to learn it and know what to do with it. Shallow instruction will produce shallow results.

I cannot count the times I have heard content area teachers tell me, "I don't have time for this stuff; I have so much content to cover." The stuff they are referring to is applications, hands-on learning, collaborative inquiry, discipline-specific strategies, and opportunities for students to reflect and puzzle over what they are learning. Many teachers respond that way because they are pressured to cover more content to prepare students for standardized testing. Covering more content will not result in improved student learning. Content is important, but the practices and processes are vital for students developing content knowledge. It does not take much preparation to give multiple-choice exams at the end of each unit, or ask the students to read each assigned chapter on their own and answer the questions at the end of the chapter. How will your students learn in your class? What will you do to ensure that they will learn? How do you know that they learned the material? And, what will you do if they do not learn?

For teachers to develop students disciplinary knowledge and literacy, they have to "teach on the diagonal"—a term coined by Cheryl Geisler (1994) which means that for specialized academic learning to take place one must use the discipline-specific habits of thinking to develop understanding of subject-matter and build disciplinary knowledge (see Figure 2.4).

What does this mean for you as a content area teacher? It means that you must design your instruction and your learning environment in such a way that when, for example, students come

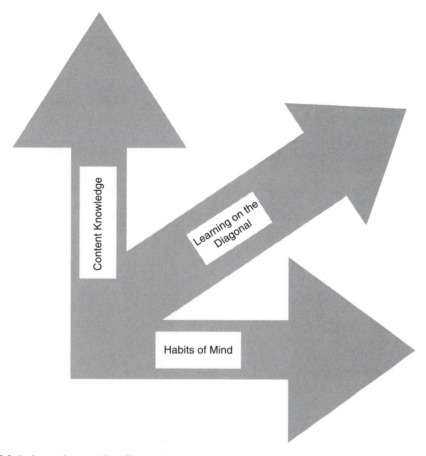

FIGURE 2.4. Learning on the diagonal.

Source: From Cheryl Geisler (1994). *Academic literacy and the nature of expertise: reading, writing, and knowing in academic philosophy*. London, UK: Psychology Press.

to your biology class, they "breathe," think about, speak, read, write about, and "taste" biology. In order for them to develop conceptual understanding of biology ideas, concepts, questions, and problems, they will need to be taught and work "on the diagonal." In other words, they will need to develop knowledge in two dimensions: (a) in knowledge of core concepts, ideas, and problems of biology; and (b) in ways of thinking, knowing, learning about, problem solving strategies, and doing biology. So, when students are asked to select two genetic disorders they are interested in and determine which one will affect the quality of people's life the most, they will have to use biologists' habits of thinking on the horizontal dimension of the model and their knowledge of the topic to evaluate the severity of the effects of each genetic disorder on people.

The statistics I reviewed in Chapter 1 show that a number of elements have to change if educators and other stakeholders are going to help adolescents meet the demands of the academic disciplines in school and beyond. Learning how to think is not just a college requirement; it is a life skill. According to the Bureau of Labor Statistics (see www.bls.gov/emp/home.htm for employment projections), of the most demanding occupations in the next decade or so, only a couple will require a college education. Occupational success will require an ability to make decisions independently, the ability to think carefully, flexibility, ability to collaborate with others, problem solving, intellectual and personal honesty, and persistence.

Digital Literacies

- QR Codes: http://www.qrcode.com/en/. Use QR codes to locate documents, link resources and solutions to problems, share text, web addresses, phone numbers, and connect to class or school website.
- ThingLink: http://www.thinglink.com. A tool for creating interactive images that support a variety of multimedia. Users can create multiple "hot spots" on specific parts of an image to build multimedia definitions that include video, images, audio, web links and more.
- Khan Academy: http://www.khanacademy.org. Khan Academy is an organization on a mission. It is a not-for-profit with the goal of changing education for the better by providing a free world-class education for anyone anywhere.

Disciplinary Literacy Learning Principles

The following are fundamental learning principles for promoting content and literacy knowledge and skills in each discipline. They include information on developing a classroom culture that values all students and promotes disciplinary, collaborative, and reflective inquiry, accountable talk, and learning. They also provide important elements for the role of the teacher and the student, and the role of rigorous instruction for development of academic knowledge and practice.

Principle 1: Learning is a Socially Constructed Process

Learning does not take place in a vacuum. People learn from and with others (Vygotsky, 1962, 1978). Teachers, students, peers, tasks, texts, processes, and social contexts, all play a role in the learning process. Literacy is also a social process. Social processes shape social languages "that are used to enact, recognize, and negotiate socially situated identities and to carry out different socially situated activities" (Gee, 2000, p. 413).

From this perspective, learning and literacy are understood only when they are viewed in relation to others. The classroom environment is foundational to student learning; student learning will not occur when the student is experiencing fear or stress (Goswami, 2008). Students need to learn in classrooms where they can trust their teacher and peers, where they experience support, are appreciated and encouraged to take risks, participate in decision-making, engage in problem-solving, and experience competence (Tschannen-Moran & Barr, 2004). Students read more when they are positively motivated, meaningfully engaged, curious, and feel a sense of self-efficacy (Wigfield, Wilde, Baker, Fernandez-Fein, & Scher, 1996).

The classroom should be set up in a flexible seating arrangement that promotes student–student discussions, cooperation, collaboration, and problem solving. The processes of creating and communicating knowledge are inherently connected. Collaboration gives students an experience in how disciplinary experts and professionals work and learn. In content area classrooms knowledge is co-constructed and reconstructed by discourse (norms, rules, grammar, syntax, vocabulary) among teachers and students. Students need to discuss, reason, argue, and support assertions, solutions, and ideas in every classroom. Learning should be practiced and shaped through accountable talk (students using norms, responses to problems, and reasoning that are appropriate for each discipline) (Michaels, O'Connor, Hall, & Resnick; 2002). "Accountable talk" is a term coined by the University of Pittsburg, it is talk that reflects students' understanding of language, vocabulary, and concepts read or discussed in class, participation in co-construction of meaning, and monitoring of meaning as it is molded from student to student in class. Accountable talk is respectful of everyone's ideas. In classrooms where accountable talk is practiced, everyone is expected to participate actively, listen attentively, and expand on each other's ideas (Zygouris-Coe, 2012).

Content area classrooms should be culturally responsive student- and knowledge-centered learning communities that facilitate disciplinary discourse, promote shared meanings of knowledge and literacy, language, accountability, reflective inquiry, and learning. Collaborative inquiry fosters critical thinking skills, problem-solving skills, motivation, and shared accountability for learning. Inquiry, experimentation, communication, collaboration, accountability, and reflection should be classroom staples, or routines.

Principle 2: Teacher as Mentor, Student as Apprentice

According to the situated cognition, or situated learning theory perspective, learning is situated in authentic activities, context, and culture. According to these theorists, usable knowledge is gained in environments that reflect the way the knowledge will be used in real life, provide learners with authentic activities, modeling of expert behavior and processes and scaffolding, promote collaboration and reflection. Lauren Resnick (1987), Jean Lave (1988), Lave and Wenger (1991), and Brown, Collins and Duguid (1989) have all introduced the concept of cognitive apprenticeship as an instructional tool. Resnick (1987) proposed that "bridging apprenticeships" could bridge the gap between classroom learning and real-life applications of the knowledge in the workplace. Brown, Collins and Duguid's (1989) research identified common characteristics of successful models of instruction including: apprenticeship, collaboration, reflection, coaching, multiple practice and articulation (McLellan, 1991). They proposed a model of cognitive apprenticeships, to "enculturate students into authentic practices through activity and social interaction," based on the successful and traditional apprenticeship model (Brown, Collins, & Duguid, 1989, p. 37). Lave and Wagner (1991) explained that in a community of practice, according to the cognitive apprenticeship model, the apprentice will move from an observer to a fully participating agent over time.

A community of practice is a group of people who share similar interests in a particular area. For example, in a mathematics content area classroom, when implementing the cognitive apprenticeship model, students will learn with their teacher (and peers) about mathematics, and over time, will be doing mathematics. In my view, apprenticeship is key to student learning in the disciplines and preparation for college, career, and the workforce. The CCSS (2010) present not only what students need to know in grades 6–12 but also what they need to be able to do to succeed in school and beyond. Deep learning and transfer of knowledge will not happen by just doing the basics, telling students what to do without presenting them with models, support, and guidance, teachers delivering content, and students passively absorbing what they can from it.

As a content area teacher, you have the choice to create the learning environment you wish to have in your classroom. There are many factors that will affect creating a culture of learning apprenticeship. Figure 2.5 highlights the key factors that will influence it. As you can see, teacher and student factors play an important role. For example, your pedagogical content knowledge (PCK) (Shulman, 1987) about your subject matter and also about how to present it in a way students can learn it and your literacy knowledge will determine what you do and how you do it to support students' content and literacy needs in your discipline. In this model, I included

FIGURE 2.5. Teacher–student apprenticeship.

Source: Model developed by Dr. Vicky Zygouris-Coe, 2014. Image created by UCF Center for Distributed Learning.

TPACK, which means, technological pedagogical knowledge (a concept coined by Mishra & Koehler, 2006) for the purpose of including technology.

Your expectations about students will affect how you relate with each student in your class. Do you believe that all students can and want to learn? Do you believe that students from diverse backgrounds and even those who have had a history of school failure can really learn? Do you have high and clear expectations and do you provide instruction that will enable them to meet those standards? What standards and criteria do you have for gauging students' progress? Is your classroom environment safe, risk-free, and motivating?

Another factor that will affect your decision to implement an apprenticeship learning model is how you perceive your role as a teacher: Do you see yourself as the sole dispenser of knowledge or as a facilitator of student learning? And, how will you design your instruction to support content and literacy learning in your classroom? Effective classroom instruction requires much planning; it is rigorous, explicit, scaffolded, and assessment-based instruction. Scaffolding refers to the support and guidance you will provide to your students to help reach a higher level of learning (Bruner, 1975, 1986; Vygotsky, 1978); your expertise matters to students. In what ways will you help students to develop the habits of thinking necessary for them to read, comprehend, learn, and apply discipline-specific knowledge? What activities will you create to meaningfully engage students in learning and motivate them to want to learn more? What role will students play in the process? Will you examine their interests, goals, background content and literacy knowledge and skills? What discipline-specific strategies will you use to help them read, talk, write, and inquire like the experts in your discipline? What will you do to examine their beliefs about learning in your discipline and how will you explain to them the role of apprenticeship in your classroom? And, how will you know that students are learning? What will you do to monitor, provide more support, and assess student learning? Rigorous, relevant, and engaging instruction is a must for disciplinary learning and preparation for college, career, and the workforce.

Principle 3: Content and Literacy Knowledge Develop in Tandem

In this chapter, I have examined the different ways disciplinary knowledge is developed, communicated, and shared in various disciplines and the habits of mind necessary for subject-matter inquiry and learning. Developing knowledge about each discipline also requires discipline-specific literacy skills for reading the texts of the discipline, writing, talking, investigating, reasoning, and representing ideas, concepts, questions, and issues associated with disciplinary standards and content requirements. In my view, disciplinary literacy is "cemented" in each discipline; mathematicians read, write, talk, and problem-solve differently than historians (and vice versa).

For example, in mathematics students might be involved in the following process of problem solving: identifying the problem, translating it into mathematical knowledge, listing essential and unknown information, coming up with a plan (and steps to solve it), solving the problem, comparing the accuracy of the solution to the problem, and reflecting on the whole process. On the other hand, a historian might problem solve about examining a historical argument in the following way: identifying the author's main argument, locating and evaluating the evidence the author offers to persuade them, evaluating the logic of the author's conclusion, identifying examples and contradictions, and comparing accuracy and credibility of evidence, with the author's view and other sources of information on the topic.

Reading, vocabulary, comprehension, writing, speaking and listening skills should not be taught or learned in isolation from disciplinary learning. Students need to learn from rigorous curricula, interact with print and non-print complex texts, and have teachers who will guide them in developing deep conceptual understanding of content and the literacies that support it.

Principle 4: Students Engage in Discipline-Specific Inquiry Learning

The terms *inquiry, critical thinking, reflective thinking,* and *problem solving* have been used to describe the *process* by which individuals find solutions to problems through reflection. Problem solving is both a way to organize and connect existing knowledge and to acquire new information. In other words, students do not first learn facts and then engage in problem solving. Instead, they use knowledge they have acquired and add new nuances to it, such as facts and concepts, as they engage in problem solving. The purpose of teaching and learning is to get students thinking about, and applying, their knowledge. All teachers want to hear and see their students' ideas, see them provide evidence for their assertions, and hear their reasons, hypotheses, interpretations, questions, and theories as they analyze and interpret information. Instruction that engages students in reflective inquiry equips them with learning knowledge and develops reflective learning tools that will serve them well with their own metacognition.

The Gradual Release of Responsibility Model (GRRM) (Pearson & Gallagher, 1983), depicts the instructional cycle during which students learn new knowledge and skills and gradually assume increased responsibility for learning. According to the model (see Figure 2.6), students gradually progress from situations in which the teacher takes all the responsibility for their successful completion of a task to situations where students take partial and later on total responsibility for learning and transfer of knowledge (Duke & Pearson, 2002). This model describes the processes, roles, and steps but depending on the task, it can play out over a day, week, month, or a year.

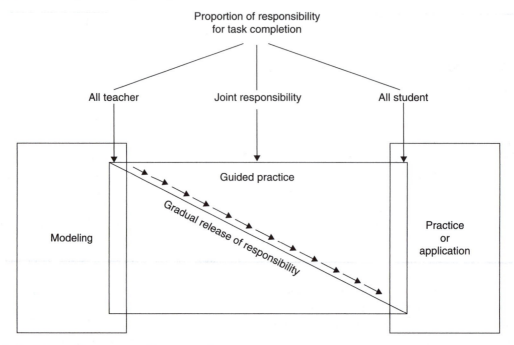

FIGURE 2.6. The Gradual Release of Responsibility Model.

Source: Reprinted from Pearson, P. D., & Gallagher, M. C., The instruction of reading comprehension, *Contemporary Educational Psychology, 8*, 317–344, Copyright 1983, with permission from Elsevier.

For example, an ELA teacher might decide to teach students how to conduct a document analysis. She begins by explaining what the purpose of this analysis is and why it is important to their understanding of the topic. She also describes the Document Analysis Strategy they will be using for analyzing the text, and explains the steps she wants them to take (modeling phase). Next, she models the process and asks the students to observe her as she is using the strategy with a document they read last week. Then, the teacher and the students work on an example together (guided practice phase). During guided practice she asks questions (What is the subject of this document?), offers clues and reminders (How about the audience? Have you located that, yet? What is the audience? How about the theme and main idea? What specific evidence do you have from the text about the purpose of this document?), and models the process again as needed. Why would this teacher use this strategy for analyzing this document? The strategy she chose to involve students in analyzing the document reflects her discipline's structure and goals. ELA deals with identifying the speaker/author and their purpose for writing the text, analyzing the occasion, setting, and format of texts, theme and main idea, and whether the author's purpose for writing this piece was to describe, inform, or persuade.

Direct explanation provides students with clear and direct instruction; cognitive modeling allows students to see and listen to how the teacher thought about the problem/task, what decisions she made (and why); and, scaffolding provides support for learning. After she monitors the guided practice, students are ready to try it on their own (practice and application phase). Collaborative learning opportunities will help students to discuss, problem solve, negotiate, reflect with their peers, and apply their learning. Independent practice will allow students to apply learning in new ways. The GRRM is not a linear model; students can move back and forth as needed. The GRRM can be used in the content area classroom to facilitate the development of knowledge, habits of mind, and discipline-specific strategies and promote transfer of knowledge.

Classrooms that operate through discipline-specific inquiry are classrooms where students learn by doing mathematics, history, art, or science. Students attend to disciplinary knowledge, teachers attend to student background knowledge and misconceptions related to inquiry, and teachers engage students in doing inquiry; they create opportunities for them to reflect and learn about knowledge development in each discipline (Donovan, Bransford, & Pellegrino, 1999). Students need to read varied print and non-print texts in each discipline, critically analyze and further explore ideas, concepts, questions, and insights, and share their understanding of text with others. They also need opportunities to defend and elaborate their thinking about texts and ideas, apply, evaluate and reflect on their learning, synthesize ideas, and express evidence-based argumentation in speech and in writing. Discipline-specific inquiry also involves knowledge, collaboration, accountable talk, metacognition, and reflection.

Principle 5: Assessment to Drive Instruction, Instruction to Drive Assessment

Assessment is an integral part of teaching and learning; it guides teacher practice and student learning. In today's content area classrooms there is a shift from "read the chapter and answer the questions at the end of it," to "show what you have learned." Effective instructional decisions are based on ongoing assessment. Teachers should use multiple types of formal and informal assessment of student progress and data to plan instruction. Formative assessment is ongoing, authentic and classroom-based, and informal; examples include observations, informal writing, problem solving, strategy use, and student generated responses. Summative assessment is more formal and it usually occurs at certain times, such as at the end of a unit or a grading period. Examples include performance assessments, group investigations, and research projects. Progress monitoring of student growth and needs is a must for student success. Teachers should assess students' content and disciplinary literacy knowledge and skills, and model and encourage students to self-regulate and manage their own learning. Teachers should also collaborate with other educators to discuss educational standards and assessments; assessments should be used as tools instead of just data-gathering instruments. Collaborative teacher inquiry on assessment issues, data interpretation, problem solving about content, disciplinary literacy, college and career readiness issues or challenges is a must for student, teacher, and school success.

Summary

- Disciplinary literacy redirects our focus from "content coverage" to "teaching in a way that is appropriate and specific to each discipline." Students in middle and high school grades are expected to comprehend texts that deal with complex concepts, problem solve in discipline-specific ways, inquire, think, talk, share, and represent their thinking in "expert" ways.
- Disciplinary literacy learning principles that are relevant to all content areas provide a pedagogical framework for teaching and learning in the disciplines. They (a) describe the characteristics of learning environments that will support, invite, and engage students in learning; (b) present learning as apprenticeship to parallel how people learn and work in

the "real" world; (c) highlight the inextricably intertwined relationship between content and literacy development; (d) support discipline-specific inquiry development and practice; and (e) emphasize the role of assessment in guiding instruction.

● Disciplinary literacy instruction is both complex and promising in turning content area classrooms into learner-centered, knowledge-centered, inquiry-based, collaborative and reflective learning cultures.

Differentiating Instruction

● All students benefit from working with, listening to, and problem solving with others in a supportive, motivating, and safe classroom environment. ELLs, in particular, will benefit from working with others in small groups, receiving feedback from peers and teacher, and being exposed to different models of talking, reading, writing, thinking, arguing, defending, questioning, evaluating, and sharing knowledge and learning.

● Struggling readers and ELLs benefit from clear objectives, rigorous and explicit instruction, clear input and much modeling, active engagement and participation, feedback, opportunities to apply new learning, sufficient practice and review, interaction with others, and frequent assessments.

● Students with varied exceptionalities may have difficulty with various discipline-specific concepts; for example, visual perception (math), hypothesis (science), time (history), 3-D relationships (art), and figurative language (ELA). Relevance is a big issue for striving readers—teachers need to provide them with meaningful and relevant activities.

● Provide modeling, support, and opportunities for students to learn and use academic language, and make necessary instructional accommodations due to language limitations (e.g., use visual clues, images, graphic organizers, provide material with familiar content, provide extra practice and time, and target language and content skills).

Reflect and Apply

1. How did you engage in discipline-specific thinking (ELA, math, science, or social studies) when you were a middle or high school student? Share your experiences with a small group, or with the class, and discuss how these experiences have framed your views about teaching and learning.

2. What insights from this chapter could you use to offer some instructional suggestions to Ms. Hilston? Use your knowledge about disciplinary literacy learning principles to help her students apply their geometry knowledge to the real-world problem or the problem at hand. Discuss your suggestions with your peers in a small group.

3. Share a lesson plan with one of your peers. Ask your peer(s) to review and identify (a) how you plan to teach select standards, discipline-specific inquiry, and habits of mind; (b) how you plan to implement the Gradual Release of Responsibility instructional model to help students develop deep understanding of the topic; and, (c) how apprenticeship is implemented throughout your instruction. Discuss areas you can improve on to make your instruction more rigorous, relevant, and effective.

Extending Learning

1. Thinking about disciplinary literacy, what three aspects of it would you like to bring to the next class or next department meeting and further discuss with your peers? Also, use insights from the chapter to help Ms. Hilston with some of her instructional challenges (see Classroom Life vignette).

2. Mentoring students as disciplinary readers, writers, thinkers, and learners is an integral part of learning in any content area classroom. Share your thoughts with your students (future or current) about learning as apprenticeship in your discipline by developing a set of norms, expectations, and routines that you will be implementing in your classroom. Exchange ideas with peers from your discipline.

3. Get together with two or three of your peers from your discipline and co-develop a classroom poster that highlights the key habits of mind that are necessary for learning in your discipline. Communicate these habits of mind in an inviting, motivating, and relevant way. Present to the rest of the class or your school and discuss what role these habits of mind will play in creating a culture of inquiry, collaboration, and reflection in your classroom.

References

Alvermann, D. E., Fitzgerald, J., & Simpson, M. (2006). Teaching and learning in reading. In P. Alexander & P. Winne (Eds), *Handbook of educational psychology* (2nd ed., pp. 427–455). Mahwah, NJ: Erlbaum.

American College Testing. (2006). *Reading between the lines: What the ACT reveals about college readiness in reading.* Iowa City, IA: Author.

Biancarosa, G., & Snow, C. E. (2004). *Reading next: A vision for action and research in middle and high school literacy.* A Report to the Carnegie Corporation of New York. Washington, DC: Alliance for Excellent Education.

Boix Mansilla, V., & Gardner, H. (1999). What are the Qualities of understanding? In Stone Wiske (Ed), *Teaching for understanding; A practical framework.* San Francisco, CA: Jossey Bass.

Brown, J. S., Collins, A., & Duguid, P. (1989). Situated cognition and the culture of learning. *Educational Researcher, 18*(1), 32–42.

Bruner, J. S. (1975). The ontogenesis of speech acts. *Journal of Child Language, 2,* 1–19.

Bruner, J. S. (1986). *Actual minds, possible worlds.* Cambridge, MA: Harvard University Press.

Burton, L. (2004). *Mathematicians as enquirers: Learning about learning mathematics.* Dordrecht, Netherlands: Kluwer.

Costa, A. (1991). The search for intelligent life. In A. Costa (Ed.), *Developing minds: A resource book for teaching thinking* (Rev. ed., Vol. 1, pp. 100–106). Alexandria, VA: ASCD.

Costa, A. L., & Kallick, B. (Eds). (2000). *Activating and engaging habits of mind.* Alexandria, VA: Association for Supervision and Curriculum Development.

Donovan, M. S., Bransford, J., & Pellegrino, J. W. (Eds). (1999). *How people learn.* Committee on Learning Research and Educational Practice. National Research Council: The National Academies Press.

Duke, N. K., & Pearson, D. (2002). Effective practices for developing reading comprehension. In A. E. Farstrup & S. J. Samuels (Eds), *What research has to say about reading instruction* (3rd ed., pp. 205–242). Newark, DE: International Reading Association.

Fang, Z., & Schleppegrell, M. J. (2008). *Reading in secondary content areas: A language-based pedagogy.* Ann Arbor, MI: The University of Michigan Press.

Fang, Z., & Schleppegrell, M. J. (2010). Disciplinary literacies across content areas: Supporting secondary reading through functional language analysis. *Journal of Adolescent & Adult Literacy, 53*(7), 587–597.

Gardner, H. (1999). *The disciplined mind.* New York, NY: Simon and Schuster.

Gee, J. P. (2000). Identity as an analytic lens for research in education. *Review of Research in Education, 25,* 99–125.

Geisler, C. (1994). *Academic literacy and the nature of expertise: Reading, writing, and knowing in academic philosophy.* Hillsdale, NJ: Erlbaum.

Goswami, U. (2008). *Cognitive development: The learning brain.* Psychology Press, Taylor & Francis.

Heller, R., & Greenleaf, C. (2007). *Literacy instruction in the content areas: Getting to the core of middle and high school improvement*. Washington, DC: Alliance for Excellent Education.

Herber, H. (1978). *Teaching reading in the content areas*. Englewood Cliffs, NJ: Prentice Hall.

Hirsch, E. D. (2006). *The knowledge deficit: Closing the shocking education gap for American children*. Boston, MA: Houghton Mifflin.

Hurston, Z. N. (1937). *Their eyes were watching God*. New York, NY: J.B. Lippincott.

Kamil, M. L. (2003). *Adolescents and literacy: Reading for the 21st century*. Washington, DC: Alliance for Excellent Education.

Kamil, M. L., & Lane, D. (1998). Researching the relation between technology and literacy: An agenda for the 21st century. In D. Reinking, M. C. McKenna, L. D. Labbo, & R. D. Kieffer (Eds), *Handbook of literacy and technology: Transformations in a post-typographic world* (pp. 323–341). Mahwah, NJ: Erlbaum.

Kamil M. L., Borman G. D., Dole, J., Kral, C. C., Salinger T., & Torgesen J. (2008). *Improving adolescent literacy: Effective classroom and intervention practices: A practice guide* (NCEE#2008–4027). National Center for Education Evaluation and Regional Assistance, Institute of Education Sciences. Washington, DC: US Department of Education.

Langer, J. (2012). *Envisioning knowledge: Building literacy in the academic disciplines*. New York, NY: Teachers College Press.

Lave, J. (1988). *Cognition in practice: Mind, mathematics and culture in everyday life*. Cambridge: Cambridge University Press.

Lave, J., & Wenger, E. (1991). *Situated learning: Legitimate peripheral participation*. Cambridge: Cambridge University Press.

Lee, C. D. (2004). Literacy in the academic disciplines and the needs of adolescent struggling readers. *Voices in Urban Education, 3*.

McKay, J. P., Hill, B. D., & Buckler, J. (1992). *A history of world societies*. Boston, MA: Houghton Mifflin.

McKenna, M. C., & Robinson, R. D. (1990). Content literacy: A definition and implication. *Journal of Reading, 34*, 184–186.

McLellan, H. (1991). Virtual environments and situated learning. *Multimedia Review, 2*(3), 30–37.

Michaels, S., O'Connor, C., Hall, M., & Resnick, L. (2002). *Accountable talk: Classroom conversation that works*. Pittsburgh, PA: University of Pittsburgh.

Mishra, P., & Koehler, M. J. (2006). Technological pedagogical content knowledge: A framework for teacher knowledge. *Teachers College Record, 108*, 1017–1054.

Moje, E. B. (2007). Developing socially just subject-matter instruction: A review of the literature on disciplinary literacy. In L. Parker (Ed.), *Review of research in education* (pp. 1–44). Washington, DC: American Educational Research Association.

Moje, E. B. (2008). Foregrounding the disciplines in secondary literacy teaching and learning: A call for change. *Journal of Adolescent and Adult Literacy, 52*(2), 96–107.

National Council for the Social Studies. (1993). *Defining social studies: The social studies professional*. Washington, DC: Author.

National Council of Teachers of Mathematics. (2009). *Guiding principles for mathematics curriculum and assessment*. Retrieved from http://www.nctm.org/standards/content.aspx?id=23273

National Governors Association Center for Best Practices (NGAC), Council of Chief State School Officers. (2010). *Common Core State Standards*. Retrieved from http://corestandards.org

National Research Council. (2013). *Next generation science standards: For states, by states*. Washington, DC: The National Academies Press. Retrieved at http://www.nextgenscience.org/next-generation-science-standards

National Science Teachers' Association. (2012). Next generation science standards for states, by states. Arlington, VA. Retrieved from: http://www.nsta.org/about/standardsupdate/default.aspx

Ness, M. K. (2007, November). Reading comprehension strategies in secondary content area classrooms. *Phi Delta Kappan, 89*(3), 229–231.

Noddings, N. (2007). *Critical lessons: What our schools should teach*. New York, NY: Cambridge University Press.

Noddings, N. (2008). All our students thinking. *Educational Leadership Journal, 65*(5), 8–13.

Pearson, P. D., & Gallagher, M. C. (1983). The instruction of reading comprehension. *Contemporary Educational Psychology, 8*, 317–344.

RAND Reading Study Group. (2002). *Reading for understanding: Toward a research and development program in reading comprehension*. Santa Monica, CA: Office of Education Research and Improvement.

Resnick, L. (1987). Learning in school and out. *Educational Researcher, 16*(9), 13–20.

Schoenfeld, A. H. (Ed.). (1994). *Mathematical thinking and problem solving*. Hillsdale, NJ: Erlbaum.

Shanahan, T., & Shanahan, C. (2008). Teaching disciplinary literacy to adolescents: Rethinking content-area literacy. *Harvard Educational Review, 78*, 40–59.

Shanahan, T., & Shanahan, C. (2012). What is disciplinary literacy and why does it matter? *Topics in Language Disorders, 32*, 1–12.

Shanahan, C., Shanahan, T., & Misichia, C. (2011). Analysis of expert readers in three disciplines: History, mathematics, and chemistry. *Journal of Literacy Research, 43*, 393–429.

Shulman, L. (1987). Knowledge and teaching: Foundations of the new reform. *Harvard Educational Review, 57*(1), 1–22.

Spoehr, K., & Spoehr, L. (1994). Learning to think historically. *Educational Psychologist, 29*(2), 71.

Torgesen, J. K., Houston, D. D., Rissman, L. M., Decker, S. M., Roberts, G., Vaughn, S., Wexler, J., Francis, D. J., Rivera, M. O., & Lesaux, N. (2007). *Academic literacy instruction for adolescents: A guidance document from the Center on Instruction*. Portsmouth, NH: RMC Research Corporation, Center on Instruction.

Tschannen-Moran, M., & Barr, M. (2004). Fostering student achievement: The relationship between collective teacher efficacy and student achievement. *Leadership and Policy in Schools, 3*, 187–207.

Venezky, R. (2000). The origins of the present-day chasms between adult literacy needs and school literacy instruction. *Scientific Studies of Reading, 4*, 19–39.

Vygotsky, L. S. (1962). *Thought and language*. Cambridge, MA: The MIT Press.

Vygotsky, L. S. (1978). *Mind in society: The development of higher psychological processes*. (M. Cole, V. John-Steiner, S. Scribner, & E. Souberman, Eds). Cambridge, MA: Harvard University Press.

Wigfield, A., Wilde, K., Baker, L., Fernandez-Fein, S., & Scher, D. (1996). *The nature of children's reading motivations, and their relations to reading frequency and reading performance*. (Reading Research Rep. No. 63). Athens, GA: National Reading Research Center.

Wineburg, S. (2001). *Historical thinking and other unnatural acts: Charting the future of teaching the past*. Philadelphia, PA: Tempe University Press.

Zygouris-Coe, V. (2012). Disciplinary literacy and the common core state standards. *Topics in Language Disorders, 32*(1), 35–50.

three
Reading Complex Texts Beyond the Textbook

Is it too much to expect from the schools that they train their students not only to interpret but to criticize; that is, to discriminate what is sound from error and falsehood, to suspend judgment if they are not convinced, or to judge with reason if they agree or disagree?
–Mortimer J. Adler

Chapter Highlights

- College, career, and workforce readiness requires students to have deep understanding of complex texts.
- Determining text complexity is a multi-faceted process involving qualitative and quantitative dimensions of text complexity, and reader factors.
- Close reading of discipline-specific complex texts is a demanding process. Students need to develop their engagement with complex texts, and teachers need to provide modeling and much scaffolded support.
- Reading complex texts through a disciplinary lens requires immersion in the discourse, texts, and habits of mind of each discipline.
- Mentoring and collaborative inquiry will facilitate students' understanding of the complex texts they read in the disciplines.

Classroom Life

Since yesterday, I have been working with my class on Edgar Allan Poe's *The Red Masque of Death*. Needless to say, I've been pulling teeth . . . My students find his writing hard; they try to wrap their heads around it but many have difficulty with several words, the author's style and tone, and how Poe explores death and vanity in his complex and morbid way. The text is a masterpiece but its plot is unpredictable and rich with complex characters. I want them to get Poe's beautiful interrogation of death but I am finding myself spending so much time on vocabulary and on prompting them to look at clues, read the text again, and again. Figurative language is "killing them"—or may be it is "killing" me . . . I am getting morbid, myself . . . They are also struggling with syntax/semantics. How can I get them to question the author more and pay attention to the context, find the big ideas in the text, and want to talk about it with their peers? I need to ask them more questions or maybe allow them to come up with questions. I am going to spend more time dissecting the text and asking them questions that will guide them toward better comprehension of the text. I am going to start with the first paragraph:

Red Death had long devastated the country. No pestilence had ever been so fatal, or so hideous. Blood was its Avatar and its seal—the redness and the horror of blood. There were sharp pains, and sudden dizziness, and then profuse bleeding at the pores, with dissolution. The scarlet stains upon the body and especially upon the face of the victim, were the pest ban which shut him out from the aid and from the sympathy of his fellow-men.

I am going to start with the first paragraph, identify the words they have been having trouble with (e.g., devastated, pestilence, fatal, hideous, profuse, dissolution, seizure, progress, termination, incidents); I will also focus on these phrases: "The Red Death," "scarlet stains," "Blood was its Avatar and its seal—the redness and the horror of blood," and on ". . . pest ban which shut him out from the aid and from the sympathy of his fellow-men." I will allow time for reading and rereading, and small and whole group discussions. I will do anything to get them to understand and appreciate the beauty of this text. Tomorrow is a new day! *(Ms. Tierney Miller, Secondary English Language Arts Content Specialist, Boston Public Schools, Massachusetts)*

New Educational Standards and Text Complexity

Since the release of the Common Core State Standards (CCSS) in 2010, departments of education, school districts, colleges of education, and publishers have been involved in a critical examination of the standards, reviews of state standards and their alignments with the CCSS, and assessment systems. As discussed in Chapter 1, many students cannot read and comprehend discipline-specific texts, and as a result, are not prepared to face the demands of college, career, and workforce reading and learning. The CCSS are designed to ensure that students graduating from high school will be college, career, and workforce ready. Students' literacy experiences will engage students in ways that are essential to their future success. According to the standards, in grades 6 through 12, students need to read and comprehend "literature and infomational texts, history/social studies, science/technical texts with scaffolding as needed at the high end of the range" (NGA & CCSSO, Appendix A, p. 10), evaluate them, gather informed evidence, reflect on and revise their understanding, formulate arguments, and negotiate and defend their understanding.

Key Ideas and Details
1. Read closely to determine what the text says explicitly and to make logical inferences from it; cite specific textual evidence when writing or speaking to support conclusions drawn from the text.
2. Determine central ideas or themes of a text and analyze their development; summarize the key supporting details and ideas.
3. Analyze how and why individuals, events, and ideas develop and interact over the course of a text.
Craft and Structure
4. Interpret words and phrases as they are used in a text, including determining technical, connotative, and figurative meanings, and analyze how specific word choices shape meaning or tone.
5. Analyze the structure of texts, including how specific sentences, paragraphs, and larger portions of the text (e.g., a section, chapter, scene, or stanza) relate to each other and the whole.
6. Assess how point of view or purpose shapes the content and style of a text.
Integration of Knowledge and Ideas
7. Integrate and evaluate content presented in diverse formats and media, including visually and quantitatively, as well as in words.
8. Delineate and evaluate the argument and specific claims in a text, including the validity of the reasoning as well as the relevance and sufficiency of the evidence.
9. Analyze how two or more texts address similar themes or topics in order to build knowledge or to compare the approaches the authors take.
Range of Reading and Level of Complexity
10. Read and comprehend complex literary and informational texts independently and proficiently.

FIGURE 3.1. College and Career Readiness Anchor Standards for Reading.

Source: Adapted from the *Common Core State Standards for English Language Arts & Literacy in History/Social Studies, Science, and Technical Subjects* (p. 35), by National Governors Association Center for Best Practices & Council of Chief State School Offices, 2010, Washington, DC: Authors. Copyright 2010 by the National Governors Association Center for Best Practices and the Council of Chief State School Officers. All rights reserved.

The CCSS include 10 college and career readiness anchor standards for reading for grades 6–12 (see Figure 3.1) (see http://www.corestandards.org/ELA-Literacy/CCRA/R for specific details on the CCSS, ELA Standards, for reading standards for literature and informational text 6–12).

According to the CCSS, Anchor Standard for Reading #10, students must read more high-quality informational text and books of increasing complexity as they get older. The CCSS define text complexity as "the inherent difficulty of reading and comprehending a text combined with consideration of reader and task variables" (see *CCSS for English Language Arts and Literacy in History/Social Studies, Science, and Technical Subjects*, Appendix A, p. 4). The CCSS call our attention to both the range and content reading students need to have and do across grade levels. For students to be college and career ready, they need to read widely and critically from a diverse range of high-quality literary and informational texts. Literary texts representing a variety of cultures and time periods (stories, poems, myths, dramas) will equip students with knowledge about narrative text structures, literary devices, how to read with a literary lens, and cultural knowledge. By reading high-quality texts in other disciplines (history/social studies, science, mathematics, etc.), students will learn how to read with different disciplinary lenses, develop knowledge about expository text structures, and content that will help them to continue to learn in each content area.

The CCSS support a curriculum that is rigorous and coherently structured to develop rich content and discipline-specific literacy knowledge within and across grades. To be college and career ready, students need to learn how to read varied complex text closely and independently. Whether your state has adopted the CCSS or not, text complexity remains a core issue for all students' postsecondary preparation.

Why Do Some Students Struggle with Reading and Comprehending Texts?

Unfortunately, in some secondary schools the majority of students struggle with reading disciplinary texts. Approximately 25–40% of students do not have developed reading, fluency, vocabulary and comprehension skills. English language learners and students with varied exceptionalities need additional support systems to help them read and comprehend. In addition, motivation, student interests, and engagement also play a role in what they read, how long they read, and how well they read and comprehend.

Several researchers have concluded that many secondary content area teachers need much preparation and professional development to develop the expertise needed to teach students how to develop disciplinary, advanced, and specialized, literacy (e.g., Berman & Biancarosa, 2005; Heller & Greenleaf, 2007; Lee & Spratley, 2010; Moje, 2008; Schleppegrell & Colombi, 2002; Shanahan & Shanahan, 2008, 2012). Several students in content area classrooms are engaged in rushed, shallow reading with teachers teaching them how to skim text for answers and focus only on details. As a result, students do not know how to read disciplinary text and fail to make inferences about the different elements, ideas and concepts in the text. Many years of these type of reading experiences can result in weakened student persistence, especially when the words are unfamiliar, the author's style is complex, and when frustration kicks in when meaning does not come right away. Years of this type of superficial reading will cause a student's reading ability, and motivation to want to read and learn, to decline over time.

All professional teacher organizations agree that adolescents need to read widely, often, critically, and have choice over what they read. Student choice, although very important for motivation and engagement with reading, does not apply to the textbooks used in content area classrooms. Content area teachers need to teach students how to read and comprehend using their textbook, and also need to introduce a variety of print and digital text(s) in their classes. For students to develop deep knowledge and critical thinking skills, they need time in class to read, analyze, discuss, and evaluate a variety of texts.

For example, The National Council of Teachers of Mathematics (NCTM) calls for students learning to solve real world problems, not just textbook problems. The National Council for the Social Studies (NCSS) asks social studies teachers to teach students how to read primary and secondary documents, and other types of texts. The Next Generation Science Standards (NGSS) focus both on content and processes. The NGSS expect students to ask questions and define problems, analyze and interpret data, engage in argument from evidence, and obtain and evaluate information from a variety of texts and sources.

The International Reading Association (IRA) stated the following in its 2012 position paper about adolescent literacy:

● Adolescents deserve content area teachers who provide instruction in the multiple literacy strategies needed to meet the demands of the specific discipline. (p. 2)

● All teachers can effectively support adolescent learners as they learn from all kinds of texts by teaching these general strategies through the discipline-specific print and nonprint materials that continue to expand rapidly (Moje, 2007b, 2008; Shanahan & Shanahan, 2008). (p. 5)

The National Council of Teachers of English (NCTE) recognized the following in their 2006 policy research brief:

> [Students across disciplines] . . . need teachers to show them how literacy operates within academic disciplines. In particular, adolescents need instruction that integrates literacy skills into each school discipline so they can learn from the texts they read.
>
> (p. 5)

The same organization, NCTE, in their 2004 position statement on adolescent literacy, called for professional development for teachers that would equip them to

> teach literacy in their disciplines as an essential way of learning in their disciplines . . . . and create environments that allow students to engage in critical examinations of texts as they "dissect," deconstruct, and re-construct in an effort to engage in meaning making and comprehension processes.
>
> (p. 3)

CCSS Connections

● The CCSS center on students experiencing and learning how to read and comprehend grade-level complex text in order to develop the domain-specific language skills, habits of mind, and knowledge they need for success in school and beyond.
● Proficiency and performance on complex texts is the strongest differentiating factor in reading between students who are more likely to be college ready and those who are less likely to be college ready.
● Anchor Standard #10: R.CCR.10: "Read and comprehend complex literary and informational texts independently and proficiently" (Common Core State Standards for English Language Arts & Literacy in History/Social Studies, Science, and Technical Subjects, p. 35).

College-Readiness and Text Complexity

The American College Testing Service in its highly influential study, *Reading Between the Lines* (ACT, 2006), determined a benchmark score on participating students' reading tests; 51% of students scored above this benchmark. According to the study, those were the students who would most likely enroll in college, earn a B or higher in their first year introductory history or psychology classes, earn a GPA of 3.0 or higher, and return for a second year at the same institution. In an effort to determine what patterns might distinguish students scoring above the benchmark from those scoring below, ACT conducted an analysis of students' responses. Here are some of the results of that analysis:

1. Literal vs. inferential question type failed to differentiate students scoring above the benchmark from those scoring below (p. 13).
2. Questions focusing on main idea/author's purpose, supporting details, relationships, meaning of words, and generalizations and conclusions also failed to differentiate those scoring above the benchmark from those scoring below (p. 14).

3. The clearest difference of performance between the two groups was the *degree of text complexity*, in the passages that acted as "sorters" within the ACT. This finding held true for both males and females, all racial groups and was steady regardless of family income levels (p. 16).

These are amazing results, aren't they? The study's results show that for 468,000 students who were tested in 2006, basic critical thinking skills did not distinguish those who are college and career ready from those who are not; competence with complex text did. The single most important predictor of student success in college is their ability to read a range of complex text with comprehension. Being able to read complex text with deep understanding is a prerequisite for college, career, and workforce success (Achieve, 2007; ACT, 2006). Based on these and other results, the CCSS call for students to read *much* complex text progressively from Grades 2–12. In addition, although high school textbooks have declined in all content areas over several years, the complexity of college and career texts has remained steady or increased (Hayes, Wolfer, & Wolfe, 1996).

According to the CCSS, the texts students read in school are not of sufficient complexity to adequately prepare them for college and career readiness. In addition, students are not reading enough infomational text, the prominent text of college and career reading. This explains the CCSS' focus on students reading more and more informational text across grade levels (Grade 8: 45% literacy, 55% informational; Grade 12: 30% literary, 70% informational). Teachers and parents need to both challenge and support students in developing their strengths as readers and "stretching" their knowledge, abilities, and skills to the next level. What students read, how they read (i.e., at a surface or at a critical and analytical level), think, and write, matters. Disciplinary literacy fits in with this context as it promotes students' reading, thinking, speaking, and writing like a disciplinarian.

What Is Text Complexity?

Have you noticed the way in which many students select texts to read? Some will select a text because peers recommended it; others will select it because it is "thin"; others will do a "book walk"—they will read the introduction, the table of contents, and the end of the book to try to get an idea about the book; on the other hand, what makes struggling readers read Stephenie Meyer's voluminous books (i.e., 544–756 pages long)? Length alone does not determine text complexity.

What are possible explanations for why so many students have difficulty understanding complex text? What makes text complex? I would first like to clarify that for the purposes of this book, the term "text" refers to print text as digital text has a different structure and patterns and requires different reading skills (Hartman, Morsink, & Zheng, 2010; Leu et al., 2008). A typical answer to this question is text readability—length and number of complex sentences and vocabulary. How are disciplinary texts organized? What aspects of their characteristics make reading and comprehension challenging? Overall, text organization and patterns, sentence structure, vocabulary, text coherence, and reader factors account for the difficulties students experience with reading disciplinary complex text.

The CCSS (NGA & CCSSO, 2010b) identify a complex three-part model for determining text complexity (see Figure 3.2). First of all, note that text complexity consists of three equally important parts.

1. *Qualitative dimensions of text complexity.* In the Standards, *qualitative dimensions* and *qualitative factors* refer to the aspects of the text that are best measured or only measurable by an attentive human reader, such as levels of meaning or purpose, structure, language conventionality and clarity, and knowledge demands.

2. *Quantitative dimensions of text complexity.* The terms *quantitative dimensions* and *quantitative factors* refer to those aspects of text complexity, such as word length or frequency, sentence length, and text cohesion, that are difficult if not impossible for a human reader to evaluate efficiently, especially in long texts, and are thus today typically measured by computer software.

3. *Reader and task considerations.* While the prior two elements of the model focus on the inherent complexity of text, variables specific to particular readers (such as motivation, knowledge, and experiences) and to particular tasks (such as purpose and the complexity of the task assigned and the questions posed) must also be considered when determining whether a text is appropriate for a given student. Such assessments are best made by teachers employing their professional judgment, experience, and knowledge of their students and the subject.

(p. 4)

The CCSS model for text complexity offers a comprehensive perspective on what makes a text complex; according to the model, a text might be defined as complex not only because of its advanced or colloquial vocabulary or because of its sentence length. Text complexity is also affected by text structure, the author's writing style and ways she communicates ideas and concepts, clarity in writing, and the cohesiveness of the text. Last (and equally important), the reader's motivation, knowledge, and experiences interact with the other two dimensions. Teachers should consider this model of text complexity to select subject-relevant texts, match readers with books, and plan for instruction that will support students' reading and comprehension of texts.

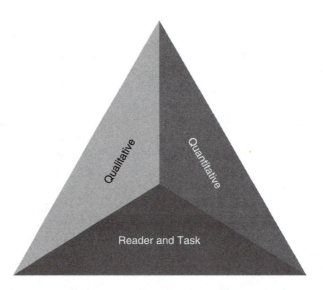

FIGURE 3.2. The CCSS three-part model for determining text complexity.

Source: The *Common Core Standards for English Language Arts & Literacy in History/Social Studies, Science, and Technical Subjects: Appendix A: Research Supporting Key Elements of the Standards and Glossary of Terms* (p. 4), by National Governors Association Center for Best Practices & Council of Chief State School Officers, 2010, Washington, DC: Authors. Copyright 2010 by the National Governors Association Center for Best Practices and the Council of Chief State School Officers. All rights reserved.

Qualitative Dimensions of Text Complexity

Levels of Meaning (literary texts) or Purpose (informational texts)

Literary texts with a single level of meaning tend to be easier to read than literary texts with multiple levels of meaning, and informational texts with an explicitly stated purpose are generally easier to comprehend than informational texts with an implicit, or unclear purpose.

Text Structure and Patterns

Text structure refers to the ways authors organize information in text. Disciplinary texts have unique text structure, patterns, and characteristics. Table 3.1 summarizes key text patterns and examples of disciplinary texts. Types of texts include narrative, informational, and expository. Narrative text often refers to fiction in which plot, characters, and values are used to explain human behavior. It involves a setting, events, and characters that are involved in interpersonal or internal conflicts; its theme could be stated or implicit. Narrative texts include autobiographies, biographies, essays, interviews, memoirs (depends on purpose and text structure), speeches, etc. Informational text's purpose is to convey factual information on specific topics or events about the natural and social world. It comes in books, magazines, the Internet, etc.

Informational text is persuasive text in which the author intends to convince the reader to adopt a particular opinion or to perform a certain action. Informational texts come in different forms such as book reviews, business letters, commercials, written debates, editorials, essays, position papers, speeches, etc. Most text structures include description, cause and effect, and order/sequence, comparison/contrast, problem/solution. Narrative texts rely predominantly on exposition, climactic actions, and denouncement. Informational text features such as headings, subheadings, bullets, captions, graphs/charts, table of contents, glossary, illustrations, and other graphic and organizational aids can be useful to readers.

Texts of low complexity have simpler and more conventional text structures whereas texts of high complexity have more complex, unconventional, and implicit (especially literary texts) structures. Simple literary texts have predictable plots and relate events in explicitly identifiable sequential order. Simple informational texts use common genre (and sub-genre) conventions. High complexity literary texts manipulate time and sequence, use flashbacks, double or multiple narrations, and flash-forwards, and demand close tracking of characters, events, plot, etc. On the other hand, complex informational texts follow discipline-specific text structures, norms, and conventions, complex graphics, and graphics that are an independent source of information in the text. Reading and comprehension of complex informational texts requires the reader to read and integrate information from print and graphics; if one source of information is eliminated, students' understanding of text will be incomplete.

Language Conventionality and Clarity

Texts that rely on literal, uncomplicated, contemporary, and conversational language tend to be easier to read than texts that rely on figurative, ironic, ambiguous, purposefully misleading or metaphorical, archaic or otherwise unfamiliar language or on general academic and domain-specific vocabulary. Each discipline has its own discourse and vocabulary. Fang and Schleppegrell (2008, 2010) recommend functional language analysis (FLA) as a method that provides a framework for analyzing how meaning is constructed in different language choices in science, history, mathematics, and language arts. Students can benefit from becoming aware of how language is used in each discipline.

TABLE 3.1. Patterns, Characteristics, and Examples of Disciplinary Texts

Discipline	Text Patterns and Characteristics	Example

1. English Language Arts	• **Patterns**
	  ○ Voice & Tone
	  ○ Figurative Language
	  ○ Traditional and Contemporary Canon of Literature
	  ○ Principles of Organization: Chronological/ Sequential, Spatial, Climactic, & Topical Order
	  ○ Characterization, Narration
	  ○ Cause/Effect
	  ○ Comparison/Contrast
	  ○ Problem/Solution
	
	• **Characteristics**
	  ○ Discourse, words & phrases, vocabulary
	  ○ Grammar, composition, writing
	  ○ Draw inferences, examine multiple themes, analyze author's choices & determine impact on plot & characters
	  ○ Determine meaning of words and phrases, figurative & connotative meanings, & impact of word choice on meaning & tone
	  ○ Analyze multiple points of view & cultural experiences
		Taylor, Mildred D. *Roll of Thunder, Hear My Cry*. New York: Phyllis Fogelman Books (1976). From Chapter 9
		
		"You were born blessed, boy, with land of your own. If you hadn't been, you'd cry out for it while you try to survive . . . like Mr. Lanier and Mr. Avery. Maybe even do what they doing now. It's hard on a man to give up, but sometimes it seems there just ain't nothing else he can do."
		
		"I . . . I'm sorry, Papa," Stacey muttered.
		
		After a moment, Papa reached out and draped his arm over Stacey's shoulder.
		
		"Papa," I said, standing to join them, "we giving up too?"
		
		Papa looked down at me and brought me closer, then waved his hand toward the drive. "You see that fig tree over yonder, Cassie? Them other trees all around . . . that oak and walnut, they're a lot bigger and they take up more room and give so much shade they almost overshadow that little ole fig. But that fig tree's got roots that run deep, and it belongs in that yard as much as that oak and walnut. It keeps blooming, bearing fruit year after year, knowing all the time it'll never get as big as them other trees. Just keeps on growing and doing what it gotta do. It don't give up. It give up, it'll die. There's a lesson to be learned from that little tree, Cassie girl, 'cause we're like it. We keep doing what we gotta do, and we don't give up. We can't."

2. Mathematics	• **Patterns**
	  ○ Description
	  ○ Problem/Solution
	  ○ Evidence/Reasoning
	  ○ Compare/Contrast
	  ○ Cause/Effect
	  ○ Sequencing
	  ○ Graphic relationships
	  ○ Symbolic Relationships & Operations
		Source: *Algebra I* (2009). Pearson Education, Inc. Retrieved from http://www. phschool.com/webcodes10/index.cfm?fuseaction=home.gotoWebCode&wc prefix=bda&wcsuffix=0511
		
		A function g(x) is defined only for negative integers. If the absolute value of the input is even, multiply the number by 2 and subtract 1. If the absolute value of the input is odd, subtract −3 from the number. If x = −2, find the result of running through the function 4 times.

- **Characteristics**
  - Conceptually dense text
  - Use of conventional and mathematical language and symbols with multiple meanings
  - Key words for solving problems
  - Complex and abstract language
  - Accuracy & precision

- **Patterns**
  - Classification
  - Process/Description
  - Factual/Statement
  - Compare/Contrast
  - Problem/Solution
  - Cause/Effect
  - Experiment/Instruction
  - Combination of all of the above

- **Characteristics**
  - Semantically dense text
  - Written in third-person, passive voice
  - Nominalization & heavy technical vocabulary
  - General phrases and relationships among concepts
  - Use of text, graphs, charts, and mathematical symbols
  - Connections among many concepts and ideas

3. Science

Source: *Earth Science: Radioactive Decay of Rocks*. Retrieved from: http://en.wikipedia.org/wiki/Radioactive_decay

Radioactive decay is the process by which an atomic nucleus of an unstable atom loses energy by emitting ionizing particles (ionizing radiation). There are many different types of radioactive decay (see table below). A decay, or loss of energy, results when an atom with one type of nucleus, called the *parent radionuclide*, transforms to an atom with a nucleus in a different state, or to a different nucleus containing different numbers of protons and neutrons. Either of these products is named the *daughter nuclide*. In some decays the parent and daughter are different chemical elements, and thus the decay process results in nuclear transmutation (creation of an atom of a new element).

The first decay processes to be discovered were alpha decay, beta decay, and gamma decay. Alpha decay occurs when the nucleus ejects an alpha particle (helium nucleus). This is the most common process of emitting nucleons, but in rarer types of decays, nuclei can eject protons, or specific nuclei of other elements (in the process called cluster decay). Beta decay occurs when the nucleus emits an electron or positron and a type of neutrino, in a process that changes a proton to a neutron or the other way around. The nucleus may capture an orbiting electron, converting a proton into an neutron (electron capture). All of these processes result in nuclear transmutation.

By contrast, there exist radioactive decay processes that do not result in transmutation. The energy of an excited nucleus may be emitted as a gamma ray in gamma decay, or used to eject an orbital electron by interaction with the excited nucleus in a process called internal conversion. Radioisotopes occasionally emit neutrons, and this results in a change in an element from one isotope to another.

(Continued)

TABLE 3.1. (Continued)

Discipline	Text Patterns and Characteristics	Example
4. Social Studies	• **Patterns** ○ Description, Enumeration ○ Definition/Explanation ○ Time Order/Sequential Events ○ Question/Answer ○ Comparison/Contrast ○ Cause/Effect ○ Problem/Solution ○ Conflict/Resolution • **Characteristics** ○ Nominalizations that reference abstract ideas and cause–effect relationships ○ Evaluative judgments ○ Language is drawn from wide range of disciplines ○ Analysis of primary (and other) sources ○ Multiple perspectives and biases ○ Analyzing graphs & images	Source: *The Great Depression (1929–1941)*, American Nation Series: Civil War to Present. Pearson Education, Inc. Retrieved from http://www.phschool.com/webcodes10/index.cfm?fuseaction=home.gotoWebCode&wcprefix=mhk&wcsuffix=1000 In October 1929, a stock market crash brought the prosperity of the Roaring Twenties to a sudden end. The period that followed, known as the Great Depression, was the worst economic disaster in United States history. Poverty, hunger, and joblessness became widespread. Believing the government should not interfere too much with the economy, President Herbert Hoover took only limited action. Seeking bolder action, Americans elected Franklin Delano Roosevelt as President in 1932. Roosevelt supported a large number of programs to restart the economy. Though Roosevelt's programs provided help for many Americans, other people criticized him for expanding the size and role of the government.

Students come to school with a varying amount of word knowledge (Graves, 1984). When reading text students come across domain-specific and more general academic words (Townsend, 2009), as well as conventional and figurative language. For example, teachers will provide vocabulary instruction for domain-specific words such as *federalism, amendment, political freedom, centralized government* but understanding of those words can also be supported by more general academic terms such as *party, government, system*, and *identity*. In addition, in the content areas, words mean more than just dictionary definitions. Application of discipline-specific concepts requires good understanding; it requires both declarative knowledge (the ability to define a term) and procedural knowledge (the ability to apply it) (Nagy & Scott, 2000). Moreover, mathematics and science require conditional knowledge (words and symbols that have multiple meanings); the words *rotate* or *translate* are used differently in these disciplines than others.

There are a number of differences in disciplinary vocabulary, and unfortunately many content area teachers assume that vocabulary instruction belongs in the English language arts classroom only. For many content area teachers, vocabulary (and comprehension) instruction is "caught, not taught;" it takes place as needed, or when the teacher notices that students do not understand certain words. General vocabulary is developed through wide reading and multiple exposures to a wide range of words (Krashen, 2004). But, general terms that are technical terms can be problematic for students in mathematics and science because they are specific to the discipline.

In English language arts, vocabulary is the "vehicle" to literary insights and experiences. English language arts teachers must teach the technical vocabulary of the discipline along with figurative language. Learning isolated in a word-by-word fashion is not an effective vocabulary practice; students need to read widely and read at times lengthy passages in order to develop vocabulary understanding (Harmon, Hedrick, & Wood, 2005).

Schell (1982) explains that reading mathematics text is particularly challenging for students because it has "more concepts per word, per sentence, and per paragraph than any other content area" (p. 544). In mathematics, if you don't know precisely what its words or symbols mean, you can't "do" math. In addition, there are several multiple-meaning words; for example, *line, mean, power, principal, product, table, times*. In addition, general terms such as *angle, difference, domain, negative, of, range* take on specific meanings in mathematics.

Science is loaded with scientific vocabulary; in a standard science textbook one might find 30–50 new words per chapter. Most students try to get a handle on scientific vocabulary through memorization. Many terms are based on Latin and Greek roots; students can benefit from morphemic analysis (examining meaningful parts i.e., prefixes, suffixes, roots, etc.). In addition, students need to understand signal words and phrases, such as "*similar to, be considered, be different from, be characteristic of, arise from*" (Harmon et al., 2005) because they provide conceptual connections among technical, subtechnical (polysemous words that have multiple meanings across disciplines: e.g., *cell, volume, degree*), and symbolic vocabulary.

The challenge with social studies is that the discipline uses text that is derived from multiple fields. For example, from anthropology (e.g., *innovation, domestication, polytheism*), economics (e.g., *currency, private property rights, oligopoly/monopoly*), geography (e.g., *biosphere, hydrosphere, indigenous*), political science (e.g., *elector, judiciary, revolution*), sociology (e.g., *counterculture, ethnocentrism, subculture*). As a result, students have to become cognizant of the connotations and denotations of words. Vocabulary in social studies centers around people, settings, and events (Harmon et al., 2005).

Knowledge Demands

Complex texts "assume" depth in students' disciplinary knowledge and literacy and cultural experiences. Background knowledge is one of the strongest predictors of reading comprehension

(Fisher & Frey, 2009; Marzano, 2004). One of the major challenges educators face is that their students have underdeveloped discipline-specific knowledge that affects what and how they teach in their classrooms. In an effort to support reader comprehension of text, teachers spend much time building students' background knowledge before they start reading the text.

Students might have topic knowledge but they lack domain knowledge (Alexander & Jetton, 2000). Domain knowledge refers to the reader's understanding of the vocabulary, concepts/ideas, processes, and ways of thinking that are characteristic of each discipline. It is important both to consider and develop the reader's background knowledge about the reading. To help students build more experiences with complex text, teachers need to allow the text to be the first source of information for students. After students have developed an understanding of the text with teacher support, prompting, and peer discussion, teachers need to help them make relevant connections with personal experiences and background knowledge.

Quantitative Factors of Text Complexity

A number of quantitative tools exist to assist educators assess aspects of text complexity accurately through algorithms. Numerous formulas exist for measuring the readability of various types of texts (e.g., Fry, Readability Formula, 2002). Such formulas, including the widely used Flesch–Kincaid Grade Level test, use word length and sentence length as proxies for semantic and syntactic complexity. The assumption behind these formulas is that longer words and longer sentences are more difficult to read than shorter ones; a text with many long words and/or sentences is thus rated by these formulas as harder to read than a text with many short words and/or sentences would be.

Some formulas, such as the Dale–Chall Readability Formula, substitute word frequency for word length as a factor, using the assumption that less familiar words are harder to comprehend than familiar words. Thus, the higher the proportion of less familiar words in a text, the harder that text is to read. While these readability formulas are easy to use, their major weakness is that longer words, less familiar words, and longer sentences are not inherently hard to read. Some, short, choppy sentences can be challenging for readers to make inferences from because they lack transition words and phrases, the things help readers make logical connections among ideas.

The Dale–Chall, the Lexile Framework for Reading, developed by MetaMetrics, Inc., uses word frequency and sentence length to produce a single measure of text complexity, called a Lexile. The most important difference between the Lexile system and traditional readability formulas is that traditional formulas only assign a score to texts, whereas the Lexile Framework can place both readers and texts on the same scale. Certain reading assessments produce Lexile scores based on student performance on the instrument; educators can use such information to make decisions about assigning texts to students.

Because the Lexile Framework also relies on word familiarity and sentence length as proxies for semantic and syntactic complexity, it may underestimate the difficulty of texts that use simple, familiar language to convey sophisticated ideas (found in high-quality fiction for older students and adults). Because readers do not have a single reading level, and their reading level depends upon what in the subject they have read before, and their interest level in the text or topic, it is important to consider other factors that might contribute to text complexity. MetaMetrics has indicated that it will release the qualitative ratings it assigns to some of the texts it rates and will investigate additional factors that may need to be added to its quantitative measure. See Table 3.2 below for a look at the original and recalibrated Lexile ranges; note the increase in levels of complexity.

TABLE 3.2. Updated Text Complexity Grade Bands and Associated Ranges from Multiple Measures

Common Core Band	ATOS	Degrees of Reading Power®	Flesch–Kincaid[8]	The Lexile Framework®	Reading Maturity	Source Rater
2nd–3rd	2.75–5.14	42–54	1.98–5.34	420–820	3.53–6.13	0.05–2.48
4th–5th	4.97–7.03	52–60	4.51–7.73	740–1010	5.42–7.92	0.84–5.75
6th–8th	7.00–9.98	57–67	6.51–10.34	925–1185	7.04–9.57	4.11–10.66
9th–10th	9.67–12.01	62–72	8.32–12.12	1050–1335	8.41–10.81	9.02–13.93
11th–CCR	11.20–14.10	67–74	10.34–14.2	1185–1385	9.57–12.00	12.30–14.50

Source: From the *Common Core Standards for English Language Arts & Literacy in History/Social Studies, Science, and Technical Subjects: Appendix A: Research Supporting Key Elements of the Standards and Glossary of Terms* (p. 4), by National Governors Association Center for Best Practices & Council of Chief State School Officers, 2010, Washington, DC: Authors. Copyright 2010 by the National Governors Association Center for Best Practices and the Council of Chief State School Officers. All rights reserved.

Other readability formulas also exist, such as the ATOS formula associated with the Accelerated Reader program developed by Renaissance Learning. ATOS uses word difficulty (estimated grade level), word length, sentence length, and text length (measured in words) as its factors. Like the Lexile Framework, ATOS puts students and texts on the same scale.

A text is coherent if it makes sense; to make sense, it has to be cohesive—meaning all of its elements (words, phrases, sentences, ideas, and concepts) have to be clearly linked together. Text coherence will affect whether a reader will be able to infer the author's communicative intentions. If the text is cohesive, it will meet the reader's expectations. A nonprofit service operated at the University of Memphis, Coh-Metrix attempts to account for factors in addition to those measured by readability formulas. The Coh-Metrix system focuses on the cohesiveness of a text—how well the text holds together. A high-cohesion text does a good deal of the work for the reader by connecting relationships among words, sentences, and ideas by using repetition, concrete language, etc. A low-cohesion text, by contrast, requires the reader to make many of the connections needed to comprehend the text. High-cohesion texts are not necessarily "better" than low-cohesion texts, but they are easier to read. (For additional resources on quantitative measure of text complexity, see Lexile Measures and the Common Core State Standards at: http://www.lexile.com/using-lexile/lexile-measures-and-the-ccssi/; Accelerated Reader and the Common Core State Standards at: http://doc.renlearn.com/KMNet/R004572117GKC46B.pdf; and, Coh-Metrix at: http://cohmetrix.memphis.edu/cohmetrixpr/index.html)

Sentence Length

Sentence structure is important for understanding text. Grammar and parts of speech, punctuation and spelling, language choices (words, phrases, idioms) all matter. For example, understanding the sentence "Remember it's a sin to kill a mockingbird" (from *To Kill a Mockingbird* by Harper Lee) depends upon how each word fits together in the context of the text. In this short sentence, from *The Joy Luck Club* by Amy Tan, "That night I sat on Tyan-yu's bed and waited for him to touch me. But he didn't. I was relieved." Simple sentences usually contain a subject and a verb, and they express a complete thought. Complex sentences include an independent and dependent clause joined by one or more dependent clauses; they also have a subordinator such as *because, since, after, although*, or *when* or a relative pronoun such as *that, who*, or *which*.

See an example of a longer and more complex sentence from *A Farewell to Arms* by Ernest Hemingway,

> They left me alone and I lay in bed and read the papers awhile, the news from the front, and the list of dead officers with their decorations and then reached down and brought up the bottle of Cinzano and held it straight up on my stomach, the cool glass against my stomach, and took little drinks making rings on my stomach from holding the bottle there between drinks, and watched it get dark outside over the roofs of the town.

Longer sentences include multiple clauses, longer phrases, at times complicated relationships and ideas that make it difficult for some readers to follow. For a detailed example of using the CCSS model for determining text quality, see Table 3.3 using *To Kill a Mockingbird*. Teachers may use this analysis as a rubric for determining text complexity of narrative texts.

In many content areas the textbook is the "Bible" as many content area teachers do not incorporate other types of genres and materials to support students' understanding of subject matter.

TABLE 3.3. Text Complexity Analysis of *To Kill a Mockingbird* by Harper Lee

Qualitative Dimensions	*Quantitative Dimensions*
Levels of Meaning/Purpose: This novel is a classic of modern American Literature dealing with issues of prejudice, social injustice, America being divided, tolerance. The story is set in a small town in Alabama during the Depression. Scout Finch struggles with issues of race and prejudice when her father, Atticus, risks everything to defend a black man wrongly accused of raping a white woman.	**Lexile:** The Lexile® measure for this novel is 870L. **Grade Level Equivalent:** The grade level equivalent is 8.1 and the interest level is grades 9–12. **Band Level:** According to the Accelerated Reader program formula, the novel is at a 5.6 grade level. Due to qualitative measures and reader-task considerations, the CCSS Text Exemplars places the novel in the 9th–10th-grade complexity band.
Structure: *Middle-High Complexity.* The novel is cohesive but several issues complicate the structure and narration of the story. Duality is reflected in the tension created by the communities, the opposition of themes, the narrative points of view, and genders. The author uses double-layered narration and flashback (i.e., Scout as an adult explicitly tells the story at the beginning of the novel and at the end. In the middle, the story is told from the perspective of Scout as a child.).	
Language Conventionality and Clarity: *Middle-High Complexity.* The author uses conversational language and colloquialism in dialogue between characters and in the description of the setting. There are many implied meanings, occasionally domain-specific language, and several metaphors (e.g., Mockingbird, Snowman, Mad dog, Boo Radley).	The text complexity of this book lies in its (a) complex ideas of rape, racism, social injustice, prejudice, (b) length, (c) content knowledge, (d) life experiences (that might not be familiar to some of the readers), and (e) deeper levels of cultural and literary knowledge and readers will need to fully understand, analyze, interpret, and transfer their comprehension of the text.
Knowledge Demands: *Middle-High Complexity.* The novel deals with critical issues of justice, prejudice, and inequality. The novel also requires appreciation for different communities' ways of life, and a contemplation of the struggles the characters experienced in a culture of racial injustice. Readers will also need to contemplate issues of fairness, justice versus the law, gender roles and stereotypes, search for identity, friendship, conformity versus individuality, and moral responsibility.	

Reader and Task Considerations

It is important to consider reader motivation, knowledge, experiences, and maturity level regarding the novel's themes and tensions. The book's theme, the context, the issues of rape, racial injustice, and moral responsibility would require higher level reading skills, intertextuality, connections between prejudice in the '30s, '50s, '60s and today in America, and critical evaluation of related social, cultural, and moral issues.

Possible Areas of Focus:
• Discuss the significance of the novel's title, citing examples from the text in which the title is either directly stated or is implied; point out the symbolic significance of mockingbirds, explain which characters can be likened to mockingbirds, and why. [RL.9–10.1]

(Continued)

TABLE 3.3. (Continued)

Qualitative Dimensions	Quantitative Dimensions

Possible Areas of Focus (continued)

- Explain how the following themes and major concepts are presented in the novel. Provide examples from the text to support your argument. Sample Themes (Ignorance and racism lead to injustice and the destruction of innocence. Or Despite its capacity for evil, humanity also has a tremendous capacity for good.) Major Concepts (The destruction of innocence, the evils of racism and classism, hypocrisy). [RL.9–10.2]
- Discuss Atticus Finch as a father, explaining how he acts as a role model for Jem and Scout; identify the moral lessons he teaches his children over the course of the novel, and point out the ways in which many of these lessons relate to the novel's major themes. [RL.9–10.5]
- Discuss how classism is presented in the novel, describing the social hierarchy that exists in Maycomb and pointing out its damaging effects. Identify explicit and implicit examples of racism in Maycomb County, taking into account the trial of Tom Robinson, the gossip among the ladies of the missionary circle, and the racial segregation apparent in the county. [RL.9–10.7]

Differentiation:

- Provide additional background information on the Great Depression and on the Civil Rights Movement.
- Provide explanations about colloquialism and offer examples; provide vocabulary assistance to students per chapter as needed. Involve students in a careful selection of key vocabulary per chapter; involve students in determining the importance of certain words for their understanding of the novel's themes and ideas.
- Select key sections from text and provide time for students to discuss, raise questions, evaluate importance, and make connections with the novel's themes. Provide supporting feedback.

Related Readings: Build students' understanding of racial injustices and the Civil Rights Movement by asking them to research (a) what it meant to be growing up black and white in the 1930s, (b) Jim Crow laws, (c) Key segregation trials, (d) women in the 1930s, (d) the Civil Rights Movement in the South (1954–1963), or (e) most important Supreme Court decisions in Black History.

Learning Extensions: Consider creating and publishing a newspaper; ask students to record their thoughts, feelings, and questions after spending a day in one of the character's shoes; writing a paper about the effects of prejudice around the world (they can select two countries/cultures to compare); or hold a debate on justice vs. moral responsibility.

On the other hand, many students struggle with reading the textbook either due to qualitative, quantitative, or reader factors. For students to be college and career ready, they need to interact with a variety of complex literary and informational texts. The CCSS provide a list of texts students should read and understand in grades 6–12 in order for them to be college and career ready, to deal with the demands of postsecondary learning and living.

Reader Characteristics and Text Complexity

The reader is the participant in the reading process. Rosenblatt (1978) viewed the act of reading as a dynamic continuously interacting act, a "transaction" between the reader and the text. Her work highlighted the reader's unique response to a given text; the reader's motivation, knowledge, language, and experiences "interact" with the reading process. Matching students with text is a "science." Simpler texts are more appropriate for struggling readers whereas more complex texts are more suitable for skilled and motivated readers. In selecting texts for readers, teachers need to consider several factors such as: the reader's cognitive abilities (attention, memory, critical analytic ability, inferencing, visualization); motivation (a purpose for reading, interest in the content, self-efficacy as a reader); knowledge (vocabulary and topic knowledge, linguistic and discourse knowledge, knowledge of comprehension strategies); and experiences (RAND, 2002). The reader's language proficiency is an important factor. Many English language learners and students with learning disabilities and language needs need additional support and interventions.

When reading complex text, students need to read, understand, and use not only conventional language, but also the language of each discipline. Disciplinary vocabulary can make reading a text challenging and even un-motivating. Reader experiences will vary according to the student's social, cultural, and economic background. Student motivation is a very important factor, especially for adolescent readers. Students will bring their personal interests to the text, to selecting texts to read, and to the reading process. Finding purpose, relevance, and developing confidence with reading and understanding complex text can promote motivation to read and persistence.

College, Career, and Workforce Connections

- "GRADES 11-CCR: By the end of grade 12, read and comprehend literature (informational texts) at the high end of the grade 11-CCR text complexity band independently and proficiently. By the end of grade 11, read and comprehend literature (information texts) in the grades 11-CCR text complexity band proficiently, and with scaffolding as needed at the high end of the range" (Retrieved from http://www.corestandards.org/the-standards/english-language-arts-standards/reading-informational-text-6-12/grade-11-12/).
- To succeed in college, career, and the workforce, high school graduates must be well equipped with the knowledge, habits of mind, and skills that come from a rigorous, rich, and relevant high school curriculum. The CCSS emphasize the role of text complexity in determining student readiness for college and careers.
- Students need to develop their information technology and media skills (e.g., how to research, gather, and evaluate information, search the web, use library and commercial databases, use survey tools, store and use records, and conduct interviews).
- *I need students with solid knowledge background in mathematics, biology, environmental science/earth science and physics, and with good technical writing skills* (Ni-Bin Chang, Professor, Engineering, University of Central Florida).

How Can Teachers Prepare Students to Read and Comprehend Complex Text?

Results have shown that many students do not have adequate experiences with complex texts (ACT, 2006). Reading complex texts should not be solely an independent reading activity; something the student does on his, or her own, quietly at his, or her desk, or at home (Fisher & Frey, 2012). By that, I do not mean that there should be time for independent reading in the classroom. What I do mean is that reading complex text should be an apprenticeship process; students need to be mentored by teachers on how to read and comprehend complex texts, and they also need opportunities to discuss their understanding with peers, generate and respond to evidence-based questions, negotiate, evaluate, and reflect on their inferences and conclusions.

Teachers should not just assign complex text; they should model how to read it and should make their thinking process visible and "tangible" for all to hear and see. Teacher think-alouds will help students learn how the teacher read the text, what she paid attention to, how she activated her background knowledge, how she connected concepts and ideas, and what decisions she made about deriving meaning from text. I will present more information and specific strategies on how to support students when reading complicated text in Chapter 8.

Sometimes teachers assume too much about students' experiences with complex texts and background knowledge on the topic (Chenoweth, 2009). Because students are in an 8th, or an 11th Grade class that does not mean that they know how to read and comprehend the texts of the discipline, or other complex texts for that matter. As a teacher, you will need to determine what your students know (in terms of content and background knowledge, vocabulary, and strategies and skills), what they need to learn, and what you will do to teach them. For example, how are students going to read and learn about operations with polynomials (8th Grade math) if they do not know what multiplication is? Formative assessment will help you make sound instructional decisions.

Applying Discipline-Specific Literacies

- All students should have (a) ample opportunities to experience grade-level complex text, and (b) teachers who scaffold disciplinary reading, thinking habits of mind.
- Disciplinary learning and knowledge development require deep, critical reading. Students need many experiences with reading complex texts in each discipline.
- Close reading of complex texts promotes understanding and appreciation for each discipline's discourse, texts, ways knowledge is organized, shared, developed, and evaluated.

Close Reading of Complex Text

When I think about this section, I am reminded of many visits I have made to some secondary content area classrooms in which students are assigned complex text, but they are not taught how to read and comprehend it. Teaching secondary grades is challenging. Content area teachers often run the "content marathon" race—they try to cover as much content as possible due to standardized testing pressures. As part of this content marathon, they at times cover content without offering students guided instruction in how to read, analyze, think about, discuss, and write about the texts they have been assigned to read.

What is close reading of text? There are a various ways to describe it—e.g., "read like a detective, write like an investigative reporter;" "sleuth reading," "analytical reading," or "critical reading." Close reading of text is a form of guided instruction that focuses on multiple readings and rich discussion about a short, complex piece of text. Did you notice my choice of words? "Guided instruction." This means that close reading is not the same as independent reading. It also means that the teacher and the student(s) play a role in the process. It requires discussion with the teacher and peers in class, and it is used for the purpose of discovering meaning from complex text. Having said that, because it requires two to three (or at times more) re-readings that are followed by discussion, you will not do close reading of text every day. Maybe every other week (depending on your purpose and your students' needs), or at least three to four times in a nine-week long unit; close reading of text can extend over a number of days.

Close reading of text can be practiced with the textbook, supplementary materials, articles, reports, etc. Although as a secondary school teacher, you will not have much control over the textbook you will use in your class, you still need to understand the importance of close reading of text. Practice it with your textbook, as well as with any additional materials you include in your subject area. Through close reading, you will be equipping students how to read complex texts.

Close reading of text keeps the reader focused on the purpose for reading (e.g., find evidence to support a claim, or examine how the author uses choice of words and structure to get his or her message across). In doing so, students ask more questions, read slower and with purpose, develop deeper understanding of the text, and use it for discussions, debates, or writing assignments.

How to Practice Close Reading of Text

Rereading of complex text is necessary in the disciplines as those texts are packed with dense information and ideas and concepts (plus graphics in informational text) that are not always explicitly or simply connected. The CCSS strongly recommend that students should read and comprehend complex text, but that they should consider the purpose of the text, what the author is trying to convey, the choices she made in how she organized the text, as well as context of the text.

Text complexity is a complex issue (no pun intended!). In earlier sections of this chapter I examined ways to determine text complexity. But complex text, however high quality it might be, won't "teach" the students, or equip them with the knowledge, lens and strategies they will need to apply to deconstruct the text. Both the teacher and the student play an important role in close reading of text. In Chapter 2, I shared about learning in grades 6–12 as an apprenticeship process and I also examined the core elements of literacy as a discipline-specific process. The text, teacher, the reader, the classroom environment, all play key roles in student reading and learning.

Step 1

To build students' experiences with close reading of complex text, start small—select a short passage, start with the first paragraph, introduce the text, and ask students to read independently. Although many students might struggle with this approach, it is important to build their experiences and confidence with reading complex text, reading the text, allowing the text to become the first source of information, and even wrestling with it a bit. All teachers want the best for our students and at times they even get a bit uncomfortable when a number of them are struggling with constructing meaning from text.

And what do most teachers do? They start developing study guides, show a lot of movies, spend much time trying to motivate them to read the text, try to find connections (text–self, text–text, text-to-world), etc.; they'll do anything to engage students with the text. But, the more they do that at the onset, the more they remove students from the text. Teachers should not leave students alone in a state of extreme frustration, but they should want them to start forming meaning first by examining the text. I am not suggesting that all reading experiences will be at a paragraph-by-paragraph level, nor do I suggest that aids and means of building students' background knowledge are not necessary. First, build the students' experiences with reading, thinking about, and constructing meaning from complex text, and later on make connections, build their background knowledge, and teach them how to access, assess, and use it.

Step 2

After students read independently, read the same text aloud as students follow along from text; ask students to pay attention—this will also support their fluency as students are being exposed to skilled reading by the teacher, or a skilled peer. Depending on need, you can direct students to do a third rereading of the same text and paraphrase in their own words their understanding of it. Ask students to annotate the text while reading, and discuss their thoughts about the text with their partner(s). Scholars make their knowledge public, they collaborate with others, consider others' views and evidence, and think carefully about what they read. Complex text requires careful reading, and evidence-based thinking, talking, and writing. As students re-read the text they can take notes, make annotations to the text (e.g., highlighting, circling key words or phrases, marking the text through symbols that indicate importance (*), or uncertainty (?), or write a more formal response as needed). Ask students to paraphrase what they understand from the text in their own words.

Step 3

Now, ask students to re-read the text for the purpose of answering a set of text-dependent questions you developed. The number and type of text-dependent questions you will ask will vary according to your goal, text, and meaning you want your students to develop. Why interact with the text again and with one another? Because thinking and learning like a scholar is a rigorous, collaborative and reflective inquiry process. Teachers write the text-dependent questions to guide students' thinking about the text, invite them to find textual evidence to support their inferences, and develop their overall understanding of the text. Text-dependent questions also become the vehicle for further class discussions about the text. Teachers should build students' background knowledge about the topic or text during reading rather than before.

The discussion can take place in a small group format or in a whole class one; it depends on your objectives and the students' needs. Accountable talk (i.e., talk that is relevant to the discipline, has good reasoning, and aims to develop everyone's knowledge in the classroom) works very well for holding evidence-based discussions. After students discuss their understanding of the text through the use of text-dependent questions and accountable talk, ask them to rewrite their "translation." This will invite them to go back to the text as needed to clarify, verify, and expand their thinking. The teacher plays a key role here as she should model how she read the text and should make her thinking and decisions visible to students through think-alouds—through verbalizing how she read the text, what she thought when she was reading, what she noted about words, language, text structure, or the author's voice, and what decisions she made using the text. At all times, the teacher should be monitoring student progress, facilitating student understanding of text, and guiding the discussion to the next text selection. In the following section, I will present more elaborations on, and examples of, text-dependent questions.

You might be thinking by now, "I don't have a whole day to read a paragraph closely!" You are correct, and I hope that you would not take a whole day to do it! This close reading sequence might take place a bit slowly at the beginning, but as you select more and more strategic parts of the text to do close reading with the students, you will be building their experiences, their proficiency, and persistence. Over time, with your support, students will become more self-efficacious. At the same time, they will learn to appreciate the importance of close reading of discipline-specific complex texts. Frontloading your instruction with slow, purposeful, scaffolded, and relevant close reading will pay off for you and your students. See Table 3.4 for a sample close reading protocol you can use (and modify as needed) for your planning.

Text-Dependent Questions

The CCSS spotlight students' ability to read closely to determine what a text says and to make logical inferences from it. The CCSS plan with the end in mind, preparing students for college and career mastery of the following standard: "Read closely to determine what the text says explicitly and to make logical inferences from it; cite specific textual evidence when writing or speaking to support conclusions drawn from the text" (R.CCR.1).

What happens when you visit some content area classrooms? You know the drill, right? A lot of times you will see the teacher give a quick introduction to the chapter/unit or topic, assign the reading and direct students to answer a couple or all of the questions at the end of the chapter,

TABLE 3.4. Sample Protocol for Close Reading of Complex Text

Step 1. 1st Reading: Read on your own (Annotation, optional)
  a. What does the text say?
  b. Think about the text, look for patterns, look for unknown words, get a feel for the text (annotate as needed)
  c. After reading, talk with a partner about the text

Step 2: 2nd Reading: Read with a pencil/pen (Option: Teacher read aloud)
  a. Read, think, & talk with your pencil: annotate the text
    i. Place a star next to key terms
    ii. Circle unknown words
    iii. Underline claims, or biases (depending on purpose)
    iv. Or, on the left margin: write notes about what the author *is saying*—example: summarize chunks of text in five words
    v. Or, on the right margin: dig deeper: write a power verb to describe what the author *is doing*
  b. Talk with your partner(s), and reread as needed
  c. Use evidence to support your thoughts: I think it means . . . because . . .

Step 3: 3rd Reading: Re-read to find answers to text-dependent questions
  a. Study the text-dependent question(s) before rereading
  b. Read with purpose
  c. Write your answer(s) and cite evidence from the text to support answer(s)
  d. Ask yourself: What evidence do I have? Is my evidence accurate and sufficient?
  e. Discuss with your partner(s)

Step 4: Additional Reading (Optional)
  a. Teacher reads with students for further discussion of text, Socratic seminar, debate, or writing

depending on how much time is available. Scan the class and you may see students read quietly (many fake reading, and a couple are sleeping in the back of the room). If there is any time left, the teacher will ask a couple of questions, three–five students might respond, the teacher might give a bit of feedback, and then the bell rings. And, to make things worst, this cycle is repeated (in some settings) day in and day out throughout the year.

Instead of just asking students questions about students' background knowledge or experiences, the standards expect students to grapple, to struggle (in a positive sense) with text-dependent, or text-based questions. Although making connections with the text or topic is important and motivating and acts as an incentive for "luring" students into reading more, a lot of times the discussion moves from one disjointed connection to the next and in a few minutes you can have an entire class that is confused and has lost interest in reading more, reading deeply, and analyzing the text. This type of questioning removes the student away from the text. In addition, many times teachers in trying to engage students with the text, ask a lot of literal questions that produce a few responses, but do not facilitate deep understanding of text. It is interesting to note that although 80–90% of CCSS reading standards require text-dependent questions, over 30% of questions in textbooks do not.

For example, note the following two questions.

1. Up to chapter 8 (in *To Kill a Mockingbird*) Boo Radley has been perceived as a madman or a monster. What evidence in the past two chapters indicates that he is not the threatening figure that people have made him out to be?
2. Do you know of anyone who might have been misunderstood by others?

The first question requires the students to locate information from the past two chapters and provide evidence from the text for their responses. Students would come to the conclusion that Boo Radley was a kind, caring, and responsible man contrary to what most townspeople believe, *after* they reread the text and considered specific evidence *from text* about his actions. Responses may vary, but here are some pieces of evidence students might use from the text on this character: Boo was responsible for kindly mending Jem's pants and folding them neatly over the fence. Evidence also points to him being behind all of the gifts that Jem and Scout found in the tree and Boo was the one who put the blanket around Scout on the night of the fire. The second question does not actually require students to read the text to answer it. Actually, it takes them away from the text. There will be time to ask this kind of question *after* students have been inundated in the text but on the onset, for students to learn from the text, they need to consider the text as their first source.

Let's examine a couple of text-dependent questions for informational text:

1. Reading the following text, what is (and isn't) the meaning of "popular sovereignty" in this text selection? Why does Monk claim that this is the form of government in America?

    The first three words of the Constitution are the most important. They clearly state that the people—not the king, not the *legislature*, not the courts—are the true rulers in American government. This **principle** is known as popular **sovereignty**.

    But who are "We the People"? This question troubled the nation for centuries. As Lucy Stone, one of America's first **advocates** for women's rights, asked in 1853, " 'We the People'? Which 'We the People'? The women were not included." Neither were white males who did not own property, American Indians, or African Americans—slave or free.

    (Source: Monk, Linda R. Words We Live By: Your Annotated Guide to the Constitution, Achieve Grade 8 Close Reading Exemplar, Retrieved from http://www.achievethecore.org/steal-these-tools/close-reading-exemplars)

2. What are your feelings about your US American heritage?

The first question is pretty clear; it does require an understanding of the remainder text analysis by the author. For students to answer the second part of question one, they will need go back to the text, read, and make inferences about "We the People" and also about the next paragraph of the Constitution's Preamble. The second question is broad and is attempting to get to the text through the students' feelings or emotions. The first three words of the first paragraph are vital to the text's message and it is asking students to think critically about the text through the text.

Benefits of Text-Dependent Questions

Text-dependent questions do not require prior knowledge of the topic nor do they elicit personal or emotional responses to questions; instead, they can only be answered by going back to the text in front of them. Text-dependent questions ask students to closely examine specific phrases, sentences, or short text selections and encourage them to think carefully about the text. They invite students to examine aspects of text that are usually overlooked when students conduct rushed reading. In other words, text-dependent questions promote scholarly reading and thinking and mirror how disciplinary experts read text carefully, systematically, and analytically in order to have informed conversations about that text.

According to the standards, students should spend time in the text, making sense of the text first, use the text as the first source of investigation, get immersed in it, and then make connections with personal experiences. Certain parts of the text will elicit connections with other texts. Text-dependent questions are not just about recall and passively reading text while waiting for the teacher to tell students what to do next. They "pull" the student back to the text to search the text for a plausible explanation. Text-dependent questions by themselves will not automatically help students read and comprehend complex texts. Through text-dependent questions and scaffolded support students can develop ownership and independence.

Text-dependent questions such as "Where in the text did you see that?"; "Show me in the text why you believe so . . ."; "What is the author up to? Why did he choose these words, perspectives, or sequence of events?"; "What is happening in this paragraph?", or "What does the author mean by . . ." will guide students to think what the text is about, think about what is stated or unstated, and pay close attention to the text. Text-dependent questions require much of the teacher and the student. Teachers need to plan for instruction that will help students read and think like scholars instead of just spectators.

Different Types of Text-Dependent Questions

As a teacher, you will have to do much careful planning about what questions are worth asking in the text. For example, in *To Kill a Mockingbird*, "Where does the author introduce the word 'mockingbird' and where does she go with that?; "Why does the author use quotations in the book?"; "What do they tell about the author's style?"; "What quotations from the text explain the concept of racial prejudice?"; "What evidence from the text supports Atticus' advice to Scout: 'You never really understand a person until you consider things from his point of view—until you climb into his skin and walk around in it.' " (Lee, 1960, p. 30); or "What evidence can you use from the text that shows that Scout puts Atticus' above advice into practice by living with sympathy and understanding toward others?" See different types of text-dependent questions followed by specific examples below.

There are three different types of text-dependent questions:

1. *Questions that assess themes and central ideas.*
    a. What evidence from the text supports positive perspectives of the Native Americans? Negative? (English Language Arts/Social Studies: European Americans and Native Americans View Each Other, 1700–1775; Text grade band: 11).
    b. What 1–3 key changes does the author of the CPR article suggest to CPR to improve success rates? (Career and Technical Subjects/Health Education: Cardiopulmonary Resuscitation (CPR); Text grade band: 9–10).
    c. What has been the most devastating impact of introducing rats to the Galapagos island ecosystem? (Science: Text grade band: 6–8).
2. *Questions that assess vocabulary knowledge.*
    a. What meaning can you infer from the use of the words "iron tyranny"? (English Language Arts/Social Studies: *John F. Kennedy: Inaugural Address* (1961); Text grade band: 11–12).
    b. The author uses the word "revolution" to describe what is happening in the world of 3-D printing. What evidence does he cite to support the use of that word in the text? (Career and Technical Subjects: Cardiopulmonary Resuscitation (CPR)/STEM: 3-D Printing; Text grade band: 6–8).
    c. How are "cloning," "genetic engineering," and "artificial selection" different? Use evidence from the text to support your answer. (Science: DNA; Text grade band: 6–10).
3. *Questions that assess syntax and structure.*
    a. According to the introductory statement in JFK's 1961 Inaugural Address, who is specifically in the audience? (English Language Arts/Social Studies: *John F. Kennedy: Inaugural Address* (1961); Text grade band: 11–12).

    b. How did the author choose to communicate the importance in the success rate of CPR at the beginning of the text? (Career and Technical Subjects: Cardiopulmonary Resuscitation (CPR)/STEM: 3-D Printing; Text grade band: 6–8).

    c. Describe how the prefix in "epigenetics" conveys the author's idea that human traits are dependent on what's in the genes. (Science: DNA; Text grade band: 6–10).

Keep in mind that one text-dependent question that is appropriate for one text might not be appropriate for another; this is a unique difference between general and text-dependent questions.

How to Construct Text-Dependent Questions

Here are some steps in planning for and constructing text-dependent questions. (And, just for fun, I will try to attach an African proverb to each step in hopes that it will serve as a mnemonic for you, and help nail the message.)

1. *Identify Key "Big Ideas" and Insights Students Need to Learn From Text.* This means that as a teacher, you need to do the preparatory work of planning, reflecting on standards, students, and text and mapping out what they need to learn from this selection and how you will get them there. Make time for the text; plan for careful examination of the text. (African Proverb: If you fail to plan, you plan to fail—Teacher planning is vital to student success.)

2. *First Steps First: Start Small to Build Student Confidence.* Craft specific opening questions that can build student confidence and promote persistence. The first questions are critical as they will orient the student into the meaning of the text and prepare her to do the work of meaning making. (African Proverb: Little by little grow the bananas—Every small step you take toward your goal, gets you closer to your goal. It takes time for students to learn how to dissect the text, analyze it, and read it like a scholar; it takes scaffolded support and practice with varied genres and degrees of complexity.)

3. *Address Vocabulary and Text Structure.* Disciplinary complex texts are loaded with technical vocabulary; identify key academic words and text structures that connect to key ideas in the text. (African Proverb: When the music changes, so does the dance—Students need to develop good understanding of words, word meanings, and text structures.)

4. *Begin with the Toughest Text First.* Many times, teachers avoid having students wrestle with the difficult texts or ideas because of reader factors. Students do not need the teacher to be doing their work; they need the teacher to be a facilitator of their learning. Start with the sections that have difficult text structure, vocabulary, and ideas. Supporting students in mastering the difficult text will also act as a confidence boost and will facilitate persistence. (African Proverb: Smooth seas do not make skillful sailors—Students learn and grow through challenges; close reading of complex text is not an easy or automatic process.)

5. *Develop Logical, Gradual, and Progressive Sequences of Text-Dependent Questions.* There has to be a progressive logic and sequence to the questions. Questions need to be building the "meaning puzzle" gradually, one question at a time and they all need to be expanding students' understanding of the text. (African Proverb: A little rain each day will fill the rivers to overflowing—Don't expect students to master everything at once. A steady pace, constantly taking small steps toward the goal will promote mastery and prevent students from getting frustrated and quitting too soon.)

6. *Identify Which Standards Are Addressed in the Text.* Identify which standards are met in the text and what students need to learn and be able to do. (African Proverb: If you understand the beginning well, the end will not trouble you—You have to have a step-by-step strategy of what you want to accomplish.)

7. *Create Quality, Thought-Provoking Culminating Assessments.* Eliminate busy work. Develop culminating activities around key ideas that reflect mastery of the standards, involve writing, give students opportunities to apply their insights, and are to be completed independently by students. (African Proverb: Knowledge is like a garden: if it is not cultivated, it cannot be harvested—What do you want students to do with the knowledge they gain from the text and the learning experience? How will they put it to use?)

Think Like An Expert

● Literary scholars read through a literary lens: for interpretation of a story, the behavior of its characters, the use of language, and the use of literary devices. (English Language Arts)
● Mathematicians read carefully, slowly, closely, attentively, analytically, and precisely. (Mathematics)
● Scientists apply an inquiry stance when they read text; they read critically, pay attention to vocabulary and mathematical and visual information, and read for explanation and prediction. (Science)
● Historians read critically, consider the author's (and their own) perspectives and biases, and look for "whys" (why events happened, why the author arrived at such conclusions) and "hows" (how they affected people; how the author developed and supported explanations). (Social Studies)

Accountable Talk

Student discussions and collaborative reflection on text are important for shaping students' understanding of text. Accountable talk can promote rich and evidence-based discussions among students and between students and the teacher. Evidence-based discussions make it necessary for students to revisit the text, and look for evidence that supports their arguments and insights in an accurate, precise, and reflective way. Accountable talk that includes text-dependent questions will facilitate careful and text-based thinking, will invite students to go back and revisit the text to collect more evidence for their assertions, and it will also over time create a culture of critical examination of knowledge and learning.

Asking students text-dependent questions should take place at all times and in each content area. There are comprehension benefits from rereading text and if close reading of text is something that students expect and experience in your classroom, they will start to view close reading as a necessity when reading a complex text in any context. I will examine accountable talk in great detail in Chapter 8, but for the purpose of this chapter, I would like to provide you with some examples of accountable talk and how it could facilitate close reading of text, rereading to clarify thinking, and discussing and prompting evidence-based thinking, reasoning, and discipline-specific discussions in the content area classroom. Figure 3.3 presents sample ways teachers can use accountable talk to promote text-dependent questioning, thinking, and talking in various content area classrooms.

English Language Arts

1. Can you give us some evidence from the text that supports your assertion?
2. Using evidence from the text, what next action should the main character take to resolve the situation?
3. What is the purpose of the metaphors used throughout the text?

Mathematics

1. Is this variable important? Can you explain why it is/isn't?
2. What information is essential to the problem?
3. Could you explain how your solution to the problem worked?

Accountable Talk

Science

1. What are the steps in your scientific method?
2. What are the advantages of this solution? Can you provide some evidence?
3. What science rules should be followed in ...?

Social Studies

1. I'm not sure I see the relevance of this point in your conclusion.... Can you help me understand it? How is it relevant?
2. What tensions (*political, economic, social, racial, etc.*) existed at that time?
3. What are five key words in this primary document and what do they mean?

FIGURE 3.3. Sample accountable talk in core disciplines.

Source: "What is disciplinary literacy and why aren't we talking more about it?" by V. Zygouris-Coe, 2012. Available from http://vocablog-plc.blogspot.com/2012/03/what-is-disciplinary-literacy-and-why.html. Printed with permission.

Digital Literacies

- Read and annotate online texts and share annotations with others: www.diigo. com.
- Free teen books and resources at the US Library of Congress: http://www.read. gov/teens/; Epic books: http://www.epicreads.com; Cool books for teens: http:// www.pulseit.com; Romance books online: http://www.publicbookshelf.com/ teen/; Free ebooks for teens: http://www.goodreads.com/list/show/23017.FREE_ Ebooks_For_Teens; Online contemporary and romance books: http://www.story-crush.com; Teen contemporary books, author interviews, and resources: http:// www.teenreads.com.
- Construct concepts maps or outlines: www.mind42.com or use Smart Art in Microsoft Word.

Text Complexity and a Disciplinary Literacy Learning Framework in Grades 6–12

In this chapter, I have examined the importance of text complexity, how to measure or determine it, what factors to keep in mind when selecting texts, and how to model and foster close reading in the disciplines. It is obvious that preparing students for school, college, career, and life learning

TABLE 3.5. Ten Guiding Principles for Implementing Text Complexity and a Disciplinary Literacy Learning Framework in Grades 6–12

1. Introduce text and establish purpose.
2. Practice close reading (careful reading, rereading, interacting with text, annotating text, identifying confusing text, self-monitoring) with a wide range of literary and informational texts of varied complexity.
   a. Students read text selection independently (students can annotate text: highlight, identify confusing parts) (1st read).
   b. Teacher reads aloud, students follow along in text (2nd read).
   c. Students reread text selection and "translate" or paraphrase in their own words (3rd read).
   d. Teacher asks text-dependent questions about text selection.
   e. Discussion (small group or whole class).
   f. Students re-write their "translation" after discussion.
   g. Teacher monitors student understanding and guides discussion on next text selection.
   h. Wrap-up.
3. Provide rigorous, rich, and relevant instruction that is aligned with standards, focuses on developing discipline-specific habits of mind, disciplinary discourse, and deep content and literacy learning.
4. Offer targeted scaffolded support that encourages student persistence with learning.
5. Model and ask critical, thought-provoking, and worthy text-dependent questions.
6. Model, practice, and foster accountable talk.
7. Expect evidence-based reasoning, thinking, and writing using varied valid, reliable, and sufficient evidence.
8. Support discipline-specific inquiry, research, and writing (from multiple texts or sources).
9. Foster student independence, curiosity, and motivation to read, write, and learn.
10. Create a culture of collaborative inquiry and reflection.

requires a lot from the teacher and the students. Although the CCSS resulted in much focus on text complexity, in my view teaching all students to read and comprehend challenging texts in grades 6–12 is not tied to the CCSS. Disciplinary thinking and learning requires reading and comprehending complex texts. Rigor, relevance, responsibility, relationships, and accountability are necessary elements. Table 3.5 above outlines important steps teachers can consider when planning to incorporate text complexity within a disciplinary learning framework. As you examine these principles, note the number of readings and rereadings of text, the role of the teacher in providing scaffolded support through the gradual release of responsibility, the role of relevant, evidence-based and informed classroom discussions, and also the fundamental importance of teacher planning.

Text Exemplars

Appendix B of the CCSS (NGA & CCSSO, 2010a) includes information on exemplars of text complexity, quality, and examples of texts for grades K–12 (see pp. 77–140 for grades 6–CCR); use it as a reference, not a mandate. For additional information on close reading exemplars, see Student Achievement Partners' *Achieve the Core*; retrieved from http://www.achievethecore.org/steal-these-tools/close-reading-exemplars).

Teachers can use these exemplars as a guide when selecting text of similar quality, complexity, and range in their classrooms. According to the CCSS, text selection should be guided by three criteria: (1) complexity, (2) quality (texts that have literary merit, cultural significance, and rich content), and (3) range (high quality texts that vary in publication date, authorship, and topic).

Summary

- Research shows that students come to secondary classes with more experiences with narrative than expository texts. The CCSS are based upon a premise that real learning comes from experiences with complex text and much teacher scaffolded support.
- Reading complex text requires teacher knowledge in how to (a) determine the quantitative measures of the text (word length, word frequency, word difficulty, sentence length, text length, text cohesion); (b) analyze the qualitative measures of the text (structure, language demands, conventions, knowledge demands, levels of meaning, purpose); and, (c) reflect on the reader and task considerations (motivation, knowledge and experiences, purpose for reading, complexity of task assigned regarding the text; complexity of questions regarding the text).
- Dynamic interactions between the reader and the text, purposeful, close, and careful (not superficial skimming) reading of text, rigorous, rich, relevant instruction that promotes discipline-specific ways for examining, evaluating, and reflecting on text, and collaborative peer inquiry play a role in reading and learning in the disciplines.

Differentiating Instruction

- To support differentiated instruction in reading, it is extremely important to measure the text complexity of content and student reading ability.
- Struggling readers, ELLs, and students with language and learning disabilities will require additional support and interventions in order to develop their capacity with reading and comprehending complex text.
- With ELLs, provide access to grade level content, build on students' first language skills and knowledge, build on effective practices used with native English speakers, make needed instructional adjustments, and promote collaboration among all students.
- Students with varied exceptionalities need much help with text structure; text features can be helpful to them for locating and following the flow of information. They also need reminders about purpose, reflecting while they are reading, and interacting with the text.

Reflect and Apply

1. How do you read complex text? Share your experiences with a small group or the entire class and discuss how your experiences might have framed your practice.
2. What insights from this chapter could you use to offer some suggestions to Ms. Miller (see Classroom Life vignette)? Apply your knowledge about reading complex text to her instructional challenge. Discuss your suggestions with a peer, or with a small group of peers.
3. Select a complex text from your content area. Use the close reading instructional sequence to map out how you will model and support close reading of text. Share

your plans with your peers, and discuss how to improve your instruction to make it more rigorous, relevant, and effective.

Extending Learning

1. You and a couple of your colleagues are working on a unit plan. What text or text selections will you select from relevant complex text to promote close reading in your classroom? Plan on your own first, identify text and/or text selections, and write five to seven text-dependent questions. You can also use the performance tasks shared in the chapter as models for creating your own assessment. Share your ideas with your colleagues, consider their perspectives, and revisit your plans. Lastly, plan to get together every couple of days to reflect on the implementation of your plan.

2. Using your insights and evidence from the text, what role do disciplinary habits of mind, apprenticeship, gradual release of responsibility, and accountable talk play in reading and comprehending complex text? Provide specific evidence from text, discuss with your peers, revisit the text as needed, and present your views to a larger group.

3. In a small group of peers from your discipline, select two examples of complex text. Work together with your peers to identify (a) qualitative dimensions of text complexity, (b) quantitative dimensions of text complexity, and (c) reader factors. Discuss challenges associated with text selection and close reading instruction and share your work and perspectives with your peers.

References

Achieve, Inc. (2007). *Closing the expectations gap 2007*. Washington, DC: Author.

Alexander, P. A., & Jetton, T. L. (2000). Learning from text: A multidimensional and developmental perspective. In M. L. Kamil, P. B. Mosenthal, P. D. Pearson, & R. Barr (Eds), *Handbook of reading research*, (Vol. III, pp. 285–310). Mahwah, NJ: Lawrence Erlbaum Associates.

American College Testing. (2006). *Reading between the lines: What the ACT reveals about college readiness in reading*. Iowa City, IA: Author.

Berman, I., & Biancarosa, G. (2005). *Reading to achieve: A governor's guide to adolescent literacy*. Washington, DC: NGA Center for Best Practices.

Chenoweth, K. (2009). *How it's being done: Urgent lessons from unexpected schools*. Cambridge, MA: Harvard Education Press.

Fang, Z., & Schleppegrell, M. J. (2008). *Reading in secondary content areas: A language-based pedagogy*. Ann Arbor, MI: The University of Michigan Press.

Fang, Z., & Schleppegrell, M. J. (2010). Disciplinary literacies across content areas: Supporting secondary reading through functional language analysis. *Journal of Adolescent & Adult Literacy*, 53(7), 587–597.

Fisher, D., & Frey, N. (2009). *Background knowledge: The missing piece of the comprehension puzzle*. Portsmouth, NH: Heinemann.

Fisher, D., & Frey, N. (2012). *Engaging the adolescent learner: Text complexity and close readings*. Newark, DE: International Reading Association.

Fry, E. (2002). Readability versus leveling. *The Reading Teacher*, 56(3), 286–292.

Graves, M. F. (1984). Selecting vocabulary to teach in the intermediate and secondary grades. In J. Flood (Ed.), *Promoting reading comprehension* (pp. 245–260). Newark, DE: International Reading Association.

Harmon, J., Hedrick, W., & Wood, K. (2005). Research on vocabulary instruction in the content areas: Implications for struggling readers. *Reading & Writing Quarterly*, 21, 261–280.

Hartman, D. K., Morsink, P. M., & Zheng, J. (2010). From print to pixels: The evolution of cognitive conceptions of reading comprehension. In E.A. Baker (Ed.), *Multiple perspectives on new literacies research and instruction* (pp. 131–164). New York, NY: Guilford.

Hayes, D., Wolfer, L., & Wolfe, M. (1996). *Schoolbook simplification and its relation to the decline in SAT verbal scores: Scholastic aptitude test.* New York, NY: Scholastic, Inc.

Heller, R., & Greenleaf, C. (2007). Literacy instruction in the content areas: Getting to the core of middle and high school improvement. Washington, DC: Alliance for Excellent Education.

Krashen, S. (1994). Why support a delayed-gratification approach to language education? *The Language Teacher, 28*(7), 3–7.

Lee, C. D., & Spratley, A. (2010). *Reading in the disciplines: The challenges of adolescent literacy.* New York: Carnegie Corporation of New York.

Lee, H. (1960). *To kill a mockingbird.* New York, NY: J.B. Lippincott.

Leu, D. J., McVerry, J. G., O'Bryne, W. I., Zawilinski, L., Castek, J., & Hartman, D. K. (2008). The new literacies of online reading comprehension and the irony of No Child Left Behind: Students who require our assistance the most, actually receive it the least. In L. M. Morrow, R. Rueda, & D. Lapp (Eds). *Handbook of research on literacy instruction: Issues of diversity, policy, and equity,* p. 321–346. New York, NY: Guilford.

Marzano, R. J. (2004). *Building background knowledge for academic achievement: Research on what works in schools.* Alexandria, VA: ASCD.

Moje, E. B. (2008). Foregrounding the disciplines in secondary literacy teaching and learning: A call for change. *Journal of Adolescent and Adult Literacy, 52*(2), 96–107.

Nagy, W. E., & Scott, J. A. (2000). Vocabulary processes. In M. L. Kamil, P. Mosenthal, P. D. Pearson, & R. Barr (Eds), *Handbook of reading research* (Vol. 3, pp. 269–284). Mahwah, NJ: Erlbaum.

National Council of Teachers of English. (2006a). *A call to action: What we know about adolescent literacy and ways to support teachers in meeting students' needs: A position statement.* Retrieved from http://www.ncte.org/positions/statements/adolescentliteracy/

National Council of Teachers of English. (2006b). *NCTE principles of adolescent literacy reform: A policy research brief.* National Council of Teachers of English: Author.

National Governors Association Center for Best Practices (NGA), Council of Chief State School Officers (CCSSO). (2010a). *Common Core State Standards.* Retrieved from http://corestandards.org

National Governors Association Center for Best Practices (NGA), Council of Chief State School Officers (CCSSO). (2010b). *Common Core State Standards. Appendix A: Research supporting key elements of the standards; Glossary of key terms.* In *Common Core State Standards for English Language Arts & Literacy in History/Social Studies, Science, and Technical Subjects.* Retrieved from http://www.corestandards.org/assets/Appendix_A.pdf

RAND Reading Study Group. (2002). *Reading for understanding: Toward a research and development program in reading comprehension.* Santa Monica, CA: Office of Education Research and Improvement.

Rosenblatt, L. (1978). *The reader, the text, the poem: The transactional theory of the literary work.* Carbondale, IL: Southern Illinois University Press.

Schell, V. (1982). Learning partners: Reading and mathematics. *The Reading Teacher, 35,* 544–548.

Schleppegrell, M. J., & M. C. Colombi (Eds). (2002). *Developing advanced literacy in first and second languages: Meaning with power.* Mahwah, NJ: Lawrence Erlbaum.

Shanahan, T., & Shanahan, C. (2008). Teaching disciplinary literacy to adolescents: Rethinking content-area literacy. *Harvard Educational Review, 78,* 40–59.

Shanahan, T., & Shanahan, C. (2012). What is disciplinary literacy and why does it matter? *Topics in Language Disorders, 32,* 1–12.

Townsend, D. (2009). Building academic vocabulary in after-school settings: Games for growth with middle school English-language learners. *Journal of Adolescent and Adult Literacy, 53,* 242–251.

four
Rigorous Instruction in the Disciplines

Instead of continuing to provide the vast majority of students with a skill-and-drill education, the United States needs to provide all students with a thinking curriculum, with writing workshops, reading clubs, research projects, debates, think tanks, and the like.
–Lucy Calkins, Mary Ehrenworth, & Christopher Lehman. Pathways to the Common Core Accelerating Achievement (2012, p. 17)

Chapter Highlights

- New educational standards do not show teachers how to teach; rigorous, effective, discipline-specific, and powerful teaching is needed to help students reach the standards.
- Rigorous instruction promotes deep learning, inquiry, metacognitive behaviors, persistence, and the ability to learn and problem-solve even in the midst of uncertainty and ambiguity.
- When planning for rigorous instruction, ask yourself, "What will all students need to know, be able to do, and what types of thinking processes will they need to engage in?" (Standards); "How will I know if they have learned it?" (Assessment); "How do I teach so that all students will learn?" (Instruction); "What will I do if they don't know, or if they come to us already knowing?" (Intervention, Differentiation, Enrichment).
- Explicit instruction helps make rigor visible to all, equips all with the tools, dispositions, skills, and knowledge needed to learn in deep and transferable ways, and facilitates mastery of learning goals.
- Rigor needs to exist in standards, expectations for all, learning goals, instruction, materials, classroom environment, learning experiences, support, and assessment.
- Rigorous instruction in the disciplines should equip all students with the specific types of thinking needed in our society, such as, analytical reasoning, interpretation, hypothesizing, problem-solving, drawing inferences, reflection, and synthesis.

Classroom Life

During an 8th grade lesson incorporating guided practice on reviewing simple algebraic expressions and the distributive property, Ms. Ferrante asks a student to complete the following simplification $8(6x + 4)$. The student hesitates and the teacher provides wait time. After 30-45 seconds, the student articulates, "I don't know! I can't do this; I am so stupid." Ms. Ferrante proceeds to do the following to resolve this situation. First she reassures the student and says, "We all have questions about what we are learning and some times things might not make sense right away; Anthony, that does not make you stupid! I don't want to hear you or anyone else say that about themselves in my class ever again! Let me go over a couple more examples to make sure we are all on the same page." She then proceeds to model the problem again through a think-aloud and makes connections with what they have already learned in class about relationships between linear equations and previous concepts or equations. She listens to the way the student is attempting to solve the problem, gives him feedback, and addresses any misconceptions. Next, she asks students to work on a similar problem with a partner, gives them time to discuss how they arrived at the solution, and walks around the classroom listening to students' conversations about the problem. She hears Anthony say, "I got it!" and watches him help his partner with the problem. She decides in the future to spend more time on guided practice before she calls on a student individually. *(Ms. Pam Ferrante, Instructional Specialist, Seminole County Public Schools, Florida).*

Classroom Instruction and Student Achievement

In Chapter 1, we examined the importance of a knowledgeable and well-prepared teacher. Since we will be discussing high impact instruction in the disciplines in this chapter, it is important that we make a couple of key connections. The No Child Left Behind (NCLB) Public Act (2002) placed the term "teacher quality" front and center in the educational arena. More recently, with President Obama's Race to the Top, there is a continued focus on teacher effectiveness.

Several studies from the Bill and Melinda Gates Foundation (e.g., *Gathering Feedback for Teaching: Combining High Quality Observations with Student Surveys and Achievement Gains*, 2012); McKinsey & Company's *Closing the Talent Gap* (Auguste, Kihn, & Miller, 2010), the Center on Education Policy's paper on the status of state K–12 education funding and reforms, *What Impact Did Education Stimulus Funds Have on States and School Districts?* (Rentner & Usher, 2012), and others are unified in their recommendations for better evaluation systems of teacher effectiveness. According to these and other reports, the quality of classroom instruction matters. Why should you consider these reports about teacher evaluation systems? Teacher effectiveness as measured through instruction evaluation and student achievement is the talk of the day in education. Marzano, Frontier, and Livingston (2011) state that student achievement in classes with skilled teachers who provide deliberate practice is better than student achievement in classes with less skilled teachers.

Teaching is highly complex. It requires effective preparation, strong content and pedagogical knowledge (Shulman, 1987), informed decision-making, professional judgment, and the ability to adapt to student learning needs. Preparation, practical practice, mentoring, support, time, reflection, professional dispositions are all necessary for making informed instructional decisions. Theory and research alone will not do it; and neither can practice alone help teachers become effective in their craft.

In this era of new educational standards, the topic of planning, providing, and reflecting on quality classroom instruction for all students is key for student learning. High quality, effective teaching has been proved to be the best predictor of student achievement (Goldhaber, 2002; Hanushek, Kain, O'Brien, & Rivkin, 2005). More specifically, a student with a very high-quality teacher will achieve a learning gain of 1.5 grade-level equivalents, whereas a student with a low-quality teacher achieves a gain of only 0.5 grade-level equivalents (Hanushek, 1992); this means that a year's worth of student growth is attributed to teacher quality differences. What you do matters for student learning and achievement.

What is needed to make the biggest positive impact on student learning? So far in this book, you have seen that the Common Core State Standards (CCSS) (2010) provide one answer to this question as they are designed for rigor, critical thinking, and deep learning. But standards alone cannot result in improved student learning. To stay competitive in the 21st century and beyond, students will need to be strategic problem-solvers, have mastery of both basic and advanced thinking skills, communicate clearly and effectively, and become independent learners.

The question, "What, from what I am doing in class today, will have the biggest impact on student learning?" needs to be a question every teacher asks himself or herself daily as he, or she plans for instruction. I used the following list of questions to reflect on my thinking about rigorous instruction and frame this chapter. All of the following elements interact with student learning, mastery, and motivation to continue to learn. I hope that you find them useful as you plan your instruction.

- How will my learning goals affect student learning?
- What impact will my instruction have on student learning?
  - How will I know what my students are learning, or what areas they need assistance in?
  - How will I assess and monitor student learning?
- What instructional strategies will I use to facilitate student learning?
- What types of scaffolded and other support will I provide to students?
- Will students work alone, or in small groups? (For what purpose? When? For how long?)
- What materials will I use to foster student learning?
- How will I organize my learning environment so it is conducive to learning?

Current teacher evaluation models around the nation continue to shed additional attention on the role of effective teaching on student performance. Why is it important to develop a common understanding of what good classroom instruction looks like? And if we do, does that mean that every teacher will teach the same way? No, it does not; that is not the goal. The goal is to create a shared vision of effective instruction and equip every teacher with knowledge and proven instructional practices that promote student learning in every classroom. Teacher, content, context, and reader factors will all create a unique and distinct learning environment. What is important for all educators to learn is how to plan and deliver classroom instruction that is rigorous, effective, and focused on student learning.

CCSS Connections

- The CCSS call for moving classroom teaching away from a focus on worksheets, drill and memorizing activities to an engaging, rigorous, and relevant curriculum that supports content acquisition requiring students to employ key cognitive strategies for learning and success in school and beyond.
- For students to graduate from high school prepared for postsecondary success in college, or career, they will need to know how to think deeply and accurately,

identify, analyze, and evaluate multiple meanings, engage in discipline-specific inquiry and thought, deal with uncertainty and work through complexity, and use knowledge, skills, and processes in known and unknown contexts.

● Reaching the rigor of the CCSS will require having high expectations for all students, rigorous instruction and support for student learning, high-level assessments, and a culture of excellence.

What Is Rigorous Instruction?

Nowadays, the word "rigor" is the buzzword in educational circles. From President Obama's speeches, to *The Bill & Melinda Gates Foundation* 2 billion dollars investments to raise college-ready high school graduation rates, to governors and school officials, to principals, teachers, and publishers—everyone is talking about rigor. Rigorous schools are presented as the antidote against industrial and economic declines.

What words come to mind when you hear the word rigor? For some, the words *austere, challenging, demanding, inflexible, rigid, strict, traditional,* or *tough* come to mind. On the other hand, others associate the word rigor with the words *critical thinking, engaging, exciting, mind opening, relationships,* and *relevance.* Rigor has also been implemented in terms of increasing credit-based graduation requirements. In my view, the following two quotes from these notable educators clarify the educational meaning of rigor, and also challenge educators to think about it in academic, environmental, and social terms.

Noddings (2007), a well-known educational philosopher who has been writing about educational reforms, defines rigor as designing instruction in which students are "asked to identify for themselves the important points in every unit of study, construct their own summary, attempt problems that have no obvious solutions, engage in interpretation, and evaluate conflicting expectations of view" (p. 32). Washor and Mojkowski (2006/2007), education reformers, perceive rigor as a learning environment that involves "deep immersion in a subject over time, with learners using sophisticated texts, tools, and language in real-world settings. In such settings, students encounter complex, messy problems for which tools and solutions may not be readily apparent or available" (p. 85). Both provide food for thought on the topic of rigorous instruction.

Rigor in teaching and learning is not a bad idea; in some classes, there is so much wasted time in busy work, in boring and meaningless worksheets, in too much high-stakes test practice, and in copying down information off the board, or the screen. Rigor is not a characteristic of a text; instead, it is a characteristic of one's behavior, interactions, attention given to, and engagement with, that text. Teachers will not intellectually prepare students for the demands of school, college, and life by "throwing them at the mercy" of difficult or painful texts.

Rigorous reading of text should result in more engagement with that text. Unproductive struggle with difficult text, words, and structures will not produce better comprehension of text. Rigorous reading should involve asking questions about the text, making inferences, expressing responses, discussing and dissecting with others text structures, meaning, author choices, and messages, identifying similarities and differences, debating and evaluating different interpretations of the text, etc. The level, depth, and breadth of student engagement with, and commitment to, the text are key ingredients of rigor. Teachers play a key role in rigor not only in selection of texts but especially in their expectations, instruction and support they provide to students, and in the environment they create for learning.

Why Focus on Rigorous Instruction?

Saying that a curriculum is rigorous does not make it so. Nearly half of ACT-tested high school graduates who earned a grade of A or B in high school Algebra II were not ready for college math, and more than half of those who earned a grade of A or B in high school physics were not ready for college science (ACT, 2009). A curriculum that reflects rigor is focused, relevant, coherent, and appropriately challenging. Rigor is not more standards, rigid standards, holding students accountable for the same level of learning, giving students more homework, or offering them hard and inflexible learning. Rigor is a trait of active thinkers and doers (e.g., teachers, students, and disciplinary experts). Last, rigor is connected to disciplinary thinking and it implies that knowledge and thinking skills and processes are developed in tandem.

For example, when there is rigorous learning in a social studies classroom, students will not only list the four causes of World War I. Rather (and in accordance with CCSS reading standards), they will need to construct their own interpretations of those events from a range of perspectives. Or, students will not simply learn the main idea of a text, but they will be able to delineate and evaluate the argument and specific claims in a text, and analyze how two or more texts address similar themes or topics in order to build knowledge or to compare the approaches the authors take.

Carol Jago (2011), in her book, *With Rigor for All: Meeting Common Core Standards for Reading Literature*, states that in academically ELA rigorous classes, students read challenging texts (classic and contemporary, fiction and non-fiction, poetry and drama). In addition, students learn how to interpret, analyze, and evaluate what they read. In terms of books, more is more; students read a lot inside and outside the classroom—one book every two to three weeks (Jago, 2011). In rigorous classrooms, there are high expectations for all: teachers and students (Blackburn, 2008). In such learning environments, teachers ask students to recall what they know and give them opportunities to apply it to solve a new problem; students are engaged in thinking and are given time to think independently and collaboratively. In rigorous classrooms one would also observe free, ongoing, and open inquiry, the willingness to challenge established norms, question ideas and each other's thinking, and open communication and collaboration. For teachers, academic rigor is planning and delivering coursework that forces students to expand their thinking, providing the support students need, and tracking student progress. For students, academic rigor means that they will perform at high levels, demonstrate in-depth mastery of complex concepts, be metacognitive about their learning, think, question, problem solve, evaluate, and reflect.

According to the above definitions of rigor, instruction that is rigorous is:

- purposeful,
- interactive,
- relevant,
- promotes inquiry and metacognitive skills,
- promotes evidence-based thinking,
- reflective,
- open for peer and public evaluation, and
- compassionate and supportive.

The goal of rigorous instruction is to help students develop the capacity to understand content that is complex and personally or emotionally challenging (Baron, 2007). Although not every learning experience will result in direct, real-world applications, students can make connections between what they are learning, and how that learning will be useful outside the classroom. Such instruction requires students to be actively involved in the learning process, make meaning of their own and others' work, tolerate ambiguity, solve problems independently and collaboratively, and apply and adapt knowledge to new situations. Rigorous instruction teaches students how to reflect on the learning process, use learning tools to recover meaning when it is lost, persist when learning is vague or frustrating and solutions cannot be achieved easily, and to know when they are learning or not.

Rigor is not associated with the amount or the length of work we assign to students. Rigor should be within reach for every student; it is important to remember that the reach will be different for every student, in each grade level, and within each discipline. Effective teachers provide rigorous instruction and challenge students' knowledge and thinking. Effective teachers do the following:

- Chunk content (break it into small parts).
- Help students stay focused on the problem or topic.
- Break down difficult problems and ideas or concepts, help students understand the problem or task.
- Challenge students to think more rigorously by asking them to explain the thinking steps they took to solve a given problem.
- Promote explanations and an attitude toward learning instead of just getting the right answer.

The CCSS and related assessments are rigorous, but what matters the most is classroom instruction. It is one thing to know what students need to understand and be able to do in each grade level to prepare them for college, career, and workforce readiness, and another to make it happen. Standards and assessments do not teach; teachers do—you, the classroom teacher, will make a big difference in your students' learning.

Not Just Academic Rigor

Beyond standards and assessments, rigor also needs to exist in many other areas, such as teacher preparation and knowledge, instruction, expectations for students, classroom environment, support, and also student performance. Rigor is creating an environment in which *each* student is learning at high levels. Part of it is encouraging students to take on the challenges associated with the standards and to not get discouraged when performance gaps occur. Another part is for administrators who evaluate teachers to understand that for teachers to provide rigorous instruction, they will need their support and understanding to make different curricular and instructional decisions. In addition, teachers need to demonstrate and help students understand the role rigor plays in college, career, and workforce. That rigor does not only relate to the academic and knowledge demands, but also to the dispositions one needs to develop for ongoing learning (e.g., tenacity, problem solving, punctuality, ambiguity, collaboration, industriousness, etc.).

Rigorous instruction and learning involves getting students to think differently about what they study and learn, to challenge themselves, to be active and reflective participants in the learning process with the teacher playing the role of the facilitator and mentor instead of the sole dispenser of knowledge. Rigor also needs to be found in the support teachers provide to *each* student so he or she can learn at high levels. Lastly, rigor should be reflected in how *each* student demonstrates learning at high levels. How do teachers use formative assessments in daily lessons so they understand what students need to learn and what they have or have not already mastered? You can use Figure 4.1 as a tool to reflect on rigor in your classroom. At a local high school,

Content	**Instruction**
Is the material complex, engaging, and relevant?	How is the teacher orchestrating the learning process?
Is the material aligned with related standards?	What is the role of the teacher and the student in the learning process?
Does it require active student engagement, perseverance, and critical thinking skills to develop meaning?	How about learning expectations, challenge, modeling, scaffolded support, and the learning environment?
Student Engagement	**Assessment**
Is the student meaningfully engaged in the learning process?	Are assessments measuring higher order thinking skills or just recall?
Does student engagement result in content and literacy learning, development of critical thinking skills, perseverance, and motivation to continue to learn?	Are assessments asking students to apply/transfer their knowledge to real-world situations?

(center: **Rigor**)

FIGURE 4.1. Reflecting on rigor.

teachers have used it to have discussions about rigor and identify instructional and other areas they would like to improve.

In addition, rigor is not just for gifted students and we don't have to wait until students have mastered the basics to provide and expect rigor in learning. For example, there are different knowledge, skills, and processes reflected in the following four learning examples:

1. Retrieve information from a graph or chart.
2. Locate and read at least two current articles on biotechnology advancements for improving amputee US Veteran soldiers' mobility.
3. Read and analyze three original newspaper articles from the recent US–Afghanistan War and identify reasons for opposition to US entry into the war.
4. Read pertinent information related to the US Financial Crisis and propose three core solutions; predict outcomes for each solution.

Let's examine the above four examples that reflect on a progressive cognitive rigor using Bloom's Taxonomy of Cognitive Process Dimensions (1956), and Bloom's revised taxonomy of educational objectives (Anderson & Krathwohl, 2001). The first example is asking the student to recall or remember knowledge. The second one is targeting comprehension and understanding of biotechnology advancements. The third is referring to application and analysis of knowledge and the fourth one is asking the reader to synthesize/evaluate information and create something new. The cognitive demands and the processes a student would use to be able to do the above vary significantly. Unfortunately, most of our instruction, and what we ask students to do as they learn new material, is located on the lowest levels of the taxonomy, in knowledge and comprehension. Students need to know how to think instead of just recall or demonstrate mastery. Teachers will need to prepare students to elaborate, make inferences, analyze and construct relationships, defend their judgment with evidence and logic, and demonstrate their thinking process. Students will need to learn how to use what they have learned in real and also unpredictable situations. In other words, rigorous instruction and learning will develop their capacity, tools, and immunity to different or unfamiliar problems or situations.

College, Career, and Workforce Connections

- Students need the same set of skills for both college and the workplace, particularly in reading and math.
- Key cognitive strategies to prepare students for college, career, and the workforce include, problem formation, research/inquiry, interpretation, academic discourse/communication, and precision/accuracy.
- Employers seek employees with professionalism/work ethic, good oral and written communication skills, the ability to work collaboratively with others, and possessing critical thinking, problem solving, and creativity skills. Employers also expect employees to know how to use quantitative tools (e.g., numbers, graphs, charts, and tables, and spreadsheet programs).
- *Incoming college students to succeed in computer science [need to meet] the usual prerequisites for admission to college, such as algebra and trigonometry. In terms of dispositions, students who are successful tend to:*
  - *Enjoy thinking logically and carefully; they have an analytical style of thinking that usually leading to success in Mathematics.*
  - *Enjoy Math and Science.*
  - *Are creative.*
  - *Are fearless about tinkering.*
  - *View Computing as a way to help the world, and extend human capabilities*
    (Gary Leavens, Professor, Computer Science, University of Central Florida).

Rigorous Instruction and Transfer of Learning

During the 2012 Olympics, I listened to a televised interview with Michael Phelps' coach, Bob Bowman, who stated that one of the ways he developed Phelps' resistance to challenging and unpredictable situations was by getting him ready for chaos! According to Coach Bowman, talent alone doesn't cut it; rather, winning requires an ability to adapt to ever changing realities and uncertainties. What separates the medalists from the competitors in the Olympics is not only their mastery of the physical fundaments, but the athletes' mental discipline and comfort with the pressures and real-life chaos of competition. During practice times, Coach Bowman hid Phelps' goggles so he would have to swim without them. On other occasions, he arranged for late pick-ups so Phelps would miss his meals and swim hungry. At times, he even cracked his goggles so they would fill with water and obstruct his vision in the pool. The coach created uncertainties for Phelps in lower risk situations so when his performance really mattered, his mental adaptability, his immunity to uncertainties and chaos gave him the best shot at winning.

Comfort with the unexpected will not just help students in the classroom; it will also prepare them for the uncertainties of summative assessments, college, career, and workforce life. Rigorous instruction and learning should also prepare students to deal with the unexpected. Learning is a complex process; problem solving takes careful thinking and time and struggling or grappling with ideas is not something to be avoided in secondary school learning. We grapple with ideas at work, don't we? Experts from different fields work independently and collaboratively to solve real life problems; and in doing so, they often deal with frustration and uncertainty. In the real world, uncertainty is the only certainty and developing an aptitude for it gives one a competitive advantage. Real-life problems do not have clear-cut solutions or right answers; there are several paths we can take to solve them.

Our challenge is to find the solution that works best given the conditions we work under. In many classrooms, the right answer is often more valued than the process students used to come up with those answers. We cannot continue to rescue our students or prevent them from feeling uncomfortable with learning complex material. I know, some of you might say, "But my students do not like to read; others cannot read well, or understand the texts of our discipline."; "Some of my students are not motivated to do anything; how am I going to get them to read, analyze text, think critically about what they read, and grapple with concepts and ideas?" One social studies teacher told me, "My students beg me, literally, to give them the answers; they don't like to take time to think or linger with unresolved questions."

I recognize that lack of student motivation, reading difficulties, underdeveloped background knowledge, lack of reading and cognitive persistence, and an intolerance of ambiguity, are all realities in many classrooms. My approach is that first you'll need to know the realities, interests, skills and knowledge of your students, and then plan strategic small steps and routines that will involve your students in new experiences and ways of learning and doing in your classroom. Less is more when done consistently, strategically, with support, and scaffolding.

Students will benefit from quality instruction, and from teachers creating challenging conditions with a high chance of failure. Such situations should be used to scaffold student learning and reflect on success or failure. Students also need to learn how to think logically (with respect to evidence), and articulate what they know and what they don't know. Last, they need to learn in an environment where they are free to ask questions without fear of ridicule, demonstrate understanding of major concepts, and apply new understandings in real-world situations.

Developing well-planned units and lessons, teaching in a way that supports deep and discipline-specific knowledge and skills, and formative and summative assessments to drive instruction will help promote rigorous learning. The CCSS have brought about instructional shifts in learning through their emphasis on the following areas in English language arts (ELA) and mathematics. All shifts reflect instructional rigor and deep learning. In ELA, the shifts include: (1) an increase in informational text (students need a balance of informational and literary text); (2) building knowledge in the disciplines (students build knowledge about the domain or content area and the world through reading discipline-specific texts, *first*, rather than through the teacher or activities); (3) progressive complexity across grades (students read the core/grade appropriate text around which instruction is centered; teachers plan for, and model, close reading of text); (4) text-based answers (students engage in rigorous evidence-based discussions about text); (5) writing from sources (writing is supported by evidence from sources to inform or make an argument); and (6) academic vocabulary (students develop the transferable vocabulary they need to access grade level complex texts).

In mathematics, the instructional shifts include: (1) focus (teachers focus on the concepts that are in the standards and narrow and deepen the scope of how time and energy is spent in the classroom); (2) coherence (educators carefully connect the learning within and across grades so that students can build new understanding onto foundations built in previous years); (3) fluency (students are expected to have speed and accuracy with simple calculations; teachers structure class and/or homework time for students to memorize, through repetition, core functions); (4) deep understanding (students deeply understand or master the math and can operate easily within a math concept before moving on); (5) applications (students are expected to use math and choose the appropriate concept for application at all times); and (6) dual intensity (students are practicing and understanding at all times with intensity).

The disciplinary literacy framework I present in this book includes all of the above instructional shifts. How? By viewing learning as apprenticeship and as a socially constructed process, by focusing on high impact and rigorous instruction, by developing discipline-specific habits of mind, and by valuing collaborative inquiry. Rigorous instruction moves away from mere lecture and passive student work. It focuses on deep learning, and it requires engaging, relevant, and complex activities, materials, assignments, and conversations. It also involves students in solving real-world tasks. Last, rigorous instruction promotes critical thinking and engages students in complex ways of analyzing, comparing, creating, and evaluating routine and other problems. This type of learning is student-centered (instead of teacher-centered) learning and the teacher is a facilitator of student learning.

Applying Discipline-Specific Literacies

- Rigorous instruction plans not only for what students will need to know and be able to do, but also plans for what discipline-specific thinking processes they will need to engage in, develop, and apply.
- Rigorous learning experiences in each discipline must relate to rigorous standards, discipline-specific thinking, promote student interests, equip them to continue to inquire rigorously, and maximize their performance on summative assessments.
- Disciplinary learning and knowledge development require rigorous standards, instruction, materials, experiences, assessment, support, and opportunities to transfer learning.

Planning for Rigorous Instruction in the Disciplines

Rigor and disciplinary teaching and learning go hand-in hand. Students will not be able to develop the knowledge, skills, and habits of mind necessary to learn and construct content-specific knowledge in non-rigorous learning environments. So, what is the first step in planning rigorous instruction? Plan with the end in mind! In other words, think of the type of learning and thinking you'd want your students to do. Select a summative task that requires students to demonstrate that thinking (e.g., project, debate, experiment). Determine what you consider mastery (baseline and top level), and determine how you will grade the assignment (rubric, etc.). And plan instruction that will develop the knowledge and skills students will need to comprehend and continue to learn about the subject matter.

Rigorous instruction in the disciplines has to be discipline-specific and relevant, and should equip students to learn in meaningful ways. Effective instruction principles apply across disciplines, but what will vary per discipline, aside from the content, structure, and goals of each discipline, are the instructional strategies that will facilitate the development of disciplinary habits of mind or ways of knowing and learning within, and for, that discipline. Schmoker (2011) reminds us of the importance of simplicity, clarity, and priority in planning instruction that will result in student learning. What will work for all students? According to Schmoker, a combination of the following:

Adequate amounts of essential subject-matter content, concepts, and topics; intellectual/thinking skills (e.g., argument, problem solving, reconciling opposing views, drawing one's own conclusions); and, authentic literacy—purposeful reading, writing, and discussions as the primary modes of learning both content and thinking skills.

(2011, p. 26)

Isn't the above quote reminiscent of disciplinary literacy? Teachers need to be developing students' content and thinking skills in tandem. The CCSS state that literacy instruction will center on "careful examination of the text itself...on students reading closely to draw evidence and knowledge from the text and...to read texts of adequate range and complexity" (Coleman & Pimentel, 2011). In mathematics, the CCSS call for balance of conceptual understanding and procedural skills and fluency, deep focus, and more authentic application in real world situations (Zimba, 2011).

Career readiness involves having the English and mathematics knowledge and skills needed to qualify for and succeed in a postsecondary training necessary for a career, employability skills such as critical thinking and responsibility, along with technical, job-specific skills related to a specific career pathway (Achieve, 2009). The 21st century workforce requires high school graduates who can locate, evaluate, synthesize, use knowledge in new contexts, solve non-routine problems, communicate and collaborate with others (Darling-Hammond & Adamson, 2010).

Instruction that promotes academic rigor engages students in complex, relevant and meaningful tasks that focus on developing deep knowledge of core concepts within each discipline. Rigorous instruction requires critical thinking, problem solving, and collaboration. Such instruction uses worthy texts and includes research projects, problem solving, essays, collaborative work, and oral presentations that enable students to develop and demonstrate abilities to find and organize information, frame and conduct investigations, analyze and synthesize data, apply learning to new situations, and evaluate their work. It is no longer how much information students know; rather, it is what students can do with their knowledge that counts (Darling-Hammond & Adamson, 2010). Teachers should model explicit problem-solving strategies, provide them with opportunities to work independently and with others to solve complex problems and tasks, and utilize technology for research and learning purposes (Conley & Barton, 2007). Rigorous instruction that holds students to high expectations and provides robust support has been shown to correlate with student success in high school and beyond (Allensworth, Nomi, Montgomery, & Lee, 2008).

Assessment of student learning should be linked to daily instruction. Ongoing assessment should inform instruction and ensure that students have a clear understanding of the performance criteria. Teachers should provide students with relevant feedback, opportunities and support to meet the assessment criteria (Chappuis, Chappuis, & Stiggins, 2009).

Think Like an Expert

- Literary experts are open-minded, comprehend and evaluate complex texts, construct effective arguments, learn through research and wide reading, question assumptions, and access the veracity of claims. (English Language Arts)
- Mathematicians identify connections between bits of mathematical knowledge, apply mathematical thinking to formulate and execute problem-solving strategies, apply mathematics in novel situations, see and use mathematics in real-world situations, and communicate and collaborate mathematically. (Mathematics)
- Scientists identify topics of interest, engage in research, develop deep understanding of related vocabulary, evaluate data sources, and carefully examine how and where data was collected and what it represents. (Science)
- Historians think deeply about the past, present, and future. Concepts of change over time, causality, context, complexity, and contingency (interconnectedness), provide the foundation of historical thinking. (Social Studies)

High and Clear Expectations for All

How do you communicate high and clear expectations for all students? Do you believe that all students can learn? Even those who have repeatedly failed in school? If your answer is "yes," how would one experience it in your classroom? Would it be reflected in how you plan your instruction, in making rigor within reach for all in your feedback, support, and encouragement, in your instructional materials, assessment, or elsewhere? Would your students attest to you having high expectations for all? Research has shown that if a teacher believes that a student can learn and succeed in school, he/she starts to behave in ways that help that student succeed. If he/she does not believe a student can learn or succeed, he/she behaves in ways that do not facilitate student learning and success (Brophy & Good, 1970; Rosenthal & Jacobson, 1968; Weinstein, 2002). At the beginning of each school year, teachers form expectations of what their students can, or cannot do based on data, past or current experiences, student appearance, gender or race, etc. Research has shown that teachers treat high-expectation students differently than low-expectation students (Ambady & Rosenthal, 1993); these differences are usually expressed in affective tone and quality of interactions with students. What are some of those differences in teachers' expectations of, and interactions with, low-expectation students? See a few examples below from Brophy (1983):

- Low expectation students receive less praise for success from teachers.
- Teachers are less friendly, smile less, and establish less eye contact and non-verbal communication with low-expectation students; they even sit them farther away in the classroom.
- They practice less wait time for low-expectation students to answer questions.
- They call less on low-expectation students to answer questions; they ask them less challenging questions.
- They demand less from low-expectation students in terms of knowledge.
- Teachers offer low-expectation students less feedback on their responses and interact with them less frequently.

Sample ways to communicate positive expectations to all students include monitoring the way you call on students, giving all students chances to participate in class, and increasing the amount of wait time between asking a student a question and moving on by either answering the question yourself, or calling on another student. Also, giving hints and reminders to help them succeed in class, correcting students in constructive ways, and telling students directly that you believe that they have the ability to do well, and celebrating small successes (Boynton & Boynton, 2005). High expectations also refer to positive teacher–student relationships. According to Thompson (1998), "The most powerful weapon available to secondary teachers who want to foster a favorable learning climate is a positive relationship with our students" (p. 6).

Showing to students that you care about them, their interests, their lives, and goals means the world to students. How?

- Create a rigorous, positive, relevant, and exciting classroom learning environment.
- Listen first, then ask questions.
- Empathize with students.
- Offer assistance and support as needed.
- Be available, and demanding.
- Let them know that they cannot get away with excuses.
- Hold everyone accountable to the same norms, rules, and expectations.
- Develop classroom pride through:

○ Displaying student work.
○ Specific feedback on student performance.
○ Positive, verbal reinforcement.
○ Showing off your class's accomplishments.
○ Showing interest and pride in students' progress and accomplishments.
○ Monitoring student success.
○ Celebrating small victories.

What should a teacher do to promote student mastery when many of his or her students are labeled as struggling and English language learners? How would one be able to differentiate instruction to meet everyone's needs? Does holding high expectations of all learners result in all being successful learners? Holding high expectations for all, means believing that all students can learn. It also means reflecting on your interactions with students, in verbal and non-verbal communications, on the quality of your instruction and scaffolded support, on assessments and monitoring of student progress, and on the classroom environment you create. When a student does not respond correctly to a question, or takes longer to answer, provide him or her with the time, and outlets he or she will need to rethink, or locate evidence.

In one Algebra II classroom I visited some time ago, the teacher had dedicated a classroom wall to communicating positive and high expectations for all students. The phrase/words: "I believe in you. Learn. Succeed. Graduate." were written in large font in the center of this wall-size poster with a picture of a high school diploma and student quotes, student photos, responses, goals, and signatures all over it. A biology teacher used a map of the US with representative colleges and universities pinned on it and students' names on each institution; the map read: "Where are you going?" In another English language arts classroom, a teacher had a high school cap and graduation gown hanging in the front of the room; she would take each student's photo and then post it on one of the classroom walls—in her own way, she was communicating to all that she believed they could all graduate, succeed, and move on. Yet, in an Earth Science classroom a teacher referred to all students as scholars. When they were not thinking, behaving, writing, or speaking like scholars, she would remind them about what they needed to do. Lee (2001, 2007) suggests building a culture of high expectations through building routines that inform students of what they are expected to do in class, how they are to do things, and why. Routines can help establish high expectations and mold students' behavior, thinking, and learning. Teachers have wonderful and creative ways of communicating high expectations for all students. Use your creativity and create a positive, supportive and challenging classroom environment that will promote learning and success for all.

Classroom Norms and Procedures

Establishing norms and procedures is a characteristic of effective classroom management (Evertson & Weinstein, 2006). Norms or rules and procedures refer to expectations of student behavior. Norms address general expectations while procedures communicate expectations for specific behaviors. Of course, the beginning of each school year is the best time to establish norms and procedures. Research shows that the implementation of rules and procedures is strengthened when students provide input in their development (Brophy & Evertson, 1976).

For example, here is one way to establish rules and procedures in your classroom about "What to do if I've missed class" (trust me, absenteeism happens regularly in secondary grades). Having pre-established procedures will buy you time to teach and provide the support students need, and will also give students a sense of control. The goal is to help them become independent thinkers and problem solvers—by establishing rules and procedures, you will be facilitating their independence. In the following example, I have included social networking options as many schools are utilizing technology for homework, checking grades, and classroom communication and updates.

- Review class rules, procedures, and rubrics for missing class, late assignments, and class participation.
- E-mail your teacher before class (include teacher e-mail address).
- If you cannot e-mail your teacher before class, e-mail teacher after class.
- Look for notes, assignments, and updates online (include URL).
- Ask classmates for information about what happened in class and ask them to share their notes with you.
- Ask three friends/classmates before you ask your teacher (on Twitter, Facebook, etc.).
- Come by before or after school prior to the next class.

Provide students with avenues for asking educated questions, asking for feedback, elaborations, and clarifications. Once you establish these ways of thinking, communicating, and learning in your classroom, students will know what to do over time. They will also start thinking differently about their own learning, assume more responsibility, speak and communicate their thoughts more clearly, and also provide support to peers in class, as needed. Adolescents often quit when they encounter complex text, concepts, words, or ideas. In an effort to facilitate persistence with reading text, or engagement with a class discussion or learning, in general, see an example below about alternatives to saying "I don't know."

- Here are my thoughts on it but I wonder what others think about it.
- May I please have more time to think about it?
- May I please have more information?
- May I consult a peer?
- May I have a clue?
- Where could I find some more information on this?
- Would you please explain this a bit more?
- Would you please go over this one more time?
- Would you please provide me with another example?
- Would you please repeat your question (or explanation)?

When designing rules and procedures, also pay attention to the physical arrangement of the classroom—is it organized for optimal teaching, learning, research, and collaboration? Do students have access to materials, technology, and equipment? Is the room pleasant and inviting? Is the room laid out for independent work, or is it laid out for discussion and collaborative inquiry? Create a clear set of classroom rules about the following: general behavior, respect of each other and property, attendance and tardiness, homework and late work, transitions and interruptions, use of materials and equipment, student participation, communication, and collaboration. Also, think about what norms and procedures you can develop to promote discipline-specific habits of mind. See Figure 4.2 for norms and procedures I developed to facilitate discipline-specific attitudes, critical thinking, and behavior that promote inquiry across the disciplines.

For reference purposes, and for saturating my classroom environment with the specific ways of knowing and learning in my discipline, I would also develop specific posters to remind students how disciplinary experts read, think, question, write, and communicate. Interact with students about classroom rules and procedures, revisit them and make changes as needed, and use

In our learning community, we value & develop *habits of learning*:

We value *effort* to learn

• We aim for personal best
• We persist
• We learn from our mistakes

We know what is *expected* of us to learn, achieve, and succeed

• We set personal goals
• We work toward academic goals
• We reflect on our goals

We *assess* our learning and progress in many ways

We *celebrate* our accomplishments—whether small or large—and enjoy learning

We value *academic rigor*

• We think critically
• We expand our knowledge
• We model our thinking
• We show our learning
• We draw on past knowledge and transfer it to new situations

We practice *accountable talk*

• We focus on the topic
• We think critically
• We show good reasoning (and provide evidence for our thinking)
• We pay attention to each other's comments
• We challenge one another to think and learn more

We are responsible for, and practice, *intelligent thinking*

• We think through tasks
• We think before we act
• We listen to others with respect and empathy
• We learn from others' thinking
• We value alternative thinking and problem-solving
• We ask critical questions
• We seek answers to our questions

FIGURE 4.2. Disciplinary learning norms and procedures.   (Continued)

We *self-manage* our learning

- We focus on our learning goals
- We are reflective
- We evaluate feedback we get from others
- We make connections between old and new information
- We are aware of our difficulties with learning
- We problem-solve
- We reflect on our goals and our progress

We see learning as an *apprenticeship* process

- We value teacher mentoring
- We are open to coaching and instruction
- We observe carefully when the teacher demonstrates or solves a task
- We learn from the teacher's thinking
- We value feedback from the teacher
- We incorporate coaching from the teacher into our learning

© Lucky Business via Shutterstock

In our learning community, we value & develop **habits of learning**
Developed by Vicky Zygouris-Coe, Ph.D., 2014

FIGURE 4.2. Disciplinary learning norms and procedures. (Continued)

classroom meetings periodically to bring up issues related to student behavior, classroom management, or rules and procedures. Create a positive and rigorous classroom environment where order, exploration and inquiry, collaboration, and discipline-specific habits of mind are developed, promoted, and implemented.

Student Engagement and Motivation

Engagement is associated with positive student outcomes, including achievement and persistence in school. On the other hand, disengagement is often associated with behavior problems, absenteeism, and eventually, high school dropout rates.

Students' engagement is high in classrooms with supportive teachers and peers, challenging and authentic tasks, opportunities for choice, and sufficient structure (Fredericks, Blumenfeld, & Paris, 2004). Engaged students show up for school. They also participate in classroom activities and processes, persist when learning gets challenging, and respond positively to teachers and peers. Last, they ask questions, are curious about learning, and show willingness to work and invest the effort necessary to master complex ideas, tasks, and skills (Blumenfeld, Kempler, & Krajcik, 2006). Engaging students in rich and exciting learning experiences will promote deeper knowledge and skill development, problem solving, creativity, and critical thinking skills—all highly desired for learning and working today.

There are a lot of ways to engage students with learning depending on the goal, objectives, task, and classroom; for example, cooperative learning, games, research, relevance, and challenging tasks. Also, complex texts, opportunities to collaborate and problem-solve with others, and choice over responses. Last, assignments, presentations, and how students will spend their time inside and outside the classroom. Many teachers use a hook, a question, or an activity that provokes students to think differently about a topic and activates their prior knowledge about the content, skill, or concept to follow. Others show quality movies, and do unpredictable things to attract students' attention, in hopes of getting some level of engagement, or response from students. But, will all of this last? There is a time and a place for watching quality movies, listening to audio (music, speeches, etc.), and even putting on a performance. Students' engagement and motivation grows when their self-efficacy, performance, and curiosity grow. A positive, rigorous classroom environment that values student learning and progress can facilitate student engagement, persistence, and motivation.

If you, the teacher, do most of the students' work for them, if you come and answer most of the questions, if you choose everything and provide no purpose and clarity over learning goals, assignments, and activities, or if you do not teach them how to make connections with past knowledge, then how (and why) would your students be engaged in learning in your classroom? Get to know your students; learn about their interests, needs, goals, and aspirations. Ask yourself: How do students engage with texts and learning? How do they interact with new knowledge? How do they practice and deepen their knowledge?

The disciplinary learning framework I present in this book (see Chapter 2) promotes student engagement and motivation in the following ways: (a) it promotes an apprenticeship learning model in each discipline that will help cultivate one-on-one relationships between teacher and student that will lead to increased motivation and engagement in learning; (b) it focuses on developing discipline-specific habits and skills that will promote deep comprehension of content and prepare students for school and beyond; (c) it makes the teacher responsible for engaging students with learning by creating a positive, rigorous, relevant, and stimulating classroom environment and providing students with the skills and processes they will need to continue to learn; (d) it values collaborative inquiry and learning relationships between teacher and student and among students; and (e) it makes learning specific, relevant, rigorous, and engaging, and stimulating.

Rigorous Materials

In many content area classrooms, teachers use a single textbook to build students' content and literacy knowledge. What types of materials do the CCSS promote for grades 6–12? According to the CCSS the range and quality of materials is rigorous. There is a greater focus on literary non-fiction texts in ELA classes in grades 6–12. According to the *Revised Publishers' Criteria for the Common Core State Standards in English Language Arts and Literacy Grades 3-12*, this blend of materials is comprised of literature (fiction, poetry, and drama), and a substantial sampling of literary non-fiction, including essays, speeches, opinion pieces, biographies, journalism, and historical, scientific or other documents written for a broad audience (see p. 57 of the Standards for more details). Most ELA programs and materials designed for them will need to increase substantially the amount of literary non-fiction they include. The CCSS emphasize arguments (such as the Founding Documents) and other literary non-fiction that contain informational text structures rather than narrative literary non-fiction that tell a story, such as memoirs or biographies (see Appendix B of the CCSS for several examples of high quality literary non-fiction) (Colemen & Pimentel, 2011).

Teachers and students are expected to analyze dense, rich and scientific, historical, or technical ideas, information, and arguments found in literacy non-fiction texts and demonstrate careful understanding of the information. This emphasis mirrors the CCSS Writing Standards that focus on students' abilities to construct an argument and write to inform or explain. The shift in both reading and writing constitutes a significant change from the traditional focus in ELA classrooms on narrative text, or the narrative aspects of literary nonfiction (the characters and the story), towards more in-depth engagement with the informational and argumentative aspects of these texts. For example, in a narrative with a great deal of science, teachers and students should be required to follow and comprehend the scientific information as presented by the text. Likewise, in a social studies text, teachers and students would focus their efforts on following chronological sequencing of events and forming personal interpretations of the trustworthiness of the text, as well as when, why, and by whom it was written instead of just memorizing key events and people.

In order for teachers to cultivate the habits of mind students will need to develop deep understanding of texts, they will need to include high quality texts that are worth reading, and provide rich and useful information. Since the CCSS emphasize close reading of text(s), select texts that are worthy of close attention, and re-reading. Select texts that provide rich ground for text-dependent questions and will sustain students' attention to the particulars of the text. Within a collection of texts on a topic, select specific anchor texts for close reading and additional texts that include challenging and informational content using multiple genres on a common topic to support students' discipline-specific knowledge and skills. The anchor text(s) will allow teachers and students to do close reading of the material, examine it from various perspectives, and demonstrate in-depth comprehension. The additional research sources beyond the anchor texts will facilitate students' curiosity to learn more about the topic, and will bolster their ability to read widely as well as in depth.

To become career and college ready, students read and comprehend texts that represent diverse genres, cultures, and eras and represent the kinds of thinking and writing students would be involved in in college, career, and work. Also, teachers should include sources that require students to read and integrate a larger volume of material for research purposes. At specific points, the CCSS require certain texts or types of texts (see Table 4.1). In Grades 9–12, the Founding Documents, selections from American Literature and World Literature, a play by Shakespeare, and an American drama are all required (see Appendix B of the CCSS for grade specific examples of texts).

TABLE 4.1. CCSS References to Multiple Texts (Grades 6–12)

Grades 6–8	Grades 9–10	Grades 11–12
Compare and contrast texts in different forms or genres (e.g., stories and poems; historical novels and fantasy stories) in terms of their approaches to similar themes and topics. (Literature, 6)	Analyze how an author draws on and transforms fictional source material in a specific work (e.g., how Shakespeare draws on a story from Ovid or how a later author draws on a play by Shakespeare). (Literature, 9–10)	Demonstrate knowledge of 18th, 19th, and early 20th century foundational works of American literature, including how two or more texts from the same period treat similar themes or topics. (Literature, 11–12)
Compare and contrast one author's presentation of events with that of another (e.g., a memoir, written by and a biography on the same person). (Informational Text, 6)	Analyze seminal U.S. documents of historical and literary significance (e.g., Washington's Farewell Address, the Gettysburg Address, Roosevelt's Four Freedoms speech, King's "Letter from Birmingham Jail"), including how they address related themes and concepts. (Informational Text, 9–10)	Analyze seventeenth-, eighteenth-, and nineteenth-century foundational U.S. documents of historical and literary significance (including The Declaration of Independence, the Preamble to the Constitution, the Bill of Rights, and Lincoln's Second Inaugural Address) for their themes, purposes, and rhetorical features. (Informational Text, 11–12)
Compare and contrast a fictional portrayal of a time, place, or character and a historical account of the same period as a means of understanding how authors of fiction use or alter history. (Literature, 7)	Compare the point of view of two or more authors for how they treat the same or similar topics, including which details they include and emphasize in their respective accounts. (9–10, History/Social Studies)	Evaluate authors' differing points of view on the same historical event or issue by assessing the author's claims, reasoning, and evidence. (History/Social Studies, 11–12)
Analyze where two or more authors writing about the same topic shape their presentations of key information by emphasizing different evidence or advancing interpretations of facts. (Informational Text, 7)	Compare and contrast treatments of the same topic in several primary and secondary sources. (9–10, History/Social Studies)	Integrate information from diverse sources, both primary and secondary, into a coherent understanding of an idea or event, noting discrepancies among sources. (History/Social Studies, 11–12)
Compare and contrast the structure of two or more texts and analyze how the differing structure of each text contributes to its meaning and style. (Literature, 8)	Compare and contrast findings presented in a text to those from other sources (including their own experiments), noting when the findings support or contradict previous explanations or accounts. (9–10, Science/Technical Subjects)	Synthesize information from a range of sources (e.g., texts, experiments, simulations) into a coherent understanding of a process, phenomenon, or concept, resolving conflicting information when possible. (Science/Technical Subjects, 11–12)

(Continued)

TABLE 4.1.   (Continued)

Grades 6–8	Grades 9–10	Grades 11–12
Analyze a specific case in which two or more texts provide conflicting information where the texts disagree on matters of fact or interpretation. (Informational Text, 8)		
Analyze the relationship between a primary and secondary source on the same topic. (History/Social Studies, 6–8)		
Compare and contrast the information gained from experiments, simulations, video, or multimedia sources with that gained from reading a text on the same topic. (Science/Technical Subjects, 6–8)		

Past standards have emphasized the reading of single texts: students had to learn how to make sense of a story, article, or book with an occasional emphasis on multiple texts. The CCSS emphasize the interpretation of multiple texts across all grade levels, and in reading, writing, and oral language. Students will still have to be able to interpret single texts, but with much more extensive emphasis on reading and using multiple texts (about 10% of the ELA standards mention multiple texts).

Select materials that are worth reading and are also needed for learning and acquiring knowledge in your discipline. Materials should be print and non-print and should include laboratory equipment, math manipulatives, video/audio recordings, calculators, technology (for reading, writing, researching, and communicating), the Internet, periodicals, newspapers, primary sources, visual aids, social networking sites and tools, and even teacher-made materials. In addition, all students will benefit from readings and materials that authentically, accurately, and relevantly represent diverse cultures (Au, 1998) and promote cultural understanding and contributions (Cazden, 2001; Ladson-Billings, 1994, 1995).

Materials should include texts that are worth reading, provide opportunities for close reading, writing, and researching, enrich students' knowledge and experiences, meaningfully involve students in learning, create interest, and build students' background information and discipline-specific skills. Whether it be literary non-fiction texts, mathematical problems, historical documents, experiments, or music, the materials you select for your class should be appropriate for the content and developmental level of your students. In addition, materials should present the subject matter from different angles, allow for different responses from different learners, offer many paths for exploration, engender conflicts, and raise new questions, and even offer surprises.

Learning Goals

Students need to have clear learning or academic goals. A learning goal is a statement of what students will understand/know or be able to do. Learning goals represent the most important learning for the year, semester, or chunk of time. Learning goals must be specific and measureable, based on prior student data, and aligned with state standards. Now more than ever, teacher effectiveness is determined by the degree to which they reached their student learning goals. Important questions for every teacher include, "What will I teach (standards) and to whom (differentiation)?"; "What do my students need (use student data)?"; and "What will count for student learning?"; "How will I know my students are or are not learning and what will I do about it?" A learning goal must be written in appropriate "student accessible language" so that students can comprehend what is expected of them. "Instructional goals narrow what students focus on" (Marzano, Pickering, & Pollock, 2011, p. 94).

Learning goals should be stated in clear, concise terms, covering an activity, lesson or unit of what students will *understand* and what they will be *able to do* as a result of instruction. Learning goals should be associated with special activities (completed in one class period), or assignments (ongoing class activities or assignments outside of class). Learning goals should explain the learning that is taking place in a lesson, unit, or semester and they should follow a specific and consistent format. "Students will understand/know_____." refers to declarative knowledge that is developed through review, revision, error analysis, and identification of similarities and differences. "Students will be able to do_____." refers to procedural knowledge, the skills, strategies, and processes the learner has developed over time through practice. Teachers can write learning goals that combine both types of knowledge: "Students will understand/know and be able to do_____." Goals stipulate desired forms of student learning, thinking/habits of mind, engagement, and behavior. Learning goals are not performance goals (e.g., scoring at a proficient level on the end of course test); they focus on learning for the purpose of gaining knowledge and increasing skill (Newell & Van Ryzin, 2008). Learning goals tend to focus on learning that takes three to ten weeks to master; a learning goal is not the same as a daily objective. Newell and Van Ryzin (2008) reported that ". . .students who perceive that their school exhibits a 'learning goal' orientation seek challenges, show persistence in the face of adversity, use more effective learning strategies, have more positive attitudes, and are more cognitively engaged in learning" (p. 467). Learning goals provide the answer to many students' question "Why bother go to school?", and they also provide feedback to students throughout the learning process.

Marzano's (2007) research on goal setting shows increases in student achievement ranging from 16 to 41 percentile points; when students know what they are expected to be learning, their performance, on average, increased by 21 percentile points. In some classrooms, the learning goal can only be found in the teacher's lesson plan; it is invisible and non-existent to the students. Learning goals must be shared with students. Many students will often ask, "Why are we doing this?" "Why do I have to do it?" or say "I will never use it in real life." Or, if you ask students who might be doing different activities in class, "What are you supposed to be learning from this?" they often say, "I don't know; the teacher asked us to read the chapter and answer the questions at the end."

There is a difference between learning activities and learning goals. Learning activities and assignments help students reach their learning goals. Learning activities are guided learning experiences that take place in the classroom. Learning assignments are learning experiences to be completed independently in class or as homework to extend classroom learning. Activities and assignments are the means by which the learning goals are accomplished. "Writing a research paper," "Presenting research on President Lincoln's assassination," or "Completing a science lab experiment," are learning activities. On the contrary, "Write arguments to support claims with clear reasons and relevant evidence," "Understand the differences between mitosis and meiosis," "Investigate and apply how the cycling of water between the atmosphere and hydrosphere has an effect on weather patterns and climate," "Decide whether a solution is reasonable in the context of the original situation," "Explain the differences between stars and plants," or "Recognize how scientists such as Copernicus, Kepler, and Galileo contributed to acceptance of the heliocentric model of the solar system," are all learning goals.

Whatever your subject area is, it is imperative that you provide a clearly stated learning goal that is accompanied by a scale, or a rubric, that describes levels of performance relative to the learning goal. Scales or rubrics can assist teachers in designing and scoring formative assessments. Marzano (2007) suggests a simplified scale for each learning goal (see adapted scale in Table 4.2). Older students, in particular, benefit from clear learning goals and purpose in learning. Not all goals need to be visible at all times, but students need to have access to them and be able to explain the learning goal and how their current activities relate to the learning goal. In some schools, principals require that all learning goals are visible at all times, usually written on the board. Some teachers post learning goals on flip charts, laminated templates (they can write on with an erasable marker) while others attach them to student notebooks and assignments. Clear learning goals also create an essential foundation for a balanced assessment system (Stiggins, 2008).

What do you expect students to learn in your class? Write goals that communicate what knowledge (declarative and procedural) students need to learn instead of just a list of activities that are not conceptually connected nor provide a clear understanding of goals, purpose, and performance for learning. Your learning goals should not only be realistic, clear, specific, and rigorous; they should also be achievable and measurable—not too easy, nor too difficult. Keep in mind the diversity of student needs and differentiate as needed. Write your learning goals in student friendly language and think about how you will monitor student understanding of the goals. When you set a learning goal do you have a picture of what mastery of that goal will look like? How will you expect your students to demonstrate their mastery of the learning goal? This

TABLE 4.2.   Learning Goal with Scale

Score 4: Demonstrates the objective *and* can apply to new situations. (Reflects a more complex learning goal.)
Score 3.5: In addition to score 3.0 performance, partial success at score 4.0 content.
Score 3: Demonstrates all the foundational knowledge of the objective. (Includes the target learning goal.)
Score 2.5: In addition to score 2.0 performance, partial success at score 3.0 content.
Score 2: Demonstrates simple knowledge; no major errors. (Reflects a simpler learning goal.)
Score 1.5: Partial success with 2.0 goal and major errors with 3.0 goal.
Score 1: With help, demonstrates partial understanding and success at score 2.0 and 3.0 goals.
Score 0.5: With help, partial success at 2.0 goal but not at 3.0 goal.
Score 0: Even with help, no success at goals.

Source: Adapted from Marzano, 2010 Research Laboratory.

will help you design assessments that match the learning goal, and it will also provide you with a rationale to share with your students about why and how they will be assessed.

Get student input—ask your students to give you feedback on the learning goal; revise it with your students, involve them in monitoring their personal growth, and in doing so, you will promote ownership of their own learning goals and performance. Students can indicate their mastery of the goal by giving you feedback such as:

4: I can show others how to do it.
3: I can do it by myself.
2: I need more practice.
1: I need help.

Use their feedback to make necessary instructional adjustments, reteach as needed, or provide additional support. Simplicity and focus (especially, in curriculum, as reflected by the CCSS), clarity, and intentional and purposeful instructional planning matter in what goes on in content area classrooms and to student learning. Effective teaching is not a "mysterious process that varies with each teacher" (Elmore, 2000, p. 16). Effective teaching across disciplines includes, clear learning objectives, modeling, guided practice, scaffolded support, formative assessment, and progress monitoring.

Examples of Learning Goals

Scales, or rubrics are useful for evaluating student performance (e.g., from critical understanding beyond the text, to critical understanding of text, to partial understanding of text, to minimum or no understanding of text). A scale or rubric is a measurement tool that includes criteria that are expected of the student, along with accompanying elements used to preview expected learning or to gauge student progress toward a learning goal. Scales are progress points; they reflect progressive steps for students to move through and arrive at the desired proficiency. They typically start with simple expectations for meeting the goal and progressively move to more complex levels. Teachers should begin by sharing the scale with students and check students' understanding of the scale by asking them to put it in their own words or to identify work that meets the criteria on the scales. Learning scales also promote reflective practice; they can help teachers plan their instruction and make necessary adjustments to help all students learn and succeed. Learning scales can include whole numbers (0–4), but teachers can add half points for partial mastery of goal (Marzano, 2009). Table 4.2 is an example of a learning scale that includes both whole and half points.

Aside from the scale, or rubric, it is important to examine what are the levels of difficulty and mental processes represented with each score. Let's examine a science example.

Score/Level 4: Knowledge Utilization

- Mental Process: Decision making; Problem solving; Experimenting/Creating; Investigating
- Examples:
  - Students will be able to select appropriate tools and technology to make observations about igneous rock specimens.
  - Students will collect neighborhood rocks and will be able to use their knowledge of igneous rocks and the rock cycle to observe the rocks and write up a story about how the rocks were formed and ended up in their hands.
  - Students will be able to create a concept map about the rock cycle, types of rocks, characteristics, and how they are formed.

○ Students will be able to investigate specimens of basalt, granite, pumice, and obsidian and connect them to their formation with geological environments.

Score/Level 3: Analysis

- Mental Process: Matching; Classifying; Analyzing Errors; Generating; Specifying
- Examples:
  ○ Students will be able to distinguish igneous from sedimentary and metamorphic rocks.
  ○ Students will be able to classify important criteria for igneous rock classification.
  ○ Students will be able to analyze information about how magmas form and are altered.
  ○ Students will be able to generate hypotheses that relate igneous activity to plate tectonic activity.
  ○ Students will be able to specify the structural relationships between bodies of intrusive rock and other rocks in the earth's crust.

Score/Level 2: Comprehension

- Mental Process: Integrating; Symbolizing
- Examples:
  ○ Students will be able to summarize information about how igneous rocks are formed.
  ○ Students will be able to illustrate the interrelationships between igneous, sedimentary, and metamorphic rocks.

Score/Level 1: Retrieval

- Mental Process: Recognizing; Recalling; Executing
- Examples:
  ○ Students will be able to identify igneous rocks by using an identification chart.
  ○ Students will be able to recall characteristics of igneous rocks.
  ○ Students will be able to use the Internet to locate pictures of igneous rocks.

Table 4.3 shows a learning scale I developed with feedback from Miriam Gregorio, an 8th Grade English language arts teacher at Neptune Middle School in Kissimmee, Florida, using the same text exemplar, *Narrative of the Life of Frederick Douglass, an American Slave*.

In addition to teachers writing scales for learning goals, students should have opportunities to write their personal goals (e.g., "Through close reading of this text I will better understand the injustices of slavery."). Students can create their own rubric for monitoring their performance, for example:

5: I exceeded my goal.

4: I met my goal.

3: I learned somewhat, but did not accomplish everything I wanted.

2: I tried, but I did not learn much; I still don't understand and I am confused.

1: I did not try to accomplish my goal.

This information can be used as a type of informal assessment, as a quick way to get an idea about where the class is with their understanding of the learning goal, and as a means of promoting student tracking of personal growth and learning (Marzano, 2010). It can also be used in teacher–student conferences for revising goals and monitoring student learning.

An effective lesson has clear focus and a clearly stated purpose. The lesson should present the class with an issue that is phrased in the form of a problem to be solved or an essential question to be analyzed and evaluated by the class. Effective lessons do not just cover information. How many

TABLE 4.3. Learning Scale Example, 8th Grade, ELA

Learning Goal: Students will explore *[or be able to understand]* the various beliefs and points of view Frederick Douglass experienced as he became increasingly aware of the unfairness of his life, and will be able to relate that experience to that of undocumented migrant workers and sweatshop laborers.
Common Core Standards: RL 8.1, RL.8.2, RL.8.3, RL.8.4; W.8.1, W.8.4; SL.8.1, SL.8.3.
Topic: Frederick Douglass, *Narrative of the Life of Frederick Douglass an American Slave, Written by Himself*
Grade: 8th Grade English Language Arts

Score 4.0	In addition to Score 3.0, in-depth inferences and applications that go beyond what was taught such as: • Student will be able to use knowledge from text, make inferences, debate, adapt and create new knowledge about issues of social justice, social reconciliation, and social transformation represented in Frederick Douglass' narrative as well as in undocumented migrant workers and sweatshop laborers.		<u>Sample Activities</u> • Using this text, write a persuasive essay about slavery's ill effects on people involved in it and the role of education in the abolishment of slavery. • Debates: Role-playing and perspective taking (e.g., president at the time, author, slave, slave master, black minister, others). • Read *Uprising* by Margaret Peterson Haddix, a book about the Triangle Shirtwaist Factory Fire and inequities in the garment industry. • Watch the *60 Minutes* documentary titled, **Harvest of Shame** about injustices in agriculture.
	3.5	In addition to score 3.0 performance, in-depth inferences and applications with partial success.	
Score 3.0	While engaged in tasks that address the text, the student demonstrates an understanding of important information such as: • The realities and unfairness of slavery as experienced and represented by Frederick Douglass. • Douglass' beliefs about cause and effects of master–slave relationships. • Douglass' perspective about physical abuse of women and separation of families. • Douglass' perspective about the role of religion in the black community. **The student exhibits no major errors or omissions.**		• Close reading of text. • Text-dependent questions. • Evidence-based classroom discussions. • Analysis of author's purpose. • Evaluation of author's point of view. • Fact–opinion analysis with evidence from text. • Cause–effect relationships with evidence from text.
	2.5	No major errors or omissions regarding 2.0 content and partial knowledge of the 3.0 content.	

(Continued)

TABLE 4.3.   (Continued)

Score 2.0	There are no major errors or omissions regarding the simpler details and processes as the student is able to: • Recognize accurate statements about, and isolated examples of, the unfairness of slavery as represented by Frederick Douglass. **However, the student exhibits major errors or omissions regarding the more complex ideas and processes.**	• Academic vocabulary instruction with focus on contextual clues. • Analysis of word choice. • Literacy devices analysis. • Text structure analysis. • Writing.
	1.5	Partial knowledge of the 2.0 content, but major errors or omissions regarding the 3.0 content.	
Score 1.0	**With help, a partial understanding of some of the simpler details and processes and some of the more complex ideas and processes.**	
	0.5	With help, a partial understanding of the 2.0 content, but not the 3.0 content.	
Score 0.0	**Even with help, no understanding or skill demonstrated.**	

Source: Scale Adapted from Marzano, 2010 Research Laboratory. Example developed by V. Zygouris-Coe, and M. Gregorio, 2014.

times have you heard teachers say, "Today I am covering. . ."? How can one just "cover," for example, European Imperialism in Africa? Effective lessons present students with core concepts and ideas and challenge students to think critically and take positions on major essential questions.

Essential Questions

What is an essential question? Essential questions are questions that probe for deeper meaning of concepts and ideas and promote further questioning. A good essential question is the principle component of designing inquiry-based learning. Once you have decided on the essential questions for your unit, post them on the classroom board for easy reference. Here are sample essential questions on the *Narrative of the Life of Frederick Douglass, an American Slave, Written by Himself*.

● In the novel *Narrative of the Life of Frederick Douglass, an American Slave, Written by Himself*, how is education related to human freedom?
● How does literature affect social justice, social reconciliation, and social transformation?
● What are core human rights issues reflected in the *Narrative of the Life of Frederick Douglass, an American Slave, Written by Himself*?

See additional sample discipline-specific essential questions in Table 4.4.

Here is one way I might present all of the above to my students. If you walked into my classroom you might see the following (see Table 4.5) on my board: the learning goal, the essential (or

TABLE 4.4.   Sample Discipline-Specific Essential Questions

English Language Arts

- How do decisions, actions, and consequences vary depending on the different perspectives of the people involved?
- What are the ideals (e.g., freedom, responsibility, justice, community, etc.) that should be honored in a utopian society?

Mathematics

- How can I use models, words and expanded formats to order and compare numbers?
- How can models help us understand the addition and subtraction of decimals?
- What are the tools needed to solve linear equations and inequalities?
- How can the mean, median, mode, and range be used to describe the shape of the data?

Music

- How is melody created?
- How does music elicit emotion?
- How does the style of music affect the mood of the audience?
- How does culture affect music?

Physical Education

- What different ways can the body move given a specific purpose?
- How does nutrition affect health and fitness?
- How can you promote the value of health and balanced living?
- How do I interact with others during physical activity?

Science

- How can I perform an experiment using the steps of the scientific method?
- How can I identify incorrect interpretation of data due to errors during the experiment?
- What affect does the Earth and moon have on the ocean's tides?
- What types of environmental conditions occur in the major biomes and how do the organisms depend on one another?

Social Studies/History (American History)

- Was colonial America a democratic society?
- Was slavery the primary cause of the Civil War?
- Does economic prosperity result from tax cuts and minimal government?
- Does the United States have a fair and effective immigration policy?

big questions related to this narrative), and even an exit question I could use as a quick writing opportunity or discussion before students leave for that day. I usually prefer to do quick writes and keep all of the class work in a notebook or folder for future reference. Remember, the learning goal specifies learning that is to take place over a period of time/days, and the essential questions can be used in a couple of ways. For example, you may use them as a framework, or guide for core ideas and understanding students are to gain from this narrative, as discussion prompts, as reference to make conceptual connections as you teach a unit of study, and as a type of informal assessment that can guide students' end of unit tests and other assignments. There is no magic formula for how many essential questions you should present or address on a daily basis. Depending on the learning goal, you might write one essential question per day or per couple of days. Students will be overwhelmed if all the essential questions on a unit of study are presented all at once. Start with the end in mind and break down, or scaffold your essential question(s).

TABLE 4.5.   Learning Goal, Essential Questions, and Exit Question Example

Learning Goal:

- Students will be able to understand the various beliefs and points of view Douglass experienced as he became increasingly aware of the unfairness of his life.

Essential Questions:

- What major injustices of slavery did Douglass present in the narrative?
- What are core Human Rights issues reflected in the *Narrative of the Life of Frederick Douglass, an American Slave?*
- In the novel *Narrative of the Life of Frederick Douglass, an American Slave,* how is education related to human freedom?"
- How does literature affect Social Justice, Social Reconciliation, and Social Transformation?

Today's Exit Question: (Short Response)

- What word choice does Douglass use to communicate his beliefs about the injustices he experienced?
  - Select one injustice from the text, identify 3 examples of word choice from the narrative, and describe the type of injustice it represents.

Create learning goals that are clear, specific, and focused so that students understand them and can see classroom activities and assignments as a means to accomplishing the goals. Use scales or rubrics to communicate expected performance to learning goals. The following can provide an essential learning goal, or question for every content area teacher: "How will my instruction prepare all students for college, career, and workforce success?"

Explicit Instruction

Rigorous instruction will promote deep learning and thinking and behaviors—in a rigorous classroom, students will be expected to construct, analyze, synthesize, and reflect on, meaning. The instructional strategies teachers will select to teach will determine how students will study, inquire about, apply meaning to new situations, and reflect on what they are learning (Jackson, 2011). For example, when students are asked to write a persuasive essay about slavery's ill effects on people using the Frederick Douglass text (see Table 4.6), and compare it with recent injustices as reflected in *The Uprising* by Margaret Peterson Haddix, and the *Harvest of Shame* documentary, they will have to go beyond factual information. Actually, they will have to find commonalities and differences across eras and injustices, synthesize all of this knowledge by extending their thinking, construct their own interpretations, and present their understanding in new ways.

Thinking in a rigorous way will not happen because of the texts or materials nor will it happen automatically. Planning for learning new material, constructing meaning from text and other resources, inquiring in discipline-specific ways, synthesizing and reflecting on learning, and transferring learning to new situations warrant explicit instruction in skills, processes, and habits of mind. Explicit instruction is a systematic and structured way for teaching academic skills, and it is clearly defined and expressed in small steps and without ambiguity. Such instruction involves scaffolds whereby the teacher guides students through the learning process with clear statements about the purpose and rationale for learning the new skill/concept, provides clear explanations, and modeling/demonstrations of the instructional target, and supports their learning through practice

TABLE 4.6.   Checklist for Designing Rigorous Explicit Instruction

Learning Goal(s)

- What will the students need to know and be able to do?
- Do I have a summative assessment?
- Do I have criteria for mastery and performance?

The Hook

- What will I do to introduce the concept or topic in a relevant way? In a way that will "hook" the students' attention, motivation, and interest?

Learning Materials

- What materials will I use to teach the skill/concept? (textbook, sources, print/non-print, resources, other)

The Lesson

- Have I reviewed important information and relevant previous learning?
- Have I reviewed prerequisite skills and knowledge?
- Have I established purpose and introduced the learning objectives?
- Have I established the context?
- What will I do to assess and build students' background knowledge?
- Do I need to introduce any key vocabulary?
- Will I present new materials in chunks (small steps)? Will I use graphic organizers?
- What will I do to model the skill/concept/procedures? What discipline-specific instructional strategies are suitable for this lesson?
- Have I identified key activities?
- Have I identified potential areas of misconceptions, struggle, or challenge for all (or some) students?
- What examples (and non-examples) and support will I offer during guided practice?
- Will I provide timely feedback?
- Are students clear on what they are to discuss, examine, and report on?
- How will I facilitate student–student collaborative inquiry on the topic?

- What higher order questioning skills will I promote? Will I ask text-dependent questions and expect students to generate evidence-based thinking?
- How much time will I allow for collaborative inquiry and sharing?
- How will I model and promote accountable talk?
- How will I promote analysis, evaluation, reflection on, and synthesis of learning?
- Will students respond independently or collaboratively? Orally or in writing?
- Will students be expected to reflect on their mastery of the concept/skill, reflect on learning goals, and explain why they are doing what they are doing?
- What opportunities will I provide for real-world applications?
- Will homework be an extension of classroom activities?
- Will I track students' progress?
- Will students practice until skills are automatic?
- What are the next instructional steps?

Closure

- Did I review what we did and learned today in class?
- What connections will I make with past and next concept/topic/skill?
- Reflection on learning goal, things we need to revisit, next steps, and homework (as needed).
- What accommodations do I need to make for students who did not master the learning goal?

with feedback until they achieve independent mastery (Archer & Hughes, 2011; Rosenshine, 1987). Having said this, explicit instruction does not mean stand up and deliver for 45–50 minutes.

What explicit instruction principles should you consider when planning for instruction? You may use Table 4.6 as a checklist for elements of rigorous explicit instruction. As you review these elements, please note the focus on step-by-step planning, clarity, learning goals, modeling, scaffolded support, guided practice, as well as the ways you would set up your classroom for collaborative inquiry and learning. In Chapter 2, I presented the Gradual Release of Responsibility Model (Pearson & Gallagher, 1983) (see Figure 2.6, p. 54) as a way of progressively releasing teacher support as students develop mastery of the skill/concept under study.

Explicit instruction will help make rigor visible to all, equip students with the tools, dispositions, skills, and knowledge needed to learn in deep and transferable ways, and will facilitate mastery of learning goals. At all times, think about what you will be doing, how, and why, and also what role your students will be playing in the learning process. Rigorous learning requires rigor, commitment, and engagement from teachers and students.

High Probability Strategies

In schools around the nation or in conversations with school educators, one will often hear the term "high-yield," or "high-probability" strategies. What are high-probability strategies? This is a term coined by Robert Marzano, who has been doing research on effective instruction and assessment, implementing standards, effective leadership, and school intervention for over 30 years. Dr. Marzano has identified nine instructional strategies (see Table 4.7) that are supported by research, and have been found to yield positive results, or have a greater effect, on student achievement. Although these strategies are effective for student learning, they should not be used by every teacher, and also should not be used all the time regardless of subject area, grade level, and context (Marzano, Pickering, & Pollock, 2001). Marzano's research has not identified whether some strategies are more effective in some subject areas, or with certain student groups. Actually, these strategies should be called higher probability strategies; some have a higher probability for working than others (Marzano, 2006). It is important to remember that strategies (no matter how effective) do not teach; teachers, do. Teaching and learning are very complex

TABLE 4.7.   High Probability Instructional Strategies

Strategies

1. Identifying similarities and differences

2. Summarizing and note-taking

3. Reinforcing effort and providing recognition

4. Homework and practice

5. Nonlinguistic recommendations

6. Cooperative learning

7. Setting objectives and providing feedback

8. Generating and testing hypotheses

9. Cues, questions, and advance organizers

Source: Adapted from Marzano, R. (2009). Setting the record straight on "high yield" strategies. *Phi Delta Kappan*, 91(1), 30–37. Retrieved from http://www.sde.ct.gov/sde/lib/sde/pdf/curriculum/cali/setting_the_record_straight_on_hield_yield_strategies.pdf

processes, and strategies are mere tools. Marzano (2006) cautions educators about strategy usage: "Until we find the answers to the preceding questions, teachers should rely on their knowledge of their students, their subject matter, and their situations to identify the most appropriate instructional strategies" (p. 9).

Unfortunately, many school administrators and districts rely predominantly on these nine instructional strategies. Some school administrators who view these strategies as the total sum of effective teaching instruction, after conducting instructional walkthroughs (short classroom visits), provide feedback to teachers on their use of these strategies in the classroom. As you select appropriate instructional strategies to help you meet learning goals, consider curricular, subject-matter, student, and contextual factors that may interfere with those goals. For example, in a situation where students have been reading complex text and have several questions about the text, but the teacher only chooses to reinforce the fact that they are reading without providing them with corrective or scaffolded feedback, well, in that case, just reinforcing student effort will not produce understanding of text or learning. There might be a situation where the use of these strategies will not produce the results a teacher had anticipated.

Marzano (2009) provides a comprehensive framework for effective teaching practices that is comprised of 41 types for strategies effective instruction (see http://www.marzanocenter.com/files/WP_CAS_AppendixA.pdf). These strategies are grouped into three areas: (1) routine strategies for communicating learning goals, tracking student progress, and celebrating student success; (2) content strategies for helping students to interact with new knowledge, practice and extend their understanding, and generate hypotheses about new knowledge; and, (3) strategies enacted on the spot for engaging students, dealing with rules and procedures, building relationships with students, and communicating high expectations for all students.

As a content area teacher teaching in times of high accountability, national efforts for evaluating teacher effectiveness, and new educational standards for college and career readiness, chances are that you will, or you have already been evaluated on your implementation of such strategies in your classroom. These strategies are "good old instruction strategies;" they have been proven effective in supporting student achievement. What is a teacher to do with these strategies? First of all, understand that they are elements of effective instruction. Second, they are not to be used all at once! Start building your routines; select one routine, content, and strategy enacted on the spot that you would like to implement each year. Both you and your students will need time to develop ownership and time to determine its effectiveness in your classroom.

The disciplinary learning framework presented in this book includes these high levels of teaching effectiveness. College, career, and workforce readiness will not happen through teacher monologue, sporadic explicit instruction, a teacher-centered approach to learning, and memorization. It takes skilled and knowledgeable preparation, a lot of intentional and consistent planning for high-impact, rigorous, and deliberate practice, and ongoing monitoring and reflection of teacher and student progress.

Digital Literacies

- Zunal Wequest http://zunal.com/. Develop rigorous scaffolded road maps that are aligned with the standards.
- Subtext: http://www.subtext.com/. Subtext is an application (app) that allows for close reading of text, citing textual evidence, and analyzing a PDF, or text (aligned with the CCSS).
- Create a video lesson: www.showme.com or www.educreations.com. Students can create and share screencasts and videotaped lessons.

Cognitive Rigor

What does cognitive rigor mean to you, especially in relation to instruction, learning, and assessment? Think about it and take a couple of minutes to write down your thoughts. Let's say that your class just read an article about coral bleaching (a sign of coral decay) around the world. What is a basic comprehension question you might ask? For example, "What is coral bleaching?" Now, what is a more rigorous question you might ask? How about, "Using evidence from the text, what is a viable solution for preventing coral bleaching?" There are many differences between the depth of thinking and mental processing required for answering each of the above questions. The first question requires mere recall of basic facts whereas the second question requires the student to describe, compare, and contrast solutions, evaluate solutions, and develop an evidence-based argument.

How has cognitive rigor been conceptualized by scholars and how would your understanding of cognitive rigor in learning goals, instruction, and assessments help you to plan instruction that will promote the rigorous knowledge and skills students need to succeed in college, career, and workforce? Bloom (1956) developed a classification system of the thinking and behavior skills important in learning. His committee identified three domains of educational activities: cognitive (knowledge), affective (attitude), and psychomotor (skills). Within the cognitive domain, Bloom identified six levels of cognitive complexity, a hierarchy that increased in terms of complexity and abstraction (from the lowest level, simple recall of facts, to the highest, evaluation). Educators have been focusing on the main action verb associated with the level of the taxonomy. Hess (2009) states that the verb alone (e.g., compare, contrast, write) is inadequate for fully describing the cognitive demand required to understand what is involved in a learning activity. Anderson and Krathwohl (2001) revisited Bloom's taxonomy by adding one more dimension: knowledge. The revised taxonomy includes both the cognitive processes (the verbs) and knowledge (the nouns) needed to fully articulate educational objectives.

Bloom's (1956) Taxonomy of Educational Objectives focuses on the type of thinking one is using when recalling, understanding, applying, analyzing, evaluating, and creating, while Webb (2002) focuses on how deeply one has to know the content and what mental processes he or she will have to engage in to be successful. According to Webb's model, curricular demands could be categorized based on the cognitive demands required to produce an acceptable response. Each grouping of tasks reflects a different level of cognitive expectation, or depth of knowledge, required to complete the task. Webb (1997) uses the word knowledge broadly to include all forms of knowledge (i.e., declarative, procedural, and conditional).

Webb's Depth of Knowledge Levels (DOK) (1997, 1999) presents a different perspective on cognitive complexity that is represented in four levels (i.e., Level 1: Recall; Level 2: Skill/Concept; Level 3: Strategic Thinking; Level 4: Extended Thinking). Level 1 skills refer to basic skills or abilities for recalling information (e.g., recalling key characters in a story or conducting basic mathematical calculations—Name the US Presidents in order.). Level 2 includes engagement beyond recalling (e.g., use context clues to identify the meaning of unfamiliar words or describe cause and effect of a particular event—Categorize the 20th and 21st century US Presidents according to their political party affiliation.). Level 3 requires higher level mental processing like reasoning, planning, and using evidence (e.g., apply a concept in other contexts or support ideas with evidence and examples—Hypothesize how President Reagan would have responded to today's US foreign policy issues.). Level 4 requires complex reasoning, planning, developing, and thinking over a longer period of time (e.g., analyze and synthesize information from multiple sources or design a solution to a practical problem—Analyze the effectiveness of President George W. Bush's war strategies in Iraq and the effectiveness of President Obama's war strategies in Afghanistan and write an article for your local High School newspaper.).

Webb's DOK attracts our attention not only to the content addressed in a test item, but also to the depth of knowledge the student will need to have to demonstrate his or her understanding of the concept(s). Depth of knowledge is determined not by the difficulty, but by the complexity of the content (e.g., simple or complex data display; reading and interpreting literal vs. figurative language) and the task required (e.g., solving a simple task vs. solving a complex task). Karin Hess's (2009) Cognitive Rigor Matrix (CRM) in Table 4.8 integrates Bloom's and Webb's models as a strategy for analyzing instruction and guiding teacher lesson planning. Difficulty only tells us how many students can answer a question correctly.

When planning lessons, it is important to consider the following questions: What level of work are the students most commonly required to perform? What is the complexity (instead of the difficulty) of the task? What are the skills and knowledge scaffolding that the students will have already needed to build the task? See sample DOK question stems in Table 4.9 below.

How might content area teachers use this information on cognitive complexity? This information can be used to explain how deeply students must understand the content to complete related tasks. States have used DOK levels and Bloom's taxonomy to (a) revise objectives, learning goals, and standards; (b) boost the rigor of classroom instruction; (c) align standards to assessments; and (d) facilitate higher level questioning that encourages students to think deeply about content, promote problem solving, encourage critical discussions, and stimulate further learning. Hattie (2002) reported that expert teachers provide all students with challenging learning goals and tasks, and structure learning in a way that all students can reach high goals and know how to enhance both surface and deep learning of content. Transfer of learning happens when students have a deep understanding of content and are presented with opportunities to apply their learning in new contexts.

Rigorous Instruction and Informal Assessment

Assessment is an integral part of teaching and student learning; it is the process of gathering, analyzing, interpreting, and synthesizing students' learning (Ferrara & McTighe, 1992). According to Johnston (1997), teachers must become assessment experts. Throughout this chapter, I have emphasized planning with the end in mind, and practicing ongoing assessment and monitoring of student progress. In Chapter 10, I will further explore the topic of assessment and CCSS assessment systems. For the purpose of this chapter, I will briefly address ways to informally assess student learning in your classroom. Formative (informal) assessment helps a teacher to identify student strengths and weaknesses (e.g., attitude and interest surveys, teacher observations, strategy applications). Summative (formal) assessment offers a summative picture of what a student has learned or done (e.g., grades, class assignments, research papers, projects, teacher-designed texts, report cards).

What are some easy ways to assess student learning on a daily basis? Bell ringer activities, paraphrasing, group answers, think, pair, share, random questioning, response cards, writing, graphic organizers, games, exit slips/exit work, are a few. After using a quick formative assessment at the end of a lesson or unit, reflect on your assessments, questions, and data. Think about what worked and what did not and whether you have sufficient information about all students' learning and progress. For example, ask yourself the following questions that can help you reflect and revise your use of assessments: Did my questions address key learning and standards? Was I able to monitor all students' progress? Did students get enough information on their progress? What else can I do to assess other areas of student learning and progress? Is there anything I would like to change next time? How else might I get some more feedback from students?

TABLE 4.8. Bloom's Taxonomy and Webb's Depth of Knowledge (DOK)

Bloom's Taxonomy (1956; 2005)	Tasks	Webb's Depth of Knowledge (2002)
Knowledge/Remembering Recalling specific information. *Can students recall information?*	Define, identify, list, locate, recall, recognize, repeat, reproduce, retrieve	**Recall** Recall a fact, information, or procedure; memorize something (simple or complex).
Comprehension/Understanding Processing information on a low level so that knowledge can be communicated without a verbatim repetition. *Can students explain ideas or concepts?*	Classify, compare, describe, discuss, exemplify, explain, identify, infer, interpret, locate, recognize, report, paraphrase, summarize	
Application/Applying Applying information in another familiar situation. *Can students use the information in another familiar situation?*	Carry out, choose, demonstrate, execute, illustrate, implement, interpret, solve, use, write	**Basic Application** Use of information, conceptual knowledge, procedures, or relationships.
Analysis/Analyzing Breaking information into parts to explore understandings and relationships. *Can students break information into parts to explore understandings and relationships?*	Appraise, attribute, compare, contrast, criticize, deconstruct, discriminate, distinguish, examine, experiment, find, integrate, organize, outline, question, structure	**Strategic Thinking** Requires reasoning, developing a plan or sequence of steps, drawing on prior knowledge; includes some complexity and can have more than one possible answer.
Synthesis and Evaluation/Evaluating and Creating Putting together elements and parts to form a whole and making judgments about the method. *Can students justify a decision or a course of action?* (Evaluating) *Can students generate new products, ideas, or ways of viewing things?* (Creating)	Appraise, argue, check, critique, defend, detect, judge, monitor, select, support, value, evaluate Assemble, construct, create, design, develop, devise, experiment, formulate, hypothesize, invent, make, plan, produce, test, write	**Extended Thinking** Requires an investigation; time to think and process multiple conditions of the problem or task. Have to synthesize information from multiple texts and then present them in a unique way.

TABLE 4.9.   Depth of Knowledge (DOK) Question Stems

DOK Level 1	DOK Level 2
• Can you recall_____?	• Can you explain how ____ affected ___?
• When did ____ happen?	• How would you apply what you learned to
• Who was ___?	develop ____?
• How can you recognize___?	• How would you compare ____?
• What is___?	• Contrast____?
• How can you find the meaning of___?	• How would you classify___?
• Can you select___?	• How are___alike? Different?
• How would you write___?	• How would you classify the type of___?
• What might you include on a list about___?	• What can you say about___?
• Who discovered___?	• How would you summarize___?
• What is the formula for___?	• What steps are needed to edit___?
• Can you identify___?	• When would you use an outline to ___?
• How would you describe___?	• How would you estimate___?
	• How could you organize___?
	• What would you use to classify___?
	• What do you notice about___?

DOK Level 3	DOK Level 4
• How is ____ related to ___?	• Write a thesis, drawing conclusions from
• What conclusions can you draw _____?	multiple sources.
• How would you adapt____to create a	• Design and conduct an experiment.
different____?	• Gather information to develop alternative
• How would you test___?	explanations for the results of an experiment.
• Can you predict the outcome if___?	• Write a research paper on a topic.
• What is the best answer? Why?	• Apply information from one text to another text
• What conclusion can be drawn from these	to develop a persuasive argument.
three texts?	• What information can you gather to support
• What is your interpretation of this text?	your idea about___?
Support your rationale.	• DOK 4 would most likely be the writing of a
• How would you describe the sequence	research paper or applying information from
of___?	one text to another text to develop a persuasive
• What facts would you select to	argument.
support___?	• DOK 4 requires time for extended thinking.
• Can you elaborate on the reason____?	
• What would happen if___?	
• Can you formulate a theory for___?	
• How would you test___?	

How Will You Know that Students are Learning?

What types of evidence will you use? Here are a few ways you can gauge whether your students are learning: Teacher observations, teacher-student mini-conferences, class/end of lesson/end of unit tests/quizzes, pre/post-tests, report cards, course assignments, portfolios, labs, informal/ formal writing, class participation, rubrics, formative/summative assessments, district/state/ national assessments. Using data from informal and formal assessment, and ongoing progress monitoring of student progress will help you plan your instruction, make accommodations and modifications to meet student needs, and have informed conversations with students, parents, and administrators about student goals and learning.

What Will You Do When Students Don't Learn?

This is a critical question. If you do not monitor your instruction's impact on student learning, you will not be able to do anything significant to meet student needs. If all the feedback students receive from you on their performance is a grade letter or a number on a quiz, without corrective feedback and new instructional steps, how will they continue to learn? The sum total of conceptual and content knowledge gaps does not equal learning, some how, in the future. Learning does not happen in a vacuum. Learning is a socially constructed process and no matter how pressed you are as content area teachers to cover content, your primary job is to teach students. One of the advantages of the CCSS is that they present teachers with a smaller, more rigorous, and more consistent list of standards that focus on developing critical thinkers.

Every teacher, depending on their context and needs, can make various decisions to help students learn. For example, some students might need more time, or because of language disabilities they might need someone to read a test aloud to them. Other students might need more feedback, or a couple more examples. Or, if a group of students have the same challenge, you might have to group them together and re-teach the concept or skill. In some cases, students might need additional materials while others have the conceptual understanding, but need more practice. Finally, depending on student needs, collaboration with other educators such as the ESE teacher, ESOL teacher, school counselor, school psychologist, or speech and language pathologist might be necessary to identify Response to Intervention (RtI) steps that would best benefit the student.

How Will You Respond If Students Already Know It?

The challenge you risk is boring advanced or gifted students who show quick mastery and require differentiated instruction to meet their needs. For example, gifted students might benefit from curricular extensions, enriching materials, independent projects, time to pursue further studying and research on topic, choice to explore or test their knowledge, and even tutoring others in class.

Teacher Reflection

Last, but not least, teacher reflection is a necessary element of student learning and success. When a teacher examines her assumptions about students, subject matter, learning theory and pedagogy, the context, and assessment data of student progress, her instruction improves. As a teacher, you will have opportunities to reflect before, during, and after your instruction. What do you reflect on before teaching? Do you reflect on your assumptions, beliefs, goals, and student characteristics/knowledge, and needs? How about your learning goal(s), instructional strategies, and reasons for choosing goals, objectives, materials, activities, assignments, and assessments? How will you make the lesson rigorous and relevant? As you deliver your instruction, you will also have opportunities to reflect and make notes about what you were able to teach. Are students on task? Do students appear to understand the concept/skill/topic? If not, what adaptations and modifications can I make? What will I need to reteach? Do some students need extra support? After teaching, think about what worked well or not, how students responded, what you'd do differently the next time, what students learned, how they learned it, and what evidence you have for their learning. What went well? What activities and strategies would you like to use again? What did not work? Did you get through the material for the lesson? What questions did you ask? How did students respond to your questions? What questions did students ask? What motivated student learning and why or why not? What planned assessments inform you of student progress and learning? What would you change or keep?

Reflection will help you identify areas of pedagogical strength and improvement, evaluate the effectiveness of your lessons/units on student learning, evaluate the effectiveness of specific pedagogical strategies and behaviors, and set goals for your professional growth. Many school districts use lesson study as a systematic way of improving instruction—a topic we will further explore in Chapter 11. During lesson study, teachers collaborate with colleagues to plan, observe, and reflect on lessons. They set collaborative goals, collect data on student learning, and follow-up with targeted discussions (Lewis, Perry, & Hurd, 2004). Start with the end in mind (what students need to understand and be able to do), and then unfold the ways you will teach, what materials you will use, what difficulties students might have with the content or strategy, what experiences will support their learning, and what students will be doing during the lesson. Plan rigorous instruction with your colleagues and use department meetings and Professional Learning Communities (PLCs) to discuss common content, and set and reflect on instructional goals and student learning.

Summary

- Rigor, relevance, and relationships are all important for improving student learning. Rigor needs to exist in standards, pedagogy, and assessment.
- Teachers who plan carefully, have clear learning goals and high expectations for all, use assessment to inform instruction, create and select relevant and stimulating materials, deliver explicit instruction that engages all in meaningful learning, provide needed support, value collaborative inquiry, and model and promote critical thinking and ownership of one's learning, are teachers who make it easy for students to take intellectual risks, persist when meaning does not come easily, and continue to learn.
- Rigorous instruction is necessary for postsecondary success in college, career, and the workforce.

Differentiating Instruction

- Increase the intensity of instruction, the time to model and provide feedback, and the feedback and scaffolded support. Utilize individual educational planning for students and provide accommodations when appropriate (e.g., extended time, assistive technology, etc.). Use multiple modalities and resources (e.g., visual, gestural, digital) to provide context to ELLs that are not language dependent.
- Use small-group instruction to reteach both students having difficulty and advanced students. Require active participation in class (e.g., questioning, discussion, explanation).
- Although ELLs and students with varied exceptionalities have unique learning needs, keep them accountable on persevering with their goals, and hold high expectations for all students. Use a timer they can see on a screen or wall to help them budget time, be flexible as they are learning, and differentiate based on their needs. Teach them how to take notes, how to discriminate relevant from irrelevant information, and prioritize the big picture, smaller parts, and details.
- Use student questions, topics, and interests to guide materials selection and instruction. Develop rubrics for success based on both grade-level expectations and individual student learning needs.

Reflect and Apply

1. What elements of rigorous instruction do you recognize in Ms. Ferrante's (see Classroom Life vignette) instructional decisions? What other suggestions could you offer? Discuss your thoughts with a small group of peers, or with the entire class.

2. Select one of the lesson plans shared in this chapter. What instructional elements might you change to further improve the rigor in goals, materials, and instruction? Discuss your suggestions with a peer from your discipline, and present your suggestions in class.

3. Write a learning goal for your content area and create a rigorous summative assessment to guide your instruction. Discuss with your peers how you will know students have mastered the learning goal in a rigorous way, and what evidence you will collect to determine their mastery.

Extending Learning

1. A peer invites you to visit her classroom, observe, and suggest ways she could improve rigorous learning. Using evidence from this chapter, develop a short observation protocol to guide your observations and peer feedback. What five to seven core instructional areas would you include in it? Defend your choice of items in your observation protocol and explain how they address rigor. Last, conduct your observation and use your notes to discuss with your peer what worked well and what she could improve.

2. What does teaching for transfer mean to you in your discipline? Select a topic, and design rigorous learning experiences that will help students acquire new information, develop the discipline-specific thinking skills to learn the information at a deep level, and apply problem-solving skills to new challenges. Provide specific examples, and present your plans to the class or a subject area colleague.

3. Gather the learning material you plan to use in an upcoming unit and analyze it for rigor. Is the material directly connected to your learning goals? Does it match the content students will face in a summative assessment? Is it grade- and age-appropriate? Is it relevant? Does it contain multiple meanings? Will it engage students over time? Can you identify ways to increase the rigor for students who are ready for more challenge? What strategies will you use to help students who are having difficulty accessing the rigorous material you have chosen? Discuss with a small group of peers how this learning material aligns with your instructional choices and student needs.

References

Achieve. (2009). *What is college and career ready?* Retrieved from http://www.achieve.org/files/CollegeandCareerReady.pdf.

ACT. (2006). *Ready for college and ready for work: Same or different?* Iowa City, IA: Author.

ACT. (2007). *Rigor at risk: Reaffirming quality in the high school core curriculum.* Iowa City, IA: ACT.

ACT. (2009). *The condition of college readiness.* Iowa City, IA: ACT.

Allensworth, E., Nomi, T., Montgomery, N., & Lee, V. E. (2008). *College preparatory curriculum for all: Consequences of ninth grade course taking in algebra and English on academic outcomes in Chicago.* Chicago, IL: University of Chicago, Consortium on Chicago School Research.

Ambady, N., & Rosenthal, R. (1993). Half a minute: Predicting teacher evaluations from thin slices of nonverbal behavior and physical attractiveness. *Journal of Personality and Social Psychology, 64*(3), 431–441.

Anderson, L. W., & Krathwohl, D. R. (Eds). (2001). *A taxonomy for learning, teaching and assessing: A revision of Bloom's taxonomy of educational objectives*. New York, NY: Longman.

Archer, A. L., & Hughes, C. A. (2011). *Explicit instruction: Effective and efficient teaching*. NY: Guilford Press.

Au, K. H. (1998). Social constructivism and the school literacy learning of students of diverse backgrounds. *Journal of Literacy Research, 30*, 297–319.

Auguste, B., Kihn, P., & Miller, M. (2010). *Closing the talent gap: Attracting and retaining top-third graduates to careers in teaching*. Retrieved from http://mckinseyonsociety.com/closing-the-talent-gap/

Baron, D. (2007). Using text-based protocols: The five Rs. *Principal Leadership, 7*(6), 50–51.

Bill & Melinda Gates Foundation. (2012). *Gathering feedback for teaching: Measures of effective teaching*. Retrieved from http://metproject.org/downloads/MET_Gathering_Feedback_Research_Paper.pdf

Bill & Melinda Gates Foundation. (2012). *Gathering feedback for teaching: Combining high-quality observations with student surveys and achievement gains*. A MET Project Research Paper: Author.

Blackburn, B. (2008). *Rigor is not a four-letter word*. Larchmont, NY: Eye on Education, Inc.

Bloom, B. S. (Ed.). (1956). *Taxonomy of educational objectives, the classification of educational goals—Handbook I: Cognitive domain*. New York: McKay.

Blumenfeld, P., Kempler, T., & Krajcik, J. (2006). Motivation and cognitive engagement in learning environments. In R. K. Sawyer (Ed.), *The Cambridge handbook of the learning sciences* (pp. 475–488). Cambridge, UK: Cambridge University Press.

Bobilya, A. J., & Daniel, B. (2009). Eleanor Duckworth: The teacher's teacher. In T. Smith & C. E. Knapp (Eds), *Beyond Dewey and Hahn: Foundations for experiential education*, Vol. I (pp. 113–122). Lake Geneva, WI: Raccoon Institute.

Boggess, J. A. (2007). The three Rs redefined for a flat world. *Techniques, 62*.

Boynton, M., & Boynton, C. (2005). *The educator's guide to preventing and solving discipline problems*. Alexandria, VA: Association for Supervision and Curriculum Development.

Brophy, J. E. (1983). Research on the self-fulfilling prophecy and teacher expectations. *Journal of Educational Psychology, 75*(5), 631–661.

Brophy, J. E., & Everston, C. (1976). *Learning from teaching: A developmental perspective*. Boston, MA; Allyn & Bacon.

Brophy, J., & Good, T. (1970). Teachers' communication of differential expectations for children's classroom performance: Some behavioral data. *Journal of Educational Psychology, 61*, 365–374.

Cazden, C. B. (2001). *Classroom discourse: The language of teaching and learning* (2nd ed.). Portsmouth, NH: Heinemann

Chappuis, S., Chappuis, J., & Stiggins, R. (2009). The quest for quality. *Educational Leadership, 67*(3), 14–19.

Coleman, D., & Pimentel, S. (rev. 2011). *Publishers' criteria for the Common Core Standards in English language arts, grades 3–12*. Retrieved from www.corestandards.org

Conley, D. T. (2008). Rethinking college readiness. *The New England Journal of Higher Education, 22*(5), 24–26.

Conley, D. T., & Barton, P. E. (2007). The challenge of college readiness. *Educational Leadership, 64*(7), 23–29.

Daggett, W. R. (2005). *Achieving academic excellence through rigor and relevance*. Rexford, NY: International Center for Leadership in Education.

Darling-Hammond, L. (2010). *Performance counts: Assessment systems that support high-quality learning*. Washington, DC: Council of Chief State School Officers.

Darling-Hammond, L., & Adamson, F. (2010). *Beyond basic skills: The role of performance assessment in achieving 21st century standards of learning*. Stanford, CA: Stanford Center for Opportunity Policy in Education.

Elmore, R. F. (2000). *Building a new structure for school leadership*. Washington, DC: Albert Shanker Institute.

Evertson, C. M., & Weinstein, C. S. (2006). Classroom management as a field of inquiry. In C. M. Evertson & C. S. Weinstein (Eds), *Handbook of classroom management: Research, practice, and contemporary issues* (pp. 3–16). Mahwah, NJ: Lawrence Erlbaum Associates.

Ferrara, S., & McTighe, J. (1992). A process for planning: More thoughtful classroom assessment. In A. Costa, J. Bellanca, & R. Fogarty (Eds), *If minds matter: A foreword to the future* (Vol. 2). Palatine, IL: Skylight.

Fredricks, J., Blumenfeld, P., & Paris, A. (2004). School engagement: Potential of the concept, state of the evidence. *Review of Educational Research, 74*(1), 59–109.

Goldhaber, D. (2002). The mystery of good teaching: Surveying the evidence on student achievement and teachers' characteristics. *Education Next, 2*(1), 50–55.

Hanushek, E. A. (1992). The trade-off between child quantity and quality. *Journal of Political Economy, 100*(1), 84–117.

Hanushek, E. A., Kain, J. F., O'Brien, D. M., & Rivkin, S. G. (2005). *The market for teacher quality* (NBER Working Paper 11154). Cambridge, MA: National Bureau of Economic Research.

Hattie, J. A. C. (2002). What are the attributes of excellent teachers? In *Teachers make a difference: What is the research evidence?* (pp. 3–26). Wellington, New Zealand: New Zealand Council for Educational Research.

Hess, K. K. (2009). *Hess' cognitive rigor matrix & curricular examples.* Retrieved from http://www.nciea.org/

Jackson, R. (2011). *How to plan rigorous instruction.* Alexandria, VA: ASCD.

Jago, C. (2011). *With rigor for all: Meeting common core standards for reading literature* (2nd ed.). Portsmouth, NH: Heinemann.

Johnston, P. H. (1997). *Knowing literacy: Constructive literacy assessment.* York, ME: Stenhouse.

Ladson-Billings, G. (1994). *The Dreamkeepers: Successful teachers for African-American children.* San Francisco, CA: Jossey-Bass.

Ladson-Billings, G. (1995). But that's just good teaching! The case for culturally relevant pedagogy. *Theory Into Practice, 34*(3), 159–165.

Lee, C. D. (2001). Is October Brown Chinese: A cultural modeling activity system for underachieving students. *American Educational Research Journal, 38*(1), 97–142.

Lee, C. D. (2007). *Culture, literacy and learning: Taking Bloom in the midst of the whirlwind.* NY: Teachers College Press.

Lewis, C., Perry, R., & Hurd, J. (2004). A deeper look at lesson study. *Educational Leadership, 61*(5), 6–11.

Marzano, R. J. (2006). *Classroom assessment and grading that work.* Alexandria, VA: ASCD.

Marzano, R. J. (2007). *The art and science of teaching.* Alexandria, VA: ASCD.

Marzano, R. J. (Ed.). (2009). *Leading edge anthology: On excellence in teaching.* Bloomington, IN: Solution Tree.

Marzano, R. J. (2010). *Formative assessment and standards-based grading.* Bloomington, IN: Marzano Research Laboratory.

Marzano, R. J., Frontier, T., & Livingston, D. (2011). *Effective supervision: Supporting the art and science of teaching.* Alexandria, VA: ASCD.

Marzano, R. J., Pickering, D., & Pollock, J. E. (2001). *Classroom instruction that works: Research-based strategies for increasing student achievement.* Alexandria, VA: ASCD.

National Governors Association Center for Best Practices, Council of Chief State School Officers. (2010). *Common Core State Standards initiative.* (2010). Washington, DC: Author. Retrieved from http://www.corestandards.org

National High School Alliance. (2006). *Increasing academic rigor in high schools: Stakeholder perspectives.* Washington, DC: Institute for Educational Leadership.

Newell, R. J., & Van Ryzin, M. J. (2008). *Assessing what really matters in schools: Creating hope for the future.* New York: Rowman & Littlefield.

Noddings, N. (2007). *Philosophy of education* (2nd ed.). Boulder, CO: Westview Press.

Pearson, P. D., & Gallagher, M. C. (1983). The instruction of reading comprehension. *Contemporary Educational Psychology, 8,* 317–344.

Rentner, D., & Usher, A. (2012). *What impact did education stimulus funds have on state and school districts?* Washington, DC: Center on Education Policy.

Resnick, L. (1987). *Education and learning to think.* Washington, DC: National Academy Press.

Rosenshine, B. (1987). Direct instruction. In M. J. Dunkin (Ed.), *The international encyclopedia of teaching and teacher education* (pp. 257–263). Oxford, UK: Pergamon Press.

Rosenthal, R., & Jacobson, L. (1968). *Pygmalion in the classroom: Teacher expectations and pupils' intellectual development.* New York: Holt, Rinehart and Winston.

Schmoker, M. (2011). *Focus.* Alexandria, VA: ASCD.

Shulman, L. (1987). Knowledge and teaching: Foundations of the new reform. *Harvard Educational Review, 57*(1), 1–22.

Southern Regional Education Board (SREB). (2004). *Using rigor, relevance and relationships to improve student achievement: How some schools do it.* (2004 Practices). Atlanta, GA: Author.

Strong, R., Silver, H., & Perini, M. (2001). *Teaching what matters most: Standards and strategies for raising student achievement*. Alexandria, VA: ASCD.

Stiggins, R. J. (2008) *Assessment manifesto: A call for the development of balance assessment systems*. Portland, OR: Educational Testing Service, Assessment Training Institute.

Thompson, J. (1998). *Discipline survival kit for the secondary teacher*. West Nyack, NY: The Center for Applied Research in Education.

Washor, E., & Mojkowski, C. (2006/2007). What do you mean by rigor? *Educational Leadership, 64*, 84–87.

Webb, N. (1997). Research Monogram No. 6: *Criteria for alignment of expectations and assessments on mathematics and science education*. Washington, DC: CCSSO.

Webb, N. (1999). Research Monogram No. 18: *Alignment of science and mathematics standards and assessments in four states*. Washington, DC: CCSSO.

Webb, N. (2002). *Depth-of-knowledge levels for four content areas*. Unpublished paper.

Weinstein, R. S. (2002). *Reaching higher: The power of expectations in schooling*. Cambridge, MA: Harvard University Press.

Zimba, J. (2011). *Criteria for resources aligned to Common Core State Standards in mathematics*. New York State Education Department. Retrieved from: http://usny.nysed.gov/rttt/docs/criteriaresources-math.pdf

five

Vocabulary Learning and Instruction in the Disciplines

*Words are not just words. They are the nexus—
the interface—between communication and
thought. When we read, it is through words that
we build, refine, and modify our knowledge.
What makes vocabulary valuable and important is
not the words themselves so much as the
understandings they afford.*
–Marilyn Jager Adams (2009, p. 180)

Chapter Highlights

- College, career, and workforce readiness requires rich, robust, and complex vocabulary knowledge that will equip students to continue to learn about the discipline, collaborate and communicate effectively with others, and create knowledge.
- New educational standards place much attention on the development of students' academic vocabulary.
- Each discipline possesses its own complex and unique discourse. Knowledge and development of that discourse is necessary for both content and literacy development and learning. Students will benefit from a language-rich, vocabulary-rich, print-rich, and collaboration-rich learning environment.
- Vocabulary development in the disciplines should be ongoing, and should be accompanied by targeted, deliberate, broad, deep, and systematic instruction that will promote vocabulary learning knowledge and independence. Engaging with the texts of each discipline will help students develop discipline-specific discourse and habits of mind.
- Students will benefit from explicit instruction, guided support, multiple exposures to words, use of effective instructional strategies, and opportunities to identify, discuss, apply, and reflect on word meanings and connections between words.
- Classroom talk should be a "staple" in each content area classroom. Learning how to hold academic conversations, provide evidentiary responses, respond to others' ideas and negotiate meaning, and practice accountable talk, will facilitate student learning.

Classroom Life

I teach 6th Grade life science, and something I've noticed my kids have challenges with is to take scientific language, understand it, and restate it in their own words. I find that they will skim a text to try and find what sounds like the right answer, but they're not really comprehending the text. I think partially the vocabulary intimidates them, but also I think they have a hard time with the density of scientific texts. I remember one of my professors teaching us that science texts will try and explain multiple concepts in just a few sentences. I think the kids try to read science texts like they would read a novel, quickly and without taking time to think between sentences. Then, when they can't get through a lot of text in as short a time as they expect, they end up picking out just a few pieces of information rather than actually digesting and understanding the text. *(Ms. Amanda Heglund, 6th Grade Science Teacher, Gotha Middle School, Orange County Public Schools, Florida)*

The Role of Vocabulary in the Context of New Educational Standards

The Common Core State Standards (CCSS) (NGA & CCSSO, 2010) require robust knowledge of academic vocabulary and domain-specific words that are found in complex texts. The CCSS indicate that one of the most important college and career readiness factors is a well-developed or robust vocabulary. Although vocabulary is addressed in the CCSS reading and language standards, the CCSS call for teachers to develop students' advanced academic vocabulary across content areas and grade levels.

The Next Generation Science Standards (NGSS), call for teachers to develop students' technical and generalized academic vocabulary. According to the NGSS, crosscutting concepts can bridge science and engineering through a common vocabulary. Students will need to develop a solid understanding of scientific vocabulary and how it applies to related fields.

Each discipline has its own discourse—the language that is used by its experts to communicate, understand, and generate word knowledge (Bruner, 1996). The amount of reading one engages in is an indicator of the vocabulary size he, or she would recognize and use in any given language (Fielding, Wilson, & Anderson, 1986). By the time most students reach school age, they can communicate pretty comfortably in their native language(s). Beck and McKeown (1991) estimated that first graders possess between 2,500–5,000 words. By the time they have finished their secondary schooling, students know about 45,000 words and have been exposed to about 85,000 word forms or families in print (Nagy & Anderson, 1984). A word family refers to a group of words in which knowing one of the words in the family helps you infer or guess the meaning of the other words you encounter while reading (e.g., biology, biologist, biological) (Stahl, 1999).

Vocabulary grows exponentially in grades 6–12. If a student reads a text without knowledge of word meanings, and without any clues about connections to other concepts of big ideas, he, or she will not be able to access the material, nor engage in the language of the discipline, or comprehend what the text is about. Studying endless word lists, memorizing, or looking up definitions and using those definitions in decontextualized sentences do not produce deep understanding of word meanings, nor text.

These approaches to vocabulary development are short lived—they will not produce the knowledge, thinking, and mastery teachers are seeking. Students will not arrive at your classroom's doorstep automatically knowing the vocabulary that matters in your discipline. Many lack experiences with the texts and habits of mind of each content area, others do not know how to identify the meaning of unknown words, and others, such as English language learners (ELLs), are developing their English language proficiency.

The three types of vocabulary include, oral vocabulary (words that are recognized and used in speaking), aural vocabulary (a collection of words a student understands when listening to others speak), and print vocabulary (words used in reading and writing). Print vocabulary poses challenges for many students because it requires quick and accurate recognition of the written word. In addition, vocabulary is also categorized according to the setting it is used in—informal or formal; vocabulary used in a formal setting is called academic vocabulary. Word identification or decoding (the ability to decipher a word out of a group of letters) and word analysis (the process involved in understanding letters, sounds, roots, prefixes, and suffixes) are the two core vocabulary development skills. Word knowledge also includes syntactic awareness (grammatical use of a word). Last, students use pragmatic awareness (how words are used to communicate) to understand the purpose of their use (Snow & Biancarosa, 2003).

Because many students have poor word identification skills and underdeveloped vocabularies that affect their motivation to read complex texts and comprehension, and also because there are so many words students need to know to be able to read, think, write, and speak in advanced ways, content area teachers find it difficult to decide which words to teach, when, and how to equip all students to learn vocabulary independently. In this chapter, I will examine how vocabulary develops, what role vocabulary plays in core academic disciplines, elements of effective vocabulary instruction, and ways to develop and extend all students' vocabulary. Aside from the information and strategies I will present, it is important to note that students also acquire word knowledge from wide reading, read-alouds, and classroom discussions and collaborations.

CCSS Connections

- Students in grades 6–12 should be able to interpret words and phrases as they are used in a text, including determining technical, connotative, and figurative meanings, and analyze how specific word choices shape meaning or tone.
- Students in grades 6–12 should be able to determine or clarify the meaning of unknown and multiple-meaning words and phrases by using context clues, analyzing meaningful word parts, and consulting general and specialized reference materials, as appropriate.
- Students in grades 6–12 should be able to demonstrate understanding of figurative language, word relationships, and nuances in word meanings, acquire and use accurately a range of general academic and domain-specific words and phrases sufficient for reading, writing, speaking, and listening at the college and career readiness level. They should also demonstrate independence in gathering vocabulary knowledge when considering a word, or phrase important to comprehension or expression.

Vocabulary and Learning

Vocabulary is generally defined as the knowledge of words and word meanings. More specifically, we use vocabulary to refer to the kinds of words students must know to read increasingly complex text with comprehension (Kamil & Hiebert, 2005). Vocabulary expands and deepens over time. Learning vocabulary is much more than memorizing words and definitions. In the content areas, "knowledge is prototypically made of language" (Halliday, 2004, p. 25) and words represent complex concepts that can be learned through meaningful interactions, repeated exposure, and application in diverse contexts (Harmon, Hendrick, & Wood, 2005).

The importance of students acquiring and developing a rich vocabulary cannot be overemphasized. The connections between vocabulary and reading comprehension is not a new discovery. Whipple (1925) empirically proved the above connection and, more recently, this relationship was re-confirmed by the National Reading Panel (National Institute of Child Health and Human Development, 2000). Many researchers have recognized vocabulary as one of the main contributing factors in academic achievement (Anderson & Nagy, 1991; Baker, Simmons, & Kame'enui, 1997; Baumann & Kame'enui, 1991; Becker, 1977; Nagy & Scott, 2000; Stanovich, 1986). Although we have had significant evidence about the role of vocabulary in reading comprehension and student achievement, vocabulary instruction does not occur frequently, nor systematically in many schools (Biemiller, 2001; Durkin, 1978–79; Lesaux, Kieffer, Faller, & Kelley, 2010; Scott & Nagy, 1997).

We have examined the fundamental importance the CCSS place on an increased emphasis on reading informational text, and an increase on the level of text complexity. What are some factors that influence text complexity? In Chapter 3, we saw that among the many factors that matter (e.g., text structure, discourse style, genre and specific text features, text format and layout, length of text, background knowledge, level of reasoning, etc.) word difficulty and language structure, including vocabulary and sentence type and complexity of words or structure is a key one (Hess & Biggam, 2004). Preparing students to progress up this staircase of text complexity will require helping students learn academic vocabulary they will encounter in texts across a wide range of topics and disciplines.

Research suggests that for students to *know* a word, to learn vocabulary and comprehend text, they need to learn them incrementally over multiple exposures in a variety of contexts to the words they are trying to learn (Stahl, 2003). Beck, McKeown, and McCaslin (1983) explain that to really know a word one would have to move it out of her receptive vocabulary (listening vocabulary), into her productive vocabulary (recognizing the word and accurately identify its correct meaning in a variety of contexts). Why doesn't vocabulary stick with just mentioning words, finding definitions, and copying them? There's so much copying of definitions that goes on in many content area classrooms!

In the disciplines, vocabulary represents concepts and knowing the vocabulary of the discipline means that you know the content of the discipline, and you are able to apply it in meaningful ways in varied contexts. For meaning to stick, students need to make *multiple* connections between a new word and their own experiences; they need to develop a nuanced and flexible understanding of the word(s) they are learning. According to McKeown, Beck, Omanson, and Pople (1985), while four encounters with a word did not improve reading comprehension, 12 encounters did!

Multiple exposure to words in meaningful ways will result in students not only knowing what a word means (definitional or declarative knowledge), but also how to use that word (procedural knowledge) in a variety of contexts, and how to use the word's meaning in order to understand the word in different contexts (contextual knowledge) and/or in combination with other ideas (Nagy, Herman, & Anderson, 1985; Nagy & Scott, 2000).

In addition, a number of terms in mathematics and science require conditional knowledge as words and symbols have multiple meanings within a discipline, across disciplines, and in common language. Words with multiple meanings are known as polysemous (or polysematic) words (Mason, Knisely, & Kendal, 1979). For example, the word *rate* means "a value" "a fixed quantity, an amount or degree of something measured per unit or something else," "a fixed ration between two things," "a charge, payment, or price fixed according to a ration, scale, or standard," and "a relative condition or quality." Examples of rate in different contexts include, "The recent floods in Tuscany affected the growing *rate* of olive crops."; "At the *rate* we are moving in this checkout lane, it will be midnight before I can get home."; "What is the interest *rate* on the car loan?"; "Regular admission to the museum is $20, the student *rate* is $12, and the *rate* for senior citizens is $10." The words "expression" and "product" mean something different in common language versus in mathematics. In common language, an "expression" can mean a saying or a facial expression and a "product" can mean merchandise or a result of something. On the other hand, in a mathematical context the words mean something totally different—*expression* refers to a group of symbols that make a mathematical statement and *product* means a quantity obtained by multiplication. Many students have difficulty with word meanings that vary according to the discipline or context.

Students who are exposed to words in multiple contexts, even without vocabulary instruction, will learn more about those words than the students who see the word in a single context (Stahl, 1991). Effective vocabulary instruction requires using a combination of approaches to ensure students encounter the same vocabulary words repeatedly through oral language and reading. Research shows that varied and multiple exposures to new words are key to word learning (Kelsius & Searls, 1990) and that dependence on a single vocabulary instruction method will not result in optimal learning (National Reading Panel, 2000).

During the early years, children learn words from oral conversations and interactions with adults and peers because such conversations are context-rich in ways that assist in vocabulary acquisition (intonation, gestures). As children reach school age, new words appear more in writing and are less frequently introduced in conversation; as a result, vocabulary acquisition eventually stagnates by Grade 4 or 5 unless students acquire additional words from written context (Hayes & Ahrens, 1988). About 5–10% of new words are grasped upon the first reading (Hayes & Ahrens, 1988; Herman, Anderson, Pearson, & Nagy, 1987; Sternberg & Powell, 1983), but for students to understand what they read, they need to grasp about 90% of the words (Betts, 1946; Carver, 1994; Hu & Nation, 2000).

Students do not grasp words and concepts through definitional learning alone; when they come across a new word, first they make some initial connections with the word (e.g., look at its orthography or spelling, connect to information from the context ("I think it has something to do with{. . .}"), or connect with a memory of the specific context ("I remember seeing it in a magazine"), but do not have a generalizable sense of the meaning of the word. After repeated exposures to the word, more connections are strengthened and the reader better understands the context in which the word's meaning is used.

To develop students' vocabulary in your subject area, help them build robust and flexible word knowledge by providing instruction about the connections and patterns in language, develop their word consciousness (interest in and awareness of words) (Scott & Nagy, 2004), foster their analytical skills about sentence structure in texts, awareness of morphology, etymology, and word relationships, and provide them with many opportunities to use and respond to words they learn through classroom talk, wide reading, and collaborative inquiry (Anderson & Nagy, 1991; Beck, McKeown, & Kucan, 2008).

Although explicit vocabulary instruction is vital to student learning and comprehension, keep in mind that most word learning will develop in your classroom indirectly, through reading, writing, listening, and speaking (Nagy, Anderson, & Herman, 1987). Talk about language use by good authors and disciplinary experts, provide scaffolded opportunities for students to experiment with language and produce it in conversations and writing, provide explicit instruction of key words, and facilitate in-depth development of new concepts. Provide the instruction your students will need to learn disciplinary content, and develop understanding of word meanings and language. Create a classroom environment that promotes word consciousness, is rich in language, reading, and classroom talk, and provide students with ample opportunities to build, comprehend, and apply language.

Because disciplinary content is accessed, learned, and assessed through the language of the discipline in the texts, language learning is a must. To construct meaning from disciplinary texts students read and analyze the language use and patterns in the text. Fang and Schleppegrell (2010) propose a framework for engaging students in disciplinary learning through functional language analysis (FLA), which recognizes that disciplinary texts are constructed in patterns of language that adolescents often find unfamiliar and challenging (i.e., content, organization, and style/voice/tone). Through FLA, students learn what a text is about by analyzing its patterns of verbs, nouns, adverbs, and prepositional phrases. In doing so, they will understand the author's word choices, perspective conveyed through those choices, and purpose. Fang (2012) proposes that for students to understand how language is used (and why) in each discipline, they will need to have many encounters with disciplinary texts, and use morphemic, syntactic, and noun analysis.

Applying Discipline-Specific Literacies

- Think about how words are conceptually related in English language arts.
- Pay attention to polysemous words. Because words are borrowed from many other fields in social studies, many terms can be abstract, metaphorical, and heavily contextualized.
- Make sure that students know words, symbols, and functions. Pay attention to words that change meaning in a mathematical context, and to subtechnical terms.
- Use Latin and Greek roots to develop students' knowledge of science technical terms.

The Vocabulary of Core Disciplines

Teaching vocabulary in the disciplines is what I call a non-negotiable—it is not a matter of *if* it needs to be taught. In my view, it is a matter of what needs to be taught, when, and how. Each content area has a large collection of discipline-specific, specialized terms that indicate important concepts. One could view each discipline as a different language; and like with every other language, to effectively communicate (orally and in writing) one has to master that language's vocabulary and symbol system. In the disciplines, some of the terms are familiar to students, like *government, equation, experiment*, or *taxation*. Other words with common meanings have specialized and contextualized meanings, such as *line, order, point*, or *root*. And, then there are those specialized, technical terms that are unique to each discipline, such as *igneous, sonnet, coefficient*, or *integers*. Each discipline poses unique challenges for students in the area of vocabulary.

Every content area teacher wishes for his or her students to develop a rich vocabulary that will enable them to access, read, and comprehend the texts of their discipline, communicate what they are learning, and continue to develop disciplinary knowledge. Students with a rich vocabulary know and use a lot of words, and continue to increase their knowledge of words daily. They have a complex understanding of many different concepts, have deep-rooted and flexible understandings of many concepts that words represent, they sort out subtle differences in word usage, and are motivated to learn new words (Baumann & Kame'enui, 2004; Graves, 2006).

Disciplinary texts can be difficult for students to read because they lack the vocabulary knowledge necessary to read them and understand them or talk and write about them. Teachers need to teach and support general academic language, analyze text for challenging and important vocabulary, and also teach the meaning of phrases, including metaphors, and nuanced meanings. In addition, teachers need to provide explicit vocabulary instruction for before, during, and after reading strategies to promote disciplinary literacy.

In a later section of this chapter, I provide examples of a variety of vocabulary strategies that can be used across the disciplines. Please note that one vocabulary strategy incorporated within a lesson does not qualify that lesson as a model for disciplinary literacy. Vocabulary learning is not merely a matter of using a few strategies. Vocabulary instruction in each discipline needs to come out of the texts and language of the discipline. It needs to help students read and comprehend the texts of the discipline, develop the language necessary to co-construct, communicate, and present disciplinary knowledge. Vocabulary development in the disciplines will develop as a result of a discipline-specific learning framework (see Figure 2.2, p. 36).

Provide support with sentence structure; fiction and nonfiction texts have different sentence structures. Guide students how to interpret complex sentences (clause and phrase analysis), help them to find the subject and verb, and deal with complex aspects of punctuation, such as split quotes. Most secondary content area teachers assume two things: (1) students have a developed vocabulary by the time they enter their class and (2) teaching vocabulary is the job of the English teacher. Well, the CCSS have removed the second assumption by placing literacy within each discipline, and by recognizing the unique reading, writing, language, and vocabulary demands of each discipline. So, what are some challenges associated with the vocabulary of various disciplines? It is important for all content area teachers to examine the vocabulary of their disciplines and the cognitive, linguistic, and academic demands it will place on students. Before you decide what words to teach, it is important to examine the nature of the words in the texts of your discipline.

Arts

Art is a tool for understanding the world, creating an interpretive community, and promoting artistic thinking. Art education texts have rich descriptions of paintings, sculptures, artistic movements, artists' backgrounds and works, as well as descriptions about the culture, the time the art was created, and the factors that could have influenced the artist's interpretation of events, objects, and ideas. Art history textbooks and related texts include many specialized words that describe artistic elements, style, artistic movements, and academic words used to describe, analyze, and critique art. Students will benefit from learning (and applying) the different meanings of academic words in the field of visual arts (e.g., *abstract, animation, balance, composition, perspective, style, movement, space, scale*, etc.) and from hands-on experiences that will help them develop and apply specialized art vocabulary (e.g., art criticism, fresco, lithograph, negative space, positive space, realism, surrealism, undertone, waterscape, etc.). Students need opportunities to discuss art movements, artistic elements, and develop art-specific vocabulary when describing or critiquing art (e.g., words to critique line, tone, movement, texture, shape, etc.).

English Language Arts

In English language arts, students read a wide range of genres and encounter many words that are contextualized, genre-and author-specific. Literature includes different genres (e.g., fiction (drama, poetry, fantasy, humor, fable, fairy tales, science fiction, short story, realistic fiction, folklore, historical fiction, tall tale, horror, legend, mystery, mythology); nonfiction (narrative nonfiction, essays, biography, autobiography, speech)). Literature often utilizes the same language people use in everyday life to express human emotions, behaviors, imaginations, and several other aspects of human life (Fang, 2012). But, in literature, authors also manipulate language to reflect perspectives in creative ways, to preserve a particular context, and in a way, to separate themselves from the real world. Each author uses language in unique ways to draw the reader into a different reality and create a dynamic contextualized interaction.

The challenge with literature vocabulary is that many of the terms students encounter in texts are not conceptually related. For example, here are some words from *The Book Thief* by Zusak (2006): *amiable, alluding, abhorrence, trepidation, gauging, unsavory, futile, castigate, unfurling, admonish*, and *irrefutable*. How are these words related to book themes about love, war, identity, literature and writing, mortality, criminality, language, communication and the Holocaust, suffering, and courage? English language arts also includes technical terms about grammar—apposition, clause, conjunction—and literary elements such as, foreshadowing, flashback, symbolism, or allusion. And, how will students learn the above and many more words in the book? Harmon et al. (2009) stated that it is not necessary for students to know each word intimately in literature study; simple acquaintance of words is sufficient. Reading widely, integrating vocabulary instruction in your curriculum, writing, peer collaborations and conversations about terms, and presentations of ideas are effective ways to bolster conceptual connections among terms. Vocabulary instruction that focuses on conceptual relationships will help students make connections between individual words and larger literature concepts.

Mathematics

Language skills are very important in mathematics classrooms. The National Council of Teachers of Mathematics' *Principles and Standards for School Mathematics* (NCTM, 2000) includes communication as a process strand. In addition, students are expected to engage in conversations about mathematical ideas and through these conversations to "develop a language for expressing mathematical ideas and an appreciation of the need for precision in that language" (NCTM, 2000, p. 60). The CCSS (2010) present a similar focus in mathematics—Standard Two in Mathematics calls for mathematically proficient students to "reason abstractly and quantitatively," Standard Three, "construct viable arguments and critique the work of others," and Standard Six, "attend to precision" (see http://www.corestandards.org/Math/Practice/#CCSS.Math.Practice.MP2).

The language of mathematics is abstract, complex, and a bit difficult to communicate to others (Kouba, 1989). Mathematics words have both general and specific meanings, while at the same time key terms must be defined in a precise manner (Shanahan & Shanahan, 2008). Mathematics involves technical, subtechnical, and symbolic terms. Here is an example of a definition of *parabola*: "A parabola is the set of all points in a plane equidistant from a fixed line (the directrix) and a fixed point (the focus) not on a fixed line." Memorization of this term will not work; drawing and illustrating the definition will.

Technical terms convey mathematical concepts that are difficult, if not impossible, to express in everyday language. Each technical term (e.g., integer, Pythagoras' Theorem) has only one meaning, which is specific to mathematics. Because these terms are encountered *only* in mathematical contexts, and are themselves often defined with other technical terms, they are difficult to learn and remember. In a way, learning technical vocabulary is comparable to learning a foreign language. One cannot learn vocabulary through mere memorization and writing definitions.

Subtechnical terms have more than one meaning that varies from one content area to another or from a content area to everyday experience(s). Students may know what the word *volume* means in everyday life, but they might not know what it means in a mathematical context (e.g., volume of a cube). Because of their multiple meanings, subtechnical terms are more difficult to learn than technical ones. Symbolic vocabulary is considered by some to be the real vocabulary of mathematics; in itself, it presents unique challenges for students as in mathematics the reader needs to recognize not only words, but also many symbols. The most common math symbols are abstract and difficult to define and can be used to convey different meanings (e.g., x, $x1$, x^2, $-x$, M, p, q, N, n, $\approx$, $<$, $>$, $\|$, Σ, $\sqrt{\ }$). Encountering words in context, providing explicit instruction, using word walls and graphic organizers, discussions, and associating words with images, will help students develop mathematics vocabulary.

Science

Science is loaded with technical vocabulary. In science, technical, subtechnical, and symbolic terms (just like in mathematics) are used to describe new concepts and many of those terms are based on Latin (e.g., adip- (fat): adipose) and Greek roots (cephal- (head): *encephalogram*). Sometimes words will have one meaning in everyday language and a very specialized meaning in science. For example, the word *image* in everyday language refers to a photograph or how a person is perceived. In science, *image* means a copy of an object formed by reflected or refracted rays of light. In addition, there are two ways in which a surface can reflect light—regular reflection and diffuse reflection. In terms of images, mirrors work by reflecting light. A plane mirror (a flat sheet of glass that has a smooth, shiny coating) shows regular reflection and forms a virtual image that is similar to the real you (details, color, same size, and upright position), but also different (the left and right of the image are the reverse of your left and right). A concave mirror (it curves inward, caves in) can also produce real and virtual images. A real image forms when light rays meet, is upside down, and may be smaller, larger, or the same size as the object.

Can you see how dense the relationships between all of these words and concepts are in science? For students to develop a solid understanding of reflection and mirrors, they will need hands-on experiences with mirrors, explicit instruction of key concepts, a discussion on how concepts are related, visuals and graphs, and opportunities to communicate with others, and support their explanations with evidence. In addition, scientific language includes syntactic ambiguity (Halliday, 2004). While verbs are action words (e.g., *to mature, to respire, to pollinate, to experiment, to delineate*), nominalizations are nouns that leave semantic information out, and contain a hidden action (e.g., *maturation, perspiration, pollination, experimentation, delineation*). Nominalizations make it difficult for students to construct meaning from text.

Because science teaching involves a lot of hands-on experiences, science teachers have an advantage in building students' vocabulary. Provide students with the hands-on experiences first and then the vocabulary to the experience. On the other hand, a challenge science teachers face is how much vocabulary to teach, especially when some words occur once and are not essential to understanding the unit or to the discipline. Identify the key vocabulary, explain to students why it is important that they all master these words, relate the words with previously learned ones or concepts, pronounce them (as many are difficult to pronounce), and allow for student–student collaboration and discussion of word meanings, usage, and science content. These suggestions also apply for Career and Technical Subjects (CTE) courses and health education courses as these disciplines draw from the sciences.

Social Studies

Social studies textbooks are packed with facts and disconnected information, ideas, and concepts that students often have to memorize. While studying history and social studies, therefore, students are exposed to new terms they will not encounter in other subjects, general academic words that have use across the curriculum, and polysemous words for which they know a common meaning, but do not know what it means in a social studies context.

How will students develop a good understanding of 10th Grade World History words such as: *anthropologists, capitalism, civilization, colonialism, communism, feudalism, genocide, imperialism, nationalism,* and *socialism*? And what are words or concepts these terms could be classified under? Have students encountered them in previous grades and topics, and have their meanings changed? For example, when students learn about American History in 11th Grade, one topic they will examine is the American Civil War; as part of that topic, they will have to remember the main figures and the dates of main events that preceded and followed other events. They will have to know about Fort Sumter, the Battle of Gettysburg, the signing of the Emancipation Proclamation, and the surrender at Appomattox. Facts around all of these events are important to know, but what is more crucial is the conceptual knowledge the students will develop about concepts that will result in a deep understanding of the events that led to the Civil War, the course and outcomes of the war, and the establishment and eventual failure of reconstruction.

Think Like an Expert

- Literary experts have well-developed, rich, and broad vocabularies and rich linguistic expression. Their vocabularies become richer and more varied over time due to wide reading and writing. They are masterful at manipulating words and language and working with the nuances of words. (English Language Arts)
- Mathematicians extract lots of information from numbers, symbols, data, and words. They strive for precision and accuracy in their use of mathematics vocabulary, and use specialized and math-specific terms to communicate their knowledge about mathematics. (Mathematics)
- Vocabulary is very important in science; it helps to advance scientific knowledge. Scientists use exact terms (and at times a lot of jargon) to describe, explain, and represent science concepts. Scientists use a lot of jargon to communicate and exchange ideas with their peers; science vocabulary is specialized, complex, and tedious. (Science)
- Historians use their own specialized vocabulary. The vocabulary of the historian includes context, chronology, artifacts, facts, movements, opinions, primary sources, interpretations, and reasoned and evidenced judgment. (Social Studies)

Vocabulary Instructional Decisions: Which Words to Teach?

In this section, I present a tiered model of vocabulary instruction, the importance of teaching general academic words (i.e., Tier Two words), what distinguishes them from other tiers of words, and why it is important to include them in instruction. Acquiring and using language is an important part of learning in grades 6–12; it also appears in the CCSS standards for reading, writing, speaking and listening, and language across grade levels. Language Standard Six in the CCSS specifically refers to "general academic words"—"Acquire and use accurately grade-appropriate general academic and domain-specific words and phrases; gather vocabulary knowledge when considering a word or phrase important to comprehension or expression" (CCSS ELA in Literacy & Literacy for History/Social Studies, Science, & Technical Subjects, 2010, p. 53).

What kind of words are "general academic words?" These are words of great importance to understanding academic writing, but they are words that many students, especially those learning English, may not comprehend because this vocabulary is neither the language of everyday conversation, nor the subject-area or domain-specific, technical, and discipline-bound words traditionally included in explicit content instruction.

Every teacher has asked this question at one time or another, "Which words should I teach?" Not all words need to be "taught" because a large percentage of them will be learned through informal everyday interactions and experiences. On the other hand, in the disciplines, students will encounter words that are "discipline-bound," appear infrequently outside of the discipline, but at the same time are important to understanding disciplinary content. Beck, McKeown, and Omanson (1987) developed the concept of "word tiers" with Tier One representing everyday, basic words; Tier Two including general academic words; and Tier Three referring to rare, domain-specific words (Beck, McKeown, & Kucan, 2002, 2008). This tiered system of vocabulary instruction categorizes words based on their frequency of occurrence in texts—from more to less frequently occurring—and applicability—from broader to narrower words.

Tier One Words

These refer to general vocabulary that is learned through spoken language and social interactions with peers and adults. These are the basic words or everyday language that need little instruction in meaning (e.g., talk, apologize, education, house). They are familiar to most students at this level, but likely to require attention for English language learners (especially words that represent figures of speech—e.g., climbing the ladder of success; racking our brains; hitting a target). These words are important, but not the focus of vocabulary instruction in secondary grades. Tier One words do not need instructional attention; instead, teachers can promote their development by making such words available through deliberate, ongoing weaving of conversational interactions in class.

Students need opportunities to hear language as well as use language. Teachers can be more talkative and playful with language at all times—they need to invite students to think how and when they'd use different words. Teachers do not have to ask for definitions of every word in the classroom. For example, while taking attendance, a teacher might say, "I am looking for faces that are happy . . . excited . . . surprised. . . today." Simple, informal, and continuous conversations matter for students' vocabulary growth—yes, even for older students! (Hart & Risley, 1995). A classroom environment that is rich in language, and uses talk, interactions, and conversations as part of the regular classroom learning processes, is a classroom where all students will continue to develop their vocabulary. The disciplinary literacy model I presented in Chapter 2 (see Figure 2.2, p. 36), views classroom talk and interactions as fundamental to learning.

Tier Two Words

These are unfamiliar vocabulary students will be less likely to learn independently. These are words they will encounter and learn through reading text and through explicit classroom instruction. The CCSS refers to these as "general academic words." Sometimes they are referred to as "rich vocabulary." These words are more precise or subtle forms of familiar words (e.g., style, function, avoid, escapade). They are particularly important because building a strong vocabulary affects comprehension of text (Baumann, Kame'enui, & Ash, 2003). "For students to become successful in academic life, they need to be able to get meaning from text, which in turn means being able to build meaning using the more sophisticated vocabulary of written language= Tier Two words." (Beck et al., 2008, p. 8).

These words are found across a variety of domains and have wide possibilities of application. Tier Two words are learned mainly from interactions with books and need to be taught explicitly because authors do not explicitly define them within the text or include them in a glossary. In other words, they require effort to learn them—many times they require precise ways to say seemingly simple things; for example, instead of using the word *scare*, one might come across the words *alarm*, *startle*, or *panic*. They can have multiple meanings, are unfamiliar to most students at this level, and can be grouped with other known ideas or words for instruction. Tier Two words are widely applicable and not particular or unique to a discipline; as a result, they are not the explicit responsibility of a particular content area teacher. A challenge with these words is that because most of these words are acquired through reading, struggling readers do not acquire them at the same rate as proficient readers. As a result, their lack of knowledge of these words, negatively affects their motivation to read more grade-appropriate material.

When it comes to selecting Tier Two words to teach, a teacher should consider introducing one word at a time and giving students sufficient time to think about, ask questions, discuss, and use the meaning of the word and its usage. Beck et al. (2002) suggest using student-friendly explanations to help students learn words, rather than relying on definitions found in dictionaries that are often confusing and vague. Vocabulary lessons should be brief, and multisensory so students can see, hear, speak, and write the words (Curtis, 2004); explicit instruction followed by targeted, short, but rich classroom discussions that facilitate students' understanding of polysemous words. Make sure that the words you select to teach, (a) are central to understanding the text (they have importance and utility); (b) have important nuances, are likely to be frequently encountered by the student, and students will use the word when writing a response to a text (have instructional potential); and (c) relate to a number of related words and concepts (provide conceptual understanding).

Tier Three Words

These words are what the CCSS refers to as domain-specific words; this is highly specific, disciplinary vocabulary that lacks generalization. Generally, these words have low frequency use, they are needed to understand the concept or topic under study, and are limited to specific knowledge domains, (e.g., meiosis, Declaration of Independence, oboe, quadratic equation). These words are best learned within the context of the content area, or domain they represent and they create cohesion in discipline-specific discourse (Zwiers, 2008). They are defined within the text, are usually taught through explanation or illustration, and they are unlikely to appear in texts of other subjects.

Because Tier Three words are apparently unfamiliar to most students, include the ideas necessary to a new topic, and are recognized as both important and specific to the subject area in which they are instructing students, teachers often define Tier Three words prior to students encountering them in a text, and then reinforce their acquisition throughout a lesson. In addition, authors will define Tier Three words in a text and include them in a glossary. For example, the definition of the word *meiosis* is: "The process of cell division in sexually reproducing organisms that reduces the number of chromosomes in reproductive cells from diploid to haploid, leading to the production of gametes in animals and spores in plants" (The Free Online Dictionary). Even if a student recited this definition that does not mean that he actually understood the process of meiosis. A student in a biology class would be expected to know (and demonstrate) how this genetic process works.

Concepts cannot be learned, deeply understood, and applied through mere definitions. And copying definitions off the dictionary does not constitute vocabulary instruction. For concepts to be learned, teachers need to explicitly explain how components of the concepts that the words represent relate or connect to each other and fit within the domain (Kucan, Trathen, & Straits, 2007). Students need explicit explanations and connections followed by further discussion on the topic. How many of your students have prepared for a unit test by trying to memorize 400 words or so, prepare index cards, and memorize the concepts but fail to apply them when asked? Many times teachers complain about their students lacking a conceptual understanding between words and concepts. Well, these vital connections will not happen through lecture alone, reading the textbook, or definitional learning. They require explicit instruction, many encounters with the words and concepts in different settings, and identifying and discussing connections among words, concepts, and big ideas on the topic.

The following are examples of Tier Three words from CCSS text exemplars that demonstrate how Tier Three words (i.e., *Jim Crow laws*, *voussoirs*, *lagging*) are text-bound, defined within the text. It is important to teach students how to do close reading of text and recognize syntax and diction clues that indicate how a term is being defined within the text.

- Freedman, Russell. *Freedom Walkers: The Story of the Montgomery Bus Boycott.* New York: Holiday House, 2006. From the Introduction: "Why They Walked"
  - Back then, racial segregation was the rule throughout the American South. Strict laws—called "Jim Crow" laws—enforced a system of white supremacy that discriminated against blacks and kept them in their place as second-class citizens. (CCSS, 2010, Appendix B, Grades 6–8, Literary Text, p. 95).
- Macaulay, David. *Cathedral: The Story of Its Construction.* Boston: Houghton Mifflin, 1973. (CCSS, 2010, Appendix B, Grades 6–8, Informational Texts: Science, Mathematics, & Technical Subjects, p. 96).
  - One by one, the cut stones of the ribs, called voussoirs, were hoisted onto the centering and mortared into place by the masons.
  - The carpenters then installed pieces of wood, called lagging, that spanned the space between two centerings.

How Many Words to Teach?

Many content area teachers find it difficult to determine which words to teach—the content is rich with many words, and a number of students have underdeveloped vocabularies. What will help the understanding of these words stick, is how many times students will have to use them, be exposed to them in different types of situations, and discuss them. Because instructional time is very precious in grades 6–12 and few vocabulary words will be taught explicitly in a year, content area teachers need to carefully determine which words will need explicit instruction, scaffolding, and attention.

So, what should a teacher consider before choosing a word to teach? Let's start with first things first. (1) Is the word important for understanding the text? What does this word choice add to the text (e.g., clarity? precision?); (2) How about the general utility of the word? Is it a word that students are likely to see often in other texts? Does it have multiple meanings? Will it be of use to students in their own writing?; and (3) How about students' prior knowledge of the word and the concept(s) to which it relates? Does it relate to other words, ideas, or experiences that the students know or have been learning? Does it have instructional potential? Are there opportunities for grouping words together to enhance understanding of a concept?

When planning vocabulary instruction, remember that vocabulary development in the disciplines is complex and demanding. Explain concepts, address the depth of word knowledge, connections with related words, and symbols (Blackowicz et al., 2006; Graves, 2006). Blackowicz and Fisher (2000) propose that the most effective vocabulary instruction builds concept knowledge, teaches words in a meaningful context, and encourages independent use of strategies. Teach vocabulary that will result in content knowledge, in quality academic discourse, in transfer to other subjects and contexts, and develop a classroom environment that is rich in discipline-specific vocabulary, in language, in classroom talk, and one that promotes an appreciation for words and further learning.

Effective Vocabulary Instruction

The goal of vocabulary instruction is to help students learn the meanings of many words so they can read and comprehend the texts of the discipline, communicate effectively, and achieve academically. Effective vocabulary instruction requires intentional planning, rich and robust opportunities for students to learn words, word meanings, and related concepts. As teachers we have a responsibility to offer "a robust approach to vocabulary [that] involves directly explaining the meanings of words along with thought-provoking, playful, and interactive follow-up" (Beck et al., 2008, p. 4). Students need to learn strategies that will help them acquire words independently.

Beck et al. (2002) advocated for vocabulary instruction that is rich and lively so that students "develop an interest and awareness in words beyond vocabulary school assignments in order to adequately build their vocabulary repertoires" (p. 13). They made several recommendations for how to design what they call robust vocabulary instruction. First, they advised that teachers should provide "student-friendly explanations" (p. 35) of the word rather than dictionary definitions. These explanations should explain the meaning of the word in everyday language, and they should characterize the word and how it is typically used. Second, teachers should engage the students in "rich and lively" (p. 13) activities that encourage deep processing of the word's meaning.

Effective vocabulary instruction teaches students the meanings of unfamiliar words and concepts, and equips students with the skills, knowledge, and tools they need to learn vocabulary independently. It also provides students with opportunities to learn vocabulary independently and nurtures an appreciation and consciousness of words and their use. Struggling readers, including English language learners, will require more explicit vocabulary instruction (Robbins & Ehri, 1994).

Nagy (1988) has also offered a similar message about the key elements of effective vocabulary instruction: integration, repetition, and meaningful use. Instruction must relate newly acquired words to other words and concepts (something that does not happen often in content area classrooms). Establishing interrelationships between already acquired and new words will help expand one's schema about the word or concept. The second element, repetition, refers to the need for students to not only acquire new word meanings but to also have sufficient practice in using the meanings so that the meaning can "grow roots" and be automatically and effortlessly accessed during reading. The last feature, meaningful use, is connected to the level of word processing needed to perform a task, or rather, the level at which students are actively engaged in using the word meanings. Naturally, the higher the level of processing, the more likely students will learn and retain word meanings.

Copying definitions does not involve a deep level of processing; students need multiple varied exposures and meaningful practice. Marzano (2004) has developed the following six-step instructional process for developing students' academic vocabulary. The first three steps deal with introducing and developing students' vocabulary and steps four through six address the importance of shaping and sharpening students' understanding of the term.

1. Teacher provides a description, explanation, or example of new term.
    a. Provide students with information about the term, descriptions and examples, but not definitions; examine what the students already know about it, and ask them to share what they know; examine (and correct) misconceptions.
2. Teacher asks students to give a description, explanation, or example of the new term in their own words.
    a. Provide more explanations, feedback, or examples as needed; monitor students' work and watch for misconceptions; students record their work in their notebooks or journal.
    b. Provide clear and understandable definitions.

      i. Students have difficulty creating sentences with words they learn simply through dictionary definitions—many interpret one or two words from a definition as the entire meaning. Teachers should use definitions and context.

      ii. Teachers must present meanings of target words through instruction that is direct; meanings should be presented using clear, consistent, and understandable wording.

      iii. Definitions can be reinforced through gestures (especially for ELLs), pictures (use Google images), objects, and examples and non-examples. The Visual Thesaurus (http://www.visualthesaurus.com) is a nice way to show relationships among words.

      iv. When introducing a new word, provide a simple definition or synonym and then model the definition within the context of a sentence or story. Also, provide examples of the word used in contexts different from the story context.

3. The teacher will ask students to create a nonlinguistic representation of the term (e.g., draw a picture, symbol, or locate a graphic to represent the new term).

    a. Students can work independently or in groups, share drawings, word maps, or images, and discuss their nonlinguistic representation choices.

4. Students will periodically do activities that help add to their knowledge of the vocabulary terms (e.g., use academic notebooks).

    a. Students restate definitions in their own words, organize their vocabulary terms, and identify prefixes, suffixes, antonyms, synonyms, and related words.

5. Students will discuss the new term with other peers in class.

    a. Provide time for students to reflect on their descriptions, discuss them with others, share aloud, and discuss misconceptions and provide corrective feedback as needed with the whole class.

    b. Provide students with opportunities to discuss words in extended discourse before and after reading. Also provide students with tasks that challenge their understanding of the word and forces students to process word meanings at a deeper, more complex level. For example, ask students to find a synonym or antonym, classify the word with other known words, or relate the definition (if applicable) to one's personal experiences.

6. Students will periodically be involved in games that provide more reinforcement of the new term.

    a. Walk around and listen for misconceptions when students are playing games.

    b. Promote use of technology for independent practice on learning vocabulary.

Research supports that the integration of explicit vocabulary within each content area improves students' ability to acquire textbook vocabulary (Baumann, Edwards, Boland, Olejnik, & Kame'enui, 2003). Explicit instruction is viewed as a means of providing direct instruction in word meaning and instruction in strategies to promote independent vocabulary acquisition skills. Direct instruction includes use of definitions, use of graphic organizers showing the relationships among words and concepts (e.g., concept mapping), and use of reference materials. Strategies that promote independent word knowledge acquisition include analyzing the semantic, syntactic, or context clues to derive the meaning of the words and the context in which they are used (Kamil et al., 2008).

Prior to teaching vocabulary, activate students' prior knowledge of content in which the new word is used and then make connections between their prior knowledge and the new vocabulary. Provide multiple repetitions of the new word—for example, use it throughout your instruction when you explain ideas, give directions, or summarize learning. Point out (or what I like to refer to as "make a fuss") and model words and phrases—e.g., keep referring to the words, *slavery, injustice, Reconstruction, secession, Confederacy, Union*, etc. Then, provide students with many opportunities to apply new word meanings across different contexts, place them in small groups to discuss their understandings of the new words (NICHD, 2000; Noles & Dole, 2004), and ask them to develop their own word maps to represent relationships among words and concepts (Kamil, 2003).

Research also supports the use of rich discussions of text(s) because discussion (a) allows students to participate as both speakers and listeners, (b) invites students to organize their thoughts (especially if they have to explain words to someone else), (c) promotes accuracy and monitoring of one's understanding, and (d) offers opportunities for repeated exposure to words which in turn, facilitate vocabulary learning (Barron & Melnik, 1973).

Introducing and Teaching Vocabulary Strategies

In the following section, I present sample vocabulary strategies all content area teachers can use in their courses to introduce and teach vocabulary. All of the strategies can be used before, during, or after reading to facilitate students' vocabulary development.

ABC Brainstorm

This is an easy and flexible strategy a content area teacher can use in many ways and for different purposes. For example, use the ABC Brainstorm as a means of assessing and activating students' background knowledge on a topic. Students can come up with as many words (that begin with a different letter of the alphabet) as they know about a topic. For example, students can write as many words (or phrases) as they know about the topic of environmental population or The American Revolution (before reading or introducing a new topic). Students can use the strategy during reading to collect words that relate to the topic at hand. Last, you can use the ABC Brainstorm after reading where students independently, or collaboratively in small groups, identify as many words about the topic. I have my students use different color pens when I use it before, during, and after reading or when I use it independently or collaboratively so they and I can see what they learned about the topic on their own or when working with others. Depending on the topic, students might not be able to come up with words that begin with certain letters; the point is not to fill the cell in; instead, it is on close reading of text, finding connections among words, and thinking carefully about the words that represent the topic. At other times teachers can use the strategy to have a discussion with the whole class on which words from those they identified are the most essential for everyone's understanding of the topic. The following example (Table 5.1) is on "Shakespeare: His Life and Work" (English language arts).

Concept of Definition Map

Many students have difficulty sharing what a definition of a word is because they do not have a developed understanding of what words mean. Word maps and charts help students expand word meanings and discover relationships among words. Vocabulary instruction must include elaboration of definitions, discussion, and writing (Beck & McKeown, 1991). The Concept of Definition Map (see Table 5.2) invites students to classify the word/concept (What is it?), describe its core features (What is it like? What are its properties?), provide examples (What are some examples of the word/concept), and also compare it with related words/concepts (What can you compare it to?). It also fosters connections between prior knowledge and the new word/concept. Before students read, list key vocabulary on the board. As part of the pre-reading discussion, brainstorm what students already know about the topic using the vocabulary map. After students read, have them fill in additional information. Ask students to present their maps for discussion.

TABLE 5.1.   ABC Brainstorm Strategy Example—Topic: Shakespeare: Sample Plays

A	G	M	S
All's Well That Ends Well	Globe Theater	Merchant of Venice	Stratford-upon-Avon
Antony and Cleopatra	ghost	Midsummer Night's Dream	sonnets
B	**H**	**N**	**T**
Born in 1564	Hamlet	"Now is the winter of our discontent."	Taming of the Shrew
Benvolio	Henry	(Richard III)	The Tempest
			Two Gentlemen of Verona
C	**I**	**O**	**U**
Comedy of Errors	"It is the east, and Juliet is the sun."	Othello	
Cymbeline	(Romeo and Juliet)	Ophelia	
Coriolanus	Inverness (Macbeth's Castle)		
D	**J**	**P**	**V**
Died in 1616	Julius Caesar	Paris	Verona
Denmark (Hamlet's home)		Prince of Tyre	Venus and Adonis
E	**K**	**Q**	**W**
Elsinore (Hamlet's Home)	King John	Quince	Winter's Tale
	King Lear	Queen Gertrude	"What is decreed must be.."
			(Twelfth Night)
F	**L**	**R**	**XYZ**
Falstaff (Henry IV)	Love's Labours Lost	Richard II	
	London	Romeo and Juliet	

Students can use their map for a guide to note taking, both from discussion and content texts. Students can also use blank maps to evaluate one another's written definitions, using a backward approach. Modify concept maps for taking notes on biographies. For example, high school students reading biographies on World War II heroes developed maps defining the unique qualities of a specific hero. Their maps served as a pre-writing material for brief reports. The Concept of Definition Map could be used during or after reading of a passage. It can be used with expository and narrative text. After you model how to work with these categories to draft a definition, give students practice, and provide opportunities for them to work in small groups and discuss their maps with others.

Semantic Feature Analysis (SFA)

Semantic feature analysis (SFA) creates bridges between students' prior knowledge and relationships among words that are conceptually related to one another (Johnson & Pearson, 1984). The SFA matrix (see Table 5.3 (biology example) and Table 5.4 (math example)) asks students to think about how words are alike and different and analyze the relationships among the given words; in a way, SFA imitates the way the brain organizes information (Fisher & Frey, 2004). This creates a true test of students' knowledge of various word or concept characteristics as students

TABLE 5.2.   Concept of Definition Map; Topic: Science Tundra

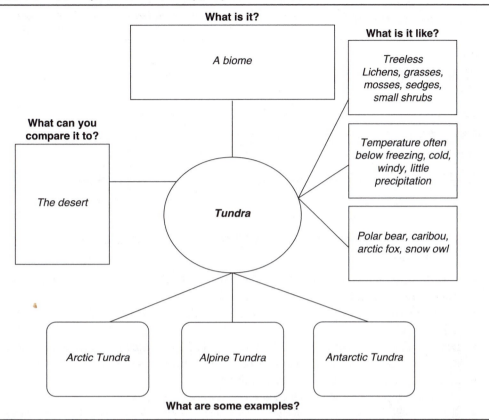

move beyond definitional knowledge to intricate, feature analysis, type of word knowledge. SFA is not an easy strategy; it works best as a during- and after-reading strategy. Because it is important for students to be actively involved in constructing meaning, teachers can use modeling, scaffolded support, and practice to guide students in creating their own list of word/concept features and relationships. SFA requires discussion and elaborations; it will result in close reading of text, and in much negotiation of meaning.

TABLE 5.3.   Semantic Feature Analysis: Biology—Vertebrates

	Vertebral Column	Endoskeleton	Internal Fertilization	Body Covering of Scales	Endothermic	Chambers of the Heart	Breathe with Lungs
Bony Fishes	+	+		+		2	
Amphibians	+	+				3	0/+
Reptiles	+	+	+	+		3	+
Birds	+	+	+	"modified"	+	4	+
Mammals	+	+	+		+	4	+

TABLE 5.4.   Semantic Feature Analysis: Geometry—Polygons

	Convex	Equilateral	Equiangular	4-Sided	3-Sided	Opposite Sides Parallel
Square	+	+	+	+		+
Rectangle	+		+	+		+
Triangle	+				+	
Quadrilateral				+		
Regular Polygon	+	+	+			
Rhombus	+	+	•	+		+
Trapezoid	+			+		

To develop a semantic feature analysis, and help students understand how to use it, consider the following steps:

- Review the material and select the major concepts students will need to use during their study of the topic at hand.
- Select the words/concepts that represent the big ideas or concepts; select the most important vocabulary.
- Develop the features during the initial teaching of SFA; for students to create their own, they will need to develop vocabulary knowledge and experiences with using the SFA over time.
- List in the first column some words in the category.
- List on the top row some features shared by some of the words.
- Students will place (+) or (-) along with numerical digits for number of shared features, a "0" for no relationship, and/or a "?" for questionable relationship beside each word and beneath each feature.
- Review the SFA matrix model with a set of familiar words/concepts, provide sufficient examples, provide guided practice, and allow for collaborative learning.
- Students will discuss (and defend) their choices in small groups and present them to the whole class for further discussion. During the review of the SFA matrices, involve students in explaining their rationale for their choices.

Vocabulary Word Box

The Vocabulary Box is a variation of the Frayer Model (a word map) that extends word knowledge beyond the definitional level (see Table 5.5). The chart is made of four sections, which hold a definition (with characteristics of the word), a synonym and antonym, an example (using the word in a sentence), and non-examples or an illustration. It will help students develop understanding of words and related concepts, draw on their prior knowledge, analyze word attributes and give examples, and make visual connections or representations. Teachers can include four copies of the template per page and use it as a during- and/or after-reading strategy. Here is how to use the strategy:

1. Explain to students the purpose of this strategy.
2. Model using the Vocabulary Word Box template by using a familiar word.
3. Provide guided practice and feedback. Ask students to work in pairs or small groups to develop their vocabulary maps. Students can present their maps to the class and discuss results.
4. After sufficient guided practice, students can use it independently.

TABLE 5.5. Vocabulary Word Box Example—Topic: Geometry

Term: Perimeter	*Synonym/Antonym*
Definition (in your own words): *The perimeter of any closed figure is the sum of the lengths of all the sides.*	**Synonym:** *Border, boundary, outline* **Antonym:** *Inside, interior, center*

Examples/Non-Examples

Example:

square = 4a   (a= side length)

rectangle = 2a + 2b
(a= length; b=width)

triangle = a + b + c

circle = *2pi* r (r is the radius)

circle = *pi* d (where d is the diameter)

Draw a Picture

Non-Examples:

$A = L.W$

$A = s^2$

Vocabulary Note-Taking Strategy

I developed this strategy as a way to facilitate deep word knowledge, during and after reading, by asking students to do the following: (a) write the text's definition about a word; (b) provide textual evidence about the definition; (c) explain how the author develops the word or idea; (d) make connections between the word and other related words the student has already learned; and (e) write a meaningful summary using the words under study. The Vocabulary Note-Taking strategy will facilitate close reading of text as students will not only have to locate what the text/author says about the word, but how he or she also develops the meaning of the word and its related ideas. Last, the student will have to make connections with his prior knowledge and other words, concepts, or ideas that he has learned so far and extend his word learning by writing a summary that includes all of the new words. In doing so, the student will be having multiple exposures to key and related words. Teachers should select key words from a topic/text, introduce the strategy, model it using familiar words, and provide feedback and support during guided practice (in Table 5.6 I used Tier Three words from a life science unit). The strategy can be used as part of small and whole class instruction and should be used with various texts prior to independent practice. Students and teacher can also use it to have discipline-specific conversations on the topic.

10 Most Important Words Strategy

The 10 Most Important Words is a vocabulary strategy that promotes deep understanding of Tier Two or Tier Three words, their meaning, and the context in which they are used (see Table 5.7). In addition, it engages the student in close reading of text, and thinking about the meaning of words in a student's own words. Then, it invites the student to explain why the words are important for his or her understanding of the topic, and last, it extends the student's understanding of the 10 words by asking him or her to write a summary using those words. The teacher can either give students the 10 most important words from the text and ask them to complete the remaining steps, or, and only after much practice with the strategy, the teacher can ask students to identify the 10 most important words collaboratively in small groups, or independently. This after-reading strategy allows for much class discussion on choice of words and evidence-based thinking from text about the significance of the words for students' understanding of the topic. Teachers can further extend the strategy by asking small groups of students to rate and evaluate each group's words according to their importance to the topic. Modeling, guided practice and support, and discussions are necessary for students to develop deep vocabulary learning.

> **College, Career, and Workforce Connections**
>
> - The CCSS indicate that one of the most important college and career readiness factors is a well-developed, or robust vocabulary. Teachers should develop students' ability to use domain-specific and academic words and be strategic about the kind of vocabulary and strategies their students will need to have and be able to use to be college, career, and workforce ready.
> - Students need to acquire and use accurately a wide range of general academic and domain-specific words and phrases sufficient for reading, writing, speaking, and listening at the college and career readiness level. They also need to demonstrate independence in gathering vocabulary knowledge when considering a word, or phrase important to comprehension or expression.
> - Learning and success in postsecondary education and life requires effective verbal communication skills (e.g., the ability to express oneself verbally, engage in conversations, communicate and collaborate with others, present to groups, and use visual displays).
> - *First and foremost the student should have a passion for understanding why and how we move, breathe, and function. Sport and Exercise Science is a broad field with many opportunities that range from coaching to medicine. However, the common learning theme for each focus area is understanding applied physiology. What makes this program most interesting is the focus on human physiology, which allows students to learn and apply concepts to the population that they will eventually work with. Students excelling in this field generally have excellent communication skills, both written and oral. In addition, they need to be comfortable and capable of learning from a broad array of sciences that include biology, chemistry, physics, physiology, biochemistry and anatomy. As such, they should be willing to take on challenges that come with this course load* (Jay Hoffman, Professor, Sport & Exercise Science, University of Central Florida).

TABLE 5.6. Vocabulary Note-Taking Strategy Example—Life Science Populations and Communities

Vocabulary Term/Idea	What does the text "say" about it? (Copy the sentence that defines/explains the term.)	Where is the information? (Include page number(s) from text.)	How does the author develop the term/idea? (Defines, redefines, gives examples, other)	What concept(s) does this term or idea relate to? (Connect it to concept(s) you have learned about so far.)
1. Organism	"An organism is a living thing."	p. 455	By giving examples of living organisms.	Life, being, animal/plant kingdom, human race
2. Habitat	"An environment that provides the things a living organism needs to live, grow, and reproduce."	p. 455	By giving examples of different environments different organisms live in.	Organisms, environment, community
3. Biotic factors	"The parts of the habitat that are living, or once lived, and interact with the organism."	p. 456	By offering examples of animals, plants and micro organisms.	Ecosystems, organisms, habitat
4. Abiotic factors	"The nonliving parts of an organism's habitat."	p. 456	By providing examples of sunlight, soil, temperature, oxygen, and water.	Climate, physical features, organisms
5. ecosystem	"The community of organisms that live in a particular area, along with their nonliving environment, make up an ecosystem."	p. 459	By explaining where one would find organisms, populations, and communities.	Organisms, habitat, population, community, ecology
6. adaptation	"The behaviors and physical characteristics that allow organisms to live successfully in their environments."	p. 469	By explaining how physical characteristics of organisms help them survive.	Competition, survival, species
7. predation	An interaction in which one organism kills another for food or nutrients."	p. 472	By explaining how organisms interact with one another and how they survive.	Population, community, predator, prey, survival, competition
8. immigration	"Moving into a population."	p. 480	By explaining how populations change in size.	Food chain, herbivore, carnivore, omnivore, scavenger, decomposer

Summary: Use a summary about the topic using the above vocabulary terms.
Organisms interact in different ways with other species and with the environment. Most organisms live with other species in their *habitat*. *Biotic* and *abiotic* factors affect the environment in which organisms live. *Adaptation* helps organism survive but *predation* and *immigration* can affect the size of a population. All of these interactions among organisms and the ways organisms interact with the environment affect the entire *ecosystem*.

Source: Interactive Science, *Florida Life Science, Unit 3*. Saddle River, NJ: Pearson Education.

TABLE 5.7.   10 Most Important Words Vocabulary Strategy—Topic: The Civil Rights Movement

Step 1: *During Reading (On My Own)* *(Identify what you think are the 10 most important words to the topic.)*	Step 2: *What the Word Means* *(Definition in my own words.)*	Step 3: *Explain Why Word Is Important To Topic* *(Complete after reading and use to discuss with others why this word is important to your understanding of the topic.)*
1. Civil rights	The rights and freedoms that belong to every citizen.	Civil Rights refer especially to the fundamental freedoms and privileges guaranteed by the 13th and 14th Amendments to the US Constitution and by subsequent acts of Congress, including civil liberties, due process, equal protection of the laws, and freedom from discrimination. Helps us understand the meanings of liberty and equality.
2. Desegregate	To eliminate segregation.	It is the focus of the Civil Rights movement.
3. Discrimination	Separating people because of personal differences.	Discrimination caused rejection, deprived Black Americans of equal opportunities and negatively affected their life.
4. Freedom riders	Non-violent civil rights activists.	They focused everyone's attention on segregation.
5. Integration	Assimilating people in a society in spite of differences.	Integration of Black Americans was the main objective and purpose of the Civil rights movement making everything accessible to all.
6. Jim Crow Laws	The Jim Crow laws were state and local laws in the US between 1876 and 1965; they mandated racial segregation in all public facilities and gave a false "separate but equal" status for Black Americans.	They were a reason for the Civil Rights movement; they denied Black Americans their dignity, rights, and privileges.
7. Prejudice	A preconceived judgment toward someone because of race, social class, ethnicity, gender, religion, and other characteristics.	Black Americans experienced prejudice for many years; they were treated with injustice, inequality, discrimination and racism.

8. Racism	Believing that race causes differences in human character or ability and that one race is superior to others.	The Civil Rights movement challenged racism in America.
9. Segregation	The practice of separating people of different races, classes, or ethnic groups, as in schools, housing, and public or commercial facilities, as a form of discrimination.	The Brown vs. Board of Education law ended segregation in public schools.
10. Stereotype	A certain idea, opinion, or image about others.	Stereotypes about Black Americans followed them through slavery and added to racism and segregation in America.

Summary: Use the words you identified to write a summary on the topic. Step 4:

By the turn of the century not much had changed for Black Americans in terms of *stereotypes, prejudice, segregation*, and *racism*. In the South *Jim Crow Laws* limited interaction between the races in public places. In the North, blacks also confronted *discrimination* in employment and housing, police harassment, and a judicial system that favored whites. The *Freedom riders* provoked the government to *desegregate* segregated seating on bus routes and terminals. The *Civil rights'* movement was a 25 yearlong movement of *integration* and giving Black Americans their rights as citizens.

Fostering Students' Independence

When students are equipped with strategies to read and understand the meaning of unknown words, their reading, comprehension, and use of these words develops. For students to become independent readers, they need to learn how to identify the meaning of words during reading. For the purpose of this chapter, I chose the following sample strategies that can promote student independence and can be used before, during, and after reading across the disciplines.

Context Clues

Contextual analysis or using context clues can help with constructing word meanings during reading. Because context clues require the reader to make inferences about relationships between unfamiliar words and the context, not all students (especially, ELLs) would be able to perceive or make those connections. In addition, depending on the text, context clues can be misleading (Beck, McKeown, & Kucan, 2002). Diamond and Gutlohn (2006) suggest the following steps for using context clues to teach vocabulary meaning:

1. Look for specific words or phrases that provide clues to the word's meaning. Choose target' words carefully for contextual analysis instruction and practice to ensure there are enough clues for students to determine the meaning of the word within the passage.
2. Look for clues in the sentence that contains the word (inside the sentence) and then look for clues in the sentences that surround the word (around the sentence).
3. Use different types of clues to infer the meaning of the word.
4. Try out the meaning in the actual sentence to see if it makes sense. For best results, support meaning from context clues with definitional information.

In addition, it is important to teach students how to recognize different types of context clues. Context clues can be semantic (aspects that give meaning and establish similarities), syntactic (order in a sentence), relationships of words in a sentence, or visual images. There are six types of context clues:

1. Definition/explanation clue
   a. A *debilitating* disease is a type of disease that impairs the strength of the body and significantly interferes with the activities of daily living.
2. Example clue
   a. Like many other *debilitating* diseases, osteoarthritis affects every aspect of daily life. In addition to the pain, stiffness, and lack of mobility, people may have trouble performing everyday activities.
3. Restatement/synonym clue
   a. Susan had to use a wheelchair to move around. She needed it because she has been suffering with the *debilitating* effects of osteoarthritis for years.
4. Contrast or antonym clue
   a. Susan's *debilitating* osteoarthritis made her feel exhausted, but Michelle felt invigorated after the walk.
5. Inference through general context clue
   a. Going to physical therapy was Susan's highlight of the week; it helped her deal with the *debilitating* effects of osteoarthritis.
6. Punctuation
   a. Susan's friend Mark suffered from muscular dystrophy, a *debilitating* disease, characterized with a progressive loss of voluntary muscle tissue and function.
   b. Susan was diagnosed with a *debilitating* disease (that impaired her strength and vitality) at age 20.
   c. Susan's *debilitating* disease also affected her family. They had to help do normal, daily functions and activities.

Model how to use context clues to construct meaning from text during reading, and encourage students to apply the strategy when reading independently.

Knowledge Rating

Teachers can use the Knowledge Rating strategy to informally assess what words their students know before and after reading (Blachowicz & Fisher, 1996). Table 5.8 includes a version of this strategy I have developed and used in various classrooms; in this particular example, I selected Tier Three words that students would not be able to define from context, from a seventh-grade text exemplar, *Mark Twain, "The Glorious Whitewasher."* The template combines a number of elements: student word knowledge before and after reading a text but also after having a discussion (in pairs, small group, or whole class) about the meaning of each, and a definition of each word in the student's own words. Using this strategy will provide the teacher with useful information about which words students have learned as a result of reading and classroom discussion. The Knowledge Rating strategy should be introduced, modeled, and practiced so students will understand the steps involved in the process. Step-by-step procedures for using this strategy include the following:

● Select the words from a reading selection that are most critical to grasping the essential concepts to be learned (could be Tier Two or Tier Three words). List the words on the Knowledge Rating chart.

- Explain to students before you start examining the new topic or text that you need to find out what they already know about the topic.
- Before reading, read each word aloud and ask students to rate their word knowledge by checking one of the columns on the chart. Use (+): I know the word (I can define it and use it in a sentence); (–) I do not know the word (I have not seen it or heard it); (?) I am not sure about the word (I have heard or seen it). This will allow you to gauge how much vocabulary instruction you will need to provide.
- During any guided-reading activities, be sure to explain and refer to the target vocabulary.
- After completing your vocabulary instruction and reading the assigned selection, have students rerate themselves; discuss answers as a class, or in small groups. Return to the text selection and discuss words that are still problematic.
- Last, ask students to rate their knowledge of the words after small group, or large group discussion, and write a definition of each term in their own words.

Etymology

Etymology is the study of the origin and history of a word; it is derived from the Greek work "etymologia" and from "etymon," which means true sense, and from "logos," meaning word. The English language has an abundance of words borrowed from other languages. Using the study of word origins can help students remember meanings and grasp the relevance of words, beyond their definition (Readence, Bean, & Baldwin, 1998). Etymologies can provide students with an

TABLE 5.8.   Knowledge Rating Strategy— English Language Arts: Topic: Mark Twain—"The Glorious Whitewasher"

Directions: Use (+): I know the word (I can define it and use it in a sentence); (–) I do not know the word (I have not seen it or heard it); (?) I am not sure about the word (I have heard or seen it)

Word	Before Reading	After Reading	After Discussion	Definition of Words (In your own words)
1. straitened	–	?	+	Having limited finances or being in a financial hardship.
2. tranquilly	+	+	+	Peacefully.
3. personating	–	–	+	To act like, to impersonate, to imitate.
4. contemplated	?	+	+	Studied carefully.
5. alacrity	–	?	+	Speed, eagerness.
6. fagged out	–	–	+	Exhausted.
7. covet	?	+	+	To desire what belongs to someone else.
8. attain	+	+	+	To get, to achieve.

TABLE 5.9.   Etymology Graphic Organizer

Word	Definition	Word Origin	Use	Related Words
core	The central or essential part of anything	Old French, *coeur*, "core of fruit," from Latin, *cor*, meaning "heart"	The earth's core has a high temperature and high pressure.	*essence, heart, gist, center*
mantle	The portion of the earth between the crust and the core.	Old English, *mentel*, "loose, sleeveless cloak," from Latin, *mantellum*, meaning "cloak"	The mantle is the area that has most of the earth's mass.	*veil, cover, blanket, screen, cloak*
magma	Molten material beneath the earth's crust.	Middle English *dregs*, from Latin, *magma*, meaning, "dregs of an ointment"	Magma that spills out of the earth is called lava.	*magmatic, magmas*
sediment	Matter that has been deposited by some natural process.	French, *sediment*, from Latin *sedimentum*, meaning "a settling, sinking down"	Small particles of gravel, sand, and mud.	*sedimentous, settle*
erosion	The gradual wearing away of land surface materials.	Latin, *erodere*, meaning, "gnaw away"	Water, wind, and ice cause erosion.	*erode, dissolution, abrasion*

appreciation for words of the present by investigating their past. "Knowing that so many words have come from mythology, literature, and historical events and figures provides important background knowledge for students' reading in the various content areas" (Bear, Invernizzi, Templeton, & Johnston, 2004, p. 263). Table 5.9 includes sample Greek and Latin roots in Science, Math, and Social Studies vocabulary.

How could you use etymology? Quality dictionaries have word entries that include an etymology reference, usually following the pronunciation and part of speech. While some etymology entries can be simple and to the point, others can provide interesting backgrounds on the words chosen. A colorful example is provided below (Readence et al., 1998). While "chauvinism," taken from a French soldier's name, once meant loyalty and patriotism, it has changed over the years to refer to men who are only loyal to their gender. When students partake in lively discussions that will often arise, a new understanding of the word will develop and provide them insight on how the word was and is currently used (e.g., F "chauvinisme," fr. Nicholas "Chauvin" fl 1815 F soldier of excessive patriotism and devotion to Napoleon). Abbreviations are often used within the entry to offer the reader a language of origin. "F" is often French, "ME" is Middle English, "OE" is Old English, and "fl" or "L" is Latin, just to name a few; "fr" often translates to "from." Remember to review the dictionaries' opening pages with students as they contain the information on how the languages are abbreviated.

An eponym is a word that reflects the name of someone or something. As in the example above, "chauvinisme" was derived from an actual person. There are many eponyms found in a

TABLE 5.10.   Sample Greek and Latin Roots in Disciplinary Vocabulary

Base	Meaning/Examples	Origin
	English Language Arts	
ab	off; from; away: abduct	Latin
annul	ring: annelida, annular	Latin
anti	opposite; against: antigen, antifreeze	Greek
glossa	tongue: hypoglossal, glossary, glossopharyngea	Greek
	Mathematics	
circa	around; approximately: circle, circumnavigate, circa	Latin
deca	ten: decimal, decameter, decathalon	Greek
kilo	thousand: kilometer, kilogram	Greek
milli	1/1,000: millimeter	Latin
	Science	
mito	thread: mitosis, mitochondrion	Greek
ov	egg: ovum, oviparous, oviduct	Latin
photo	light: photosynthesis, photograph, photon	Greek
ren	kidney: renal, adrenalin, renin	Latin
	Social Studies	
chrono	time; chronic, chronology, chronological, synchronize, chronicle	Greek
homo	human; man: Homo sapiens	Latin
post	behind; after; rear: posterior, postmortem	Latin
tax	arrangement: taxon, taxonomy, ataxia	Greek

variety of subject matter. The word "boycott" is derived from Charles C. Boycott, a snooty Irish landlord. The word "dahlia" comes from Anders Dahlia, a Swedish botanist. Why do these matter? Discussion of words and their origins can impact vocabulary learning by connecting words to background knowledge, and integrating new information into the students' schemas. The following graphic organizer (Table 5.10) is one way to investigate and discuss the etymology of words.

Morphemic Analysis

Morphemic analysis is a vocabulary strategy that can help students learn the meaning of words by examining morphemes, the meaningful word units or parts (roots, prefixes, suffixes). Morphology also includes related concepts, such as cognates and derivations (e.g., determine, determination). Morphemes can be free or bound. Free morphemes carry meaning on their own (e.g., boy, girl) and bound morphemes (i.e., parts of words) must be attached or bound to other morphemes to make words. Morphemic analysis involves teaching students the meanings of morphemes and how these meanings combine within words to form new meanings. Morphemic analysis also involves teaching learners, during and after reading, how to disassemble and reassemble words to understand their meanings. Adolescents know more morphemes, including Greek and Latin roots and increasingly sophisticated affixes—all of which are bound morphemes that cannot stand alone. Students need direct instruction in morphemic analysis—learning how to isolate the root word and think about its meaning, and then isolate any affixes (prefixes and/or suffixes) and think about their meanings. Finally, learners need to be

TABLE 5.11.   Morphemic Analysis Template—Topic: US Immigration in the 1900s

Word	Prefix	Root	Suffix	Related Words with Same Root Word	Meaning from Context	Definition in my Own Words
Immigrants	Im- (into)	migrate (to travel)	-s (more than one)	Migration, transmigrate, emigrate	People who came from a different country.	People who move to another country to stay.
Naturalization		Naturalize (to put on an alien the rights and privileges of a citizen)	-tion (condition, action, process)	Naturalized, naturalizer, unnaturalizing	Naturalized citizens in the US are entitled the same rights and privileges of natural-born citizens.	Legal process of granting citizenship to one of who was not born in this country.
Pluralism		Plural (multiple, many)	-ism (action, process, result)	Pluralist, Pluralistic	The existence of different ethnic, religious, or cultural groups within a society.	The US is a "melting pot" of people, cultures, and customs.

shown how to put those meanings together to determine the meaning of the entire word. Some students find use of a graphic organizer to be a helpful tool for morphemic analysis, such as the one shown above (see Table 5.11). Morphemic analysis does not always work. Some prefixes carry multiple meanings, and sometimes removal of affixes doesn't leave recognizable root words, or the meaning of the root that is left isn't related to the meaning of the whole word. Yet, morphemic analysis can be more effective when used in conjunction with context clues. Teach morphemic analysis in the context of rich vocabulary instruction; it should not be used as a memorization list. Instead, hold class discussions to analyze the word and its parts, and infer its meaning.

Target Word Analysis

I like to use a variation of morphemic analysis and etymology through the Target Word Vocabulary Analysis strategy I developed and used in various classes (see Table 5.12). This strategy can be used during and after reading. It is more advanced than simple morphemic analysis and etymology, as it invites students to think about the meaning of each word (What I think it means); conduct morpheme analysis of a target word, but also examine its origin (Are there any word parts I recognize?); think about where the student might find the word (context and usage); identify other related words (Does it relate to any other words I know?); think about

TABLE 5.12.   Target Word Vocabulary Analysis Strategy; Topic: World War II-Holocaust

Target Word: *Genocide* 1. I think it means. . .	*Massive destruction/killing of people.*
2. Are there any word parts I recognize? (Root, prefix, suffix)	*geno- (Greek, "geno,"=race)* *-cide (Latin, "cidium"=killing, to cut down)*
3. Where might I find this word?	*History book; e.g., unit on the Holocaust.* *Human rights organizations.* *Museums.*
4. How does it relate to other words I know?	*Annihilation, carnage, decimation, ethnic cleansing, Holocaust, mass execution, massacre, race extermination, slaughter*
5. Why is it important for me to know this word?	*Understand what happened during the Holocaust.* *Understand World War II.* *Understand that genocide continues around the world.*
6. How does it add to my understanding of the topic?	*How propaganda, political and financial reasons, and prejudice led to the slaughter of six million Jews (from 1933–1945). It also helps me understand reasons for and events related to World War II. Last, similar causes apply to genocide around the world today.*
7. Actual word definition (include page #s).	*"The deliberate and systematic killing of an entire population." (McGoudall Littell, The Americans: Reconstruction of the 21st Century, 2005, p. 544)*

why it is important to know this word (What does it add to my knowledge about the topic?); and last, use the actual definition from the text. In a way, it is using a backwards approach; most teachers start with the definition of a word located in a dictionary. This strategy will invite the student to think very carefully about the meaning and significance of the word, and will facilitate deep learning. Careful selection of target words is important—select words that are core to all students' understanding of a topic, model the strategy with a familiar word first, allow time for sufficient guided practice and discussions, and use collaborative inquiry to discuss the importance of the word to the topic and other related concepts.

Vocabulary Self-Selection Strategy

Haggard (1982, 1986) developed a simple way for helping students become more involved with, and aware of, words. As students are reading, they identify words they think everyone in class should learn, mark them, use a post-it note to mark them, or record them in their notebook. After reading, the teacher places students in groups where they can discuss their word choices. The following are steps involved in vocabulary self-selection.

1. As students read a text selection, ask them to identify a couple of words that they find interesting or challenging.

2. Ask students to mark or record their choices so that they can discuss them later with the class.
3. After reading, place students in small groups of four, and ask them to discuss their word choices. Each group will vote and contribute one word everyone has to learn for the week. Depending on the number of groups, students will learn four to six new words from their reading for that week.
4. Students discuss and extend word meanings and record them in their journal or notebook.
5. These agreed-upon words can be used for follow-up class activities, writing assignments, games, and even practice tests.

As students practice the strategy, they can continue to collect vocabulary from other sources, and record it in their notebooks or journals. The teacher can also model her ways for selecting vocabulary and how she uses context clues, text features (e.g., bolded text, side-bar definitions, glossaries), morphemic analysis, or reference materials to determine word meanings (Blackowicz & Fisher, 2000). The vocabulary self-selection strategy can also aid ELLs' vocabulary knowledge because it provides them with choice, interactions, and discussions. This simple strategy can help students become metacognitive about their word choices, promote connections with their prior knowledge, facilitate word consciousness, and actively engage them in word learning.

Reinforcing and Extending Vocabulary Knowledge

Providing students with opportunities to play with, and manipulate words and word meanings, can enable them to develop a metacognitive and flexible understanding of words in every content area classroom (Blachowicz & Fisher, 2004). Research has shown that students learn vocabulary and vocabulary strategies through repeated and varied exposure and practice (Juel & Deffes, 2004). The following activities can also be used to assess student understanding of multiple-meaning words.

- Ask students to verbalize how they are learning new words.
- Ask students to describe pictures or objects. Ask them to explain different definitions for words that have multiple meanings.
- Ask students to illustrate various meanings of a word.
- Ask students to locate sentences for passages from text(s) that provide evidence for the multiple meanings of a word.
- Create word webs to record different meanings, sentences, or related concepts to a targeted polysemous word.
- Promote word consciousness.
- Use the Semantic Feature Analysis strategy.
- Use word puzzles and games. There are several ways to develop your own word puzzles using words from a current topic under study.
- Vocabulary self-collection is another way for students to select, collect and review words independently after they already worked with the words and their meanings.

Solid comprehension of new vocabulary requires practice, review, and multi-layered, comprehensive processing over time. Instruction that includes practice (followed by support) and review activities that require the students to process, manipulate, reflect upon, and think deeply about a word and its relationships, is more likely to be effective. Review must be distributed over time, with vocabulary integrated into more complex tasks, and be varied so vocabulary use can be applied to a wide range of contexts and used to illustrate a comprehensive application of student understanding. Students can begin by putting word definitions into their own words, include practicing using the word in a variety of contexts, drawing illustrations, graphics, or semantic maps to show relationships among related words, participating in discussions and games that link new words to words that students already know, and other reinforcing and extending strategies distributed over time.

Word Analogies

Word analogies are useful ways to increase students' vocabulary and comprehension (Readance, Bean, & Baldwin, 1998). They can be used before, after, or during reading. An analogy is a comparison of the similarities of two concepts (e.g., electricity is like flowing water). The familiar concept is called the analog and the unfamiliar one is called the target. Both the analog and the target have features or attributes. If the two concepts share similar features, an analogy can be drawn between them. Analogies provide elaborations between what is known and what is not known (Glynn, 2007). The most effective analogies are those that elaborate.

The *Teaching-With-Analogies Model* (Glynn, Duit, & Thiele, 1995; Glynn, 2007) provides a step-by-step approach for teachers.

1. Introduce the target concept.
2. Remind students what they already know about the analog concept.
3. Identify relevant features of the target and analog concepts.
4. Map similar features or attributes of the target and analog concepts.
5. Indicate where the analogy between the two concepts breaks down
6. Draw conclusions about the two concepts.

If you use word analogies, remember to model how to formulate and analyze the analogy, and how students can create their own word analogies (Vacca & Vacca, 1999). Create opportunities for students to create word analogies independently and collaboratively and encourage discussions where they would have to defend their answers.

Word Consciousness

Good vocabulary instruction makes students excited, curious about, and more attentive to words (Stahl & Shiel, 1999). Are your students intrigued by the words of your discipline? Do their vocabularies seem rich and varied? Do they like learning about words? Are they motivated to understand the nuances of words they encounter in texts? If so, your students might be word conscious. How about your classroom environment? Is it language-rich? Do you get excited about words? Do you talk about words in everyday classroom interactions and facilitate students' vocabulary? According to Graves and Watts-Taffe (2002), a successful vocabulary program should also provide opportunities for fostering word consciousness. Word consciousness refers to an understanding of and interest in words, how they are used, and their importance in communicating and learning.

Students who possess word consciousness enjoy learning new words, use them creatively, and understand how words and concepts are related across different contexts. A student who is word conscious knows a lot of words well, is interested in words, enjoys conversing with others about words, and uses words skillfully. Also, he, or she is on the lookout for precise words, is responsive to the nuances of word meanings, and realizes that words could promote clarity and/or confusion. Word consciousness will draw the reader to the language of the text (Graves, 2006). To increase word consciousness in your classroom, model using quality, discipline-specific, and elaborate language. Also, draw students' attention to words, their meanings, and use, read aloud good literature and informational text, communicate your appreciation and love for words, and be playful with words and language.

See the following ways to promote word consciousness in the content area classroom:

● Show an interest in words—become a logophile.
● Use the words of your discipline and other complex words in your classroom interactions.
● Create a language-rich and print-rich environment.
● Create opportunities for students to learn more words and share ideas with one another.
● Model adept word choice—consider the difference between asking students if their lunch was tasty or delectable.
● Allow students to hear unknown words to describe familiar concepts. "By the end of the weekend, I was so tired." Or, "By the end of the weekend, I was drained."
● Model a word-of-the-day. A new word that is interesting and describes either something students have been learning about or going through—anything that makes connections with what they are learning will have a longer "shelf life." Or, create a word wall with novel or complex words and have students participate in it. The teacher and students take turns posting a word-of-the-day on the word wall, explain why they selected it, provide some clues and ask the class to guess what it means, or explain what it means. Everyone in class refers to or, uses the word-of-the-day, and at the end of the week, students can either find connections among posted words (classify them), or select the "best" word they liked and explain why. There are a lot of ways a teacher could play with the word-of-the-day.
● Promote word play. This is not a waste of time, nor is it something for younger readers. Through word play students can create new words, reflect metacognitively on words, word parts, and context, and engage in relationships among words. Idioms, clichés, and puns are also nice ways to facilitate word play and build the vocabulary knowledge of all, especially, that of English language learners.
● Dramatization can help clarify words and their meanings.
● Investigations about how words are used in different texts or publications. Students could analyze language structure, word choice, and usage.

Word Sorts

A word sort is a very simple, non-intimidating vocabulary strategy that has hidden potential for creating semantic relationships among words and reasoning skills of classification and deduction. It can be used before, during, or after reading. The teacher identifies a list, or group of words from a unit or multiple (preferably) related units of study, and asks students to sort the words out into logical arrangements. Gillet and Kita (1979) describe two types of word sort: open word sort and closed word sort. In closed word sorts, the teacher selects the words and also gives students a number of categories they can use to group related words under. In open word sorts, the teacher gives students the words, but asks students to create categories and sort the words under each category. In either case, the goal is for students to identify shared conceptual features among words, and can be used as an after-reading strategy. Students can work on their word sorts in groups and discuss their choices. The following (Table 5.13 and Table 5.14) are examples of closed and open word sorts.

TABLE 5.13.   Closed Word Sort Example—Science

Categories: metals, nonmetals

Words: nickel, bohrium, sulfur, mercury, bromine, lithium, krypton, cobalt

Student Work Sample:

Metals	Non Metals
nickel	lithium
bohrium	bromine
mercury	krypton
cobalt	sulfur

TABLE 5.14.   Open Word Sort Example—Business

Words: Salaries and wages, tools and furniture, land, finance costs, goodwill, buildings, insurance costs, patents, taxes, depreciation, interest, copyrights, machinery, trademarks, vehicles

Student Work Sample:

Expenses

Salaries and wages, finance costs, insurance costs, taxes, depreciation, interest

Tangible Fixed Assets

Land, buildings, machinery, vehicles, equipment, tools and furniture

Intangible Fixed Assets

Goodwill, patents, copyrights and trademarks

Word Walls

Word walls in a secondary classroom? Aren't word walls for young readers only? Well, not exactly. Word walls can promote a print-rich environment in any content area classroom (Readance, Bean, & Baldwin, 2004). A word wall is an ongoing, display of words that is used for reference purposes throughout the study of a topic or unit (see Figure 5.1—developed by Mr. J. Foley, Biology/Zoology teacher, Lake Mary High School, Lake Mary, FL). Word walls can be used in a number of ways to promote development, reinforcement, and extension of vocabulary. Having a word wall will not do anything for students. Allowing students to interact with a word wall, will. Effective word walls are interactive in nature. They can support the teaching and understanding of key discipline-specific terms, promote independence in reading and writing by building students' vocabulary, be used as a reference for language learners, and can also be used to strengthen connections between words and concepts.

Teachers can build word walls in a variety of ways; for example, use different color card stock to distinguish concepts that belong to previous topics of study, use pictures and visuals to help ELLs, or write clues, definitions, and characteristics of the word on the back of the card. In secondary classrooms where different teachers often share the same classroom, making the word

FIGURE 5.1. Word Wall Example—Science

wall as "mobile" as possible might be useful (i.e., create it on chart paper). The word wall should be visible to all students. Make access to the words easy by using tape to mount the words so students can move individual words, group and classify words as needed. Students can also use technology to create online word walls and access them from anywhere, anytime through online platforms Padlet (see http://padlet.com). Students can also use www.Wordle.net and www. Tagxedo.com to turn their words into word clouds.

Word wall topics or themes can vary according to class and topic. Sample ideas include (and are not limited to) the following: SAT/ACT words, prefixes/suffixes, Greek and Latin Roots, graffiti words (words students are interested in), frequently misspelled words, discipline-specific/ topic-specific words, etc. Word walls can also be used as vocabulary games. A word wall in itself cannot teach vocabulary (Harmon, Wood, Hedrick, Vintinner, & Willeford, 2009). However, if used effectively, word walls can be used as tools for supporting word learning. They can provide students with multiple exposures to key words, and actively and meaningfully engage them in analyzing, connecting, and evaluating word meanings, and applying words in different contexts.

Digital Literacies

- Online Etymology dictionary: http://www.etymonline.com/ is an online resource explaining the meaning of word parts.
- Wordle: http://www.wordle.net/create, or Tagxedo: http://www.tagxedo.com/ are advanced word organizers that can be used to identify main idea before reading or to share their interpretation of the text after reading.
- Padlet: http://padlet.com is a free and user-friendly digital tool that allows users to create a digital wall of multimedia sticky notes, which can include text, images, links and videos. Teachers can create a vocabulary word wall and embed it into a webpage, blog or wiki for quick and easy access 24/7.

Summary

- Language is core to knowledge and vice versa. For students to be ready for college, career, and the workforce, they will need to know and use words beyond the definitional level. New educational standards emphasize the need for students to engage in systematic, purposeful, and collaborative discussions and conversations about what they are reading, researching, and learning.

- Explicit vocabulary instruction should focus on strategies that promote independent word knowledge acquisition and equip them with ways to analyze the semantic, syntactic, or context clues to derive the meaning of the words and the context in which they are used.

- Discipline-specific vocabulary instruction has to take place in authentic and meaningful ways. Students will benefit from instruction that will help them learn disciplinary content, develop their understanding of word meanings and language, enable them to participate in academic conversations and express their learning in writing, and provide them with ample opportunities to build, comprehend, and apply language.

Differentiating Instruction

- The CCSS support English language development through the basic design of the standards. The Speaking and Listening standards provide opportunities for students to listen to language and engage in collaborative conversations, while practicing using newly acquired vocabulary. The language standards provide a focus on learning language conventions in both writing and speaking. Often, ELLs approach the language as if it were math or science by trying to equate one word precisely to another. The concept that one word can have more than one meaning doesn't make sense to these students, causing confusion when they encounter multiple meaning words in text. In addition, they often try to spell the words differently in different contexts. This notion is further reinforced in that many words with identical pronunciations but different meanings— such as no and know—are spelled differently.

- Learning vocabulary is a challenge for ELLs, as well as those students who speak non-standard dialects such as African American Vernacular English (AAVE), Bahamian English, or Gullah. Here are some steps in teaching new words to ELLs and other special needs students.
  - Say the word. The teacher, or other fluent reader, models how the word is pronounced. Students then repeat the pronunciation.
  - Analyze the word. Examine root words and affixes. Make connections to related words students may know.
  - Discuss the word. Discuss denotations, connotations, and etymologies of target words to broaden students' understanding, and help them make connections between target words and known words.
  - Write the word. Teachers write the word on the classroom word wall. Students write the word and its meanings, using their own words, in their journal, personal dictionary, or notebook.
  - Involve the use of their senses during word study. The more senses they use, the better they understand and remember.
  - Involve concrete objects that are labeled with target words. Teachers often begin by labeling objects in their classrooms.

○ Provide an experiential base for the concept or target words (e.g., the Internet, videos, photographs, can help provide experiences that students can then write and discuss using the target vocabulary).

○ Provide students with many opportunities to use the word in meaningful situations.

○ ELLs and others benefit from collaborative learning activities in class.

● In addition to carefully selecting words to teach as part of vocabulary instruction, teachers should also balance direct teaching of word meanings in meaningful contexts and teaching word-learning strategies (e.g., context clues, dictionaries, glossaries). ELLs will also benefit from strategies that draw on cognate knowledge meaning, an understanding of words that have similar orthographic structures in English and the ELLs' native language (e.g., English–Spanish cognates: information–información, artist–artista).

● Provide opportunities for active and collaborative explorations of words, ideas, and interpretations. ELLs and students with varied exceptionalities, will need more practice with applying word knowledge in multiple contexts, and support in being able to distinguish which meanings of words make sense in certain contexts. Media and technology can be very useful for vocabulary support.

Reflect and Apply

1. What elements of your current practice (if you are an inservice teacher), or your future instruction (if you are a preservice teacher) are aligned well, or would be aligned well with the shift toward more emphasis on general academic vocabulary? Use your knowledge from this chapter to discuss one to three ideas about this shift with a partner, or a small group of your peers. Share your ideas and perceived challenges associated with this instructional shift in your discipline.

2. How can content area teachers teach vocabulary effectively? What suggestions could you offer to Ms. Heglund (see Classroom Life vignette)? Discuss your suggestions with a small group of peers.

3. Use what you learned in this chapter about the importance of academic conversations and accountable talk for strengthening vocabulary, language, and thinking, and come up with a few specific accountable talk moves you would like to implement in your classroom. If you are currently not teaching, write a note to a friend who is teaching, and explain to her how to use accountable talk in her classroom. Discuss with your peers key factors that will promote, or inhibit, accountable talk in content area classrooms.

Extending Learning

1. Interview a disciplinary expert about the ways he or she learns and uses vocabulary to apply and generate knowledge in their discipline. Write five questions about the unique structure and vocabulary demands of the discipline, and seek feedback on how to promote students' discipline-specific vocabulary. Summarize the interview responses, and present your findings to the class.

2. Select one topic from your discipline, identify the words that are worthy of teaching, and develop an explicit vocabulary instruction plan. Outline your steps, provide a

rationale for your choice of words to teach and describe one or two ways you will teach them. Be sure to also specify how students will learn these words. Present your plan to the class or a subject area colleague, and defend it using principles of effective instruction from this chapter.

3. Choose a topic of study from your content area textbook (e.g., lesson or unit). Study the text and work with a partner (preferably from your community of practice) to identify Tier Two and Three words in the text. Together, identify a couple of ways you will teach Tier Two and Tier Three words, and also consider the needs of ELLs and other struggling readers in the classroom. Present your topic, list of words, and vocabulary strategies to the class and practice a focused academic conversation on your choices.

References

Adams, M. J. (2009). The challenge of advanced texts: The interdependence of reading and learning. In E. H. Hiebert (Ed.), *Reading more, reading better: Are American students reading enough of the right stuff?* (pp. 163–189). New York, NY: Guilford.

Anderson, R. C., & Nagy, W. E. (1991). Word meanings. In R. Barr, M. L. Kamil, P. Mosenthal, & P. D. Pearson (Eds), *Handbook of reading research, Vol. II*. White Plains, NY: Longman.

Applebee, A. N., Langer, J. A., Nystrand, M., & Gamoran, A. (2003). Discussion-based approaches to developing understanding: Classroom instruction and student performance in middle and high school English. *American Educational Research Journal, 40*, 685–730.

Baker, S. K., Simmons, D. C. & Kame'enui, E. J. (1997). Vocabulary acquisition: Research bases. In D. C. Simmons, & E. J. Kame'enui, (Eds), *What reading research tells us about children with diverse learning needs: Bases and basics*. Mahwah, NJ: Erlbaum.

Barron, R. F., & Melnik, R. (1973). The effects of discussion upon learning vocabulary meanings and relationships in tenth grade biology. In H. L. Herber & R. F. Barron (Eds), *Research in reading in the content areas, second year report* (pp. 46–52). Syracuse, NY: Syracuse University, Reading and Language Arts Center.

Baumann, J. F., & Kame'enui, E. J. (1991). Research on vocabulary instruction: Ode To Voltaire. In J. Flood, J.J. Lapp, and J.R. Squire (Eds), *Handbook of research on teaching the English language arts* (pp. 604–632). New York, NY: MacMillan.

Bauman, J. F., & Kame'enui, E. J. (2004) (Eds). *Vocabulary instruction: Research to practice*. New York, NY: The Guilford Press.

Baumann, J. F., Kame'enui, E. J., & Ash, G. (2003). Research on vocabulary instruction: Voltaire redux. In J. Flood, D. Lapp, J.R. Squire &, J. Jensen, (Eds), *Handbook of research on teaching the English Language Arts* (2nd ed.) (pp. 752–785). Mahway, NJ: Lawrence Erlbaum.

Baumann, J. F., Edwards, E. C., Boland, E. M., Olejnik, S., & Kame'enui, E. J. (2003). Vocabulary tricks: Effects of instruction in morphology and context on fifth-grade students' ability to derive and infer word meanings. *American Educational Research Journal, 401*(2), 447–494.

Bear, D. R., Invernizzi, M., Templeton, S., & Johnston, F. (2004). *Words their way: Word study for phonics, vocabulary, and spelling instruction* (3rd ed.). Upper Saddle River, NJ: Merrill Prentice Hall.

Beck, I., & McKeown, M. (1991). Conditions of vocabulary acquisition. In R. Barr, M. Kamil, P. Mosenthal & P. D. Pearson (Eds), *Handbook of reading research (vol. 2)*. White Plains, NY: Longman.

Beck, I. L., McKeown, M. G., & Kucan, L. (2002). *Bringing words to life*. New York, NY: Guilford.

Beck, I. L., McKeown, M. G., & Kucan, L. (2008) (2nd ed.). *Bringing words to life*. New York, NY: Guilford.

Beck, I., McKeown, M. G., & McCaslin, E. (1983). Vocabulary development: All contexts are not created equal. *The Elementary School Journal, 83*, 177–181.

Beck, I. L., McKeown, M. G., & Omanson, R. C. (1987). The effects and uses of diverse vocabulary instructional techniques. In M. G. McKeown & M. E. Curtis (Eds), *The nature of vocabulary acquisition* (pp. 147–163). Hillsdale, NJ: Erlbaum.

Becker, W. C. (1977). Teaching reading and language to the disadvantaged––What we have learned from field research. *Harvard Educational Review, 47*, 518–543.

Betts, E. A. (1946). *Foundations of reading instruction, with emphasis on differentiated guidance*. New York, NY: American Book Company.

Biemiller, A. (2001). Teaching vocabulary: Early, direct, and sequential. *The American Educator, 25*(1), 24–28.

Blachowicz, C. L. Z., and Fisher, P. J. L. (1996). *Teaching vocabulary in all classrooms*. Saddle River, NJ: Merrill/Prentice Hall.

Blachowicz, C. L. Z., & Fisher, P. J. L. (2000). Vocabulary instruction. In M. J. Kamil, P. B. Mosenthal, P. D. Pearson, & R. Barr (Eds), *Handbook of reading research* (vol. 3) (pp. 503–523). Mahwah, NJ: Lawrence Erlbaum Associates.

Blachowicz, C. L. Z., & Fisher, P. J. L. (2004). Vocabulary lessons. *Educational Leadership, 61*(6), 6–69.

Blachowicz, C. L. Z., Fisher, P. J. L., Ogle, D., & Watts-Taffe, S. (2006). Vocabulary: Questions from the classroom. *Reading Research Quarterly, 41*(4), 524–539.

Bruner, J. (1996). *The culture of education*, Cambridge, MA: Harvard University Press.

Carver, R. P. (1994). Percentage of unknown vocabulary words in text as a function of the relative difficulty of the text: Implications for instruction. *Journal of Reading Behavior, 26*(4), 413–437.

Cazden, C. B. (1976). Play with language and meta-linguistic awareness: One dimension of language experience. In J. S. Bruner, A. Jolly, & K. Sylva (Eds), *Play: Its role in development and evolution* (pp. 603–608). New York, NY: Basic.

Cazden, C. B. (1986). Classroom discourse. In M. Wittrock (Ed.), *Handbook of research on teaching* (3rd ed.) (pp. 9–21). New York, NY: Macmillan Publishing Co.

Cazden, C.B. (1988). *Classroom discourse: The language of teaching and learning*. Portsmouth, NH: Heinemann.

Cazden, C. B. (2001). *Classroom discourse: The language of teaching and learning* (2nd ed.). Portsmouth, NH: Heinemann.

Chamot, A. U., & O'Malley, J. M. (1994). *The CALLA handbook: Implementing the cognitive academic language learning approach*. Reading, MA: Addison- Wesley.

Chapin, S., O'Connor, C., & Anderson, N. (2003). *Classroom discussions: Using math talk to help students learn: Grades 1–6*. Sausalito, CA: Math Solutions Publications.

Curtis, M. (2004). Adolescents who struggle with word identification: Research and practice. In T. Jetton and J. Dole (Eds). *Adolescent literacy research and practice*. New York: Guilford.

Diamond, L., & Gutlohn, L. (2006). *Vocabulary handbook*. Baltimore, MD: Brookes Publishing Co.

Durkin, D. (1978–79). What classroom observations reveal about reading comprehension instruction. *Reading Research Quarterly, 14*, 481–533.

Fang, Z. (2012). Language correlates of disciplinary literacy. *Topics in Language Disorders, 32*(1), 19–34.

Fang, Z., & Schleppegrell, M. J. (2010). Disciplinary literacies across content areas: Supporting secondary reading through functional language analysis. *Journal of Adolescent and Adult Literacy, 53*(7), 587–597.

Fielding, L., Wilson, P. & Anderson, R. (1986). A new focus on free reading: The role of trade books in reading instruction. In R. Raphael and R. Reynolds (Eds), *Contexts in literacy* (pp. 149–160). New York: Longman.

Fisher, D., & Frey, N. (2004). *Improving adolescent literacy: Strategies at work*. Upper Saddle River, NJ: Merrill/Prentice Hall.

Fisher, D., and Frey, N. (2008). *Word wise and content rich: Five essential steps to teaching academic vocabulary*. Portsmouth, NH: Heinemann.

Flynt, E., & Brozo, W. G. (2008, March). Developing academic language: Got words?. *The Reading Teacher, 61*(6), 500–502.

Gillet, J. & Kita, M. J. (1979). Words, kids, and categories. *Reading Teacher, 32*, 538–542.

Graves, M. F. (2006). *The vocabulary book: Learning and instruction*. New York: Teachers College Press.

Graves, M. F., & Watts-Taffe, S. M. (2002). The place of word consciousness in a research-based vocabulary program. In A. E. Farstrup & S. J. Samuels (Eds), *What research has to say about reading instruction* (3rd ed.) (pp. 140–165). Newark, DE: International Reading Association.

Glynn, S. (2007). Teaching with analogies model. *Science and Children*, 52–55.

Glynn, S. M., Duit, R., & Thiele, R. B. (1995). Teaching science with analogies: A strategy for constructing knowledge. In S.M. Glynn and R. Duit (Eds). *Learning science in the schools: Research reforming practice* (pp. 247–273). Mahwah, NJ: Erlbaum.

Guan Eng Ho, D. (2005). Why do teachers ask the questions they ask? *RELC, 36* (3), 297–310.

Haggard, M. R. (1982). The vocabulary self-selection strategy: An active approach to word learning. *Journal of Reading, 26*, 203–207.

Haggard, M. R. (1986). The vocabulary self-collection strategy: Using student interest and world knowledge to enhance vocabulary growth. *Journal of Reading, 29*(7), 634–642.

Halliday, M. A. K. (2004). The language of science (Vol. 5 in *The collected works of M. A.K. Halliday*, J. Webster (Ed.)). London, UK: Continuum.

Harmon, J. M., Hendrick, W. B., & Wood, K. D. (2005). Research on vocabulary instruction in the content areas: Implications for struggling readers. *Reading & Writing Quarterly, 21*, 261–280.

Harmon, J., Wood, K., Hedrick, W., Vintinner, J., & Willeford, T. (2009). Interactive word walls: more than just reading the writing on the walls, *Journal of Adolescent and Adult Literacy, 52*(5), 398–408.

Hart, B., & Risley, R. T. (1995). *Meaningful differences in the everyday experience of young American children.* Baltimore, MD: Paul H. Brookes.

Hayes, D. P. and Ahrens, M. G. (1988). Vocabulary simplification for children: A Special case of "motherese"? *Journal of Child Language, 15*(2), 395–410.?

Herman, P. A., Anderson, R. C., Pearson, P. D., & Nagy, W. E. (1987). Incidental acquisition of word meaning from expositions with varied text features. *Reading Research Quarterly, 22*, 263–264.

Hess, K., & Biggam, S. (2004). A discussion of "increasing text complexity." *Vermont State Board of Education,* R45–R48.

Hu, M., & Nation, I. S. P. (2000). Unknown vocabulary density and reading comprehension. *Reading in a Foreign Language, 13*(1), 403–430.

Johnson, D. D., & Pearson, P. D. (1984). *Teaching reading vocabulary* (2nd ed.). New York, NY: Holt, Rinehart & Winston.

Juel, C., & Deffes, R. (2004). Making words stick. *Educational Leadership, 61*, 30–34.

Kamil, M. L. (2003). *Adolescents and literacy: Reading for the 21st century.* Washington, DC: Alliance for Excellent Education.

Kamil, M., & Hiebert, E. (2005). Teaching and learning vocabulary: Perspectives and persistent issues. In E. H. Hiebert and M. L. Kamil (Eds), *Teaching and learning vocabulary: Bringing research to practice* (pp. 1–23). Mahwah, NJ: Lawrence Erlbaum.

Kamil, M. L., Borman, G. D., Dole, J., Kral, C. C., Salinger, T., & Torgesen, J. (2008). *Improving adolescent literacy: Effective classroom intervention practices: A practice guide* (NCEE#2008-4017). Washington, DC: National Center for Education Evaluation and Regional Assistance, Institute of Educational Sciences, US Department of Education. Retrieved from http://ies.ed.gov/ncee/wwc/pdf/practice_guides/adlit_pg_082608.pdf

Kelsius, J. P., & Searls, E. F. (1990). A meta-analysis of recent research in meaning in vocabulary instruction. *Journal of Research and Development in Education, 84*(3), 226.

Kouba, V. L. (1989). Common and uncommon ground in mathematics and science terminology. *School Science and Mathematics, 89*(7), 598.

Kucan, L., Trathen, W. R., & Straits, W. J. (2007). A professional development initiative for developing approaches to vocabulary instruction with secondary mathematics, art, science, and English teachers. *Reading Research and Instruction, 46*, 175–195.

Lesaux, N. K., Kieffer, M. J., Faller, S. E., & Kelley, J. G. (2010). The effectiveness and ease of implementation of an academic vocabulary intervention for linguistically diverse students in urban middle schools. *Reading Research Quarterly, 45*(2), 196–228.

Marzano, R. J. (2004). *Building background knowledge for academic achievement: Research on what works in schools.* Alexandria, VA: Association for Supervision and Curriculum Development.

Mason, J. M., Knisely, E., & Kendall, J. (1979). Effects of polysemous words on sentence comprehension. *Reading Research Quarterly, 15*, 49–65.

McCann, T. M., Johannessen, L. R., Kahn, E., & Flanagan, J. M. (2006). *Talking in class: Using discussion to enhance teaching and learning.* Urbana, IL: National Council of Teachers of English.

McConachie, S. M., & Petrosky, A. R. (2010). *Content matters: A disciplinary literacy approach to improving student learning.* San Francisco, CA: Jossey-Bass.

McKeown, M. G., Beck, I. L., Omanson, R. C, & Perfetti, C. A. (1983). The effects of long-term vocabulary instruction on reading comprehension: A replication. *Journal of Reading Behavior, 67*, 254–262.

McKeown, M. G., Beck, I. L., Omanson, R. C., & Pople, M. T. (1985). Some effects of the nature and frequency of vocabulary instruction on the knowledge and use of words. *Reading Research Quarterly, 20*, 522–535.

Michaels, S., O'Connor, M. C., Hall, M. W., & Resnick, L. (2002). *Accountable talk: classroom conversation that works.* Pittsburgh, PA: University of Pittsburgh.

Moje, E. B. (2008). Foregrounding the disciplines in secondary literacy teaching and learning: A call for change. *Journal of Adolescent and Adult Literacy, 52*(2), 96–107.

Nagy, W. (1988). *Teaching vocabulary to improve reading comprehension.* Newark, DE: International Reading Association.

Nagy, W. E., & Anderson, R. C. (1984). How many words are there in printed English? *Reading Research Quarterly, 19*, 304–330.

Nagy, W. E., & Scott, J. A. (2000). *Vocabulary processes.* In M. L. Kamil, P. Mosenthal, P. D. Pearson, & R. Barr (Eds), Handbook of Reading Research (Vol. 3) (pp. 269–284). Mahwah, NJ: Erlbaum.

Nagy, W. E., Anderson, R. C., & Herman, P. A. (1987). Learning word meanings from context during normal reading. *American educational Research Journal, 24*, 237–270.

Nagy, W. E., Herman, P., & Anderson, R. (1985). Learning words from context. *Reading Research Quarterly, 20*, 233–253.

National Council of Teachers of English (NCTE). (2011). *Literacies of disciplines: A policy research brief.* Urbana, IL: NCTE.

National Council of Teachers of Mathematics (NCTM). (2000). *Principles and standards for school mathematics.* Reston, VA: NCTM.

National Governors Association Center for Best Practices, Council of Chief State School Officers. (2010). *Common Core State Standards initiative.* (2010). Washington, DC: Author. Retrieved from http://www.corestandards.org

National Governors Association Center for Best Practices, Council of Chief State School Officers. (2010). *Common Core State Standards: Appendix A.* (2010). Washington, DC: Author. Retrieved from http://www.corestandards.org

National Governors Association Center for Best Practices, Council of Chief State School Officers. (2010). *Common Core State Standards: Appendix B.* (2010). Washington, DC: Author. Retrieved from http://www.corestandards.org

National Governors Association Center for Best Practices, Council of Chief State School Officers. (2010). *Common Core State Standards: English language arts and literacy in history/social studies, science, and technical subjects standards.* (2010). Washington, DC: Author. Retrieved from http://www.corestandards.org

National Governors Association Center for Best Practices, Council of Chief State School Officers. (2010). *Common Core State Standards: Mathematics standards.* (2010). Washington, DC: Author. Retrieved from http://www.corestandards.org

National Institute of Child Health and Human Development. (2000). *Report of the National Reading Panel. Teaching children to read: An evidence-based assessment of the scientific research literature on reading and its implications for reading instruction* (NIH Publication No. 00-4769). Washington, DC: US Government Printing Office.

National Reading Panel. (2000). *Teaching children to read.* National Institute of Child Health and Human Development.

Noles, J. D., & Dole, J. A. (2004). *Helping adolescent readers through explicit strategy instruction.* In T. L. Jetton, & J. A. Dole (Eds). Adolescent literacy research and practice. New York, NY: Guilford Press.

O'Brien, D. G., Moje, E. B., & Stewart, R. A. (2001). Exploring the context of secondary literacy: Literacy in people's everyday school lives. In E. B. Moje & D. G. O'Brien (Eds), *Constructions of literacy: Studies of teaching and learning in and out of secondary classrooms* (pp. 27–48). Mahwah, NJ: Erlbaum.

Palincsar, A. S. (2003). Collaborative approaches to comprehension instruction. In A. P. Sweet & A. E. Snow (Eds), *Rethinking reading comprehension* (pp. 99–114). New York, NY: The Guilford Press.

Palincsar, A. S., & Brown, A. L. (1984). Reciprocal teaching of comprehension-fostering and comprehension-monitoring activities. *Cognition and Instruction, 1*, 117–175.

Pearson, P. D., & Gallagher, M. C. (1983). The instruction of reading comprehension. *Contemporary Educational Psychology, 8*, 317–344.

Readence, J. E., Bean, T. W., & Baldwin, R. S. (1998). *Content area literacy: An integrated approach* (5th ed.). Dubuque, IA: Kendall/Hunt.

Readence, J. E., Bean, T. W., & Baldwin, R. S. (2004). *Content area literacy: An integrated approach* (8th ed.), Dubuque, IA: Kendall/Hunt.

Resnick, L. & Nelson-LeGall, S. (1999). Socializing intelligence. In L. Smith, J. Dockrell, & P. Tomlinson (Eds), *Piaget, Vygotsky, and beyond.* London, UK: Routledge.

Robbins, C., & Ehri, L. C. (1994). Reading storybooks to kindergartners helps them learn new vocabulary words. *Journal of Educational Psychology, 86*, 54–64.

Scott, J. A., & Nagy, W. E. (1997). Understanding the definitions of unfamiliar words. *Reading Research Quarterly, 32*, 184–200.

Scott, J. A., & Nagy, W. E. (2004). Developing word consciousness. In J. F. Baumann & E. J. Kame'enui (Eds), *Vocabulary instruction: Research to practice* (pp. 201–217). New York, NY: The Guilford Press.

Shanahan, T., & Shanahan, C. (2008). Teaching disciplinary literacy to adolescents: Rethinking content area literacy. *Harvard Educational Review, 78*(1), 40–61.

Snow C. E., & Biancarosa, G. (2003). *Adolescent literacy and the achievement gap: What do we know and where do we go from here?* New York, NY: Carnegie Corporation of New York.

Stahl, S. A. (1991). Beyond the instrumentalist hypothesis: Some relationships between word meanings and comprehension. In P. Schwanenflugel (Ed.), *The psychology of word meanings* pp. 157–178. Hillsdale, NH: Lawrence Erlbaum Associates.

Stahl, S. A. (1999). *Vocabulary development.* Newton Upper Falls, MA: Brookline Books.

Stahl, S. A. (2003). Vocabulary and readability: How knowing word meanings affects comprehension. *Topics in Language Disorders, 23*, 241–247.

Stahl, S. A., & Shiel, T. R. (1999). Teaching meaning vocabulary: Productive approaches for poor readers. In *Read all about it! Readings to inform the profession* (291– 321). Sacramento, CA: California State Board of Education.

Stanovich, K. E. (1986). Matthew effects in reading: Some consequences of individual differences in the acquisition of literacy. *Reading Research Quarterly, 21*, 360–407.

Sternberg, R. J., & Powell, J. S. (1983). Comprehending verbal comprehension. *American Psychologist, 38*, 878–893.

Vacca R., & Vacca, J. (1999). *Content area reading: Literacy and learning across the curriculum* (6th ed.). Menlo Park, CA: Longman.

Vygotsky, L. S. (1962). *Thought and language.* Cambridge, MA: The MIT Press.

Vygotsky, L. S. (1978). *Mind in society: The development of higher psychological processes.* (M. Cole, V. John-Steiner, S. Scribner, & E. Souberman, Eds). Cambridge, MA: Harvard University Press.

Whipple, G. (Ed.). (1925). *The twenty-fourth yearbook of the national society for the study of education: Report of the national committee on reading.* Bloomington, IL: Public School Publishing Company.

Zusak, M. (2006). *The Book Thief.* New York, NY: Knopf Books.

Zwiers, J. (2008). *Building academic language: Essential practices for content classrooms* (2nd ed.). San Francisco, CA: Jossey-Bass.

Zwiers, J., & Crawford, M. (2011). *Academic conversations: Classroom talk that fosters critical thinking and content understandings.* York, ME: Stenhouse.

Zygouris-Coe, V. (2012). Disciplinary literacy and the common core state standards. *Topics in Language Disorders, 32*(1), 35–50.

Zygouris-Coe, V. (2012). What is disciplinary literacy and why aren't we talking more about it? *Vocabulogic, 1–6.* Retrieved from http://vocablog-plc.blogspot.com/2012/03/what-is-disciplinary-literacy-and-why.html

six
Questioning and Comprehension in the Disciplines

*I am not smart; I just stay with
the problems longer.*
–Albert Einstein

Chapter Highlights

- Schools must prepare students for the skills, knowledge, and habits of mind they will need to learn and succeed in college and in tomorrow's careers and workplaces.
- Comprehension is a complex, active, and interactive process of constructing meaning from text. It involves the reciprocal interaction of three factors—the reader, the text, and the context in which the text is read.
- The Common Core State Standards (CCSS) recognize the importance of students becoming active learners and effective questioners.
- Each discipline has its own inquiry process. Learning how to think, reason, ask questions, and communicate in discipline-specific ways will help students meet the demands of each discipline and will prepare them for college, work, and life.
- Text-dependent questions, open-ended questions, and essential questions will facilitate close reading of text, deeper comprehension, and transfer of knowledge to new situations.
- Teachers need to provide explicit instruction in comprehension and questioning, scaffolded support, adequate practice and feedback, progress monitoring, and opportunities for students to discuss what they are learning with others.

Classroom Life

In my High School Social Studies class-room, the most common challenges in content area literacy are vocabulary, comprehension, and recognizing and understanding point of view. The students I work with, mainly seniors, are largely lower-quartile students and struggle with reading and writing. The obstacles these students face in the classroom stem from learning disabilities and a lack of progression in the skills they have. The vocabulary level of my students is perhaps the most obvious issue in their writing, speech, reading, and comprehension. I have found that even basic terms are not a part of their vocabulary and are not recognized when they read and write. For example, when I used the term "characteristic" in a short prompt, a significant number of students were unable to answer the question, because they did not know what it meant. Before we could continue, I had to explain the term charac-teristic into even more elementary terms like "something that describes something else."

Underdeveloped vocabulary becomes a major obstacle for reading and compre-hending historical texts. Another challenge my students face in content area literacy is comprehension, particularly when using primary sources. They have difficulty reading and analyzing primary sources. Higher-order questions are extremely difficult for the majority of the students in my classes, unless the answer is phrased almost exactly like the question. In a recent lesson, students were asked to evaluate the bias of a contemporary of Napoleon Bonaparte and the majority of the class was unable to understand another point of view. They come to class not knowing how to identify point of view, biases, and assumptions in texts, and they give up when it comes to evaluating different perspectives. Point of view is very important for historical thinking. *(Mr. Chase Fults, 12th grade Economics (standard and honors) and 10th grade World History Honors, Lake Mary High School, Lake Mary, Florida)*

The Importance of Critical Thinking Skills and Processes in the 21st Century

The jobs of today (and tomorrow) require complex mental knowledge and mental work. The skills will keep changing as societies' and world needs change. A strong education for students is the surest way to build them a strong foundation for the future. The Program for International Student Assessment (PISA) 2009 results show that the reading skills of 15 year olds vary widely around the world; they also show that we need to do more to give students a running start to their careers. Due to global financial crises, many young people are unemployed (e.g., 50% in Greece and 20% in Italy, Ireland, the UK, and France) (OECD, 2010).

In addition, workers with less training and skills have suffered more from the changing economies. Despite the unemployment rates, many jobs are still going unfilled; 40% of employers in Australia, Mexico, Japan, and Poland reported they could not find employees with the skills they were looking for. Even employed people report that they underuse their skills and are seeking more challenging work. Educational efforts should focus on building the right skills, and turning them to better jobs and better lives. Schools must prepare students for the skills, knowl-edge, and dispositions (the habits of mind) they will need in college and in tomorrow's careers and workplaces. Our greatest challenge is to prepare students to work, live, and continue to learn and innovate in a global world that is changing 24/7.

Learning, working, and living in the 21st century also require reading and comprehending digital, or online text(s). The Common Core State Standards (CCSS) also recognize that for students to succeed in a technologically advanced world, they will need to master new ways to read, write, communicate, and collaborate in face-to-face, and virtual environments. For example, the CCSS *Reading Standards for Informational Text, Integration of Knowledge and Ideas, Standard 7, for Grades 11–12* state: "Evaluate the advantages and disadvantages of using different mediums (for example, print or digital text, video, multimedia) to present a particular topic or idea." Technology should not be viewed as an "add-on" in today's classrooms. Unfortunately, we use it as an instructional supplement.

The answer to the question "What does it mean to be literate in a connected world?" is ever changing. Research shows that reading online is a very complex process that requires knowledge of search engines, how information is organized and accessed in websites, and inferential and comprehension monitoring skills (Coiro, Knobel, Lankshear, & Leu, 2008; Richardson, 2013). Students need new comprehension skills, strategies, dispositions, and social practices of the Internet and Information Communication Technologies (ICTs) to effectively read and comprehend multimodal text on the Internet and develop New Literacies (Coiro, 2003a, 2003b; Leu et al., 2008, 2009; Wilson, Zygouris-Coe, Cardullo, & Fong, 2013).

Because preparation for college and career readiness is demanding and multi-faceted, and much focus is placed on helping students develop deep learning, I decided to dedicate two chapters to the topic of comprehension. Making meaning from texts does not just happen when students show up for class. The content and literacy demands of each discipline, as well as reader characteristics, and other factors make comprehension of texts in middle and high school grades a challenge for both teachers and students. In addition, all of the topics, information, data, and models I have introduced in this book so far, point to the need for improving students' critical thinking, meaning-making, and metacognitive skills. In this chapter, I present the importance of questioning in comprehension, and in Chapter 7, I will examine effective comprehension instruction principles, and discipline-specific strategies to promote students' learning.

CCSS Connections

- The CCSS expect that students are involved in critical examination of texts, use evidence from texts to present careful analyses, well-supported claims, and clear and logical information.
- Text-dependent questions require deep understanding of texts that extends beyond knowledge of basic facts.
- The CCSS call for instruction that will help students not only acquire facts and information but develop knowledge, prepare them to question what they read, and equip them with knowledge, skills, and dispositions that will enable them to learn throughout life.

The Role of Comprehension in College, Career, Workforce and Life Readiness

College, career, and workforce readiness, and lifelong learning, involve both convergent and divergent learning. Creativity and learning require an interchange between convergent and divergent thinking. New educational standards promote a common definition of what our students need to know and be able to do to be college and career ready. According to the CCSS, upon high school graduation, students should have strong content knowledge, skills, and habits of mind that will prepare them to be successful in postsecondary education and career. A student who is college and career ready can qualify for, and succeed in, entry-level, credit-bearing college courses without needing remedial or developmental work (Conley, 2010, 2013).

The jobs that are growing today have two common characteristics: expert thinking and complex communication skills. According to the *2012 US News and World Report's Best Jobs*, the top three jobs in business include market research analyst, financial adviser, and accountant. In creative services, public relations specialist, architect, and art director. In health care, dentist, registered nurse, and pharmacist. In science and technology, computer systems analyst, database administrator, and web developer. In social services, school psychologist, interpreter, and substance abuse counselor.

These and other jobs require the ability to think deeply and carefully and solve new problems (e.g., doing different types of research, creating a new gluten-free menu in a restaurant, or designing sustainable communities) that cannot be solved by standard rules. The second skill 21st century jobs require is complex communication; the ability to interpret information (from multiple sources and perspectives) to others in public relations, industry, technology, teaching, etc. Teachers can, and should, play a key role in preparing students not only to develop solid knowledge, but also transfer it and apply it to new situations. Expert thinking and complex communication skills should be taught and developed in each content area (Levy & Murnane, 2004).

What are some advantages of well-prepared high school students who can succeed in college, in their respective careers, and in the workforce? Aside from national economic growth, another benefit will be the quality of living—college-educated workers will earn twice as much as high school graduates by 2025 (Carnevale & Rose, 2011). And, what do the CCSS and the New Generation Science Standards (NGSS) have to do with all of this? The new educational standards are designed with all students' college and career readiness in mind! The CCSS promote accuracy and logic (especially in math) but they also promote transferable learning, finding different solutions to problems, supporting one's viewpoint with evidence, exchanging ideas about different solutions and discoveries, and collaborating and problem solving with others. The NGSS science and engineering practices place much emphasis on asking questions and defining problems (i.e., Practice #2—see http://nstahosted.org/pdfs/ngss/20130509/AppendixF-ScienceAndEngineering PracticesInTheNGSS_0.pdf), developing and using models, planning and carrying out investigations, analyzing and interpreting data, using mathematics and computational thinking, and constructing explanations and designing solutions.

One of the main shifts resulting from the CCSS is leading high-level, text-based discussions in the classroom. The CCSS call for a shift from "What is the main idea?" type of questions to questions that require a closer reading of text. Students are asked to use evidence from what lies within the text and make valid claims that can be proven with the text. The CCSS promote more text-dependent questions that might start with the author's choice of words and organization of ideas, and move toward connections among ideas among texts. Coleman and Pimentel (2011) suggest the following about how to hold effective classroom discussions:

> An effective set of discussion questions might begin with relatively simple questions requiring attention to specific words, details, and arguments and then move onto explore the impact of those specifics on the text as a whole. Good questions will often linger over specific phrases and sentences to ensure careful comprehension and also promote deep thinking and substantive analysis of text.
>
> (p. 7)

This emphasis of the CCSS designers on text-dependent questions should not remove questions about one's opinions, background experiences, or other personal connections and reactions.

Coleman and Pimentel (2011) suggest that we should start first with the text, help students develop a "good" understanding of the text, its details, and ideas, and later on engage in opinions and broad questions. Starting with narrow, specific, and text-based questions will help develop text understanding that can lead to a discussion of broader issues and ideas. Often, we spend too much time on the personal opinions, which are important to the reading transactions between reader and text (Rosenblat, 1969, 1978), and unintentionally create a longer distance between the reader and the text. In addition, the New Generation Science Standards (NGSS) view the ability to ask questions and define problems as an essential learning element—questions about data, evidence, biases, relationships, and problem solving. According to NGSS, asking questions, especially scientific questions that are supported by evidence, leads students to further investigations, further involvement with science, and further learning. Students need to learn how to ask many questions about what they read and learn, and teachers can play a key role in how they scaffold their questioning skills and comprehension.

College, Career, and Workforce Connections

- College, career, and workforce readiness require that students read and analyze texts through the use of text-based questions. Students need to become independent thinkers, be able to identify critical information in written texts or oral presentations, communicate their ideas effectively, ask relevant questions, and consider others' perspectives.
- College, universities, and employers want students to apply their knowledge to solve real-world problems. Teachers need to teach more than "how to get the answer." They need to support students' ability to question what they are learning, think critically and reflectively, and access concepts from a number of perspectives.
- Students need to learn how to ask and answer questions, pay attention to details, identify essential versus non-essential information, apply knowledge, and evaluate actions and responses.
- *Students ideally should have excellent communication skills (written and oral), the ability to comprehend things that they read, and the disposition to improve all those skills in the course of their university education. They should also have the disposition to be open to new ideas, texts, and experiences and the willingness and ability to analyze—or, at least, the willingness and ability to learn to analyze— all those new things they encounter* (Anna Maria Jones, Associate Professor, English, University of Central Florida).

What Does It Mean To Comprehend?

I have asked many students from different subject area classes, "What does it take to do well in American History, in Health Education, in Algebra 2, or in Psychology classes, etc.?" Their answers have been, "Memorizing lots of facts." "You've got to know how to take tests!" "You have to like the course." "A good teacher who teaches you how to think!" "Lots of hard work and studying!" "Knowing how to study." Very seldom have I heard a student say that reading is a success factor in their subject area learning or performance. I think because reading is not directly "evaluated" in subject areas, students do not think about reading, or learning how to read and comprehend in the disciplines. As a result, they do not know what to do when they have problems reading and comprehending texts.

Reading involves more than just opening a book, moving your eyes up and down the page, recognizing words, and reading sentences. Reading is thinking; reading is an active process. Comprehension is a complex, interactive process of constructing meaning from text—in other words, reading, identifying important ideas, evaluating them, and applying them. It involves the reciprocal interaction of three factors—the reader, the text, and the context in which the text is read (RAND, 2002). For comprehension to develop and improve, teachers have to consider all three factors.

The interactive process of reading includes a sophisticated interplay of many elements such as: word decoding; word relationships; monitoring of understanding across words, sentences, paragraphs, sections, pages, and other texts; interpreting the literal, figurative, technical, and subtechnical meanings of written language; identifying and comparing conceptual relationships; "combing" through text to identify essential and non-essential information; making connections with experiences and prior knowledge and schema; considering the purpose, task, text, and context; and forming and monitoring one's meaning from text.

In every class, readers vary in terms of language experiences and knowledge, prior knowledge about content and reading, reading ability and skills, strategies they know and use, attitudes and motivation toward reading, and also in terms of reading and study habits. A student's past and present experiences in and out of the classroom shape his or her background knowledge (Fisher & Frey, 2009). A reader's reasoning ability consists of his or her attention, memory, and the ability to critically analyze, infer, and visualize what is read. A reader's knowledge entails linguistic ability and knowledge of vocabulary, topic, discourse, and comprehension strategies (Anderson & Freebody, 1981; Baumann, Kame'enui, & Ash, 2003; Blachowicz & Fisher, 2000; Hiebert & Kamil, 2005; NRP, 2000; RAND, 2002; Ruddell, 1994; Stahl, 1999; Stahl & Kapinus, 1991). Reader motivation refers to the desire and interest to engage in a reading activity. Motivation affects one's self-image as a reader, his or her self-efficacy (the readers' estimations of their abilities to apply skills and strategies to literacy learning) (Alvermann, 2001), and the student's engagement with reading text (Guthrie & Wigfield, 2000; Wigfield & Tonks, 2004).

Texts vary in genre, topic, structure and style, level of complexity, and also appeal. Text characteristics affect reader comprehension (RAND, 2002). We have examined text differences from different subject matter areas. For example, English classes use predominantly narrative texts, whereas, science and social studies use mainly expository texts. Each discipline has a unique text structure and organizational patterns. In addition, many of the texts students use nowadays are digital; print text follows a linear process whereas digital text does not (Coiro, 2003a, 2005; Coiro & Dobler, 2007; Leu et al., 2004). In addition, when students read digital text, they have to use evaluation of text and self-regulation at the same time (Coiro & Dobler, 2007). Texts used in secondary grade subject area classrooms are dense, complex, and have varied vocabulary, text structure, style and ways of communicating information (Heller & Greenleaf, 2007). It is important to teach students how to read and comprehend informational text with greater proficiency (Torgesen et al., 2007).

The context refers to when reading happens, where (inside and outside class, or school), and why a text is being read (for efferent or aesthetic purposes). A reader will approach a text he or she is reading for fun versus a text he or she has to read in class, like a textbook, or a research article. Also, readers will approach a science text that includes lots of graphs, data, symbols and numbers, very differently from a text that has many hidden and abstract concepts (e.g., *The Odyssey*). In addition, if a reader reads and learns in a supportive and motivating classroom, and in a place where critical thinking, accountable talk, and collaborative inquiry are "nonnegotiables," the entire reading process and outcomes will be different from those in a teacher-directed, "stale," and uninviting classroom. We also need to consider that adolescents' literacies are complex and extend beyond the classroom and school walls (Alvermann, 2001; Moje & Tysvaer, 2010). Our goal is to create classroom environments that support their needs, and prepare them to become lifelong learners.

Proficient Readers

A student who has "good" or proficient comprehension is someone who uses existing knowledge to make sense of new information, asks questions about the text before, during, and after reading, draws inferences from text, monitors his or her comprehension, uses fix-up strategies when meaning breaks down, determines what is important, and synthesizes information to create sensory images (Harvey & Goudvis, 2000; Keene & Zimmermann, 1997; Pearson, Roehler, Dole, & Duffy, 1992).

Blachowiscz and Ogle (2001) reported that a proficient comprehender previews, predicts from preview, sets purposes for reading, chooses appropriate strategies, checks understanding, integrates new information with known, monitors comprehension, continues to predict and question as he/she works through text, summarizes and synthesizes, responds appropriately, cross-checks with other information, checks for fulfillment of purpose, and uses what is read. Proficient readers monitor their learning, and have well-developed vocabularies (Nagy, Anderson & Herman, 1985). When students are taught vocabulary in depth, their comprehension improves (Beck, Perfetti, & McKeown, 1982).

If proficient comprehenders have these characteristics, and use the aforementioned processes, what does it actually mean to understand? I am finding it difficult to put in a few words, but here is my attempt. To understand is to retain, to recall what you are reading, to explain, to infer, to interpret, to conclude, to answer literal and inferential questions, to generate questions, to rethink through big ideas, to learn new vocabulary, to apply or transfer, to take other's perspectives, and to have self-knowledge. Understanding means using content effectively for transfer and meaning.

Grant Wiggins (2010) states that knowledge refers to facts and usable information, whereas understanding refers to opinions about what the facts mean, to debatable conclusions that are based on our interpretations of facts as filtered through our prior experiences and beliefs. Here's one example: "Fracking has been used in more than one million US wells, and has produced more than seven billion barrels of oil and 600 trillion cubic feet of natural gas" (facts). "The massive water requirements for fracking and the potential conflicts with other water needs, including for agriculture and ecosystems, create major challenges. Methane contamination of drinking water wells is a much more serious challenge" (understanding).

Teachers need to help students acquire facts and information, and especially, learn how to apply them in critical ways. All content area teachers have students in their classes who have acquired knowledge but do not know what to do with it. The evidence I presented you with calls for a shift from covering facts and knowledge, to understanding them deeply. For example, science teachers need to stop presenting science as a bunch of facts, laws, theories, and terms to be memorized. Instead, they should teach science in a way that helps students discover how the world works. Effective comprehension instruction in all content areas should focus on how the teacher engages the reader to think critically about texts, and demonstrate and use his or her understanding.

Now, let us examine the role of questioning in reader comprehension. In the following section, I present information on different types of questions and how to use them to promote student understanding in the disciplines, and explore various questioning strategies and practices for content area classroom instruction.

Applying Discipline-Specific Literacies

- Questioning is part of learning in each discipline. Facilitate the development of discipline-specific inquiry in your classroom.
- Teach students how to recognize different types of questions, how to look for textual evidence to support their answers, and how to generate questions that will promote discipline-specific discussions and further exploration of the topic.
- Teach students discipline-specific ways to question texts and perspectives, and teach in a way that promotes higher order thinking and questioning skills that are inherent to, and are needed, for learning in each discipline.

Questions, Questioning, and Comprehension

My mother made me a scientist without ever intending to. Every other Jewish mother in Brooklyn would ask her child after school: "So? Did you learn anything today?" But not my mother; "Izzy," she would say, "did you ask a good question today?" That difference — asking good questions — made me become a scientist.

Isidor Isaac Rabi

I love this quote by Isidor Isaac Rabi, a Ukrainian-born American physicist and Nobel laureate recognized in 1944 for his discovery of nuclear magnetic resonance. I applaud his mother for encouraging her son to ask "good" or effective questions in school. Why ask questions? Questions play a very important role in facilitating comprehension. They can help students develop their schemata, promote better understanding, and increase motivation. The questions we ask of students will influence what they learn in class. Questions should not be used as "time fillers" in class; instead, teachers should plan questions carefully. It is important that teachers ask questions that help students see relationships among ideas and concepts, and promote focused academic discussions in class. Questions asked before reading, give students purpose. Questions generated by students while they read, facilitate comprehension of text. Questions asked after reading can help monitor students' understanding of text and can also be used to challenge their thinking.

Asking "good" or effective questions is more important than knowing the right answer. Effective questions increase student engagement; they hook them, and raise their curiosity about learning. When students are meaningfully engaged, learning takes place. Most students are accustomed to answering questions at the end of the chapter, article, or activity. They usually skim the text, rush through the material, pick a word or idea here and there, rarely go back to the text to search for meaning or connections between ideas in a systematic and careful manner, and then try to answer the questions and be done—"getting done" is the driving force for many instead of "getting meaning." They don't even have time for alternative perspectives; they skip meaning, important details, and others' viewpoints. In a way, they are "trained" to do that— several years of schooling, a repeated focus on content, lack of opportunities to reflect on what they are reading and learning, and the endless battle with the clock, have cultivated the skimming approach to learning.

Our students have learned how to apply a textbook approach to questioning and they do not know how to implement an inquiry, a discipline-specific approach to questioning. In addition, many students come to class with varied academic and sociocultural experiences. Lisa Delpit, a well-known educator, has been writing for years about education and race. In her recent book, *"Multiplication is for White People." Raising Expectations for Other People's Children* (2012), she calls for students, especially students from low income socioeconomic backgrounds, to learn not to blindly accept what they read in books and just regurgitate facts. Instead, they need to learn to provide sufficient and clear arguments to support their thinking. Developing critical thinking skills is a goal for all, not just middle-class students, and learning to question is learning to wonder. As Grant Wiggins stated, "Students cannot possibly learn everything by the time they leave school, but we can instill in them the desire to keep questioning throughout their lives." (1989, p. 44).

Our students are used to answering "what" questions, finding basic facts, and identifying low-level information; they operate at the lowest levels of Bloom's taxonomy (1956) [and revised by Anderson & Krathwal, 2001], or classification levels of intellectual behavior. In other words, a lot of what we teach them and what they know how to do is reflected in the knowledge and comprehension levels of the taxonomy—our teaching and many of our assessments are based on those two lower levels. On the other hand, college and career readiness, as reflected in the CCSS and NGSS, call for learners who can competently (and independently) operate in the more advanced levels of thinking (i.e., application, analysis, creating/synthesis, and evaluation). Table 6.1 shows

TABLE 6.1.   Bloom's Revised Taxonomy and Questioning

Bloom's Taxonomy	Sample Questions
Creating • *create, construct, develop, plan, invent, change, design, produce, modify, propose*	• What is your theory about_____? • Construct a model that would change_____. • Predict the outcome of_____. • How would you modify the plan/experiment/ • design/plot/events_____? • What could be done to minimize/maximize/eliminate/prevent_____? • Propose an alternative solution to _____. • In what way would you design_____? • How would you test_____? • What is your original solution for_____? • Propose a model for_____.
Evaluating • *evaluate, appraise, judge/ critique, check, hypothesize, decide, defend, experiment, debate/argue, rank*	• What is your opinion about_____? • What would you recommend about_____? • How would you rate____? • How would you evaluate_____? • How would you prioritize/rank_____? • How would you justify_____? • What data/evidence did you use for your conclusion/appraisal of_____? • What criteria did you use to evaluate_____? • How did you assess the importance of_____? • Why did you select_____over_____?
Analyzing • *analyze, categorize, identify similarities/ differences, compare, classify, investigate, integrate, organize, distinguish, test*	• How is _____ related to_____? • What is the theme_____? • What inferences did you make about_____? • What conclusions can you draw about_____? • How would you classify/categorize_____? • What evidence can you provide about_____? • What are similarities/differences between_____ and_____? • What is the function of_____? • What is the pattern here? • How can you further investigate_____?

Applying
- *apply, use, construct, implement, practice, execute, model, transfer, experiment, solve*

- Show your thinking.
- How did you come up with this idea/solution/
- conclusion/experiment?
- How would you use_____?
- What examples/evidence can you provide to support_____?
- How would you use what you learned in_____?
- In what ways would you show your understanding of_____?
- What other ways would you plan to_____?
- What elements/factors would you change to_____?
- What questions do you have about_____?

Understanding
- *discuss, infer, expand, summarize, explain, clarify, interpret, give main idea, review*

- Summarize/State/_____.
- Restate/Paraphrase _____ in your own words.
- What is the main idea of_____?
- What can you say/
- explain about_____?
- What does the author mean by_____?
- Which is the best answer_____?
- Why is _____the best answer/solution/idea for_____?
- What facts/ideas support_____?
- What did you infer from the readings/
- presentations/resources about_____?
- Could you clarify
- about_____?

Remembering
- *define, recall, list, describe, recognize, recite memorize, locate, remember*

- Who/what/where is_____?
- Why did _____?
- When did _____?
- How is_____?
- How would you describe _____?
- How would you explain/show _____?
- What can you recall/remember/tell _____?
- What is the main idea?
- List 3 reasons for_____.
- Describe what happened.

Bloom's revised taxonomy of cognitive domain (Anderson & Krathwal, 2001) accompanied by sample questions per level.

In some of my classes, I have used a couple of YouTube video clips from the movie, *Ferris Bueller's Day Off* as examples of teacher monologue, how teachers can waste time in class (i.e., Ben Stein, the economics teacher, takes 10 minutes for attendance), lack of student engagement due to lack of background knowledge, lack of connections, and overall, lack of teaching! In one of the clips, Ben Stein is sharing information about economics. The class literally looks like they have "checked out"—some are bewildered, others look like they are listening to him speak in a foreign language, while some are sleeping or blowing bubble gum. In summary, none of the students are engaged; Ben Stein keeps talking and occasionally asks a couple of questions (i.e., the infamous, "Anyone, anyone?" question stem) and proceeds to answer them himself. This is indeed a humorous and very realistic representation of "learning" in some classrooms. In this learning framework, the teacher is doing all or most of the talking, and asking, and, actually, even most of the answering. Yes, there might be four or so students in a class who answer the teacher's questions, but what happens to the rest of the students in class?

One of the major shifts of the CCSS in thinking involves moving away from just single correct answers, to the possibility of multiple correct answers that are supported by evidence. This shift requires deep comprehension, moving away from mere memorization, simplistic thinking, and single perspectives to complex understanding and reasoning, and multiple perspectives. See Table 6.2 below for sample CCSS reading standards for grades 6–12 and the types of questions associated with those standards. The CCSS explicitly call for the development of students' comprehension, questioning skills, and habits of mind that will help them learn and succeed in school and beyond.

TABLE 6.2.   Sample CCSS Reading Standards and Related Questions

Reading Standards for Literature (Grade 6)	Related Questions
6RL2--Determine a theme or central idea of a text and how it is conveyed through particular details; provide a summary of the text distinct from personal opinions or judgments.	• What is the theme or central idea of this text? What details in the story/poem/drama help the reader determine this theme? • How does the author of this text help you understand the theme of the story? What details/evidence from the story support your answer? • How does the author use the way the protagonist responds to his situation to develop the theme of the story? • What is your summary of the story/drama/poem? Summarize without including personal opinions/judgments.
Reading Standards for Informational Text (Grade 7)	**Related Questions**
7RI5--Analyze the structure an author uses to organize a text, including how the major sections contribute to the whole and to the development of the ideas.	• How does the cause/effect structure contribute to the development of the author's central idea? Use examples from the article in your analysis. • In your view, why did the author decided to organize the text the way he or she did? Use information from the text in your analysis. • Is the structure of the paragraph(s) effective? Why or why not? Use examples from the article to support your analysis. • How do the major sections of the text contribute to the whole and to the development of ideas? Use examples from the article in your analysis.
Reading Standards for Literature (Grade 9)	**Related Questions**
9RL6--Analyze a particular point of view or cultural experience reflected in a work of literature from outside the United States, drawing on a wide reading of world literature.	• What is the author's point of view on this issue? Use evidence from the text to support your answer. • How is the author's cultural background and experiences reflected in _____ (a work of literature from outside the U.S.)? Use examples from the text in your analysis. • How is the author's viewpoint reflected in _____ (a work of literature from outside the U.S.)? Use examples from the text in your analysis. • Are there any biases or prejudices in the author's perspective about_____?

Reading Standards for Informational Text (Grade 10)	*Related Questions*
10RI3--Analyze how the author unfolds an analysis or series of ideas or events, including the order in which the points are made, how they are introduced and developed, and the connections that are drawn between them.	• How does the author organize his ideas/argument(s) in the text? How does he or she help you understand the connections between ideas or concepts presented in the text? Use examples from the text in your analysis. • What is the most likely reason the author presents a series of ideas in the order he/she does? Use examples from the text in your analysis. • How does the author develop his/her analysis of a concept in order to help you understand the material being presented? Use examples from the text in your explanation. • How does the author introduce, develop, and draw connections between ideas and events? Use examples from the text in your analysis.

Reading Standards for Literature (Grades 11–12)	*Related Questions*
11RL4--Determine the meaning of words and phrases as they are used in the text, including figurative and connotative meanings; analyze the impact of specific word choices on meaning and tone, including words with multiple meanings or language that is particularly fresh, engaging, or beautiful. (Include Shakespeare as well as other authors.)	• What does the word _____ mean in paragraph___? Why do you think the author used the word ____ in paragraph____? Which word(s) help you understand the meaning of _____ in paragraph___? What does the author's use of the word _____ reveal about his/her attitude/purpose toward the topic? Use examples from the text in your answer. • What is the tone of the text? How does the author create this tone? Use examples from the article in your analysis. • What does the phrase _____ (figurative language) mean? How does the use of that phrase enhance your understanding of the text? Use examples from the text in your answer. • What is the connotation of ____ as it is used in the text? How does the use of that word enhance your understanding of the text? Use examples from the text in your answer.

Reading Standards for Informational text (Grades 11–12)	*Related Questions*
11-12RI1--Cite strong and thorough textual evidence to support analysis of what the text says explicitly as well as inferences drawn from the text, including determining where the text leaves matters uncertain.	• What is the text stating explicitly about_____? Use evidence from the text to support your answer. • What message(s) or idea(s) does the author convey implicitly? Use evidence from the text to support your answer. • What questions remain unanswered in this text? Use evidence from the text to support your answer. • What would happen if_____? Use evidence from the text to support your answer.

Throughout this book, I have proposed a discipline-specific framework to learning in grades 6–12, and I have been presenting you with evidence and examples about the benefits of such a learning framework for college, career, and workforce readiness. So, in the context of deep learning in the disciplines that will prepare students for college, career, and the workforce, and also in the context of advanced educational standards (i.e., CCSS and NGSS), what role should questioning play in the preparation of students for school, college, and beyond?

What Makes a "Good" Question, "Good"?

What are the key characteristics of a "good" or effective question? Effective questions:

- Have more than one answer.
- Frame and focus inquiry efforts.
- Do not result in obvious and immediate answers.
- Are realistic, relevant, and important to the student's immediate and future learning.
- Promote persistence with reading and learning; they motivate the student to really want to find the answer.
- Challenge students to dig deeper and think more about what they read, about their understanding of a topic, and about their learning, in general.
- Facilitate connections among ideas and concepts and deeper understanding.
- Promote reflection, metacognition, going back to the text, conducting further research, and collaborating with others.

Maybe the questions I should ask are, "What questions do you want students to answer and learn about in your class?"; "Why do you ask the questions you ask of your students in your class?"; "What is your purpose with questioning them about the text, the topic, or something that happened inside or outside the class?" Effective questions will vary depending on the learning goal, the topic, and student characteristics. Usually, "good" questions are those that are clear, open-ended, and thought-provoking. They expand and challenge students' comprehension of text(s) and knowledge, and involve them in analysis, evaluation, collaboration, and synthesis. The CCSS require close reading of complex text. In Chapter 3, I presented the purpose and benefits of text-dependent questions and steps to constructing them. It is important to note that not all of the texts students are going to read are going to be complex. Close reading and text-dependent questions become particularly important for reading and comprehending complex texts because those types of texts do not explicitly state the meaning, ideas, or concepts.

"Good" text-dependent questions are not designed to seek "yes, or no" type answers. Instead, they are designed to challenge the reader, the text, and even the entire classroom's understanding of the text or topic at hand. They require time for the reader to go back to the text and seek evidence; in a way, they will make the reader linger over words, phrases, sentences, and paragraphs, and will help him or her discover new insights from the text. In addition, text-dependent questions will take some time for others to respond and engage in accountable talk.

Text-dependent questions can be used throughout the close reading of a text. They help the student read and examine the text, analyze the way the text is written, think about the author's word choices, and "slice and dice" the text for the purpose of building deep comprehension of the text and providing textual evidence to support his or her assertions. Here is an example of a non-text-dependent question: "In the Gettysburg Address" Lincoln says the nation is dedicated to the proposition that all men are created equal. Why is equality an important value to promote? (see www.achievethecore.org). On the other hand, a text-dependent question on the same issue would read as follows: "The Gettysburg Address" mentions the year 1776. According to Lincoln's speech, why is this year significant to the events described in the speech? (see www.acievethecore.org). The non-text-dependent question is distancing students from the text; they can answer this question using their background knowledge without reading the text. For students to answer the text-dependent question, they will have to think about 1776, the events that surrounded it, the decisions Lincoln made, and the connections between the year and the choice of words and concepts Lincoln used in his address. Chances are, students will have to go back to the text and they will also have to synthesize information, and present textual evidence to support their answer.

Text-dependent questions' goal is to keep the student inside the text for the purpose of figuring out the text. Use them to help facilitate deep understanding of text, to help students think outside of the text concepts and parameters, and to encourage them to make connections with other texts, concepts, or ideas. The goal is to use "good" questions to promote deep understanding that is transferable and applicable to new situations. Answering and generating text-dependent questions can facilitate critical thinking habits and evidence-based argumentation that includes, but also goes beyond, personal experience. Use text-dependent questions and encourage students to develop their own and use them to have engaging, accountable talk (see Chapter 8) in your classroom.

What Questions to Ask?

There are different types of questions. In each classroom there should be room for convergent and divergent questions (Ciardiello, 1998). Convergent questions involve straightforward, at times even literal, thinking and result in a single answer. When involved in convergent thinking, students consider material from a variety of sources to arrive at one "correct" or best possible answer. Convergent thinking emphasizes speed, accuracy, and logic whereas divergent thinking involves examining a problem from a variety of perspectives and discovering possible solutions to a given problem. It helps students see and follow the evidence and reasoning that led to the original expert opinion. Most of the thinking that takes place in schools is convergent, as school learning requires students to gather and remember information and make logical and appropriate decisions accordingly.

On the other hand, divergent thinking is creative, and it involves multiple solutions to problems; it is aimed at generating many diverse ideas about a topic in a short amount of time. Divergent thinking "asks" students to come up with their own understanding and ask their own questions. For example, thinking of different ways to solve an equation, design an experiment, or interpret an event are examples of divergent thinking. Divergent questions are critical in nature, involve speculative inferencing, and result in a range of answers. In many classrooms, the tendency is to ask many convergent questions. In addition, because students tend to like one word, simple, and clear-cut answers, they tend to complain and give up when a teacher asks divergent type questions. Even when teachers ask students to generate their own questions about a text or topic, they tend to generate convergent questions.

Closed or close-ended questions elicit short, usually one-word, responses (see Table 6.3) whereas open or open-ended questions prompt a long response or responses (more than one- or two-word answers). Close-ended questions use *when, where, who, is, can,* or *do* type question starters. On the other hand, open-ended questions starters begin with *why, what,* or *how*. For example, if you ask students "What do you like about the *Hunger Games*?" by Suzanne Collins (2008), they would respond in a variety of ways. Some would talk about the action, while others would focus on the love story. Yet, others would talk about the war and survival. There are many possible responses to open-ended questions (see Table 6.3); many times open-ended questions elicit new ways of looking at a text, problem, or phenomenon. Open or open-ended questions

TABLE 6.3.   Sample Close-Ended and Open-Ended Questions from Various Subject Areas

Discipline/Subject Area	Close-Ended Questions	Open-Ended Questions
Art	• What is a characteristic of charcoal you see in self-portrait B? • What are contemporary colors? • Who was Picasso? • What is impressionism?	• What did you think about the artist's choice of design principles in her artwork? • What is the message of this abstract sculpture? • What art elements "spoke" to you in this still composition? • If you could redesign any package of food to make it more visually appealing, what would you draw? What would be an example of changes you would make?
English Language Arts	• What is the title of this book/article? • Who is/are the main character(s)? • What is the setting of the story? • Who is the author of this text?	• What unknown or interesting words can you identify? • What do you think about the author's style? • What do you think will happen next in the story? • What did you like or dislike about the text?
Mathematics	• What is 10% of 300? • What is a triangle with three equal sides called? • Have you solved a problem like this before? • What is the Pythagorean theorem?	• What is this diagram saying? • What information do you have about the problem? • What is an alternative explanation or solution? • What patterns did you notice?
Physical Education	• What is aerobic exercise? • What is the difference between "warm" up and "cool" down? • What is this food consumption log "saying"? • What is the ideal body weight of a 5 foot, seven inches tall, 15 year old male and female?	• What is the relationship between flexibility and overall fitness? • Why is it important to follow PE safety practices? • What is an example of peer pressure? • How does conflict hinder team communication?
Science	• What is your hypothesis? • Who was Galileo? • What is an eclipse? • What is photosynthesis?	• What clues did you use to determine what this text is about? • What else might have caused_____? • What are the effects of environmental pollution on mankind? • How do astronomers measure distances to the stars? • How is _____ different than _____?

Social Studies	• What is your ethnicity? • What is a difference between democracy and monarchy? • Who was George Washington? • What is the 1st Amendment of the US Constitution?	• What did you learn about President's Lincoln's Assassination from these primary and secondary sources? • What questions do you have about Imperial Colonialism? • What were the effects of World War I on humankind? • What is the relationship between peace and stability in the Middle East and in the US?

also promote a respect for each student's perspective, ideas, and ways of thinking. They allow for multiple interpretations, stimulate student talk and interactions, and extend student thinking.

What are other types of questions? In the following section, I examine essential questions, Question-Answer-Relationships (QAR), self-questioning, and asking questions through a disciplinary lens.

Essential Questions

"Big ideas" are the fundamental and recurring themes of each discipline; they categorize and help us make sense of many (and at times seemingly unrelated) facts (Wiggins, 2010). For example, the study of biology includes the following big ideas: the cellular basis of life; information and heredity; matter and energy; growth, development, and reproduction; homeostasis; evolution; structure and function; unity and diversity of life; independence in nature; and science as a way of knowing. There are numerous questions associated with these big ideas. Essential questions can help students develop a thorough and deep understanding of each big idea.

Essential questions are the essence of the issue; they are broad, open-ended, guiding questions that provide the foundation or big ideas of a lesson; they frame effective instruction. They are important questions that require thinking beyond basic reading and understanding; they point to a greater issue or challenge, result in forming a decision, and tend to recur throughout one's life. They give teachers direction to what they are expected to teach and students a purpose for what they are expected to accomplish. Essential questions help organize content in a way that challenges what students have learned.

Essential questions help students understand the purpose or theme of the lesson, make connections between concepts or ideas, approach the answer in a variety of ways, expand their thinking, and guide inquiry and discussion. Essential questions are higher-order questions that often do not have a simple "yes" or "no," or "right" answer. They are meant to be argued, they promote student inquiry, stimulate rethinking of big ideas, assumptions, and prior lessons, ongoing collection of information or data, making connections among concepts, and focus on deep learning. Sometimes the question evolves and at times it could remain unanswerable. The term was introduced by Grant Wiggins and the *Coalition of Essential Schools* in the 1980s (Wiggins & McTighe, 1998) and since then it has been used for designing lessons and curricula. See Figure 6.1 for sample essential questions about academic and life issues.

Each academic discipline is characterized by its own, unique, essential questions. Essential questions used before, during, and after reading, will help students make connections with the big ideas of each discipline. For example, here is an essential question from a high school earth space science class: "To what extend is hydraulic fracturing/fracking helping or harming

- What kinds of questions do scientists ask?
- How does culture influence what and how we think?
- How do authors challenge our understanding of issues?
- Why do some communities rise above tragedy with grace and forgiveness while others cannot recover?
- What is the relationship between science and religion?
- What factors contribute to a healthy lifestyle and promote overall wellness?
- What are the characteristics of a good leader?
- What makes a country globally competitive?
- What is justice?
- Which political world figure (i.e., president, prime minister, leader), of the 20th century did the most to advance civil rights and liberties?
- What should be done to end childhood hunger in the US?
- What is the best way to deal with illegal immigration issues in US states that border with Mexico?
- What is the price of technological advancements?
- What can be done to protect our environment?
- What do people need to know and be able to do to learn, work, and live in the 21st century?
- How can you be ready for careers that do not exist, yet?

FIGURE 6.1.   Sample essential questions about academic and life issues.

humankind?", or "To frack or not to frack?" (to put it in plain terms). This essential question should also help students make connections with one of the big ideas in earth science, that of matter and energy, and how matter and energy affect our environment and impact our health, humankind, and the planet. Further study, research, and discussion on a topic many students do not think has any practical, or real life applications, will help them develop a deeper understanding of the material, what happens to our environment through hydraulic fracturing, how it impacts our groundwater, air, and climate conditions such as drought, and also make conceptual connections with big ideas in science.

What essential questions underlie the thinking of various experts? See examples of discipline-specific essential questions in Figure 6.2.

Arts
- Should we ever sensor artistic expression?
- How do people express themselves through art today?
- How do artists find inspiration?
- In what ways can we foster human creativity?

Health
- What is the relationship between wellness, fitness, and longevity?
- What prevents people from making healthy food choices?
- In what ways can we prevent eating disorders?
- How can drug use affect human learning?

Language
- What can we learn about our own language from studying another?
- In what ways are language and power connected?
- How can we effect social change through our words and actions?
- In what ways does effective communication affect our relationships?

Literature
- What is the relationship between popularity and greatness in literature?
- Is conflict an inevitable part of the human condition?
- How does our sense of self affect our relationships?
- Can literature effect social change?

FIGURE 6.2.   Sample discipline-specific essential questions.   *(Continued)*

Mathematics
- How does math help us make sense of the world?
- How can we create, test, and validate a model?
- How do we translate real world problems to algebraic expressions?
- How does math as a universal language help us to communicate?

Science
- How can organisms, places, and ideas change over time?
- What chemical processes underlie living things?
- In what ways can we safeguard our environment?
- How has the earth's surface changed?

Social Studies
- How are we connected to people in the past?
- Why should we recognize and seek multiple points of view?
- How should we balance the rights of individuals with the common good?
- What goods and services should the government provide?

Technology
- How can technology improve our lives?
- In what ways is technology affecting the learning process?
- What are ethical uses of technological advancements?
- How is technology effecting social awareness, justice, and human rights around the world?

FIGURE 6.2. Sample discipline-specific essential questions. *(Continued)*

Complex Questions

Students also need to grapple with complex questions. They need to think about, and discuss with others, questions that examine interrelated concepts, themes, and ideas that do not have immediate or tangible answers. Students need to grapple with questions that motivate them to think carefully and deeply about text, characters, events, problems, and issues. Complex questions do not have just one answer; the answers cannot be easily located in a literal fashion in the text; they require lots of inferencing about the text (or across texts) and lots of reflecting about their understanding as it is filtered through their personal experiences. At other times, in novels, characters might ask complex questions that expose their inner conflicts (Beers & Probst, 2013). For example, see the sample complex questions in CCSS text exemplars below (see Table 6.4).

Complex questions arise from each topic of study. They can be teacher- or student-generated, and can require a long time to answer; some will not have immediate or tangible answers. The point is to progressively engage students with complex questions, but before you construct them consider the complexity of the texts, the abstractness of some ideas, and student characteristics. Just like essential questions, complex questions can be examined over and over again as students build more complex schemata, build their background knowledge and comprehension strategies and skills, and develop their overall thinking skills.

Question-Answer Relationships

Question-Answer Relationships (QAR) is a framework for helping students understand how to self-question using different types of questions (Pearson & Johnson, 1978; Raphael & Pearson, 1982). Research has shown that QAR supports students' reading comprehension (Raphael, Wonnacott & Pearson, 1983), teaches them how to ask questions about the text (and images), and where and how to locate answers to them, and promotes critical thinking skills and metacognition (Buehl, 2001).

TABLE 6.4. Examples of Complex Questions for Sample CCSS Text Exemplars (Grades 6–12)

Grades 6–8 Text Exemplars	Complex Questions
Poetry: Hughes, Langston. *I, Too, Sing America*	• Why do you think Langston selected domestic imagery (i.e., the house, the kitchen, the eating, the table) to represent the theme of this poem? • How is "America" presented in this poem, and how does it make you feel about the country? How does this poem make you think about what it means to be an American? • How did Langston manage to address two periods in the same poem—America in the time of slavery and the America of 1994? How are those two periods similar? How are they different? • How does this poem reflect White and African Americans' relationships today?
Informational Text (Science, Mathematics, & Technical Subjects): Katz, John. *Geeks: How Two Lost Boys Rode the Internet Out of Idaho*	• What is Jesse Dailey's message to geeks in the following excerpt? ". . . It makes no sense to try, or even to want, to fit into a place where you don't belong. . . . It's not going to happen, and if it ever did, it's not what you would want anyway. . . . It's a delusion. The trick is to take something that's painful, and to make it so trivial that it's inconsequential. Just walk away and make it trivial. My advice to geeks? If you don't like it, leave, leave fast, make it trivial. Come to terms with who you are." (p. 3) • How does the author deal with paradoxes such as, connection and removal, alienation and community, or inclusion and exclusion in the book? • How can "life on the screen" be "real life"? • What message does this book offer for people who interact with the world through technology, and for relationships between mainstream and marginalized cultures?
Grades 9–10 Text Exemplars	Tough Questions
Stories: Steinbeck, John. *The Grapes of Wrath*	• Steinbeck portrays the powerful and the powerless during The Great Depression years (1930s). What similarities and differences can you identify between the migrant labor problem in the 1930s and in today's America? • What physical, emotional, social, and intellectual conflicts did you identify in the book? • Why do you think Steinbeck chose this book title, "The Grapes of Wrath?" • Which people in the book grow to see a larger purpose in life? What factors contribute to this shift in their perspective?
Informational Text (English Language Arts): Wiesel, Elie. *Hope, Despair, and Memory*	• In what ways did Wiesel's personal experiences impact his perspective about the importance of hope, despair, and memory in life? • Which aspect of Wiesel's speech affected you the most? What further questions did it raise for you? • How does Wiesel tie hope, despair, and memory together? • How did the world remain during the Holocaust? How has the world remained silent in recent genocide?

Grades 11-12 CCR Exemplars	Tough Questions
Drama: Wilde, Oscar. *The Importance of Being Earnest*	• In what ways is Wilde criticizing the Victorian society in this drama? • Wilde uses wit and humor to bring out which damaging effects of societal hypocrisies on people? • What are the (physical, intellectual, social, or moral) conflicts in *The Importance of Being Earnest*? How do these conflicts dominate this play? How does the final scene resolve all these conflicts? • Wilde uses a number of objects that gain more meaning as the action develops. Choose two of the following symbols: cucumber sandwiches, bread-and-butter, the German language, French music and language, "the chapter on the fall of the Rupee," bottles of champagne, teacake, muffins, and the capacious handbag. How do your choices relate to the plot and especially to the characters?
Informational Text (History/ Social Studies): McCullough, David. *1776*	• Why did McCullough choose to write about 1776? What is the significance of that time and events for American history and also for America, as we know it today? • What leadership qualities enabled George Washington to turn a lost cause into victory? What can today's political leaders learn from him? • Read the following excerpt: "Permit me then to recommend from the sincerity of my heart, ready at all times to bleed in my country's cause, a Declaration of Independence, and call upon the world and the Great God who governs it to witness the necessity, propriety and rectitude thereof." (p. 68). What impact did the Declaration of Independence have on the army and on the events that followed?

QAR can be used with narrative and informational text. Content area teachers can use QAR to develop students' ability to answer questions (Raphael & Au, 2005). QAR teaches students to use information sources: text and prior knowledge. In the context of the CCSS, close reading, and evidence-based argumentation, QAR can facilitate students' inferential skills (see Table 6.5).

The four question–answer relationships fall under the following two categories.

A. *In The Book:* Answers are usually literal and can be found in the text.
   1. "Right There" (or level I) Questions: these are literal questions whose correct answers can be found "right there" in the text (or website, video, etc.). Sample "Right There" question stems include: "What is . . .?" "When is . . .?" "Who is . . .?" "Where is . . .?" "How many . . .?" "According to the passage . . ." "Could you name or list . . .?"
   2. "Think and Search" (or Level II) Questions: the answer to these questions can be found from more than one phrase, sentence, or paragraph but it is stated in the text. Students have to put information together and think a bit more about how ideas are connected in the text. Sample "Think and Search" question stems include: "Could you describe . . .?" "What is the main idea of the passage?" "What caused . . .?" "What are similarities and

differences between . . ..?" "What do these details add to this story, text, or image?" "Can you explain . . .?" "Can you summarize . . .?" "What two examples from text can you use to support your statement?" "Could you calculate . . .?"

   B. *In My Head*: Answers are inferential and span beyond the text; they require connections between students' understanding of the text and his or her prior knowledge.

     3. "Author and Me" (or Level III) Questions: the answers are inferred; they require the readers to think about what they have read and formulate their own ideas. Sample "Author and Me" question stems include: "What does the author imply by . . .?" "What is the author's purpose?" "What is the tone of this text?" "What is the message of this text?" "How do you know . . .?" "What biases or beliefs did you identify in this text?" "How do you know . . .?" "What can you conclude about . . .?" "What inferences did you make about . . .?" "How could you differentiate between____ and ___?"

     4. "On My Own" (or Level IV) Questions: the answers to these questions are dependent on the reader's prior knowledge. Sample "On My Own" question stems include: "What is your opinion about . . .?" "Which character interests you the most?" "What do you know about . . .?" "Why do you believe . . .?" "Have you ever . . .?" "What does this remind me of?" "What conclusions can you draw from this text/image?" "What questions do you still have about . . .?"

See sample discipline-specific QAR examples in Table 6.6.

To teach students how to develop these question–answer relationships, consider the following steps. Keep in mind that the following sequence might take a few periods or weeks depending on student abilities and needs. In many secondary schools, QAR is part of everyday instruction. Use QAR not in a checklist, or in decontextualized way where students just label questions. In addition, use it in interdependent, not linear, ways—in other words, when constructing meaning readers do not start with literal information, then connect the dots, and finally come up with their own opinions. Last, a student might answer a question by using "Think and Search" and "Author and Me" when the information was actually "Right There." This is not a wrong approach; students will use the strategy differently than the teacher intended. "Right There" and 'Think and "Search" questions

TABLE 6.5.   QAR Example—8th Grade Human Body Unit

In the Book	In My Head
Right There: What is the circulatory system? The bodily system that consists of the heart, blood vessels, and blood that circulates throughout the body, carries nutrients and oxygen to the body's cells, and removes cellular waste (carbon dioxide).	*Author and Me: Why are sedentary people prone to cardiovascular problems?* Sedentary people do not get the recommended level of physical activity (30 minutes of walking five days a week). Long periods of physical inactivity raise people's risk of developing heart disease, diabetes, cancer, and obesity.
Think and Search: What are similarities and differences between, arteries, veins, and capillaries? Arteries carry oxygen-rich blood away from the heart. Veins carry blood containing waste products to different organs (kidneys, liver, etc.) and then back to the heart. Capillaries enable the exchange of water and chemicals between the blood and the tissues.	*On My Own: What are some strategies you can use to prevent cardiovascular disease?* Adhere to an exercise regimen, lower blood pressure, quit smoking, eat a heart-healthy diet, maintain a healthy weight, and get regular health screenings.

TABLE 6.6. Discipline-Specific QAR Examples

	Art	English Language Arts	Mathematics	Physical Education	Science	Social Studies
			In the Book			
Right There	What color is the moon in Van Gogh's *Starry Night*?	What was the Dust Bowl?	What are multiplicative inverses?	What does vigorous or moderate-intensity physical activity mean?	What is the circulatory system?	What was the Underground Railroad?
Think and Search	What are three main art elements Van Gogh used in *Starry Night*?	What do the images in Elizabeth Partridge's (2002) book, *This Land Was Made for You and Me: The Life and Songs of Woody Guthrie*, tell about life during the Dust Bowl, California during the Great Depression, and the people who fled Oklahoma?	What is the simple interest for $500 invested in a savings account at 3.25% for 3 years?	According to the author, what are three key health-related services all schools should provide to all students?	What are similarities and differences between, arteries, veins, and capillaries?	What are key differences between Islam and Christianity?
			In My Head			
Author and Me	What mood does Van Gogh try to arouse in *Starry Night*?	What message is Elizabeth Partridge trying to convey about Woody Guthrie's songs during that time of American history?	How would you represent this data using percents, decimals, and fractions?	How is the author trying to persuade you to become more physically active?	Why are sedentary people prone to cardiovascular problems?	What key services does local government provide for your community?
On My Own	If you were to choose three colors to make a painting, which ones would you choose and why?	What other musicians do you know who have used their voice or lyrics to give voice to the oppressed of their time?	What types of graphs do you suggest the basketball team uses to display information on the team's performance record (or statistics)?	If you could crate a more nutritious menu for your school cafeteria, what types of foods and drinks would you include and why?	What are some strategies you can use to prevent cardiovascular disease?	What project could you design to educate adolescents about the importance of voting?

will help students identify important information and make connections among ideas. "Author and Me" questions will help students evaluate text and reflect on their own learning. Teachers should adapt QAR to fit their discipline's goals and topics. Make sure that you provide sufficient feedback and hold class discussions where these and other situations can be examined. QAR will provide the teacher and students with a common language for building comprehension of text (Raphael & Au, 2005) and preparing for students to take tests. QAR steps include the following:

- Select a short passage from a narrative or informational text and read it aloud to students.
- Introduce related questions and explain how to generate and use questions to guide our thinking. Introduce the QAR questions and terms.
- Model how to use QAR with a text. Use a think-aloud to model the appropriate QAR strategy (i.e., in the text, in your head), how you located the information, and write the answer or say it aloud.
- Place students in groups of four or five and guide them to collaborate with their group members to use the QAR with the assigned text and related questions. Encourage students to think and explain their choice of QAR strategy.
- After students have had sufficient time, practice, and feedback with QAR, ask them to generate their own questions using QAR, and discuss their decisions and answers as a class.
- At all times, invite students to reflect on what they have learned and how to use QAR in this and in other classes.

Questioning the Author

Questioning the Author (QtA) is an approach to comprehension instruction that is designed to meaningfully engage students with the text and help them construct meaning from the text (Beck & McKeown, 2006; Beck, McKeown, Sandora, Kucan, & Worthy, 1996; Beck, McKeown, Hamilton, & Kugan, 1997). QtA allows teachers to ask specific questions of students that will help them create meaning and reflect on the text while they read. Through the use of classroom discussion, teachers will assist students in going beyond just sharing their opinions and ideas about a text they have read. Instead, teachers will engage students with *queries* that ask students to consider the meaning of the text and not just retrieve information (Beck, et al., 1997).

Queries are different from traditional questions in a number of ways. First, they are used during initial reading instead of before or after reading; they help the student develop meaning in the course of reading. Second, the teacher's role shifts from the question generator and evaluator to the discussion facilitator. Through queries, the teacher will be encouraging students to examine the author's ideas and also interpret and respond to one another's ideas about the text. QtA can change the classroom climate from a competitive, teacher-directed environment to a collaborative inquiry one. Last, QtA and query-driven classroom discussions facilitate student engagement, classroom discussions, and more comprehensive answers in the student's language.

There are three types of queries: initiating, follow-up, and narrative (see Table 6.7). Within each of these main types of queries there are specific prompts that are used to help launch a discussion, focus students in a specific area of the content, or focus students on a particular characteristic of the text. The main purpose of initiating query prompts is to help open up the discussion and help students identify the main messages or ideas presented by the author.

Follow-up queries promote connections among sections of the text and also between the reader's and others' ideas about the text; they help focus and direct class discussions. They will help students discover the difference between what the author "says" and what he or she means and how the author selects and "weaves" words and ideas to present his or her perspective on the

TABLE 6.7. Sample QtA Querries

Initiating Queries	• What is the author trying to say here? • What is the author's message? • What is the author talking about? • What do you think the author wants you to know?
Follow-Up Queries	• What does the author mean here? • Does the author explain this clearly? • Does this make sense with what the author told us before? • How does this connect to what the author told us here? • Does the author tell us why? • Why do you think the author tells us this now? • How is the author presenting the characters? • What is happening with the character(s) so far? • What is the author up to?

Narrative Queries	• Characters
	  ○ How do things look for this character now?
	  ○ What is the author trying to do with these changes in the character(s)?
	• Plot
	  ○ How has the author let you know that something has changed?
	  ○ How has the author settled this for us?

topic. Narrative queries follow and address narrative text structure, authorship, and purpose. These queries may often deal with characters, themes, how the author developed the plot and "molded" the characters to get his or her message across.

In order for students to feel able to construct meaning, through the use of QtA the teacher would need to assist students with understanding that the text is written by someone who is imperfect and has a particular purpose and viewpoint on the topic at hand, offer them specific, open-ended probes, and request that they consider those probes while they read, and provide opportunities for collaboration (Beck et al., 1996). By seeking to understand what the author is trying to say in a text and questioning the material during reading, students become more aware of their own meaning-making processes, and are actively engaged in constructing meaning from text (Beck et al., 1997).

How to Use the QtA Technique

The QtA technique has three main components: planning the implementation, creating queries, and developing discussions. Before you begin, select the text and decide what you want your students to understand or analyze from this text. Identify any potential difficulties in the text that might interfere with student comprehension (i.e., vocabulary, background knowledge, specific concepts or ideas, or text structure and organization). Chunk the text into manageable sections (i.e., a sentence, paragraph, or set of paragraphs that include an idea) and plan queries for each segment. Explain to your students that they will be taking part in a different kind of reading. Tell them that you understand that it will take time to adjust but that you will be with them every step of the way to help guide them through the new process of reading. Introduce the passage selection and clarify any difficult vocabulary before students read the text.

The second step should include deposing the authority of the text their students will be reading. The author may have a strong background in the subject matter, but the content may still not be expressed in the clearest or easiest manner. Letting students know that the content presented is someone's ideas, a regular person that can sometimes makes mistakes, will provide students the opportunity to understand they have the right to question the author. Tell students directly that it is fine for them to question the author and that you know this may be new for them.

Third, use a think-aloud about the text. Provide students with the opportunity to see parts of QtA modeled by first selecting a piece of text and then demonstrating the kinds of thoughts and considerations a reader should make when reading. When you first introduce the technique, do a read-aloud and provide students with a copy of the text so that they can follow along; over time, students can read the first segment silently and then discuss it with the teacher and others. The read-aloud will allow the teacher to stop at difficult or interesting parts, and speak aloud about anything that is confusing. Saying aloud when the author's writing is confusing, when it is clear, and how you are trying to figure it out what is meant is an important part to this mini-lesson. This will also provide students with an opportunity to share their own feelings about the text and add if it is confusing to them.

Fourth, after students have interacted with the text, a discussion should be initiated to help students note the features of the experience that just occurred. Some of the specific features include reading and stopping to consider what was read, noting any breakdown in the construction of meaning, thinking about what the author meant, why the author wrote that particular section, and why it is important to know. Last, upon completion of the think-aloud/discussion activity, take some time to explicitly tell your students that many of the techniques used today will be expected of them. Offer them support by going over some of the steps or doing another think-aloud/discussion in the following days. The goal is not to use the QtA with an entire, long, passage, but to equip the reader with a method of developing meaning from text as they read.

Using the QtA with short text selections and powerful modeling, feedback, guided practice, and class discussions, will make QtA use more student-initiated and directed over time. Teachers should remind and encourage students to use the same processes they used in QtA sessions when they read independently so they internalize this thinking process of building understanding from text as they read. Students should "pause occasionally during reading, ask themselves what's going on, consider what they have read, reread sections as needed, consider what connects to what and whether it all makes sense." (Beck & McKeown, 2006, p. 120).

How to Develop QtA Discussions

The teacher can help students develop meaning from text by using the following six QtA moves: marking, turning back, revoicing, modeling, annotating, and recapping (see Table 6.8 for examples of QtA moves).

TABLE 6.8.   Examples of QtA Moves

QtA Moves	Example
Marking	Student: "Poverty and unemployment also can cause crime in a society. Not having enough money or not knowing how make a living legally could cause some people to steal or hurt someone. Some people without money may feel like society's rules aren't working for them so why should they care?"
	Teacher: "So, what you are saying is that if some people feels society's rules aren't working for them, that the society has let them down through poverty or unemployment and as a result they are often less likely to obey the rules or laws of that society."

Turning Back

Teacher: "What is the author trying to tell us by writing about the barge that is full of trash that keeps floating up and down the coast?"

Student 1: "He's telling us no one wants the trash near them."

Teacher: "Is that a big deal—no one wanting or being able to dispose of the trash?"

Student 1: "Yes, we've got too much trash. I see bags and bags of it every Monday by the curbs in my neighborhood."

Student 2: "I don't understand why we have all this trash around. Almost everything is recyclable today. Everyone I know recycles their plastic, metal, and paper."

Teacher: "As Americans, do we recycle enough of our waste? What does the author tell us is the amount of waste we recycle?"

Student 2: "Oh, he does say it's only 27%. That isn't that much. It just feels like more to me because I see all those recycling bins around."

Revoicing

Student: "James Madison didn't get enough credit. He was important and put a lot of his ideas into the constitution. He liked the idea of government."

Teacher: "It seems you are saying that James Madison played an important role on the formation of our government and that many ideas like having a strong government were championed by him."

Modeling

Teacher: "What do you think the author is trying to tell us?"

Student 1: "He provides us a quote by Franklin Roosevelt about government. I think he's trying to tell us this lesson is going to be about government."

Teacher: "Why did the author use this quote?"

Student 1: "He might like using quotes. It's easier to write with quotes so you don't have to write the ideas yourself."

Student 2: "I think the quote is about government and that it matches what he's going to write about."

Teacher: "Those are interesting thoughts. When I read this quote I thought about how Roosevelt compares the three branches of government to three horses. I like that the author included this quote because it is easier for me to picture three horses than the judicial, legislative, and executive branches of government. Comparing the actions of the horses to actions of the government in the line "so that their field might be plowed" helps me understand that these branches are vital to the workings of our federal government."

Annotating

Teacher: "While it is true that Jefferson thought doubling the size of the United States a good thing, the author didn't tell us that Jefferson was not fond of the idea of having to purchase the Louisiana Territory from France. Having to purchase it would give the idea that France had a right to be in Louisiana."

Recapping

Teacher: "Yes, good thoughts here from everyone. You figured out from the text that in a market economy, individuals make major economic decisions and their thoughts on what should be produced, how much should be produced, and how it will be produced."

Marking involves the teacher highlighting an important part of a student's comment. In turning back, the teacher turns the students' attention back to the text for more information, clarification, or to correct a misunderstanding. Revoicing means using rephrasing or interpreting to help students clearly express what they are trying to say. In modeling, the teacher shows how he or she constructed meaning from text—it can be used especially when dealing with a difficult text or when the majority of the class is having difficulty understanding a text selection. The teacher may model or clarify a difficult passage, map out his or her thinking process, show how he or she used context clues, or draw a conclusion using different parts of information from the text. During annotating, the teacher provides information to fill in any gaps whether from the class discussion or from what the author failed to include in the text. This move is particularly useful when students do not have sufficient background knowledge to understand the author's message. Recapping involves the teacher highlighting and summarizing key points.

Reciprocal Teaching

Reciprocal teaching is a type of cognitive apprenticeship that is based on four strategies proficient readers use to comprehend text: predicting, questioning, clarifying, and summarizing (Palinscar & Brown, 1984). In a reciprocal teaching scenario, the group reads a text selection and group members take turns leading the discussion. In order for reciprocal teaching to be effective, certain instructional foundations must be in place. Teacher scaffolding provides readers the support they need in order to become successful at using all four strategies. Students view the teacher modeling each of the strategies, try the strategies out for themselves in a supported environment, and work independently using the strategies to comprehend text. At any time, students can and should receive teacher support, which helps them move through more difficult texts and reading tasks.

Start by explaining to students the four reciprocal teaching comprehension strategies (Duke & Pearson, 2002). Proficient readers predict before and during reading the text. Model how to make predictions looking at the title, author, illustrations, or graphics in the text. Model for students how to use what they have read or clues from text and images to help them predict what will happen next in the text. Proficient readers ask questions before, during, and after reading. Explain to students that questioning builds comprehension and model different types of questions. When proficient readers read something that does not make sense, they stop and clarify. After reading a text, proficient readers are able to recall and put in their own words important details and ideas from the text. Model for students how to summarize effectively.

Next, model the strategies through the use of think-alouds. Reciprocal teaching was designed as a discussion technique in which think-alouds play an integral part. During a think aloud, the reader talks aloud as they use each of the four strategies. Both teachers and students should conduct think-alouds each time they are engaged in reciprocal teaching lessons (Oczuks, 2003). Thinking aloud helps students clearly see the steps to creating understanding while reading and the teacher is able to see the reading processes the students are using. Provide guided and collaborative practice, scaffold student learning, and move toward independent use. Provide feedback as needed during small group and whole class discussions and monitor student progress.

Table 6.9 includes an example of how reciprocal teaching can be used in the classroom. In addition, another way to use reciprocal reading during small group time is in a group of four students, each student playing a different role (and switching roles over time)—e.g., the predictor, the questioner, the clarifier, and the summarizer. In this way, students can gain experiences with each type of strategy, play an active role in collaborative learning, and be accountable to one another for learning. Metacognition is an essential component of reciprocal teaching. Using the

TABLE 6.9. Reciprocal Teaching Example. Topic: The Coldest Journey: Sir Ranulph Fiennes to Undertake a Six-Month Antarctic Expedition at Temperatures of –90C

Prediction: Before you read this selection, look at the title or cover, the headings, find our who the author is, and look at any graphics or images. Make a prediction about the text.	
Prediction: *I think the article will be about the British explorer Sir Ranulph Fiennes' experiences, record, and future plans with Antarctic expeditions.*	**Support:** *The title, photos, and commentaries are about the oldest and greatest living explorer in the world.*
Main Ideas: After reading the text, what are a couple of main ideas in this text?	**Questions:** For each main idea listed, write down a question or two about it.
Main Idea 1: *Indeed, Sir Ranulph Fiennes is the greatest living explorer in the world. A six-month Antarctic expedition takes knowledge, experience, fearlessness, team skills, and lots of determination.* **Main Idea 2:** *There are many dangers involved with surviving one of the world's most inhospitable environments.*	**Question 1:** *Do the benefits of expeditions outweigh the dangers and losses? Explain.* **Question 2:** *How long would one train to be able to participate in such an expedition?* **Question 3:** *How do the severe weather conditions and isolation affect people psychologically?* **Question 4:** *What are some contributions of these expeditions for science?*

Summarize: *Crossing the Antarctic Continent is a significant achievement! The 68 year old British explorer lead a team in 2012 on foot across the Antarctic during the coldest time of the year. The team will carry out measurements for scientists and will collect data on marine life, oceanography, and meteorology. Sir Ranulph Fiennes has dedicated his life exploring the world's most remote regions. He has an amazing record and has been helping us understand what it takes to cross Antarctica and how important it is that we continue to learn about it.*

Clarify: Select words, phrases, or sentences in the passage that are unclear. Then explain how you clarified your understanding.

Word or Phrase:	**Clarify:**
1. inhospitable terrain 2. equinox 3. "Between 1979–82 he circumnavigated the world via both Poles."—what does this mean?	1. I used context clues that described the Antarctic terrain and I understood how difficult it is for humans to survive there. 2. I had to look it up in a dictionary—Either of the two points on the celestial sphere where the apparent path of the Sun crosses the celestial equator. 3. He went completely around the world—I used context clues; I thought about the two Poles.

Source: Article retrieved from: http://www.dailymail.co.uk/news/article-2204415/Sir-Ranulph-Fiennes-undertake-month-Antarctic-expedition-temperatures-90C.html.

reciprocal teaching strategies, students learn to consciously think about, monitor, and reflect on their strategy use. Throughout instruction, students should engage in reflective thinking and answer the question, "How did the reciprocal teaching strategies help me comprehend the text?"

Student-Generated Questions

Why should you teach students to generate questions? Questions stimulate new ways of analyzing, evaluating, and thinking; they generate new questions. Self-questioning shifts the control to the students; it gives them the responsibility to generate questions they could use to question others in class, to further discuss the topic, or questions they could raise about what they do not understand or would like to learn more about. How can you help students learn how to generate questions? First, question formulation involves the expression of ideas; it can lead to new ideas, more engagement, problem solving, and more responsibility for one's own learning. Many students say that they don't know what to ask; when they do come up with a question they often ask, "Is this the right one?" "Is this what you wanted?" Although finding the "right" answer is important, finding what questions are "right" to the reader in the context of various texts and situations might be more significant. Teaching students how to formulate questions can easily be part of classroom practice. In the context of new educational standards and a global need for solving problems that affect the entire planet, generating (not just answering) questions could also be viewed as a means of college, career, and workforce readiness.

Self-Questioning Strategy

Table 6.10 includes an example of a self-questioning strategy I developed to promote comprehension of text. This strategy combines questions that follow the goals, structure, and habits of mind of science and is also aligned with Bloom's revised taxonomy of the cognitive domain (Anderson & Krathwal, 2001). This strategy aims to help the student to (a) critically question what he or she is reading and understanding from science text; (b) question the author's purpose and credibility; (c) provide textual evidence for all answers; (d) make connections among concepts and ideas from this and other topics examined so far; (e) reflect on his or her knowledge about the topic; and (f) seek further examination of the topic. This strategy can be used across subject areas. Teachers should model it, discuss it with students, and use it with various pieces of text collaboratively before students use it independently. It is packed with many critical thinking skills that require class discussions, feedback and guidance from the teacher, and practice.

TABLE 6.10. Self-Questioning Strategy—Science Example (Grades 6–8)

Topic: Electromagnetic Spectrum	*Class/Period: Ms. Wilson—4th period* *Name: Ryan Millford Date: 2–20–2013*
1. What 3 key pieces of information do I need to know about this topic? *(Remembering)*	*1. An electromagnetic wave is made up of electric and magnetic fields that move through space (or some medium) at the speed of light.* *2. Electromagnetic waves travel at the same speed in a vacuum but have different wavelengths and frequencies.* *3. An electromagnetic spectrum is made up of radio waves, microwaves, infrared rays, visible light ultraviolet rays, X-rays, & gamma rays.*

2. What does the author want me to understand about the topic? Present evidence (include page #s or quotes as needed). *(Understanding)*	*To understand the properties of electromagnetic waves; to learn how they are similar and different; to tell how waves make up the electromagnetic spectrum (p. 286).*
3. What do I need to do to better understand what the author is telling me about the topic? *(Applying)*	*Explain to my parents how microwaves work. How do microwaves work? How come the doctor can see my bones using X-rays? Why do astronauts have to wear space suits? How come the doctor could tell I had broken my ankle when he looked at my X-ray?*
4. How is this information similar (or different) from other material I have read on the topic? *(Analyzing)*	*Similar:* • *Energy exists in many forms.* • *Our eyes can see light because they are sensitive to this frequency.* *Different:* • *Waves transfer energy without a transfer of matter.* • *Light waves can travel through light and through matter.*
5. What evidence does the author present for his or her assertions? *(Evaluating)*	*Examples, graphs and pictures, reports from NASA.*
6. How has this information changed what I understand about the topic? *(Creating)*	*Our lab experiment helped me better understand how light waves interact with matter.*
7. 1 question I still have about the topic.	*If gamma rays diagnose and treat cancer, why do we have an increase in cancer rates?*

Question Formulation Technique

Question Formulation Technique (QFT) (Rothstein & Santana, 2011) can be used to teach students to formulate their own questions. QFT includes four steps: (1) produce questions, (2) improve questions, (3) prioritize questions, and (4) use questions. What can these steps do for student thinking, collaboration, and co- construction of knowledge?

First, QFT promotes metacognition (thinking about one's own thinking and learning). Second, these four steps facilitate habits of mind that will help students ask as many questions as they can about a topic, learn to be open to others' ideas, differentiate between statements and questions, turn statements into questions, know the difference between closed and open-ended questions, transform closed-ended questions into open-ended questions, and reflect on questions. Last, as students learn to ask their own questions, they delve deeper into their understanding of topics or issues, make connections, and assume greater ownership of their learning.

The QFT (Rothstein & Santana, 2011) results in an interplay between the teacher and students in class in the following ways: (1) the teacher designs a question focus and asks the students to formulate questions using the rules for generating questions; (2) students think about the questions they generated and improve them; the teacher sets the rules for prioritizing questions and students rank the top three questions; and (3) the students use the questions and move on to learning more about the topic, text, or project at hand. The focus of the following example I developed is on Franklin Delano Roosevelt's (FDR's) State of the Union Address, 1941; the speech is available in Appendix B of the CCSS (see http://www.corestandards.org/assets/Appendix_B.pdf, p. 124). My goal is to demonstrate how to use the QFT (Rothstein & Santana, 2011) to teach students to generate "good" questions.

Roosevelt, Franklin Delano. "State of the Union Address." (1941)

For there is nothing mysterious about the foundations of a healthy and strong democracy. The basic things expected by our people of their political and economic systems are simple. They are:

Equality of opportunity for youth and for others.
Jobs for those who can work.
Security for those who need it.
The ending of special privilege for the few.
The preservation of civil liberties for all.
The enjoyment of the fruits of scientific progress in a wider and constantly rising standard of living.

These are the simple, basic things that must never be lost sight of in the turmoil and unbelievable complexity of our modern world. The inner and abiding strength of our economic and political systems is dependent upon the degree to which they fulfill these expectations.

Many subjects connected with our social economy call for immediate improvement. As examples:

We should bring more citizens under the coverage of old-age pensions and unemployment insurance.
We should widen the opportunities for adequate medical care.
We should plan a better system by which persons deserving or needing gainful employment may obtain it.
I have called for personal sacrifice. I am assured of the willingness of almost all Americans to respond to that call.

A part of the sacrifice means the payment of more money in taxes. In my Budget Message I shall recommend that a greater portion of this great defense program be paid for from taxation than we are paying today. No person should try, or be allowed, to get rich out of this program; and the principle of tax payments in accordance with ability to pay should be constantly before our eyes to guide our legislation.

If the Congress maintains these principles, the voters, putting patriotism ahead of pocketbooks, will give you their applause.

In the future days, which we seek to make secure, we look forward to a world founded upon four essential human freedoms.

The first is freedom of speech and expression—everywhere in the world.

The second is freedom of every person to worship God in his own way—everywhere in the world.

The third is freedom from want—which, translated into world terms, means economic understandings, which will secure to every nation a healthy peacetime life for its inhabitants-everywhere in the world.

The fourth is freedom from fear—which, translated into world terms, means a world-wide reduction of armaments to such a point and in such a thorough fashion that no nation will be in a position to commit an act of physical aggression against any neighbor—anywhere in the world.

Step 1: Produce Questions

First, before students can generate questions, establish the rules associated with this process. Encourage students to write down as many questions as they can think of about FDR's speech. There is no need to stop, think, discuss, or address anyone's questions (no matter how easy, difficult, or peculiar) at this point. Students can record their questions in their journal or notebook. They can also use statements and turn them into questions. At the beginning students may act frustrated or confused about the task simply because they are used to having the teacher generate all of the questions; in their view, the teachers tells you what to think, what to learn, or what to ask and the student's role is to do it. Through a classroom discussion, help students understand the expectations associated with generating questions. Following these rules for generating questions will help get the process flowing.

Second, place students in groups of four to six depending on your class size. Small group work will facilitate more targeted dialogue and interactions. A student either volunteers, or is selected, to act as a group scribe; he or she, is the one who will record (and contribute to) the group's questions. Last, the teacher will give students the question focus, meaning the only topic or item they are allowed to generate questions about. The question focus helps keep them absorbed, fixated, or concentrated on that topic only. The teacher will write the question focus on the board or on an overhead sheet, will give students a few minutes and will monitor their time (about five minutes) and discussions, and will also remind them of the question generating rules. The question focus, of course, will vary according to task, topic, text, or project. The question focus needs to a) be clear; b) not reflect the teacher's preference or bias; c) stimulate diverse thinking and discussion; and d) not be stated as a question because the goal is to invite students to generate their own questions. Using FDR's 1941 speech, after students had read it on their own, I gave them the following question focus: "Freedom of speech, freedom of worship, freedom from want, and freedom from fear are universal rights." See sample student-generated questions below.

- Who is giving this speech?
- Who is the audience of the President's State of the Union Address?
- Where was the speech given?
- When did F. D. Roosevelt (FDR) give this speech?
- Did FDR have to say what he said in his speech?
- Was America in war in the 1940s?
- Was the world in war in the 1940s?
- Did FDR's speech influence the moral climate of the world in the 1940s?

- Was his speech about the Four Freedoms important to America in 1941?
- Was his speech about the Four Freedoms important to the world in 1941?
- Is FDR's Four Freedoms message important to America today?
- Is FDR's Four Freedoms message important to the world today?
- Were freedoms lost in the 1940s?
- Were some nations being aggressive against others in the 1940s?
- Who was the main world aggressor in the 1940s?

Step 2: Improve Questions

Now that students have generated some questions, what's next? Ask them to look at the questions they generated—what is the message of their questions? What type of questions did they generate? Open- or closed-ended questions? Higher order or literal questions? Easy or complex questions? Rhetorical, factual, or hypothetical questions? Having a class discussion on the types of questions students generated and on the kinds of information each type of question can produce will be helpful to students to reflect and think further about questions, thinking, and learning. During this phase, explain to students what open- and closed-ended questions are, what are their advantages (in terms of what information they can provide), model how to change questions from one type to another, and give them time to categorize their questions. For example, "Did FDR have to say what he said in his speech?" to "Why did FDR choose to say what he said in his speech?" Students can also review their questions and mark them as "O" for open-ended and "C" for closed-ended. A class discussion can follow on categorizing and evaluating each other's questions and selecting which open-ended and closed ended questions to complete. See sample improved (open-ended) questions below.

- What was FDR's State of the Union Address about?
- What was happening with the American economy in the 1940s?
- What was happening with American medical care in the 1940s?
- How were these freedoms relevant to America's political and economic system in 1941?
- Why did FDR address four specific freedoms?
- What do you think about the Four Freedoms? Are they all a "good" idea? Are they possible?
- What turmoil in the world was FDR talking about?
- What was the world facing in 1940s?
- Why was peace around the world especially important in 1941?
- Why do you think FDR placed so much emphasis in his speech on personal sacrifice and on Americans to respond to that?
- Why did FDR call for four specific immediate improvements in America's 1941 economy?
- Why did FDR ask Congress to put "patriotism ahead of pocketbooks"?
- How would the freedom of speech make America a stronger and healthier country in the 1940s?
- Why was the freedom of worship essential to democracy in the 1940s and why is it important now?
- How would freedom from wants make America a stronger and healthier country in the 1940s?

Step 3: Prioritize Questions

This is the phase where more critical thinking, metacognition, collaboration, and fun can all take place. The ability to prioritize tasks, thinking, ideas, steps, etc. is vital to learning, problem solving, and living. Students in school, college, work, and life will have to organize their thinking, time, resources, or finances, and will have to think about prioritizing steps, projects, experiments, decisions, etc. Prioritizing is an important skill to college, career, and workforce success—one many students do not have. Many do not know how to rank the steps to writing an essay or conducting a lab experiment. Prioritizing questions according to importance will not be easy for many students. To learn to do so, they will need many experiences with different texts and tasks, scaffolded support, and opportunities to compare, reflect, evaluate, negotiate, and decide on which questions, from all available ones, are the most important for their understanding of the topic.

How can you help students prioritize their questions? First of all, the students need to do the prioritizing, not the teachers. The teacher can play the role of the facilitator, one who asks questions about the prioritizing students make, but at the same time remaining neutral about their choices. The teacher can remind students of the criteria for selecting priority questions, and monitor the small and whole group discussions on the types and number of questions they select. It is essential that students continue to work in groups and are given time to go back to the text, review their questions, think about what they know and what they need to learn, and then select or rank their questions.

Ask students to select the top three questions from their list. Which ones can qualify as top ones? Any of the following criteria can be used and modified depending on the purpose of the activity, the expected outcomes, and where the students are with their knowledge of questioning and content. Students can choose the three most important questions; meaning the ones that will provide the most critical information about the text, topic, project, or task, or the top three questions that are measurable, or even those that will help you develop a successful experiment. The criteria will vary according to content area, topic, and task. Students can also select the top three questions that most interest them (this will address choice, motivation, and engagement). Many times students have difficulty selecting only three questions; with more practice and evaluation of the types of information each question provided them with, students will continue to learn how to generate, improve, and prioritize questions.

I have used both sets of criteria for different reasons. At times I asked students to select the three most important questions for our knowledge of the topic, or completion of the project. On other occasions, I asked them to select the top three questions they are interested in and explain why and how they'd add to their knowledge or project success. Next, students review their questions and select the top three ones. They then have to get into an agreement with their group about their choices, and discuss, explain, negotiate, and come to a consensus about the top three choices. As a group, they have to explain their reasoning for their ranking to the entire class. If you wish, you can have further voting and agreement across groups on the top three questions the entire class will explore. This further analysis, comparison, and evaluation of questions stimulates more engagement with the topic, more collaboration, and more evidence-based thinking. See the prioritized questions on the topic below.

- What was FDR's State of the Union Address about?
- Why did FDR address Four specific Freedoms?
- How were these freedoms relevant to America's political and economic system in 1941?

Step 4: Use Questions

Aside from generating questions, even "good" ones, what else can students do with the questions they formulated? Is the purpose of student-generated questions to only help them deeply understand a topic, text, or project? Yes, students need to engage with learning, and we wish for them to develop deep understanding of text/topic. In addition, they need to learn from their own thinking (metacognition) and from their peers' thinking and knowledge. Finally, students need to approach a new topic of study, a text, and a research project, or experiment with their own questions, and not just respond to teacher-generated questions.

When students reflect on their own knowledge and understanding, on their own questions, on others' ideas, and on the overall learning process, they develop a deeper understanding and a different mindset about learning. Creating a classroom of inquiry will motivate and prepare students to pursue their own interests and use their creativity to improve and present their work. See sample reflective questions that can stimulate further learning and application on the topic below:

- What makes a society healthy, moral, and strong?
- What does freedom mean to you?
- What does freedom of speech, worship, want, and fear mean to you?
- Which freedom is most important to you? Why?
- Is it possible for everyone in the world to have the four freedoms? Why/ Why not?
- Is FDR's speech as relevant today as it was in 1941? Please explain.
- What were the effects of Roosevelt's Four Freedom ideas on the Atlantic Charter declared by Winston Churchill and FDR in August 1941, on the Universal Declaration of Human Rights (1948), and on what is known today as the United Nations (1942)?
- How is our current President's administration measuring up to FDR's Four Freedoms?
- What can we as citizens do to help maintain a healthy, moral, and strong America today and in the years to come?

The ultimate goal of all teachers is to help students become independent thinkers and learners and prepare them to succeed in school, college, career, and life. Students need to learn to generate, evaluate, and reflect on their questions (and those of others), to consider others' viewpoints, to communicate and collaborate, to use evidence to support their thinking, and to problem solve in academic and real-life contexts. The reflection process of this last stage of the QFT (Rothstein & Santana, 2011) is very important; do not skip it. Plan for it to happen in your classroom, and discuss with students not only what they learned but how they can use their questions in other courses and situations. Ask students to reflect on what they learned about FDR's State of the Union (1941) speech, about America and the world in the 1940's, about their understanding of these events for 1941 and for now, about generating, improving, prioritizing, and using questions, and about learning from and with others in class. And, encourage them to continue to use their question generating skills in all courses, and in learning in general.

The QTF can be used in other content areas. For example, in a health education class, the teacher may focus the QFT on cigarette smoking to guide students' research on the topic and encourage them to generate questions about it from the text(s) and their research. A mathematics teacher may ask students to not only explain the steps they took to solve a problem, but to also generate as many questions as possible about the problem-solution process and alternative ways to solve it. A science teacher may choose to focus on the "Radiation effects from the 2011 Fukushima Daiichi Nuclear Disaster on Japan today" to guide their research on environmental pollution.

All content area teachers need to put the students in the "driver's seat," and support and mentor them as they navigate their own learning journey. Remember what you have been learning in this book? Reading and learning are apprenticeship processes with you, the classroom teacher, as the mentor, and your students as your apprentices. Yes, it will take some time for them to start developing the mindset of generating, evaluating, negotiating, and reflecting on their questions and understanding, but it sure is worth it. These are core skills and core habits of mind and dispositions students need to develop in secondary grades to prepare them for the learning demands of college, career, and the workforce.

Think Like an Expert

- Literary experts ask many questions when they read. They question who is speaking, what is the intended audience, what is the author's background and how his or her background affects the writing, how language is organized and presented, how the author presents the characters and conflict(s) in the text, and how this work relates with other similar works on the subject. They also engage in problematizing the topic of the novel by raising critical questions about the text, the author, its message, and the impact of the work on humanity. (English Language Arts)
- Mathematicians use inductive reasoning to solve new problems; they ask many questions and take risks. Students need to learn multiple ways to solve and represent problems, explain their steps to solving the problem, and consider others' approaches to solving the problem. To solve mathematical problems accurately, students need to have good understanding of mathematical content, thought, and language. (Mathematics)
- Scientists also ask many important questions. They often ask questions about the significance, validity, accuracy, and soundness of other scientists' work. Scientists do that because they are skeptical about other scientists' work. They are often skeptical of others' work and invest much time on examining the implementation of the scientific method, the use of hypothesis and data collection, and carefully examining the conclusions others draw about their research. (Science)
- Historians are deeply involved in historical explanation; they question everything and everyone. They compare, contrast and evaluate evidence from multiple documents (cross-checking) as it relates to setting and time (contextualization), perspective (sourcing: who made it, when, why, and is it believable?), and use corroboration among primary and secondary sources and others' interpretations. (Social Studies)

Discipline-Specific Habits of Mind and Questioning

Throughout this book I have been discussing the importance of developing students' discipline-specific knowledge, skills, and habits of mind. I have presented much evidence that supports the development of ways of thinking and knowing that are unique and essential to each discipline, to reading, writing, inquiring, learning, communicating, and writing in ways that promote further engagement and learning (Shanahan & Shanahan, 2008, 2012; Zygouris-Coe, 2012a, 2012b).

Effective questions, questioning text, questioning others and one's self-knowledge, can help shape students' reading, thinking, studying, and learning behaviors; in a way, they can produce ways to read and learn that are helpful and specific to each discipline. Every teacher wants his or her students to be attentive as they read, engage with texts, discussions, and learning, to take responsibility for themselves, and to reflect on what they are learning. All students should ask important questions, and be willing to share and revise their thoughts or conclusions in conversation with others.

Table 6.11 shows the different lenses sample disciplinarians use—i.e., how they read and think, what questions they ask, and how they write, and communicate. In literature, authors question others' interpretations. Mathematicians' questions focus on problem-solution, accuracy, and explanations. For example: What is the question you are trying to answer?; What information do you have that can help you answer the question?; What information do you need to answer the question? How could you show the information in the problem a different way? How is this problem like another problem you've solved? Scientists question hypotheses, data, solutions to

TABLE 6.11. **Disciplinarian Experts' Habits of Mind**

Authors (ELA)	Historians (Social Studies)
How do they read and think? • Do close reading of texts. • Read a lot and from various genres. • Appreciate texts. • Pay attention to, and analyze text elements and structures. • Analyze literary elements and types of genres. • Seek to construct meaning from texts. • Think analytically and creatively. • Make connections. • Identify and represent problems, conflicts, and solutions. • Make interpretations using evidence from multiple sources; include perspective-taking. • Use literacy criticism. • Are persistent, curious, flexible, and reflective.	**How do they read and think?** • Do close reading of texts (images, and artifacts). • Carefully examine source information/evidence and multiple viewpoints (sourcing). • Understand Historical context (contextualization). • Analyze primary and secondary sources; compare and contrast; recognize cause-effect. • Read multiple accounts and perspectives (corroboration). • Look for connections and biases among sources. • Evaluate interpretations. • Use evidence to support claims.
What questions do they ask? • Who is the author/speaker? • Who is the audience? • What is the author's purpose? • What, who, when, where, why, how? • What is the big idea? • What is happening? • What is the significance? • What is the conflict-resolution? • What is/are cause(s)-effect(s)? • What arguments does the author use? • What figures of speech, style and tone does the author use?	**What questions do they ask?** • Who, what, where, when, why, how • What matters and why? • What were key causes-effects? • What counts as evidence? • What has changed (or has not)? • How does the past help us make sense of the present? • Whose perspective is represented (under-, mis-, or missing)? • Ask evidence-based questions.
How do they write? • Use language beautifully and creatively. • For different purposes and audiences (describe, inform, entertain, persuade). • Independently and collaboratively. • Systematically.	**How do they write?** • Identify a topic of interest and focus on it. • Do lots of research; gather evidence from trustworthy sources; find supporting evidence for argument. • Pay attention to purpose, context, audience, and clarity. • Avoid restating or paraphrasing others' ideas—they add personal interpretation of historical facts/evidence. • Cite evidence (specific, exact) to support arguments. • Peer review of writing. • Revise and edit.
How do they communicate? • Orally (language). • Through writing. • Media, technology. • With others.	**How do they communicate?** • Oral communication. • Writing/Publications. • Historical analysis. • Media and technology.

Mathematicians	Scientists
How do they read and think?	*How do they read and think?*
• Do close reading of text and math proofs.	• Do close reading of texts and data.
• Slowly, examining all information, precisely.	• Read critically—do not automatically accept others' conclusions.
• Analyze information and proofs and look for connections.	• Do scientific process analysis.
• Seek patterns and logical explanations.	• Identify the question.
• Make predictions.	• Collect information/data.
• Describe, compare, investigate, interpret, and explain results.	• Form hypothesis.
• Problem-solve.	• Test hypothesis.
• Are persistent and methodical thinkers.	• Design experiment, establish procedures.
• Are reflective.	• Observe and record data.
	• Make evidence-based conclusions, arguments.
	• Communicate results.
What questions do they ask?	*What questions do they ask?*
• Why?	• Why? How?
• Is it clear?	• What methods to use?
• Do I understand what is asked?	• What prior work affected current events?
• What is the overall pattern of . . .?	• How did other scientists examine topic/issue/problem?
• Can you justify your statements?	• What empirical evidence did one cite?
• Can you explain your process/steps taken to solve . . .?	• Are the experimental data sufficient/convincing?
• Did you investigate every variable?	• Were data analyzed and interpreted fairly?
• Did you notice anything unusual?	• What are implications?
• Did you identify any patterns?	• What is/are cause(s)-effect(s)?
• Can you prove . . .?	• What are major conclusions?
• Are conjectures supported by evidence?	
• What can be done to improve or change . . .?	*How do they write?*
	• Use the scientific method.
How do they write?	• Cite evidence.
• Write a lot; write well; write precisely.	• Keep science notebooks (anecdotal notes, facts, observations, questions).
• Write coherent reports.	• Write about experiments, data, and thinking.
• Provide details; explain steps, solutions.	• Revise and edit.
• Write math proofs clearly and logically.	
• Take notes, write summaries, and descriptions.	*How do they communicate?*
• Keep journals.	• Writing/Publications.
	• Media and technology.
How do they communicate?	• Exhibitions/demonstrations/simulations.
• Use everyday and mathematical language to communicate.	
• Express ideas clearly verbally and in writing.	
• Solve real world problems.	
• Through reports and proofs.	
• Verbally summarize.	
• Explain advantages/disadvantages of each method or solution orally and in writing.	

(Continued)

TABLE 6.11. (Continued)

Artists: Musicians	Health and Fitness Experts
How do they read and think? • Recognize that music is the key to reading well. • Read horizontally and vertically at the same time. • Read music notation (i.e., the representation of sound with symbols, from basic notations for pitch, duration, and timing, expression, timbre, and special effects). • Read rhythm, note durations, and time signatures. • Read notes, keys, and spaces. • Notice emerging patterns. • Read ahead several bars, recognize the music, and play it while at the same time anticipate what is about to happen in the coming notes. • Move slowly and fluidly from note to note. • Listen carefully and critically to others' music and learn from other musicians and composers.	*How do they read and think?* • Read carefully, analyzing words and data. • Analyze data, reports, and results. • Examine evidence. • Collect information/data from a variety of sources. • Form and analyze hypotheses, procedures, multiple factors, measurements, instruments used, and results. • Question claims and evaluate the data/ evidence to support them. • Collect data over time. • Think of ways to improve performance, health, and fitness.
What questions do they ask? • Did the music catch the listener? • How did the composer use the notes to make music enjoyable for the listener? • What increased the power of the music? • How do I compare to other artists? • How creative is the piece or performance? • What is the quality of the artistic expression? • What is the technique? • How did the music represent the culture?	*What questions do they ask?* • What happened? How? How fast? What was the time/performance? • What methods were used? • What has been done to address the issue? • What data was used to propose a different approach? • What are cause-effects? • What factors interact with the result/ performance? • What are implications for health and fitness?
How do they write? • Write in notes, keys, symbols, and spaces. • Express their ideas, feelings, and emotions through music. • Write lyrics, melody, note length, and timing. • Think about the audience, message, purpose, and context. • Use music composition software. • Write and re-write. • Practice writing music.	*How do they write?* • Collect observations, field notes, and data. • Write research and other reports. • Cite evidence. • Keep careful, accurate records. • Use informational/explanatory and argumentative writing.
How do they communicate? • Through performance and critique. • Express emotions, feelings, intentions, and their interpretations of human phenomena and complex ideas through music. • Use artful delivery as a medium. • Playing instruments, singing, composing, and conducting. • Employ a variety of technical means and cognitive techniques.	*How do they communicate?* • Sharing plans, studies, and results. • Creating models to promote health and fitness. • Research data and advancements. • Media and technology.

problems, and accuracy of evidence. Historians question perspective and point of view and the validity and quality of evidence in interpretations of the past.

To use questioning effectively, think about the questions you are asking, why you are asking them, ask questions of all students, give them sufficient time to think, provide feedback as needed, and encourage collaboration. When providing explicit instruction on, for example, a skill, vocabulary word, or comprehension strategy, ask quick, closed, and right or wrong questions to get as much feedback from all as possible. Inform students that during that part of instruction, you will be calling on various students. If students do not know the answer, repeat the questions, rephrase it and focus it as needed, and also encourage students to seek help from others in class. After a student arrives at the answer either alone, or with someone else's help, it is important to check and make sure that the student really understands the answer before moving on.

Avoid embarrassing students and create a classroom environment where learning and collaboration are expected and experienced. Students should never feel ridiculed about their answers, about making mistakes, and about having different perspectives. Also avoid giving away the answers to right or wrong questions. Many times teachers give the answers away because they are pressed for time—they do not have time to check or correct students' understanding. Encourage participation from all students and establish classroom norms about student questioning, sharing, and classroom discussions.

Digital Literacies

- Discuss text or topics, share comments, feedback, and links: http://todaysmeet.com, or www.voicethread.com.
- Chartle: http://www.chartle.net/. A chart-making tool that can help organize and synthesize concepts. Summarize text through word clouds: http://tagul.com.
- Flashcard Stash: http://flashcardstash.com. A dictionary-based website for helping students learn vocabulary and more. Rewordify: http://rewordify.com is a free, online reading comprehension and vocabulary development software.

How to Create a Disciplinary Inquiry Classroom Culture

What will your students learn in your class? How will your students demonstrate their understanding? What counts for learning in your class? How will you know your students mastered the knowledge, processes, and skills they need to succeed and continue to learn in your subject area—what does that look, sound, and "feel" like in your class? Coaching students to engage in collaborative inquiry means that essential habits and norms are taught and learned.

When students learn how to inquire, they find purpose in studying and learning, they explore questions and issues that are important to them, and become more engaged with their learning. They also read, write, listen, speak, research, collaborate, inquire, explain, communicate and collaborate, and ask new questions. Discipline-specific inquiry knowledge, skills, and practices will not only help students understand what they are reading, it will propel their motivation and learning beyond the walls of the classroom.

Inquiry is not only about developing questions, but also about examining how these questions impact the world around them. In an inquiry-oriented classroom, the teacher is the facilitator of the learning process, the one who cultivates student curiosity and challenges students to think like discipline experts as they explore questions. It is a place where the teacher models disciplinary habits of mind, curiosity, self-reflection, flexibility and openness to new ideas, theories, or models, and respect for evidence. Last, it is a classroom environment where diverse ideas are valued and students feel safe to share, support, and debate their thinking. It is a place where students:

- Ask: THEY find questions that matter.
- Investigate: THEY conduct research to gather information about their questions.
- Create: THEY expand their schema about a topic through creating a product (a presentation, a paper, a model, a design).
- Discuss: THEY share their discoveries with others and consider their perspectives.
- Reflect: THEY look back on their insights, on what they have learned, on what worked or did not work, and develop new questions (as needed).

Developing an inquiry-based classroom takes vision, commitment, planning, and practice, and patience. To create such an environment, you also need to practice and foster accountable talk. In Chapter 8, I will examine accountable talk in detail, and I will present it as a great way to promote academic questioning and discourse in the classroom that is inherent to each discipline, and support more disciplinary talking, thinking, and learning. Throughout this book I have invited you to view learning in the academic discipline. When students' ideas, interests, questions, and perspectives are valued, student motivation, collaboration, self-efficacy, and persistence grow (Guthrie & Wigfield, 2000; Margolis & McCabe, 2003). School, after all, should teach students how to learn, how to think critically, and how to open their minds to new ideas.

Assessment and performance are very important factors in student learning, but let us not forget that school is not about just passing the test, getting into college, or entering the workforce. School should be about learning how to live and contribute to a society. Our classes should not be silos of information; instead, each content area class should be a lens through which students can make sense of the world. Teachers have to teach students how to read, think, ask questions, evaluate one another's thinking, and reflect on learning. Although close reading of text can promote comprehension and text-based questions can help students use textual evidence to support their assertions, students (and teachers) should also ask questions that are beyond the text pages or the school walls. Students need to learn that teachers don't have all of the answers to all of the questions and some questions still remain unanswered. Questioning is helpful for learning in class, in college, at work, and in life!

I was recently working with a group of high school science heads of departments at a school district disciplinary literacy meeting in science; one of the topics we worked on was questioning and how to promote student-generated questions as a means of promoting student comprehension. One discussion item focused on the fact that many times teachers come up with the questions (teacher-generated), ask the questions, give many of the answers, all in hopes to get students engaged, help them out, and have some sort of discussion (even with a handful of students) in class. Everyone in the room was discussing ways to facilitate student-generated questions. One of the participants who taught biology and Advanced Placement biology, asked me the following question: "If my students do not pass the End of Course (EOC) science exam, they will not graduate. Many of them will not ask any questions, and when they do that, they are not learning. I cannot afford to wait a month or two for them to come up with questions; I cannot afford to not have them learn. What would you do in that situation?"

This was a great, and very realistic question! In the context of high school science (or any other subject area for that matter) where there is so much to learn in terms of content, and so many examinations and demands for high school students, every second of instruction counts. My response focused on four areas: (1) creating a classroom culture of inquiry takes time; (2) scaffolding questioning in the classroom is a must as many students are not used, or do not know how, to ask effective questions; (3) monitoring instruction and student learning is necessary for the teacher to decide when to start relinquishing control or providing extra support as needed; and (4) building in time for collaborative inquiry in the classroom is an instructional decision; teachers should decide when, at which part of a lesson students will generate questions and whether that will happen independently or collaboratively.

As a teacher, you cannot expect that your students will start asking questions about what they read and learn, challenge the text(s), or challenge each other's thinking because standards, exams, or learning, in general, require it. Question generation should not occur only at the end of a topic of study, lesson, or unit. If students are to learn how to inquire about text, others' perspectives, and learning, they should be expected to generate questions before reading, during reading, and after reading. Why not collect student questions about a topic before they start reading about it? And how about asking students to mark the text or use post-it notes to write down questions they have about what they read (i.e., vocabulary, or ideas). Last, if you start by giving them five questions to respond to about what they are learning, how about asking them to generate one question for themselves, or for class discussion, or further research on the topic.

Additionally, teachers can collect different types of questions (open, closed, etc.) from small or whole class discussions and ask to evaluate them; or, throughout a unit, students can be generating all kinds of effective questions they can later sort out, categorize, collect further information, and evaluate as a small group or class. The point I am trying to make is that questioning as a habit of mind needs to be valued, developed, and supported throughout the learning process through quality feedback and with various texts and contexts. This is not an "all or nothing" issue—it takes scaffolding; questioning skills will develop over time if they are expected, valued, integrated, taught, supported, challenged, and evaluated in each content area classroom. Needless to say, we had a great time coming up with ideas about how to integrate quality questioning skills in high school classrooms to help all students not only master the content, but also want to learn more about science on their own, inside and outside the classroom walls.

Summary

- Comprehension is a complex, active process that requires the reader to be actively and meaningfully involved in constructing meaning from text. New educational standards expect students to acquire knowledge and apply knowledge to new situations. Good thinkers are also good questioners; they ask questions that build and extend their thinking and knowledge, and they also ask questions that have no immediate answers.

- One of the major instructional shifts resulting from the CCSS is the focus on having high-level, text-based discussions in each discipline and grade. Students need explicit instruction in questioning, in identifying different types of questions, in collecting evidence from text to support their answers, and in asking questions that will challenge others' thinking. Effective questioning promotes meaningful and deep student engagement with reading and learning.

- Effective comprehension instruction will focus on questioning, text-dependent questions, and in meaningful engagement of the reader with texts and with learning. Questioning does not have to be an individual act; collaborative inquiry works especially well in content area classrooms to promote sound reasoning, accountable talk, and discussions that will strengthen and extend students' knowledge and learning.

Differentiating Instruction

- Use hands-on learning. Allow students to collaboratively work on examining texts, problem solving, and questioning and checking each other's ideas, perspectives, and solutions. Students' reading comprehension skills will improve when you provide modeling on how to ask good questions, how to evaluate answers, and how to provide evidence from text to support one's claims.
- Vary questioning strategies to build exceptional education students' comprehension. Teach questioning strategies explicitly, provide immediate feedback, and encourage students to generate their own questions about what they are reading or learning.
- Learning to comprehend text is an essential skill for all students. Balance teacher-generated and student-generated questioning. Use questioning to motivate students, identify their misconceptions, encourage involvement of passive learners, evaluate students' thinking processes and knowledge, gain insight about students' interests, help students how to construct meaning from texts, and provide student feedback.
- Create a print-rich, language-rich, and learning-rich classroom environment that supports each student's learning, is inviting, safe, accepting, empathetic, respectful, motivating, and challenging. Promote student-student collaboration through flexible grouping, accountable talk, and project-based learning. Hold high expectations for all learners, and provide needed support.

Reflect and Apply

1. What suggestions can you offer to Mr. Fults (see Classroom Life vignette) from what you learned in this chapter? Provide a rationale about your choices, and discuss them with peers in a small group.
2. Questioning plays an important role in comprehension. What role will questioning play in your instruction? Use information from this chapter, and identify one to three ways you plan to teach questioning and foster student question generation. Discuss your ideas with a peer, or peers from your own discipline.
3. Using your knowledge of your discipline and how students' comprehension develops, what are one to three areas that are particularly challenging for students when it comes to higher-order questioning skills, text-dependent questions, or student-generated questions? Select information from the text to plan instruction that will address those challenges. Discuss with a peer, or peers and record any additional ideas or questions that emerged from the peer, or group discussion.

Extending Learning

1. Select one topic from your discipline, and plan a lesson on discipline-specific questioning to promote students' comprehension of topic. Present your plan to the class or a subject area colleague, and use evidence from this chapter on questioning and comprehension to support your instructional decisions.
2. Visit a classroom from your own discipline. Pay particular attention to the role of the teacher and the students in the learning process. Who does the questioning? What types of questions are asked? Which types of questions students have difficulties

with? Analyze your observations, look for patterns, and use information from the text to offer some discipline-specific suggestions to the classroom teacher about ways to promote students' questioning skills and comprehension.

3. Think about your own discipline and suggest five to seven ways to build struggling readers' questioning and comprehension skills. Collaborate with an ESOL and an exceptional education teacher. Share your ideas, incorporate theirs, and present the collaborative suggestions to your peers.

References

Alvermann, D. E. (2001, May). Reading adolescents' reading identities: Looking back to see ahead. *Journal of Adolescent & Adult Literacy, 44*(8), 676–690.

Anderson, L. W., & Krathwohl, D. R. (Eds) (2001). *A taxonomy for learning, teaching, and assessing: A revision of Bloom's taxonomy of educational objectives.* New York, NY: Longman.

Anderson R. C., & Freebody P. (1981). Vocabulary knowledge. In Guthrie J. T. (Ed.), *Comprehension and teaching: Research reviews* (pp. 77–117). Newark, DE: International Reading Association.

Baumann, J. F., Kame'enui, E. J., & Ash, G. E. (2003). Research on vocabulary instruction: Voltaire redux. In J. Flood, D. Lapp, J. R. Squire, & J. M. Jenses (Eds), *Handbook of research on teaching English language arts* (2nd ed., pp. 752–785). Mahwah, NJ: Erlbaum.

Beck, I. L., & McKeown, M. G. (2006). *Improving comprehension with questioning the author: A fresh and expanded view of a powerful approach.* New York, NY; Scholastic.

Beck, I. L., McKeown, M.G., Hamilton, R.L., & Kugan, L. (1997). *Questioning the author: An approach for enhancing student engagement with text.* Newark, DE: International Reading Association.

Beck, I. L., McKeown, M. G., Sandora, C., Kucan, L., & Worthy, J. (1996). Questioning the author: A year-long classroom implementation to engage students with text. *Elementary School Journal, 96*(4), 385–414.

Beck, I. L., Perfetti, C. A., & McKeown, M. G. (1982). Effects of long-term vocabulary instruction on lexical access and reading comprehension. *Journal of Educational Psychology, 74*(4), 506–521.

Beers, K. & Probst, R. (2013). *Notice and note: Strategies for close reading.* Portsmouth, NH: Heinemann.

Biggs, J. (1999). *Teaching for quality learning at university.* Buckingham, UK: Society for Research into Higher Education and Open University Press.

Blachowicz, C. L. Z., & Fisher, P. J. L. (2000). Vocabulary instruction. In R. Barr, M. L. Kamil, & P. B. Mozenthal (Eds), *Handbook of reading research* (Vol. 3, pp. 503–523). Mahwah, NJ: Erlbaum.

Blachowicz, C. L. Z., & Ogle, D. (2001). *Reading comprehension: Strategies for independent learners.* New York, NY: Guilford.

Block, C. C., & Pressley, M. (Eds), (2002). *Comprehension instruction: Research-based best Practices.* New York: Guilford Press.

Buehl, D. (2001). Question-Answer Relationships. In *Classroom strategies for interactive learning* (2nd ed., pp. 106–108). Newark, DE: International Reading Association.

Carnevale, A., & Rose, S. J. (2011). *The undereducated American.* Washington, DC: Georgetown University Center on Education and the Workforce.

Ciardiello, A. (1998). "Did you ask a good question today? Alternative cognitive and metacognitive strategies." *Journal of Adolescent & Adult Literacy, 42,* 210–219.

Coiro, J. (2003a). Reading comprehension on the Internet: Expanding our understanding of reading comprehension to encompass new literacies [Electronic version]. *Reading Teacher, 56*(5), 458–464.

Coiro, J. (2003b). Rethinking comprehension strategies to better prepare students for critically evaluating content on the Internet. *The NERA Journal, 39,* 29–34.

Coiro, J. (2005). Making sense of online text. *Educational Leadership, 63*(2), 30–35.

Coiro, J., & Dobler, E. (2007). Exploring the online reading comprehension strategies used by sixth grade skilled readers to search for and locate information on the Internet. *Reading Research Quarterly, 42,* 214–257.

Coiro, J., Knobel, M., Lankshear, C., & Leu, D. J. (Eds). (2008). *Handbook of research on new literacies* (pp. 1–22). Mahwah, NJ: Lawrence Erlbaum.

Coleman, D., & Pimentel, S. (2011). Publishers' criteria for the Common Core State Standards in English language arts and literacy, Grades 3–12. The National Association of State Boards of

Education, Council of Chief State School Officers, Achieve, and the Council of the Great City Schools.

Conley, D. T. (2010). *College and career ready: Helping all students succeed beyond high school.* San Francisco, CA: Jossey-Bass.

Conley, D. T. (2012). A complete definition of college and career readiness. The Educational Policy Improvement Center. Retrieved from https://www.epiconline.org/readiness/definition.dot

Conley, D. T. (2013). System approach to improving college and career readiness. A presentation given at the Confederation of Oregon School Administrators (COSA) Annual Superintendents Meeting, February 1, 2013, Glenenden Beach. Retrieved from http://www.epiconline.org/publications/document-detail.dot?id=a4d97dae-f7f3-46ac-82f2-354b6e0d488c

Delpit, L. (2012). *Multiplication is for white people. Raising expectations for other people's children.* New York, NY: The New Press.

Duke, N. & Pearson, D. (2002). Effective practices for developing reading comprehension. In A. Farstrup, & S. Samuels, (Eds), *What research has to say about reading instruction* (pp. 205–242). Newark, DE: International Reading Association.

Fisher, D. & Frey, N. (2009.) *Background knowledge: The missing piece of the comprehension puzzle.* Portsmouth, NH: Heinemann.

Guthrie, J. T. & Wigfield, A. (2000). Engagement and motivation in reading. In M.L. Kamil, P.B. Mosenthal, P.D. Pearson, & R. Barr (Eds), *Handbook of reading research:* Volume III (pp. 403–422). Mahwah, NJ: Erlbaum.

Harvey, S., & Goudvis, A. (2000). *Strategies that work: Teaching comprehension to enhance understanding.* Portland, ME: Stenhouse.

Heller, R., & Greenleaf, C. (2007). *Literacy instruction in the content areas: Getting to the core of middle and high school improvement.* Washington, DC: Alliance for Excellent Education.

Hiebert, E. H., & Kamil, M. L. (2005). *Teaching and learning vocabulary: Bringing research to practice.* Mahwah, NJ: Lawrence Erlbaum Associates.

Keene, E., & Zimmerman, S. (1997). *Mosaic of thought: Teaching comprehension in a reader's workshop.* Portsmouth, NH: Heinemann.

Knoester, M. (2010). Independent reading and the 'social turn': How adolescent reading habits and motivation relate to cultivating social relationships. *Networks: An On-line Journal for Teacher Research, 12*(1), 1–13.

Lankshear, C. & Knobel, M. (2003). *New literacies.* Maidenhead: Open University Press.

Leu, D. J., (2006). New literacies, reading research, and the challenges of change: A deictic perspective. In J. Hoffman, D.L. Scharlett, C.M. Fairbanks, J. Worthy, & B. Maloch (Eds). *Fifty-fifth National Reading Conference Yearbook* (pp. 1–20). Oak Creek, WI: National Reading Conference.

Leu, D. J., Jr., Kinzer, C. K., Coiro, J., & Cammack, D. (2004). Toward a theory of new literacies emerging from the Internet and other information and communication technologies. In R.B. Ruddell & N. Unrau (Eds), *Theoretical models and processes of reading,* (5th ed.) (pp. 1568–1611). International Reading Association: Newark, DE.

Leu, D. J., O'Byrne, W. I., Zawilinski, L., McVerry, J. G., & Everett-Cocapardo, H. (2009). Expanding the new literacies conversation. *Educational Researcher, 38*(4), 264–269.

Leu, D. J., McVerry, J. G., O'Bryne, W. I., Zawilinski, L., Castek, J., & Hartman, D. K. (2008). The new literacies of online reading comprehension and the irony of no child left behind: Students who require our assistance the most, actually receive it the least. In L. Mande- Morrow, R. Rueda, & D. Lapp (Eds). *Handbook of research on literacy instruction: Issues of diversity, policy, and equity,* (pp. 321–346). New York, NY: Guilford.

Levy, F., & Murnane, R. J. (2004). *The new division of labor: How computers are creating the next job market.* Princeton, NJ: Princeton University Press.

Margolis, H., & McCabe, P. (2003). Self-efficacy: A key to improving the motivation of struggling learners. *Preventing School Failure, 47*(4), 162–169.

Moje, E., & Tysvaer, N. (2010). *Adolescent literacy development in out-of-school time: A practitioner's guidebook.* New York: Carnegie Corporation of New York.

Nagy, W. E., Anderson, R. C., & Herman, P. A. (1985). Learning words from context. *Reading Research Quarterly, 20*(2), 233–253.

National Governors Association Center (NGA) for Best Practices, Council of Chief State School Officers (CCSSO). (2010). *Common Core State Standards.* National Governors Association Center for Best Practices, Council of Chief State School Officers. Retrieved from http://corestandards.org

National Reading Panel. (2000, April). *Report of the National Reading Panel: Teaching children to read*. Washington, DC: National Institute of Child Health and Human Development, National Institutes of Health, US Department of Health and Human Services

Oczuks, L. (2003). *Reciprocal teaching at work: Strategies for improving reading comprehension*. Newark, DE: International Reading Association.

Organization for Economic Cooperation and Development (OECD). (2010). *PISA 2009 results: What students know and can do: Student performance in reading, mathematics, and science (Vol. I)*. Retrieved from http://www.oecd-ilibrary.org/education/pisa-2009-results-what-students-know-and-can-do_9789264091450-en

Palincsar, A. S. & Brown, A. (1984). Reciprocal teaching of comprehension-fostering and comprehension monitoring activities. *Cognition and Instruction, 1*(2), 117–175.

Pearson, P. D., & Johnson, D. D. (1978). *Teaching reading comprehension*. New York: Holt, Rinehart and Winston.

Pearson, P. D., Roehler, L. R., Dole, J. A., & Duffy, G. G. (1992). Developing expertise in reading comprehension. In S. J. Samuels & A. E. Farstrup (Eds), *What research has to say about reading instruction* (2nd ed., pp. 145–199). Newark, DE: International Reading Association.

Pellegrino, J. W., & Hilton, M. L. (Eds) (2012). *Education for life and work: Developing transferable knowledge and skills in the 21st century*. National Research Council. Retrieved from http://www.nap.edu/catalog.php?record_id=13398.

Pressley, M. (2000). What should comprehension instruction be the instruction of? In M. L. Kamil, P. B. Mosenthal, P. D. Pearson, & R. Barr (Eds), *Handbook of reading research: Volume III* (pp. 545–561). Mahwah NJ: Erlbaum.

RAND Reading Study Group. (2002). *Reading for understanding: Toward a research and development program in reading comprehension*. Santa Monica, CA: Office of Education Research and Improvement.

Raphael, T. E., & Au, K. H. (2005). QAR: Enhancing comprehension and test taking across grades and content areas. *The Reading Teacher, 59*(3), 206–221.

Raphael, T. E., & Pearson, P. D. (1982). *The effect of metacognitive training on children's question-answering behavior*. Urbana, IL: Center for the Study of Reading; Cambridge, MA: Bolt, Beranek and Newman.

Raphael, T. E., & Pearson, P. D. (1985). Increasing students' awareness of sources of information for answering questions. *American Education Research Journal, 22*(2), 217–235.

Raphael, T. E., & Wonnacott, C. A. (1985). Metacognitive training in question-answering strategies: Implementation in a fourth grade developmental reading program. *Reading Research Quarterly, 20*, 282–296.

Raphael, T. E., Wonnacott, C. A., & Pearson, P. D. (1983). *Increasing students' sensitivity to sources of information: An instructional study in question-answer relationships* (Tech. Rep. No. 284). Urbana, IL: University of Illinois, Center for the Study of Reading.

Rasinski, T., Padak, N., McKeon, C., Krug-Wilfong, L., Friedauer, J., & Heim, P. (2005) Is Reading Fluency a Key for Successful High School Reading? *Journal of Adolescent and Adult Literacy, 49*, 22–27.

Richardson, W. (2013). Students first, not stuff. *Educational Leadership, 70*(6), 10–14.

Rosenblatt, L. (1969). Towards a transactional theory of reading. *Journal of Reading Behavior, 1(1)*, 31–51.

Rosenblatt, L. (1978). *The reader, the text, the poem: The transactional theory of the literary work*. Carbondale, IL: Southern Illinois University Press.

Rothstein, D,. & Santana, L. (2011). *Make just one change: Teach students to ask their own questions*. Cambridge, MA: Harvard Education Press.

Ruddell, M. R. (1994). Vocabulary knowledge and comprehension: A comprehension-process view of complex literacy relationships. In R. B. Ruddell, M. R. Ruddell, & H. Singer (Eds), *Theoretical models and processes of reading* (4th ed., pp. 414–447). Newark, DE: International Reading Association.

Shanahan, T., & Shanahan, C. (2008). Teaching disciplinary literacy to adolescents: Rethinking content area literacy. *Harvard Educational Review, 78*(1), 40–59.

Shanahan, T. & Shanahan, C. (2012). What is disciplinary literacy and why does it matter? *Topics in Language Disorders, 32*(1), 7–18.

Snow, C. E., Griffin, P., & Burns, M.S. (Eds). 2005. *Knowledge to support the teaching of reading: Preparing teachers for a changing world*. San Francisco: Jossey–Bass.

Stahl, S. A. (1999). *Vocabulary development*. Cambridge, MA: Brookline Books.

Stahl, S. A., & Kapinus, B. A. (1991). Possible sentences: Predicting word meanings to teach content area vocabulary. *The Reading Teacher, 45*, 36–38.

Torgesen, J. K., Houston, D. D., Rissman, L. M., Decker, S. M., Roberts, G., Vaughn, S., Wexler, J., Frabcis, D., Rivera, M. O., & Lesaux, N. (2007). *Academic literacy instruction for adolescents: A guidance document from the Center on Instruction.* Portsmouth, NH: RMC Research Corporation, Center on Instruction.

Wigfield, A., & Tonks, S. (2004). The development of motivation for reading and how it is influenced by CORI. In J. T. Guthrie, A. Wigfield, & K. C. Perencevich (Eds), *Motivating reading comprehension: Concept Oriented Reading Instruction* (pp. 249–272). Mahwah, NJ: Erlbaum.

Wiggins, G. (1989). The futility of trying to teach everything of importance. *Educational Leadership, 47*(3), 44–59.

Wiggins, G. (2010). *What is a big idea?* Retrieved from http://www.authenticeducation.org/ae_bigideas/article.lasso?artid=99

Wiggins, G., & McTighe, J. (1998). *Understanding by design.* Alexandria, VA: Association for Supervision and Curriculum Development.

Wilson, N. S., Zygouris-Coe, V., Cardullo, V., & Fong, J. (2013). Pedagogical frameworks of e-reader technologies in education. In J. Keengwe, *Pedagogical applications and social effects of mobile technology integration,* (pp. 1–24). Hersey, PA: IGI Global.

Zion, M., Michalsky, T., & Mevarech, Z. R. (2005). The effects of metacognitive instruction embedded within an asynchronous learning network on scientific inquiry skills. *International Journal of Science Education, 27*(8), 957–983.

Zygouris-Coe, V. (2012a). Disciplinary literacy and the common core state standards. *Topics in Language Disorders, 32*(1), 35–50.

Zygouris-Coe, V. (2012b). What is disciplinary literacy and why aren't we talking more about it? *Vocabulogic,* 1–6. Retrieved from http://vocablog-plc.blogspot.com/2012/03/what-is-disciplinary-literacy-and-why.html

seven
Discipline-Specific Comprehension Instruction

We now accept the fact that learning is a lifelong process of keeping abreast of change. And the most pressing task is to teach people how to learn.
–Peter Drucker

Chapter Highlights

- The Common Core State Standards (CCSS) are designed to help all students promote and develop deep comprehension of complex text.
- The most effective comprehension strategies identified by research include: instruction in questioning, story and text structure, summarizing, using graphic organizers, multiple strategy instruction, and comprehension monitoring.
- Although generalized literacy strategies such as KWL, QAR, prediction guide, anticipation guides, and note-taking are particularly beneficial for struggling readers, for students to develop deep understanding of disciplinary texts and concepts, content area teachers need to use instructional strategies that are reflective of the specialized nature, structure, discourse, and habits of mind of each discipline.
- Taking a discipline-specific approach to deeper learning will ensure that students learn how to read, think, write, argue, communicate, and evaluate in ways that are unique to each discipline.
- Transfer of learning does not happen automatically. Students need to learn in environments that are rigorous, supportive, and are also conducive to inquiry, exploration, and deep learning.
- Teach students to how to read carefully, purposefully, and closely, analyze the text, look for patterns in text structure, ask questions about the text, summarize, discuss and argue with others, synthesize, and reflect on information.
- To develop students' metacognitive skills, teachers need to provide them with many opportunities to monitor their own progress, reflect, work collaboratively with peers (take the perspective of others, listen, and talk), and formulate and share their thinking, knowledge, and explanations.

Classroom Life

I am telling you, comprehension instruction is tough. It is not something you can pigeonhole for 15 minutes a couple of times per week. If you just touch and go, students are going to be floundering. You have to plan for it, you have to integrate it throughout your instruction, and you have to be deliberate and creative with it. I use whole class instruction to teach and model new information; I usually spend 12–15 minutes or so on it. I do a lot with partner work and collaborative activities because kids need to process what they are reading, writing, and learning. Some weeks, when I have more time, I might devote a whole period on a collaborative inquiry activity.

My students fought me for a while at the beginning of the year—they don't like to make their thinking public and they didn't like to work with others. I decided to use some strategies that would challenge them to think! One of them I have used over and over again with my history classes is, Take a Stand. I spent much time at the beginning of the year modeling it, explaining what kinds of thinking we would be doing, and why we were going to use them in our groups. I usually select 2–3 primary documents, ask students to read them, discuss them, raise questions about them, and then Take a Stand as a group about the issue or topic at hand; they have to collaborate together, find evidence from all documents to support their stand, and they also have to defend it to the other groups. I have seen them grow so much! They talk, they do close reading, they argue, they negotiate, and they get a deeper understanding of the texts and the ideas in them.

I look for comprehension strategies that will "hit a couple of birds with one stone." History is not something to be memorized; it has to read carefully, it has to be processed deeply, and it has to be discussed and argued in order for students to understand that perspectives shape our interpretations of life. Comprehension instruction is something I continue to learn about; I want to make history real and I also want to motivate my students to continue to learn and stimulate their curiosity. *(Ms. Erin Foley, 10th grade Social Studies, Hagerty High School, Oviedo, Florida).*

Teaching Comprehension

The purpose of reading is understanding. Dolores Durkin's landmark work in 1979 showed that teachers spent much time on assessment and worksheets rather than on comprehension instruction. Comprehension instruction varies from class to class; actually, in some classes, there is no explicit comprehension instruction.

So, what do we know from research (e.g., Fielding & Pearson, 1994; National Reading Panel, 2000; RAND, 2002) about effective comprehension instruction?

- Reading vocabulary and fluency affect comprehension.
- Students can benefit from vocabulary instruction in Tier II words, wide reading, and promoting word consciousness.
- Students can benefit from developing a repertoire of strategies for developing and monitoring comprehension.
- Explicit instruction makes a difference in learner outcomes, especially for struggling readers.
- Discipline-embedded comprehension instruction promotes reader comprehension.
- Students benefit from reading large amounts of various types of text, student choice in text selection, reading texts of optimal challenge, and practicing multiple readings.

- Teachers who provide students with choice, challenging tasks, and collaborative inquiry opportunities, strengthen their motivation to read and comprehend text.
- Effective teachers use a variety of instructional practices to foster reader comprehension.

There is a myriad of comprehension strategies (from accessing text, to note-taking, to questions, and to comprehension monitoring). In some of the schools I visit, comprehension instruction is comprised of a set of graphic organizers students use independently or collaboratively. Comprehension instruction needs to be explicit, strategic, purposeful, integrated, and ongoing in secondary school classrooms. It should also promote student engagement and self-regulated learning. Teachers should use text-based collaborative learning for both high- and low-ability students. In order to foster development of new knowledge, students need opportunities to engage in guided interactions with texts in groups (Kamil et al., 2008). Teaching and learning in an era of higher and globally aligned educational standards warrants quality comprehension instruction and development. Although there are several effective comprehension strategies available, remember that strategies are a means to an end; they are tools students can use to construct meaning from text (Block & Pressley, 2002).

What comprehension strategies work? The National Reading Panel Report (NRP, 2000) emphasized the importance of comprehension strategy instruction, and it also provided research evidence on the following eight reading comprehension strategies:

1. Comprehension monitoring in which the reader learns how to be aware or conscious of his, or her understanding during reading and learns procedures to deal with problems in understanding as they arise.
2. Cooperative learning in which readers work together to learn strategies in the context of reading.
3. Graphic and semantic organizers, which allow the reader to represent graphically (write or draw) the meanings and relationships of the ideas that underlie the words in the text.
4. Story structure from which the reader learns to ask and answer who, what, where, when, and why questions about the plot and, in some cases, maps out the time line, characters, and events in stories.
5. Question answering in which the reader answers questions posed by the teacher and is given feedback on the correctness.
6. Question generation in which the reader asks himself or herself why, when, where, what will happen, how, and who questions.
7. Summarization in which the reader attempts to identify and write the main or most important ideas that integrate or unite the other ideas or meanings of the text into a coherent whole.
8. Multiple strategy instruction in which the reader uses several of the procedures in interaction with the teacher over the text. Multiple strategy teaching is effective when the reader, or the teacher, in naturalistic contexts, uses the procedures flexibly and appropriately.

(p. 4–6)

Research on effective comprehension instruction points to teaching comprehension instead of mentioning comprehension. It also points to teaching students how to become active and meta-cognitive readers, to teaching a variety of strategies that will build deep understanding of text, and to creating a classroom environment that promotes and focuses on understanding rather than just surface-type knowledge (National Institute of Literacy, 2007). In spite of the evidence, many secondary teachers, especially in areas like science, are reluctant to provide explicit reading comprehension instruction due to fear of losing valuable content time, or due to beliefs about whose responsibility it is (i.e., reading or English teachers) to teach students how to read and comprehend (Greenleaf, Schoenbach, Cziko, & Mueller, 2001; Greenleaf, Brown, & Litman, 2004; Ness, 2009; O'Brien, Stewart, & Moje, 1995). Content area teachers are well positioned to teach discipline-specific comprehension strategies and foster critical comprehension development (Fang & Shleppegrell, 2008).

CCSS Connections

- Students in grades 6–12 need to read and comprehend disciplinary texts critically, independently, and proficiently. They should be able to cite strong textual evidence to support their analysis and interpretation of the text(s), determine central themes and ideas, identify relationships among ideas, and provide objective summaries of text(s).
- Students in grades 6–12 will need to learn how to compare and contrast the structure of two or more texts, analyze how the structure of each text contributes to its meaning and style, determine the author's choices and point of view or purpose in a text, and analyze how the author acknowledges and responds to conflicting viewpoints, provides explanations, discusses procedures, or discusses results in a text.
- Students in grades 6–12 need to read text(s) critically and be able to determine the argument and claims in the text, distinguish between fact, opinion, and reasoned argument, analyze the relationships among concepts in a text, analyze the author's purpose, and assess the evidence the author provides to support his, or her claims.

Teaching Comprehension Approaches

There are two main approaches to teaching comprehension—strategy and content instruction. Strategy instruction encourages the reader to employ his or her mental processes, and use certain strategies to interact with the text. On the other hand, ". . .content instruction attempts to engage students in the process of attending to text ideas and building a mental representation of the ideas, with no direction to consider specific mental processes." (McKeown, Beck, & Blake, 2009, p. 219). McKeown, Beck, & Blake (2009) argue that strategy approaches teach students cognitive processes and how to use these processed to read and understand text. For example, during reading, students can use monitoring reading and summarizing. They can use before, during, and after reading strategies such as reciprocal teaching (Palinscar & Brown, 1984), transactional strategies (i.e., predictions, connections to background knowledge, questioning, ask for clarifications, visualizing, and summarizing) (Pressley et al., 1992), or collaborative strategic reading (Vaughn et al., 2011).

Both approaches can be combined for best results. Vaughn et al. (2013) found that when a content approach was combined with essential questions and vocabulary, appropriate text-based instruction and reading (using the text as a source for reading and discussion), text-based discourse, and collaborative learning activities that focus on comprehension checks and application, eighth grade students' comprehension abilities and content knowledge in social studies improved. In this study, not only students' comprehension of social studies text improved, but also there was significant improvement in their broader reading for understanding abilities.

In this chapter, I present discipline-specific strategies that use combined strategy and content instruction to read and understand text, use the text as a basis for reading and accountable talk, and promote content and comprehension growth. These strategies will help all content area teachers deliver the content in discipline-specific ways that foster good understanding of text and promote critical thinking.

In order for secondary students to sufficiently learn content, it is vital that they learn certain literacy strategies in tandem with content in their content-area instruction. This supports student efforts in thinking critically about content before, during, and after text reading in their content-area classes. This is not an easy feat, considering the vast differences in text and text-reading across their content area classes. Comprehension strategies are tools to guide thinking and they work best when taught and practiced in meaningful contexts. Discipline-specific materials often require advanced skills such as understanding conventions, text structures, and content-specific ways of thinking and writing. Although content teachers may feel unqualified to teach literacy skills, they are the experts in their subject matter. Their strong technical knowledge plays a powerful role in helping students become critical readers of domain-specific texts.

Content teachers can improve their students' learning of key content area concepts and facts by explicitly teaching a few, specific instructional routines for reading strategically, considering the unique ways that information can be presented, and making connections to that information. Strategy instruction should be embedded within content-focused texts and not practiced out of context. Teaching only generic strategies might suggest to students that all texts are similar in structure, and that skills can transfer from one text to another without considering different discourse patterns or discipline-specific ways of communicating. The most effective comprehension strategies identified by research include instruction in questioning, story and text structure, summarizing, using graphic organizers, multiple strategy instruction, and comprehension monitoring. The following comprehension strategies can benefit all students and are integral to independent comprehension monitoring and development of critical thinking.

Fluency and Comprehension

Fluency is "freedom from word identification problems that might hinder comprehension in silent reading or the expression of ideas in oral reading" (Harris & Hodges, 1995, p. 85). Fluency is more complex and essential to comprehension than most of us realize. It is not about learning to read faster; it is about the time it provides the reader for constructing meaning from text as she or he is reading—the ultimate goal of reading. Fluency has two components: accuracy and automaticity. Automaticity refers to recognizing words without attention or conscious effort. Fluency involves three major components: rate (measured in words per minute), accuracy (decoding text without errors), and prosody (intonation, expression, and phrasing). The more time a student saves by fluent decoding, the more time she or he has to monitor the text for meaning, and the more likely she or he will correctly interpret text. Fluency is a complex, lengthy, developmental process that involves all the early phases of reading acquisition. Fluency is dependent upon the text type and the reader's familiarity with vocabulary; it continues to expand just like vocabulary and comprehension. All adolescent readers must be given opportunities to move beyond automatic decoding of words and strategies to develop their reading fluency (National Institute of Child Health and Human Development [NICHD], 2004). Wide, independent reading, teacher read-alouds, listening to peers read, and repeated reading of complex text (something that close reading of text will facilitate), all benefit fluency development.

Modeling fluent reading will help students understand how they should sound when they read. All subject areas include vocabulary that is technical—students will benefit from listening to the teacher offer the correct pronunciation of technical and unknown words. The ability to read orally and with expression is part of public speaking. Most adolescents do not like to read aloud in class or be put on the spot by the teacher to read orally. To promote oral reading in content area classrooms, have students read to others in pairs or small groups, give them time to go over the text or the problem silently before calling on them to do oral reading, and use oral reading strategically. Repeated reading, shared reading, paired reading, and other similar procedures are referred to as guided oral-reading procedures. The re-reading of text until the student reaches a certain level of proficiency, one-on-one tutoring, peer tutoring, and use of audio-recorded material are means of guided oral-reading practice. Struggling readers and English language learners (ELLs) in content area classrooms need to be in reading fluency—they need to hear fluency modeled, they need to practice with a fluent reader, and they also need to independently practice reading with fluency.

Read aloud in class and model the process of smooth and expressive reading. Explain to students how you read text, how you use your voice to express the author's meaning, and how you read at a pace that is not too fast for listeners to keep up with. Reading along silently with a recorded version of a text can also build fluency. For example, in English Language Arts, teachers can read aloud excerpts of award-winning novels and literary works. Students can listen to sonnets that are inherently rich in prosody and rhythm, and view films related to the novels they have been reading. In mathematics, students can read word problems together and explain how they arrived at their solutions. In science classes, students can listen to audio recordings of selected passages from their science textbooks. In a social studies class, students can download and listen to Dr. Martin Luther King's "I Have a Dream" speech (and the speeches of other historical figures), and compare the message they received from listening to him deliver it, to his intonation and prosody, versus reading it from the text.

Accountable talk will facilitate fluency because it is based on using the language of each discipline to communicate ideas, question each other, expand on meaning, and facilitate collaborative learning. To build students' fluency in English Language Arts, engage them with reading, give them opportunities to talk about, question, respond to, and reflect on what they are reading and understanding, encourage them to use the language of the era the literary selection represents, and use plays and drama when appropriate. Understanding and using the language of mathematics is necessary for explaining the steps involved in a solution. In science, students will need to use its language to read and interpret data, formulate hypotheses, plan and conduct research, and present their solutions. In social studies, students need to become articulate in analyzing and evaluating multiple documents and need to engage in conversations about history. When students are engaged in accountable talk in the disciplines, they discuss their own and others' understanding of the material and as a result their fluency, comprehension, critical thinking and reasoning skills grow.

Applying Discipline-Specific Literacies

- Build students' experiences with reading, discussing, and responding to a wide variety of texts. Develop students' understanding of texts through discipline-specific text structure instruction.
- Use discipline-specific strategies that promote understanding of text(s), are aligned with the structure, questions, processes, and habits of mind of your discipline, facilitate metacognitive thinking, and foster deep learning.
- Make disciplinary learning fun and also make it challenging, relevant, collaborative, and reflective. And be there, as a facilitator, to provide support, guidance, and feedback to students—implement a disciplinary literacy learning framework that views learning as an apprenticeship process.

Independent Reading

The National Council of Teachers of English (NCTE) stated the following in their 2004 position statement, *Call to Action: What we Know About Adolescent Literacy and Ways to Support Teachers in Meeting Students' Needs.* Adolescents need:

> Sustained experiences with diverse texts in a variety of genres and offering multiple perspectives on real life experiences. Although many of these texts will be required by the curriculum, others should be self-selected and of high interest to the reader. Wide independent reading develops fluency, builds vocabulary and knowledge of text structures and offers readers the experiences they need to read and construct meaning with more challenging texts. Text should be broadly viewed to include print, electronic, and visual media.
>
> (http://www.ncte.org/positions/statements/adolescentliteracy)

In order for students to be college and career ready, they need to read quality texts that expose them to a wide variety of content, structures, and genres. Reading independently helps students develop their fluency skills (Archer, Gleason, & Vachon, 2003). In addition to content area instruction for building fluency, comprehension, and content knowledge, teachers should also encourage students to practice wide, independent reading. Many school districts have invested in reading software programs that monitor independent reading. Although such programs can provide teachers with an amount of reading a student has done, what do they do for promoting a love for reading? Some studies point to the fact that independent reading is connected to social practices and identity rather than to solitary practice (Gee, 2000; Heath, 1983; Smith, 1998). Students who enjoy reading discuss books, read in areas of interest among family members and friends, and read aloud to others (Knoester, 2010). Students who achieved high on reading assessments had high intrinsic motivation and chose to read (voluntarily or independently) on a regular basis outside of school (Ivey & Broaddus, 2001; Krashen, 2004).

One way to foster independent reading in the classroom is by creating a classroom library that offers a wide selection of discipline-related books, magazines, electronic media, and comfortable places to read and talk with others about books (Krashen, 2004). Offering a wide range of diverse, multicultural fiction and non-fiction literature, comic books, graphic novels, and other materials and resources are necessary to maximize student independent reading. Find out your students' interests in topics, areas, and genres, give them choice, and collaborate with your school's library media specialist and literacy coach—they can help with book recommendations for your classroom or school library. Last, create a classroom environment where reading and learning are valued, expected, modeled, supported, and where students are provided with options, choice, and guidance to pursue their own interests and goals.

Building Comprehension through Text

Many students in secondary grades skim text; in other words, they move quickly, "get the gist" of what the text is about, and then they are done. When the teacher asks them specific questions about the text, many simply respond by saying, "I don't get it." By definition, skimming implies a quick passing over a surface; it means to read or glance through quickly or superficially. Skimming does not promote a transaction, an exchange or relationship between the reader and the text (Rosenblatt, 1986).

On the other hand, careful reading of text involves the reader in a process of paying attention to how the text is written, to its meaning, and its purpose. When students are involved in close reading of text, they notice a lot of things about the text itself. They question the purpose of the author, they question what they are reading, and they also compare the text with other texts they have read, with personal experiences, and with their background knowledge on the topic, in general. In Chapter 3 I addressed the topic of close reading of complex text, and how teachers can facilitate and organize it. In Chapter 4, I made the case for rigorous learning and instruction, and the importance of ongoing student engagement with text, close reading of text, a critical, purposeful, and relevant approach to the text, and deep, metacognitive thinking.

The goal is not to ignore reader characteristics, background knowledge, and personal opinions about what students read and learn. Instead, by teaching students how to read, analyze, evaluate, and reflect on text, they would be making connections between new and already acquired knowledge, as well as personal experiences, easier. As a reminder, according to CCSS guidelines about reading complex text, students should first develop their text-reading and text-analyzing skills, learn how to answer and evaluate text-dependent questions, build their knowledge of academic vocabulary found in the text, and provide evidence for their arguments before they start on what the event, word, or character reminds them. The aim is to keep them in the text through engaging, relevant, and guided instruction before they distance themselves from the text—make the learning a shared experience for all. By focusing classroom discussion on the text, all students have opportunities to engage. Of course, it is easier to talk about personal experiences than to analyze text (especially text that is complex). Building perseverance through complex reading and thinking will help students develop the critical thinking skills they need to be successful in college, career, and life.

Text Structure and Comprehension

The CCSS place significant emphasis on comprehension and text structure instruction for increasingly more complex text that is both narrative and informational (NGA & CCSSO, 2010). The College and Career Readings Anchor Standards for Reading, standard five, specifically addresses sentences and paragraphs: "Analyze the structure of texts, including how specific sentences, paragraphs, and larger portions of the text (e.g., a section, chapter, scene, or stanza) relate to each other and the whole." (NGA & CCSSO, 2010, p. 10).

The adoption of these standards by most states has drawn attention to the need for all teachers to explicitly teach text comprehension. In the past few years a number of resources have become available that provide information about research regarding comprehension literacy instruction for students in Grades 4–12, including those who struggle with reading (Biancarosa & Snow, 2004; Heller & Greenleaf, 2007; Kamil et al., 2008; National Institute for Literacy, 2007; Scammacca et al., 2007; Torgesen et al., 2007). Being literate in science means something different than being literate in English, or other subject areas. Each discipline has its own discourse, habits of mind, and ways of accessing, constructing, evaluating, and communicating knowledge.

So where, in which content area class, should students learn how to read and comprehend texts? A consistent recommendation of intervention studies is that content literacy skills taught by content-area teachers using discipline-specific reading materials is vital for improving comprehension skills. Torgesen et al. (2007) state that in order to meet adolescent literacy goals *all teachers* must be involved, especially since most middle and high school students spend most of their time in content-area classes and must learn to read expository, informational, discipline-specific texts with proficiency. "Although reading strategies might be taught explicitly in a designated reading support class, students are unlikely to generalize them broadly to content areas unless teachers also explicitly support and elaborate the strategies' use with content-area texts" (p. 12).

Interventions for students in secondary grades usually include decoding, vocabulary, comprehension, and text structure (Torgesen et al., 2007; Kamil et al., 2008). In terms of comprehension instruction, research has shown that older struggling readers benefit from explicit instruction in comprehension strategies that help them become more active and strategic readers (Torgesen et al., 2007). Strategy instruction should include modeling, guided practice, collaboration with others, feedback, and scaffolding. In terms of text structure, the use of graphic organizers and direct instruction on text structures and organizational patterns have also been helpful for struggling readers (Torgesen et al., 2007).

College, Career, and Workforce Connections

- According to David Conley (2012), there are four keys to college and career readiness. First, students need to know and be able to use key cognitive strategies, such as: formulating hypotheses, problem-solving, identifying sources and collecting information, analyzing and evaluating findings and viewpoints, organizing and constructing work products in a variety of formats, and monitoring and confirming the precision and accuracy of all work produced. Second, students need to have deep understanding of content knowledge, the ways knowledge is structured, accessed, and constructed in each discipline, and the habits of mind that enable students to interact with the knowledge and others. Third, students need to have key learning skills and techniques, such as: ownership of learning (motivation, self-awareness, progress monitoring, self-efficacy) and specific learning techniques (strategic reading, study skills, collaborative learning, technology skills, and self-monitoring). Fourth, students need to have key transition knowledge and skills that will provide course planning during high school to prepare them for higher education or career pathways.
- Employers want future employees who can identify problems, and plan, develop, and implement solutions.
- *In order to learn history at the college level, incoming students need to abandon dogmatic beliefs they cannot defend with evidence, allow themselves to be challenged (though not brainwashed) by new ideas, and possess the skills needed to convey written information clearly and concisely to a variety of audiences* (Daniel Murphree, Associate Professor, History, University of Central Florida).

Text Structure Instruction

Narrative text tends to be organized around literary elements such as setting, characters, problem/solution, plot, and theme. A key to comprehending narrative involves how all of these organizational elements are related. Narrative text follows a structure often referred to as "story grammar" that provides a predictable sequence. Authors manipulate story structure for literary effect in their own unique ways. The setting establishes the environment, where and when the events take place. A character is a person or persons depicted in the narrative. Characters include the protagonist, antagonist, and other major and minor characters. Characters are usually examined through appearance, actions, and attitude. A conflict is usually visible between two or more characters (usually a protagonist and an antagonist), but can occur in different forms. Conflicts are usually internal, external, and relational. The plot is a series of episodes throughout the story. The plot includes an exposition that introduces how the main characters relate to one another in the story. Rising action is the place where the protagonist understands his or her goal(s) and begins to work toward it. The climax is the turning point in the story where the main character makes the single most important decision that defines the outcome of his or her story. Falling action is when things go wrong or loose ends are put together. Resolution is the final confrontation in the story between the protagonist and the antagonist. Last, the theme is outside the plot and is used to describe an issue that runs through the story, such as love, racism, etc.

Informational text tends to be based on a hierarchy of main ideas and subordinate main ideas, often reflected through the use of headings and sub-headings. It uses a variety of text patterns such as, description, chronological sequencing, compare/contrast, problem/solution, and cause/effect. Students need explicit instruction on the ways in which authors choose and use words, how they express their ideas through syntax (sentence structure) and paragraphs, and how in general, they present and organize ideas and information in the text. Knowledge of text structure affects access to, and understanding of, text.

In addition, knowledge of informational text features can aid students' comprehension. Point features (e.g., table of contents, index, glossary, appendix) guide students through text organization. Organizational aids (e.g., bold/italicized/color print, bullets, titles, headings, subheadings, captions, labels, sidebars) help students locate important information. Graphic aids (e.g., diagrams, tables/charts, graphs, figures, maps, cross-sections, overlays, illustrations/photos/images, timelines) represent information in different ways and expand the meaning of text.

The syntactic structure (i.e., the pattern in a particular sentence) of texts and the syntactic (i.e., how ideas and information are represented) and lexical (i.e., sentence length coupled with vocabulary difficulty) complexity can also interfere with students' comprehension. For example, science texts have twice the number of rare words in texts than any other discipline. Syntax refers to the study and understanding of grammar—the system and arrangement of words, phrases and clauses that make up a sentence. In order to comprehend a sentence, the reader must read it, process it, integrate a variety of syntactic and word meaning information, and store it in his or her working memory (Paris & Hamilton, 2009). Each sentence communicates ideas the reader has to integrate to construct meaning. The level of a text's syntax is one predictor of a text's comprehensibility (Snow, Griffin, & Burns, 2005); effective readers have a developed knowledge of phrase structures, parts of sentences, and how they work (Scott, 2004). Syntactic awareness develops through exposure to oral and written language; many readers (e.g., English language Learners and other struggling readers) with reading difficulties find it challenging to understand complex sentences because of the large number of ideas and unusual (specialized, figurative, or technical) vocabulary in them.

Helping students manipulate and "play" with words and parts of sentences orally, and in writing, can help build fluency in sentence writing and comprehension. Sentence combining, anagrams, deconstruction and expansion, and coding have been found to improve reading comprehension and writing skills (Graham & Perrin, 2007; Graham & Hebert, 2010). To construct meaning from text structure, students also need to know about paragraph structure (i.e., identify main ideas and key supporting details). Students need to know that discipline-specific texts at times includes unstructured paragraphs that hold more than one idea or have a main idea that is not explicitly stated and it must be inferred. Use the texts of your discipline to teach paragraph instruction.

Textbook Organizational Patterns

Text structure helps to guide students' comprehension of text. Generally, informational text includes signal words and phrases that cue the reader to the text's structure and purpose. Explicit teaching of text structures helps students access text and understand its purpose. Common organizational patterns in textbooks include the following.

- *Analysis:* Analysis takes a key idea (superordinate information) and examines the relationship of the parts of that idea (subordinate information) to the whole. This organizational pattern is used frequently in mathematics and social studies textbooks. Signals words include: *consider, analyze, investigate, the first part suggests, this element means.*

- *Cause/Effect:* The text describes events and identifies or implies causes for why the event happened or is happening and predicts what probably will happen. At times many different causes can be responsible for one effect and many different effects can be produced by a single cause. For example, why have many college graduates recently moved back to live with their parents? This organizational pattern is used frequently in science, social studies, and English language arts. Cause signal words include: *cause, because, the reason for, on account of, bring about, give rise to, created by, contributed by, led to, due to, since.* Effect signal words include: *as a result of, outcome, finally, consequently, therefore, for this reason, hence, effect, then, so.*

- *Comparison/Contrast:* Describes how two or more events, places, characters, or ideas may be similar and/or different in multiple ways. Authors also use similes, metaphors, and analogies. For example, let's identify similarities and differences between President Obama's and Former President Bush's agendas on war. This organizational pattern is used frequently in English language arts and health textbooks. Comparison signal words include: *like, alike, same as, similar to, similarly, likewise, additionally, in addition, to, neither/nor, in/by comparison, most, in common, but also, not only.* Contrast signal words include: *in/by contrast, different from, difference between, on the other hand, unlike, however, rather than, instead, instead of, yet, but, nevertheless, as opposed to, on the contrary, although, as opposed to, opposite, compared with, in comparison to, even though, either/or, otherwise, whereas, in spite of, despite.*

- *Description:* Describes a specific topic; sensory details help the reader visualize information. For example, what information do the parameters, or combinations of parameters, provide about the graph of the quadratic function? This organizational pattern is used frequently in science, social studies, English language arts, fine arts, career and technical education, and health textbooks. Signal words include: *for/an example, to begin with, in particular, for instance, most importantly, to illustrate, characteristics are/include, such as, is/looks like, most important, another, can be defined, appears to be.*

- *Definition/Example:* The author introduces terms and provides examples. For example, in Earth Science, the term "inertia" means the tendency of an object to resist a change in motion. This organizational pattern is used frequently in science, mathematics, health, fine arts, and career and technical education textbooks. Signal words include: *refers to, thus, in other words, described as, equals.*

- *Explanation of Concepts:* The author introduces and explains or clarifies a new concept. This is similar to definitions/examples. For example, in a chapter on humans in the biosphere, the author will also explain the concepts of monoculture, renewable and nonrenewable resources, and sustainable development. This organizational pattern is used frequently in science, fine arts, career and technical education, and health textbooks.

- *Listing and Enumeration:* Lists connected information, outlines a series of steps, and orders ideas in a hierarchy; for example, the presentation of different steps included in an experiment. This organizational pattern is used frequently in mathematics, social studies, career and technical education, and health textbooks. Signal words include: *first, second, third, last, then, at that time, during, immediately, next, until, while, soon, after, now.*

- *Problem/Solution:* The text includes a problem, presents one or more solutions, and finally, the actual solution is selected. Sometimes, there is not one solution to a problem. For example, how can the government prevent drivers from texting and driving? This organizational pattern is used frequently in science, social studies, English, and health textbooks. Signal words include: *the problem is, a reason for the problem is, the dilemma is, the solution is, to solve this, one/an answer is, alternative, one idea/question/challenge is, evidence is, the difficulty is, it is possible to, if/then, therefore, since, as a result of, so that, consequently, in response to, in order to, thus, fortunately, unfortunately, results, the result, resolved, resolution, conclusion, outcomes, efforts.*

- *Sequence or Time Order:* Includes a series of events from beginning to end that lead to a conclusion or a sequence of events related to a particular event. An example includes listing the events that led to the American Revolution. This organizational pattern is used frequently in science, mathematics, social studies, fine arts, career and technical education, and health textbooks. Signal words include: *first, next, last, at last, another, then, when, while, finally, before, preceding, after, afterwards, as, initially, following, simultaneously, meanwhile, not long after, much earlier/later, soon/soon after, in tandem, tomorrow, next day/week/year, previously, additionally.*

Because authors organize their texts in different ways and students come with varied knowledge of text structure, teachers should help them learn how to recognize these organizational patterns in disciplinary texts. How can you provide text structure instruction?

- Show students how to recognize a new organizational pattern of text before they start reading the text.
  - Select the passage, and use a printed copy or a projector for all students to see your demonstration.
  - Read the passage aloud, and highlight significant/relevant signal words/phrases while reading.
  - During instruction, do a think-aloud to describe your thinking process behind identifying signal words and what decisions you made.
- Model for students how to use text structure information to organize and comprehend text using a graphic organizer.
  - Draft a brief summary statement using important information from the graphic organizer.
  - Generate questions about the text selection that match the text's structure.
- Post on the wall for future reference.
- Provide collaborative opportunities for student practice to identify a text structure that has been taught.
- Allow students to demonstrate understanding of text structure through the use of graphic organizers or summarizing text with a specific text structure that has already been taught.

Table 7.1 on the next page shows examples of text structure with related graphic organizers and sample text that can help you and your students use text structure patterns to promote comprehension of text.

TABLE 7.1. Text Structure Instruction Examples

Text Structure	Format with Graphic Organizers	Text Example
Definition		A pollutant is a harmful material that can enter the biosphere.
Sequence		The Under World Journey (*Odyssey*) The journey of the dead began with Thanatos, God of Death, who would cut a lock of hair from them at the moment of death. Hermes, who would lead them to the River Styx, then guided their souls to Hell. There those who had been buried were permitted to approach Charon. Those lacking a coin were not allowed to accompany Charon until after 100 years of wondering had passed. Those who were ferried across the river would pass Cerberus, the three-headed dog that guarded the Underworld. After the Styx was crossed, the dead would travel until they found themselves in the Asphodel Fields, a place of apathy where they forgot who they were and drifted aimlessly until they were called to the next part of their journey. Continuing along the road, the dead would come to a fork in the road, where they would be judged. The judges – Minos, Rhadamanthys and Aeacus1 – had a choice of three verdicts. The good would head forward to Elysium, the bad would head forward to Tartarus, while those who were neither good nor bad would head back to the Asphodel Fields.
Comparison/ Contrast		A rational number is a number that can be written as a ratio. Every whole number is a rational number, because any whole number can be written as a fraction. An irrational number can be written as a decimal, but not as a fraction. An irrational number has endless non-repeating digits to the right of the decimal point. Here are some irrational numbers: $\pi = 3.141592...$ $\sqrt{2} = 1.414213...$
Cause-Effect	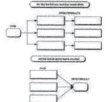	The causes of World War I began in central Europe in late July 1914 and included intertwined factors, such as the conflicts and hostility of the four decades leading up to the war. Militarism, alliances, imperialism, and nationalism played major roles in the conflict as well. The political changes effected by World War I were reflected best in the decline of the empires. While the Ottoman Empire and Austria-Hungary completely collapsed, the Great War also sounded the death knell for monarchies in Germany

(Continued)

TABLE 7.1.   (Continued)

Text Structure	Format with Graphic Organizers	Text Example
		and Russia, which became republics. World War I was also the cause for a rise in nationalistic tendencies leading to the demand for independence in many British colonies of outside Europe.
Problem/ Solution	Problem | Solution (blank table rows)	Most children with cancer miss at least some school, especially during the year immediately following diagnosis. Unfortunately, a few encounter extreme absenteeism for diagnoses or treatment (which may itself require hospitalization) or because of post-treatment illness or lethargy. Besides loss of entire days, some students leave class if feeling ill or lethargic, adding to their total of missed classroom time. Fortunately, treatment advances may lessen some of these problems. However, it is still unknown if today's advanced medical treatments help current students achieve regular attendance. Second, it is imperative that school, parents, and medical professionals assess the student's ability to attend class. A clear statement from health providers about when/if it is permissible for a student to stay home may thus help avoid unwarranted absences. Third, to prevent parental overprotection emphasize to parents the necessity of regularly attending school—for all of its academic and social advantages—is advised. Fourth, if attendance becomes problematic, it makes sense to secure homebound services and assure that missed academic content (e.g., critical skills in math or essential vocabulary) is sent to the student and checked for completion. Fifth, addressing each student's fear of peer ostracism (e.g., due to hair loss or classmates' misbeliefs that cancer is contagious) can facilitate regular school attendance. Last, tackling potential logistical barriers can aid some students, such as when families lack transportation or babysitters. Helping families access community (or hospital-based) supports should not be overlooked. If necessary, teachers can contact their own school's social worker, if one exists, or reach out to hospital or community workers to guarantee appointments are kept and that transportation is available to permit return to school.

Text Marking, Annotating, and Text Coding

Students who use text marking such as, highlighting, underlining, and marginal annotating to interact with text and note important facts, questions they have about the text, reminders, or unknown words, read with a pencil or, a pen in their hand. Students also use sticky notes to mark important facts, or note their questions for texts that cannot be marked directly. In many schools students use text coding, or "marking the text," as they read text by circling unfamiliar words, placing a question mark next to the text they have a question about, or using different codes to interact with the text and write notes in the margins. Text marking, annotating, and coding helps students get in the habit of interacting with text as they read and ask questions such as, "What does this mean?" "Is this important?" "Can I connect it with what I already know?" "I don't know this word; what does it mean?", etc. This practice functions as a reminder of "unfinished business" the reader still has with the text—something to go back to later, discuss with others, ask questions, or do further reading.

Teachers can develop a variety of text codes (see Table 7.2 for sample Text Codes) to help students actively "code" fiction or informational text as they read. Use overhead transparencies, LCD Projectors, Interactive White Boards, or other means to model how to use text marking, annotating, and coding. Text coding can be used with print and digital text.

Text coding or marking of digital text usually involves two processes: highlighting and sticky notes. For example, standard print text codes for questions "?" or important information "!" are often replaced with more visual representation of the code. Students often replace symbols in text coding of digital text with color representation. Students often code specific information using color highlighting, and often follow up with a sticky note to support their discussion.

Annotating is an interactive reading process that allows the student to comment or reach meaning as he or she is reading. In a way, annotation helps the student keep track of his or her thinking during reading or re-reading of text. Annotating also makes the readers' thinking process visible. For example, a student might mark or circle a place in the text where a word definition is found, or circle words that are used frequently in the text, or use brackets to mark an example. Another may use numbers to number lists of ideas, events, causes, or effects. Students can also write notes to themselves in the margins (e.g., "Check definition in secondary document."), note similarities or differences, mark summary statements, or draw arrows between text sections to note relationships.

To model text coding and annotation, select high-interest reading materials your students will enjoy (e.g., short stories, newspaper or magazine articles, or book excerpts). Introduce text coding to your class and explain to students that using these codes will help them focus their reading and make it active. Share with them that in order to make notes next to what they read, they have to be thinking about it. Start with introducing your list and over time then invite students to add or

TABLE 7.2. Text Coding Examples

Text Code	Meaning
✓	Correct, or I agree
–	I disagree
?	I have a question
!	Wow! New, or interesting information
⬭	Circle unknown words
→ ←	Making connections
☆	Important Information
P	Predictions
V	Visualize, create mental images
MI	Main Idea

create new text codes as a class. Model text coding using a think aloud and ask students to follow along from their copy. As you code the text on your copy, you'll want to say things like, "I put a question mark here because I don't understand what the author is trying to say." Or "Oh, I don't know this word; I am circling it." Practice it several times, answer students' questions, and then have them try it on their own.

If students are unfamiliar with text coding, it might take them a while to get used to it. Students will need to see you practicing text coding if you'd like them to use the technique, too. Students do not have to use all of the codes at once; explain to your students that the text coding is meant to help them read more carefully and comprehend the text better. As you review their work, choose what you want to look for; text coding is not to be graded but you can emphasize that you are looking for underlined or highlighted text and for using codes to denote questions, or connections, and making notes in the margins.

Note-Taking

Do content area teachers need to teach students about how to take notes? Well, yes. Many students do not know how to take effective notes. Just like many would highlight an entire page because they think everything on the page is important, others do not know how to take notes from lectures, collaborative group discussions, or whole class discussions. Note-taking about what is important helps with retrieving important information. Better note-takers usually perform better in school and certain types of note-taking produce better results. Forms of note-taking include outlining (main idea, key details), patterning (using flow charts and diagrams), and listing, margin notes, and highlighting. The process of encoding (recording notes) and product function (reviewing notes later) facilitates multiple levels of processing of material, promotes attention during lectures, allows students to transform the information, and review it at a later time when they need to further research it or prepare for a lab, or written assignment, or test (Stahl, King, & Henk, 1991). In addition, note-taking practices may vary from course to course. For example, biology, chemistry, and earth science teachers could ask students to have more structure in their notes to reflect observations, steps, variables, measures, elements, and observations. Mathematics teachers could also ask students to examine a word problem and highlight essential information in green color and non-essential information in blue color. Although the ways one could take notes from texts, experiments, viewing of films or images, etc. may vary from discipline to discipline, note taking remains an essential and basic, level of processing and interacting with text. Table 7.3 includes guidelines for successful note-taking teachers may use with all students and especially with struggling readers and students with disabilities.

In this section, I provide some examples of note-taking graphic organizers for your consideration. All of the graphic organizers are designed to help students engage with text(s), organize their notes, and strengthen their understanding of text. The first example is the Double-Entry Journal (DEJ) (see Table 7.4). The rationale behind this graphic organizer is to help students interact with text while reading, introduce some writing, clarify and organize their thoughts, make connections, and think about concepts and ideas in the text(s). The left column is designed for key quotes and facts the student selects from the text; the second column is used for notes and comments the student makes about the quote, fact, or selected passage. Examples of what students can include in the right column include: "This makes me think of. . ."; "This reminds me of. . ."; "I wonder. . ."; "This is important because. . ."; I infer. . ."; "I am confused because. . ."; "I would like to learn more about. . ."; "I agree/disagree because. . ." Model the process through a think aloud, provide guided practice, and invite small or whole class discussion on students' understanding of the text.

TABLE 7.3. Note-Taking Guidelines

Self-Monitoring Questions	• Am I using complete sentences? • Are my notes clear or confusing? • Did I capture the main points? • Did I abbreviate? • What help do I need?
Guidelines	• Concentrate on the lecture or reading material. • Pay attention—the speaker is making important point if he, or she: pauses before and after an idea; uses repetition; uses introductory phrases to introduce an idea; writes an idea on the board. • Take notes consistently. • Do not write down every word; be selective and brief. • Use symbols (+, −, ×, >, <, /, &, =, etc.); use numbers for words (1, 2, 3, etc.); abbreviate words. • Paraphrase: Translate ideas into your own words. • Organize your notes in ideas or categories; include date and label. • Do not be concerned about grammar and spelling but write legibly. • Mark or highlight your notes to show importance and key details.

TABLE 7.4. Double Entry Journal—Topic: *The House on Mango Street* by Sandra Cisneros (1984)

Direct Quote (With Page Number)	Makes Me Think Of . . .
1. "We didn't always live on Mango Street. Before that we lived on Loomis on the third floor, and before that we lived on Keeler. Before Keeler it was Paulina, and before that I can't remember." (p. 3).	She moved around quite a bit with her family.
2. "I knew then I had to have a house. A real house. One I could point to. But this isn't it. The house on Mango Street isn't it" (p. 5).	She was still dissatisfied with her new home.
3. "eyes like Egypt" (p. 25).	In different cultures, people see beauty differently; make up is also looked at differently.
4. "Their strength is secret" (p. 66).	This reminds me of power. Esperanza obviously identifies with the trees in this chapter.
5. "with lungs powerful as morning glories" (p. 90).	Esperanza is upset that her mother's potential for singing is overweighed by her obligation to stay home and take care of the family.
6. "When we win the lottery . . ." (p. 85).	She's hopeful that better times will come their way; however, she is tired of having it rubbed in her face that they have no money.
7. "for the ones who cannot get out" (p. 110).	There are people in the barrio that will never change and never become what they dream of for themselves.
8. "You will always be Esperanza. You will always be Mango Street. You can't erase what you know. You can't forget who you are"(p. 103).	You are who you are. Be proud of yourself and everything you have.

The second example, Three Column Note-Taking, is a modified Cornell Notes strategy that also encourages the reader to interact with the text during reading and to also reflect on his or her thinking (see Table 7.5). The first column asks the student to paraphrase what he or she has learned from reading the text; in the second column, the student writes what he or she learned from being involved in a small group discussion (it can also be changed to a whole class discussion); in the third column, the student writes questions, thoughts, or observations he or she has about the topic. This template can be changed in a variety of ways. For example, the first and second columns can be used for students to do the following: Main Idea-Details/ Evidence; Opinion-Proof; Hypothesis-Proof; or Problem-Solution. This graphic organizer can be used during and after reading depending on objectives and goals. It can also be used collaboratively and independently. I particularly like the third column because it encourages the reader to delve deeper into the topic, and think metacognitively about their comprehension of the text or topic.

The last example is the Inquiry Chart (I-Chart). The I-Chart is an instructional procedure that fosters critical reading and thinking (Hoffman, 1992). It uses more than one source of information and allows the student to collect supporting or contradicting information on a topic. Within the I-Chart, students (or the teacher) identify a topic, document what they already know, collect information from different sources, and also bring their perspective through new questions and insights about the topic (see Table 7.6). When using this graphic organizer, consider the following three phases: planning, interacting, and integrating/evaluation.

During planning, the teacher can select the topic, or use information from student interests. The topic can be broad or very specific. After you or your students have identified the topic, start forming key questions about the topic; it is useful to involve the class in generating topic-related questions. Use the actual graphic organizer and model how to use it. The sources can also be teacher- or student-generated. During the interactive phase, students think about what they already know about the topic and then address any new facts from additional sources as they relate to the guiding questions. Interesting facts and new questions will result from further study on the topic and may not be related to the initial guiding questions. Learning more about the topic through additional sources can span over a few days or weeks. Students can record in their I-Chart any information that relates to the guiding questions.

TABLE 7.5.   Three Column Note-Taking Example—Topic: Unusual Behavior of Floating Ice

What I Have Learned from the Text	What I Have Learned from Small Group Discussion	Questions, Observations, and Thoughts I Have
• When water freezes, oxygen is removed from the water. • Most liquids get heavier as they freeze, so they sink. For example, cubes of frozen alcohol would sink to the bottom of a glass. • As liquid cools, the molecules in the liquid get closer together. Because they are closer, more molecules can fit into a space, and liquid gets heavier.	• Water is different, instead of getting smaller and heavier as it freezes, water suddenly expands, or takes up more space than liquid water. • When frozen water expands, it gets lighter.	• If ice did sink instead of floating on top of water, ponds and streams would freeze solid. Fish would be trapped in the ice. • In what other instances could floating ice be helpful? • This must be the reason why mariners can see floating icebergs.

TABLE 7.6.   I-Chart Example

Topic: Global Warming	Question 1: What is global warming?	Question 2: How is global warming affecting the climate?	Question 3: What are some key effects of global warming on human health and agriculture?	Question 4: How can we prevent further global warming impact on the earth?
What Do I Already Know?	*Global warming is the increase in the average measured temperature of the Earth's near-surface air and oceans.*	*The climate continues to warm up. We have more floods and droughts.*	*Water pollution and changes in agriculture, farming, and fishing.*	*Reduce environmental pollution; impose fines to high polluting countries.*
Source 1: US Environmental Protection Agency (EPA): http://www.epa.gov/climatechange/	*Increasing gas emissions warm the planet. Humans are responsible for global warming.*	*Polar regions warm more than any other parts of the world. Melting of highly reflective snow and ice reveals darker land and ocean surfaces, which increases absorption of the sun's heat & warms the planet.*	*Heat-related illnesses; cold-related deaths; rise in infectious diseases (due to parasites).*	*Reduce greenhouse gas emissions; find alternative sources of energy; live a greener lifestyle.*
Source 2: Stop Global Warming: http://www.stopglobalwarming.org/	*More carbon dioxide is now in the atmosphere than has been in the past 650,000 years. This carbon stays in the atmosphere, acts like a warm blanket, and holds in the heat — hence the name 'global warming.'*	*Glaciers are melting 10 times faster; we have longer drought seasons and catastrophic storms.*	*Doctors at the Harvard Medical School have linked dengue fever, malaria, hantavirus, etc. to climate change. The global food crisis is also related to climate change.*	*Use compact fluorescent bulbs. Inflate your tires. Change your air filter. Use recycled paper. Plant trees. Buy a fuel-efficient car.*
Source 3: Stop Global Warming: http://www.stopglobalwarming.org/	*In 2007 The US Supreme Court ordered the federal government to take a fresh look at regulating carbon dioxide emissions from cars.*	*The oceans of the world have gotten warmer because of the fast ice melting rates; we've had the tsunamis, hurricanes and more typhoons.*	*Use your muscles; get exercise; buy locally; make your home energy efficient.*	*Take action! Use solar heating. Do not use plastic grocery bags. Reduce garbage. Carpool.*

(Continued)

TABLE 7.6. Continued

New Questions About the Topic:	*What about our future?* *How can we get everybody involved?* *Shouldn't countries that are high pollutants pay the price for the damage they are causing to the earth and atmospheric system?*
Other Interesting Facts I Found:	*Buy products with less packaging and recycle paper, plastic and glass. Save 2,000 lbs. of carbon dioxide per year. Composting helps reduce greenhouse gas emissions by reducing the number of trips trucks must make to the landfill as well as the amount of methane released by our landfills.*
What I learned About the Topic:	*The Earth's atmosphere is overloaded with heat-trapping carbon dioxide, which threatens large-scale disruptions in climate. We must act now to spur the adoption of cleaner energy sources at home and abroad. At the current rate of retreat, all of the glaciers in Glacier National Park will be gone by 2070. Unless we act now, our children will inherit a hotter world, dirtier air and water, more severe floods, droughts, wildfires, and health risks.*

The final phase, integrating and evaluating, involves summarizing and synthesizing information. The teacher can discuss with the students the information they learned from additional sources; this comparison can also take place in small groups. Students can examine any unanswered questions they still have and conduct further research on the topic. Last, they can use the I-Chart to report on what they have learned, and/or use the information for a research paper. Discussion on the quality of sources, supporting, or contradicting evidence, and reflection on their learning about the topic should be facilitated through the use of the I-Chart procedure.

Summarizing

Summarizing is a difficult skill for many students across grades and content areas. In order to summarize a text or texts, a discussion, or a research project, students have to "restate the essence of text or an experience in as few words as possible or in a new, yet efficient, manner" (Wormeli, 2005, p. 2). In order for summarization to be effective, the student must be able to process the ideas in a passage and/or across texts and consider how they are connected to one another. Summarizing can be highly effective, across subject areas, for helping students identify main ideas, generalize, remove redundancy, integrate ideas, and improve their memory of what is read. It is especially worthwhile when used with other strategies such as generating questions and answering questions (NRP, 2000) as it provides students with an opportunity to understand and restate the text (Harvey & Goudvis, 2000). As a content area teacher, you need to consider that perhaps your students were never directly taught to summarize effectively; therefore, use explicit instruction and provide students with opportunities to discuss their understanding of text with others and use summarizing as a means of improving their comprehension of text. Students will benefit from teachers modeling how to write effective summaries, from collaborative work, and from class discussions. Throughout all summarization steps, teachers should emphasize the importance of textual evidence, clarity, and the purpose of writing a summary to promote better understanding of text(s).

To teach summarization effectively using these (and other) graphic organizers, preview the passage and ask the students to think about what they expect the passage to be about. After reading the text, have students generate the main idea in their own words and support it with text details. After students write their summary, ask them to share with a partner or other peers in a small group, go back to the text(s) as needed, and polish their thoughts. Remind them that the first sentence should include the thesis of their summary; they can use words like "in summary," or "in conclusion," or "the main point or idea," toward the end of their summary.

The following two are examples of summarization graphic organizers; both graphic organizers can be used with narrative and informational texts. The first one is a T-Chart (see Table 7.7)

TABLE 7.7. Summarization: T-Chart Example

Topic: Legislative Branch (Civics)

Main Idea	Details/Evidence/Examples
Congress is made out of Senate and The House of Representatives.	*The Senate is made of two senators from each state (100 Senators). The House of Representatives (435 House members) has proportional representation, depending on its population. (p. 97)*
Congress represents the legislative branch of the government.	*Congress makes the federal laws that affect all Americans. They are elected by constituents to make laws for the nation (p. 96)*
Congress's main function is to be a "servant to the people" and defend the Constitution.	*Congress exists to be the representative of people's interests; they make sure their state or district gets a fair share of federal money. (p. 96, 106)*
Congress has a lot of powers.	*The most powerful people in Congress are the Majority Leader of the House of Representatives and the Senate Majority Leader. The Vice President has the title, President of the Senate. The Speaker of the House is next in line to become President in case the President and Vice President die.* • *The Constitution gave Congress expressed and enumerated powers (to make laws, coin and regulate money, and manage commerce).* • *Congress also has implied powers and nonlegislative powers (suggesting amendments to the Constitution, approve/reject the President's choices for Supreme Court Justices/judges/ambassadors, & impeach federal officials & a President).* • *The President can veto or ignore a bill that has been approved by both houses of Congress. (p. 98–99; 101–102, 109–111)*
There are specific qualifications for becoming a member of Congress.	*For Senate: 30 y.o. and older; have US Citizenship (for at least 9 yrs.), and live in the state they plan to represent.* *For House: 25 y.o. and older, have US Citizenship (for at least 7 yrs.), and live in the state you plan to represent.*

Summary: *The Constitution requires top government officials to support and defend it and its citizens. Congress is of The Senate and The House of Representatives. Each member of Congress is elected by his or her constituents to make laws for the country. Congress leads the legislative branch of the government. Although Congress has a lot of powers (expressed, enumerated, implied, and nonlegislative), The Supreme Court checks whether laws are constitutional and at the end, the people, decide whether Congress members really represent them (through re-election) and support and defend their interests and The Constitution of the United States of America. The terms on members of Congress is another way to make sure people's rights are represented and protected.*

students can use to identify main ideas and supporting details from text. The T-Chart can be useful to students for whom you are still providing scaffolding with regard to reading for understanding. You may begin with a partially completed T-Chart, where you have given students the main ideas and their task is to go back to the text and look for supporting details. As students progress, you can offer them a blank T-Chart and ask them to find, with others or on their own, the main ideas and supporting details, and then build a summary using that information.

The second example (see Figure 7.1) is a bit more complex as it is gives the student a progressive pattern—i.e., main idea from the text, supported by three subtopic main ideas, and each subtopic idea is supported by one to three pieces of evidence from text—then students have to incorporate information from subtopic main ideas and write a concise summary. This graphic organizer involves many steps that invite the reader to "dissect" the text and identify the subtopic ideas that support the main idea from the entire text. This can be used as a productive means for collaborative work and negotiation of meaning. It promotes close reading of text supported by textual evidence at many levels and it fosters good understanding of text.

Think Like an Expert

- Literary experts critically examine the role of the author in interpreting a text, focus on identifying and analyzing the conflicts, have many questions about the author's purpose, biases, and ways of organizing the text, and hold conversations about literature, its context, and its relationship to the world. (English Language Arts)
- Mathematicians focus on precision and accuracy, and they work hard to understand solutions. They engage in problem solving, they ask a lot of questions, pay attention to details, and are focused on concepts rather than just on formulas. (Mathematics)
- Scientists understand the deeper meanings of concepts, systematically observe natural phenomena, they develop hypotheses and plan experiments or research, collect, critically question, analyze, and interpret data in order to problem-solve, evaluate the validity of conclusions, and work collaboratively with others. (Science)
- Historians read inside and outside the text, look for corroboration from other sources, think about which perspectives are represented in documents and which ones are left out, analyze images and contextualize information, and evaluate the trustworthiness of sources. (Social Studies)

Strategies for Discipline-Specific Comprehension Instruction

Why consider discipline-specific comprehension strategy instruction? A body of research has demonstrated that explicit teaching of strategies that help students understand what they read improves their comprehension of text (e.g., Block & Duffy, 2008; Block & Pressley, 2002; Duffy, 2002; Duke & Pearson, 2002; NRP, 2000). Students will achieve independence in strategy use if they have learned and practiced the strategy in a meaningful context and if the strategy is related to the material they are learning (Gambrell, Kapinus, & Wilson, 1987).

One caution about strategy instruction is that too much emphasis on strategies can direct the teacher's and the students' attention to the surface aspects of the strategies themselves rather than to the meaning of what is being read. Learning how to use a strategy effectively takes a lot of time and effort; as students become more proficient, the strategies become more automatic and require less effort. Strategy instruction works best when the strategy is applied to a specific text selection, when the teacher provides modeling, when students have many opportunities to use the strategy with varied text, discuss and reflect on what the meaning they are constructing with text, and when the teacher makes necessary instructional adaptations to meet all students' needs (Duffy, 2002).

Name: _____

Topic: World News (Grades 8–12)

SUMMARIZATION

MAIN IDEA (TOPIC):
2008 Olympic Games Challenges

MAIN IDEA (SUBTOPIC 1):

Several reports state that awarding the Olympic Games to a country with severe environmental issues like China was not in the best health interests of any of the athletes.

SUPPORTING DETAILS/EVIDENCE

1. Ten thousand five hundred athletes are expected in Beijing in summer 2008.

2. Ethiopian runner Haile Gebrselassie, pulled out of the Beijing Olympic marathon because of air smog and his problems with asthma.

3. The 2008 Summer Olympic Games will feature participating athletes wearing charcoal masks with team trainers and doctors close by with ibuprofen and asthma suppository.

MAIN IDEA (SUBTOPIC 2):

Among the major challenges facing Chinese authorities, looking after athletes' health and protecting sports ethics promise to be some of the toughest.

SUPPORTING DETAILS/EVIDENCE

1. Authorities are ensuring that athletes meet all requirements and are eligible to participate in the Olympics.

2. Testing athletes for performance-enhancing drugs is common practice.

3. Avoiding any political or other controversial international issues is a major goal.

MAIN IDEA (SUBTOPIC 3):

The Olympic Games organizers fear a repeat of the drug scandals that plagued Athens 2004.

SUPPORTING DETAILS/EVIDENCE

1. Athletes will be fed organic food in order to avoid contamination with substances that could fake doping tests.

2. An estimated 4,500 samples will be collected from the 10,500 athletes taking part, considerably higher than the 2004 games in Athens.

3. Chinese authorities hope to organize a clean event to avoid cheating.

SUMMARY:

The 2008 Olympic Games is the largest sports event the world has ever known. The race to ensure that Olympic athletes are not using performance enhancing drugs or undergoing genetic manipulation is a constant challenge. The location of the games has been a major controversy due to the levels of environmental pollution in Beijing. As a result, some world class athletes will not be participating in these games. In addition, organizers are very cautious about ethical, political, and internationally-sensitive issues. Controversy, safety, protests, security concerns, and fears of doping are some of the challenges surrounding the 2008 Olympic games.

FIGURE 7.1.   Summarization Strategy.

Comprehension instruction should guide students in reading text for the purpose of understanding and it should also encourage critical discussions of the text. Implementing the Gradual Release of Responsibility Model (GRRRM) (Pearson & Gallagher, 1983), will help students develop strategy independence over time and transfer of knowledge, skills, and processes. Research I reviewed in this chapter shows that summarizing while reading, asking questions about the text and answering questions, recognizing and using narrative and informational text structures, visualizing, comprehension monitoring, and other active ways of thinking about the ideas in a text are especially helpful with texts that a reader finds challenging. Students need to learn how to use such strategies independently, so they can eventually interpret text independently. In summary, to support student comprehension of text(s), engage them in close and critical reading of reading high-quality texts, teach students effective reading comprehension strategies using the Gradual Release of Responsibility Model (GRRM) (Pearson & Gallagher, 1983), guide students to apply strategies when reading challenging texts, and create a classroom climate of accountable talk and collaborative inquiry.

In the following section, I present examples from six discipline-specific comprehension strategies I developed per core academic subject area (i.e., English language arts, mathematics, science, and social studies). Each strategy follows the structure, literacy and learning demands, and habits of mind that are unique to each discipline. I combined subject area standards, CCSS standards, and CCSS recommended texts to construct examples from the above four subject areas. These strategies are not designed to take away from content. Rather, they are aimed at building students' critical and discipline-specific thinking skills that will enable them to better read, comprehend, evaluate, and reflect on what they are learning; they will also help students become more aware of their own understanding (metacognition).

Content coverage is not an end in itself; it is the subject matter you will use to develop students' disciplinary habits of mind. Instead, plan with the learner in mind: What should the students know, understand, and be able to do as a result of taking your class? How will you know if students have developed the necessary knowledge and skills? What will each student do to demonstrate his or her understanding? What will you do if they are not learning? When using these (and other) strategies, please consider your learning goals and student abilities and needs. All strategies can span over a period of a few days; they are designed to be used with modeling, close reading of text, guided practice, much discussion and collaborative inquiry. The following strategies will also promote development of discipline-specific discourse. Teachers can use them to informally assess students' historical understanding of the subject matter and development of comprehension processes, and use data from student growth to plan for further instruction. Consider the following core steps of effective strategy instruction I have presented so far in the book:

- Identify texts that are aligned with your content instruction and promote understanding of big ideas.
- Make learning experiences relevant to current events and everyday life.
- Chunk the text (in meaningful conceptual "bites").
- Identify key words from text selection and discuss their meaning and importance.
- Have materials ready (copies of text or projector, copies of strategy template).
- Introduce the strategy and make sure that students understand that the goal is to understand the content of the text.
- Demonstrate and model the strategy (with different texts, not just one text).
- Model your own thinking (using a think-aloud), how you used the strategy, the information you used, and the decisions you made.

- Provide appropriate amount of guided practice depending on the complexity of the text, the strategy, and students' needs.
- Provide collaborative practice and promote accountable talk.
- Discuss how students used strategy, when and where to apply it, and what they learned about content and comprehension skills (i.e., ask students to share, discuss challenges with content and/or strategy, encourage negotiation of meaning, and reflection on student learning).
- Move to independent practice.
- Allow for application and transfer (especially in real word situations).
- Assess and re-teach, as needed.
- Practice ongoing reinforcement and implementation with varied texts.

Use the GRRM (Pearson & Gallagher, 1983) and progressively release the control of the learning to the student. Students need to become not only independent readers and thinkers, but they also need to self-monitor their own thinking and learning processes. All of the following strategies are designed to promote collaborative inquiry and deep learning. Disciplinary thinking, learning, and doing, is not about just content coverage; instead, it is about uncovering the content, examining it with a discipline-specific lens, and mentoring the students in identifying and using the assumptions, the forms of inquiry, and the habits of mind that transform facts into understanding and into formulating new knowledge. For instruction to result in deep learning, teachers have to enable students to read and comprehend the texts of each discipline and also question texts, themselves, and others, consider diverse views, and build informed judgments.

Literary Studies

Literature provides us with a better understanding of the world through dialogue, many conversations, questions, and negotiation—it actually teaches conflicts (Graff, 1992). Literature involves reading and comprehending texts, interpreting texts, and criticism (determining the significance and implications of texts). In English studies, content areas teachers' goal should not be to promote student dependence on teacher knowledge. Instead, teachers should guide students to examine the role of the author in interpreting a text, to make their own interpretations and use conversations about literature, about its context, and about its relationship to the world as a guiding instructional principle.

Table 7.8 includes an example of Literary Analysis that includes the major discipline-specific processes, skills, and types of analysis students will need to do to understand and analyze text. Notice that there is a progressive movement toward the theme through a careful analysis of literary elements. Literary Analysis can be used during and after reading; it is also a nice tool for small and large group discussions; students can also use information from literary analysis for essays and other topic-related projects.

Story Mapping (see Table 7.9) is very useful tool for helping students "map" the entire novel; it is equivalent to using a storyboard that can help students understand the context, the characters, the main events of the story, the conflict, and the theme. This strategy can be used for prewriting activities, during, and after reading; it can guide their thinking, discussions, and writing.

The Main Idea strategy (see Table 7.10) I am sharing below is different to just identifying the main idea in a passage or book. Students are asked to start with the theme, identify the main idea, and then take three more steps: (1) provide three pieces of supporting evidence for the main idea; (2) identify three subordinate ideas; and (3) make connections with other main ideas they have identified so far from the same book or related books.

TABLE 7.8.   Literary Analysis Strategy—Topic: *Jane Eyre* by C. Brontë (1847)

1. Conflict • What is the primary cause of this piece? • What is the nature of the conflict? (internal, external?) • How does this work present its core conflict?	• *Jane's conflicts are mainly internal but we see a combination of internal and external in the book. Jane is a poor orphan girl who only has some nasty relatives, her education as a teacher of music, drawing, and French, and her will to survive.* • *Jane falls in love with her new employer, Mr. Rochester, but she is conflicted because he is her boss and he is also superior to her socially. She finds out that Mr. Rochester is married to a madwoman!* • *Jane runs away from Thornfield so that she won't be tempted to live in sin with Rochester and thinks about going to India with St. John Rivers to do missionary work. She decides to return back to Mr. Rochester and they get married.*
2. Character(s) • Who is the protagonist? The antagonist? Explain their conflict. • What did you learn about this character through his/her thoughts, words, actions, and interactions? • What is his/her core conflict? • How does he/she resolve the conflict?	• *Protagonist: Jane Eyre. The antagonists are: Aunt Reed, Mr. Brocklehurst, Bertha Mason, Mr. Rochester (when he urged Jane to ignore her conscience and surrender to passion), and St. John Rivers.* • *Jane is not the traditional Victorian female character. She is "simple and plain" and she is a strong woman. Jane is presented as equal to the male character in emotional strength and maturity.* • *Rochester is the ideal hero of the Victorian times (he is romantic, charming, would not divorce his mentally ill wife); later on he resolves his conflict by marrying Jane.* • *The main conflict for both is the struggle between passion and moral responsibility to God and society.*
3. Setting • How does the time period in which this piece takes place affect the character and his/her conflict(s)? • What is the atmosphere of the story?	• *1847, Victoria era; many people were hungry; the period affects both Jane's decisions and conflict but she goes against what was expected for women at that time.* • *The atmosphere is very tense, mysterious, gothic, and tragic. Jane moves from place to place (Gateshead, Lowood, Thornfield, Moor House, and Ferndean). Atmosphere, character, experience, and location are all connected.*
4. Imagery • What kinds of language, sounds, and objects does the author use in this piece?	• *Jane addresses her reader directly. . . . 'Reader, I married him'.* • *She shifts between past and present tense.* • *The language is very difficult—it is 19th century language.* • *The sentences are long and complicated and the vocabulary is difficult.*

5. Symbolism
* What do objects or images mean in the story?

* *The red room where Jane's uncle died causes her hysteria; what she experiences in the future, takes her back to the red room.*
* *Gross porridge in Lowood and later on when she is homeless.*
* *Fires set by Bertha. Jane refers to herself as "fire" when talking to St. John Rivers.*
* *Ice; when she left Rochester she tells herself, she "must be rock and ice for him." St. John Rivers is icy. Jane likes ice.*
* *The splintered chestnut tree symbolizes how Rochester and Jane will never completely recover from their separation.*
* *The madwoman in the attic (Bertha) who later commits suicide.*
* *Drawing portraits—Jane drew four (one of herself, one of what she imagines Blanche Ingram will look like, one of Rochester, and one of Rosamond Oliver).*

6. Plot and Structure
* What are the most significant events in the story?
* What is the most intense event?
* What is the least intense event?

* *The novel's climax happens after Jane receives her second marriage proposal, now from St. John Rivers, who asks her to go with him to India as his wife and missionary. Jane almost accepts when she hears Rochester's voice calling her and she knows that she must return to him.*
* *She returns to Thornfield and finds it burned to the ground. She learns that Bertha Mason set the fire and died in the flames; Rochester is now living at his home in Ferndean. Jane goes to him there, rebuilds her relationship with him and marries him. She claims to enjoy perfect equality in her marriage.*

7. Point of View
* Who is telling the story? (1st, 2nd, or 3rd person narration?)
* What is the narrator's tone and agenda?
* Is the story told from a certain point of view?
* Does the point of view affect the meaning, theme, or interpretation of the story?

1st person narration from the point of Jane. All of the events are told from Jane's point of view. Sometimes she narrates the events as she experienced them at the time, while at other times she focuses on her retrospective understanding of the events. She presents her strengths, her weaknesses, and her decisions in a way that makes the reader empathize with her.

8. Tone
* How does the author feel about the subject matter, the events, and the characters?

The tone is Gothic, romantic, and confessional, creating an atmosphere of mystery, secrecy, or even horror.

9. Theme
* What does the story say about humanity, moral/ethical ideas, etc.

Love versus autonomy; religion; social class; gender relations. It brings attention to women's morality and sensuality.; It presents a "new woman" (who was based off the main character, Jane) who is independent, strong, forward, and radical (for her time) about marriage, sex, and contraception.

TABLE 7.9.   Story Map Example

1. Author & Title	*Louisa May Alcott; Little Women*
1. Place, Time, & Setting	*1868–1869; Concord and Boston, Massachusetts; During and after the Civil War (1861–1876)*
2. Characters	*The majors characters are: Jo March (protagonist), Beth March, Amy March, Meg March, Laurie Lawrence.*
3. Narrator	*Omniscient. The narrator knows everything and provides analysis and commentary about the characters and their lives.*
4. Point of View	*Third person. The narrator focuses on all the different characters in turn.*
5. Tone	*Sympathetic, real, and sometimes very moral*
6. Foreshadowing	*When Laurie presents the March sisters with a postbox, the narrator hints that love letters will pass through the box in years to come. Laurie's promise to kiss Amy before she dies foreshadows their future marriage.*
7. Event #1	*Jo refuses to marry Laurie*
8. Event #2	*Beth becomes sick and later on dies*
9. Event #3	*Meg gets married*
10. Event #4	*Laurie marries Amy*
11. Event #5	*Jo marries Professor Bhaer*
12. Major Conflict	*I think being poor, being female, and trying to juggle life is a conflict for the whole family. Also, the girls are growing up and are having trouble accepting not having the comforts they used to have, making adult choices that mean sacrificing independence, and trying to fit into society's stereotypes for women: Jo wants to become a great writer instead of a conventional adult woman.*
13. Rising Action & Climax	*The sisters begin to mature; they meet Laurie, their next-door neighbor; Meg gets married. (rising action) Jo turns down Laurie's marriage proposal, confirming her independence. (climax)*
14. Falling Action & Ending Event(s)	*Beth dies, and Amy marries Laurie; Jo marries Professor Bhaer; Jo starts a school for boys and puts her writing career on hold.*
15. Motifs	*Music (signing; Laurie wants to be a musician); teaching (many characters are teachers); language (proper)*
16. Symbolism	*Umbrellas (protection of a man over a woman), burning (burnt dress, burning Jo's writings)*
17. Theme(s)	*Family love; Poverty vs. wealth; Sibling rivalry; Women's struggle with family duty and professional growth; Gender stereotypes; Female independence; The importance of being genuine*

TABLE 7.10.   Main Idea Strategy—Topic: *The Gift of the Magi* by O. Henry (1905)

Theme(s): *Poverty, generosity, love, and wisdom*

Main Idea: *The main idea is that human emotion, love, and affection are the best gifts to give or receive because they come from someone's heart.*

Supporting Evidence for Main Idea (Use page numbers from text as needed.)		
1. *Della sells her hair to buy Jim a chain for his watch. Jim sells his watch to buy Della pretty combs for her hair.*	2. *The gifts that the two loving spouses exchange are symbols of their love for one another and those gifts can never be taken away by their poverty.*	3. *They were wise to sell their most valuable possessions for the person they loved. They were like the three wise men — the Magi—who brought presents for Jesus Christ after he was born.*

Subordinate/Less Important Ideas (Use page numbers from text as needed.)		
1. *Fear about their future and how they will survive it financially.*	2. *Lack of pride (Della put her pride aside and sold her beauty, her hair; Jim sells his most prized possession).*	3. *Beauty comes from within, not from possessions or appearance.*

Connections to Other Main Ideas We Have Identified So Far (Use page numbers from text as needed.)		
1. *Wisdom at times means doing the silly thing for the right reason.*	2. *Identity and love: when someone truly loves, he or she loves the other person for who they are, for their true identity.*	3. *Sacrifice is not a negative word; I guess, it could be seen as a gift that is very expensive and worthy.*

Character analysis is another key element of story understanding and analysis of conflict. The Use Your Adjectives (see Table 7.11) strategy invites students to describe a book, or a key character in the book using relevant adjectives. Because the strategy limits students to five adjectives, they will have to think very carefully about adjective choice; they will also have to go back to the text, think on their own or discuss their choices with peers, review their notes, and make interpretations using evidence from the text. Students will also have to explain their choices and give examples from the text to support them. Last, they will use the information to write a summary on the main character. Teachers can use the strategy with the protagonist and the antagonist, do a nice side-by-side comparison of the two, and hold wonderful small and whole class discussions on the main characters and students' interpretations of them in the text.

The Questions-Connections strategy (see Table 7.12) can be useful in a variety of ways. Students can respond to questions generated by the teacher, by themselves, or from collaborative work with peers. Students have to provide text evidence to support their answers, and they also have to go a step further and connect what the question is asking with the overall theme or topic. This is not easy work; it requires much processing of text, making interpretations and making connections among ideas that may not be explicitly stated in the text. The strategy also asks students to write one question they still have about the topic—it gives them an opportunity to generate more questions and also gives them the message that there is a lot more to think about, or beyond, the text. Last, students write a summary that highlights their understanding of how key ideas and concepts are connected in the text.

The Viewpoint Analysis (see Table 7.13) provides a relevant format for informed argumentation. It facilitates perspective taking and critical thinking. After reading a text, students are

TABLE 7.11. Use Your Adjectives Strategy
Directions: Select 5 adjectives to describe the book or character(s) and explain how they apply.

Book: *Eleven* by Sandra Cisneros	✓ Character(s): Rachel

5 Adjectives	*Explanation*
1. EMBARRASSED	She expected a great birthday but was embarrassed and humiliated and wants to disappear into the sky.
2. IMAGINATIVE	She thinks things up in her head all the time about the birthday, the sweater, people, and herself.
3. TIMID/SHY	She does not want to wear the ugly red sweater that is not hers; she is too shy in from of her teacher.
4. DEFIANT	But she keeps saying "not mine"; she wants to "bunch it up."
5. INSIGHTFUL	She knows that she does not know enough; she understands that people' experiences affect how they act. She understands that although she is eleven, she can still be scared like she is five, or cry like she is three.

Summary: **Use the above adjectives to write a summary about the book or the character(s).**
Rachel is the main character in the book. She is narrating what happened at her 11th birthday and what it means to be eleven years old. She did not get the birthday she had expected and she felt embarrassed and helpless and starts crying. She imagines what she can do to the ugly read sweater and although she is defiant in her head, she is pretty shy in front of others. She is insightful about why she and other people acted the way they did. She wishes she was 102 years old because then she would have more wisdom and respect to stand up for herself.

TABLE 7.12. Questions-Connection Strategy—Topic: *The Killer Angels* by Michael Shaara (1974)

Questions	Answers with Evidence from Text(s)	Connections with Theme/Overall Topic
3 Key Questions about the Topic: Assigned by Teacher ☐ Identified by Me ☐ Generated from Collaborative Work? ☐ (Check appropriate box.)		
1. One of the major conflicts in the novel is the disagreement between Lee and Longstreet on how they should fight the battle. What does each man think the army should do? Should Longstreet have acted differently?	Longstreet understands modern nature of warfare and believes that fortified, defensive positions are the best way to win a battle; he suggests that Lee moves the Confederate army to a position southeast of Gettysburg, so the Confederates come between the Union army and the Union capital, Washington, D.C. Robert E. Lee, is a more traditional soldier, and he believes he can destroy the Union army—even in a fortified, high ground position—if he simply puts his men in the right places. But Lee underestimates the	It relates to the importance of strategic planning for winning wars. The battle also relates to a divided nation.

Union artillery, secured in the high ground of Cemetery Ridge, which utterly demolishes the Confederate soldiers as they attempt to cross the field. Pickett's Charge was the last great infantry charge—never again would so many men slowly march across a field to strike their enemies.

2. What error did General Lee make that cost him the victory?

He was not specific enough to General Ewell about weather to attack or not Culp's Hill and Cemetery. "Tell General Ewell the Federal troops are retreating in confusion. It is only necessary to push those people to get possession of those heights. Of course, I do not know his situation, and I do not want him to engage a superior force, but I do want him to take that hill, if he thinks practicable." (Chapter 3)

It relates to loyalty, and to command errors, and to Southern aristocracy.

3. Why do you think the Confederate army lost the Battle of Gettysburg?

General John Buford, the Union cavalry commander, seized the high ground and tried to protect Seminary Ridge and the hills around it. This helped the officers to see much of the area, they were covered with rocks and trees that can block bullets, and the artillery had a greater range when fired from high positions. Robert E. Lee is annoyed with General Ewell for not seizing Culp's Hill or Cemetery Hill. I think the high ground was the major cause of the Union victory.

It relates to technological advancements and strategic war planning for winning wars and to the high cost of lives lost in wars; this was the bloodiest battle in the history of the Civil War.

Lee, without J. E. B. Stuart, Lee could not plan strategically—he had no information about the movements of the Union army or an area he does not know. The Union artillery took down the advancing Confederate soldiers, and killed or wounded almost 60% of them.

1 Question I Have About the Text/Topic

Should Longstreet have tried to try to take command from Lee or get help from other generals to help him change Lee's mind?

Summary: Write a summary using knowledge you have about the topic and include connections to the greater theme.

In The Killer Angels, Michael Shaara tells the story of the Battle of Gettysburg. On July 1, 1863, the Army of Northern Virginia or Confederate army, and the Army of the Potomac, or Union army, fought the largest and bloodiest battle of the American Civil War. When the battle ended, 51,000 men were dead, wounded, or missing. The main characters are key historical figures— General Robert E. Lee, commander of the Confederate army; General James Longstreet, Lee's second in command; and Union Colonel Joshua L. Chamberlain, who participated in one of the most famous parts of the Battle of Gettysburg, the fighting on Little Round Top. Lee underestimated the Union Army's position and equipment advantage and did not take Longstreet's advice. At the end, the Confederate attack begins as the troops start marching across the open field toward the Union troops. The Union begins firing cannons, blowing huge holes in the Confederate line and killing hundreds of men. When the Confederates come within range, the Union soldiers open fire with their guns, killing hundreds more. Pickett loses sixty percent of his division. The Confederates retreat, and the Battle of Gettysburg come to a bloody end.

TABLE 7.13. Viewpoint Analysis Strategy

Supporting Evidence		Opposing Evidence
1. It is the right thing to do (moral duty).	**Question/Point of View:**	1. It offends our values as Americans.
2. It allows us to get information from enemies.	Is war prisoner torture ever justified?	2. Torturing prisoners endanger US troops.
3. It can help us save lives.		3. It makes us look bad to the world.
Decision: I believe "yes, torturing war prisoners is okay" because it is morally right to do that for our national security.		
Rationale: Well, we have been trying to secure our country and freedom around the world; we need to do what we need to do to get information from our enemies so we can save lives. I trust the laws and the system and that our government will do it within limits for national security purposes.		
Summary: Torture is debated because everyone has their own point of view; some people see it as a moral and ethical act and others do not. Some people think that endangering troops is part of being at war and that we should prevent prisoner abuse; others think that saving lives and protecting our national freedoms is a just reason for torturing war prisoners.		

Source: Is torture ever justified? Retrieved from *http://teacher.scholastic.com/scholasticnews/indepth/upfront/debate/index.asp?article=d0130.*

asked to provide evidence for a certain point of view on a topic (for or against), provide supporting and opposing evidence on the issue or dilemma at hand, make a decision on their viewpoints, provide a rationale, and write a summary that covers diverse viewpoints on the topic. This format is conducive to small and whole class discussions and much negotiation of meaning.

Mathematics

Mathematicians experiment and use knowledge and inductive reasoning to solve new problems. Teachers need to engage students in doing, rather than, hearing about mathematics and help students see the connections between what they are learning in class and the world they live in. They need to challenge students' misconceptions that there is just one approach or solution to a mathematical problem. Students need to learn multiple ways to solve and represent problems, reason through a problem, and also consider how peers explain solutions using different approaches. Solving mathematical problems requires deep understanding, not just memorization of formulas and application of known procedures.

The Anticipation Guide (see Table 7.14) presents debatable statements about a topic on which students indicate whether they agree, or disagree with each statement before they read about the topic. The Anticipation Guide will activate students' prior knowledge on the topic, and will also give them a purpose for reading. It will also help clarify students' ideas by comparing the before and after reading decisions they made. In addition, it will help them consider others' responses by listening to, or discussing, their decisions. Deeper processing will be fostered as students provide an explanation for their decisions, especially after reading. Students can use the strategy individually, in pairs, in small groups, or with the entire class. Teachers should introduce the anticipation guide before they introduce a new topic, and revisit it after reading with the entire class.

TABLE 7.14.   Anticipation Guide—Geometry Example

Directions:

- Check "Agree" or "Disagree" beside each statement below before you start the task.
- Compare your choice and explanation with a partner.
- Revisit your choices at the end of the task. Compare the choices that you would make after the task with the choices that you made before the task and be ready to provide an explanation.

Before Reading Agree	Before Reading Disagree	Statement	After Reading Agree	After Reading Disagree
X		1. The *Pythagorean Theorem* is statement: "In any right triangle, with the hypotenuse of a length c and the sides of lengths a and b, the sum of the squares of a and b will equal the square of the hypotenuse, c."	X	
Explain why you agree or disagree **after** *reading:* *This is the definition of the Pythagorean Theorem.*				
X		2. In algebraic terms, $a^2 + b^2 = c^2$, c is the hypotenuse and a and b are the legs/sides of the triangle.	X	
Explain why you agree or disagree **after** *reading:* *I know that* $a^2 + b^2 = c^2$				
X		3. The *Pythagorean Theorem* can be used to calculate right angles only.		X
Explain why you agree or disagree **after** *reading:* *This is not a true statement. The Pythagorean Theorem is used to calculate the length of the sides of a right triangle.*				
	X	4. The *Pythagorean Theorem* is true for some right triangles but not all.		X
Explain why you agree or disagree **after** *reading:* *This statement does not make sense to me. It is used to find the lengths of one of the sides when the other two sides are known.*				
X		5. *Pythagorean Triples* are groups of three whole numbers or integers that make the *Pythagorean Theorem* true.		X
Explain why you agree or disagree **after** *reading:* *I thought that they could be used for any real number greater than zero. But, I read that the definition of a Pythagorean triple consists of three positive integers. Example: (3, 4, 5) would be one. (1, 1 √2) would not be a Pythagorean triple.*				

Many students have difficulties understanding word problems and converting problems into equations. The Key Words strategy (see Table 7.15) can be used to promote students' understanding of both the problem and how to convert it into an equation. Teachers can select key words, or concepts per topic, model, and provide guided and collaborative practice.

In mathematics, it is particularly important for students to make distinctions between information that is important to the understanding of the problem or topic, and information that

TABLE 7.15.   Key Words for Converting Problems to Equations Strategy—Algebra 1 Example

Word	Operation	Example	As an Equation
Sum	Addition	The sum of my age and 10 equals 59.	$y + 10 = 59$
Difference	Subtraction	The difference between my age and my younger brother's age, who is 44 years old, is 5 years.	$y - 44 = 5$
Product	Multiplication	The product of my age and 12 is 168.	$y \times 12 = 588$
Times	Multiplication	Three times my age is 147.	$3 \times y = 147$
Less Than	Subtraction	Seven less than my age equals 42.	$y - 7 = 42$
Total	Addition	The total of my pocket change and 10 dollars is $10.87.	$y + 10 = 10.87$
More Than	Addition	Thirteen more than my age equals 62.	$13 + y = 62$

is not. The following strategy, Determining Essential and Non-Essential Information (see Table 7.16), can be used to address how to read and comprehend mathematics text. Students will identify essential and non-essential information, and then restate the problem in their own words before they proceed with solving it. This will allow the teacher to provide feedback to the entire class, or to individual students. Students will also learn from each other's understanding of the problem, and it will promote student self-awareness and comprehension monitoring.

The Problem-Solution (see Table 7.17) is a multi-layered strategy that promotes critical thinking about problem solving. It involves the reader in identifying and interpreting the problem in mathematical language, listing essential and unknown information, identifying steps planned to solving the problem, solving the problem, reflecting on what worked, or did not work (meta-cognitive), and what the student will need to pay attention to in the future. Students will benefit from the step-by-step and reflective approach to problem solving.

TABLE 7.16.   Determining Essential vs. Non-Essential Information Strategy

Problem: Nancy, who lives in Los Angeles, wants to send a package to her sister in Miami. It is approximately 2348 miles (3778 km) from Los Angeles to Miami. The package contains a picture that she drew, some cookies that she made and a book she thinks her sister will like. The package weighs 3.5 pounds and is 12″ by 6″ by 8.″ The company has a special; any size box will be sent for $11.25 for the first pound and $6.25 for each additional pound or portion of a pound. How much will it cost for Nancy to send her package?	
Essential Information	**Non-Essential Information**
• *First pound costs $11.25* • *2.5 pounds will be calculated at $6.25 a pound or portion of.*	• *It is approximately 2348 miles (3778 km) from Los Angeles to Miami.* • *The package is 12″ by 6″ by 8.″* • *The package contains a picture that she drew, some cookies that she made and a book she thinks her sister will like*
Write the problem in your own words. $C = (1)(\$11.25) + (2.5)(\$6.25)$	

TABLE 7.17.   Problem-Solution Strategy—Algebra 1 Example

1. What is the problem? (Read it carefully, read it again aloud, and reword it.). Write the problem in your own words.
Discount Lumber gives contractors a 15% discount on all orders. After the discount, a contractor's order cost $578. What was the original cost of the order?
Rewording: The original cost minus 15% discount cost is order cost.

2. Translate the problem in mathematical language.
Let c = the original cost of the order, in dollars.   Translating: c – 0.15c = $578

3. List essential information for solving the problem. *15% discount* *Order cost: $578*	What information is unknown? *Original cost of order*	

4. What is my plan? Step 1 *Equation—combine like items*	What is my plan? Step 2 *Multiply both sides by 1*	What is my plan? Step 3 *Simplify*

5. Solve it; state solution clearly; check your answer with the original problem.
1.00c – 0.15c = 578 Equation
0.85c = 578 Combine like terms
c = 578/0.85
Divide both sides by 0.85
c = 680 Simplify
The contractor's discount on the lumber costing $680 would be (0.15)($680)=$102. When this is subtracted from $680, we have $578. So, $680 works in the original problem.
The original cost of the order is $680.

6. Reflection: What worked? What did I miss? What do I need to pay attention to next time?
I read the problem carefully, found out what I knew and what was missing. I need to keep reading word problems very carefully; some words can be tricky.

Source: Example adapted from Northern Nebraska Community College.

The KWNSR strategy (see Table 7.18) can be used to directly instruct students about a new math concept/topic. "K" stands for "What facts do I know about the problem?"; "W" stands for "What is the problem asking me to do?"; "N" stands for "which information is needed to solve the problem?"; "S" stands for "What strategy operation or tools will I use to solve the problem?"; and "R" stands for "Reflection—What do I need to do next time?" The example I provided (with the help of Margaret Cubero, a Florida math educator) shows a step-by-step approach to organizing one's thoughts and putting down what he or she knows about the problem, selecting the appropriate operations, and reflecting on the outcomes of the solution. In the example below, I have also added, for demonstration purposes, two additional columns in part five of the strategy in which I model my thought process and use the Gradual Release of Responsibility instructional model. The KWNSR is also a nice strategy for exam review.

TABLE 7.18. KWNSR Strategy (with Teacher Modeling Component)—Math Example

Find the inverse function of this problem:
$$f(x) = \frac{7-5x}{2}$$

1. What facts do I *Know* about the problem?	2. *What* is the problem asking me to do?	3. Which information is *Needed* to solve the problem?	4. What *Strategy*/Operation or Tools will I use to solve the problem?
1) It is a straight line because of the power of the equation. 2) Passes the Horizontal Line Test (A function f has an inverse function if and only if no horizontal line intersects the graph of f at more than one point.) 3) Need to have the equation in the form of y=ax + b	1) Find the inverse of the function $f(x) = (7-5x)$ divided by 2.	1) Decide if problem has an inverse by using the Horizontal Line Test. 2) Need to replace the f(x) by y. 3) Substitute x for y and y for x. 4) Replace y by $f^{-1}(x)$ in the new equation. 5) Verify that f (x) and $f^{-1}(x)$ are inverse functions.	1) Algebraic calculations such as substitution, multiplication, properties (associative, distributive, etc). 2) Know rules of inverse functions – domain of f is equal to the range of f^{-1} and range of f is equal to the domain of f^{-1}. 3) Know that $f(f^{-1}(x)) = x$ and $f^{-1}(f(x)) = x$. 4) Know how to do inverse operations. If the equation is adding terms, know how to subtract terms. 5) Know how to manipulate fractions.

5. Solve it!

Step #	Left side of eq.	Right side of eq.	Modeling the Thought Process	Gradual Release of Instruction
1	f(x) =	$\dfrac{7-5x}{2}$	Write the problem down.	What is the first step always? Write the problem down.
2	y =	$\dfrac{7-5x}{2}$	Make substitution of f(x) with y.	What substitution do we need to make so we can work the problem? Make substitution and solve for y.

Step	Equation		
	$x =$	$\dfrac{7-5y}{2}$	Switch or interchange x and y (setting it up for the inverse).	What is the next step? Since we are looking for inverse, we need to switch the x and y in the equation.
3	$2x =$	$\dfrac{2(7-5y)}{2}$	Multiply both sides of the equation by 2. Because: The denominator on the right side of the equation had a 2. So, multiplying it by 2 would eliminate the fraction. Then because I am eliminating the fraction on the right side of the equation, I need to multiply the left side of the equation by 2 also.	What do we need to do now? We want to eliminate the fraction. How do we do that? We need to multiply both sides of the equation by 2. Is it in its simplest form? No.
4	$2x =$	$7-5y$	Equation simplified.	Is it simplified now? Yes.
5	$2x + 5y =$	$7 - 5y + 5y$	Need to have y on the left side of the equation and all other terms on the right. So, y would be on the left and x would be on the right. To do that, I need to add 5y to both sides of the equation. How did I know that? Because in step 4 the 5 y had a subtraction sign in front and we need to use the opposite signs.	What is the next step? Need to get have the equation in y=ax + b format. Need to move y to the left side of the equation. How do we do that? Add 5y to both sides of the equation. How did we know to add 5y? Because the sign in front of 5y is negative (subtraction).
6	$2x + 5y =$	7	Simplified the equation but is not in thecf y=ax + b. This now has x and y on the left side of the equation, but x needs to be on the right.	What do we do here? Simplify.
7	$2x-2x + 5y =$	$7-2x$	Need to have x on the right side of the equation. To do that, I need to subtract 2x from both sides of the equation.	Is it in the correct format? No. We need to have it in y=ax+b format. What do we need to do? Need to subtract 2x from both sides of the equation.

(Continued)

TABLE 7.18. (Continued)

8	$5y =$	Simplified the equation. It is very close to the form $y - ax + b$, but the coefficient of y is not 1, it is 5.	What do we do here? Simplify.
9	$\dfrac{5y}{5} =$	Need to divide both sides of the equation by 5.	Is it in the correct format? No. We need to have it in $y=ax+b$ format. What do we need to do? Need to divide both side of the equation by 5.
10	$y =$	Simplified the equation. It is in the format of $y = ax + b$. Now to write it in inverse function format.	What do we need to do in this step? We need to simplify and write it in the $y=ax+b$ format.
11	$y=$	Putting the equation in $y=ax+b$ format by using the Communitive Property.	Written in $y=ax+b$ format by using the Communitive property.
12	$y=$	Multiplied the numerator and denominator by (-1) to make $-2x$ positive. This is the same thing as multiplying by 1 so it does not change the value of the equation.	What is the step we need to do to just make the equation in the format of $y=ax+b$? Need to make x positive.
13	$y=$	Used the Distributive Property to simplify the equation and "clean up the signs."	What is the property we need to use to simplify the equation?
14	$f^{-1}(x)$	Written in inverse function format by replacing the y with $f^{-1}(x)$.	Complete with the calculations so what do we need to ask? We need to ask if it is written in function format?
15		f and f^{-1} have domains and ranges consisting of the set of real numbers.	What can we say about the domains and ranges? The domain and range consists of the set of real numbers.

For the equation expressions in rows 8–13:
- Row 8: $7 - 2x$
- Row 9: $\dfrac{7 - 2x}{5}$
- Row 10: $\dfrac{7 - 2x}{5}$
- Row 11: $\dfrac{-2x + 7}{5}$
- Row 12: $\dfrac{(-1)(-2x + 7)}{(-1)(5)}$
- Row 13: $\dfrac{2x - 7}{-5}$
- Row 14: $\dfrac{2x - 7}{-5}$

6. Did I solve it correctly? Yes but could have made several simple calculation errors.

If not, what did I miss?

These are the areas I could have made a mistake:

1) Steps 4 and 5 – could have selected the wrong operation to do. This is a very common mistake.

2) Steps 6 and 7 – could have selected the wrong operation to do a second time.

3) Step 12 – could have made calculation error, not multiply by (−1) divided by (−1).

4) Step 14 – could have forgotten to write it as an inverse function.

7. *Reflection:* What do I need to do next time?

1) Be aware of my calculation skills. (Know when to add/subtract or multiply/divide values.)

2) Be aware of simplification skills. (Know when to simplify to see the next steps to be completed.)

3) Remember the formula for a line and the relationship of the formula for its inverse.

TABLE 7.19. Math Journal—Algebra 1 Example

Equation/Problem (include pg. number as needed)	Solve It	Explain Solution

1. (i) = x
    (ii) = 3y
    (iii) = 612 ÷ d; where d = distance (rounded to the nearest whole foot)
	(i) + (ii) = (iii)
	x + 3y = 612 ÷ d
		I substituted the value of each variable into the equation.

2. The length of a rectangle is 6″ longer than the width. The perimeter is 32″. Find its length and width.	$2(l + w) = P$ Let x = width. Let x + 6 = length. $2((x + 6) + x) = 32$ $2x + 12 + 2x = 32$ $2x + 2x + 12 = 32$ $4x + 12 = 32$ $4x + 12 - 12 = 32 - 12$ $4x = 20$ $4x/4 = 20/4$ $X = 5$	I used the formula for perimeter of a rectangle. I created variables for the length and width based on the word problem. I then substituted the values into the formula and worked the problem.
3. Simple Interest $96 interest paid in 4 years at a rate of 3%. Find the principal.	i = prt $96 = p(.03)(4)$ $96 = .12p$ $96/.12 = .12p/.12$ $800 = p$	I used the simple interest formula i=prt which is interest = principal times the rate times the time. I substituted in the known values and worked the problem.
4. Simplify: 15ab – 6ac – 21ad	$15ab - 6ac - 21ad$ $3(5ab - 2ac - 7ad)$ $3a(5b - 2c - 7d)$	I looked at the coefficients and found that they were multiples of 3 so I could factor out the value 3. I then looked at the variables and found that the variable a was common to all three terms so I could factor out the a.
5. Solve the following quadratic equation: $x^2 + 8x + 16 = 0$	$x^2 + 8x + 16 = 0$ $(x + 4)(x + 4) = 0$ $x + 4 = 0$ $x = -4$	I looked at the equation and saw that 16 was a perfect square (4 × 4). And saw that 2 × 4 = 8. I know the quadratic formula is $x^2 + 2xy + y^2$ factors to $(x + y)(x + y)$. I then substituted and solved for x.

Table 7.19 includes a template I developed for a Math Journal that focuses not only on solving the problem, but also on explaining the solution and approach taken to solve it. The Math Journal can be used as a standards template for solving mathematical problems in class, and also as part of homework.

Science

Scientific thinking is not produced through rote memorization; it is a rigorous, evidence-based method of inquiry about the world humans live in. Students need to actively engage in scientific inquiry, understand the deeper meanings of concepts, and critically question and analyze data in order to problem-solve, and work collaboratively with others. Scientific teaching should be active, engaging, rigorous, collaborative, evidence-based, and it should connect classroom learning to life.

TABLE 7.20. Read Like a Scientist Strategy—Interactive Science: Chromosomes and Heredity

1. What is the text about?	Chromosomes and inheritance.
2. Who is the author? *(Provide evidence on author's scientific or other expertise.)*	*A number of scientists, and professors who teach science. I looked it up in the front of the textbook (About the Authors, p. 13-15)!*
3. What is the author's perspective on the topic? *(Use evidence from text.)*	*I think it is neutral because they present + and – points; they also present reports and studies that question what we know. (Evidence: Lesson 4).*
4. What concepts do you need to know to understand this topic?	*1. DNA replication, mitosis* *2. Heredity, genetics (DNA replication), fertilization, purebred, hybrid, allele (dominant, recessive)* *3. Probability, Punnet square, pedigree, phenotype, genotype, homozygous, heterozygous* *4. Meiosis, sexual and asexual reproduction*
5. What scientific ideas(s), problem(s) or dilemma(s) does this text address? *(Use evidence from text.)*	*1. How chromosomes, genes, and inheritance are related.* *2. What happens during meiosis and fertilization?* *3. How traits are passed from human parents to children.* *4. How chromosomes relate to disease.* *5. Is it ethical to the DNA of an organism?* *6. How far should genetic research go?* *(Evidence: Lesson 4 on chromosomes)*
6. To what 1-3 broader scientific idea(s) does this text relate?	*1. The Genetic Code* *2. The science of heredity* *3. DNA is the genetic material!*
7. What are 1-3 scientific questions raised by this text?	*1. How can we prevent chromosomal deficiencies?* *2. How can science help us understand human behavior?* *3. How can science help people understand which diseases are hereditary and which ones are not?* *4. What is the future of genetic research?*
8. What possible experiment or research can be developed to solve the problem or address the dilemma? *(Explain why it is appropriate for this problem.)*	*In the lab, we can show the movement of chromosomes during meiosis.* *I think we need more research on meiosis to help prevent miscarriages and birth defects; my sister has had two miscarriages in the past three years. This is appropriate because many people with deal with many physical and emotional difficulties; science can help.*
9. 1 question I still have about this text/topic.	*What difficulties do people (and their families) with Down's Syndrome face? How can we help them?*

The Read Like a Scientist strategy (see Table 7.20) reflects major scientific thinking and learning habits of mind that will help students critically question and analyze text, and problem-solve in science. The strategy also asks students to evaluate the credibility of the author's statements and evidence he or she presents. Through this approach, students will also make connections with other scientific concepts, will determine what experiment or relevant steps are necessary for solving the problem, or addressing the dilemma, and will generate a question for further study.

The Scientific Problem Method Organizer (see Table 7.21) provides a science-specific lens for hypothesis formulation, collection of data, solutions, analysis of results, and reflection on the problem and its solution. In every step, the student is asked to provide evidence for his or her decisions, think critically about data collection, observations, and results, and evaluate the entire process. Students will also benefit from discussing with others their hypothesis, results, and recommendations. The last part of the strategy asks students to generate a question that still remains unanswered in an effort to foster critical thinking, and further research, and engagement with the text, or topic.

The Problem-Solution strategy (see Table 7.22) can be used for a systematic and evidence-based analysis of a scientific problem. Students will state the problem in their own words, examine what or who caused the problem, and use evidence from the text(s) to explain why the problem is a problem (i.e., its significance and effects). Students will also design, discuss, and evaluate two solutions to the problem, and will summarize the best solution using evidence from the text(s).

Claim-Evidence-Reasoning (see Table 7.23) is a way for students to understand, analyze, and evaluate scientific claims. Students will identify the source(s) of the claim, evidence that supports or does not support the claim, and then summarize their opinion about this scientific claim using evidence from text(s).

Teachers can use the Engaging in Argument from Evidence strategy (see Table 7.24) to promote understanding of perspective taking and critical evaluation of scientific evidence in a topic. This strategy will also foster collaborative inquiry; teachers can split the class into four groups and assign a different perspective on the same scientific issue or concept per group. Students within each small group will examine what the concept or issue means to different groups of people and use evidence to argue for it through that perspective. A whole class discussion on the same topic following small group inquiry will expand students' understanding of the topic at hand, and will promote text-based argumentation.

The Summarization strategy (see Table 7.25) takes a multi-layered approach to developing a well-developed summary of a scientific topic. Before students start writing their summary, they have to identify three key insights, connect the concepts at hand with other scientific concepts or theories, use evidence from text and graphs, charts or tables, make further connections with prior knowledge, and think of implications of this topic for science and life. This process will help students self-monitor and regulate their understanding and will result in a quality summary of the topic.

Social Studies/History

Historians argue . . . all the time! Historians are not in the business of memorizing a bunch of unrelated facts and events. The study of history helps students "develop their capacities to synthesize information, weigh evidence, evaluate points of view, and think analytically" (Manning, 2006, p. 24). Historical thinking involves questioning, connecting, sourcing, making inferences, considering alternative perspectives, and recognizing one's own knowledge (Calder, 2006). Historical practice is evidence-based argumentation about the human past. Students must draw upon their skills of historical comprehension in order to engage in historical analysis and interpretation. Teachers need to teach them how to reconstruct meaning from historical documents, identify the main questions, and also analyze the intentions of the people involved and the complex ways in which they interacted with their complex world.

TABLE 7.21. Scientific Problem Organizer Strategy—Solar Energy Example

1. Define the problem (State it in the form of a specific and testable question.)	*Do solar panels supply electricity to anything?*
2. Conduct research on the problem and re-state the question, if needed.	*Can one size solar panel do the work of any batteries?*
3. Formulate a hypothesis.	*I predict that a 2.5-inch solar panel produced more electrical power to the rechargeable battery compared to the alkaline non-rechargeable AA, C, and D batteries.*
4. Think about your hypothesis. (How can you support it? State if research or controlled experiment will be used. Then, test your hypothesis, collect your data, and keep good records.)	*Experiment; Materials: 1, 2.5 solar panel; 4 miniature screw-base lamps; 4 lamp holders; 3 battery holders; 3 alkaline non-rechargeable AA, C, D batteries; 1 rechargeable AA battery; 1 voltage meter. Procedures: I measured the voltage on the 3 alkaline non-rechargeable batteries AA, C and D, and the AA rechargeable battery with a voltage meter. I took the red (positive) and black (negative) electrical wire, from the battery holders and connected the positive and negative connections to the light bulb lamp holders to the non-rechargeable batteries. I repeated the same procedure with electrical wires from the solar panel to the AA rechargeable battery. I put the solar panel with rechargeable battery to a sunny area in my back yard. I measured the voltage of the batteries with a voltage meter for 9 days and I recorded my data.*
5. Conduct systematic observations and collect data. (What data did you collect? From where? For how long? How did you organize it—in table, chart, graph, other?)	*I recorded the voltage for each battery for 9 days and logged in in my observation notebook. I organized it in a bar graph to show changes. On day 4, AA non-rechargeable battery voltage dropped from 1.48 volts to .66 volts and lost its potency. The C non-rechargeable dropped from 1.60 volts to 1.29 volts; on day 6, it dropped to .04 volts and lost its potency. The D non-rechargeable dropped from 1.59 volts to .09 volts on day 9, lost its potency. By day 9, the AA rechargeable battery with solar panel continued to have potency and varied from 1.23 volts to 0.96 volts. The AA rechargeable battery continued to recharge because the solar panel produced more electrical power to it because it was exposed to direct sunlight every day.*
6. Draw conclusions from data. (What conclusions can you draw from your data? Did data support or not support your hypothesis? How did you analyze your results? Formulate your report, conclusions, and make recommendations.)	*My results supported my hypothesis that the 2.5-inch solar panel produced more electrical power to the rechargeable battery compared to the alkaline non-rechargeable AA, C, and D batteries. I was very excited to see the results and how the data I collected supported my hypothesis. I analyzed my results by hand; I examined differences in the measurements I took and I made close observations throughout. It made me think more about uses of solar energy and how they can help make our environment more green and healthy. Recycling and using energy from the sun is free, clean, and powerful. I recommend using solar energy; it does not take much to maintain and install. Although big solar panels can be expensive, the fact that solar energy is renewable means that we can have steady power source for our needs.*
7. Unanswered question(s) you still have and next steps.	*How would solar energy work in places with heavy rainfall?*

TABLE 7.22. Problem-Solution Organizer Strategy—Earth Science: Climate and Climate Change Example

---

1. Problem: What is it? (Write the problem in your own words.)
Global sea levels have risen fast over the past century.

2. Who or what caused this problem? (State evidence from text(s).)
One main cause has been greenhouse-gas emissions. If we can slow down the carbon dioxide emissions, we can slow down the rate of sea level rise.

3. Why is the problem a problem? (State evidence from text(s).)
Warmer oceans have been expanding. Rising global sea levels coastal regions and make storm surges worse (like the Venice, Italy, historic flood of 2008 and Hurricane Sandy of 2012). They cause destructive erosion, huge flooding, and loss of human, animal, and plant life. Whole islands around the world are at risk of been swallowed by oceans.

4. Discuss or Design 2 solutions to this problem (using evidence from text):

Attempted Solution #1:	**Attempted Solution #2:**
Slow down greenhouse-gas emissions by creating strict global environmental laws.	*Increase people's awareness and encourage them to live a carbon lifestyle that can help stabilize warming.*
Details:	**Details:**
Enforce strict plans for checking emissions around the world and especially in high pollutant countries.	*Develop a campaign to help people make low carbon lifestyle easy for all. Campaign should include information about home, work, leisure, and daily activities for all ages.*
Results:	**Results:**
Reduced greenhouse-gas emissions will slow down glacier and ice cap meltdown into the ocean.	*Existing campaigns have created new products, vehicles, have promoted recycling, and are creating changes in housing, work environments, schools, and public transportation.*
Pros (1-3):	**Pros (1-3):**
Save human lives especially in low-lying areas. *Save billions.*	*More people are becoming educated about the benefits of a low carbon lifestyle; there are new greener appliances and materials; more choices in clothing and foods.*
Cons (1-3):	**Cons (1-3):**
Sea levels will continue to rise anyway. *Laws and taxation.*	*We don't have enough change!* *We need more people living a low-energy lifestyle!*

5. Summarize the best solution for this problem (Provide reasons/rationale for your choice of best solution.).
The best solution is to global water levels rising is to slow down and prevent them from rising! The best solution is to create international cooperation to reduce global greenhouse gas emissions, to restore forests that work as carbon sinks and reduce greenhouse gas emissions. We need to work together to save our planet!

TABLE 7.23.   Claim-Evidence-Reasoning Strategy—Health Example

1. What is the claim? State it.	*Sodas are bad for your health; they contribute to obesity, elevated blood pressure, stroke, kidney damage, and certain cancers.*
2. Who is making this claim?	*Laura Martin, an MD.*
3. Are there any biases, prejudices, or interests related to the person(s) or agency that is making this claim?	*Well, she is a medical doctor who sees a lot of patients; she also writes for WebMD. She is interested in preventing disease and she also reports results from studies.*
4. What evidence do you have from text(s) that supports this claim?	*A recent study from the University of Miami reported a 48% increase in heart attack and stroke risk among daily diet soda drinkers, compared to people who did not drink diet sodas at all or did not drink them every day.*
5. What evidence do you have from text(s) that contradicts or disproves this claim?	*There's debate among researchers about the issue and the types of studies. Rachel K. Johnson, RD, PhD, MPH, is a professor of nutrition at the University of Vermont and an American Heart Association spokeswoman who does not believe limiting sugar-sweetened drinks is the only solution. She says, "But to me, it is an important step in the right direction."*
6. Find 2 additional resources that back up the claim.	*David Ludwig, MD, Director of OWL Child Obesity Clinic and Author of: Ending the food fight http://children.webmd.com/video/child-obesity-epidemic* *Dr. Oz: The Food Industry and Child Obesity: http://www.doctoroz.com/videos/food-industry-child-obesity*

7. Write your opinion about this claim and use evidence to support it.
I have mixed feelings about this claim; I need to research it more. I get the impression that soda drinking is a reason for obesity but not the main one. I don't think we can stop teenagers from drinking soda all together. What we can do is educate them about the risks of drinking too much soda (sweet, diet, or zero calories). The evidence points to adolescents drinking too much soda per day and the dangers of developing obesity and diseases. Some adolescents consume 1,000-2,000 calories per day just from drinking soda. Childhood obesity is a national issue that threatens our society. I am going to be recording how much soda I drink per day!

TABLE 7.24. Engaging in Argument from Evidence Strategy—Earth Science: Matter and Energy Example

Scientific Concept: *hydraulic fracturing or fracking*

1. What does this scientific concept mean to a policy maker? *Argue using evidence from text(s).* *It means policies, taxes, public disclosure, jobs, environmental and public protection, the potential for state and local government and budgets.*	*2. What does this scientific concept mean to a* gas company CEO? *Argue using evidence from text(s).* *It means, project, profit, and shareholder value increases. It means lots of profit!*
• What argument might a *policy maker* present about the importance of this concept or topic? Use evidence from text(s).	• What argument might a *gas company CEO* present about the importance of this concept or topic? Use evidence from text(s).
He or she would argue about job creation, laws about quality, water and public protection, and changes in taxes and consumer benefits and costs.	*He or she would argue about products, profits, stock prices, and the benefits of the company, greener energy, and ways to deal with taxes and laws.*
3. What does this scientific concept mean to a consumer? *Argue using evidence from text(s).* *It means job creation, taxes, reduced gas prices, and savings.*	*4. What does this scientific concept mean to an* environmentalist? *Argue using evidence from text(s).* *It means potential environmental disaster! It means fluid spills, groundwater and air pollution, well casings failure, and dangerous waste disposal.*
• What argument might a *consumer* present about the importance of this concept or topic? Use evidence from text(s).	• What argument might an *environmentalist* present about the importance of this concept or topic? Use evidence from text(s).
He or she would argue for cheaper natural gas and savings for the family budget.	*He or she would argue how fracking will affect the environment now and in the future, the dangers for air pollution and water contamination, and impact on human health.*

TABLE 7.25. Summarization Strategy—Biology: Animal Behavior Example

Topic: Animal behavior and evolution

1. What 3 key things (from the text) did you learn about this topic?	*1. If a behavior that is influenced by genes increases an individual's fitness, that behavior will tend to spread through a population.* *2. Some adaptive behaviors can affect the survival of populations and species. Behaviors that are not adaptive become less common.* *3. Learning behaviors are, habituation, classical conditioning, operant conditioning, and insight learning.*
2. What scientific concepts, theory, or scientific evidence does this topic relate to?	Concepts: • *Evolution* • *Characteristics and traits of animals.* • *How animals descended from earlier forms through the process of evolution.* • *How animals interact with one another and their environments.* **Theory:** *Darwin's theory of evolution*

3. What evidence from graphs, charts or tables do you have about this topic?	*Many photos, charts, and images about different species, their characteristics, and behaviors.* *Charts mapping seasonal animal behavior.* *Data graphs from field studies of the short-tailed shearwater and its reproductive success.* *Graphs showing a ground squirrel's body temperature throughout a year.* *I learned about how natural selection affects animal behavior; I also learned how scientists study, track, and report animals' adaptive behaviors.*
4. What evidence from past knowledge (texts) or experience(s) have helped you better understand this topic?	*What we learned about evolution, animal traits and characteristics, animal diversity and systems, helped me to understand the adaptive behaviors of animals.* *How I trained my dog to let me know when he wants to go out helped me understand operant conditioning.*
5. What are future implications of this topic for science and life?	*Should marine mammals be kept in captivity?* *How animals' respond to their environment affects their survival.* *Animal behavior changes can be early signs of environmental changes.* *Research can also help us understand interactions between humans and their environment.*

6. Summary: Write a summary about this topic using information from items 1-5.

Animals, their characteristics, fitness, and behavior have all evolved over time. Innate and learned animal behaviors affect animal reproduction and survival. Animals respond to changes in their environment. Social behaviors affect an animal's evolutionary fitness. Research in how animals interact with their environment and how the environment can predict their survival can be useful for both animals and humans.

Figure 7.2 reflects the discipline-specific habits of mind historians are involved in as they attempt to analyze and argue about the past and its implications for the present and the world. Teachers can use each element of Thinking Like a Historian to promote students' critical understanding of historical evidence and text-based argumentation. Each element can be used in close reading of texts, examination of evidence, questioning like a historian, and arguing about history in small and whole class discussions. I recommend also including it in students' notebooks, and teaching students how to use sourcing, contextualization, corroboration, do close reading, and make critical connections across historical concepts, events, or ideas.

Evidence-based argumentation is the "bread and butter" of history. Table 7.26 can be used to guide students' understanding of primary or secondary documents using the Examining the Author's Argument strategy. This strategy includes many steps that can be broken down and used over time in class in a small or whole class format. Through it, students will develop a comprehensive understanding of a document by identifying: the author, his, or her purpose with this document, the author's biases, or errors in his, or her writing, and evaluating the credibility of the evidence he or she provides to persuade the reader about the topic or event.

Historical documents also include artifacts, images, maps and charts that contain important information about a person, event, or place. The Image Analysis strategy (see Table 7.27) will help students to critically examine, analyze, evaluate, discuss, and reflect on historical images; it will help build their understanding of the purpose of the image(s), the message it "communicates," evaluate the source, and reflect on how the image analysis added to, or challenged, their

Thinking Like a Historian

✓ **Sourcing**

- Examine source information.
- Who is the author of this document?
- When was the document developed?
- For what purpose(s) was the document created?
- How trustworthy is the document source?
    - o What makes this document source trustworthy?

✓ **Contextualization**

- Situate the document and its event(s) in time and place (historical context).
- What are the major current events?
- What are the key events that preceded them?
- What are the key themes?
- Who are the key players/people that distinguish the period the document was created?

✓ **Corroboration**

- Gather and a sk questions about important details across multiple sources, accounts, and perspectives.
- Compare and contrast details across multiple sources to determine agreement and disagreement.
- What other primary sources might corroborate or refute this interpretation?
- Were the documents accurate, complete, inclusive, biased, relevant, or well supported?

✓ **Close Reading**

- Read the text independently; read closely and pay attention to language, text, and sentence structure.
- Annotate the text (highlight, circle, or underline) for unknown words, things that are unclear/confusing, questions you might have, and important facts.
- Pay attention to text during teacher read-aloud.
- Answer text-dependent questions.
- Use evidence to support claims.
- Read what is said and what is not said.
- Read with a critical eye, like a historian—pay attention to explicit facts and facts or information that are missing.
- Analyze primary sources (i.e., texts, images, music/film, artifacts, data).
- Ask good questions: What is the purpose of this document? What is the document's author not mentioning? Whose voices are heard, silenced, or not heard in this document or historical account? Which perspectives are missing, overrepresented, underrepresented, or misrepresented?

✓ **Use Background Knowledge**

- Use your historical knowledge to read and understand the document.
- Ask yourself: What else do I know about this topic? How can I use the knowledge I already have to understand this document/topic and other topics, themes, and ideas?

FIGURE 7.2. Thinking Like a Historian.

TABLE 7.26. Examining the Author's Argument Strategy—World History Example

1. Who is/are the author(s) of this document? *A reporter for CNN News.*

2. What is the author's purpose with this document? *To inform the public about child soldiers in Somalia.*

3. What is the author's main point or conclusion in this document? *More children are abducted and abused in war-torn Somalia.*

4. What 2 reasons does the author offer to persuade you to agree with his/her conclusion?
- *The author offers testimonials about a serious child abuse issue.*
- *The Human Rights Watch reports persuaded me; they look credible; I researched it more about found out that their mission is to defend human rights worldwide (http://www.hrw.org)*

5. Are the author's premises clear? True? Are they supported by evidence? *Yes*

6. Does the conclusion follow logically from the premises? *Yes; "for children in Somalia, nowhere is safe."*

7. Does the author make any logical errors *(Circle all that apply: generalizations, faulty causes and effects, false analogies, going in circles without providing evidence, false either/or argument, etc.)*? **Provide 1 piece of evidence from the document for your choice(s).** *No, I don't think so.*

8. Does the author clearly define terms in the document? *Please provide 1 piece of evidence. Yes, the term of abuse, abduction, and human rights.*

9. Does the author use single meaning sentences or vague ones? *Please provide 1 piece of evidence.*
Single meaning sentences.

10. Does the author contradict himself/herself? *Please provide 1 piece of evidence. No, I do not think so.*

11. Does the author provide relevant examples? *Please provide 1 piece of evidence. Yes; examples from camps, statistics about the increase of children soldiers, and deaths. Example: "Dozens of recruits, mostly ages 14 to 17, are driven by truckloads to the front line, where they are told to jump out only to be mowed down by gunfire while Al-Shabaab fighters launch rockets from behind, according to Hassan."*

12. What type(s) of evidence does the author provide? *Provide 1 piece of evidence.* **Is the evidence relevant to the main point of the document? If yes, explain the relevance.**
Reports from the Human Rights Watch; diplomatic efforts to solve the problem.
Evidence: A 15-year-old boy recruited by Al-Shabaab from his school in Mogadishu in 2010 told Human Rights Watch "out of all my classmates — about 100 boys — only two of us escaped, the rest were killed."
This evidence is relevant because it supports the problem.

13. Is the evidence from trustworthy people/sources? *Yes! From reports that global organizations that protect human rights.*

14. What types of people/sources/authorities does the author rely upon? (e.g., politicians, religious leaders, scientists, historians, economists, writers, everyday people, other). *Circle or identify all that apply.*
Politicians, reporters, everyday people, military leaders, and human rights global organizations.

15. How much of the evidence persuades you that the author's conclusions/points are correct? *Provide 1 example.*
All of it! And especially, this: "The 104-page report, released two days ahead of a Somalia conference hosted by the British government, grimly details countless violations against children based on more than 160 interviews conducted over the last two years with Somali youngsters who escaped from Al-Shabaab forces, as well as parents and teachers who fled to Kenya."

Source: *More Child Soldiers in Somalia Fighting. Retrieved from: http://articles.cnn.com/2012-02-21/africa/ world_africa_somalia-child-soldiers_1_al-shabaab-child-soldiers-human-rights-watch?_s=PM:AFRICA.*

TABLE 7.27.   Image Analysis Strategy—Salem Witchcraft Trials of 1692 Example

Image	Analysis
1. Observe the image. What is the image showing?	*It is showing the Salem witchcraft arrests in 1692 and a man on his way to the gallows.*
2. What is the setting/period for this image?	*Puritan New England in 1600s.*
3. List people in the image; What are unique characteristics of the people? (e.g., gender, dress, age, race, social class, etc.)	*Puritan soldiers and farmers. Men and women. Wealthy people and farmers.*

(Continued)

TABLE 7.27. (Continued)

Image	Analysis
4. List objects in the image; What are unique characteristics of the objects?	*Weapons, an ox cart, an ox, horses, and rocks.*
5. List activities in the image; What are unique characteristics of the activities?	*Puritan soldiers leading a chained man to the gallows.* *Some Puritans are on horses.* *Farmers look like they are coming to the rescue of the arrested man.* *The scene is out in the country; looks like it is on a hill.* *The wind is blowing and the sky is dark.* *The arrested man does not look like he is trying to escape.* *A woman (may be the wife?) is trying to hold on to the arrested man.*
6. How are people and objects arranged in this image?	*The Puritans are standing straight; the farmers are bent over and look afraid and angry. There are women, men, and animals in the image.*
7. What are the motives of the image developer? What is the image "telling"?-- What can you conclude from it?	*To show the fear and uproar these accusations caused. These trials affected the farmers' and others' lives.*
8. What is the image not "telling"?	*Why was this man arrested and led to the gallows? Did men have the same symptoms as the women?*
9. What clues do you have from the image to suggest what is happening?	• *The sky is dark and ominous.* • *The villagers/farmers look afraid, are hunched over, and look helpless.* • *The Puritan soldiers are using weapons are keeping them away or under control. Some soldiers are on horses.* • *The arrested man's hands are in chains. His wife is trying to hold on to him. The accused man's gaze is toward the sky as if he is pleading with God for his innocence.* • *There are farm animals in the picture and lots of people—this arrest looks like it stirred trouble.* • *The villagers look skinny and tired; the Puritans look determined, more confident, and healthier.*
10. How does this image support or contradict what you have learned about the topic so far?	*It supports what I have learned about The Salem Witchcraft—people had fears of disease, like smallpox, were afraid of Native Americans, and were suspicious of outsiders. Over 200 people were accused of practicing witchcraft; later the colony admitted the trials were a mistake and compensated the families of the accused.*
11. What 1 question does this image raise about the topic?	*Were people falsely accused because of fear of witchcraft or because others wanted their land and that was one way to take it away from them?*

Source: Image: "Witchcraft Victims on the Way to the Gallows," by F.C. Yoyan, appeared in the *Boston Herald, May 14, 1930*. Retrieved from: http://edsitement.neh.gov/lesson-plan/understanding-salem-witch-trials.

TABLE 7.28. Identifying Point of View Strategy—World History: "We Shall Fight on the Beaches" speech by Winston Churchill, July 4, 1940, Example

1. What is the purpose of this document?	*To give a report on the military situation and evacuation from France, to praise the British Army, Air Force, and Navy, and to warn Britain about the collapse of France and the danger of standing alone to face a German invasion. He also appealed to the US to enter the war against Germany.*
2. What is the target audience of this document?	*The British House of Commons.*
3. What are main points and assumptions in the document?	Main points*: the state that Europe is in during the Battle of France; the valor of the British Armies; Britain in danger of German invasion.* Assumptions: *England is alone in the fight against the Nazis; rallying national support against them.*
a. Do they have a theme or pattern? If yes, what is it?	*a. "We shall fight in France, we shall fight on the seas and oceans, we shall fight with growing confidence and growing strength in the air, we shall defend our island whatever the cost may be. We shall fight on the beaches, we shall fight on the landing grounds, we shall fight in the fields and in the streets, we shall fight in the hills. We shall never surrender!"'*
4. What are key words that are repeated throughout the document?	• *"we shall fight on"; "we shall fight in"; "we shall go on"; "we shall never"; "we shall not flag or fail"; "British"; "French"; "the House"; "The enemy"; "German"; "Air Force"; "Navy"; "Army"; "This island"; "Europe"; "Nazi"; "beaches"; "landing grounds"; "fields"; "streets"; "hills"*
a. Do they form any concepts? If yes, specify.	• *struggles, hardship, sense of duty, inspiration, determination, national pride, courage, valor, sense of duty, hope, victory, danger*
5. What authorities does the author use as examples? And why?	• *World War II, the great military loss British in Belgium and France, thousands of British and French soldiers being stranded at Dunkirk, the efforts of the British Army, Air Force, and Navy, the plans of Nazi Germany, the potential danger of German invasion of Britain.*
6. What issues and assumptions do the main points address? (e.g., freedom vs. authority)	• *Victory over Nazi Germany, the bravery of the British military, patriotism, and the hope of Britain rising up and defeating Germany.*
7. What is the author's point of view? (e.g., scientific, progressive, feminist). Provide evidence from text to support your perspective.	• *Churchill's point of view is patriotic, authoritative, and progressive. Evidence: see speech for how he praises the British Armies, his call to Britain to stand against Germany, and his absolute determination as Prime Minister to lead, bring hope, and bring victory.*

understanding of the person, place, or event. It can also stimulate the development of student-generated questions and further research on the topic.

Through the Identifying Point of View strategy (see Table 7.28), students will be able to analyze and interpret the intentions of the author, the author's word choices and organization of ideas, the author's orientation, and his or her motives and beliefs about the historical event, person, place, or concept. This strategy will particularly help students learn how authors organize and present their perspectives on various topics, learn how to appreciate historical perspectives, and compare and contrast differing sets of ideas, values, and personalities. Last, students will have to conduct close reading of the text(s) in order to provide evidence that supports their interpretations of the author's point of view as reflected in the document(s).

The Fact versus Opinion (see Table 7.29) strategy will help students differentiate between historical facts and interpretations and the ways in which historical evidence and people's interpretations are represented in historical documents. Students will also pay close attention to the words, phrases, and evidence the author(s) presented to support facts and opinions and will have to provide evidence for their opinions. Last, students will also be given an opportunity to develop their own interpretations of the evidence presented in the documents, and generate questions that warrant further study on the

TABLE 7.29.   Fact vs. Opinion Strategy—American History: The March to Washington, August 28, 1963, Example

1. List 3-5 top facts from the document(s). (Facts are statements that can be proven true.)	2. What words or phrases did the author use to inform the readers that an idea was a fact?	3. What evidence did the author(s) include to support statements of fact?
1. August 28, 1963 over 250,000 people (including 73,000) whites met in Washington, DC to demand the passing of the civil rights bill.	• The date, the numbers of people, the location, the legislation	• Photos, articles, speeches, video
2. This was the largest demonstration in the history of the US with lots of unity among different types of civil rights organizations.	• Evidence from reports about lack of violence, estimated numbers, and organizations uniting (marching together hand in hand)	• Photos, articles, reports, video
3. At the end of the day, President J.F. Kennedy and the march leaders met in the White House.	• JFK met with the top six leaders	• Photos from the JFK Presidential Library and Museum; statement by JFK
4. Malcolm X called it the "Farce in Washington."	• The role of the government in the march, the absence of violence	• His observations
5. Malcolm X said, " 'integration' can weaken the black man's movement."	• The unity among civil rights organizations and the cooperation with the government	• His beliefs, knowledge, and perspectives

4. Do you have any questions/comments about the fact(s) in the document(s)? (e.g., clear/unclear, complete/incomplete, biased/unbiased)

It was helpful to have different perspectives and not just what was in the textbook. In a way, each author has his or her own biases because of their experiences, race, and perspective. I want to read more testimonials from blacks and whites who marched and not just from leaders of the movement.

5. What opinion(s) did you identify in the document(s)? (Opinions are statements that describe someone's judgment, belief, feelings or way of thinking about a topic.)	6. What words or phrases did the author use to inform the readers that an idea was an opinion?	7. Did fact(s) or authority support the opinion(s)? Please specify.
1. "Marching united for the pursuit of the dream of equality." (Textbook)	• Marching united; dream of equality	• Facts about the way the march was done
2. "We have witnessed today in Washington tens of thousands of Americans—both Negro and white—exercising their right to assemble peaceably and direct the widest possible attention to a great national issue." (JFK Statement)	• We have witnessed; exercising their right to assemble peacefully	• Facts about the right to assemble peacefully
3. "The executive branch of the Federal Government will continue its efforts to obtain increased employment and to eliminate discrimination in employment practices, two of the prime goals of the March." (JFK statement)	• will continue its efforts; two of the prime goals of the March	• Opinion about the role of the government and the goals of the march
4. "This was a national bitterness; militant, unorganized, and leaderless. Predominantly, it was young Negroes, defiant of whatever might be the consequences, sick and tired of the black man's neck under the white man's heel." (Malcolm X speech)	• a national bitterness; militant; unorganized; defiant; sick and tired	• Facts about who participated; opinions about how the march was done and why and the role of blacks and whites
5. "Yes, I was there. I observed that circus. Who ever heard of angry revolutionists all harmonizing "We Shall Overcome . . . Suum Day . . ." while tripping and swaying along arm-in-arm with the very people they were supposed to be angrily revolting against? Who ever heard of angry revolutionists swinging their bare feet together with their oppressor in lily-pad park pools, with gospels and guitars and "I Have A Dream" speeches?" (Malcolm X speech)	• I observed a circus; tripping and swaying; were supposed to be angrily revolting against	• Facts about people holding arms, singing, and MLK, Jr.'s speech; opinion about all of the above

8. What opinion did you form about the topic/document(s) as a result of these facts?

The March in Washington was courageous! It brought so much national attention that forced the government to ban discrimination against blacks in public places and in voting rights.

9. What 1 question do you still have about the document(s)/topic?

Did JFK's signing of the Civil Rights Act of 1964 become his death sentence?

topic. This strategy presents a scaffolded approach to developing historical understanding about historical facts, multiple perspectives and interpretations, and supported or unsupported expressions of opinion versus informed hypotheses that are grounded in historical evidence.

The Take a Stand strategy (see Table 7.30) will promote the development of students' historical thinking by inviting them to formulate an informed position on an issue. Use it to teach

TABLE 7.30. Take a Stand Strategy—War on Terrorism Example

1. State your stand on the topic.	*The US plans for war on Terrorism since 911 have not been successful.*
2. Prepare a short paragraph that puts the issue in context (explain who, what, where, when, and why).	*Since September 11, 2001, when terrorists brought down the Twin Towers, attached the Pentagon building, and crashed the plane in Pennsylvania, the US has been trying to remove Al-Qaeda. We invaded Iraq, we have been in war with Afghanistan, we captured Sadam Hussein, executed Osama bin Laden, and have not managed to eliminate the sources of terrorism. These wars have cost over 4000 soldiers' lives and over 30,000 seriously wounded; the wars have cost us billions of dollars and have affected our national budget, many nations hated us, and our national security is still threatened.*
3. What are 1-3 key terms or concepts that support your stand on the topic?	• *The huge casualties of war* • *The US national budget* • *The growing influences of Al-Qaeda and Islamic extremism in the Middle East* • *The threat of nuclear war*
4. List any underlying assumptions, beliefs, and values you have about the issue.	• *I don't like war!* • *My cousin and a neighbor were killed in Afghanistan.* • *I don't think we can control the growth of Islamic extremist in the Middle East.* • *Many of my friends' families have lost their homes—why are we fighting other people's wars and our own people are suffering?*
5. What evidence do you have from the document(s) to support your stand?	• *The number of US Soldier casualties.* • *The cost of the wars in trillions (over $1,428,069, 632, 956 and growing by the minute).* • *In 12 years of war on terror, the U.S. has been trying to destabilize Al Qaeda and remove its leaders but more and more Al-Qaeda camps are growing in the Middle East.*
6. What other points of view, evidence, and conclusions might be possible on this topic?	Other points of view: • *It is not easy to eliminate terrorism; The cost of the wars is worth it when compared with the cost of national security; We needed to protect the oil fields; The US has improved aviation security and homeland security.* Conclusion: *The war on terror cannot be won the way we have approached it; actually, I do not know if it can be won at all. May be educating people is the best solution to national and world problems.*
7. What implications does your stand suggest?	*My stand suggests that we bring our soldiers back home, honor those who lost their lives and support war veterans whose lives are forever changed, work with other countries to get their commitment on global threats to terrorism. It seems like a war on terrorism is a war without end! It also implies that we focus on rebuilding our country financially.*

students how to comprehend a variety of historical sources and perspectives on an issue, identify underlying motives, beliefs, and assumptions, use evidence from texts, and discuss implications of the topic for current events and the world. This strategy can be used to facilitate informed small and whole class discussions, and evidence-based argumentation on a topic.

Metacognition and Comprehension Monitoring

Metacognition

Metacognition is the act of thinking about thinking. Metacognition refers to the cognitive processes of monitoring and self-regulation that relate to how well one learns and performs various tasks (Pintrich, 2002). Metacognition plays an important role in communication, reading comprehension, problem solving, language acquisition, attention and memory, self-control, self-learning, writing, and personality development (Flavell, 1979). How do students learn? According to NRC (2000), students (a) come to the classroom with preconceptions about how the world works; (b) must have a deep foundation of usable knowledge, understand facts and ideas in the context of a conceptual framework for each discipline, and organize knowledge for retrieval information; and (c) must be taught explicitly metacognitive skills (i.e., be aware of their own learning, set goals, and monitor their progress toward them).

Everything I have presented so far in this book reflects the importance of eliciting and challenging students' preconceptions, organizing instruction around a discipline-specific conceptual framework, connecting new information to the framework, providing relevant examples for context, and integrating metacognitive skill development into content. In Chapter 2, (see Figure 2.6), I presented the view of learning as apprenticeship and I also attempted to illustrate the interactions of several processes that affect the learning process, including teachers' and students' preconceived ideas about learning and how it takes place, as well as the role of metacognition, self-awareness, and self-monitoring in the learning process.

To prepare students for college and career readiness, teachers must encourage all students to believe that they can indeed grapple with complex disciplinary text and ideas, and solve complex problems. Teachers should assess students' beliefs on their learning prior to attempting to teach metacognitive tasks because the learners' beliefs and assumptions about learning impact self-regulated learning. They should also teach students self-regulated strategies that will help them become more aware of their strengths, weaknesses, and how to adapt to learning tasks. To develop students' metacognitive skills, teachers need to provide them with many opportunities to monitor their own progress, reflect, work collaboratively with peers (take the perspective of others, listen, and talk), and formulate and share their thinking, knowledge, and explanations.

A number of science and mathematics educators have been researching the role of metacognition through teaching IMPROVE, a set of metacognitive steps, on students' mathematical achievement (Mevarech & Kramarski, 1997; Kramarski, Mevarech, & Amari, 2002) and scientific inquiry skills (Zion, Michalsky, & Mevarech, 2005). IMPROVE steps include the following: Introducing the new concepts, Metacognitive questioning, Practicing, Reviewing, Obtaining mastery, the Verification, and Enrichment. Metacognitive questions involved (a) comprehension questions: What's the problem asking? What is it giving you? What type of problem is it? What are the essential features?; (b) Connection questions: How are . . . and . . . similar or different?; (c) Strategic questions: What strategy is most appropriate? Why is this strategy most appropriate? How can the suggested plan be carried out? and (d) Reflection questions: How do you know it's right? How could you have solved it differently?

Eggert, Ostermeyer, Hasselhorn, and Bögeholz (2013) in a recent study with senior high school science students examined the effects of cooperative training strategies to enhance students' socio-scientific decision making (i.e., describing socio-scientific issues and developing and evaluating solutions) and metacognitive skills. Providing students with cooperative-metacognitive training can help them grapple with complex problems, develop self-regulatory skills, and improve learning. Their study carries implications for instruction that is aligned with the CCSS, the discipline-specific approach to literacy presented in this book (see Figure 2.2). Do you want your students to develop deep understanding of concepts, problems and ideas, develop solutions, evaluate them, and make informed decisions in your discipline? Create a classroom learning environment that reflects your discipline's habits of mind, engage them in critical thinking, equip them with needed tools, model desired processes and outcomes, provide quality feedback, promote collaborative inquiry, and teach them how to monitor and regulate their own thinking and problem-solving processes.

Comprehension Monitoring

Comprehension monitoring is a metacognitive strategy that involves the ongoing evaluation of a reader's understanding of the text. Comprehension monitoring strategies help students monitor their understanding as they read and repair meaning when it breaks down. Monitoring teaches students to be aware of what they do understand, identify what they do not understand, and use appropriate "fix-up" strategies to resolve comprehension problems (Armbruster, Lehr, & Osborn 2001). "Fix-up" strategies, such as re-reading, re-stating, predicting, visualizing, and using context clues and decoding skills to figure out unknown words or ideas, help students do the job of repairing. Many struggling readers are neither aware when meaning breaks down nor know what to do to repair it. "Teaching metacognition helps students to monitor their learning, develop a deeper understanding of text, and think at a higher level. . . . Metacognitive students are strategic in their learning, asking focused questions, sharing how they solved problems, and engaging with each other." (Wilson, 2001, p. 33)

Teach students how to read carefully, purposefully, and closely, analyze the text, look for patterns in text structure, ask someone questions about the text, consider graphs, images, and charts, and think about what they are reading. Also, teach students how to identify unknown, confusing, or complex parts, stop after each paragraph or two and summarize, ask questions before, during, and after reading, and synthesize information (Collins & Smith, 1980; Pressley, 2000; Tovani, 2000). Teachers can use think-alouds to model how they monitor their comprehension when reading complex text; for example, the teacher could stop and say something like, "This doesn't make sense to me. I think I need to go back and reread that passage (or think about the word, or study the graphics more carefully, etc.) to make sure I understand." Then, he or she would think aloud as he or she models the particular fix-up strategy.

Digital Literacies

- Wix: http://www.wix.com/. Develop a classroom homepage that supports comprehension instruction and offers links to resources. Wikispaces: http://www.wikispaces.com/. Great places to post meaningful questions for classroom collaboration inside and outside of the classroom.
- Digital Docs in a Box: http://www.digitaldocsinabox.org. Allows teachers and students to access digital documentary kits and create digital documentaries.
- Storify: http://storify.com. Students can follow current events, speeches, and presentations, and turn them into stories using social media.

The Goal: Deep, Transferable Learning

What is deep or deeper learning? Deep learning involves the critical analysis of ideas, making connections to already known concepts and principles; it leads to long-term retention of concepts so they can be used for problem solving in new contexts. The main characteristics of deep learning include: looking for the meaning, focusing on the key argument or concepts, distinguishing between argument and evidence, relating new and previous knowledge, and linking the subject matter content to real-life situations (Biggs, 1999).

Deep learning is the process of learning for transfer—taking what one has learned in one situation and applying it to another (The William and Flora Hewlett Foundation, 2010). Isn't that the goal of comprehension, also? Isn't every teacher's goal to develop students who are critical, independent thinkers, and life-long learners? To transfer learning means to apply it to new situations. Deep learning prepares students to (a) master core academic content; (b) think critically and solve complex problems; (c) work collaboratively; (d) communicate effectively; and (e) learn how to learn (e.g., self-directed, metacognitive, learning). This definition of deeper learning is also supported by the National Research Council's (NRC) recent report, *Education for Life and Work: Developing Transferable Knowledge and Skills in the 21st Century* (2012). According to this report (Pellegrino & Hilton, 2012), deeper learning is the outcome of three, intertwined, important domains of competencies for college, career, and life: cognitive (e.g., critical thinking, analysis, reasoning/argumentation, problem solving); intrapersonal (e.g., self-management, learning to learn, metacognition, flexibility, perseverance); and interpersonal (e.g., expressing ideas/communicating, negotiation, empathy/perspective-taking, collaboration).

So, if deeper learning is our goal, can it be taught? If yes, how? What kind of instruction will develop it? What is the relationship between deep learning and content? For example, can a student compare and contrast the English and Spanish settlements in the New World without having some knowledge of the content? Comprehension instructional strategies that promote deep learning of content should be taught in tandem with content development—that is the "beauty" of disciplinary literacy. Deep learning cannot happen without content; comprehension of content cannot take place without interacting, analyzing, discussing, raising questions about, and writing about the content. The essence of learning is its transferability.

What teachers do, how they teach, the learning environments they create, and the ways in which they manage the curriculum, all impact the learning process. The following figure (see Table 7.31) uses information from three learning theorists (Biggs, 1999; Entwistle, 1988; Ramsden, 1992) and showcases the factors that lead to deep and surface learning approaches. These factors also reflect an alignment with the CCSS, 21st century knowledge skills, and dispositions, and disciplinary literacy habits of mind.

How Can Teachers Promote Deep Learning?

Just talking about students learning the thinking habits and dispositions of disciplinary experts without rigorous content, instruction, support, and modeling and nurturing of related processes, will not result in deep learning. In this last section of the chapter, I would like to share with you the work of Ken Bain and invite you to make your own inferences about effective ways to teach and prepare our students.

Ken Bain, in his first book, *What the Best College Teachers Do* (2004), concluded that the best instructors created engaging learning environments, put the learner's questions and interests in the forefront, facilitated collaboration between advanced and novice learners, and gave students ways to learn through trial and error before they "graded them;" they provided students with opportunities to "do the discipline" before they fully "knew the discipline." They provided

TABLE 7.31.   Deep vs. Surface Learning

Characteristics	Deep Learning	Surface Learning
	• Focuses on what is important • Connects previous to new knowledge • Makes interdisciplinary connections • Connects theoretical ideas to real-life experiences • Distinguishes evidence from argument	• Focuses on unrelated parts of the learning task • Connections between facts and ideas are loosely connected • Information is memorized for assessment purposes • Task is viewed as an external imposition • Cannot distinguish evidence from argument
Student Factors	• Learning motivation is internal • Looks for connections between new and prior knowledge • Seeks ways to put ideas or concepts together • Is actively involved in learning • Shows personal interest in learning, asks questions, and takes time to reflect on learning	• Learning emphasis is external • Not recognizing new information as building on prior one • Perceives material as a series of unrelated facts or ideas that have to be memorized • Is passive • Shows negative feelings toward the material (e.g., boredom, excessive complaining, being distracted, or unfocused)
Teacher Factors	• Connects ideas or concepts into a coherent whole; makes connections between new material and prior knowledge • Engages students in active learning • Examines students' misconceptions • Encourages risk-taking and rewards effort • Uses materials, assessments, and creates classroom tasks that require thought and reflection	• Focuses on content coverage without making necessary connections among ideas • Allows students to be passive; does not address student misconceptions • Focuses on student performance on closed questions and mostly independent assignments • Assigns much busy work that is not discussed or reflected upon • Assessments focus on knowledge of independent facts

students with opportunities to learn inductively (from specific example and experience to general principles) in a "natural critical learning environment." Great teachers were committed to fostering a deep approach to learning, used a variety of teaching approaches and helped students develop their minds, their knowledge interests, and intellectual and personal abilities.

So, how can you, a current or future content area teacher create a great learning environment for the students in your class? Bain (2004) suggests first, have great insight in what it means to learn in your field. Second, learn how adolescents learn and what are the personal and social factors that can interfere with learning. Third, think about what questions might engage students actively, meaningfully, and deeply. And, last, develop your ability to ask important and intriguing questions that will engage your students in learning more deeply about your subject area.

In his second book, *What the Best College Students Do* (2012), he researched key characteristics and dispositions of college students who made a significant impact in their discipline. First, they believed that all people can learn and that intelligence and ability are malleable, not fixed. They had a "meta-cognitive" understanding of their own ways of thinking, and looked for ways to problem solve instead of just look for the right answers. Success was an outcome of intrinsic motivation, tenacity, intellectual curiosity, solving useful problems, and taking risks that helped them learn and grow.

Transfer of learning does not happen automatically or easily. It does happen when teachers ask big questions that fascinate their students, provide students with the tools to pursue answers to their own questions and interests, encourage conceptual connections between information and the big questions or ideas, help them organize information in meaningful ways like a disciplinary expert, promote reflection and collaborative inquiry, and create a learning environment that is conducive to inquiry, exploration, and learning (Ambrose et al., 2010; Zull, 2002). Encourage your students to bring their own questions to learning and help them find connections between their questions and what they are learning in your class.

The distinction I am making here is that throughout this book I have espoused the belief that cognitive competencies such as, looking for and evaluating evidence, thinking, and reasoning, and evidence-based arguments, discourse, and other habits of mind vary from discipline to discipline. Taking a discipline-specific approach to deeper learning will ensure that students learn how to read, think, write, argue, communicate, and evaluate in ways that are unique to each discipline. In addition, it is my goal that the framework of disciplinary literacy learning as an apprenticeship proposed in this book will help pre-service and in-service content area teachers understand the importance of intrapersonal and interpersonal competencies in deep learning. Last, discipline-specific habits of mind will not deprive or place the student in a deficit; instead, they will equip the student to think and continue to learn in trans-disciplinary ways.

Randi Weingarten, president of the American Federation of Teachers (AFT), shared how she would teach one of her favorite lessons, the moral dilemma of dropping the atomic bomb on Hiroshima during World War II, in the context of the Common Core. In a May 2013 interview (see http://stateimpact.npr.org/ohio/2013/05/13/aft-president-randi-weingarten-explains-how-she-would-teach-the-common-core/), she stated that years ago she would have had students read the section in their textbook before coming to class and she would divide them into teams to debate the question, "Was it right or wrong to bomb Hiroshima?" The next day in class, she would have spent a couple of days covering the entire topic and the teams would have had about 20 minutes to discuss their views with their peers; last, she would have used a written assignment for them to summarize their learning.

On the other hand, and in the context of the Common Core, she stated that she would probably give students three to four days, or possibly the entire week to explore the same topic. Weingarten would put together a packet of related primary documents for students to study from the US and Japan and she would also give students a lesson on locating primary documents. Students would work collaboratively in small groups, and would spend a day coming up with answers to key questions about the US's decision to bomb Hiroshima. On the second day, they'd work again in small groups to critique, evaluate, and refine each other's arguments. On the third day, the class would have a whole group oral debate. On the fourth day, after students had built their knowledge about the topic and listened to others' perspectives, Weingarten might have students switch sides in the debate, provide evidence for their conclusions, and challenge each other's perspective on the topic. Weingarten stated that the common core lesson would take more time to teach because teachers would have to teach a combination of critical thinking skills that require deeper, multi-layered thinking instead of just skills that focus on memorization of unrelated facts from textbook passages.

Comprehension is a complex process, and teaching in discipline-specific ways that promotes deep learning is neither a quick, nor an easy process. Deep learning requires different roles from teacher (i.e., facilitator of student learning) and the student (i.e., active participant in the learning process), rigorous instruction, complex texts and complex knowledge, time and different decisions about content organization, curricular goals, and assessment, and different experiences, activities, and learning environments.

Summary

- Comprehension is a complex, active, and interactive process that involves the reader, the text, and the context. Comprehension is regulated by cognitive, emotional, and social experiences. Comprehending involves activating a schema, a unit of organizational knowledge. Deep comprehension requires the student to read critically, make inferences, ask questions, provide evidence to support his or her assertions, make connections among knowledge, and transfer knowledge to new situations.
- Deep learning of disciplinary content will not happen through mere teacher lecture, student note taking, and memorization. Students need to learn how to develop knowledge, how to analyze text, how to think about text, how to support their thinking with text evidence, how to questions what is said and what is not said in the text, how to consider others' interpretations and processes, and how to reflect and monitor their own understanding and learning. Comprehension monitoring, summarizing, graphic organizers, question answering and question generation, text structure, multiple strategy instruction, and comprehension monitoring are effective ways to promote good comprehension of texts in content area classrooms.
- Effective comprehension instruction will focus on how the teacher engages the reader to think critically about texts and to demonstrate, use, and reflect on his, or her understanding. Essential comprehension instruction elements include knowledge of students and content, critical engagement of students with texts, discipline-specific instruction, monitoring of student learning, and assessment. In addition, comprehension development requires a classroom climate of rigor, disciplinary inquiry, apprenticeship, collaborative inquiry, and accountable talk.

Differentiating Instruction

- Before starting a unit of study, use an informal assessment, like a survey, to pre-assess the students' prior knowledge of the topic. Take into account the students' language proficiency and use pre-reading activities that assess and build upon students' background knowledge. Use formative assessment data effective comprehension instruction strategies and create a positive learning environment.
- Students with varied exceptionalities require explicit comprehension instruction. Use related graphic organizers, provide scaffolded teaching and learning, demonstrate fix-up strategies, and use guiding questions, think-alouds, that provide an active model for thinking during the reading process. Choose reading materials that are culturally relevant, and use media and technology.
- Summarization helps students' comprehension (August & Shanahan, 2006). Teach ELLs how to summarize and provide them with feedback, diverse models, and peer support. Encourage summarizing with short text selections, promote use of journals for note taking, and monitor students' summarization skills.
- Collaborate with English as a Second Language (ESL) teachers and literacy coaches about how to make text more accessible to ELLs—e.g., create

scaffolded outlines, study guides, rewritten texts, audio texts, and leveled texts. ELLs benefit from using computers and technology to locate information, research, synthesize, and communicate with others. Use a structured approach when teaching ELLs. Engage them in reading and learning by explaining directions, developing purpose questions, pre-teaching vocabulary, obtaining assistance from native language speakers, and using discussion. The CCSS steers teachers away from placing too much emphasis on activating and building students' background knowledge through films and lengthy introductions before students read the text. Guide students' thinking during reading through teacher read-alouds of short text sections, partner reading, using text-based questions, discussions, and informal writing. Extend ELLs' thinking after reading by making connections with their experiences, summarizing, using informal writing, discussion, and collaborative learning activities.

Reflect and Apply

1. What three insights from the text do you plan to implement in your instruction to support and extend students' comprehension skills and knowledge of subject matter? Provide a rationale about your choices, and discuss your insights, reflections, and plan with a peer.

2. Using your knowledge of your discipline and how students' comprehension develops, what suggestions could you offer to Ms. Foley (see Classroom Life vignette)? Discuss your ideas with a peer, or peers in a small group.

3. Select one of the discipline-specific strategies presented in this chapter and teach it to a group of students (in grades 6–12). After you model it and provide sufficient guided and independent practice and feedback, collect some feedback from the students about how the strategy supported their learning and any challenges they had with using it. Share your personal observations and the students' feedback with a group of peers. Last, suggest ways to improve the strategy and/or its implementation.

Extending Learning

1. Develop a classroom poster on the thinking skills and processes necessary for students to develop understanding in your content area. Focus on five to seven key thinking skills all students need to develop in order to learn and succeed in your discipline. Include tips or short explanations for students. Use your creativity to construct your poster, and present it to the class or to a group of peers.

2. Visit a content-area classroom for a few days and take notes about the role comprehension instruction plays in that classroom. Is it specific, explicit, and deliberate? What discipline-specific strategies does the teacher use to support students' comprehension development? Using information from this chapter, select one discipline-specific strategy you think will work well with the students in that class. Provide a rationale, share it with the teacher, explain he or she can use it, and follow-up with some more classroom observations. Do a before and after comparison on student engagement, learning, challenges, and instruction, and share with the classroom teacher and your peers.

3. Choose a topic of study from your content area textbook (e.g., lesson or unit). Study the text and work with a partner (preferably from your community of practice), and select one or two discipline-specific strategies to implement. Present your instructional plan using specific examples from the topic. In your plan, also consider areas of challenge for your students, demonstrate your modeling and scaffolded support, and specify how you will monitor their understanding of text.

References

Ambrose, S. A., Bridges, M. W., DiPietro, M., Lovett, M. C. & Norman, M. K. (2010). *How learning works: 7 research-based principles for smart teaching.* San Francisco, CA: Jossey-Bass.

Archer, A. L., Gleason, M. M., & Vachon, V. L. (2003). Decoding and fluency: Foundation skills for struggling older readers. *Learning Disability Quarterly, 26*, 89–101.

Armbruster, B. B., Lehr, F., & Osborn, J. (2001). *Put reading first: The research building blocks for teaching children to read, kindergarten through grade 3.* Washington, DC: National Institute for Literacy.

August, D., & Shanahan, T. (2006). *Developing literacy in second-language learners: Report of the National Literacy Panel on language-minority children and youth.* Mahwah, NJ: Lawrence Erlbaum Associates. Retrieved from http://www.cal.org/projects/archive/nlpreports/Executive_Summary.pdf

Bain, K. (2004). *What the best college teachers do.* Cambridge, MA: Harvard University Press.

Bain, K. (2012). *What the best college students do.* Cambridge, MA: Harvard University Press.

Biancarosa, C., & Snow, C.E. (2004). *Reading next—A vision for action and research in middle and high school literacy: A report to Carnegie Corporation of New York.* Washington, DC: Alliance for Excellent Education.

Biggs, J. (1999). *Teaching for quality learning at university.* Buckingham, UK: Society for Research into Higher Education and Open University Press.

Block, C. C. & Duffy, G. (2008). Research on teaching comprehension: Where we've been and where we're going. In C. C. Block, S. Parris, *Comprehension instruction research-based best practices* (2nd ed.) (pp. 19–37). New York, NY: Guilford.

Block, C. C., & Pressley, M. (Eds), (2002). *Comprehension instruction: Research-based best Practices.* New York: Guilford Press.

Calder, L. (2006). Uncoverage: Toward a signature pedagogy for the history survey. Journal of American History. Retrieved from http://www.iub.edu/~tchsotl/part3/calder%20uncoverage_files/Content-Server_data/20248906.pdf

Collins, A., & Smith, E. (1980). *Teaching the process of reading comprehension.* (Tech. Rep. No. 182). Urbana: University of Illinois, Center for the Study of Reading

Conley, D. T. (2012). *A complete definition of college and career readiness.* Portland, OR: Educational Policy Improvement Center. Retrieved from www.epiconline.org

Duffy, G. G. (2002). The case for direct explanation of strategies. In C. C. Block & M. Pressley (Eds), *Comprehension instruction: Research-based best practices* (pp. 28–41). New York, NY: Guilford.

Duke, N. & Pearson, D. (2002). Effective practices for developing reading comprehension. In A. Farstrup, & S. Samuels, (Eds), *What research has to say about reading instruction* (pp. 205–242). Newark, DE: International Reading Association.

Eggert, S., Ostermeyer, F., Hasselhorn, M., & Bögeholz, S. (2013). Socioscientific decision making in the science classroom: The effect of embedded metacognitive instructions on students' learning outcomes. *Education Research International.* Retrieved from: http://www.hindawi.com/journals/edu/2013/309894/

Entwistle, N. (1987). *Understanding classroom learning.* London, UK: Hodder & Stoughton.

Fang, Z., & Schleppegrell, M. J. (2008). *Reading in secondary content areas: A language-based pedagogy.* Ann Arbor, MI: University of Michigan Press.

Fielding, L., & Pearson, P. D. (1994). Reading comprehension: What works. *Educational Leadership, 51*(5), 62–68.

Flavell, J. H. (1979). Metacognition and cognitive monitoring: A new area of cognitive-developmental inquiry. *American Psychologist, 34*, 906–911.

Gambrell, L., Kapinus, B., & Wilson, R. (1987). Using mental imagery and summarization to achieve independence in comprehension. *Journal of Reading, 30*, 638–642.

Gee, J. P. (2000). Identity as an analytic lens for research in education. *Review of Research in Education, 25,* 99–125.

Graff, G. (1992). *Beyond the culture wars: How teaching the conflicts can revitalize American education.* New York, NY: Norton.

Graham, S. & Hebert, M. (2010). *Writing to read: Evidence for how writing can improve reading. A Carnegie Corporation Time to Act Report.* Washington, DC: Alliance for Excellent Education.

Graham, S., & Perrin, D. (2007). *Writing next: Effective strategies to improve writing of adolescents in middle and high schools—A report to Carnegie Corporation of New York.* Washington, DC: Alliance for Excellent Education.

Greenleaf, C., Brown, W., & Litman, C. (2004). Apprenticing urban youth to science literacy. In D. Strickland & D. Alvermann (Eds), *Bridging the gap: Improving literacy learning for preadolescent and adolescent learners in grades 4–12.* Newark, NJ: International Reading Association.

Greenleaf, C. L., Schoenbach, R., Cziko, C., & Mueller, F. L. (2001). Apprenticing adolescent readers to academic literacy. *Harvard Educational Review, 71*(1), 30–39.

Harris, T. L., & Hodges, R. E. (1995). *The literacy dictionary: The vocabulary of reading and writing.* Newark, DE: International Reading Association.

Harvey, S., & Goudvis, A. (2000). *Strategies that work: Teaching comprehension to enhance understanding.* Portland, ME: Stenhouse.

Heath, S. B. (1983). *Ways with words: Language, life, and work in communities and classrooms.* Cambridge, UK: Cambridge University Press.

Heller, R., & Greenleaf, C. (2007). *Literacy instruction in the content areas: Getting to the core of middle and high school improvement.* Washington, DC: Alliance for Excellent Education.

Hewlett Foundation, William and Flora (2010). Education program strategic plan. Menlo Park, CA. Retrieved from http://www.hewlett.org/uploads/documents/Education_Strategic_Plan_2010.pdf

Hoffman, J. (1992). Critical reading/thinking across the curriculum: Using I-charts to support learning. *Language Arts,* 69(2), p. 121–27.

Ivey, G. & Broaddus, K. (2001). Just plain reading: A survey of what makes students want to read in middle school classrooms. *Reading Research Quarterly,* 36(4), 350–77.

Kamil, M. L., Borman, G. D., Dole, J., Kral, C. C., Salinger, T., and Torgesen, J. (2008). *Improving adolescent literacy: Effective classroom and intervention practices: A Practice Guide* (NCEE #2008-4027). Washington, DC: National Center for Education Evaluation and Regional Assistance, Institute of Education Sciences, US Department of Education.

Knoester, M. (2010). Independent reading and the 'social turn': How adolescent reading habits and motivation relate to cultivating social relationships. *Networks: An Online Journal for Teacher Research, 12*(1), 1–13.

Kramarski, B., Mevarech, Z. R., & Arami, M. (2002). The effects of metacognitive instruction on solving mathematical authentic tasks. *Educational Studies in Mathematics, 49*(2), 225–250.

Krashen, S. (2004). *The power of reading: Insights from the research.* Portsmouth, NH: Heinemann.

Manning, P. (2006). Presenting history to policy makers: Three position papers. *Perspectives: The Newsmagazine of the American Historical Association, 44*(3), 22–24.

McKeown, M. G., Beck, I. L., & Blake, R. G. K. (2009). Rethinking reading comprehension instruction: A comparison of instruction for strategies and content approaches. *Reading Research Quarterly, 44*(3), 218–252.

Mevarech, Z. R., & Kramarski, B. (1997). IMPROVE: a multidimensional method for teaching mathematics in heterogeneous classrooms. *American Educational Research Journal, 34*(2), 365–394.

National Governors Association Center (NGA) for Best Practices, Council of Chief State School Officers (CCSSO). (2010). *Common Core State Standards.* National Governors Association Center for Best Practices, Council of Chief State School Officers. Retrieved from http://corestandards.org

National Institute for Literacy. (2007). *What content-area teachers should know about adolescent literacy.* Jessup, MD: National Institute of Child Health and Human Development. Retrieved from http://lincs.ed.gov/publications/pdf/adolescent_literacy07.pdf

National Institute of Child Health and Human Development. (2004). *Report of the National Reading Panel. Teaching children to read: An evidence-based assessment of the scientific research literature on reading and its implications for reading instruction.* Washington, DC: US Government Printing Office. Retrieved from http://national.readingpanel.org

National Reading Panel. (2000, April). *Report of the National Reading Panel: Teaching children to read.* Washington, DC: National Institute of Child Health and Human Development, National Institutes of Health, US Department of Health and Human Services

Ness, M. (2009). Reading comprehension strategies in secondary content-area classrooms: Teacher use of and attitudes toward reading comprehension instruction. *Reading Horizons, 49*(2), 143–166.

O'Brien, D. G., Stewart, R. A., & Moje, E. B. (1995). Why content literacy is difficult to infuse into the secondary curriculum: Strategies, goals, and classroom realities. *Reading Research Quarterly, 30,* 442–463.

Palincsar, A. S. & Brown, A. (1984). Reciprocal teaching of comprehension-fostering and comprehension monitoring activities. *Cognition and Instruction, 1*(2), 117–175.

Paris, S. G., & Hamilton, E. E. (2009). The development of children's reading comprehension. In S. E. Israel & G. G. Duffy (Eds). *Handbook of research on reading comprehension.* New York, NY: Routledge.

Pearson, P. D., & Gallagher, M. C. (1983). The instruction of reading comprehension. *Contemporary Educational Psychology, 8,* 317–344.

Pellegrino, J. W., & Hilton, M. L. (Eds) (2012). *Education for life and work: Developing transferable knowledge and skills in the 21st century.* National Research Council. Retrieved from http://www.nap.edu/catalog.php?record_id=13398.

Pintrich, P. R. (2002). The role of metacognitive knowledge in learning, teaching, and assessing. *Theory into Practice, 41*(4), 219–225.

Pressley, M. (2000). What should comprehension instruction be the instruction of? In M.L. Kamil, P.B. Mosenthal, P.D. Pearson, & R. Barr (Eds), *Handbook of reading research: Volume III* (pp. 545–561). Mahwah NJ: Erlbaum.

Pressley, M., Wood, E., Woloshyn, V. E., Martin, V., King, A., & Menke, D. (1992). Encouraging mindful use of prior knowledge: Attempting to construct explanatory answers facilitates learning. *Educational Psychologist, 27*(1), 91–109.

Ramsden, P. (1992). *Learning to teach in higher education.* London, UK: Routledge.

RAND Reading Study Group. (2002). *Reading for understanding: Toward a research and development program in reading comprehension.* Santa Monica, CA: Office of Education Research and Improvement.

Rosenblatt, L. (1986). The aesthetic transaction. *Journal of Aesthetic Education, 20*(4).

Scammacca, N., Roberts, G., Vaughn, S., Edmonds, M., Wexler, J., Reutebuch, C. K., & Torgesen, J. K. (2007). *Interventions for adolescent struggling readers: A meta-analysis with implications for practice.* Portsmouth, NH: RMC Research Corporation, Center on Instruction.

Scott, C. (2004). Syntactic contributions to literacy development. In C. Stone, E. Stillman, B. Ehren, & K. Apel (Eds). *Handbook of language and literacy* (pp. 340–362). New York: Guilford Press.

Smith, F. (1998). *The book of learning and forgetting.* New York, NY: Teachers College Press.

Snow, C. E., Griffin, P., & Burns, M. S. (Eds). 2005. *Knowledge to support the teaching of reading: Preparing teachers for a changing world.* San Francisco: Jossey-Bass.

Stahl, N. A., King, J. R., & Henk, W. A. (1991). Enhancing students' note taking through training and evaluation. *Journal of Reading, 34*(8), 614–622.

Symonds, W. C., Schwartz, R. B., & Ferguson, R. (2011). *Pathways to prosperity: Meeting the challenge of preparing young Americans for the 21st century.* A Report issued by the Pathways to Prosperity Project, Harvard Graduate School of Education. Cambridge, MA: Author.

Torgesen, J. K., Houston, D. D., Rissman, L. M., Decker, S. M., Roberts, G., Vaughn, S., Wexler, J., Frabcis, D., Rivera, M. O., & Lesaux, N. (2007). *Academic literacy instruction for adolescents: A guidance document from the Center on Instruction.* Portsmouth, NH: RMC Research Corporation, Center on Instruction.

Tovani, C. (2000). *I read it, but I don't get it: Comprehension strategies for adolescent readers.* Portland, ME: Stenhouse.

Vaughn, S., Klingner, J. K., Swanson, E.A., Boardman, A. G., Roberts, G., Mohammed, S. S., et al. (2011). Efficacy of collaborative strategic reading with middle school students. *American Educational Research Journal, 48*(4), 938–964.

Vaughn, S., Swanson, E. A., Roberts, G., Wanzek, J., Stillman-Spisak, S. J., Solis, M., & Simmons, D. (2013). Improving reading comprehension and social studies knowledge in middle school. *Reading Research Quarterly, 48*(1), 77–93.

Wilson, N. S. (2011). The heart of comprehension instruction: Metacognition. *California Reader, 44,* 3.

Wormeli, R. (2005). *Summarization in any subject: 50 techniques to improve student learning.* Alexandria, VA: ASCD.

Zion, M., Michalsky, T., & Mevarech, Z. R. (2005). The effects of metacognitive instruction embedded within an asynchronous learning network on scientific inquiry skills. *International Journal of Science Education, 27*(8), 957–983.

Zull, J. (2002). *The art of changing the brain?: Enriching teaching by exploring the biology of learning?*. Sterling, VA: Stylus Publishing.

eight
Disciplinary Literacy Learning Environments

Whether speaking in small groups or large groups, [students] should be the audience for one another's comments . . . they should speak to one another, aiming to convince or to question their peers.
–National Council of Teachers of Mathematics (NCTM), Professional Standards for Teaching Mathematics

Chapter Highlights

- College and Career Readiness (CCR) warrants deep learning, critical reasoning supported by evidence, and application of knowledge and skills. The ongoing technological advancements of the 21st century also require students to know how to collaborate with others, problem-solve, inquire, and communicate effectively.
- Each discipline possesses its own complex and unique discourse. Knowledge and development of that discourse is necessary for both content and literacy development and learning. Students will benefit from a language-rich, conversation-rich, information-rich, and collaboration-rich classroom environment.
- Accountable talk is the talk of each discipline that fosters disciplinary habits of mind and learning.
- Students need opportunities to learn, develop, and use communication, reasoning, problem solving, perspective taking, and collaboration in authentic disciplinary learning environments.
- Collaborative learning, problem solving, and inquiry are necessary for college, career, and workforce readiness, as well as for life.
- Disciplinary learning environments should include rigor, inquiry, apprenticeship, accountable talk, collaboration, and support.

Classroom Life

As a Social Studies teacher, my classroom is arranged for cooperative learning groups. Early in the school year, rules were set for movement, transitions, and voice levels. My students work in pairs (shoulder partners) or in groups of four. Having a majority of English Speakers of Other Languages (ESOL) or Language Students (LS) in my classroom has been a big challenge.

My first language is Spanish and most of my ESOL and LS students talk the same language. You may think is easier since I can translate and they can understand the lesson but the reality is it is not. I learned throughout the years, that work created with a group is just as important as individual performance. It is very difficult to get the ESOL or LS students to perform with their group or individually.

My pacing guide is moving at a very quick pace and covers a lot of material. The ESOL and LS students have great difficulty understanding the vocabulary and content required to be covered by the pacing guide. I understand that I have to accommodate the lesson to their needs and I do; but my concern is that most of the times they leave the classroom not knowing the lesson for that day. My other concern is that it is not fair to the other students since most of the times I have to teach the lesson in two languages. I have to continually engage in formative assessments to make sure no one is left behind. For that reason, I do not ask many higher order questions, since I know it will take me double the time to explain what it means.

One resource that helps me in my classroom, especially with cooperative learning activities, is a graphic organizer that is part of their book. My students seem to enjoy it and actually compete with each other to complete questions; it helps to guide their conversations and thinking. Anything that has structure—helps them to stay focused while in groups, stimulates their thinking with higher order questions, and supports good conversations—works for them and for me! I also use a variety of other graphic organizers to address the different needs of my students. Getting them to work in cooperative learning groups without planning, structure, and support does not work for my students. I work hard at building their proficiency in the English language as well as their academic vocabulary and thinking skills and I incorporate whole group, small group, and partner talk activities. *(Ms. Maria Rodriguez Negroni, 6th grade History/Geography, Kissimmee Middle School, Kissimmee, Florida).*

The Role of Discourse and Collaboration in the Common Core State Standards (CCSS)

To prepare students to learn and work in the 21st century, our educational system needs to enable all students to learn. A student-centered approach to learning will respond to each student's needs, goals, and interests. New educational standards (e.g., the CCSS, and the New Generation Science Standards [NGSS]), are causing major shifts in our perspectives about teaching and student learning in the 21st century. In this book, I have presented the need for a shift from "covering content" to promoting disciplinary inquiry and knowledge.

The ongoing technological advancements of the 21st century also require students to know how to collaborate with others to problem-solve, inquire, and communicate effectively. College and Career Readiness (CCR) needs to take place in a discipline-specific culture of inquiry, collaboration, and apprenticeship. Teachers need to facilitate student learning, and help them become independent, reflective, and self-regulated learners. Students need teachers who are not only disciplinary experts, but who also know how to listen, question, provide appropriate praise and feedback, and mentor students in the learning process.

The CCSS place a lot of emphasis on communication, reasoning, argumentation, perspective taking, and collaboration. For example, according to the CCSS, one way to deepen mathematical conceptual understanding is through the communication students have around concepts, problems, strategies, and representations. Problem solving, reasoning and proof, communication, representation, and connections are also National Council of Teachers of Mathematics (NCTM) (1995) process standards. Both the CCSS and NGSS call for making student thinking visible through classroom talk, argumentation, and other forms of representation.

CCSS Connections

- Students in grades 6–12 are expected to engage, initiate and participate effectively in varied collaborative discussions with peers to discuss, question, interpret, and evaluate texts, and one another's understanding of them.
- Students in grades 6–12 need to know how to have good communication skills, and be able to present claims and findings, support them with evidence, discuss them with others, consider others' diverse perspective, and negotiate meaning.
- Students in grades 6–12 are expected to respond respectfully and thoughtfully to diverse perspectives, summarize points of agreement and disagreement, and, when needed, qualify, or justify their own views and understanding and make new connections in light of the new evidence and reasoning presented.

What Is Academic Language?

> Our teachers come to class, and they talk and they talk, 'til their faces are like peaches; we don't; we just sit like cornstalks.
>
> (Cazden, 1976, p. 74)

Academic language is the essence of thinking and learning. What are some definitions of academic language?

- Academic language is "the language that is used by teachers and students for the purpose of acquiring new knowledge and skills . . . imparting new information, describing abstract ideas, and developing students' conceptual understandings" (Chamot & O'Malley, 1994, p. 40).
- Academic language refers to "word knowledge that makes it possible for students to engage with, produce, and talk about texts that are valued in school" (Flynt & Brozo, 2008, p. 500).
- "Academic language is the set of words, grammar, and organizational strategies used to describe complex ideas, higher-order thinking processes, and abstract concepts" (Zwiers, 2008, p. 20).

Academic language, or academic discourse is essential for learning and success in school, and it has always been part of classroom life. Academic discourse means communication of thought through words, talk, conversation, and/or a formal discussion on a topic. It refers to both the way ideas are communicated and exchanged and also what the ideas involve. Discourse also involves questions such as: Who is talking? About what? In what ways? What do they write about? What questions are important? How does knowledge change? Whose ideas, opinions, questions, and perspectives are valued? Who starts, ends, moves, and controls the discussion? How often do discussions take place?

Walk into most secondary grade classrooms, and whom will you find doing most of the talking in class? Yes, you are correct . . . the teacher! Teachers talk a lot and students talk very little—according to the disciplinary learning framework presented in this book, the opposite should be happening in content area classrooms. Students must talk, listen to others, and consider others' perspectives on topics, negotiate meaning, provide evidence for their arguments, and must interact with the teacher and with peers in class. Each discipline has its own discourse; it is co-constructed and reconstructed by people within an intellectual community. In this chapter, I examine the verbal aspect of discourse, and how it should be facilitated in discipline-specific ways in grades 6–12. Students in each subject area need to learn the vocabulary, the habits of mind, and the tools of each discipline's discourse (i.e., special terms, symbols, etc.).

For students to master the discourse of each discipline they not only need to develop and understand the vocabulary of the disciplines, but they also need to interpret what they read, express themselves orally and in writing, explain and support their answers clearly and with evidence, exchange ideas during whole-group instruction, collaborate with others, and have many opportunities to learn and use academic language. The teacher needs to not only create the appropriate classroom climate that facilitates all students' disciplinary thinking, discourse, and collaborative inquiry, but he or she will also need to monitor the classroom culture. For example, he or she will have to look for low expectations, low or nonparticipation patterns, dominance, and inequality. Engaging students in the discourse of each discipline, and giving them opportunities to use it and develop it takes much planning, monitoring, and a learning pedagogical framework that supports disciplinary literacy and learning.

Academic Language in the Content Areas

Why is academic discourse, language, or talk important in disciplinary learning and college, career, and workforce readiness? For that matter, why is it important for learning, in general? In Chapter 2, I examined Vygotsky's (1962, 1978) theory about learning being a socially constructed process. In that same chapter (and throughout this book) I have also examined various core academic disciplines, and uncovered their characteristics, with the most prevalent being the unique discourse of each discipline. Knowledge is not developed in a vacuum; disciplinary experts, college students, and professionals all exchange ideas with their peers and share their thinking through discipline-specific discourse.

Unfortunately, in many secondary classrooms, academic discourse is something we "sprinkle," and use sparingly to quickly assess comprehension (Durkin 1978/1979), instead of using it to develop students' discipline-specific habits of mind through it. In Chapter 4, we also saw that many teachers hold lower expectations of struggling readers and English language learners (ELLs). The students who need to talk more and express their understanding of a topic, are asked easier questions (usually in the teacher initiates-student responds-teacher evaluates format, Cazden, 1988), and are given less time to respond, or in other cases they are not given any opportunities to respond (Guan Eng Ho, 2005).

Many of the visible manifestations of academic language used in the classroom come from the exchanges between teacher and students, and on occasion (when time allows . . .) among students. Most instructional patterns involve the teacher initiating a topic (I) usually by asking a question, a student responding (R), the teacher evaluating (E) the response or providing feedback (F), followed by another teacher-generated question (Cazden, 1986; 2001). Most of the time, the teacher asks the questions, evaluates one or two student responses (while the rest are passively listening or looking around), and elaborates on them. Who needs to be developing and practicing academic language in the classroom? Who needs to be developing critical thinking skills, reflecting, and expanding on their understanding of the text or topic? The students do. And who is doing most of the work, and carries the cognitive load in the above scenario? The teacher does.

Teachers can alter the discourse patterns in their classrooms by creating authentic opportunities for students to develop and practice academic language. Vocabulary and comprehension in the content areas is connected to concepts; the more a student discusses his understanding of words and listens to others' understanding, the more his, or her vocabulary and thinking will improve. Again, a teacher's perspective, attitudes, and beliefs about how adolescents will learn at a deep and rigorous level in his or her discipline, will also determine how he or she will plan instruction, use time, reflect on the teacher's and the students' role in the learning process, and create a classroom learning environment that either promotes academic discourse and collaborative inquiry, or promotes teacher talk and a teacher-centered approach to learning.

Because adolescents do not naturally engage in academic talk in the classroom, teachers should model the behaviors, skills, patterns, responses, and strategies they expect to see from students during academic discourse. For example, how does an expert (i.e., an author, historian, a mathematician, or a scientist) talk with other experts? How do they exchange knowledge and ideas and together generate new knowledge? What questions do they ask? What evidence do they provide? How do they prompt each other to get more information about each other's thinking?

During guided instruction teachers can provide additional examples, and provide specific feedback that will help students learn how to have academic conversations with peers in the classroom. Teachers should allow for collaborative inquiry to take place in many ways—e.g., students working in pairs, in small groups and in whole class groups. During collaborative tasks, students will need to have opportunities to discuss ideas, question one another, negotiate meaning, and clearly communicate their ideas to others. Last, students should use academic talk should as a means of self-monitoring during independent tasks, and also as a way of receiving more feedback from the teacher and others.

Academic discourse is an essential process for learning and doing in each discipline (Moje, 2008; O'Brien, Moje, & Stewart, 2001). Through communication, students reflect upon, clarify and expand their thinking and understanding of discipline-specific conceptual relationships and arguments. Classroom talk that is discipline-specific, challenging, and promotes academic learning will help students articulate their knowledge about the subject matter, and it will also build their knowledge, confidence, and ability to engage in intellectual conversations (Chapin, O'Connor, & Anderson, 2003).

Does Academic Talk Belong Only to Certain Disciplines?

Many teachers believe that classroom talk fits better in other disciplines than in mathematics. After all, mathematics involves figures, symbols, functions, equations, graphs, and data, and not many words, right? On the contrary, mathematics learning and doing requires using mathematics language fluently and accurately. The following are sample CCSS-aligned suggestions for teachers of mathematics to consider for involving students in academic discourse in their classrooms.

- Create a classroom environment that is founded on high expectations for all and on what counts in learning and doing mathematics—establish the mathematical habits of mind (e.g., accuracy, careful listening, asking questions and formulating conjectures, setting hypotheses, validating and supporting ideas with mathematical argument, working independently and collaboratively), and discourse norms.

- Respect and value students' ideas and ways of thinking. Listen carefully to students' questions, ideas, and steps to problem solving. Promote accountable talk.
- Practice talk moves that engage students in discourse. Chapin, O'Connor and Anderson (2009) suggest the following five talk moves:
  - Revoice: "So you are saying . . ."
  - Restate someone else's reasoning: "Could you repeat what Mark said in your own words?"
  - Apply reasoning to someone else's: "Do you agree or disagree with Adrienne? Why?"
  - Prompt for further participation: "Can you expand on Adrienne's idea? Would you like to add anything else?"
  - Practice wait time: Don't answer your own questions; give students sufficient time to think about the question and formulate an answer.
- Use a variety of ways to reason, make connections, solve problems, and communicate. Make conjectures and present solutions, explore examples and counterexamples to investigate a conjecture.
- Pose questions that will elicit, engage, and challenge each student's thinking; challenge them to think of alternative solutions, discuss their steps and decisions with others in class, and consider others' solutions and processes. For example, "How did you reach your conclusion?" "Is this true all the time?" "How can you prove that?" "Can you think of a counter example?" "Do you see a pattern?" "What would happen next?"
- Ask students to clarify and justify their ideas orally and in writing. Also, ask them to use mathematical evidence to argue and persuade others of the validity of their representations, solutions, conjectures, and answers. Use students' thinking to discuss misconceptions.
- Listen carefully to student discussions, and decide on what to expand upon or revisit from among the ideas that students bring up during a discussion.
- Decide when and how to attach mathematical notation and language to students' ideas. Encourage students to use symbols, written hypotheses, explanations, arguments, oral presentations, pictures, diagrams, graphs, tables, computers, calculators and other technology.
- Decide when to provide information, when to clarify a step, law, theory, or issue, when to model, when to lead, when to take the back seat, and when to let a student struggle with a problem.
- Monitor students' participation in discussions, and create a climate of inquiry, support, safety, and rigor that encourages all to participate.

Suggestions for Developing Academic Language in the Disciplines

How can content area teachers create a discipline-specific academic discourse-oriented classroom? What are teaching practices associated with creating such an environment? How can one start to elicit meaningful student talk in the subject areas? And, what role do the teacher and students play in the process?

- Create and maintain a respectful, motivating, challenging, and supportive classroom environment. Arrange desks so students can see one another's faces instead of speaking to the back of their heads. Teach them how to communicate with others in a professional manner.
- Plan authentic student engagement in academic discourse (orally and in writing) and explain your expectations about academic discourse in your classroom. Focus classroom

conversations on the subject matter and choose tasks that motivate students to discuss their thinking.

- Create a common language in your classroom that reflects, and uses disciplinary habits of mind that promote deep learning. For example, the following might be common academic discourse elements:
  - ○ Thinking and talking together helps us understand the material better.
  - ○ Talking together about our thinking helps us think better; complex texts and ideas require collaborative thinking.
  - ○ Each person's thinking is different and unique; we will all learn from one another and everyone has a right to participate.
  - ○ Students make reference to text to support ideas, and provide evidence for claims and arguments.
  - ○ Students make reference to knowledge they gained from class discussions.
  - ○ Students connect ideas, paraphrase others' comments, clarify or define terms or ideas under discussion, and synthesize information.
  - ○ Students use challenging questions, indicate when ideas need more evidence, and challenge each other's evidence and reasoning.
  - ○ Students present their arguments in logical ways, use examples, and think critically about discussions.
  - ○ Students listen to others and show respect and interest in others' comments.
- Classroom talk is about issues and learning, not about individuals.
- Listen carefully to students' comments (orally and in writing), and provide feedback that will challenge them, direct them, and encourage them to think about the topic at hand in different ways. Listen to the conversations for evidence of rigorous thinking.
- Identify, model, expect, promote, and scaffold discipline specific habits of mind and academic talk moves for learning; start small: less is more when done well and is sustained over time. Introduce students to talk-centered instruction and learning—e.g., present arguments/responses in clear, logical, informative ways and support claims with textual evidence, and how to listen and respond to classmates' ideas.
- Rotate between individual responses, small-group collaborations, and whole class discussions; create many diverse opportunities for students to engage with texts and learning through academic discourse. Start with whole class discussion, provide feedback, and then transition to small group discussions.
- Use essential questions, and ask high-level questions that promote connections among ideas/topics, and create academic discourse that relies on varying evidence-based perspectives. Encourage students to pose questions, and encourage others to elaborate and go back to the text(s) to support their thinking.
- Establish frames for effective academic discourse that create opportunities for students to co-construct meaning from text(s) through targeted academic conversations with others (classmates, teacher, others outside the classroom).
- Engage students regularly in specific, targeted, academically focused, and sustained discussions in small and whole class groups about what they are reading, questions they are having, and connections and reflections they are making between texts and topics.
- Use questioning and grouping strategies that facilitate ongoing discussions about text(s) and learning; students in your class should know that academic discourse is a routine, and a key element of learning.
- Select questions that do not have easy answers but require students to think critically about the issue at hand. To facilitate classroom talk, choose questions that require small group

collaboration, and give students adequate time to think about and respond to complex questions (McCann, Johannessen, Kahn, & Flanagan, 2006).

● Encourage students to use the vocabulary of the discipline. This will help them to apply their understanding of discipline-specific vocabulary, and use it to communicate in disciplinary ways.

● Seek student feedback; involve students in evaluation of class discussions and self-evaluation (orally and in writing).

● Monitor academic conversations and student behavior, and make instructional changes as needed.

Applying Discipline-Specific Literacies

● All disciplines have a unique discourse, habits of mind, communication, and collaboration. Help your students develop deeper understanding of subject matter and critical thinking skills, through the use of accountable talk and collaborative inquiry.

● Expect, model, support, and monitor students' use of discipline-specific discourse in small and whole group settings.

● Create a classroom environment that is positive, safe, motivating, organized, rigorous, reflective of disciplinary ways of learning and knowing, and one that promotes accountability and collaborative inquiry.

Disciplinary Literacy and Classroom Talk

In Chapters 2 and 3 of this book, I examined disciplinary literacy in detail. By now, you know that disciplinary literacy is at the heart of the CCSS; also, the CCSS call for deep and specialized knowledge and ways of knowing and learning or habits of mind. What do CCSS instructional shifts require students to have, or be able to do, in the areas of reading, speaking and listening, and vocabulary and language in the disciplines?

● Reading
   ○ Deep understanding of text.
   ○ Reason abstractly and quantitatively.
   ○ Metacognitive processes and behaviors.
   ○ Ability to locate, critically examine, integrate and carry meaning across texts and sources.
   ○ Develop evidentiary arguments, and provide text-based answers to support conclusions or arguments.
● Speaking and Listening
   ○ Initiate and participate in discussions; engage in collaborative conversations.
   ○ Plan and deliver information clearly and precisely.
   ○ Generate and respond to questions to clarify, connect, expand, and/or elaborate on others' remarks.
   ○ Identify/summarize the reasons for evidence a speaker or source provides to support points.
   ○ Adapt speech and presentation for specific tasks, setting, and purposes.
   ○ Set and follow group norms and goals for speaking, listening, and thinking.
   ○ Respond thoughtfully, honor and evaluate diverse perspectives.

- Vocabulary and Language
  - ○ Engage in the study of discipline-specific vocabulary (academic, domain-specific) needed to access complex texts.
  - ○ Use knowledge of strategies to discern meaning of words in the context they are used.
  - ○ Understand figurative language, word relationships, and nuances.
  - ○ Use knowledge of language and conventions of Standard English grammar when writing, speaking, listening, and reading.

Students can benefit from setting personal goals and co-constructing classroom norms, or goals for speaking, listening, and thinking. For example, what does "being respectful to others" look like? What collaborative and intellectual dialogue skills will students need to have and develop in grades 6–12? Modeling, role-playing, feedback, and classroom discussions will help them develop effective communication and thinking skills. Table 8.1 includes sample speaking, listening, and thinking norms and goals.

TABLE 8.1. Sample Speaking, Listening, and Thinking Norms or Goals

Skills	Sample Goals
Speaking	• Speak loudly enough so everyone in class can hear you. • Establish meaningful eye contact. • Speak clearly, concisely, and respectfully. • Speak at a comfortable and inviting pace. • Make clear and accurate statements. • Provide evidence to support your statements. • Use appropriate grammar and vocabulary. • Use an enthusiastic and collaborative tone. • Disagree with others in a neutral tone. • Use verbal and non-verbal communication.
Listening	• Make eye contact—look at the person speaking. • Practice active listening. • Do not interrupt—wait for your turn to talk. • Do not talk while someone else is speaking. • Respond respectfully to what you hear someone say. • Don't change the subject—concentrate on what is being said. • Empathize. • Respond verbally and non-verbally. • Ask a question. • Paraphrase what you hear someone say.
Thinking	• Share your understanding of the text or task. • Make inferences. • Identify biases, assumptions, or fallacies. • Use evidence from the text(s) to support your assertions. • Explain the relevance and accuracy of your perspective. • Be prepared (materials marked, responses written, and questions prepared) • Acknowledge others' perspectives and identify differences. • Identify positive or negative implications. • Make connections with other texts or concepts. • Elaborate on your own or on others' statements.

What role do academic conversations play in your classroom, in your specific content area or discipline? Talk is a fundamental part of learning and developing students' thinking (Bruner & Haste, 1987; Vygotsky, 1978). The ability to communicate clearly and precisely is needed for school, college, career, and life (National Council of Teachers of English [NCTE], 2011). All learners use talk to make sense of their ideas, observations, interactions with texts and others, and experiences. Talk forces learners to think about what they are learning, articulate their ideas, and reflect on what they do and do not understand. We know that each discipline has its own words and many of those words have precise, specialized meanings. What happens in content area classrooms? Do teachers systematically and intentionally plan for collaborative inquiry and academic conversations in your course? Do they plan for extended conversations that involve co-constructing academic knowledge (Cazden, 2001)? What would make academic conversations "a classroom staple" instead of an occasional event in your learning environment? In many content area classrooms, academic conversations happen either between the teacher and a couple of students who can carry the conversation, or occur whenever there is time or nothing better to do.

Classroom Talk, Inquiry, and Collaboration

Many educators view collaborative and academic dialogue and inquiry as something they could do when time allows. Face it, in content area classrooms time is of the essence and very often there is not much to spare. After all, we, as content area teachers, spend most of our time lecturing, presenting our expert knowledge, "covering" content, and preparing students for the demands of the subject area and for success in assessments. Collaboration is not a deficit, or a waste of time; it is a problem-solving, a communication, and a critical thinking skill; it facilitates deeper learning. Planned, systematic, and involved academic conversations should not be seen as an "add-on," or an oxymoron in grades 6–12. Instead, if we are to help students develop the knowledge, skills, and dispositions needed for success in secondary grades, college, and beyond, we need to re-evaluate our views about academic and collaborative discourse, and adjust our instruction accordingly. We also need to teach students how to develop discipline-specific effective communication skills. Academic language will benefit both your advanced and struggling readers.

Zwiers (2008) and Zwiers and Crawford (2011) have developed six ways to develop and sustain academic conversations that will promote deep understanding of text(s) and academic discourse in the content areas. His five essential academic conversation skills are as follows:

1. Elaborate, clarify, and question (e.g., Can you elaborate? What makes you think that?).
2. Support ideas with examples and evidence (e.g., Can you gives us an example from the text? In the text it said . . .).
3. Build on or challenge others' ideas (e.g., Can you add to this idea? I would like to add . . .).
4. Paraphrase and summarize (e.g., In other words, you are saying . . .; This is what I heard you say . . .).
5. Synthesize key ideas from conversation (e.g., What have we learned so far? The main idea from our discussion is . . .).

Classroom talk is not only an instructional medium but it also plays a key role in balancing students' background knowledge and "socializing intelligence" (Resnick & Nelson-LeGall, 1999). Social interaction promotes co-construction of meaning and student learning, and should be considered as an important element of comprehension instruction in secondary grades (Applebee, Langer, Nystrand, & Gamoran, 2003; Palinscar, 2003; Palinscar & Brown, 1984). As you reflect on the role classroom talk plays in your discipline, also think about the ways in which you will model the desired interactions and outcomes, provide support and feedback as students practice these steps, and gradually release the responsibility to the students to lead the dialogue (Pearson & Gallagher, 1983).

Learning through Talk and Argument

Disciplinary argumentation involves sharing, processing, and learning about ideas and is governed by shared norms of participation. Argument in each discipline should take place for the purpose of critiquing, evaluating, and reflecting on each other's ideas instead of "attacking" others. So, how do we promote disciplinary argumentation? In Chapter 6, I examined the importance of asking good, open-ended, and challenging questions. I also discussed how to facilitate student-generated questions and grapple with questions that do not have direct, tangible, or immediate answers. Students need opportunities to engage in discipline-specific forms of communication.

Classroom talk can take place in various ways: partner talk, in small-group and whole group discussions, and also in presentations. Keep in mind that some teachers do not like to use these talk formats because they fear that students will get off task, or the classroom environment might appear as disorderly, noisy, and unproductive. They especially fear how it will appear to administrators, or others who are involved in classroom walkthroughs and teacher observations. Others feel uncomfortable with how to deal with student conflicts in the classroom.

Students need to learn, *and* practice, disciplinary communication norms and skills in the classroom. It is each teacher's responsibility to teach students how to disagree with an idea and how to disagree with a person in civil and productive ways. English language learners will also benefit from classroom talk and argument—they will help show them how to share their knowledge, ideas, and evidence in specific ways. Teachers should promote student-mediated discussion in small groups, and practice teacher-mediated discussion in whole groups.

Think Like an Expert

- Literary thinking experts engage in ongoing conversations, questions, and debates about the discipline. They also evaluate and negotiate diverse interpretations, theories, critical responses, and contexts about literature and the discipline. (English Language Arts)
- Communication, problem solving, reasoning, and considering others' perspectives, and dialogic inquiry are central to mathematical learning. (Mathematics)
- Scientific research is collaborative and multidisciplinary in nature. Scientists also use collaborative inquiry as a method for deepening their understanding, furthering their research, and co-developing knowledge. (Science)
- Historical thinking and inquiry involves questioning ideas, perspectives, evidence, connecting ideas and concepts, sourcing, making inferences, considering alternative perspectives, and making interpretations based on evidence across multiple sources. To understand the past and disseminate historical research to audiences, historians engage in collaborative inquiry with experts from their discipline, with diverse audiences, and also with various agencies. (Social Studies)

Characteristics of Discipline-Specific Learning Environments

To develop students' discipline-specific knowledge, skills, and habits of mind, all content area teachers need to think about their discipline, curricula, and learning goals to organize their learning environment, instruction, and content. When teachers tell me that they want their students to learn deeply, I often ask them about what in their classroom environment (aside from instruction, materials, processes, feedback, etc.) will facilitate that. I see far too many content area classrooms that look like "sad" storage rooms with tattered cardboard boxes for storing books, dictionaries, or materials, with sparse books on bookcases, and a sterile atmosphere. Students learn when they are in a positive, safe, organized, challenging, collaborative, and motivating environment. Every learning environment should be a conversational, thinking, hands-on, creative, relevant, and inviting space for students to learn. Color, visible inspiration, technology, materials and tools for "tinkering," opportunities for students to make their thinking visible, along with high expectations, support, and respect, are all helpful environmental elements. Moreover, students' attitudes toward a subject area and attendance are affected by the classroom's learning environment. In the following section, I present sample ways for learning in different content area classrooms.

Career and Technical Subjects (CTE)

CTE courses provide learning spaces where career, technology, and culture meet. There are a lot of courses that fall under the CTE umbrella such as, accounting, family and consumer sciences, health occupations, architectural drafting, automotive services, computer programming, culinary arts, hospitality and tourism, etc. Any of the above learning environments will need to include many resources and technology, means of teaching, models of learning, and hands-on, relevant applications and connections to career and societal contexts. Infusion of information and communication technologies plays a key role in these learning environments along with partnerships, internships, and on-the job experiences. Students need rigorous career-focused instruction, delivered by qualified and enthusiastic teachers, many subject relevant opportunities with authentic and emerging learning activities that extend beyond the school walls to develop career-specific knowledge, skills, and dispositions, varied experiences, and problem solving.

Teachers need to model and encourage students to synthesize knowledge from different disciplines to solve problems, have high expectations for all students, use innovative and creative techniques to teach content, and use school- and problem-based learning. Peer cooperation and collaboration, teacher feedback, and opportunities to analyze, reflect, and evaluate solutions to everyday problems are a must. Students also need an apprenticeship model of learning—they need to learn from and with more knowledgeable others, receive feedback, and be encouraged to raise critical questions, think carefully about their goals and aspirations, monitor their progress, and become prepared for postsecondary success.

English Language Arts

Reading, writing, questioning, and discussing, should be daily routines in English language arts classes. Students will learn to read and write critically, widely, and for long periods of time when they are encouraged, when they have the freedom to express themselves, and when they receive support, and feedback. High expectations for all students, rigor, cognitive persistence, critical questioning, collaboration, and choice contribute to students' engagement with language, literature, and writing. Small group discussions about the texts student read and their perspectives on the texts will help create an atmosphere of inquiry. Present students with a variety of reading materials beyond the standard textbook—students thrive on choice over books, genres, and ways to present and share what they are learning.

Allow time for inquiry, encourage students to examine topics, texts, characters, authors, etc. in depth, practice close reading of texts, and argue orally and in writing by providing relevant evidence to support their claims. Provide them with opportunities to express their reasoning, view, and analyze texts from different perspectives. Teacher prompting, constructive feedback, and higher-order questioning will help guide students' thinking and facilitate subject-specific habits of mind. Plan rigorous instruction and model key strategies and processes. Offer extra credit for projects and students' interpretations of texts. Deliver abstract ideas and language in creative and practical ways—support the development of students' domain vocabulary, writing, and speaking and listening knowledge and skills. A risk-free, intimidation-free, supportive, flexible, and challenging learning environment promotes student participation, collaboration, and oral and written self-expression. Models and rubrics for long writing assignments work well. Teacher feedback on reading, use of language, conventions, literary elements and techniques, and teacher enthusiasm especially for texts students do not easily relate with, are necessary for student learning. Availability of texts, resources, technology, digital writing tools, display of students' artwork and writing, and other visual inspiration contribute to the effectiveness of the learning environment.

Fine Arts

Students on fine arts courses need time to practice, inside and outside the class, in focused and precise ways. They need a balanced instruction that is interdisciplinary and focused on meaning and inspiration, purposeful activities, a positive, collaborative, and creative community, and instruction that helps them master related concepts and techniques, and encode visual art. Teachers need to help students develop academic and artistic inquiry knowledge, skills, and dispositions. Students will benefit from a learning environment that develops their critical thinking and problem solving skills, and fosters creativity, imagination, experimentation, visual literacy, and artistic accomplishment and expression.

A collaborative, supportive, organized, well equipped (with art and other supplies, musical instruments, etc.), and innovative learning environment will also facilitate the development of students' self-confidence, social competence skills, oral and written communication skills, visual skills, and artistic expression. Experiment with new techniques, interpretations, and approaches to music and visual arts, use digital tools, social media, and technology to support students' artistic inquiry, and provide diverse outlets for self-expression. Students need opportunities to apply knowledge, practice, experiment, play, take risks, critique and evaluate with others the form (how the work is), the theme (what the work is), the context (where, when, by/for whom, and why the work was created), and exchange perspectives and ideas.

Mathematics

All students will benefit from an environment where they are actively involved in doing mathematics. They will also benefit from being engaged in solving relevant and challenging problems in small groups. Collaborative problem solving will facilitate the development of mathematical habits of mind, perseverance, decision-making, curiosity, self-monitoring, and success in learning and doing mathematics. Give students worthwhile tasks that help them to discover the importance of mathematics in everyday life, and in other content areas, and give them opportunities to discuss their mathematical understanding and solutions with others.

To help students develop a positive disposition toward math, show enthusiasm for, and enjoyment of, learning and doing mathematics. Provide concrete models, encourage students to ask questions, stimulate their curiosity, make your thinking and theirs visible, and make mathematical inquiry, communication, and collaboration a daily activity. Create effective daily routines—for example, start each class with a five-minute warm-up activity such as a drill, computation, or solving the math problem of the day. Organize calculators and materials to maximize instructional time, and use creative ways to take attendance that don't eat up your time. Last, create an atmosphere that prevents the mathematical anxiety some students have about the subject.

Physical/Health Education

Physical education teachers provide quality developmentally appropriate instruction that helps students to achieve and maintain a healthy and active lifestyle. Teachers need to hold high expectations for all students developing in psychomotor, cognitive, and affective domains. A positive physical education learning environment is safe, inclusive, and physically challenging and enjoyable. In such an environment, students learn skills and develop an understanding of, and appreciation for, the benefits and importance of physical activity. They also engage in learning movement activities that develop their positive self-image, motivation, confidence, communication, collaboration, and social skills.

Teachers need to also encourage students to be active inside and outside of the school setting, and prepare them to participate in a variety of extramural activities including athletic, intramural, and club programs. Students need opportunities to take risks, try, fail, and try again, free of harassment from the teacher and other students. Teachers need to develop learning activities that help all students understand the nature and different types of competition, give students choice over their competitive environment, and encourage positive competitive activities through personal goal setting and team play. Teachers provide students with adequate time to practice and develop their skills and feedback that is based on skills analysis. Teachers emphasize critical thinking skills and problem solving strategies through higher-order questioning. Fair and consistent classroom management techniques, good use of time, class organization, teacher enthusiasm, feedback, and support help create a positive learning environment.

Science

Laboratory work is part of various science courses (i.e., biology, chemistry, physics). For lab learning environments to be effective, they need to be engaging and challenging instead of prescriptive. Investigation, equity, rigor, cooperation and collaboration, teacher support, and active engagement in science learning influence students' attitudes toward science as well as learning, and development of scientific knowledge, inquiry, and dispositions. Students need the freedom to explore and exercise their curiosity, investigate, observe, and collaborate. Students will benefit from a learning environment that encourages active involvement, class discussions, problem solving, and the autonomy to explore personal scientific thoughts and questions. In addition, science teachers need to show enthusiasm about teaching science, construct science lessons that are practical and interactive, and provide hands-on science experiences. They also need to model scientific habits of mind, model how to implement the scientific method, conduct research, measurements, and experiments, use technology, present results, and promote collaboration.

Social Studies

Social studies teachers engage students in the study of history, geography, economics, government, and civics. Social studies instruction draws on other disciplines such as anthropology, sociology, political science, psychology, religion, law, archaeology, philosophy, art, literature, and other humanities subjects and the sciences. Social studies classes should help students become active and responsible citizens. Students need to learn in learning environments that help them to develop their critical thinking skills, master content, challenge ideas and assumptions, ask, discuss, and answer higher-order questions. They also need to learn how to take a critical stance toward arguments, acquire, organize and evaluate information from multiple sources and perspectives, draw conclusions, and examine topics, issues, and events from a variety of perspectives.

Teachers need to instruct students in researching and interpreting varied primary sources (e.g., original documents, speeches, cartoons, artifacts, images, literature, biographies, journals, oral histories, etc.). For students to develop social studies-related inquiry skills, they need to ask questions, identify problems, collect evidence, present interpretations, defend conclusions, and collaborate with others. Students will also benefit from visiting different learning sites such as government and health agencies, cultural institutions and using technology for long distance activities, visits, and accessing databases and repositories.

Accountable Talk in the Disciplines

Accountable talk is an important component of a disciplinary literacy-learning framework (McConachie & Petrosky, 2010). It is talk that reflects careful reasoning and the ability to verbalize one's thinking in a way that everyone understands the ideas and positions or arguments during whole-group discussion (Michaels, O'Connor, Hall, & Resnick, 2002). Lauren Resnick at the University of Pittsburg coined the term. The accountable talk lens is based on Vygotsky's theoretical framework that stresses the importance of social interaction in the development of a person's mental processes. What does accountable talk have to do with conversations that matter in the disciplines? Accountable talk requires everyone (teacher and students) to be accountable for constructing meaning in class; meaning is co-developed by all and for all! It is talk that responds to, and builds on, what others have said in class. It is demanding talk because it requires all to participate and bring accurate and relevant knowledge to the topic under discussion. Accountable talk involves three important elements of academically productive classroom talk: (1) accountability to the learning community; (2) accountability to quality reasoning; and (3) accountability to knowledge.

For students to be accountable to the learning community, they need to be attentive, listen carefully, paraphrase and summarize as needed, ask clarifying questions, add to everyone's understanding of the topic, make connections and partial concessions (yes . . . but . . .), provide reasons when they agree or disagree with others, and expand everyone's thinking as needed. This is pretty easy to implement in a classroom. Teachers introduce students to the idea and use a number of conversation openers or extenders to suggest the desired features of student talk. Also, selecting interesting ideas to examine, talk and argue about will make accountable talk happen in a classroom. Using the following accountable talk moves will help teachers access students' thinking, knowledge, processes, misperceptions, and reasoning abilities.

- Ask Students to Say More/Clarify
  - What do you mean by that?
  - Could you give an example?
  - Can you say more about that?
- Wait time
  - Take your time.
  - We'll wait; we want to hear from you.
  - Wait; let Carson finish his thought.
- Paraphrase/Repeat
  - Who can put in their own words what Mike just said?
  - Angela, could you repeat what Gustavo said?

- Ask for Evidence/Reasoning
  - Why do you think that?
  - How did you arrive at that conclusion? What evidence did you use?
  - What in the text(s) made you think that?
- Counter Example
  - Is this always the best solution? Is there another way you could solve this?
  - How does your idea support or not support Enrique's idea?
  - What if this factor had been eliminated? What would have happened then?
- Agree/Disagree with Others
  - Do you agree? Why?
  - Do you disagree? Why?
  - Are you saying something similar or different from what Tiffany is saying? How so?
- Add On
  - Who can build onto the idea Jackie is building?
  - Is there anything else you'd like to add?
  - Who can expand, or push further the idea Jackie is building?

Accountability to quality reasoning is reflected through defending one's answers against others' points of view, challenging the speaker to provide evidence for his statement, synthesizing information, and drawing logical and reasonable conclusions about what is needed next for the development of further knowledge. This type of talk involves explanation and self-correction. Finding the logic in classroom discussions is not an easy task. Some students present incomplete thoughts while others can interrupt or disrupt the discussion. Rigorous thinking requires rigorous knowledge and reasoning.

Being accountable to knowledge means that students will verify statements and results, explain clearly how they arrived at their conclusions, provide evidence to support their answers, and highlight relationships between prior knowledge, topics, and ideas. This type of accountability is the most difficult one. Why? Because it requires students to have the needed facts and information from texts to hand. Students will need to have appropriate evidence to support their explanations. They will challenge each other when the knowledge is lacking, incomplete, or unavailable. This type of accountability will also reveal students' misunderstandings and areas of need.

All three of these elements are aligned with the types of thinking students will need to meet CCSS requirements; they can be used as a framework for conducting text-based discussions, and are also aligned with disciplinary literacy learning. Accountable talk can help develop students' content knowledge, as well as academic language and deliberate discourse, reasoning, and speaking and listening skills (Michaels, O'Connor, Hall, & Resnick, 2002; Zygouris-Coe, 2012a). All three elements of accountable talk are interdependent, and all three must happen if we will use discourse to promote academic learning. If students are not accountable to the learning community, discussions might be polite but students will not risk sharing their complete, incomplete, erroneous, or provocative ideas that can build, expand, adjust, and challenge their own and others' thinking. Let's not forget that disciplinary knowledge and scholarship advance through peer review, critique, publication, reflection, and refinement.

Create a learning environment where all students are expected, and entitled to contribute and everyone's contributions matter. Encourage risk-taking and explicitly model and practice different talk moves. Over time students will develop new forms and norms of discourse, begin to listen to each other, build on each other's ideas, and participate productively in deliberate practices (Michaels, O'Connor, & Resnick, 2007). It will take time to internalize academic discourse norms, and it will take commitment from the teacher and the students. Table 8.2

TABLE 8.2. Ways to Promote Accountable Talk

Reason	I understand . . .
	I predict . . . because . . .
	My evidence about . . . is . . .
	When you said . . . it helped me understand . . .
	How do you know that?
	Can you give me some examples?
	An example of . . . is . . .
	Where did you find that information?
	Where in the text(s) does it "say" that?
	I know/believe/support that because it says . . .
	What points are you trying to prove?
	What information do you have?
Explain	Why do you think that?
	What do you mean?
	Can you explain more?
	Can you explain . . . in your own words?
	Say more about . . .
	Based on my evidence, I think . . .
	I don't know what you mean by . . .
	This is the same/different . . . because . . .
	How does your evidence support . . .?
	What evidence do you have to support . . .?
	What do you need to find out in order to solve the problem?
	Which idea would you reject/accept, and why?
Connect	This reminds me of . . .
	I agree/disagree with . . . because . . .
	Who agrees/disagrees with what . . . said?
	I want to add on what . . . said
	I can connect this to . . .
	Your evidence is the same/different because . . .
	What do you think caused the . . . to . . .?
	Based on what you know, what can you predict about . . .?
	What is the relationship between . . . and . . .?
	What are some possible solutions to this problem?
	Does this information align with what we know?
	Here is how I can relate . . . to . . .
Question	Could you clarify your statements?
	A question I have is . . .
	I am confused by . . .
	Who can repeat . . .?
	Could you repeat what you said?
	Is there another way to say . . .?
	Could you say more about . . .?
	So, are you saying . . .?
	Is this your main point?
	What questions did . . . create?
	I wonder about . . .
	What did . . . mean by that?
	Are you saying that . . .?

presents sample ways to use accountable talk or moves to have academic conversations that will matter in your classroom.

The following are discipline-specific examples of accountable talk or moves that follow each discipline's habits of mind (Zygouris-Coe, 2012b). Accountable talk uses evidence that is reflective of, and appropriate to, the discipline (e.g., precision and accuracy in mathematics, data from investigations in science, specific details in literature, evidence from multiple sources in history), and follows established academic norms. Teachers could use the following (and other) examples to create the norms, procedures, routines, skills, and expectations of accountable talk in their classrooms.

English Language Arts Discourse

Students must articulate their text comprehension, summarize, make inferences, and justify claims using complex sentences, precise vocabulary, and grammatical accuracy. They analyze text structure, language, and organization of ideas in texts, identify main ideas, analyze characters, setting, conflict, and plot, question the author, ask a lot of questions, argue about and negotiate meaning from texts, present evidence for their claims, and consider and evaluate others' perspectives. The following are sample ways to promote accountable talk in English language arts classrooms (see Figure 8.1).

- In my opinion…
- I agree with _____ because…
- I disagree with _____ because…
- I have something to say…
- I have something to add to what _____ said…
- Let me see if I understand what you are saying; Are you saying that...?
- What do you mean when you say…?
- Is this your main point?
- What is your thesis?
- Could you give an example of…?
- I noticed that…
- Another example of that is…
- How can you prove that…?
- I wondered about…
- I have a question for _____ about…
- Could you say more about that?
- I'm not sure I see the relevance of this point on your conclusion. Can you help me understand it? How is it relevant?
- I am having trouble understanding this part of the text…could someone explain it to me?
- What do we know about…?
- What caused…in the story?
- What were key effects of the main character's…on...?
- Can you give us some evidence from the text that supports your assertion?
- Using evidence from the text, what next action should the main character take to resolve the situation?
- What is the purpose of the metaphors used throughout the text?
- Why do you think…was the author's purpose with this book?
- Explain more why these significant events are worth remembering from this book.

FIGURE 8.1. Sample accountable talk moves in English language arts classrooms.

Mathematics Discourse

Mathematical language includes not only specialized vocabulary (new words and new meanings for familiar words), but also syntax and organization. During mathematics, students are expected to describe patterns with clarity, present data, make generalizations, explain and justify a

- This is true because…
- This is not true because…
- I agree with your results because…
- I disagree with your results because…
- I know this is an accurate answer because…
- My answer is different because…
- What is another way to show this relationship?
- What if you changed…? What would happen then?
- Could you give me another example? I am not sure I see what you see.
- Explain the problem in your own words.
- Defend your solution.
- What information do we have in this problem?
- What is essential information in this problem?
- What is non-essential information in this problem?
- What pattern(s) do you see?
- Can you draw your solution?
- Why does your solution make sense?
- Could you explain how you arrived at this solution?
- What is another strategy we could use to solve this problem?
- Can you prove your results another way?
- Why is the definition of this variable important?
- What makes a whole difference of…?
- What does the expression mean?
- Can you show me how you figured this out?
- I have a different approach. Can I show you what I did?
- Is this variable important? Can you explain why it is/isn't?

FIGURE 8.2. Sample accountable talk moves in mathematics classrooms.

solution, express a mathematical argument in oral and written forms, and use representations to support their claims. Students are involved in actively using mathematical language to communicate about and negotiate meaning for mathematical situations, construct viable arguments and critique the reasoning of others, attend to precision, understand multiple representations of mathematical concepts, and justify their reasoning. The above are sample ways to promote accountable talk in mathematics classrooms (see Figure 8.2).

Scientific Discourse

Scientific discourse refers to the processes and methods used to communicate, and debate scientific information and build scientific knowledge. The discourse focuses on how to arrive at and how to present scientific ideas to multiple audiences (e.g., peers, general public, or other potential audience that may benefit or contribute to scientific knowledge). Science talk uses data and models as evidence in developing explanations. The scientific method exemplifies scientific discourse. Science requires that we change our ideas as new, valid and relevant evidence emerges. Scientists are concerned about converging toward claims that are accurate and can be generalized. They consider new ideas and evidence, and focus on converging on common representations or understandings. The following are sample ways to promote accountable talk in science classrooms (see Figure 8.3).

- What do we know about…?
- What is…? What isn't?
- What are the uses of…?
- What is the formula of…?
- What is the difference between a…variable and a… variable?
- What does…mean and how does it work?
- What are the some of the major accomplishments of…?

FIGURE 8.3. Sample accountable talk moves in science classrooms. *(Continued)*

- Name two important functions of....
- What happens when you accidently place... in... and then you...?
- What are the advantages of this solution? Can you provide some evidence?
- What are the disadvantages of this solution? Can you provide some evidence?
- What are the steps in your scientific method?
- What science rules should be followed in...?
- Where can you find...?
- Why can't this... stop the reaction in...?
- Why does X change to Y after this action?
- Will this development do more good or harm? How?
- Do you have a solution for...?
- Does the ability to do X increase or decrease with Y?
- Does the size of... affect how...?
- How does...function?
- How much does...weigh and how will its weight affect...?
- How can you make...in a science experiment?
- How do you calculate...?
- Is this... an accepted solution or practice in...? Why?
- Is it safe to put... in...? Why?

FIGURE 8.3. *(Continued)*

Social Studies—History Discourse

In history classrooms, students are involved in analyzing and writing historical arguments. Their discussions focus on identifying and evaluating the author's claims, and the evidence used to support them. They look for facts and interpretations, and consider multiple interpretations in the process of constructing meaning—they use questioning, historical inquiry, sourcing, corroboration, and contextualization. The following are sample ways to promote accountable talk in history classrooms (see Figure 8.4).

- Explain how...and why...
- How are... and... similar?
- How could... be used to...?
- How do you know that...?
- How does... apply to everyday life?
- How does...connect with what we have already learned from...?
- If...is true, what else is also probably true?
- List some reasons, in statements beginning, "Because..."
- Outline the reasoning (premises and conclusions) in...
- Restate in your own words...
- What are the implications of...?
- What are the strengths and weaknesses of...?
- What do we already know about...?
- What do you think causes...Why?
- What does...mean?
- What is a counterargument for...?
- What is a new example of...?
- What is another way to look at...?
- What is being silently taken for granted here?
- What are some differences between...and...?
- What is the nature of...?
- What would be the opposite viewpoint of...?
- What would happen if...?
- Why is...important?
- What tensions (political, economic, social, racial, etc.) existed at that time?
- What are five key words in this primary document and what do they "tell" you about the topic?

FIGURE 8.4. **Sample accountable talk moves in history classrooms.**

Engaging all students in meaningful and accountable academic conversations is not an easy task, nor will you see positive results right away. It is not easy, but it is worthwhile. Many adolescents don't like to talk in class, collaborate with others, and share their thinking. We've done a nice job of conditioning them to teacher-talk in content area classrooms. Practicing meaningful discussions over time will foster improvement, and will result in making academic discourse a common learning mode in content area classrooms. Nurture academic discourse and collaborative inquiry that matter and reflect the conversations students will be having in college, career, and the workforce.

College, Career, and Workforce Connections

- Students need to know how to problem-solve, interpret results, and construct quality products on their own, and with others. Students need to have knowledge, skills, and strategies for collaborative inquiry and learning.
- Disciplinary learning environments should prepare students for the types of thinking, doing, and collaborating they will be required to know and do in postsecondary education.
- Working effectively with others, building professional relationships, working in teams, and teaching others are all important for postsecondary learning and success.
- *Students entering our undergraduate pre-licensure BSN (baccalaureate in nursing) program need to like people, have the ability to accept and work with individuals with a wide variety of beliefs and behaviors, some of which will be different from those valued by the student. They must also enjoy taking responsibility for their own learning and going beyond the minimum level of knowledge needed to simply "pass" a course. They must be well prepared with deep knowledge of the sciences (chemistry, anatomy, physiology and human nutrition) and statistics as well as the social sciences (psychology and sociology) and be able to apply that knowledge when assessing patients and providing nursing care. For optimal effectiveness, they should seek to develop a wide view of the health are system, and how its different components relate to each other and impact the health of both individuals and communities and the world. Since nurses are educated, not trained, their chances of success in their education as a nursing professional also depend on their holistic view of the patient and their family, and the community in which the patient lives and works* (Diane Wink, Professor, Nursing, University of Central Florida).

Collaborative Inquiry

Collaborative inquiry deepens students' understanding of concepts, socializes intelligence (Resnick & Nelson-Le Gall, 1999), promotes evidence-based explanations, and engages students in rich forms of scientific evidence. Students can ask each other questions and problem-solve as a group before they ask the teacher. Collaboration is an instructional and learning strategy that involves students getting together in pairs, or in larger groups of four (or up to six if the class size is large) to interact about their reading, writing, and thinking; they discuss ideas, generate questions, set goals, and learn. The groups can be homogeneous or heterogeneous in structure. Collaborative learning provides students with opportunities to express their thinking orally, to listen to others, and consider, question, and evaluate one's own thinking and that of others.

Bruner (1999) views collaboration as a strong pedagogical tool that helps students . . . learn that truths are the product of evidence, argument, and construction, rather than authority, textual or pedagogical" (p. 57). Through discussion with others, students develop what he calls, "intersubjective interchange." Collaborative learning helps students build and expand their understanding, practice and develop language, develop critical thinking and social skills, and self-monitor speaking and listening. Such experiences will also equip students with the college, career, workforce, and life readiness skills of discussion, collaboration, interpretation, negotiation, disagreement, compromise, argument, problem solving, and self-evaluation. Collaborative learning can take many forms. Students can benefit from learning social skills such as: share time, resources, and space; debate an idea in a respectful manner; elicit participation from all group members; and, evaluate group efforts. Collaborative learning is also beneficial for ELLs and students with disabilities (Slavin, 1984).

Teachers assign students to groups on the basis of interests, topic of study, book, project, birth order, birthdate (e.g., month, or 1st–10th of the month, etc.), or by randomly numbering students. If the groups are going to be working together for several weeks on projects that require them to meet after school, consider asking students to choose their own groups so they can work with others who have similar schedules or live in the same area. Assigning students to groups also depends on the teacher's purpose and the class dynamics. Students who work in pairs can sit side by side and students who work in groups of four or more students should sit facing one another, and as close to one another as their desks will permit. It is important to note that sometimes a group will not be able to meet their goals for different reasons; they may even decide to "divorce" themselves from some group members. This is okay as long as the group has made an effort to solve their problem and have proposed how they will meet the goals and objectives of the task. The more experiences students have in conflict resolution, and the more teachers monitor the in-class collaboration, the easier collaboration will become.

Barriers to Collaboration in Middle and High School

Although the impact of student collaboration on student learning has been documented, collaboration learning does not take place often in grades 6–12. Why not? There are several barriers to using collaboration in the upper grades. Some teachers worry that if they give students control over their own learning, they will not learn a lot. Some content area teachers perceive themselves as the dispenser of information in the classroom. Others are concerned that students will spend more time on irrelevant topics, rather than on the task; yet others believe that some students will dominate discussions, and others will not learn. Last, some teachers argue that collaborative groups take too much class time away from the curriculum, and they cannot afford to "waste" any time. In addition, students and parents can also have issues with collaboration.

Some students do not like group work because it is more work—"We have to think, talk, participate, pay attention to what others are saying, and take notes. I like it better when I just sit back and listen." Other students say, "I hate doing group work; I have to wait on others and then I end up doing all the work by myself."; "I don't like to talk in public; I want to keep my thoughts to myself and I don't particularly care what others think!" Teachers can use team-building activities throughout the year for community and bonding purposes, and for helping students learn how to collaborate with others in a risk-free and emotionally safe environment. Some groups come up with their own cheer, protocol, flag, etc. Team-building activities at the beginning of the year will make it easier for students to collaborate on more complicated collaborative activities toward the end of the school year.

Many students do not know how to effectively collaborate with others. Some will arrive in your class having collaborative learning experiences since early elementary grades, while others will arrive with no experience with collaborative groups. Collaboration involves clear communication and expression of ideas, negotiation of roles, meaning, and timelines, questioning, perspective taking, and creating a positive and respectful environment for, and with, all. Students need to learn how to collaborate with others, they need to have clear expectations about learning, be given opportunities to evaluate their role in the success or failure of the group, and be expected to discuss what worked or did not work as a group. For students to learn how to collaborate with others, collaboration has to be part of classroom learning. Students can collaborate before, during, or after any assignment or any time the teacher feels students need an opportunity to build, expand, challenge, or assess their thinking and learning. Some teachers use collaborative groups to check students' understanding, build their background knowledge, review material, teach writing, problem solving or question generation, and even conduct group assessments.

How to Create Effective Collaborative Groups

Collaborative groups work well when the teacher implements the following principles:

- *Sets clear expectations for student behavior.* Students can benefit from having collaboration norms; you can either develop them yourself, or include all students and invite them to co-develop them. Collaboration norms help to keep everyone accountable. Here is a set of norms from a science class. Over time, these norms become habitual behaviors; when a peer violates a norm, the group is responsible for helping the peer adjust his or her behavior and keep each other accountable.
  - We will be prepared for our discussions.
  - We will begin and end our discussions on time.
  - We will stay engaged throughout each discussion.
  - We will ask good questions, and will provide evidence-based answers.
  - We will focus on the group discussion; we will stay on task.
  - We will stick to the goals and get to the point.
  - We will listen respectfully, we will respect, and we will consider matters from another's perspective.
  - We will agree or disagree in a civil, prepared, and thoughtful manner.
  - We will maintain a positive tone during our discussions.
  - We will not complain about a problem unless we can offer a solution.
  - We will contribute equally to the workload of this team.
  - We will have fun!

  In addition, teachers give students clear directions about assignments and at times depending on the assignment, they post the directions on chart paper or project them on the board for all to use as a point of reference. Anything you can do proactively in terms of clarity and planning will help the process. Allow students to set up expectations for their group, negotiate how they will meet assignment requirements, divide tasks and responsibilities, and even form their own sub-deadlines.

- *Models what is expected prior to placing students in groups.* Model what you would like students to do, whether it is to discuss a book they are reading, problem-solve, answer questions, come up with alternative solutions, conduct experiments, or complete a graphic organizer.

- *Requires student accountability.* Collaborative groups provide students with opportunities to teach one another and learn the material. To promote accountability, teachers assign roles to different students. Possible roles include, and are not limited to, the following (roles can vary according to subject matter and task): data keeper (keeps track of information generated by the group); noise and discussion monitor (monitors noise level and helps group stay on task); scribe, questioner (asks questions of group members, of the teacher, or of other groups); reporter (gives a report on behalf of the group); summarizer (summarizes what the group did or outcomes of their work); word analyst (provides vocabulary information to the group), etc. Students produce an artifact that keeps them on task during collaborative learning.

- *Monitors each group.* Teachers drop in on each group, sit on the periphery of the group and listen in, and make themselves available for feedback. They also monitor students' participation, use of accountable talk, follow the flow of the collaboration, make formative assessments of students' understanding, and provide additional explanations or directions as needed. Teachers should observe, monitor, listen, be close enough to help as needed, and move on; they should not use collaborative learning time to grade student homework. On the other hand, they should not interfere with students' discussions, solutions to problems, and processes.

- *Assesses and evaluates students' group work.* Students put more effort and will assume more responsibility if they know that their work will be assessed and evaluated.

- *Asks students to evaluate their own and others' performance and reflect on the group learning process.* Self-evaluation promotes more responsibility of one's own learning and it also facilitates metacognition. It is helpful to have certain criteria in place for evaluating others' work. For example, students can evaluate one another's participation and contributions; they should be confidential and teachers should use them for conference purposes with students. Reflection is an important component of collaborative learning. It helps students develop ownership of their own learning and engages them in the process. Reflection can focus on project directions and goals, group participation, challenges with the project, areas of improvement, as well as group contributions and next steps.

Cooperative Learning

Cooperative learning is a specific type of student-student collaboration. It refers to an instructional technique that uses small, heterogeneous groups of students working together toward achieving a common goal. It means much more than just having students working in groups. Cooperative learning can be used to teach academic, social, and interpersonal skills (Johnson & Johnson, 1990, 2009; Kagan, 1992; Slavin, 1983). Cooperative learning is associated with Roger and David Johnson who have been guiding educators about how to implement cooperative learning in the classroom. Cooperative learning involves five key components: positive interdependence, promotive (face-to-face) interaction, individual and group accountability, social skills development, and group processing (Johnson, Johnson, & Holubec, 2008).

Positive interdependence is a process of creating relationships in which each member of the group relies on the knowledge and talents of others to accomplish a goal; in other words, students "sink or swim together." Positive interdependence can be achieved through common goals, division of responsibilities and roles within each group, shared contributions, and shared performance—each student's grade is dependent upon the performance of the rest of the group. Students will have to accept each other's contributions in order for them to meet a common goal.

Promotive interaction refers to every student supporting each other by encouraging, supporting, and eliciting each person's contribution and learning. Individual accountability means that everyone is responsible for doing all of the work—no "freeloading," or "hitch-hiking" and each individual's effort and determination are rewarded. Cooperative learning provides a support system, a mechanism for helping every student learn, and a climate of shared responsibility for all students. Collaborative learning skills are learned behaviors; knowing how to work with others includes many social skills such as communication, active listening, willingness to help or work together, taking turns, sharing materials and ideas, respecting others' views, and reaching consensus. When heterogeneous cooperative learning is effectively implemented, all students benefit academically, socially, and emotionally. Cooperative learning is an important component of inclusive classrooms; teachers can use cooperative learning to provide additional help to students with varied exceptionalities and needs.

Think-Pair-Share and Jigsaw are two cooperative learning activities frequently used in content area classrooms. Frank Lyman (1981) developed Think-Pair-Share. It provides students with personal time to independently think about a problem or question. When prompted by the teacher, the student pairs up with a peer and discusses his or her ideas and also listens to the ideas of his or her partner. Teachers can assign partners or invite students to choose their own partner. Following the pair dialogue, the teacher gives all students an opportunity for discussion with the whole class or with another pair (see Table 8.3 for a sample template students can use during a Think-Pair-Share activity).

Jigsaw is an effective strategy to use when you want to increase students' mastery of a topic, boost their concept development, enhance targeted discussions among students, and foster group project participation and learning (Kagan, 1994). Because each student is seen as invaluable to the collaborative process this leads to a shared responsibility model of learning that focuses on both interpersonal, and intrapersonal components (Gregory & Chapman, 2007). Jigsaw is seen as a powerful differentiated instruction strategy because it gives all students the ability to contribute to the topic, discussion, or task in meaningful ways (Crawford, 2008). The following are steps for implementing Jigsaw (Schlemmer & Schlemmer, 2008):

- Divide students into 4–6-person Jigsaw groups. These will be the "home base groups" (see Figure 8.5 for a Jigsaw Grouping Chart).
- Give the home base group information on the goals and overall tasks of the assignment. Will they be learning about the causes of the Civil War? Will students be creating a report, presentation, or concept map?
- Divide the lesson into segments that are comparable to the number of students you have in each group. For example, if you have four students in each group divide the information into four groups.
- Assign each student in a group to learn one segment of the topic or subject.
- If providing students with information to read (e.g., examining multiple texts) give them time to read over their segment in order to become familiar. They may want to take notes of the important parts or parts they plan to share. If this is based on students' research, consider using an Inquiry Chart to assist them with preparing.
- Form "expert groups" by having students from each home base group join other students assigned to the same segment of information. In these expert groups, the students should discuss the main points of their segment, check their understanding of the topic, and select the important elements they would want to share with their home groups. They will return

to their home groups to teach their group mates what they learned in their "expert" group (see Table 8.4 for a Jigsaw Note-Taking Template students can use to organize their thoughts and learning).

● At the end, the entire class comes together to examine, assess, and reflect on their preparation, group processes, and understanding of the material. At times, teachers use quizzes to assess student understanding.

TABLE 8.3. Think-Pair-Share—Chemistry Example-What Element Am I?

Question	What I Thought	What my Partner Thought	What we Decided to Share
I am a very active metal. I react violently with water. Which element am I?	*I am not sure about this one. I think it might be sodium because sodium reacts with water and makes a gas.*	*My partner thinks it is potassium because it is a metal and it reacts very violently with water. In fact, last week he thinks one of his class experiments demonstrated how potassium and water made a gas in mere seconds.*	*After reading, we decided it is potassium. Potassium seems like a more active metal.*
I am a common part of the atmosphere and have 5 electrons. Which element am I?	*I think it's nitrogen because I know that nitrogen occupies 78 percent of our atmosphere.*	*My partner agrees and states that it does have only 5 electrons.*	*This one is definitely nitrogen.*
I have a melting point of 3287 K, am a hard metal, and am part of the acid earth family. Which element am I?	*I think it's tantalum because it's part of the acid earth family. I am not sure about the melting point, but it is a hard metal.*	*My partner said he thought it was tantalum too. He found in our book that tantalum has a melting point of 3287 K.*	*We're pretty sure it's tantalum and have enough info to prove it. This one was an easy one.*
I am an inert gas that has blue and green illuminations. Which element am I?	*I think it's either neon or argon because they are both inert gases that have illuminations in their emissions.*	*My partner thinks it is argon because he remembers one of his science teachers doing an experiment and that he saw green and blue emissions.*	*I think we'll share that it is argon because I think my partners experience gives us a good idea.*
I am the most abundant element in the universe. I am flammable. What element am I?	*I think it might be oxygen because it's very abundant. I also think it might be carbon because I've read that carbon is in so many things.*	*My partner thinks it is hydrogen because hydrogen is flammable and when we look up hydrogen on the Internet we found that it was in many things in this world and other worlds.*	*The answer is hydrogen. I can see from our search my partner is right. It is very flammable.*

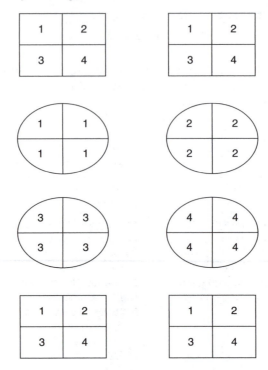

FIGURE 8.5.   Jigsaw grouping chart.

* Square tables indicate Home Base Groups Round tables indicate Expert Groups

Sometimes, cooperative learning can be stereotyped as a method where more capable students help those less prepared. The following are sample ways teachers can differentiate learning within cooperative groups to meet all students' needs (Schniedewind & Davidson, 2000):

Differentiate Tasks by Complexity and Quantity

In a Jigsaw activity where students are reading a biography of Martin Luther King, Jr., each student can receive a version of the book, a portion of the book, or additional resources that will appropriately challenge them. Each student plays a vital role in the group's learning and success without feeling awkward or anxious. They can study, research, and summarize their reading, report to one another, review their findings together as a group, and become responsible for knowing many aspects of Martin Luther King Jr.'s life. Students can demonstrate their knowledge by completing a group project, or taking a quiz, answering questions, using technology to create resources on the topic for the class, or hold a debate. This way, aside from the material's level of complexity, each student's contribution becomes essential to the group's success.

Use Heterogeneous Cooperative Groups to Enhance Individualized Work

For example, during a biology unit on the human body, teachers can utilize cooperative learning groups in a variety of ways. One example includes using this group structure to expand students' understanding of subject matter vocabulary. I like to use technology to help expand students' vocabulary knowledge and understanding. Students can choose 10 of the most important words from the unit to learn more about or teach the class about them. In groups of four, they each select key words, assess their understanding of the words, and think of ways to make connections with other related concepts, or use those words to make a case about their importance for

TABLE 8.4. Jigsaw Activity Note-Taking Template—American History Example

Expert Group	Home Group
I am an expert on the topic of: *Christopher Columbus*	What were the other topics covered by my home group: • *Our topic as a group was "Voyages of Portugal and Spain."* • *I covered Christopher Columbus while other topics included Vespucci, Balboa, and Magellan.*
Points of discussion I want to talk about in my expert groups about the topic. • *Christopher Columbus was a Genoan navigator that was financed by the King and Queen of Spain to partake in a voyage in the search of trade routes heading West instead of around the tip of Africa.* • *He actually discovered the Americas.* • *His interaction between old and new world led to the Columbian Exchange.*	How do the topics and information from my home group partners connect with my topic? • *Columbus was the one of the first explorers out of Spain. He believed the Earth was round.* • *His explorations led the way for other sailors/navigators to explorers such as, Vespucci (1497–1504), Balboa (1513), and Magellan (1519).*
What did I learn in my expert group? • *Columbian Exchange was good for trade but Indians (Native Americans) were burdened with new diseases such as small pox.* • *Many of them died.*	Write a group summary about the home group's subject. • *Explorers and traders sailed the ocean from Spain and Portugal during the late 1400s into the early 1500s in search of new trade routes.* • *Columbus' voyages led to the Columbian Exchange and furthered travel by other explorers. He led the way for other explorers such as Vespucci, who did not believe the new land was Asia, Balboa who named the South Sea, and Magellan who renamed the South Sea the Pacific Ocean.* • *Trade was expanded along with contact with natives of the new land.*

understanding the human body, etc. Students take some time examining each group member's words and rationale for their importance and then decide as a group about the 10 words they will present to the class and also how to present them so every student in class develops a solid understanding of them. This way, students not only learn more about the words they have chosen, but they also have to negotiate, use evidence from text to support their choices, and learn more words from their group members' choices. Students' choices have varied from using PowerPoint Presentations, Animated films, or photography and images to explain the words, etc. One of my favorite ones is Wordle (http://wordle.net), using a word cloud to demonstrate the prominence or importance of certain words within a text (see Figure 8.6). You could also turn this into a Jigsaw activity where different groups are responsible for studying a different system (e.g., digestive and excretory, nervous, etc.) and teaching others either about the system and its functions or about vocabulary related to each system.

Use Peer Tutoring to Challenge both Tutors and Tutees

When writing a quadratic function to model three different graphs, tutees learn more about writing different quadratic functions and tutors learn more about how to use the appropriate

FIGURE 8.6.   Wordle—Topic: Human Body, Biology Unit.

mathematics language, how to write a quadratic function in a certain way, and how to best explain it so the tutee understands it. The tutee learns about the advantages of a quadratic function in vertex and standard forms, and how the real solutions of the quadratic equation relate to the graph of the related quadratic function.

Other Approaches

Differentiate by giving alternate homework assignments, research projects, enrichment activities, and projects. Effective heterogeneous cooperative groups will promote equity by respecting student diversity, needs, learning styles, and interests.

Socratic circles, or a Socratic seminar, is another way to facilitate student-generated dialogue and self-directed involvement. The strategy derives its name from the Greek philosopher Socrates who created a teaching method that focused on questioning, critical thinking, and discussions. Socrates believed that the answers to all human questions reside within us and that through disciplined conversation we can discover the ultimate truth. The 2012 US Teacher of the Year, Rebecca Mieliwocki, is a seventh-grade English teacher at Luther Burbank Middle School, in suburban Los Angeles. Ms. Mieliwocki was selected for this prestigious award for inspiring and motivating her students, making learning fun, and also for using the Socratic method of questioning to stimulate students' critical thinking and create dynamic lessons. The Socratic seminar is an approach that includes an inner and an outer circle to engage students in a formal conversation about essential questions and other topics. Its purpose is to lead students in a deeper understanding of complex ideas (Copeland, 2005).

Basic procedures for using the Socratic seminar include:

1. On the day before the Socratic seminar, hand out the text. The text should not be too long, but should challenge students' thinking as they read it.
2. Students should spend that evening, as homework, reading and analyzing the text.

3. The next day during class, the teacher randomly places students either in the inner or outer circle.

4. The students that form the inner circle read the passage aloud and then engage in a discussion of the text for 10 minutes. The leader asks peers in the inner circle open-ended questions; for example, "What do you think this text means?" Students in the outer circle observe silently and take mental notes. Students learn to work cooperatively and to question others' perspectives in civil and intelligent ways.

5. After students in the inner circle conclude their discussion, the outer circle assesses the performance and gives feedback on the group or on an individual.

6. Students in the inner circle exchange positions and roles with peers in the outer circle. The new inner circle holds a 10-minute discussion and then receives feedback from students in the new outer circle.

Before teachers implement the Socratic seminar, they will want to consider the classroom dynamics and students' needs as well as think carefully about the role of the teacher in the process. The classroom environment needs to be conducive to the Socratic seminar; consider both the physical classroom and emotional climate in planning for a successful session. Desks or chairs need to be arranged into an inner circle and an outer circle—some teachers have students sit directly on the floor. The goal is for members of the inner circle to have an outer circle member directly behind them.

The teacher's role during the Socratic seminar has four different parts:

1. Select the text for the discussion. Make sure to select high quality text that will expand the topic and thinking. Teachers can also select what types of discussions students will discuss in both circles. Questions can range from factual (what is said), interpretive (what is meant), and evaluative (why is it important). For example, in mathematics and science classrooms, teachers can present students with a problem or experiment that will raise many questions. In a history class, select two to three primary documents students can analyze, discuss, and examine how they add to their understanding of the event, person, or historical issue. Select materials and questions that will challenge students' thinking.

2. Keep the discussion of the inner circle focused. The teacher takes on the role of facilitator or coach and directs the conversation. After a brief instruction, he or she retreats to the sideline and observes and listens carefully as students engage in collaborative inquiry. The teacher's role is not to overly bombard students with questions, but to allow for a flow to be created by student conversations and dialogue. Students should take ownership of the material. During the beginning stages, teachers will need to model what is expected. The Socratic seminar provides students with the opportunity to learn about self-regulated and collaborative inquiry with the teacher providing support through cues and prompts.

   Sample questions include the following:
   ● What evidence from the text(s) do you have to support your idea?
   ● What do you think the author is trying to say here?
   ● Who is the audience for this text?
   ● What factors shaped our interpretations of the text?
   ● What did this word or phrase mean to you?

3. Direct the feedback of the outer circle. The feedback provided by students in the outer circle is extremely important. Teachers should spend time modeling what quality feedback sounds like, and allow time for practice in other settings. At first, the comments of the outer group can be basic observations and the teacher can highlight specific points made.

4. Monitor, assess, and evaluate individual and group performance. Assessment can be done formally or informally. The teacher can use and develop a rubric that will allow a type of

scorecard that students can review (see Table 8.5). But, the most important type of feedback the teacher can provide is at the conclusion of the activity, verbally describing the level of achievement of the learning goals and ways to improve the discussion. Students need an opportunity to evaluate the seminar especially in terms of their own performance, contributions, engagement, and comfort level. Sample relevant questions for self-reflection include the following:

- Was there a point when the seminar reverted into a debate/discussion rather than a dialogue? If yes, how did you or the group handle this?
- What evidence did you see of peers actively listening and building on others' ideas?
- How has your understanding of this text, problem, or issue been affected by the ideas explored in the seminar?
- What would you like to do differently as a participant the next time you are in a Socratic seminar?

TABLE 8.5. Sample Socratic Seminar Rubric

	Outstanding (3)	Average (2)	Below Average (1)
Read the text and was prepared to discuss it	Responses reflect a critical understanding of the text.	Responses reflect a basic and incomplete understanding of the text.	Responses reflect lack of preparation; student did not read the text.
Engaged in the discussion	Actively participated throughout the Socratic Circle time.	Actively participated in at least 50% of the Socratic Circle time.	Sporadic participation; was mostly off-task.
Supported ideas with textual evidence	Supported ideas with evidence from text(s).	Supported some ideas with evidence from text(s) and only when asked to.	Does not support ideas with evidence from text(s).
Expressed thoughts in complete sentences	Expressed thoughts with clarity and logic; made connections between ideas; moved the discussion forward.	Comments are logical, but ideas are not connected.	Comments do not flow logically in the discussion.
Used logical reasoning in questioning	Raised thoughtful, logical, and critical questions that engaged others in the discussion.	Raised basic questions that did not further engage others in the discussion.	Questions do not address nor guide the discussion.
Accepted many points of view	Accepted and reflected on others' viewpoints.	Acknowledged others' viewpoints but did not consider them to expand understanding.	Did not accept others' points of view.
Listened carefully and respected others	Paid attention to details, took into account other participants' points, and addressed faulty logic or evidence respectfully.	Paid attention to some details, but personal perspective distracted the student from the ideas of others.	Was inattentive and misinterpreted others' points of view.

The advantages of the Socratic seminar include the fostering of critical thinking skills, vocabulary, listening and speaking skills, and it also allows for student voice and agency. The disadvantages of the strategy include the time involved to conduct the Socratic seminar (15–30 minutes), the fact that the discussion may provide no tangible answers, and also the whole activity may appear a bit unstructured to someone who is not familiar with its principles and goals.

Motivation, Engagement, and Student Voice

Motivation, engagement, and student voice are key learning filters. There are a number of factors that affect student motivation to learn, to engage in learning, to participate in classroom discussions, or even show up for school. One of the characteristics of a disciplinary learning environment is that it helps to socialize intelligence through the use of accountable talk and collaborative inquiry. Resnick and Nelson-Le Gall's (1999) view of "socialized intelligence" is very relevant to the disciplinary learning framework proposed in this book. If students in a subject area classroom believe that they are supposed to be asking questions, providing evidence, thinking deeply about concepts, and discussing their thoughts with others, then they will practice all of these habits of learning and will keep striving to learn. They will also learn how to develop such habits of thinking through socialization and interactions with others. See Table 8.6 for practices of teachers who promote student motivation for learning.

If students believe that intelligence is "fixed," or determined at birth and is resistant to change or external influence, then when they have difficulty in a subject area, they will probably interpret it as lack of intelligence in that domain (e.g., "I am dumb at science; I don't get it"). On the other

TABLE 8.6.   Sample Practices of Teachers Who Motivate Students

What Teachers Do	What Teachers Do Not Do
• Celebrate students' diversity in culture, language, reading, family, apparel, etc. Adolescents need to be recognized as individuals.	• Use sarcasm.
	• Draw negative attention to a student's culture or language.
	• Limit instruction to one learning style.
• Set high expectations and provide scaffolds to help students meet their goals.	• "Keep score."
• Create a classroom that encourages risk.	• Have unannounced quizzes.
• Create opportunities for students to participate in large- and small-group discussions, and choose with whom, and how, they would like to share their thoughts and reflections.	• Lack resources.
	• Give unforgiving deadlines.
	• Lack cooperative learning practices.
	• Use assessments that do not inform instruction.
• Make sure everybody knows each other in your classroom by names. This is particularly difficult but absolutely essential in the secondary classroom.	• Grade everything.
• Promote wide reading and discuss differences (e.g., text structure, purposes, organization) between aesthetic (live through the text) and efferent (carries information from text) reading.	
• Provide class time for aesthetic reading and encourage it inside and outside the school.	

hand, if students believe intelligence is largely a matter of effort, then they are more likely to put in more effort, attempt difficult tasks, and persist even after failure (Dweck, 1999). In Chapter 2, I discussed the importance of teachers' and students' beliefs in learning (see Figure 2.2); a student's motivation to persist is affected by the student's belief about whether he or she can improve on existing skills and acquire new ones through effort. Dweck (1999) advises teachers to not praise students by using blanket statements about their inherent abilities (i.e., "You are so good at English"). Instead, they should reinforce the belief that effort will result in increases in proficiency (i.e., "I can see that your chemistry scores have gone up in the last several weeks; have you been studying more?"). Praise is best applied when it is specific to a skill the student is developing.

Vygotsky (1978) called our attention to the "sociocultural mind." In other words, the more a student is exposed to another's thinking, the more his or her thoughts are influenced. Literacy and learning are socially constructed processes. Meaningful and supportive relationships in the classroom become important forces of external motivation. The more students interact with people who value them, respect them, prepare them, challenge them, and support them in their interests and learning, the more likely they are to internalize those motivators as their own. This is one major reason for creating a supportive learning environment that promotes meaningful student to teacher and student-to-student relationships. Motivating students to learn also includes being supportive and demanding at the same time. Challenge that is followed by support is motivating to adolescent learners (Eccles & Wigfield, 1995)—making things easy for students will actually backfire on their motivation to continue to learn.

Low student engagement with learning is a major barrier to providing all students with a rigorous education. In most states, the heavy focus on high-stakes testing that is also coupled with a lack of active learning opportunities has resulted in an increasing number of disengaged students. Increasing student engagement is not a simple or quick matter. Teachers need to implement persistent efforts, collaborate with colleagues, and plan with student engagement in mind. Student engagement involves cognitive, emotional, and social factors and requires a learning environment that is safe, motivating, challenging, supportive, inclusive, and emotionally safe, and risk-free. A positive learning environment will also promote a mastery-goal (seeking to improve and learn) versus a performance-goal orientation (looking smart and focusing on grades).

What does engaging work look like? Results from research with students and teachers showed that in their view, engaging work is work that stimulates people's curiosity; it is work they are good at, allows them to use their creativity, and fosters positive relationships with others. Work that is repetitive, requires little effort and thought, and is forced on people by others, is work people dislike (Strong, Silver, & Robinson, 1995). Students who are engaged display three characteristics: (1) they are drawn to their work; (2) they persist despite challenges or obstacles; and (3) they take pleasure in completing their work (Schlecty, 1994). External rewards have a short "shelf" life; they do not produce long lasting results. According to Strong, Silver, and Robinson (1995), four forces drive students to become engaged in learning are success, curiosity, originality, and relationships.

Students will flourish when teachers hold high expectations for them, convince them they can succeed, make the criteria for success clear, model the skills they will need to be successful, and provide clear, immediate, and supportive feedback. Students will also become engaged and learn when the work they do in the classroom fuels their curiosity and propels them to further understanding. Teachers need to provide adolescents with activities and assignments that give them choice to express their autonomy, originality, and creativity and will foster peer relationships (Strong, Silver, & Robinson, 1995). If you would like to have more student engagement in your classroom, create tasks that have the following characteristics:

- Are rigorous and move at a brisk pace; they require high levels of thinking, questioning, problem solving, inquiring, and reflecting.
- They do not result in right or wrong answers.
- Are student-centered, relevant to real-world applications, and meaningful to students' lives, goals, or interests.
- Chunk lecturing (up to 15 minutes at a time or as needed), and utilize the teacher as a facilitator of the learning process.
- Are connected to the essential question and provide purpose and intentionality.
- Involve student-student collaboration, teach students how to collaborate with others, and permit student mobility in the classroom.
- Are authentic and include student input and choice.
- Are challenging and attainable.
- Allow for student choice (expression and presentation).
- Consider different learning styles.
- Include use of key comprehension strategies for inquiry, higher order thinking questions, discipline-specific vocabulary, problem solving, and accountable talk.
- Are "moldable," meaning, they can be changed, or expanded by the student.
- Incorporate media and technology.
- Promote learning beyond the classroom walls.

How are students going to engage in learning if they have no agency? Give students a voice in how activities are carried out, in constructing meaning, and in what they think about the learning process. Make space for student voice in your classroom, and students will give you access to their thinking, their feelings about learning, and their goals, interests, and aspirations. Give students opportunities to express themselves, seek and value their opinions, promote collaborative decision-making, encourage them to identify problems and generate solutions, and hold them accountable for their learning (Fielding, 2007; Mitra, 2009; Toshalis & Nakkula, 2012).

Personalization and choice in curricular and instructional tasks play an important role in student learning. In addition, studies of social development have shown that creating a sense of community in classrooms and schools has a strong impact on adolescents' social development. Resnick et al. (1997) found that community and a sense of belonging are ways to prevent at-risk adolescent behaviors—her study showed that is it very important for adolescents to feel connected to individuals at school and to the school as a whole. Environments that promote student motivation and engagement also have the following characteristics (Toshalis & Nakkula, 2012):

- Personalization and Choice in Curricular Tasks
  - Help students develop personal learning plans.
  - Offer students lots of choice in curricular tasks.
  - Provide students with opportunities to show mastery in a variety of ways.
  - Allow (and encourage) independent projects that build on students' special interests.
- Developing Students' Social and Emotional Growth
  - Get to know your students well.
  - Focus on educating the "whole" student: academically, emotionally, socially.
  - Promote student reflection.
  - Engage students in peer collaboration.
  - Coach students on how to communicate with others and present their ideas clearly, effectively, and appropriately.

- Fostering Autonomy and Lifelong Learning.
  - Build students' skills around planning, time management, self-pacing, persistence, self-organizing, and taking initiative.
  - Help students learn how to learn.

In addition, positive, productive learning environments are inclusive. In inclusive classrooms, students are comfortable with diversity, are thoughtful and engaged, have conflict resolution skills, and are aware of their interconnectedness. Students learn to think about, *we* rather than *I*, make decisions that benefit the entire classroom community, and interact with each other in culturally responsive ways. They also become aware of differences, talk and address uncomfortable issues of race, gender, poverty, stereotypes, prejudices, justice, disease, loss, bullying, and disabilities, and have a repertoire of communication and interaction skills. Discussions, support, community, fairness, equity, justice, and how to live, work, and learn together in a democratic society are important components of inclusive classrooms.

Teachers who create inclusive learning environments see *all* students as *their* students (Delpit, 1995). All children can learn in the right learning environment. Poverty, disabilities, cultural and other differences are not deficits; instead, students need well prepared and culturally competent educators, high quality instruction, instructional accountability, and support systems that will help meet their needs, challenge them and support them to meet their academic aspirations (Delpit, 1995).

I like this quote by Lisa Delpit as it speaks about the power of teachers' perceptions and beliefs about students from diverse socio-cultural backgrounds; it highlights the need for inclusive learning environments.

> We do not really see through our eyes or hear through our ears, but through our beliefs. To put our beliefs on hold is to cease to exist as ourselves for a moment — and that is not easy. It is painful as well, because it means turning yourself inside out, giving up your own sense of who you are, and being willing to see yourself in the unflattering light of another's angry gaze. It is not easy, but it is the only way to learn what it might feel like to be someone else and the only way to start the dialogue.
>
> (1995, pp. 46–47)

The following are suggestions for creating an inclusive learning environment (Sapon-Shevin, 2008):

- To build classroom community, start early and continue throughout the year.
- Teach positive social skills, conflict resolution, and peer mediation skills.
- Collaborate with the school counselor and provide students with outlets, resources, and effective interpersonal communication skills.
- Bring the following concepts to life—community, inclusion, friendship, support, caring, empathy, and kindness. Use real-life examples, role-play, and discussions inside and outside the classroom.
- Adopt zero-tolerance and zero-indifference policies toward bullying and any type of abuse. Students need to know what is and is not acceptable and be responsible to face school policy consequences for inappropriate and unacceptable behavior.
- Share your beliefs about diversity and inclusion and discuss their impact on learning. Provide real life examples from everyday life—e.g., language (ways you or others describe different people), music, media, books, materials, portrayal of diversity in the arts, etc.
- Create many opportunities for students to work together, assist one another, listen to each other's thinking and ways of learning, and learn from each other.

- Seize teachable moments for social justice and hold discussions about perceptions, beliefs, and gender, social, and cultural differences in norms, verbal and non-verbal communication, and experiences.
- Create a classroom atmosphere of acceptance, respect, connectedness, collaboration, and positive learning.

The Classroom Environment and How Students Learn

What role does the classroom environment play in student learning? Gleaning from various learning theories, such as, Cambourne (1988, 1994, 1995), Resnick & Nelson-LeGall (1999), and Gee (1996, 2001), a classroom environment that uses a disciplinary literacy learning framework has the following characteristics: a) is rich in language and disciplinary discourse; b) is rich in disciplinary habits of mind and ways of inquiring and learning; c) is student-centered, collaborative, and barrier free; and, d) is a place where students embrace what Resnick & Hall (1998) refer to as a scholarship of effort and teachers embrace learning as apprenticeship. In that classroom environment learning is expected, encouraged, supported, and promoted.

There are various theories about how students learn. In this chapter, I present two different theories about student learning—Cambourne's (1995) conditions of learning and Resnick's (1999) principles of learning. Both theories propose that in-school learning should be similar to out-of-school learning. First, Australian linguist Brian Cambourne (1995) became interested in language acquisition. His theory focuses on seven non-hierarchical and interactive conditions of learning that address acquisition of knowledge. According to Cambourne (1995), there are seven conditions of learning: immersion, demonstration, engagement, expectation, use, approximation, and response.

- *Immersion.* To learn, students must become immersed in the subject to be learned. Teachers need to present the material many times, in a variety of ways, and create conditions that are pertinent to the object of study.
- *Demonstration.* Demonstrations are essential parts of classroom learning; teachers and students demonstrate their knowledge to one another.
- *Expectations.* Teachers establish clear expectations about the material and how it is to be learned. Students know what they are expected to learn and accomplish.
- *Responsibility.* Students are responsible for their own learning and also for the learning of others—teachers create opportunities for them to research, report, and collaboratively learn with, and from, others. Students are encouraged to go after their own interests and goals, share their learning with the class, and monitor their learning.
- *Practice.* Students have opportunities to practice learning inside and outside the class and learn from knowledgeable others.
- *Response.* Students need timely and informative feedback from teachers to master new skills and strategies. Teacher feedback should also inform students about the criteria used for assessing their learning and performance.
- *Application.* Teachers should provide students with opportunities to apply their knowledge and learning to authentic situations and encourage students to think metacognitively about their work.
- *Engagement.* Engagement occurs naturally when students are interested in the subject, when students believe that they are capable of learning, when they find purpose and relevance in the task, and when they learn in an environment of trust.

These conditions of learning can happen during the same lesson and promote barrier-free learning regardless of the subject matter or student skills. Cambourne suggested that engagement is multi-layered and involves holding a purpose, seeking understanding, self-efficacy, and taking responsibility for learning. Engaged learners take what they are learning and make it meaningful and relevant to their lives. To create forceful learning, teachers must appeal to their students on a personal and emotional level. Students must see learning as their own (Lent, 2006). For learning to take place, students will have to get immersed in discipline-specific learning and in the habits of mind and dispositions that make learning effective.

To create a discipline-specific learning environment, a classroom also needs to be a place where learning is encouraged and supported. Lauren Resnick (1999; Resnick & Hall, 1998), a cognitive psychologist, focused on how students learn, and viewed intelligence as a result of effort instead of aptitude. Her theory focused on effort-based learning and principles of learning that socialize intelligence. These principles are:

- *Institute Effort-Based Learning.* Both teachers and students believe that getting smarter is more a matter of hard work than aptitude. Teachers need to teach students both what and how to learn.
- *Set Clear Expectations for Learning.* Teachers need to make expectations about learning, student behavior, performance, preparation, and responsibility clear to all students, parents, and the community.
- *Recognize Achievement.* Schools should recognize student achievements and successes in a variety of ways. Students thrive in environments that celebrate student progress, learning, and success.
- *Institute Fair and Credible Evaluations.* All assessments should be aligned with expectations. Students should know the assessment standards in advance and their progress should be assessed on the basis of how closely they meet the standards.
- *Join Knowledge and Thinking with Learning.* Knowledge and critical thinking should not be separated; students need to value both.
- *Require Discipline-Based Talk with Learning.* Students need to learn to use the language of each discipline in accurate and meaningful ways. Each discipline is a language itself. This means that they need to learn and use the vocabulary of each discipline and the habits of mind that will help them to problem-solve disciplinary subject matter. In English language arts, students need to use the language of interpretation; in mathematics, the language of accuracy and precision; in science, the language of research and inquiry, and in social studies, the language of argumentation.
- *Promote and Model Discipline-Based Thinking and Learning.* Students need to learn that each discipline has its own structure, demands, expectations, and ways of acquiring knowledge and research. They also need to learn how to respond to one another's thinking through discipline-specific accountable talk.
- *View Learning as an Apprenticeship.* When students learn as apprentices, they have ample opportunities to observe how their mentors problem solve, think, and learn. Mentors scaffold their learning, provide quality feedback, create opportunities for them to apply their knowledge, support them toward mastery, and hold them accountable for their learning.

Gee (1996) stated that whereas a primary discourse, or someone's first social identity, is acquired almost unconsciously through an apprenticeship in "families within their socio-cultural settings" (p. 137), secondary discourses can be difficult to learn depending on how far the secondary discourse is removed from, or is in conflict with, the primary discourse. Shirley Brice Heath (1990) demonstrated that some discourse communities better prepare children to succeed in a school environment. Villanueva (1993) found that middle-class students have a better understanding of school discourse than working-class students. Some students are conflicted when the school discourse contradicts their social identity.

Content area teachers should teach students that school is just a secondary discourse among the many they will learn throughout their lifetime and especially help ELLs to embrace multiple discourse communities. In each content area classroom, students should learn the discourse, ways of thinking and learning, specialized vocabulary, and other ways each discipline and its community identify itself or themselves. For students to acquire a secondary discourse, certain conditions have to be in place.

Another way to promote disciplinary literacy learning in each content area classroom is by utilizing the classroom wall space to display student work and use it as reference material. Such text can include student notes, solutions to problems, outlines, timelines, illustrations of words, characters, or scientific relationships, pictures, norms, or student-generated graphic organizers. Student-generated text is different from teacher or commercially produced bulletin boards, charts, agendas, learning goals, or rules and announcements. Student-generated text can be used in the classroom as a learning aid. Students can use technology and their own creativity to show their understanding of processes or tasks. The following figures provide some examples of wall text from various content area classrooms. Figure 8.7 is an example of a group semantic web on the concepts sound speed, pitch, and loudness. Figure 8.8 is an example of a group-generated flow map on physical science concepts (both examples of wall text are from Ms. Swalina's Environmental Science classes, in Lake Mary High School, Lake Mary, Florida).

In my view, CISCO Systems' motto about technological collaboration reflects the importance of collaboration for learning, working, and living and it supports the view point presented in this chapter about socializing intelligence, building collaborative inquiry, and creating collaborative discipline-specific learning environments in grades 6–12. This American multinational corporation, which specializes in manufacturing network equipment and network management software, has developed a collaboration architecture that enables other companies to have borderless

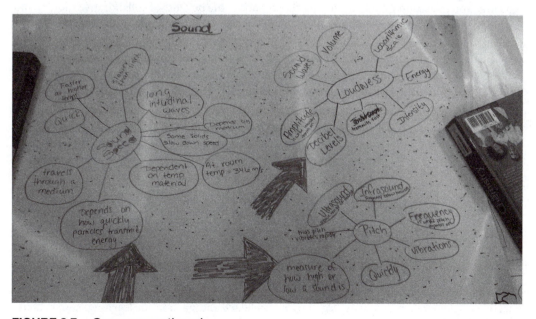

FIGURE 8.7. Group semantic web.

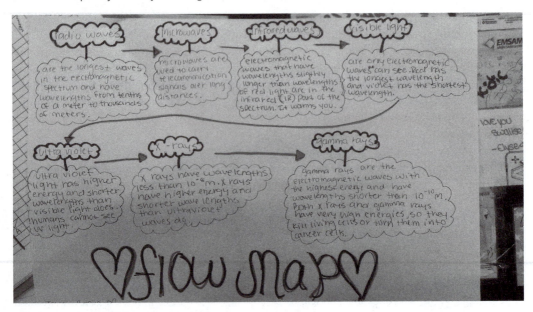

FIGURE 8.8.   Group-generated flow map.

collaboration and many other application advantages. Their motto is, "Collaborate better: meet today's business challenges and build your competitive advantage. Collaboration makes the expertise of one the expertise of all."

Let's revisit our pedagogical beliefs about how adolescents learn best, and let's choose to embrace collaborative learning in our classrooms. Let's use it at the right time, for the right length of time, and for the right reasons to support, extend, and expand students' knowledge and learning. You have ample evidence in this chapter about the benefits of collaborative inquiry and learning, and how best to implement it in the classroom—I hope that you give collaboration a chance!

Jeff Charbonneau, the 2013 US Teacher of the Year, teaches chemistry, physics, and engineering at Zillah High School in Zillah, Washington. His peers described him as a teacher who both challenges and engages his students. President Obama described him as a teacher who

> creates accessible, interactive lessons that help convince kids that the science classes most students consider hardest are worth diving in to, not running away from. . . . When Charbonneau began his teaching career at Zillah High School 12 years ago, the school had no science curriculum, and no engineering curriculum. Students had to go off-campus for technology classes, and computer resources were lacking. But Jeff was determined to turn that around. He wanted to convince kids that something like quantum mechanics wasn't something to run away from. It was something to get excited about. . . . He is also the founder and director of ZHS Robot Challenge, a robotics competition that has involved hundreds of students across the state of Washington. . . . Basically there is nothing that Jeff won't try to give students the best education in every respect.

Effective teachers relate, motivate, teach with excellence and passion for learning, support, and also celebrate their students' accomplishments, however small or big.

To increase student motivation and meaningful, sustained, engagement in your classroom, establish meaningful learning goals around the essential ideas of your discipline and the specific tools and habits of mind students will need to access and develop those ideas. Provide a learning environment that promotes student autonomy and self-regulation. Make learning relevant to students' interests and goals, and make connections with everyday life or important current events. Help students set their goals and monitor their own progress. Create a classroom environment where all students learn and use disciplinary discourse. Use collaborative learning to engage students in the process and prepare them for learning, work, and life post-graduation. Last, assess what matters (Kamil et al., 2008).

Digital Literacies

- Zoom: http://zoom.us/, or Google Hangout http://www.google.com/+/learnmore/hangouts/. Use for cloud-based collaborative meetings and learning.
- Videolicious: https://videolicious.com. Make video, share, and communicate, or create a class newsletter and host a class website: http://www.weebly.com.
- Glogster: http://www.edu.glogster.com. Students can create class posters on topics, books, people, and events with text, photos, video, and sound files.

Celebrating Student Success

When teachers offer verbal, specific praise to students for effort instead of intelligence, students are more likely to be in a mindset of growth (Dweck, 2006). According to Dweck (2006), it is more effective to praise children for work and persistence. People nearly always perform better if they focus on things they can control, such as their effort, rather than things they cannot. For example, provide students with specific feedback on their efforts, persistence, and curiosity: "Andrea, you've been working hard on collecting evidence to support your arguments, and your class contributions and last paper show it." Recognize students for creative expression, scientific thinking, effective collaboration, and persuasion.

In upper grades, ownership of work increases when student work is open to public review; preferably when someone other than the classroom teacher such as a disciplinary expert evaluates it. Honor rolls and recognition for students who have the biggest increase in their grade point average have been used in high schools as an effective way of recognizing academic achievement (Westerberg, 2009). Other teachers utilize technology to share, promote, and publicize, and recognize student achievement and success (e.g., e-portfolios, blogs, Twitter, etc.).

In secondary grades, celebrate students who are working consistently and effectively toward a goal and are showing improvement. Recognize students for their progressive knowledge gain and skill relative to the learning goal. Acknowledge them when they have achieved a certain score on a scale or rubric of learning progress. Use a variety of ways (certificate, parent notification, applause, etc.) to recognize and celebrate the final status and progress of the entire class. Make your classroom environment a positive, rigorous, scholarly, and supportive community of learning. Make your class a place where students are expected, and are supported to succeed, where everyone values learning, where accommodations and modifications are provided to help all learn, and where adolescents' needs for group membership, peer acceptance, admiration, respect, and growth are met.

Summary

- College, career, and workforce readiness goes beyond content knowledge, critical thinking skills, and dispositions. It also includes having, and using, communication skills to exchange ideas, problem-solve, and create/co-create knowledge. Learning in school, beyond school, and in life, also requires collaborating with others, learning how to consider others' perspectives, and working with others in various learning environments.

- Academic discourse requires knowledge of subject matter, use of disciplinary vocabulary, effective ways to express one's understanding, and communication skills. The CCSS place a strong emphasis on providing instruction that actively involves the learner in speaking, listening, using academic discourse, and participating in collaborative inquiry.

- Create learning environments that have rigor, relevance, apprenticeship, accountable talk, and collaborative inquiry. Accountable talk supports disciplinary learning and promotes co-construction of meaning by all in the classroom. Accountable talk involves three important learning aspects: (1) accountability to the learning community; (2) accountability to accurate knowledge; and (3) accountability to rigorous thinking.

Differentiating Instruction

- Create safe, supportive, inviting, accepting, and culturally and linguistically responsive classroom environments for all students. Assess and monitor students' progress and use classroom observation, one-on-one conferencing, and peer tutoring for extra feedback and support.

- Provide ELLs and students with exceptionalities with opportunities to socialize with peers, practice academic vocabulary, and learn from other's perspectives, reasoning, and explanations. Include a wide range of motivating and culturally relevant materials, and use technology to provide additional communicative support.

- Students with varied exceptionalities need learning environments that engage them in learning, but do not over-stimulate them, or distract them. Create a motivating learning environment by having posters of disciplinary experts with learning exceptionalities.

- Collaborative learning opportunities are natural contexts for meaning-making and authentic communication. Build students' academic language skills, encourage students to use academic discourse, and provide them with instruction. Give students feedback and support on how to effectively communicate, collaborate, and negotiate meaning with others.

Reflect and Apply

1. Describe the ideal disciplinary learning environment. What does it look like? How are desks, materials, and equipment arranged? What learning conditions, expectations, norms, and ways of knowing and learning would one see and experience in that space? Support your choices with evidence from this chapter, and share with a peer or colleague.

2. What does accountable talk mean to you and how will you implement it in your classroom? Select key accountable talk moves that are specific to your discipline, and explain to a peer or colleague how you will model, encourage, support, and develop students' disciplinary knowledge and thinking through accountable talk.

3. Using your knowledge of this topic, offer some suggestions to Ms. Rodriguez Negroni (see Classroom Life vignette), and discuss your ideas with your peers in a small group.

Extending Learning

1. Observe a content area classroom, and collect information on the classroom learning environment, on the presence or absence of academic discourse and accountable talk, and on the role collaboration plays in student learning. Compare and contrast your observations with insights from this chapter, and present them to your class or subject area colleagues. Offer key suggestions to the teacher for ways to improve, or extend all of the above in that classroom.
2. Create a presentation you can give at a department meeting (choose the subject area) about the relationship between developing a deep understanding of subject matter, and collaborative learning. Include two to three specific examples to help teachers reflect on their instruction and on student learning, and think of ways to promote collaborative inquiry in their classroom.
3. Develop a lesson plan on a topic of your choice. Study the material, design your learning goals, and work with a partner (preferably from your community of practice) to identify ways to promote accountable talk and collaborative inquiry. Present your lesson plan to the class or a subject area colleague, consider others' suggestions and ideas, negotiate on meaning, and make related adjustments to your lesson plan as a result of collaborative inquiry.

References

Applebee, A. N., Langer, J. A., Nystrand, M., & Gamoran, A. (2003). Discussion-based approaches to developing understanding: Classroom instruction and student performance in middle and high school English. *American Educational Research Journal, 40*, 685–730.

Bruner, J. (1999, April). *Keynote address.* In *Global perspectives on early childhood education* (pp. 9–18). A workshop sponsored by the Committee on Early Childhood Pedagogy, National Academy of Sciences, and the National Research Council, Washington, DC. PS 027 463.

Bruner, J., & Haste, H. (Eds) (1987). *Making sense: The child's construction of the world.* London, UK: Methuen.

Cambourne, B. (1988). *The whole story: Natural learning and the acquisition of literacy.* Auckland, AU: Ashton Scholastic.

Cambourne, B. (1994). The rhetoric of "the rhetoric of whole language." *Reading Research Quarterly, 29*(4), 330–332.

Cambourne, B. (1995). Towards an educationally relevant theory of literacy learning: Twenty years of inquiry. *The Reading Teacher, 49*(3), 182–192.

Cazden, C. B. (1976). Play with language and meta-linguistic awareness: One dimension of language experience. In J.S. Bruner, A. Jolly, & K. Sylva (Eds), *Play: Its role in development and evolution* (pp. 603–608). New York, NY: Basic.

Cazden, C. B. (1986). Classroom discourse. In M. Wittrock (Ed.), *Handbook of research on teaching* (3rd ed.) (pp. 9–21). New York, NY: Macmillan Publishing Co.

Cazden, C. B. (1988). *Classroom discourse: The language of teaching and learning.* Portsmouth, NH: Heinemann.

Cazden, C. B. (2001). *Classroom discourse: The language of teaching and learning* (2nd ed.). Portsmouth, NH: Heinemann.

Chamot, A. U., & O'Malley, J. M. (1994). *The CALLA handbook: Implementing the cognitive academic language learning approach.* Reading, MA: Addison-Wesley.

Chapin, S., O'Connor, C., & Anderson, N. (2003). *Classroom discussions: Using math talk to help students learn: Grades 1–6.* Sausalito, CA: Math Solutions Publications.

Chapin, S., O'Connor, C., & Anderson, N. (2009) (2nd ed.). *Classroom discussions: Using math talk to help students learn: Grades K–6.* Sausalito, CA: Math Solutions Publications.

Copeland, M. (2005). *Socratic circles: Fostering critical and creative thinking in middle and high school.* Portland, ME: Stenhouse Publishers.

Crawford, G. B. (2008). *Differentiation for the adolescent learner: Accommodating brain development, language, literacy, and special needs.* Thousand Oaks, CA: Corwin Press.

Delpit, L. D. (1995). *Other people's children: Cultural conflict in the classroom.* New York: New Press.

Durkin, D. (1978/79). What classroom observations reveal about reading comprehension instruction. *Reading Research Quarterly, 14,* 481–533.

Dweck, C. S. (1999). *Self-theories: Their role in motivation, personality and development.* Philadelphia: Psychology Press.

Eccles, J. S., & Wigfield, A. (1995). In the mind of the achiever: The structure of adolescents' academic achievement related-beliefs and self-perceptions. *Personality and Social Psychology Bulletin, 21,* 215–225.

Fielding, M. (2007). Beyond "voice": New roles, relations, and contexts in researching with young people. *Discourse, 28*(3), 301–310.

Flynt, E., & Brozo, W. G. (2008, March). Developing academic language: Got words? *The Reading Teacher, 61*(6), 500–502.

Gee, J. P. (1996). *Social linguistics and literacies: Ideology in discourses* (2nd ed.). London, UK: Taylor & Francis.

Gee, J. (2001). Identity as an analytic lens for research in education. *Review of Research in Education, 25,* 99–125.

Gregory, G. & Chapman, C. (2007). *Differentiated instructional strategies: One size doesn't fit all.* Thousand Oaks, CA: Corwin Press.

Guan Eng Ho, D. (2005). Why do teachers ask the questions they ask? *RELC,* 36 (3), 297–310.

Heath, S. B. (1990). The children of Trackton's children: Spoken and written language in social change. In J. W. Stigler, R. A. Shweder, & S. H. Gill (Eds), Cultural Psychology: *The Chicago symposia on human development* (pp. 496–519). New York, NY: Cambridge University Press.

Johnson, D. W. & Johnson, R. T. (1990). Cooperative learning and achievement. In S. Sharan (Ed.), *Cooperative learning: Theory and research* (pp. 23–37). New York: Praeger.

Johnson, D. W., & Johnson, R. T. (2009). *An overview of cooperative learning.* Edina, MN: Cooperative Learning Institute.

Johnson, D. W., Johnson, R. T., & Holubec, E. (2008). *Cooperation in the classroom* (8th ed.). Edina, MN: Interaction Book Company.

Kagan, S. (1992). *Cooperative learning.* San Juan Capistrano, CA: Resources for Teachers, Inc.

Kagan, S. (1994). *Cooperative Learning.* San Clemente, CA: Kagan Publishing.

Kamil, M. L., Borman, G. D., Dole, J., Kral, C. C., Salinger, T., and Torgesen, J. (2008). *Improving adolescent literacy: Effective classroom and intervention practices: A Practice Guide* (NCEE #2008–4027). Washington, DC: National Center for Education Evaluation and Regional Assistance, Institute of Education Sciences, US Department of Education.

Lent, R. (2006). *Engaging adolescent learners: A guide for content area teachers.* Portsmouth, NH: Heinemann.

Lyman, F. (1981). *The responsive classroom discussion: The inclusion of all students.* Mainstreaming Digest. College Park, MD: University of Maryland.

McCann, T. M., Johannessen, L. R., Kahn, E., & Flanagan, J. M. (2006). *Talking in class: Using discussion to enhance teaching and learning.* Urbana, IL: National Council of Teachers of English.

McConachie, S. M., & Petrosky, A. R. (2010). *Content matters: A disciplinary literacy approach to improving student learning.* San Francisco, CA: Jossey-Bass.

Michaels, S., O'Connor, C., & Resnik, L. (2007). Deliberative discourse idealized and realized: Accountable talk in the classroom and in civic life." *Studies in Philosophy and Education, 27*(4), 283–297.

Michaels, S., O'Connor, C., Hall, M., & Resnick, L. (2002). *Accountable talk: classroom conversation that works.* Pittsburgh, PA: University of Pittsburgh.

Mitra, D. L. (2009). Strengthening student voice initiatives in high schools: An examination of the supports needed for school-based youth-adult partnerships. *Youth and Society, 40*(3), 311–335.

Moje, E. B. (2008). Foregrounding the disciplines in secondary literacy teaching and learning: A call for change. *Journal of Adolescent and Adult Literacy, 52*(2), 96–107.

National Council of Teachers of English (NCTE). (2011). *Literacies of disciplines: A policy research brief.* Urbana, IL: NCTE.

National Council of Teachers of Mathematics (NCTM). (1995). *Assessment standards school mathematics.* Reston, VA: Author.

O'Brien, D. G., Moje, E. B., & Stewart, R. A. (2001). Exploring the context of secondary literacy: Literacy in people's everyday school lives. In E. B. Moje & D. G. O'Brien (Eds), *Constructions of literacy: Studies of teaching and learning in and out of secondary classrooms* (pp. 27–48). Mahwah, NJ: Erlbaum.

Palincsar, A. S. (2003). Collaborative approaches to comprehension instruction. In A. P. Sweet & A. E. Snow (Eds), *Rethinking reading comprehension* (pp. 99–114). New York, NY: The Guilford Press.

Palincsar, A. S., & Brown, A. L. (1984). Reciprocal teaching of comprehension-fostering and comprehension-monitoring activities. *Cognition and Instruction, 1*, 117–175.

Pearson, P. D., & Gallagher, M. C. (1983). The instruction of reading comprehension. *Contemporary Educational Psychology, 8*, 317–344.

Resnick, M. D., Bearman, P. S., Blum, R. W., Bauman, K. E., Harris, K. M., Jones, J., et al. (1997). Protecting adolescents from harm: Findings from the national longitudinal study of adolescent health. *Journal of the American Medical Association, 278*(10), 823–32.

Resnick, L. B., & Hall, M. W. (1998). Learning organizations for sustainable education reform. *Daedalus, 127*, 89–118.

Resnick, L. & Nelson-LeGall, S. (1999). Socializing intelligence. In L. Smith, J. Dockrell, & P. Tomlinson (Eds), *Piaget, Vygotsky, and beyond*. London: Routledge.

Sapon-Shevin, M. (2008). Learning in inclusive classrooms. *Educational Leadership, 66*(1), 49–53.

Schlecty, P. (1994). Increasing student engagement. *Missouri Leadership Academy*, 5.

Schlemmer, P., & Schlemmer, D. (2008). *Teaching beyond the test: Differentiated project-based learning in a standards-based age.* Minneapolis, MN: Free Spirit.

Schniedewind, N., & Davidson, E. (2000). Differentiating instruction with cooperative learning: Challenging all students in heterogeneous groups. *Educational Leadership, 58*(1), 24–27.

Slavin, R. E. (1983). When does cooperative learning increase student achievement? *Psychological Bulletin, 93*, 429–445.

Slavin, R. E. (1984). Team assisted individualization: Cooperative learning and individualized instruction in the mainstreamed classroom. *Remedial and Special Education, 5*(6), 33–42.

Strong, R., Silver, H. F., & Robinson, A. (1995). Strengthening student engagement: What do students want (and what really motivates them)? *Educational Leadership, 53*(1), 8–12.

Toshalis, E., & Nakkula, M. J. (2012). The integration of motivation, engagement, and voice in student-centered learning. Invited paper for the *Students at the Center: Teaching and Learning in the Era of the Common Core* project, sponsored by Jobs for the Future and funded by the Nellie Mae Foundation. Retrieved from www.studentsatthecenter.org.

Villanueva, V. (1993). *Bootstraps: From an American academic of color.* Urbana, IL: National Council of Teachers of English.

Vygotsky, L. S. (1962). *Thought and language.* Cambridge, MA: The MIT Press.

Vygotsky, L. S. (1978). *Mind in society: The development of higher psychological processes.* (M. Cole, V. John-Steiner, S. Scribner, & E. Souberman, Eds.). Cambridge, MA: Harvard University Press.

Westerberg, T. (2009). *Becoming a great high school: 6 strategies and 1 attitude that makes a difference.* Alexandria, VA: ASCD.

Zwiers, J. (2008). *Building academic language: Essential practices for content classrooms* (2nd ed.). San Francisco, CA: Jossey-Bass.

Zwiers, J., & Crawford, M. (2011). *Academic conversations: Classroom talk that fosters critical thinking and content understandings.* York, ME: Stenhouse.

Zygouris-Coe, V. (2012a). Disciplinary literacy and the common core state standards. *Topics in Language Disorders, 32*(1), 35–50.

Zygouris-Coe, V. (2012b). What is disciplinary literacy and why aren't we talking more about it? *Vocabulogic, 1–6.* Retrieved from http://vocablog-plc.blogspot.com/2012/03/what-is-disciplinary-literacy-and-why.html

nine

Writing in the Disciplines

Writing is easy. All you have to do is cross
out the wrong words.
–Mark Twain

Chapter Highlights

- College and Career Readiness (CCR) requires good writing skills; writing is a must for learning, working, collaborating, problem solving, and living in the 21st century global economy.
- The Common Core State Standards (CCSS) Anchor Standards for Writing focus on three types of writing (i.e., argument, informative/explanatory, and narrative), and present writing as a learning, thinking, communication, and knowledge-building process that is essential for knowledge development in each discipline.
- Argument is a key feature of academic writing and learning. Students will benefit from intensive, explicit, and effective writing instruction within each content area.
- Writing for a variety of purposes, increasing students' knowledge about writing, writing about the texts students read and the interests they have, and using technology and assessment, will help students become strategic writers.
- Students need to write routinely, they need feedback from the teacher, peers, and others, and they also need opportunities to collaborate with peers in the writing process.
- Collaborative inquiry and writing as an apprenticeship are important elements of college, career, and workforce readiness.
- With guidance and support, students need to learn how to use technology, digital tools, and the Internet to create, share, refine, and publish their writing. They need to learn how to use technology strategically to create, refine, and collaborate in writing. They also need to learn how to use technology accurately to collect, evaluate, and cite sources.

Classroom Life

As a teacher, primarily focusing on writing, there are many struggles faced each and every day. Our school has a high population of non-English speakers, low-income families as well as homeless and highly transient students. These factors cause many struggles in the classroom. In addition, many of my students not only have inconsistent educational histories, lack of academic background knowledge and vocabulary, but behavioral issues as well. Many of the issues pertaining to writing would focus primarily on lack of vocabulary and background knowledge.

When asking students to write an essay to address a prompt, they are often confused about what the prompt is and they have difficulty coming up with good evidence to support their claims. Recently our school administered a monthly essay assessment and the prompt asked students, "How do you feel about your parents supervising you when you use the Internet?" Many students did not write a good essay because they were unsure of what the word "supervised" meant. I think as teachers, we work hard to teach our students new words and help students learn and apply new information, but at times we forget that most of our students do not speak or use academic language outside of the classroom.

Another contributing factor to students' struggles with writing is their lack of background knowledge; this becomes particularly challenging when they have to produce the writing in a limited time frame. Many students have an extremely hard time thinking of supporting evidence to back up any claim they want to make in their writing. This seems to be the hardest for teachers to address since there is no way of knowing what a standardized or summative type assessment prompt might ask them to write about. If a class works for a month on a specific topic, or a piece of literature, and the teacher involves students in routinely writing, most students will produce a substantial amount of support for their writing because they have been exposed to the information which can be used. However, without that background knowledge on a topic, students have a very hard time developing specific levels of support for their claims or conclusions. Writing about the texts they read helps their comprehension of text and their writing. We need to be engaging our students in wide reading and routine writing in each content area classroom. *(Ms. Nicole Colabella Dunham, 7th grade English Language Arts, Kissimmee Middle School, Kissimmee, Florida).*

Writing for Postsecondary and Life Success

Writing is important for college, career, workforce, and civic engagement. Writing permeates every facet of living and learning. Good writing skills are "a marker . . . and a gatekeeper of high-wage, professional jobs" (National Commission on Writing, 2004, p. 7). Writing improves student cognition by leading them to deeper thinking—it is a tool for learning subject matter (Shanahan, 2004); it also prepares students for the postsecondary world.

The knowledge and skills needed for college and for employment are now considered to be identical (American College Testing [ACT], 2005). More professions require good writing skills than those typically associated with writing; any time a profession requires written communication, good writing becomes important. In 2004, the College Board, commissioned a report by The National Commission on Writing for America's Families, Schools, and Colleges titled, *Writing: A Ticket to Work . . . or a Ticket Out: A Survey of Business Leaders.* Survey results of 120 major American corporations employing about eight million people concluded that writing is a "threshold skill" for hiring and promotion among salaried employees (p. 5). Over 40% of responding companies reported that they "frequently" or "almost always" produce technical reports (59%), formal reports (62%), and memos and e-mail documentation and correspondence (70%). In addition, over 40% of the companies provide training for employees with writing deficiencies, amounting to an annual a cost of $3.1 billion (National Commission on Writing, 2004).

In schools, we use writing in a number of ways. For example, if students have been reading a book, an article, or some type of text, we have them write a summary, a reflection, or questions they have in order for us to assess what they thought or learned or what they did not learn. More importantly, writing generates more thinking about the topic at hand *as* students write about it. Writing is " 'a composing process' that requires preparation, planning, and revision" (Howard, 1983, p. 5). Writing is a reflection of one's thinking; actually, writing is more organized, clear, precise, and thoughtful than speaking. Writing is an effective communication, self-expression, and learning tool that enables us (a) to collect, analyze, preserve, and transmit information with detail and accuracy, and (b) generate ideas.

Although there is much evidence on the importance of writing for learning, writing instruction does not take place consistently in content area classes, including English language arts (Applebee & Langer, 2006; Kiuhara, Graham, & Hawken, 2009). Kiuhara, Graham, and Hawken (2009) found that high school students who participated in their national survey reported that they were rarely asked to complete writing assignments that involved analysis and interpretation. In addition, 60% of science teachers reported that they did not feel prepared to teach writing. The National Commission on Writing (2006) report titled, *Writing and School Reform*, was the result of five hearings held across the country on the importance of writing. It addressed the following national writing priorities:

- Make writing central to the school reform agenda.
- Ensure that curricula in schools provide the necessary time for students to use writing to learn and to learn to write
- Advance writing assessment that is fair and authentic.
- Guarantee that students have access to, and opportunities to compose with, current technologies, including digital technologies.
- Provide comprehensive professional development for all teachers to improve classroom practice.

Writing is a promotion tool in college, and in the corporate world—most Fortune 500 companies provide ongoing professional development for their employees to help them write better. On March 7, 2013, the New York Post reported that 79.3% of New York City high school students entering the City University's community college system required remediation in English (reading, writing) and mathematics. Writing is not just about writing a five-paragraph essay or a research paper. It is a thinking and communication tool that should be used for reflection and learning across grade levels, content areas, and contexts.

Today, messages are created, sent, and received in multimodal ways; writing takes place in paper and pen/pencil, and it also takes place in the form of e-mails, blogs, Wikis, Nings, Facebook, Twitter, and on websites. Twenty-first century literacy and learning includes interactions with multimodal, multimedia texts (Kress, 2003; Serafini, 2011). Multimodal texts include written text, visual images, graphic elements, hyperlinks, video clips, audio clips, and other modes of representation that require different reading, comprehension, writing, and communication skills (Kress, 2003). Multimodal communication involves multiple "modes" or communicative forms (i.e., digital, spatial, musical, visual).

Knobel and Lankshear (2008) invited teachers to learn and teach about the digital literacies of the 21st century. Students need to learn a) how to write with different tools; b) what language (e.g., words, video, audio, images) to use to communicate through writing; and c) how to develop knowledge, present it, access it, and share it through digital tools and technologies. Writing in today's digitally connected world involves remixing and hybridization (i.e., "remixing a video game with video-editing tools to create narratives via writing with moving images and sound for do-it-yourself entertainment purposes" (Knobel & Lankshear, 2008, p. 25). Teachers need to teach students how to write well, engage them in writing in order to teach and learn content, and prepare them for college, career and workforce, and citizenship.

College, Career, and Workforce Connections

● College instructors use writing to evaluate students (to some degree) in post-secondary courses. Arguments, expository, and narrative are key types of college writing. Students are expected to write routinely and in relatively short amounts of time; they need to know how to pre-write, edit, and re-write before, and often after, their writing is submitted for feedback. College writing requires students to present arguments clearly, substantiate claims, utilize the basics of a style manual when writing a paper, and produce writing that is largely free of grammatical and usage errors. College writing and learning also includes research and identifying and using appropriate strategies and methodologies to explore and answer problems. Students need to know how to access different types of information, evaluate that information, synthesize it, and incorporate it into a paper, or report.

● Students who are college and career ready know how to demonstrate independence, and know how to respond to the varying demands of the audience, task, purpose, and discipline. They also value evidence when offering written interpretation of text, and use technology and digital media strategically and capably.

● In order for students to succeed in rising global market challenges, they need to be prepared for diverse writing types and formats, written communication and collaboration, and use of technology and online writing tools and communications.

● *In order to learn history at the college level, incoming students need to abandon dogmatic beliefs they cannot defend with evidence, allow themselves to be challenged (though not brainwashed) by new ideas, and possess the skills needed to convey written information clearly and concisely to a variety of audiences* (Daniel Murphree, Associate Professor, History, University of Central Florida).

Transitioning from High School to College Writing

Many educators and others believe that American students cannot write. Others, although they embrace technological advancements, "blame" the availability of so many tech-distractions for students' aversion toward formal writing, and poor writing and verbal skills. And to complicate this matter more, although nowadays students write all the time, according to the Common Core developers and other researchers, they are not writing properly. Many teachers are concerned about students' diminishing grammatical skills and vocabulary, the presence of "text writing" in formal writing, and short forms of expression.

Although with the implementation of the CCSS, students will be responding more frequently to what they read or write, is that enough for their writing development? In this chapter, I propose that to get students ready for the writing demands of college, career, and the workforce, all teachers will need to engage students in rigorous inquiry about how to best express their ideas in writing. Explicit, systematic, and targeted writing instruction improves all students' writing ability. Students need opportunities to express themselves about what they are learning in logical, detailed, complex, and creative ways. To do so, they need to read and write all kinds of literary and the expository texts, and they also need writing assignments that help them to connect with the "real" world.

Making the transition from high school to college writing can be daunting and overwhelming for many students. Students can become intimidated by the types, demands, and length of writing, the freedom to choose topics, and by their lack of confidence in their writing abilities to meet the demands of college writing. In college, writing is used to fulfill many tasks from writing an accurate summary of a text students are reading, to presenting an argument by analyzing readings and supporting one's claims with evidence and good reasoning. High school content area teachers, especially, need to teach students to write like they will in college.

College writing involves explaining the results of an analysis and making the "point" or claim of the paper or report clear to the reader. A good point, or claim usually "says" something important about a) what the student read; b) something that will help the reader to better understand the topic; c) something that is not obvious; d) something the reader did not already know; e) something that is contestable, and no one would agree with by reading it; and f) something that a writer can present in four to five pages.

Argument is a key feature of college writing that includes the following: (a) a claim and (b) evidence that encourages the reader to agree, test, or think about the claim and reflects that the writer has considered possible limits or objections to the claim. Defending one's claims with relevant, valid, current, and credible evidence is a college student's (and a professional's) "duty." College students practice writing in the context of their courses. They are expected to do research, gather data, analyze it, think about it, and communicate it to readers who can assess it and use it. In a way, all college writing that expresses a thesis is an "argument" because the writer is persuading the reader to accept his or her perspective or position (Hjortshoj, 2009).

Writing and Writing Instruction

Characteristics of Proficient Writers

Proficient writers are not born; they are made. Some students have difficulty expressing themselves, while others feel that they were born bad writers and are terrified by the blank page. Writing is not just the task of putting words on paper; a good writer thinks of writing as a process and not just as a product. First the writer has to figure out what to say. There is a difference between writing as an act, and the thinking that underpins it. Some students do not know how to make an argument. Yet, others who manage to write a few hundred words, view their first draft as the final one. Proficient writing requires skill and knowledge about writing, reading, metacognition (thinking about one's own thinking) to support the writing, mentors and others who can offer feedback, and practice drafting, revising, and getting feedback again.

A proficient writer balances thinking about a subject, thinks about purpose, audience, and word choice, looks for multiple meanings, is aware of his or her own biases and influence of others, and is willing to make his or her thoughts available to others for feedback. A proficient writer takes time to think about the "what," and the "how," takes time to think, rethink, and to think about how to organize and present his, or her thoughts about the subject. Proficient writers take time to prewrite, draft, revise, edit, tighten arguments, polish words, and also take time to check spelling, mechanics, style, clarity, and organization. Last, they also develop their ideas as they write, use concise language, keep the audience in mind, and use grammar to help the reader understand their ideas.

Writing as a Process

The process approach to writing has been associated with high writing proficiency scores on the National Assessment of Educational Progress (NAEP) assessment in writing (Goldstein & Carr, 1996), higher scores in timed testing situations (Worden 2009), time spent on writing and improved writing achievement (Pritchard & Honeycutt, 2006). The writing process is linear in the sense that sentence A must follow sentence B. It is also recursive (writing/revising) in the sense of the five stages in the process that become the focus of writing instruction. The following stages can take place on paper or on the computer, independently, or collaboratively.

1. *Pre-writing or planning.* This stage involves deciding on a topic, generating ideas, gathering information, organizing one's thoughts and notes, making lists, creating graphic organizers, deciding on the audience and the purpose for writing, and thinking about how to write about what is to be said on the topic.
2. *Drafting.* Another way to describe this stage is: "Write without stopping or worrying about grammar, form, spelling, etc." The purpose is to get as many words, phrases, and thoughts on paper (or on the computer screen) as possible. The first draft is not the last one; a piece of writing will go through several drafts before it is "finalized."
3. *Revising.* James Ellison (2000), author of *Finding Forrester: A Novel*, said, "You write your first draft with your heart, and you rewrite with your head." Revising allows the student to look at his or her writing again, through the eyes of the reader. Peers or the teacher can offer feedback about clarity, meaning, organization, ask clarification questions, or suggest deleting or adding more information that would help the writer with meaning or content.
4. *Editing.* This stage focuses on form, spelling, punctuation, mechanics, usage, and grammatical errors.
5. *Postwriting/Presenting/Publishing.* During this stage students make their writing public either by submitting a completed piece of writing to the teacher, uploading it on a class Wiki, or a school newspaper, or sharing with parents, community members (e.g., local businesses and agencies), or other experts (e.g., professional organizations).

Writing is not an isolated act; we write to an audience for a particular purpose. Writing is a social act; it is a means of documenting, communicating, generating, and refining our ideas about people and the world around us. Chunking of especially long-term writing assignments, modeling, guidance, and scaffolded support with all stages of the writing process, especially pre-writing and revising, are necessary for student learning. Feedback from the teacher and peers is vital to student writing and learning. Teachers should focus on the content of students' writing (i.e., ideas, organization of ideas, word choice and sentence fluency) first and view form (i.e., conventions and presentation) as an important but secondary focus.

The following informal writing activities can be used across the content areas. They facilitate reflective thinking, and involve the writer to monitor his, or her thinking and learning about a topic (Cunningham & Allington, 2011; McLaughlin, 2010; Tompkins, 2010).

- Journals (double entry, dialogue, or personal journals, etc.).
- Learning logs, laboratory notes, informal response activities (e.g., "Write any questions you have about the reading, video, lecture, or discussion.").
- Collaborative note-taking (e.g., "Write down three main points, or a summary, from this text and discuss them with you partner(s).").

- Quick writes (e.g., "Write what you know about the topic for 2 minutes.").
- Admit/exit slips (e.g., "Write down on a post-it note, scrap paper, or index card something you learned or a question you have from today's lesson and hand in before you leave.").

When students write about what they are learning, they make connections, summarize, question their understanding, problem solve, look for evidence, and analyze and become more reflective about what they are learning.

Teachers need to understand that students will come to class with a wide range of writing abilities, experiences, styles, strategies, and interests. Depending on these factors, each student will have a preference when writing. Informal and formal writing should exist in each content area classroom. Good writing is not produced in "one sitting" or in one draft; writing well is hard work. Students need to be taught how to take a writing project through the stages of planning, drafting, revising, and editing.

Research on Writing Instruction

Writing improves cognition in a number of ways. Different kinds of writing produce different kinds of thinking. For example, analytical writing sharpens students' reasoning skills; summarizing helps students to focus on the big picture of the text; short answer questions requires them to focus on particular information. Writing is closely connected to reading. Reading and writing are language (Tierney & Shanahan, 1991), cognitive (Shanahan, 2006; Tierney & Pearson, 1983), and sociocultural processes (Gee, 1996; Vygotsky, 1978).

Judith Langer's research reports titled, *Beating the Odds: Teaching Middle and High School Students to Read and Write Well* (2000a) and *Guidelines for Teaching Middle and High School Students to Read and Write Well: Six Features of Effective Instruction* (2000b) were an outcome of long-term research conducted in English programs in 44 classrooms, in 25 (high and low performing) schools, in 4 states. All high performing schools actively and meaningfully engaged students and teachers in academically rich classrooms. Students in those schools were learning a lot about language and how it works, they were learning grammar, spelling, organizational structure, and vocabulary, and were involved in much reading, writing, and oral language. Schools that "beat the odds" had the following characteristics:

1. Systematic use of separated, simulated, and integrated skills instruction.
2. Test preparation integrated into ongoing goals, curriculum, and regular lessons.
3. Explicit connections made among knowledge, skills, and ideas across lessons, classes, and grades, and across in-school and out-of-school applications.
4. Explicit teaching of strategies for planning, organizing, completing, and reflecting on content and activities.
5. When a learning goal was met, teachers moved students beyond the goal to deeper understanding and generation of ideas.
6. Students worked collaboratively with others to develop depth and complexity of understanding.

The *Reading Next* (2006) and *Writing Next* (2007) reports have documented the importance of the interdependent nature of the reading-writing connection—good readers are often good writers, and vice versa; students who write well often read more than those who do not write well; wide reading improves writing; students who perceive themselves as good readers and writers tend to engage in independent reading and writing.

In *Reading Next*, a report by the Carnegie Corporation of New York (Biancarosa & Snow, 2006), the authors presented a call for action for improving middle and high school literacy and achievement. Their report included 15 elements (nine instructional and six infrastructural elements) of effective adolescent literacy programs. Number seven was, "Intensive writing, including instruction connected to the kinds of writing tasks students will have to perform well in high school and beyond" (p. 12). According to the report, students who have opportunities to write along with reading reflect more critical thinking about reading. In addition, knowledge of grammar and spelling strengthens students' reading skills. Instruction in sentence combining, summarization, and writing strategies improves students' writing. Students benefit from intensive writing instruction that has clear objectives and expectations, and challenges all students to engage with academic content at high levels of reasoning.

In 2007, the Carnegie Corporation of New York published a report titled, *Writing Next*, that focused on how to improve the writing performance of adolescents (i.e., students in Grades 4 through 12) and writing instruction in those grades (Graham & Perin, 2007a). *Writing Next* highlighted that writing as a literacy component has been neglected and our adolescents are underprepared to face the demands of 21st century writing. According to Graham & Perin (2007a),

- 70% of students in Grades 4–12 are low-achieving writers.
- 50% of high school graduates are not prepared for college-level writing.
- 35% of high school graduates in college and 38% of high school graduates in the workforce believe that their writing does not meet expectations of quality.
- 50% of private employers and 60% of state government employers state that writing skills impact promotion decisions.
- Poorly written applications are likely to doom candidates' chances for employment.

In that report, Graham and Perin (2007a) conducted a meta-analysis, a method that provides a quantitative measure of effectiveness using statistical analysis to determine the strength and consistency of the effects of different instructional practices, on the quality of student writing. Results of their analysis of 142 separate, but related, scientific studies, identified 11 instructional strategies that had a significant impact on student writing performance; they sorted the research by effect size (ES) to judge the performance difference between the experimental and control group. An effect size is a measure of the estimated strength of a phenomenon without making any statement about whether the relationship in the data reflects a true relationship in the population. Effect size measures are important in meta-analysis studies that summarize findings from a particular area of research, and in statistical power analyses. The stronger the effect size, the greater was the impact of the intervention on the writing performance of adolescents. Graham & Perin (2007a) suggest that the following 11 instructional practices should be used together for an "optimal mix" in order for them to have the greatest effect (p. 11).

- *Writing strategies* involve explicitly teaching adolescents strategies for planning, revising, and editing (ES=0.82).
- *Summarization* involves explicit and systematic instruction in the summarization process and providing models of well-written summaries for students to emulate (ES=0.82).
- *Collaborative writing* involves adolescents working together to plan, draft, revise, and edit their work (ES=0.75).
- *Specific product goals* involve assigning students specific, reachable goals for the writing they are to complete (e.g., identifying a purpose for the essay, offering examples to support one's point of view, or writing a persuasive essay) (ES=0.70).
- *Word processing* involves the use of word processing software to complete writing assignments—they are particularly helpful to low-achieving students (ES=0.55).

- *Sentence combining* involves teaching students to construct more complex, sophisticated sentences (ES=0.50).
- *Prewriting* engages students in brainstorming, gathering information, constructing outlines, and organizing thoughts and information (ES=0.32).
- *Inquiry activities* involve students in collecting, and analyzing data to help them develop content for their writing (ES=0.32).
- *Process writing* approach is a multi-faceted approach that provides students with (a) extended time for writing; (b) stresses the importance of keeping the audience in mind; (c) fosters discussion and interaction among students about the writing task; (d) creates an environment that supports writing; (e) provides individualized instruction based on student needs; and (f) encourages students' ownership of their written work (ES=0.32).
- *Study of models* provides students with opportunities to read, analyze, and emulate models of good writing (ES=0.25).
- *Writing for content learning* is used as a tool for advancing students' learning in an academic content area (ES=0.23).

Graham and Perin (2007a) offer seven recommendations for teaching writing:

1. *Dedicate time to writing and involve students in writing over time.* Students need to spend time daily in class planning, revising, authoring, or publishing text for on-demand writing, short-term, or long-term projects. Students need to learn to write for a variety of purposes (Graham & Perin, 2007b). For example, they write to learn content material (e.g., summarize, use learning logs, or journals), communicate with others (e.g., personal/business letters, notes, cards, e-mail), inform (e.g., writing reports; explain how to do something; describe a person, object, place, or event), and persuade others (e.g., expressing an opinion about a controversial topic). They also write to respond to literature (e.g., book evaluations, analyzing authors' intentions), entertain others (e.g., writing stories, plays, or poem), reflect about one's self (e.g., autobiography, writing about personal events), and demonstrate knowledge (e.g., classroom/state/other tests that involve writing).

2. *Increase students' knowledge about writing.* Students need to read widely and regularly a variety of texts from different genres and disciplines. Teachers need to provide students with a vehicle for learning the different forms and purposes of writing (Graham & Perin, 2007a). For example, after reading a story, a speech, or an article, direct the students' attention to text structure, organization, the ways the author selected and used language to communicate his or her perspective on the topic, and follow-up with a discussion on what the author was trying to achieve and how they could use the same procedures to their own writing. Introduce students to different models of writing. For example, when introducing students to argument, read various types of argumentative writing, identify the common features across texts, and ask students to apply those features to write their own argument.

3. *Foster students' interest, enjoyment, and motivation to write.* Make sure that writing assignments are worthwhile and serve a realistic and meaningful purpose—find ways to connect writing to their lives, aspirations, and goals and ensure that assignments are appropriate for students' aptitudes and interests. Use peer collaboration for brainstorming, drafting, revising, editing, and publishing. Set high and realistic writing expectations for all students and celebrate their achievements.

4. *Help students become strategic writers.* Treat writing as a process, model it, teach it, and engage students in the same processes skilled writers engage in (i.e., draft, revise, edit, share). Make writing assignments clear for students; they need to know exactly what is expected of them within a given assignment, purpose, and time frame. Model your writing

process. Do the writing assignment yourself before assigning it to the students—estimate how reasonable the assignment is and anticipate, and provide for, common student challenges with it. Use graphic organizers and writing strategies to help students develop their writing. Provide purpose for the strategy (e.g., summarization), model it, provide sufficient guided practice and feedback, monitor independent use of the strategy, and encourage students to reflect on the impact of the strategy on their writing.

5. *Teach basic skills* (e.g., handwriting, typing, spelling, punctuation, capitalization) to mastery. Provide guided practice with sentence combining and all of the above.

6. *Take advantage of technological writing tools.* Use technological tools to meet the needs of all writers.

7. *Use assessment to gauge students' progress and needs.* Use rubrics to evaluate different types of writing. Use clear criteria for evaluating their assignment and validate your criteria by sharing a sample. Read for what the student actually wrote, not what he or she meant to say. Focus on development and organization of thoughts, word choice (diction), clarity, and coherence. Grammar, misspellings, and form should play a secondary role. Share your criteria and evaluations with students. With students' permission, remove their names from the papers and let students evaluate each other's papers using the rubric/criteria. Follow-up with a class discussion on the peer evaluation process and any themes related to areas all students might need to pay attention to in their next writing assignment. Class discussions should focus on the following: Are ideas in the text clearly developed and presented? Is the text clear and coherent? Is the text's organization and style appropriate to the task, purpose, and audience? Are words used precisely and clearly? Did students write in complete sentences, using their own words? Are there any spelling, grammar, and usage errors?

Grade students' assignments using rubrics and set criteria and make instructional adjustments for struggling writers. For example, provide extra instruction in planning, revising, text organization, sentence construction, handwriting, or spelling, re-teach skills and strategies as needed, allow extra time to complete assignments, provide more feedback, and monitor struggling writers' progress, and encourage students to self-monitor their writing progress.

In a more recent report by the Carnegie Corporation of New York titled, *Writing to Read: Evidence for How Writing Can Improve Reading*, Graham and Hebert (2010) identified the following group of closely related effective writing instructional practices that improve students' reading across the content areas.

● Have students write about the texts they read.
  ○ Respond to a text in writing (writing personal reactions, analyzing and interpreting text).
  ○ Teach students how to summarize texts.
  ○ Write notes about a text (e.g., structured note-taking, concept mapping).
  ○ Answer questions about a text in writing, or create and answer written questions about a text.
● Teach students the writing skills and processes that go into creating text.
  ○ Teach the process of writing, text structure for writing, and paragraph or sentence construction skills (improves comprehension).
  ○ Teach spelling and sentence construction skills (improves reading fluency).
  ○ Teach students strategies for planning, revising, editing, and publishing their writing.

    ○ Engage students in pre-writing activities to help them generate and organize ideas about writing.

    ○ Teach spelling skills (improves word reading skills).

- Take a process approach to writing across the content areas.
- Study models of good writing from different disciplines.
- Increase how much content students write (e.g., daily writing about self-selected and other topics).
- Involve students in collaborative writing activities.
- Use technology and digital writing tools in the writing process.

Results from all of the aforementioned reports indicate that all teachers should use writing to promote students' learning. Writing instruction that strengthened students' reading and writing skills included both process writing and skills instruction. In order for students to learn how to write well, they need to (a) write about the texts they read; (b) receive explicit instruction in spelling, in writing sentences and paragraphs, in text structure, and in the basic forms of composition; (c) write routinely across the curriculum; (d) receive feedback from teacher and peers and have opportunities to revise their writing in-school; and (e) write more at home. Writing won't just happen. It needs to be taught explicitly, effectively, and consistently. We should be teaching students writing for reasons that go beyond the walls of the school. When students graduate from high school, they will move into the college, career, and workforce worlds that require the ability to write.

Writing can be a really useful learning tool for each of the disciplines and students need to be involved in writing that is representative of each discipline's goals and structure. For example, in English language arts students need to write about conflict, the author's view, and they also need to write with English themes. In history, students need to write historical essays that synthesize information from diverse and even conflicting viewpoints. In mathematics, students need to write how they made sense of problems and the steps they took to solve them. In science, students need to write up replicable experiments, summarize their steps, observations, data, and limitations of the experiment(s).

The Role of the Teacher in the Writing Process

Kelly Gallagher (2011) reminds us of the following about the role of the teacher in the writing process:

> [O]f all the strategies I have learned over the years, there is one that stands far above the rest when it comes to improving my students' writing: the teacher should model by writing—and think out loud while writing—in front of the class.
>
> (p. 15)

Donald Graves (1983) advised all teachers to "ask questions that teach." He proposed the "process-conference" approach to teaching writing. He encouraged all teachers to write with their students, to demonstrate what they did when they wrote, and to also show students how to use their time. According to Graves (1983),

- Voice drives writing.
- A student must own his/her writing.
- Writing is a process and revision is a major sub-process.
- Variation in writing quality from week to week is normal.
- Learning to write is a developmental process.

Teachers need to teach students not only how to read books, but also how to read their own writing; to not only check their spelling, but to also teach them to examine their own writing with insight, looking for strengths and weaknesses, noticing what is working or not working and why, and identifying what needs revision (Graves, 2003). Let us use language that is important to writing development and improvement, and let's not focus only on grades. The teacher's instruction, modeling, guided support, questions, and feedback, are key in directing students' writing.

CCSS Connections

- Students in grades 6–12 need to write routinely over extended periods of time for a range of tasks, purposes, and audiences. Students need to learn how to write (a) arguments to support claims using valid and sufficient evidence; (b) informative/explanatory texts to examine and convey complex ideas and information clearly and accurately; and (c) narrative texts using well-chosen details and well-structured event sequences.
- Students in grades 6–12 need to produce clear and coherent writing, engage in all phases of the writing process, and use technology, including the Internet, to produce and publish writing, interact, and collaborate with others.
- Students in grades 6–12 need to conduct short and sustained research projects, gather and evaluate information from print and digital sources, and use information to support analysis, reflection, and research.

Writing and the Common Core State Standards (CCSS)

The CCSS demand that all students have access to high-quality instruction that will prepare them to meet college and career ready expectations. In writing, students must be able to demonstrate proficiency at their grade level in the Grade 6–12 Standards for Literacy in history/social studies, science, and technical subjects. The message about "shared responsibility in developing college and career ready students" also applies to writing—all content area teachers will be held responsible for increasing students' writing proficiency.

The CCSS reposition writing at the core of K–12 education. The CCSS for writing include standards for text types and purposes (e.g., arguments, informative/explanatory and narrative texts), production and distribution of writing, research to build and present knowledge, and range of writing. The standards place much emphasis on an important element of college and career readiness: the ability of a student to write sound arguments on key disciplinary topics and issues. The CCSS also place writing across all disciplines, and call for writing for real purposes. According to Graff (2003), by the time students' graduate from high school they should know how to engage in oral and written argument. In any field of study and profession students pursue, they will not only have to read and think critically, but they will also have to conduct research, think about what they find, organize findings in a certain manner, explain the entire process, and share it with peers and others who will evaluate its soundness.

The Anchor Standards for Writing (NGA & CCSSO, 2010) are divided into four categories (see Table 9.1). Teachers should use the 10 College and Career Readiness Anchor Standards for Writing for lesson planning.

The CCSS strongly emphasize the need for students to learn to write about the information they find in text(s), and research, and present the results of their research in writing and multimedia formats. Good writing comes from good reading. Writing about texts students read increases reading comprehension (Graham & Hebert, 2010). According to the CCSS, students

TABLE 9.1.   College and Career Readiness Anchor Standards for Writing

Text Types and Purposes

W.CCR.1: Write arguments to support claims in an analysis of substantive topics or texts, using valid reasoning and relevant and sufficient evidence.

W.CCR.2: Write informative/explanatory texts to examine and convey complex ideas and information clearly and accurately through the effective selection, organization, and analysis of content.

W.CCR.3: Write narratives to develop real or imagined experiences or events using effective technique, well-chosen details, and well-structured event sequences.

Production and Distribution of Writing

W.CCR.4: Produce clear and coherent writing in which the development, organization, and style are appropriate to task, purpose, and audience.

W.CCR.5: Develop and strengthen writing as needed by planning, revising, editing, rewriting, or trying a new approach.

W.CCR.6: Use technology, including the Internet, to produce and publish writing and to interact and collaborate with others.

Research to Build and Present Knowledge

W.CCR.7: Conduct short as well as more sustained research projects based on focused questions, demonstrating understanding of the subject under investigation.

W.CCR.8: Gather relevant information from multiple print and digital sources, assess the credibility and accuracy of each source, and integrate the information while avoiding plagiarism.

W.CCR.9: Draw evidence from literary or informational texts to support analysis, reflection, and research.

Range of Writing

W.CCR.10: Write routinely over extended time frames (time for research, reflection, and revision) and shorter time frames (a single sitting or a day or two) for a range of tasks, purposes, and audiences.

Source: National Governors Association Center for Best Practices & Council of Chief State School Officers. (2010). *Common Core State Standards for English language arts and literacy in history/social studies, science, and technical subjects.* Washington, DC: Authors. Retrieved from http://www.corestandards.org/ELA-Literacy/CCRA/W.

need to learn how to summarize text, critically analyze information reported in texts, synthesize information from multiple texts, and use what they draw from sources as evidence for supporting their own ideas. The CCSS also place an emphasis on digital writing and editorial tools. Students will need (a) opportunities to write in response to reading across the curriculum; (b) opportunities to read print and digital texts, and write in response to reading; and (c) instruction in using digital writing and editing tools, and opportunities to use them. This is a major shift from current writing standards that require explicit writing instruction and teacher professional development about how to teach students to write about text (NCTE Framework for 21st Century Curriculum and Assessment, 2013).

Three Types of Writing in the CCSS

The CCSS expect students to master three types of writing: writing to argue, writing to inform and explain, and writing to tell a story (narrative writing) (see Table 9.2). By the time students reach high school level, writing instruction should focus more on argument and informational writing; students should be able to write 80% of the time to explain or make arguments and 20% of the time to write narratives. In order to be college and career ready, students should show mastery and precision in arguments, informative/explanatory texts, and narratives; they need to learn how to argue using evidence and make complex ideas and information clear in writing.

Argument Writing

The writers of the CCSS provide specific explanations of the three types of writing emphasized in the CCSS for English language arts and literacy in history/social studies, science, and technical subjects Appendix A (NGA & CCSSO, 2010, p. 23–25). Writing Standard 1 of the CCSS-ELA calls for students to "Write arguments to support claims in an analysis of topics or texts, using valid reasoning and relevant and sufficient evidence." An argument is "convince me with evidence, logic, and reason" writing. It is clear writing, supported with relevant evidence or definitions for support, and writing that reflects a logical way of showing that the writer's position, belief, or conclusion is valid. Argument is a form of conversation and inquiry; it is something we do on a daily basis. We confront an issue, we take a stand, and support what we think with what we believe are good reasons or evidence. Making an argument involves providing good reasons to support your viewpoint, creating counterarguments, and recognizing how and why readers might object to your ideas.

Disciplinary experts view writing as a form of inquiry in which they convey their understanding of the claims people make, the questions they raise, and the conflicts they address. As a form of inquiry, writing begins with problems, conflicts, and questions the writer identifies as important. Writing is meant to advance a scholarly conversation and not reproduce others' ideas. Disciplinary experts read others' work with a "critical eye"—they examine the reasons others use to support their arguments,

The purposes of arguments are to (a) change the reader's point of view; (b) persuade the reader to a particular action or new behavior; or (c) persuade the reader to accept the writer's conclusion, evaluation of a situation, concept, problem, or solution.

Argument writing is different from persuasive writing. Persuasive writing depends on the writer-reader relationship where the writer uses emotional or moral appeals to connect with the reader's interests, beliefs, character, or emotions. On the other hand, in argument writing, the writer seeks to convince the audience based on logic and reasoning, and on credible facts and

TABLE 9.2. Distribution of Communicative Purposes by Grade in the 2011 NAEP Writing Framework

Grade	To Persuade	To Explain	To Convey Information
4	30%	35%	35%
8	35%	35%	30%
12	40%	40%	20%

Source: Adapter from: National Assessment Governing Board. (2007). *Writing framework for the 2011 Assessment of Educational Progress, pre-publication edition.* Iowa City, IA: ACT, Inc.

Student Sample: Grade 6, Argument

This argument was written as homework after a class in which grade 6 students viewed a movie titled *Benchwarmers* and discussed how movie writers and producers promote smoking. The letter is addressed to the producer of a film in which smoking appears.

Dear Mr. Sandler,

Did you know that every cigarette a person smokes takes seven minutes off their life? I mentioned this because I just watched the movie, Benchwarmers, and I noticed that Carlos smoked. Why did you feel the need to have one of the characters smoke? Did you think that would make him look cool? Did you think that would make him look older? It did neither of those things. As a matter of fact, I think it made him look stupid and not very cool. Especially when he put out a cigarette on his tongue.

If I were producing a movie, I would want my characters to be strong, healthy and smart. I would not have any smokers in my movies for many reasons. The first reason is it sets a bad example for children. An estimated 450,000 Americans die each year from tobacco related disease. In fact, tobacco use causes many different types of cancers such as lung, throat, mouth, and tongue. Another reason not to promote smoking is it ages and wrinkles your skin. Who wants to look 75 if you are only 60? It turns your teeth yellow and may lead to gum disease and tooth decay. Lastly, smoking is a very expensive habit. A heavy smoker spends thousands of dollars a year on cigarettes. I can think of better things to spend money on.

So Mr. Sandler, I urge you to take smoking out of all future movies you produce. Instead of having your characters smoke have them do healthy things. That will set a positive influence for children instead of poisoning their minds. Thanks for reading my letter. I hope you agree with my opinion.

Sincerely, _____

P.S. 1 love your Chanukah song.

FIGURE 9.1. Student sample: Grade 6, argument.

claims supported by sufficient evidence. Figure 9.1 includes a Grade 6 argument example provided by the CCSS for English Language Arts & Literacy in Social Studies/History, Science, and Technical Subjects, Appendix C: Samples of Student Writing (NGA & CCSSO, 2010, p. 36).

Discipline-Specific Argument. Types of argument writing include: advertisement, advice column, editorial, historical essay, literary essay, op-ed column, personal essay, petition, political cartoon, political speech, and review. Artists view art as inquiry, as an open-ended process of investigation, experimentation, and imagination—they experiment with new techniques and make artistic inquiry visible and audible. Students in fine arts (music and visual arts), should be arguing about the role of fine arts (e.g., music, dance, visual arts, theatre) as ways of knowing, as exploration and discovery. Literary experts argue by taking a position on a debatable topic and attempt to change the reader's mind about it by analyzing the topic and providing valid reasoning and relevant evidence. In English language arts (ELA), students should make claims, interpretations, or judgments using evidence from text(s) about the meaning and worth of a literary work or works.

Historians work backwards—they start with the answers, search for the questions, and present several arguments from primary sources before they make an overall argument for a particular interpretation of events. In history, students should analyze evidence from primary and secondary sources to support a claim about a historical event, topic, or situation. Mathematicians use proofs to argue that something is true. In mathematics, students should use proofs to convince others that something is true. Scientists always follow the scientific method when inquiring or arguing.

In science, students should make claims that are supported by data/evidence and their knowledge of scientific concepts to argue their claims. Sports and science experts focus on understanding physical health, and the development of lifelong habits. In physical education/health classes, students should be arguing about factors that will strengthen their physical performance in sports and promote a healthy lifestyle, and they should be providing evidence to support their claims.

How to Organize Argument Writing. There are different ways to organize an argument essay. The basic essay format includes an introduction, the body of the argument (with first, second, and third points and supporting information), and a conclusion.

Toumlin's (1958) method for argumentative writing includes the following steps:

1. *Claim:* the position or claim being argued for; the conclusion of the argument. Which claim is right for your arguments?
   - Claims of fact or definition
   - Claims of cause and effect
   - Claims about value
   - Claims about solutions or policies
2. *Grounds:* reasons or supporting evidence that bolster the claim.
3. *Warrant:* the chain of reasoning that connects the claim and evidence/reason. There are six main argumentative strategies via which the relationship between evidence and claim are often established.
   - Argument based on generalization
   - Argument based on analogy
   - Argument via sign/clue
   - Causal argument
   - Argument from authority
   - Argument from principle
4. *Backing:* support, justification, and reasons to back up the warrant.
5. *Rebuttal/Reservation:* exceptions to the claim; description and rebuttal of counter-examples and counter-arguments.
6. *Qualification:* specify the limits to claim, warrant and backing.

Scientific Argumentation. Llewellyn (2013) presents the following structure and organization of a scientific argumentation that can be very useful to science teachers and students—it follows the goals of science and the process of scientific inquiry. He states that the goal of scientific argumentation is to generate, verify (through empirical and experimental data), communicate, debate, and modify explanations for the purpose of refining and building consensus about scientific ideas or phenomena. A scientific argument includes the following six parts:

1. *Question:* a question about an observable event, phenomenon, or a subject of dispute that provokes a discussion or investigation.
2. *Assumption:* using prior knowledge to construct a tentative explanation to the question.
3. *Claim:* an assertion generated from observations and measurements from findings/data that support the claim.
4. *Evidence:* observations and measurements from findings/data that support the claim.
5. *Explanation:* a summary based on the claim that provides interpretation and validation of the evidence.
6. *Rebuttal:* a counterclaim (supported by evidence) provided by others about the legitimacy or validity of the original claim.

Claim: What do you think?

    Important questions to ask about a claim:

- Does the claim declare something?
- Can someone contest your claim?
- Is the claim supported by evidence?
- Is the claim a well-structured statement that challenges the status quo on the topic?

Reason: Why do you think that?

    Important questions to ask about a reason(s):

- Do your reasons explain why you think the audience should accept your claim?
- Are your reasons supported by evidence?

Evidence: How do you know that is true?

    Important questions to ask about evidence:

- Could someone check your evidence?
- Is your evidence accurate?
- Is your evidence sufficient/enough?
- Is your evidence representative?
- Is your evidence reliable?

Warrant: Why do the reasons/evidence support the claim?

    Important questions to ask about warrants:

- What is your warrant?
- Is it clear/obvious?
- Is it true?
- Does your warrant include both your reasons and your evidence?
- Is there a logical connection between your reason/evidence and your claim?

Acknowledgement/Response: What about alternative views or contrary evidence?

    Important questions to ask about acknowledgement/response:

- Are you raising alternative views, claims, or warrants?
- Are you accepting/rejecting or explaining problems within your own argument?

FIGURE 9.2.   Argument review.

What Makes Argumentative Writing Difficult?.   One of the reasons many students have difficulty with argumentative writing is because they have had limited experiences with reading argumentative texts. In addition, students in grades 6–12 are more accustomed to summary and worksheet writing than they are to argumentative writing (Applebee & Langer, 2006; Kiuhara, Graham, & Hawken, 2009). As a result, many students do not know how to differentiate between claims, reasons/evidence, and warrants (see Figure 9.2) nor do they view different genres such as editorials, reports, essays, etc. as arguments (Chambliss & Murphy 2002). Verbal arguments differ from written arguments.

    Students need to have collaborative reasoning experiences where they disagree with others or engage in debates for the purpose of developing solutions. They need to learn how to argue in a collaborative and productive manner in a culture of collaborative inquiry. Learning to argue will help students learn how to formulate their thoughts, express themselves clearly, take turns, listen to the others' perspective, and provide evidence that will convince others of the validity of the point of view. Over time, learning to argue should result into *argue to learn*—engaging in dialogic discussions with peers by challenging each other's beliefs, for the purpose of expanding everyone's understanding of a topic (Andriessen, 2006).

Informational/Explanatory Writing

Informational/explanatory writing is used to describe, give information, explain, or inform in an accurate manner; it focuses on why or how. Students use details, facts, and examples in their writing to define, describe, or compare and contrast ideas, concepts, etc. Types of informational/ explanatory writing include: application, blog, directions, fact sheet, feature article, how-to book or manual, lab or other reports, news article, nonfiction book, recipe, resume, and website. Figure 9.3 includes a grade 8 informational/explanatory writing example provided by the CCSS Language Arts & Literacy in Social Studies/History, Science, and Technical Subjects Appendix C: Samples of Student Writing (NGA & CCSSO, 2010, p. 47).

For example, in ELA, students describe the different parts of poetry. In mathematics, students explain mathematical concepts. In history, they compare and contrast the three branches of the government. In science, they explain the migration route of salmon.

Student Sample: Grade 8, Informative/Explanatory

This essay was written about a favorite activity. The writer wrote for one entire class period the first day and revised his essay the second day after discussing ideas for revision with a partner.

Football

What I like doing best is playing football, mainly because it is one of my best sports. One of the greatest things about it, in my opinion, is the anticipation, wondering what the other players are thinking about what you might do. Football is a physical game, of course, but it's the mental aspect that I appreciate the most.

At times football can get grueling, which makes the game even more exciting. The first time you make contact with another player (even with all that equipment) you get very sore. That is true for everyone, but in time you get used to the aches and pains. After a while, you develop mental disicipline, which allows you to ignore some of the pain. The mental discipline then allows you to go all out, to unload everything you have, every play. That's how you win games, everyone going all out, giving 110%.

The game takes concentration, just as much as any other sport, if not more. You develop this aspect in practice. That is why it is so important to have hours and hours of it. Mentally, you have to get over the fear, the fear of eleven madmen waiting for the chance to make you eat dirt. And that comes through practice. Once you overcome the fear, you can concentrate on the more important things, like anticipating the other guy's next move. Studying the playbook and talking with other players also helps.

During the game, your mind clears of all thoughts. These thoughts become instinct. You have to react, and react quickly, and you develop reactions and instinct in practice. For example, when you're carrying the ball or about to make a tackle, you want to make sure you have more momentum than the other guy. If you don't you'll be leveled. But, you should react instinctively to that situation by increasing your momentum.

Playing defense, all you want to do is hit the man with the ball, hit him hard. Right when you upload for a stick, all your body tightens. The you feel the impact. After you regain your thoughts, you wonder if you're all right. You wait for your brain to get the pain signal from the nerves. Even so, if you do get that signal, which is always the case, you keep right on playing. You can't let that experience shake your concentration.

On offense, while playing receiver, you can actually "hear" the footsteps of the defensive back as you're concentrating on catching the ball. What separates the men from the boys in the one who "hears" the footsteps but doesn't miss the ball. That's mental discipline, concentration.

Football is very physical or else it wouldn't be fun. But it is also a mental game and that is why it's challenging. You can get hurt in football if you screw up and ignore the right way to do things. However, mental discipline and concentration, which you develop during hours of practice, helps you avoid such mistakes.

FIGURE 9.3.   Student sample: Grade 8, informative/explanatory.

Narrative Writing

Narrative writing conveys fiction or nonfiction experiences and is used to inform, instruct, persuade, or entertain. In ELA, students provide details about characters, scenes, events, or objects. In history, students write narrative accounts about historical figures. In mathematics, students can use narrative writing to write songs and poems about a concept, law, or theorem. In science, they write narrative descriptions of procedures they followed in their investigations so they can replicate their procedures and steps. Types of narrative writing include: autobiography, biography, fable, fantasy, fiction, folk tale, historical fiction, narrative memoir, narrative nonfiction, and personal narrative.

Extensive Practice with Short, Focused Research Projects

The CCSS also call for extended practice with short, focused research projects. Through short, focused research, students will build a gradual and more comprehensive understanding of the research process. According to Writing Standard 7, short, sustained research projects that typically take about a week to complete, and occur on a quarterly basis will help students to repeat the research process several times and learn how to conduct research independently. To build students' confidence with extended writing, break the writing into smaller chunks. Many times students feel very frustrated about writing—the blank page intimidates them and they find it difficult to translate in writing what is in their heads about a topic.

To make writing a bit less scary, use small groups to develop persuasive writing skills. For example, in pairs or in groups of three, ask students to answer the following question: "What ultimately is the message in *Of Mice and Men*? What essential truth does Steinbeck want to convey? The discussion will help them verbalize what they are going to write about and how they will write it; they will determine what is important to the thesis. What piece(s) of evidence are important? In these small groups, one student would be starting a first draft and then reading it out loud, to pick up things that might not sound right. If time allows, they can do a second draft—they can edit and revise together; this way, when they receive feedback from each other and later on also by the teacher, they will feel more confident about writing an essay on their own at home. Building students' confidence with writing is a fundamental step in helping them become independent writers.

Research Paper/Report Format

Research paper and report writing requires specialized research and writing skills. It involves identifying and collecting information from multiple sources, analyzing, organizing, synthesizing, generalizing, and applying knowledge in writing. Teachers can use the following process to guide students' research and report writing.

- *Identify a research topic.*
  - If your assignment defines the topic, begin your search for materials.
  - If a topic is not assigned, choose a topic and narrow it before you begin.
- *Develop a research question.*
  - Think and learn about your topic.
    - Free writing and brainstorming can help.
    - What questions can you ask yourself about your topic?
    - What key words and ideas relate to your topic?
    - Look for similarities, patterns, and connections among sub-topics, word, and phrases.

○ Phrase your topic as a question. Choose the question you think you can find an answer to through research.

○ Narrow your topic.

○ Develop a tentative thesis.

● *Develop a research strategy.* Ask yourself the following questions:

○ What am I trying to accomplish? What is my (rhetorical) purpose?

○ What questions am I trying to answer?

○ What are the most important words or phrases associated with my topic?

○ Where will I find sources for my paper/report?

● Will I go to the library?

● What kinds of databases and search engines will I use to research information on my topic?

○ How long will it take me to do the research and the writing? (Set a schedule.)

● *Locate sources using the library, catalogs, indexes, and the Internet.*

○ Are you looking for popular or scholarly information?

○ Are you looking for magazine, periodical, and newspaper articles, or articles from scholarly journals/sources?

● *Evaluate sources.*

○ What is the goal of the website?

○ Is the website produced by a reputable organization?

○ Does it include contact information and invite inquiries?

○ Do the developers identify themselves? Do they provide any evidence of their expertise or credibility?

○ Do the authors distinguish between opinion and fact?

○ Do they provide non-anecdotal evidence to support their claims?

○ When was the website created? How often is it updated? When was it last updated?

● *Cite what you find using a standard format.*

○ See assignment format specifications (e.g., Modern Language Association (MLA), American Psychological Association (APA), or other as specified)

● *Carefully read, take notes, analyze, and synthesize information across sources.*

● *Develop an outline and organize your research; plan your research paper/report.*

○ Introduction

○ Body

○ Conclusion

○ References

● *Write the paper in past tense following the writing process stages (planning, drafting, revising, editing, and publishing).*

Laboratory Report Format

The purpose of a laboratory report is to provide a formal analysis of results of a controlled study. Most teachers expect students to type their lab reports, submit them electronically, and use APA format. Laboratory reports can be completed independently or collaboratively; when written collaboratively, only the data can be identical in the students' reports. Laboratory reports must be written in students' own words. Students are expected to cite any outside sources. Table 9.3 shows an example of a laboratory report format and Table 9.4 includes a rubric for assessing the laboratory report that reflects the structure and goals of science and promotes scientific inquiry thinking and writing.

TABLE 9.3.   Sample Laboratory Report Format

Title	Include the independent and dependent variables with the effect observed in the laboratory. Include your name, instructor's name, section/period, and date.

Purpose	This is an introduction that states the reason for doing the lab. Use your own words to state the problem.
	Purpose must be measurable.
	Purpose is usually stated as a question.
	Must include variables—state specifically what you will be measuring.
	   • Include independent variable(s) and the conditions.
	   • State dependent variable(s) and discuss how it will be measured.
	   • Identify the control and experimental groups.
	Include any pre-laboratory activity and any additional information you researched, collected, or learned before conducting the lab.

Hypothesis	Write each pre-lab question as a statement with your guess. Write your educated guess in the form of s statement that begins with "I think . . ." or "If . . . then . . ." Explain why you wrote the hypothesis you did.
Procedure	In paragraph form, and in past tense, provide a thorough description of what you did. Write a separate paragraph for each step of the procedure. Use titles for each section of the procedure. Include materials in procedural steps. Use the proper names of equipment used in the experiment. Identify the independent and dependent variable(s), control, constants, and if trials were repeated.

Observations/Data	Include data tables, graphs, or charts.
	Graphs and charts should be computer-generated.
	All graphs should be based on class data.
	Include the following in your graph:
	   • Title
	   • Label axes with title and units
	   • Plot all points
	   • Add a line or curve of best fit—NOT a connect dots graph
	   • Include a legend if more than one set of data is on the same graph

Analysis/Results	Write a clear interpretation and summary of the results in your experiment.
	Create a graph(s) of your data.
	In paragraph form, answer the following questions:
	   • What data did you gather from the experiment?
	   • Why did you gather this data?
	   • Did you have an unusual or outlier results?
	   • What is the percent error?

Conclusion	Relate the results to any hypotheses or questions raised in the introduction in the form of a summary statement.
	Discuss and explain the following in separate paragraphs in your conclusion.
	   • Did the data support or did not support your hypothesis?
	   • Did you meet the purpose of the lab? What is your claim—what did you discover by doing this lab?
	   • Make specific references to your data and explain why your evidence supports your claim.

- What is the scientific explanation of how the independent variable was affected by the dependent variable? Make connections to a scientific concept and what we are learning in class.
- Explain any specific sources of error. What could be done in the future to correct or reduce the error? What needs to be done to improve this lab?
- How could you further investigate what you learned form this lab? What are possible applications of this lab in the real world?

| References | Cite any sources, including textbook(s), Internet sources, and lab partners' full names. |
| | Use APA citation format for all references. |

TABLE 9.4.   Sample Laboratory Report Rubric

	1 *Beginning or* *Incomplete*	*2* *Developing*	*3* *Accomplished*	*4* *Exemplary*	*Score*
Title	Most identifying aspects are missing; incomplete/ erroneous	Some identifying aspects are presented; partially complete	Most identifying aspects are presented; partially complete	All identifying aspects are clearly presented; well-written	
Purpose	Purpose is not stated or is unclear; no information on variables	Purpose is stated; information on variables is missing	Purpose is clearly stated; information on some variables is missing	Purpose is clearly stated; includes all variables	
Hypothesis	The question to be answered is irrelevant/ missing	The question to be answered is partially identified; written in unclear manner	The question to be answered is stated; written in unclear manner.	The question to be answered is clearly stated and written	
Procedure	Missing many important procedures; not written in paragraph format	Written in paragraph format; most important steps are presented; several steps are missing	Written in paragraph format; important steps are presented; some are missing	Well-written in clear paragraph format; all procedures are clearly presented	
Observations & Data	All figures, graphs, & tables contain errors and are poorly constructed; have missing/ incorrect information	Most figures, graphs, & tables are presented; some have missing/ incorrect information	All figures, graphs, & tables are correctly presented; some need improvement	All figures, graphs, & tables are correctly presented and all contain accurate information	

(Continued)

TABLE 9.4.   (Continued)

	1 Beginning or Incomplete	2 Developing	3 Accomplished	4 Exemplary	Score
Analysis/ Results	Incomplete/ incorrect interpretation of data; shows lack of understanding	Some of the results have been partially addressed; shows incomplete understanding	Almost all of the results have been correctly interpreted and discussed	All important results have been correctly discussed; shows good understanding of results	
Conclusion	Conclusion is missing; or, conclusion is incomplete	Conclusion is stated; points reflect lack of understanding and many gaps	Most conclusion items are clearly and adequately addressed	All important conclusion items are clearly and adequately addressed	
Spelling & Grammar, Style	Frequent spelling & grammar errors; writing style is very rough	Occasional spelling & grammar errors; writing style is choppy	A couple of spelling & grammar errors; readable, appropriate style	Correct spelling & grammar; well-written	
Appearance & Format	Sections are not in order; poor formatting; illegible	Most sections are in order; some formatting is readable; readable	All sections are in order; formatting needs improvement; readable	All sections are in order; well-formatted; legible, readable	

I-Search Paper

A personal and alternative approach to research writing is the I-Search paper, a paper that is less formal than the traditional research paper, and is about a topic that is important to the writer (Macrorie, 1998). I-Search papers differ from traditional ones in the methods of topic selection, the research process, at times in the sources used, and in the informal and personal look and tone of the final product. The I-Search paper is inquiry-driven; it motivates students to do independent research and communicate through writing because the focus of the research stems from their personal questions. Students should have time during class to write about their progress, questions they have and challenges associated with the process, and changes they would like to make to the process. Teachers should monitor student progress through each phase. The main components of an I-Search project/paper include:

- *Search Focus/Story*
    - Why am I interested in this topic? Explain why learning more about this topic is personally important to you (e.g., I have had asthma since I was three years old. I am very active and involved in sports; I would like to learn more about how I can manage my asthma and have a safe and active life.).
    - Explain what you know about the topic before you start researching it.

- ○ State your main research question, what you want to learn and why, and sub-questions to support it.
  - ● Main question: How can I manage my asthma so I can have a safe and active life?
  - ● Sub-questions: What can I do to keep playing sports? Is there a physical activity I should not participate in? What environmental conditions affect my asthma? What kinds of medications are best at controlling asthma? What foods should I avoid?
  - ○ Plan your research. Where will you find information on this topic? What key terms will help you find answers to these questions?
  - ○ Review your sources and reflect on what information you have; organize it.
  - ○ Share your most significant findings.
- ● *Search Results*
  - ○ Describe your results and provide support.
  - ○ Use quotes, paraphrasing, and summarizing to develop your ideas.
  - ○ Cite information from sources.
- ● *Search Reflections*
  - ○ Discuss what you learned from your research experience. Reflect on how this research will affect your life or decisions in the future.

Writing From Sources

This is a major CCSS shift in ELA/literacy. As a result, writing needs to emphasize the use of evidence to inform or make a logical argument about ideas, facts, or events presented in the books students read instead of just writing about personal experiences. Standard 9 requires students to present a careful analysis of evidence from the text(s), well-defended claims, and clear information through their writing. Students will generate reports from research and write from multiple sources.

The quality of effective writing also depends on the student's ability to cite relevant, credible, accurate, and sufficient information as evidence to support their claims or explanations. Teachers need to provide students with instruction, direction, feedback, and practice on how to formulate keyword topics, use search engines and library databases, analysis of sources, and how to evaluate information. Students often take whatever is available on the Internet as "truth." Google, Yahoo, or Wikipedia searches often do not produce scholarly results. On other hand, library sites such as InfoTrac Junior Edition, Academic Search Premier, CQ Researcher, or General Reference Center Gold, or Google Scholar (for more advanced students) will provide them with credible and relevant information.

Students also need to learn how to cite references; in literature or the arts, students need to learn the Modern Language Association (MLA) (2009) format and in social sciences, the American Psychological Association (APA) format. There is a variety of free tools available to help them develop their skills with these style guidelines (e.g., StudentABC Citation Creation, Citation Builder, Citation Machine, Evernote, CiteULike, Connotea, or Zotero).

On-Demand Writing

Teaching students to produce on-demand writing is one of the most important things teachers can do. Students write on demand while attending a class, or taking a course or state assessment, or a college entrance exam. Many jobs require on-demand writing. On-demand writing requires a different skill set and different cognitive processes than process writing. With process writing you have the luxury of taking it home, revising it, bringing it back to class and sharing it with others, receiving feedback from others, etc. On the other hand, on-demand writing is timed; students need strategies on how to respond to on-demand writing. For example, students need to first understand what they have to do, what is the purpose, or what the writing demand is. Many times, adolescents do not have a clear plan of action when it comes to writing; they just jump into it and hope for the best. Students will benefit from strategies that will help them plan before they start writing. If they have 45 minutes to write an essay, taking five minutes to plan their response will help them produce a more focused essay.

Gallagher (2006) developed the ABCD strategy for on-demand writing. The steps of the strategy are as follows:

- *Attack the Prompt (1 minute)*
  - ○ Circle the words that ask you to do something.
  - ○ Draw an arrow from each circled word to what it specifically asks you to do.
  - ○ Rewrite and number the circled words. Rewrite what the word asks you to do.
- *Brainstorm Possible Answers (4 minutes)*
  - ○ Create a graphic organizer to help gather your thoughts.
  - ○ Give yourself time to do this. You may need to narrow your topic later.
- *Choose the Order of Your Response (1 minute)*
  - ○ Number the parts of your brainstorming you will use first, second, etc.
  - ○ Cross out any ideas you have decided not to use.
- *Detect Errors Before Turning the Draft In (1 minute)*
  - ○ Carefully read your writing.
  - ○ Reread to make sure what you have written makes sense and is complete.
  - ○ Look for punctuation, capitalization, and grammatical errors.

Applying Discipline-Specific Literacies

- Writing is interconnected with knowing and learning. Each discipline has its own specialized vocabulary, conventions, style, genres, and uses for texts. A health professional will follow a different writing style than an accountant. Students need to understand how conventions are used in each discipline.
- The purpose of writing in the disciplines is to empower the student to communicate effectively in clear and correct prose in a style appropriate to the subject, task, occasion, and audience.
- Disciplinary writing is also a form of communication for the members of each discourse community. Collaboration and feedback from peers is important for writing development, revision, sharing, and publication.

Writing in the Disciplines

The CCSS expect all students to learn many ways to represent data and information. Their writing will have to meet expected standards of clarity, coherence, and grammar and conventions, but the format and organization will look very different in English language arts, mathematics, science, or social studies. Writing is a powerful tool for discovering meaning, and writing is the responsibility of each content area teacher. In the disciplines, we write differently both in terms of form (e.g., a lab report in science versus an interpretive argument to primary sources in history) and conceptually in terms of content (e.g., math uses facts whereas English seeks the story in everything).

What is the connection between writing and learning within a discipline-specific framework? How do disciplinarian experts use writing to promote critical understanding of texts and encourage the making of evidence-based arguments? What does it mean to develop students' discipline-specific writing? It means to teach students a way of thinking, researching, doing, and writing accepted in each discipline. Discipline-specific genres of writing (e.g., essays, lab reports, research papers, etc.) need to be taught alongside informal writing assignments designed to foster critical thinking and active learning. To teach students how to write in discipline-specific ways, teachers need to scaffold writing assignments that will guide students through a series of learning and writing tasks.

Effective writers develop their discipline-specific writing skills by reading and analyzing the works of others in their fields or disciplines. Disciplinarian experts use a "read-analyze-write" approach to writing. Non-English language arts content area teachers need to approach writing from the perspective of their respective discipline instead of the perspective of an English teacher. For example, most English language arts teachers bear the burden of teaching plagiarism and fair use, whereas the responsibility should be shared by all content area teachers, and especially by social studies and science teachers. There are two ways one could approach disciplinary writing: writing in the disciplines and writing to learn.

Writing in the Disciplines (WID) is a component of academic writing that builds students' knowledge of various genres and helps them to become proficient academic writers. In college, students encounter academic reading and writing. Most of the writing they will do in college will require them to write about what they read in various texts and other sources. Key writing on various college courses includes: response to text, summary, abstract, critical analysis, rhetorical analysis, comparative analysis, literacy analysis, visual analysis, exploratory synthesis, interpretive essays, position papers, literature review, position papers, thesis-driven synthesis, argument-synthesis, journal articles, project proposals, journal articles, lab and field reports, and research papers.

WID focuses on discipline-specific writing, on helping students learn the specific, typical writing formats, vocabularies, conventions, styles, and genres of a discipline. Although there are certain aspects of academic writing that cut across all disciplines, we know that each discipline has its own unique writing forms, styles, and conventions that students must learn and apply in their WID assignments. All disciplines value writing that is clear, well developed, has a logical progression and organization of ideas, is carefully worded, and is grammatically correct. Each student's writing reflects his or her ability to engage in the language and the content of a discipline.

English Language Arts

Authors in English language arts are involved in literature (fiction) analysis. They read widely and critically, use language beautifully, creatively, and precisely, use strategies and devices to convey meaning, make arguments and counter-arguments, use conventions, grammar, and literary devices, and write to describe, inform, entertain, and persuade. Most common writing formats/forms for ELA include: essay, I-search paper, journalistic writing, informational writing, narrative writing, argument writing, poetry, literature reviews, thesis-driven synthesis, research paper, report writing, critical analysis, comparative analysis, rhetorical analysis, process analysis, take a stand, character analysis, summaries, critique of a visual argument (i.e., photo, film, video, or visual text), and responses to reading.

Fine Arts (Music, Visual Arts)

Artists represent their ideas visually; they explore, create, experiment with new techniques, and respond through a variety of multi-sensory modes. Artists communicate their ideas through critique and analysis of the artwork, the genres, media use, and artistic intent. Because artists use medium-specific language, they are naturally involved in reading, writing, observing, listening, speaking, critical thinking, and performing/exhibiting their work. They critique their own work, and the work of others. Sample writing in fine arts includes, observations, description and analysis of artistic elements and genres supported by evidence, analysis of artist's purpose and primary and secondary ideas in the piece, comparison of artistic elements in the piece to other artwork, argumentative writing, research paper or report, biographies, and essays.

History/Social Studies

Historians study the past to discover how specific cultural developments affected the people, cultures, and societies. They collect clues and analyze ideas in primary and secondary documents and they also revise past information by offering alternative perspectives and an interpretation that answers a question about a past event. They explain why the question is important, they present the sources they found and how they analyzed them, and they discuss how their interpretation of an event is valid and significant. As we have seen in this book, historians pay attention to content, corroboration, sourcing, bias, and perspective taking. Typical forms of formal writing involve research papers and reports, analytical/argumentative writing, narrative writing, response paper to a film, documentary, or reading, book reviews, analysis of visual information, evaluation of sources (e.g., credibility, reliability, limitations, bias) annotated bibliographies, timelines, and historical essays.

The Document-Based Questions (DBQs) Project started around 2000 for the purpose of helping students in elementary through secondary grades read primary and secondary sources critically, discuss and debate their own ideas, and write evidence-based arguments clearly. DBQs are used in many social studies classrooms to help students write with power (i.e., support, evidence) and skill. DBQs promote historical habits of mind and address and support CCSS in language, reading, writing, and speaking. DBQs also help students make inferences, identify point of view and assess its importance as they evaluate evidence from texts, address conflicting perspectives, and examine how different documents support claims, and use factual evidence from texts to write evidence-based argument essays.

Mathematics

Mathematicians actually spend much time writing and communicating their ideas to others. Being able to write clearly is as important a skill as it is to be able to solve equations. Being able to write mathematical explanations clearly and correctly improves the mathematical understanding of ideas. Mathematical writing is about showing how well one understands the mathematical concepts and ideas instead of just "showing the work." In mathematics classrooms, students use facts and evidence to explain their thinking, justify their answers and processes, and make logical conclusions. Sample writing includes record keeping of what students are learning or doing in math journals, learning logs, or blogs, writing to explain mathematical ideas in solving math problems, free writes, biography and autobiography reports, summaries, and formal research projects or reports.

Writing plays an important role in mathematics learning. Students are expected to not only understand mathematical concepts, and use strategies, they are also expected to explain and justify their mathematical actions and thinking through writing. The CCSS for mathematics stress the importance of students explaining their reasoning, justifying their thinking, arguing for or against, constructing viable arguments and critiquing the reasoning of others, constructing different ways of solving problems, summarizing and describing distributions.

Talk to the average mathematics teacher about writing and you will probably hear this response: "Writing? I don't have enough time to teach and do the mathematics; where am I going to find time to do writing?" The advantage of writing in mathematics is that it allows the student to reflect on his or her own ideas, as well on the ideas from the class, and use writing to think about the process of solving equations by writing about it. Writing can also be used as a catalyst for developing academic discourse. Writing, especially in the form of math logs, or journals, can be particularly beneficial to students as they explain their thinking and steps taken to solve a problem, and receive feedback from the teacher or peers. The following are sample ways to incorporate writing in the mathematics classroom.

- *Student Logs.* Student logs are formal ways of reporting learning about specific items—e.g., writing about new topics, concepts, definitions, or interesting facts they did not know, or learned about during the math lesson, or important steps they took to solve a problem with an explanation of how to solve the problem. Students have to provide information on each category; the teacher can set up the log to follow the topic at hand.
- *Student Journals.* Math journals can be used to assess students' background knowledge, give students opportunities to map out their thinking and steps taken toward solving a problem, or write questions they have about a topic. For example, students can write about something confusing in math, write an explanation of a math concept, or write a paragraph about a pattern, a graph, or a problem you present them with. Math journals are informal ways of communicating what students are learning or the experiences they are having with learning. When using math journals, teachers should provide daily feedback to students about how to help shape their understanding of math.
- *Exposition*
  - ○ *Explain a concept.* Explain why every integer is also a rational number.
  - ○ *Explain relationships.* Describe the relationships among these three sets of numbers: natural numbers, whole numbers, integers, rational numbers, irrational numbers, and real numbers.
  - ○ *Explain a concept or geometrical figure through poetry.* Although a lot of math teachers do not make time for poetry in their class, because poetry also relies on patterns, it can facilitate mathematical understanding of concepts and language skills. For example, here is a Haiku poem (three lines, five syllables, seven syllables, five syllables) on geometry:
    Obtuse angles
    Are greater than ninety degrees
    Less than one eighty
  - ○ *Explain an algorithm or describe a process.* Explain how a particular algebraic expression can be simplified.
  - ○ *Explain a theorem.* "The Pythagorean Theorem says that for any right-angled triangle, the square of the hypotenuse is equal to the sum of the squares of the other two sides: $a^2 + b^2 = c^2$. In other words, if you take the length of the longest side of a right-angled triangle and square it, you will always get the same amount as you get if you square the lengths of the other sides and then add them together."
  - ○ *Describe a geometric figure.* Describe a trapezoid and a rectangular prism to a friend.
  - ○ *Describe or interpret a graph.* Students are given a statistical graph from a newspaper article and are asked to interpret what is being presented, what the graph "tells" the reader, or what the graph "does not tell" the reader. Ask them to write about what they notice or what questions they have.

○ *Describe the solutions to a problem.* After you solve the problem, write an explanation of your solution.

○ *Write a problem.* Think of an everyday situation and write a word problem and provide a solution for it. For example, watch an upcoming basketball game; examine the team's record and write about the probability of the team that can win the game.

○ *Connect the mathematical significance with a real-life event or phenomenon.* For example, the Domino's website allows you to build your own pizzas, but doesn't specify how much they cost. Use linear equations to find the base price (y-intercept), and cost per additional topping (slope) to figure out how much Domino's is really charging for pizza (source: http://www.mathalicious.com/lesson/domino-effect/).

○ *Rewrite an unclear textbook explanation.* Re-write the textbook explanation of a concept, solution, or steps in your own words.

○ *The mathematics report.* Possible topics for a mathematics report include: (a) writing about different aspects of the history of mathematics—e.g., non-Euclidean geometry, or investigate the history of mathematical notation; (b) students conduct a survey on a topic of their choice, select appropriate statistical measures to analyze results, and write a detailed summary of the process and their findings; (c) students research areas of study or careers that require mathematical knowledge and use; students can do interviews with professors, career professionals, or employers, research related college courses, and read scientific or other related articles on each career; students will write and present a report on their findings; or (d) students can research biographies of famous mathematicians—e.g., Newton, Pascal, Euclid, Einstein—and write a report or an obituary about the mathematician of their choice.

Physical Education/Health

Sports and science experts have high research standards. They collect much data, conduct careful observations, form hypotheses, experiment with new techniques, use various instruments, and use specific evidence to support their claims, observations, or proposals. They collaborate with other scientists in the investigation of human performance, athletic training, physical fitness, wellness, and health promotion.

Because the discipline draws from many other areas such as science, physiology, biology, anatomy, chemistry, etc., most writing in physical education/health classes follows an inquiry-based pattern. Students will benefit from writing assignments that invite them to communicate their thinking and collaborate with others for learning. Sample writing assignments include description of rules and directions for different sports and routines; reports on hypothesis, plan of action, observations and results; evaluation and analysis of exemplars, case studies, and movement activities; interpretations of graphs, charts, and data; and, argumentative writing about the importance of health and wellness.

Science

In science and technology, researchers discover, collect, and organize information through the scientific method. They question, observe, experiment, and theorize; they generate scientific questions and they often challenge commonly accepted scientific beliefs, as well as the conclusions of other scientists. They confirm scientific ideas through verifiable observation. In social sciences (e.g., psychology, sociology, geography, economics), experts start their inquiry by asking questions or identifying problems related to phenomena, form a hypothesis based on certain assumptions, try to verify the hypothesis by making careful observations, they assemble and analyze data, and determine a clear pattern of response.

Most scientific writing follows a problem-solution pattern. The writer usually establishes authority by providing concrete evidence and verifiable observations. Their evidence comes from scientific investigation and, at times, from informal observations or anecdotes. In science, students describe experiments that could be replicated, summarize their procedures, observations, and results, and provide evidence that supported or did not support their hypothesis. Other writing assignments include (and are not limited to) translating chemical equations to words (e.g., photosynthesis, or cellular respiration), lab notes that document accurate and objective descriptions of lab procedures, results, and issues, observation notes, summarizing experiments, topics, chemical and other processes, laboratory reports, research papers, short essays, short reports, taking a stand, poems, creative writing, interactive science notebooks, and collecting and interpreting data. Scientific writing is characterized by precision, clarity, and objectivity.

Think Like an Expert

- Literary experts "play" with language in creative ways. They use language, strategies, and devices to convey meaning, make arguments and counter-arguments, and write to describe, inform, entertain, and persuade. (English Language Arts)
- Mathematicians use writing to show how well they understand the mathematical concepts and ideas, use facts and evidence to explain their thinking, justify their answers and processes, and make logical conclusions. (Mathematics)
- Scientists observe carefully and write down their ideas and observations. They conduct experiments, and write down their hypotheses, procedures, and observations. They also communicate with others through writing and share and publish their results, reports, observations, and questions. (Science)
- Historians conduct evidence-based writing. They evaluate sources, provide interpretations based on valid and adequate evidence, and offer alternative perspectives on historical issues, questions, events, and figures. (Social Studies)

Writing to Learn

Writing to Learn (WTL), focuses on using writing to better understand and learn information (e.g., summarizing, analyzing, or synthesizing information). Students learn from what they read and write. In this section, I present a few WTL strategies and show through examples how to use them in various disciplines to support students' writing development.

Academic Journals and Learning Logs

Journal Writing

Good readers and writers use a variety of tools to generate and organize information and ideas; they also take notes in all sorts of places, including mental notes and notes they write in their journals and notebooks. What is the purpose of journal writing and how is it used in schools? Journals can be used in a variety of ways and for different purposes. The main purpose of journal writing is to record important ideas and concepts. Journal writing can be structured or unstructured.

Journal writing can take many forms and it can be used for a variety of writing purposes in every content area. For example, ELA science teachers might structure journals to reflect observations and student memos, or questions about an experiment, whereas social studies teachers might ask students to write questions about an event, period, or unit of study. Some teachers use journal writing to help students start or organize their writing while others ask students to write daily responses to learning, answer questions, discover their own voice as writers, brainstorm ideas about writing assignments, or record personal thoughts, questions, key vocabulary, or reflections about learning. Journal writing is not usually graded. Teachers can provide feedback to students through written comments in their journals and they can also use the journals as a means to learn more about students' lives, interests, and aspirations. For journal writing to be most effective, students need to write daily.

Sometimes teachers will assign a writing prompt and give students a few minutes at the beginning or at the end of a class to write in their journals. Journal entry sharing will vary according to task and way in which it is used in the classroom. Students should also be given the opportunity to write their private thoughts and feelings without fear of criticism and share them on a voluntary basis.

Character Journals

ELA teachers should explain to students that they will be keeping a character journal on one of the main characters in a story (this same approach can be used in a history class where students can create a historical figure journal). They will write their journal entries from the character's point of view, using language the character would have used. Students will write in their Character Journals throughout the duration of the novel or unit. It is important to give students choice over their character, time to write daily, and opportunities to share and discuss their Character Journal entries with peers. Students should also include information in their journal entries about the character's motivations, actions, emotions, reactions to other characters, personal reflections on major events or themes, how the character's beliefs influenced his or her reactions, and character developments as they move through the text.

Students can write in actual paper journals, decorate their journal cover according to reflect the character, or write journal entries in an online journal or blog. When students finish reading the novel or text, it is also useful to ask them to reflect on all of their journal entries and on character changes throughout the book. For example: How do your journal entries present this character? How did your own perceptions of the character change throughout the course of the book?

Cornell Notes

Cornell Notes are a (two column) note-taking system developed in the 1950s by Walter Paulk, an education professor at Cornell University. The left column includes key questions, words, or ideas and the right column is for related note taking from text or lectures. Cornell notes can be used across content areas. Table 9.5 shows an example of a Modified Three-Column Note-Taking Strategy I developed; this strategy incorporates the Cornell Note-Taking system and also gives the student an opportunity to make connections with the topic/text, ask questions about it, and write a summary. This strategy can be used across the content areas to facilitate students' writing and learning.

Learning Logs

Students in grades 6–12 use learning logs or content area journals in a variety of ways to informally write about what they are learning, take notes during class, or record ideas, questions, and feelings about learning in class. Learning logs are useful for pre-writing and drafting purposes, preparing for tests, or responding to a wide range of prompts. Similarly to double-entry journals, students use learning logs to keep an ongoing record of learning and reflections as they happen in a notebook. Students write in their own language, to themselves, about what they are learning, what is confusing or interesting to them, or what they like or dislike about the topic, process, or class.

Interactive Notebooks

A variation of a learning log is the interactive notebook, a tool for students to make connections with new learning, reflect on their learning, and deepen their understanding of text, task, or

TABLE 9.5. Modified Cornell Note-Taking Strategy—English Language Arts Example, Grade 11: *Because I Could Not Stop for Death* by Emily Dickinson (1890)

Words, Concepts, or Ideas	Notes from Reading the Text	Class Notes (e.g., Lecture, Discussion, Small Group)

• *Words*
  ◦ *Gossamer*
  ◦ *Tippet*
  ◦ *Tulle*
  ◦ *Cornice*
• *Concepts/Ideas*
  ◦ *Death*
  ◦ *Dying*
  ◦ *We should not fear death; it is part of an endless life.*
	• *Words*
	  ◦ *A thin, light cloth*
	  ◦ *A woman's fur scarf*
	  ◦ *A soft material (silk, cotton, nylon) used for making veils and dresses*
	  ◦ *The molding around the top of a building*
	• *Concepts/Ideas*
	  ◦ *The poem has lots of imagery to create a scene about the speaker traveling with death to the grave*
	  ◦ *The author uses repetition ("We passed . . ."—3 times in stanza 3*
	  ◦ *Alliteration*
	    ▪ *"Recess . . . Ring"*
	    ▪ *"Grazing Grain"*
	    ▪ *"Setting Sun"*
	    ▪ *"Gossamer . . . Gown"*
	    ▪ *"Tippet . . . Tulle"*
	    ▪ *"Horses' Heads"*
		• *The author uses metaphors (e.g., the character of death; the house as a metaphor for a grave).*
		• *Personification—(a) death is personified as a guide leading the speaker to eternity:*
		  ◦ *"He kindly stopped for me"*
		  ◦ *"He knew no haste"*
		  ◦ *"His civility"*
		  ◦ *"We paused before a house . . ."*
		(b) "The Dews grew quivering and chill"
		• *The author capitalizes certain words to show importance, uses lots of dashes for long pauses, and lots of references to religion that reflect her religious beliefs (e.g., "He" = God; "Immortality" = her belief that life after death is eternal in heaven.*
		• *Diction: she uses a simple writing style that shows her acceptance of death; presents death as a friend and she accepts dying.*
		• *The tone is accepting and shocking—she makes death sound like a good thing. She also accepts death as part of life. But, death came in the middle of her busy life and she was unprepared—"Because I could not stop for death."*

2 connections I made with what I already know about the topic.
  1. *My grandfather kept saying that he was ready to go and we should not be sad; he was starting a new life. I never fully understood that . . .*
  2. *My friend, Erin, died from a car accident at age 16. She laid there in a coffin, dressed in a white wedding gown. Why?*

1 unanswered question I have about the topic.
Can anyone really prepare for death?

Summary:
Emily Dickinson presents a different view on death in this poem from beyond the grave—she presents death as kind, civil, and human. The speaker is too busy for death, so death "kindly" takes the time to stop her. Death's "civility" makes the speaker reflect and give up those things that made her so busy so she can enjoy the ride. There are reminders of the world the speaker is leaving behind and the speaker is no longer active but is now part of the landscape. The carriage stops at her new "house," a grave, and a resting place as the speaker travels to eternity. In this poem, the speaker is dressed in a gossamer gown, which represents a new beginning rather than the end. The poem endorses eternity and shows how the speaker has obtained immortality.

subject. Scholars and scientists use notebooks and learning logs to record their notes, steps, or observations (print or electronic). Interactive notebooks are a way for students to take notes and organize their learning from class lectures, labs, or textbooks.

Interactive notebooks allow students to creatively organize ideas and information provided in class or in labs. On the left side of the notebook students use color to record any of the following (input): brainstorming, diagrams, concept maps, flow charts, pictures, or reflections. On the right side, they write information they were given in class—notes from lectures, labs instructions/materials/procedures; notes from books and videos; or, teacher questions and sample problems (output). The interactive notebook is a culmination of a student's work throughout the year that shows both the content they learned, their thinking and learning processes, as well as the role of reflection in developing knowledge. Students can share their work (interact) with teachers, peers, and parents. Teachers use interactive notebooks across the content areas to informally assess, monitor, and reflect on students' learning, and differentiate instruction.

Cubing

Cubing is a strategy developed to support students' reading and writing (Cowan & Cowan, 1980; Vaughn & Estes, 1986). In writing, it can be used as a pre-writing activity to stimulate students' thinking about a topic. Each side of the cube represents a different thinking skill; the strategy incorporates both Bloom's Taxonomy and Webb's Depth of Knowledge (DOK). The strategy invites students to look at a topic from the following six different angles. For example, students can write about their understanding of the concept of democracy in a US Government class.

- *Describe it:* How would you describe the topic/event/person/issue? Describe key characteristics.
  ○ Describe the concept of democracy.
- *Compare it:* What is it similar to?
  ○ Compare it with other forms of government we have learned about.
- *Associate it:* What does it make you think of? How does the topic connect to other topics/events/people/issues?
  ○ What does US democracy make you think of?
- *Analyze it:* What is it made or composed of? How would you break the topic/issue/problem/decision into smaller parts?
  ○ What are key characteristics of a democratic society?
- *Apply it:* What can you do with it? How is it used? How does it help you to understand other topics/events/people/issues?
  ○ How do you apply elements of democracy in your everyday life?
- *Argue for or Against it:* Take a stand and list reasons for supporting or not supporting it. Example: Take a stand for or against the benefits of democracy.
  ○ I support it because . . .
  ○ I do not support it because . . .
  ○ I agree with it because . . .
  ○ I disagree with it because . . .
  ○ This works because . . .
  ○ This does not work because . . .

Teachers often create a visual cube that serves as a starting point when they want students to analyze or consider various aspects of a topic. Cubes can be used as an after-reading and writing strategy because students need to have developed sufficient knowledge about a topic to start thinking and writing critically about a topic. Almost any topic can be cubed and teachers modify the

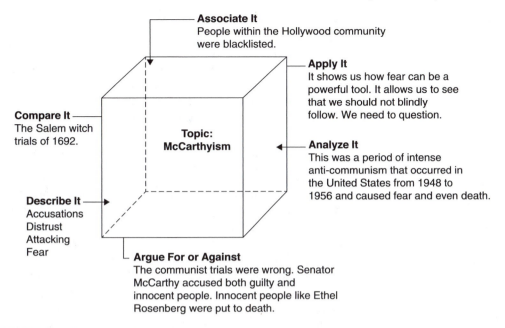

Associate It
People within the Hollywood community were blacklisted.

Apply It
It shows us how fear can be a powerful tool. It allows us to see that we should not blindly follow. We need to question.

Compare It
The Salem witch trials of 1692.

Topic: McCarthyism

Analyze It
This was a period of intense anti-communism that occurred in the United States from 1948 to 1956 and caused fear and even death.

Describe It
Accusations
Distrust
Attacking
Fear

Argue For or Against
The communist trials were wrong. Senator McCarthy accused both guilty and innocent people. Innocent people like Ethel Rosenberg were put to death.

FIGURE 9.4. Cubing strategy example.

Created by Zygouris-Coe, 2004-present, University of Central Florida

strategy to use as needed according to student needs and task. Figure 9.4 offers an example of the cubing strategy on the topic of McCarthyism. Although this example refers to social studies, cubing is used across the content areas. For example, in science, on the topic of energy sources, the six sides of the cube can focus on: list and define energy sources; explain how the energy source is produced; compare and contrast to energy sources; classify the sources as renewable or nonrenewable; categorize the energy sources as pollutants or non-pollutants; present the information to the class.

Teachers can scaffold the use of this strategy by modeling, and providing guided and independent practice on each side of the cube with different texts before they use all six tasks at once. After students have had sufficient practice with the strategy, teachers could divide the class into six groups and assign a perspective per group, or place students in small groups of six and assign (or allow each student to choose) a different perspective. Students in either scenario can use collaborative discussions, make revisions, and share their final writing with the entire class. Students can also tape their writing to an actual paper cube and display it in the classroom.

RAFT

RAFT is an acronym for a pre-writing strategy that stands for Role, Audience, Form, and Topic (Holston & Santa, 1985). It can be used across the content areas; it allows the teacher to create writing assignments from various points of view, for different audiences, and in different formats. It is a useful differentiation tool. RAFT can help students focus their thoughts on a topic, elaborate on it, and create a thoughtful piece of writing that reflects their understanding of role, audience, form, and topic (Strayer & Strayer, 2007). It promotes student motivation about writing and can also be used to facilitate discussions.

● *Role of the Writer:* Reporter, scientist, artist, historian, authority figure, or writer. Writing from a different perspective facilitates the development of critical thinking skills.

- *Audience:* Who is the target audience and what does the audience need to know? An audience could be one's self, a person, a fictional character, or a group of people (i.e., a peer group, a committee, an agency, a government), or objects.
- *Format:* The writing format should correspond with the role of the writer, the audience, and the topic; e.g., a poem, a letter, a speech, a critique, a biographical sketch, a booklet, a report, an article, a cartoon, a video, a song, a game, etc.
- *Topic:* The topic can stem from the research or study students are doing within a subject, a topic of personal interest, a related topic, or subtopics that need more clarification; the topic needs to be narrow or specific enough. What's the subject or the topic of this piece?

Table 9.6 includes an RAFT example for a foreign language class. Figure 9.5 is an example of a letter following the RAFT strategy (Role: writer; Audience: readers; Format: Letter; Topic: Edgar Allan Poe's life). RAFT is used across the content areas. For example, in mathematics, R: Parts of a graph; A: classmates; F: How to read the graph; T: why are graphs important in math. In Science, R: an environmentalist; A: the public; F: a persuasive letter; T: the harmful effects of deforestation on our planet.

Teachers need to explain to students how and when to use the strategy, model it, provide examples, practice it, and discuss it. Students need to understand that the role, audience, and format they choose must be aligned with the topic. When working on the format, explain to students that they must consider the purpose or goal for how they present their information. Is their purpose to describe, inform, persuade, encourage, critique, or clarify? Help students with the statement of purpose and suggest to them to include a strong verb that will help them to focus on their writing. For example, is the purpose to persuade parents to offer five to nine servings of fruits and vegetables to their children daily? Or, is it to inform pet owners how to prevent heartworm disease in dogs? Remember to provide students with time to practice, receive feedback, discuss, and revise as needed. Peer collaborations in small groups will help facilitate discussions and revisions.

Summarizing

Summarizing is an important skill for comprehension development as well as for writing. Sometimes content area teachers forget that students need to be taught how to summarize, especially long text. Summarizing is not the same as paraphrasing and retelling. Summarizing depends on some level of paraphrasing (restating ideas in one's own words) and retelling (telling again orally what is remembered from the text). But, summarizing is not just a quick retell. It involves higher order thinking skills such as comprehending, analyzing, and synthesizing ideas in text(s), and is important for comprehension building in every discipline.

TABLE 9.6.   Sample Foreign Language RAFT Assignment: Foods Unit

Role	Audience	Format	Topic
Chef	Customer	Menu	Detailed description of menu items, including preparation
Customer	Restaurant Owner	Letter/E-mail	Appreciation for menu choices and service
Travel Writer	Magazine Reader	Article	Travel tips, good things to eat on a budget, what to avoid
Cookbook Writer	Cooks/Chefs	Recipe	Instructions on food selection/ quality and food preparation
Student Traveling Abroad	Friends	Letter/E-mail/ Video	Describe a typical meal you would eat at a local restaurant

Let me introduce myself…

I am the second child of two actors. My parents named me Edgar after the legitimate son of Gloucester in *King Lear.* Allan is the name of my foster family, the Allans of Virginia. When I moved to Boston, I worked as a clerk and a newspaper writer. Because my wages were meager, I lied about my age and at the age of 18, I enlisted on the army. I served for five years and later on I enrolled at the West Point Military Academy but was dismissed of my military duty at age 22 for neglect of duty and disobedience to orders from superiors.

I depended entirely on writing for my living and I could not have picked a worse time to do it. I published poems, stories, articles, and I also edited magazines and became a critic of others' work. My best-known work throughout my lifetime was my poem, *The Raven.* It made me an overnight success, but I only received $9 for it. When I was 27 years old, I married my 13 year-old cousin, Virginia Eliza. We did not consummate the marriage for several years, but we were very happy; poor and happy. My wife put up with me and with the several ladies that were after me; my scandals made me the talk of the town. The saddest day of my life was when Virginia developed tuberculosis and later died at the age of 24.

I was viewed as twisted man, an alcoholic and a drub abuser, and a gambler. In my view, I lived my life the way I wanted to live it and I wrote about what people wanted to read—spiritualism was in vogue in 19th century America. People loved my tales of macabre, detective stories, and putting cryptographs into newspapers and magazines.

My death has been a mystery … no one really knows how I died. I was missing for five days; it didn't help my case that I was found delirious, disheveled, and wearing cloths that did not belong to me. Once I was hospitalized, I never regained consciousness. Did I die because of drugs or alcohol overdose? Was I poisoned? Was I sick and mad? Or did I die because of cooping? Oh, you will never know… I could not even die the proper way … the first time they buried me at Old Westminster Burying Ground in Baltimore, there were nine people present. In1873, 24 years after my death, Paul Hamilton Hayne, a poet and critic, published a newspaper article about the sorry condition of my graveside and raised $1500! with Baltimore schoolteacher Sara Sigourney Rice to build me a monument. A monument for Poe! That's a kicker! I was reburied closer to the church and in 1885 Virginia's and my remains shared the same gravesite.

Well, that's it; dear reader, you decide about who I was and before you believe what others have said, make sure you dig deeper; someone has to tell my story the way it should be told …

FIGURE 9.5.   Using the RAFT strategy to write a letter on Edgar Allan Poe's life.

Student reading and writing skills, higher order thinking skills, text structure and complexity, and number of texts, all play a role in students writing effective summaries. Some students will include everything and others will include nothing of relevance in their summaries—they do not know how to summarize. Routine summarizing of written text(s), of labs, procedures, presentations, and class activities need to exist in every content area classroom. Modeling, think-alouds, guided practice, and feedback from the teacher and peers are also necessary for students to learn how to summarize well. To summarize well, students need to learn how to be able to do the following:

- Identify essential information.
- Remove/delete redundant and irrelevant information.
- Focus on the main idea(s)/purpose/message/gist of the text.
- Identify key words/phrases that capture the main idea(s)/purpose/message/gist of the text.
- Save the main ideas and important details that support them.

Summary Guide. Table 9.7 shows a summarizing strategy I developed called Summary Guide. The Summary Guide can be used in discipline-specific ways for students to summarize in writing what they are reading from texts or learning in class.

TABLE 9.7. Summary Guide Strategy Example—Topic: *Refraction and Lenses* (Middle School Science)

1. Write a short summary (with no more than five sentences) of the assigned reading section.

When light hits an object, it can be reflected, refracted, and/or absorbed. Refraction can make you see something that is not there. Some mediums cause light to bend more than others; they have a different index of refraction. The type of image formed by a lens depends on the shape of the lens and the position of the object. The speed of light through a substance depends on how that substance interacts with electric and magnetic fields.

2. List the words, concepts, ideas, symbols, formulas, or visuals that are particularly important in this reading section. Explain whey they are important.

Refraction, index of refraction, and concave and convex lenses are very important for this section because they help us to understand the ways in which light interacts with matter, what determines the image formed by a lens, and the factors that affect the speed of a wave.

3. List the words, concepts, ideas, symbols, formulas, or visuals that are either unfamiliar to you or that you still have questions about.

I need to study the diagram about how light travels through water, glass, and air again.

For example, in English language arts and social studies, a teacher could ask students to summarize a reading section and then identify words, concepts, ideas, or visuals that are important to that section and/or unfamiliar to students. In mathematics and science (see Table 9.7), they could respond to the above as well as to a formula or vector.

The GIST. The GIST acronym stands for Generating Interactions Between Schemata and Text (Cunningham, 1982; Frey, Fisher, & Hernandez, 2003). This strategy can be used to scaffold summary writing and help students learn how to progressively write more concentrated summaries about a text (i.e., identify the GIST of the text selection). It is particularly useful for ELA, social studies, and science courses. See the following steps for implementing the GIST strategy:

1. Identify a short piece of text that is divided into four to five sections or summarization points.
2. Explain the GIST strategy. Begin with summarizing sentences before you move onto paragraphs. Read the first sentence of a paragraph, stop, and ask students to write a summary for each text portion in 15–20 words. Write the students' summaries on the board, edit, and discuss them with the whole class.
3. Show students the next sentence of the paragraph. Now, ask students to summarize two sentences in 15–20 words.
4. Continue the process with the entire text portion or paragraph until the group has summarized the entire paragraph in 15–20 words.
5. Practice as much as needed and then ask students to summarize an entire paragraph at once in 15–20 words. Once students have shown mastery of the GIST strategy, ask students to summarize text individually.

One-Word Summaries. One-Word Summaries (Wormelli, 2005) help students get into the habit of summarizing text routinely by identifying key concepts and ideas in the text(s). Asking students to write a one-word summary about a text, a procedure, a problem, a presentation, etc. is not an easy task; it requires good understanding of the text or task at hand and it promotes critical thinking skills. When practiced over time with close reading of short text selections, it can promote active engagement with learning. Although they can be used across the disciplines, they are particularly useful for social studies and science texts. Here are some suggestions on how to use One-Word Summaries.

Following a reading of text, a lesson, a presentation, a lab demonstration, or a discussion, ask students to:

1. Write one word that summarizes the topic, task, or event.
2. Write one sentence that explains their one word choice.
3. Ask students to share their word choices and explanations with others in class in a small or whole group format.
4. Encourage students to discuss, argue for, and support their word choices.

Writing Frames

A Writing Frame consists of a skeleton outline to scaffold students' fiction or non-fiction writing (Nichols, 1980). Writing Frames help struggling writers to use text structure (e.g., comparison-contrast) for summarizing content area information. Many students have difficulty getting started and staying focused on a topic when asked to respond in writing to text they have read. The Writing Frames contain key language information to help students organize their thoughts and writing about the major ideas of a narrative or informational text. The connectives in writing frames (i.e., first, then, finally) guide students in transitioning from one idea to the next and give them a structure for developing logical and coherent writing. Table 9.8 includes an example of different types of Writing Frames.

TABLE 9.8.   Types of Writing Frames

Procedure-Sequence Frame	I would like to explain how . . . It begins with . . . Next . . . Then . . . As a result . . . The final step/result is . . .
Summarizing Writing Frame	I found ____ interesting for these reasons . . . I learned new facts about . . . I also learned that . . . The most important/interesting thing I learned was . . . Finally, . . .
Problem-Solution Writing Frame	I would like to explain why . . . is a problem The main reason for it is . . . Other reasons include . . . The best solution for the problem is . . . The reason why this is the best solution is . . . Finally, . . .
Cause-Effect Writing Frame	There are various explanations as to what, why, how, and when . . . One explanation is . . . The evidence for that is . . . A second explanation is . . . The evidence for that explanation is . . . Based on the evidence presented, I think the best explanation is . . .

(*Continued*)

TABLE 9.8. Types of Writing Frames (Continued)

Comparison-Contrast Writing Frame	*Comparison* Although . . . and . . . are different in . . . they are similar in . . . They are also similar in . . . . . . is the same as . . . Finally, they both . . . *Contrast* Although . . . and . . . are both . . . they are different in . . . . . . has . . . and . . . has . . . Another way they differ is . . . Finally, . . .
Opinion Writing Frame	The issue we are discussing is . . . Arguments for it include . . . Evidence to support the arguments is . . . People who support this argument claim that . . . Arguments against it include . . . Evidence to support this include . . . People who do not support this argument claim that . . . Based on the evidence provided for the different points of view, my conclusion is . . .
Persuasion Writing Frame	I think that . . . because . . . The first reason for my thinking is . . . Another reason is . . . Moreover, because of this evidence, . . . These facts show that . . .

Creative Writing

Different forms of creative writing are used across the content areas such as poems, riddles, songs, business cards, menus, travel brochures, epitaphs, postcards from the past, etc. Figure 9.6 presents a variety of ways students can use creative writing to respond to literature in English language arts courses.

Students can use biopoems to describe the lives of historical figures, characters in stories, fictional characters, or inanimate objects. Table 9.9 presents both the steps to writing a biopoem and an example.

1. Book TV: Have a student act as host, another one as author, and others as a cast of characters; allow for questions about the book, event(s), or character(s) from the audience (rest of the class).

2. Character analysis: Describe a character from a psychologist's, a politician's, an authority figure's, an investigator's, or other's (specify:_____) perspective. What would the character be like? Give a couple of examples and explanations.

3. Sing a song: Write the lyrics and sing us a song about a character, story, or event.

4. Reality show: Create a reality show around the book and its characters. What would it be called and why? What would viewers expect to see? Describe an episode in writing.

5. Business card: Place your name and the title of the book on one side of the card. Summarize the story in the most gripping way you can on paper the size of a business card.

6. Text or tweet about it: Send a daily text message or Tweet update (to your teacher and classmates) about your book, events, or character(s) in the book.

7. Then and now: Create a Then (Book Era)/Now (21st Century) list to compare the ways in which characters or places (settings) compare across time.

FIGURE 9.6. Sample creative writing responses to literature—English language arts.

TABLE 9.9. Steps to Writing a Biopoem, and Example

Steps to Biopoem Writing	*Example*
• Line 1: First name of the person.	• Abraham
• Line 2: Three or four adjectives that describe the person.	• 16th US President, exceptionally astute politician, a self-taught strategist, great character, gloomy
• Line 3: Important relationship (son of . . ., friend of . . ., resident of. . .).	• Son of Nancy and Tom, husband of Mary Todd, father of Robert, Edward, Willie and Tad
• Line 4: Two or three things, people, or ideas that the person loved.	• Dedicated to nationalism, equal rights, liberty, and democracy
• Line 5: Two or three feelings the person believed or experienced.	• Who felt committed to preserving the Union, sad most of the time, and alone in the world
• Line 6: Two or three things the person experienced.	• Who experienced criticism, opposition, isolation, assassination
• Line 7: Accomplishments (who composed . . ., who discovered . . . etc.).	• Who led during the American Civil War, preserved the Union, modernized the economy
• Line 8: Two or three things the present wanted to see happen or wanted to experience.	• Who wanted to preserve the Union, see liberty for all
• Line 9: His or her residence.	• Past resident of 1600 Pennsylvania Avenue, Washington, DC
• Line 10: Last name of the person.	• Lincoln

Quick Writes

A Quick Write is a writing strategy that can be used before, during, or after reading in any content area to develop writing fluency, to promote reflection, and to informally assess student thinking. Teachers will give students a prompt or an open question and students will write for a limited amount of time (1–3 minutes). Quick Writes can be used to write predictions about what would happen next in a story, to synthesize ideas about a text by quickly writing about them, write or respond to a word problem, or to reflect on confusing parts of a text. Teachers can also use this type of writing to informally assess students' understanding of a text, topic, or task. Examples include:

● List one or two terms, or concepts you cannot define clearly.
● Write one question you have from today's lesson.
● List key similarities and differences between the two main characters in the book.
● Write the problem in your own words.
● Define in your own words what a biosphere is.
● What 1–3 questions do you have about the Great Depression?

Admit/Exit Slips

Admit slips are brief, informal written comments students write on a piece of paper, an index card, or a template (see Table 9.10 for a 3-2-1 admit slip template) before or at the beginning of a class. Students submit their responses as they enter the class, which allows the teacher to do a quick review on what questions students have and make necessary instructional adjustments. Students' comments may include any of the following:

- What worked best with this assignment/lesson?
- What was confusing about this assignment/lesson?
- What was challenging about this assignment/lesson?
- What one main question do you have about the assignment/lesson?

Exit slips are also quick and informal written responses to a prompt or a question, but they are collected at the end of a lesson or a class. They help students reflect on what they are learning in class. Teachers use them for informal assessment purposes, and for addressing content issues and questions in class the next day. Teachers usually give students up to five minutes to write an exit slip before the class ends. Students can use an index card, a piece of paper, or a template the teacher has provided (see Table 9.11 for the 3-2-1 exit slip template).

- Write something you learned in class/lab today.
- Write a question you have about today's lesson.
- Write what was confusing from today's lesson.
- Write what else would you like to learn from today's lesson.
- Write three words that summarize today's lesson.
- Write the formula we learned today.
- Which graph type did you like the most? Why?
- Solve this problem.
- Write one prediction about what will happen next in the story.
- Write how you could use what you learned in class today in the real world.
- What is the main cause of this event?
- What is the main effect of this event on the nation's economy?
- What did you enjoy from the group work today?
- What changes would you like to see in the group work?

TABLE 9.10.   3-2-1 Admit Slip

Student Name:	Class/Period:
3	Three things that were challenging for me with this assignment/lesson . . .
2	Two things I need help with . . .
1	One question I still have . . .

TABLE 9.11.   3-2-1 Exit Slip

Student Name:	Class/Period:
3	Three things I learned today . . .
2	Two things I found interesting . . .
1	One question I still have . . .

The Role of Collaboration in Writing
Socio-Cultural Differences in Writing

Writing is a socially constructed process; it is an outcome of dynamic interactions among the writer, texts, audience, language, and the social context. For example, what is considered an effective argument in a culture is shaped by the rhetoric of that culture. The influence of language and culture shows in the students' writing in terms of word choice, grammatical structure, and organizational patterns.

Cultural differences are also reflected in how language is used pragmatically. For example, in some cultures people learn new skills through observation whereas in Western cultures, verbal instruction tends to be the main learning tool. Heath (1983) reported communication in working class Caucasian and African-American families as well as among middle class families from both ethnic groups. Hart and Risley (1995) reported on the importance of the amount of parental talking (i.e., language diversity, feedback tone, symbolic emphasis, guidance style, and responsiveness) for children's "meaningful differences" in language, vocabulary knowledge, growth, and use.

Chinese composition structure is characterized by a beginning, following and amplifying, turning, and conclusion whereas the basic English composition is characterized as introduction, body, and conclusion. Chinese writing delays the introduction of the theme, and ends with a statement that is unrelated to the thesis and its tone is reserved. On the other hand, English writing's tone is straightforward; English writing introduces the theme too early and ends with a conclusion that reasserts the thesis in different words (Chen, 2006). Chinese writing reflects collectivism, while English writing reflects individualism. Chinese writers tend to cite proverbs and fixed phrases in their writing (Wu & Rubin, 2000). Arabic speakers argue by presentation—by repeating arguments, paraphrasing them, and exaggerating them (Hatim, 1997). Western argumentation is characterized by counterarguments (a claim to oppose, opposition, substantiation of counterclaim, and conclusion). Learning about contrastive rhetoric between Chinese-English or Arabic-English, for example, can help teachers and students to become aware of these rhetorical differences for the purpose of improving students' writing.

Although in each content area classroom teachers will have students with diverse linguist and sociocultural backgrounds who will need to develop mastery with standard English, it is important to understand, respect, and appreciate those differences (Delpit, 1995). Create a safe and culturally inclusive classroom environment that is founded on collaborative inquiry. Provide students with meaningful writing experiences and authentic writing tasks. Integrate writing instruction with content learning.

Allow time for writing and provide routines and support for students to become comfortable with the writing process. Provide modeling in text structure, drafting, revising, and editing, as well as in spelling and mechanics. Support students' vocabulary development and provide modeling (especially with multi-paragraph writing) and feedback in the organization of ideas, word choice, and conventions. Use teacher-student conferences to monitor student growth. Encourage students to develop their own voice, share their writing with others, and receive peer feedback. Use technology to support students' writing, editing, and publishing.

Peer Collaboration

Two key elements of effective writing instruction in any content area classroom are the opportunity to read and write with peers, and meaningful feedback from both the teacher and peers (Gallagher, 2006). "Real" or academic writing is an outcome of collaboration; disciplinarian experts and professionals collaborate with others in many levels before they produce their final report, research, story, or article. Although that is the case, in many classrooms students view peer collaboration in writing as a waste of time because the teacher is the one who "does the grading!" Students need to learn in classrooms where collaboration is valued and practiced; they need ongoing opportunities to help them discover the benefits of peer collaboration on their writing. Collaboration will take place differently depending on the task.

Collaborative writing can take place in many ways. For example, students can work in pairs to read and evaluate each other's outline, thesis, or hypothesis. Or, they can sit in front of a computer co-writing their introduction or citing references. Students can work in small groups, and as a group they divide up the labor of a particular project (e.g., research project or report); they develop their part, and come together as a group to update, share work, and revise their work. Using outlines, goals, and rubrics, will help each student to be accountable in the writing process.

Larger collaborative writing projects take time and ongoing communication among all members. Technology (computers, digital writing, sharing, and publishing tools) and the Internet can facilitate such collaborations. E-mails, chat rooms, instant messaging, and group editing software and sites make it possible for students to collaborate with each other. To facilitate smooth online collaborations, students should learn how to collaborate online, and should also be familiar with the media and technology they will be using for their project. For example, students should make sure that everyone is included in the online discussion—include everyone's e-mail address if you are sending an e-mail. Everyone in the group should follow the same communication format, and use netiquette rules for writing messages. Everyone is responsible for responding to e-mails and other messages in a timely fashion. Students should come to a consensus about when they need to meet for "face-to-face" discussions, meetings, or updates. One of the most common types of writing collaboration is in the form of in-class peer review/evaluation, which we will examine in the next chapter.

Digital Literacies

- Sample websites for digital writing, sharing, and web publishing tools:
  - Blogger (http://www.blogger.com).
  - Edmoto (http://edmoto.com).
  - Google Docs (http://docs.google.com).
  - Google Sites (http://sites.google.com).
  - Kidblog (http://kidblog.org).
  - Twitter (http://twitter.com).
  - Padlet (http://padlet.com).
  - Wiggio (http://wiggio.com).
  - Wikispaces (http://wikispaces.com).
  - Tumblr (http://tumblr.com).
- Sample digital presentation tools include the following:
  - Glogster (http://edu.glogster.com).
  - Prezi (http://prezi.com).
  - Slideshare (http://www.slideshare.net).
  - Wordle (http://www.wordle.net).
- Blurb: http://www.blurb.com/. A digital storytelling platform that allows the user to import photos, videos, and text, and share through social networking such as hashtags, Facebook, Twitter, Tumblr, or e-mail.

Digital Writing: Writing on the Screen

What role does writing play in a digital, interconnected world? Today's technologically advanced world requires the use of digital tools for composing, creating, sharing, and publishing ideas. What it means to write in the 21st century and beyond is shifting as a result of new technologies, globalization, and changes in college, career, and the workforce. Digital writing involves use of digital tools for creating and sharing writing, and different ways of interfacing with the world—it involves new ways thinking and communicating ideas and information that inherently require critical thinking skills. The National Writing Project (NWP) has created a *Technology Liaisons Network* (see http://www.nwp.org/cs/public/print/programs/tln), a forum for ideas on the role of technology in writing. In 2010, NWP also developed *Digital Is*, a website dedicated to learning more about digital writing and to exploring ways to write, publish, connect, and share with others.

Mobile devices, social media, and other Web 2.0 (i.e., a second generation of the World Wide Web with more features and functionality) applications have been integrated widely in classrooms across the nation. Many of our students are digital consumers, but school should also be the place where they learn how to be critical, reflective, and transformative digital citizens. Although today's students are comfortable with technology that does not mean that they have the skills necessary for them to be critical and thoughtful writers or consumers of media and technology. In order to prepare students to do that, teachers need to teach them how to read, write, search, and evaluate sources and information, and collaborate with others with a broad access to a diverse range of Web 2.0 tools.

Results from a 2013 survey of 2,462 advanced placement (AP) and NWP teachers surveyed by the Pew Research Center's Internet and American Life Project were presented in a NWP report titled, *The Impact of Digital Tools on Student Writing and How Writing is Taught in Schools* (Purcell, Buchanan, & Friedrich, 2013). Results showed that, overall, digital tools allow students to effectively organize and structure their writing assignment and they also facilitate their ability to consider and understand multiple perspectives on a topic. In addition, they reported that digital tools provide students with a broader audience for their work, result in more feedback from peers, and encourage greater student engagement with writing.

More specifically, results showed that (a) 78% of the teachers reported that digital tools such as the Internet, social media, and cell phones, encourage student creativity, personal expression, and give students a purpose to write; (b) 96% agree digital technologies make it possible for students to share their work with a broader and more diverse audience; and (c) 79% agree that these digital tools encourage greater collaboration among students. On the other hand, teachers were displeased by their students' use of "cell phone/texting" quick and careless abbreviated writing (46%), navigating issues of fair use and copyright in composition, and their difficulty with reading and comprehending long or complicated digital texts. Only 18% of teachers said that digital technologies make writing more difficult; 40% reported that they have students share their work on wikis, websites, and blogs; and 29% have students edit others' work using collaborative web-based tools such as GoogleDocs and Moodle.

The CCSS expect students in grades 6–12 to use digital tools to create, share, and publish their writing. Digital technologies require one to be a critical (and clear) thinker and a good communicator. In learning more about, and using, digital technologies we cannot forget that technology (no matter how effective or advanced) cannot replace quality writing instruction, or a strong literate community in the classroom. Technology facilitates learning but in itself it cannot instantly improve students' writing and learning.

Digital tools require a strong pedagogical framework. Posting a document online does not make it a better document; uploading a research report in GoogleDocs does not make it an effective report. On the other hand, using GoogleDocs for collaborative brainstorming, drafting, revising, and editing purposes can be an effective way to use technology for collaborative purposes. Students can use GoogleDocs for collaborative research reports and other writing, access documents from anywhere, share their work, co-edit, and receive more immediate feedback from the teacher. Students need authentic reasons for writing and outlets for publishing their work, but they also need to learn how to write well, manage deadlines, conduct research, collaborate with others, and select the right digital tool for the task.

Teaching students to take time, think things through, think critically, take time to organize thoughts in a logical and coherent manner, take time to write in clear and effective ways, proofread and revise one's work and produce multiple drafts, is a challenge. In the context of a digitally networked world, the CCSS, and the aforementioned report, "the question is not whether we should use technology to teach writing; instead, we must focus on the many ways that we must use technology to teach writing." (Hicks, 2013, p. 12). There is a need for teachers to teach students how to effectively and thoughtfully use digital tools, how to do research, and how to select, analyze, and evaluate information in today's digital world—students need to learn and also take time to craft writing with digital tools. Students need much help first with writing, and then with technology. They also need to discuss and provide feedback and guided practice on concepts of citation and plagiarism, fair use and copyright.

We know that literacy has changed in the digital age, but how are we catching up in schools? What does it mean to engage in digital literacy? Many schools across the US are still struggling with basic print resources let alone technological ones. In 2013, President Obama called for an overhaul of the federal E-rate program in an effort to improve schools' technological capabilities. President Obama's program called, *ConnectED*, is designed to connect all schools to the digital age through updated connectivity, improving the technological skills of all teachers, and building on private sector innovation.

College and career readiness also includes digital literacies. Although technology cannot "fix" our students and schools, it can certainly help teachers use their time differently and help make teacher-student writing interactions, conferences, feedback, and work more productive, motivating, and easier to progress monitor. Teachers can assess their students' writing needs, and provide them with tutorials that can help them improve their writing. Technology will never replace literacy, but it will continue to shape it. Digital technologies also provide students with opportunities to practice writing through participation and collaboration and share their work with a wider audience. They also encourage student creativity and personal expression, and make it possible for them to write, edit, and publish, anytime, anywhere. On the other hand, the easy access to information can become overwhelming for students who do not know how to evaluate sources to determine whether they are appropriate for the topic, valid, and reliable. Many students will just download pages upon pages of information on a topic, print them, and then highlight key information, instead of taking notes from sources.

Teachers should be very specific about their expectations concerning digital presentation tools, as at times students can combine slides and information from different presentations and create "hodge-podge" type presentations. To reduce unoriginal writing content in your classroom, I suggest using Turnitin, an Internet-based plagiarism-prevention service (http://turnitin.com)—check with your school to see if they have a license agreement.

What Is the Best Approach to Improve Students' Writing?

This is a tough question. Everyone agrees on the importance of writing skills for academic and professional success. We also find agreement on the role of critical thinking on students' ability to express their thoughts in coherent, well-crafted sentences, paragraphs, and essays. Teachers and students have various misconceptions about writing. Writing is not independent of content, purpose, and audience, and it is not just about syntax and mechanics. In my view, the answer to this question is not one-sided: Students need to learn about the mechanical aspects of writing, but they also need to keep in mind the dialogues between the author and the reader. They also need "big doses" of all types of writing—argumentative, explanatory/informational, and narrative on discipline-specific content.

Think of every writing assignment you use in your class as a data point; analyze it, and use that information to plan for future writing instruction and support. Do not expect your students to catch up with writing as they move from grade to grade or class to class—writing is not "caught," it needs to be taught! Students do not automatically know how to write well, and especially, how to write in ways that are important to your discipline. Create a learning environment in your classroom that communicates the message to students about writing being a way to study, learn, express oneself, construct, and communicate new knowledge. Teach your students about the rules of good writing, provide them with many opportunities to write and receive feedback from you and from their peers, and make critical thinking, discipline-specific accountable talk, evidence-based discussions, peer editing, and writing part of your classroom routines. Collaborate with your peers to discuss your department's focus on writing, examine student writing samples, analyze student data, share resources, and plan for writing instruction.

Students need to see you, the classroom teacher, read and write with them. They also need you to model your thinking, your struggles, and your writing. For students to become college and career ready in writing, there needs to be a paradigm shift in content area teachers' beliefs and practices about writing. Writing cannot be something we do when we have time. Writing cannot continue to be a mechanical act. Students will need to write formal writing assignments, but they also need to write daily for different purposes, audiences, and in different ways (e.g., in journals, exit slips, short responses, research papers, multimedia assignments, opinion pieces, etc.). In addition, students need to write in every content area course—for example, they need to write out mathematical problems or proofs, write up lab reports, write music or lyrics, plays, and computer games.

Writing should not be something teachers make students do. Students should learn about the value of practical writing and the ways writing will help them in postsecondary college and career experiences, and in civil life, in general. I believe that students enjoy writing—look at how they are expressing themselves through social media. Writing is thinking—let's provide our students with opportunities to write formally and informally and to practice expressing themselves and their ideas in clear, critical, analytical, reflective, and informative ways.

Summary

- College, career, and workforce readiness require students to have good writing skills. Writing in the disciplines requires students to learn how to inquire, read, think, speak, and write in ways that are appropriate for each discipline.
- The CCSS for writing emphasize three types of writing (i.e., argument, informative/explanatory, and narrative) and pay particular attention to argument writing. Writing effective arguments about claims and counter-claims, that are supported by valid and sufficient evidence, is a must for college and career readiness. Students are expected to develop and use different types of claims and collect, evaluate, and present quality evidence to support their claims.

- Research on effective writing instruction shows that students need to write about the texts they read, write routinely in each content area, receive explicit instruction in writing, receive feedback from teacher and peers, have opportunities to revise their writing, and use technology and digital tools for writing, sharing, and publishing purposes.

Differentiating Instruction

- Demonstrate how reading and writing are connected, and use a variety of strategies to attract students' attention to differences in style and genre. Involve English language learners (ELLs) in writing frequently and explain to them how writing is a tool for thinking, communicating, sharing, and learning. Give students opportunities to write for different purposes, build their vocabulary, and allow them to write in both languages.
- Expose ELLs and struggling writers to extensive modeling. Explicitly demonstrate the writing process and encourage revision and editing. Model topic selection that is meaningful, interesting, and relevant. Provide step-by-step instruction, which includes academic vocabulary, organization of ideas, and writing. Teach grammar in the context of the actual writing, present mini-lessons, and provide guided writing practice, and much feedback.
- Some students may have dysgraphia (a writing disability). Some students freeze when it comes to writing due to having difficulty encoding a word, a thought, accurate language, connected thoughts, and accurate composition. They require a lot of scaffolding, encouragement, and feedback. Many students who are language impaired and/or have limited experiences, may not have the range of vocabulary, and/or language-expressive skills required in your discipline.
- Create a culture of collaboration. Encourage collaboration throughout the writing process and encourage peer sharing and editing. Use learning logs, journals, and technology to support ELLs' writing.

Reflect and Apply

1. Reflect on what you have learned from this chapter. What types of writing have you produced so far (e.g., lab report, essay, research paper, poem, etc.)? What type of writing do you enjoy the most? What aspects of your writing would you like to improve? Discuss your answers with your peers, and provide evidence to support your conclusions.
2. Tap into what you learned about writing and writing instruction from this chapter to offer some suggestions to Ms. Dunham (see Classroom Life vignette). Use technology, the Internet, or a digital tool to share your ideas with a small group of peers.
3. The message of writing in the disciplines is that writing and content learning need to take place in tandem. Using information from this chapter, find three pieces of evidence from the chapter that support this thesis and discuss them in a small group.

Extending Learning

1. Visit a content area classroom for at least a week. Use a learning log to record your observations about the role of writing in that classroom. Categorize your observations using the following categories: (a) time spent writing; (b) types of writing genres;

(c) writing to learn strategies; (d) writing instruction (modeling, guided practice, feedback); (e) collaboration; (f) technology use; (g) formative assessment. Organize your findings and write a report. Include suggestions to improve writing in that class and evidence to support your suggestions from course readings. Last, share your suggestions with the your class or colleagues.

2. Think about your own discipline, select a type of writing you would like to introduce or strengthen in the classroom, and write a lesson plan. Make sure that you include pertinent lesson plan information such as: grade level, subject area, objective, related CCSS, procedures, materials, and related activities. Share the first draft of your lesson plan with a content area teacher, receive feedback, revise, and present your planned lesson to the class.

3. Conduct research on digital writing tools and uses of technology to develop writing in grades 6–12. Use a research paper format to share your research with your class or your colleagues.

References

American College Testing (ACT). (2005). *College readiness standards.* Iowa City, IA. Retrieved from http://www.act.org

Andriessen, J. (2006). Arguing to learn. In K. Sawyer (Ed.). *The Cambridge handbook of the learning sciences* (pp. 443–459). New York, NY: Cambridge University Press.

Applebee, A., & Langer, J. (2006). *The state of writing instruction: What existing data tell us.* Albany, NY: Center on English Learning and Achievement.

Biancarosa, G., & Snow, C. (2006). *Reading next—A vision for action and research in middle and high school literacy: A report to Carnegie Corporation of New York.* Washington, DC: Alliance for Excellent Education. Retrieved from http://www.all4ed.org/files/ReadingNext.pdf

Chambliss, M. J., & Murphy, P. K. (2002). Fourth and fifth graders representing the argument structure in written texts. *Discourse Processes, 34*(1), 91–115.

Chen, C. (2006). Why does my English sound so Chinese? *Proceedings of the CATESOL state conference.* Retrieved from http://www.catesol.org/06Chen.pdf

Cowan, G., & Cowan, E. (1980). *Writing.* New York, NY: Wiley.

Cunningham, J. (1982). Generating interactions between schemata and text. In J. A. Niles & L. A. Harris (Eds), *New inquiries in reading research and instruction* (pp. 42–47). Washington, DC: National Reading Conference.

Cunningham, P. M. & Allington, R. L. (2011). *Classrooms that work: They can all read and write* (5th ed.) Boston, MA: Allyn & Bacon/Pearson.

Delpit, L. D. (1995). *Other people's children.* New York, NY: New Press.

Dietiker, L., Kysh, J., Sallee, T., & Hoey, B. (2007). *Geometry connections* (3.1 Version). Sacramento, CA: CPM Educational Program.

Ellison, J. (2000). *Finding Forrester: A novel.* New York, NY: Newmarket Press.

Frey, N., Fisher, D., & Hernandez, T. (2003). What's the gist? Summary writing for struggling adolescent writers. *Voices from the Middle, 11*(2), 43–49.

Gallagher, K. (2006). *Teaching adolescent writers.* Portland, ME: Stenhouse.

Gee, J. (1996). *Social linguistics and literacies: Race, writing, and difference.* London, UK: Taylor & Francis.

Goldstein, A., & Carr, P. (1996). *Can students benefit from process writing?* Washington, DC: US Department of Education Office of Educational Research and Improvement.

Graff, G. (2003). *Clueless in academe: How schooling obscures the life of the mind.* New Haven, CT: Yale University Press.

Graham, S. & Hebert, M. (2010). Writing to read: A meta-analysis of the impact of writing and writing instruction on reading. *Harvard Educational Review, 81*(4), Winter.

Graham, S. & Perin, D. (2007a). *Writing next: Effective strategies to improve writing of adolescents in middle and high schools* (Carnegie Corporation Report). Washington, DC: Alliance for Excellent Education. Retrieved from http://www.all4ed.org/publications/WritingNext/WritingNext.pdf

Graham, S. & Perin, D. (2007b). What we know, what we still need to know: Teaching adolescents to write. *Scientific Studies in Reading, 11*, 313–336.

Graves, D. (1983). *Writing: Teachers and children at work*. Portsmouth, NH: Heinemann.

Graves, D. (2003). *Writing: Teachers and children at work* (20th Anniversary edition). Portsmouth, NH: Heinemann.

Hatim, B. (1997) *Communication across cultures. Translation theory and contrastive text linguistics*. Exeter, UK: University of Exeter Press.

Hart, B., & Risley, R. T. (1995). *Meaningful differences in the everyday experience of young American children*. Baltimore, MD: Paul H. Brookes.

Heath, S. B. (1983). *Ways with words: Language, life, and work in communities and classrooms*. New York, NY: Cambridge University Press.

Hicks, T. (2013). *Crafting digital writing: Composing texts across media and genres*. Portsmouth, NH: Heinemann.

Hjortshoj, K. (2009). *The transition to college writing* (2nd ed.). New York, NY: Bedford/St. Martin's.

Hoffman, J. (1992). Critical reading/thinking across the curriculum: Using I-charts to support learning. *Language Arts, 69*(2), 121–127.

Holston, V., & Santa, C. (1985). A method of writing across the curriculum that works. *Journal of Reading, 28*, 456–457.

Howard, J. (1983). *Writing to learn*. Washington, DC: Council for Basic Education.

Kiuhara, S., Graham, S., & Hawken, L. (2009). Teaching writing to national students: A national survey. *Journal of Educational Psychology, 101*, 136–160.

Knobel, M., & Lankshear, C. (2008). *Digital literacies: Concepts, policies, and practices*. New York, NY: Peter Lang.

Kress, G. (2003). *Literacy in the new media age*. London & New York: Routledge.

Langer, J. (2000a). Beating the odds: *Teaching middle and high school students to read and write well* Retrieved from http://www.albany.edu/cela/reports/langer/langerbeating12014.pdf

Langer, J. (2000b). *Teaching middle and high school students to read and write well: Six features of effective instruction*. Albany, NY: National Research Center on English Learning and Achievement. Retrieved from http://www.albany.edu/cela/publication/brochure/guidelines.pdf

Llewellyn, D. (2013). *Teaching high school science through inquiry and argumentation* (2nd ed.). Thousand Oaks, CA: Corwin.

Macrorie, K. (1998). *The I-search paper: Revised edition of searching writing*. Portsmouth, NH: Heinemann-Boynton/Cook.

McLaughlin, M. (2010). *Content area reading: Teaching and learning in an age of multiple literacies*. Boston, MA: Allyn & Bacon/Pearson.

National Commission on Writing. (2004). *Writing: A ticket to work . . . or a ticket out: A survey of business leaders*. New York, NY: College Board. Retrieved from http://www.collegeboard.com/prod_downloads/writingcom/writing-ticket-to-work.pdf

National Commission on Writing. (2006). Writing and school reform. New York, NY: College Board. Retrieved from http://www.collegeboard.com

National Council of Teachers of English. (2013). *Framework for 21st century curriculum and assessment*. Retrieved from: http://www.ncte.org/library/NCTEFiles/Resources/Positions/Framework_21stCent_Curr_Assessment.pdf

National Governors Association Center (NGAC) for Best Practices, Council of Chief State School Officers. (2010). *Common Core State Standards*. National Governors Association Center for Best Practices, Council of Chief State School Officers. Retrieved from http://corestandards.org

National Governors Association Center (NGAC) for Best Practices, Council of Chief State School Officers. (2010). *Common Core State Standards Common Core State Standards for English language arts & literacy in history/social studies, science, and technical subjects: Appendix A*. National Governors Association Center for Best Practices, Council of Chief State School Officers. Retrieved from http://corestandards.org

Nichols, J. N. (1980). Using paragraph frames to help remedial high school students with writing assignments. *Journal of Reading, 24*, 228–231.

Pritchard, R. J., & Honeycutt, R. L. (2006). The process approach to writing instruction: Examining its effectiveness. In C. A. MacArthur, S. Graham, & J. Fitzgerlad (Eds), *Handbook of writing research* (pp. 275–290). New York, NY: Guilford.

Purcell, K., Buchanan, J., & Freidrich, L. (2013). *The impact of digital tools on student writing and how writing is taught in schools.* Washington, DC: Pew Research Center's Internet & American Life Project. Retrieved from http://pewinternet.org/~/media//Files/Reports/2013/PIP_NWP%20Writing%20 and%20Tech.pdf

Serafini, F. (2011). Expanding perspectives for comprehending visual images in multimodal texts. *Journal of Adolescent and Adult Literacy, 54*(5), 342–350.

Shanahan, T. (2004). Overcoming the dominance of communication: Writing to think and to learn. In T. L. Jetton & J. A. Dole (Eds), *Adolescent literacy research and practice* (pp. 59–74). New York, NY: Guilford.

Shanahan, T. (2006). Relations among oral language, reading, and writing development. In C.A. MacArthur, S. Graham, & J. Fitzgerald (Eds), *Handbook of writing research* (pp. 171–186). New York, NY: Guilford.

Strayer, B., & Strayer, T. (2007). *Strategies for differentiating in the content areas.* New York, NY: Scholastic.

Tierney, R. J., & Pearson, P. D. (1983). Toward a composing model of reading. *Language Arts, 60*(5), 568–580.

Tierney, R. J., & Shanahan, T. (1991). *Research on reading-writing relationships: Interactions, transactions, and outcomes.* In P. E. Pearson, M. Barr, & P. B. Mosenthal (Eds). *Handbook of reading research Volume II* (pp. 246–280). New York, NY: Longman.

Tompkins, G. E. (2010). *Literacy in the middle grades.* (2nd ed.) Boston, MA: Allyn & Bacon/Pearson.

Toumlin, S. (1958). *The pattern of an argument: Data and warrants.* New York, NY: Cambridge University Press.

Vaughn, J., & Estes, T. (1986). *Reading and reasoning beyond the primary grades.* Boston, MA: Allyn & Bacon.

Vygotsky, L. S. (1978). *Mind and society.* Cambridge, MA: Harvard University Press.

Worden, D. L. (2009). Finding process in product: Prewrting and revision in timed essay responses. *Assessing Writing, 14,* 157–177.

Wormelli, R. (2005). *Summarization in any subject: 50 techniques to improve student learning.* Alexandria, VA: Association of Supervision and Curriculum Development.

Wu, S.-Y., & Rubin, D. L. (2000). Evaluating the impact of collectivism and individualism on argumentative writing by Chinese and North American college students. *Research in the Teaching of English, 3,* 148–178.

ten

Assessing Student Learning in the Disciplines

If assessment is to be a positive force in education, it must be implemented properly. It cannot be used to merely sort students or criticize education. Its goals must be to improve education. Rather than 'teach to the test,' we must 'test what we teach.'
–McLean, J. E. & Lockwood R. E.

Chapter Highlights

- Assessment of student learning plays an important role in informing and improving student learning and instruction, and in preparing students for college and career readiness.
- Standardized assessment provides a general picture of a student's performance, and has been used for accountability, funding, and comparison purposes. Authentic Assessment captures, in detailed ways, student content knowledge, skills and processes, in naturalistic settings and contexts.
- The No Child Left Behind Act of 2001 brought about sweeping assessment and curricular changes. Accountability implications of the policy have resulted in narrowing the curriculum.
- The Partnership for Assessment of Readiness for Colleges and Careers (PARCC), and the Smarter Balanced Assessment Consortium (SBAC) are the two federally funded assessment consortiums that are aligned with the Common Core State Standards (CCSS).
- Assessment should be an ongoing, flexible, and collaborative process that uses multiple types of information to gauge student learning and progress.
- Implementation of the CCSS and the new generation assessment systems will require more effective systems of accountability, engaging, relevant, and rigorous curricula and materials, and focused teacher preparation and ongoing professional development.

Classroom Life

One of the challenges that content area teachers face in regards to assessment is how quickly what is being assessed is changing. Many teachers in the content areas continue to assess students with tests that strictly test their ability to recall facts in regards to a topic. As we move deeper into the Common Core era, the transition to close reading and critically thinking about the text and questions will be an obstacle that is sure to impact their teaching. Students must be taught to actively engage with the text and read and reread text in order to extract the meaning of text. Students must also be able to support their answers with text-based evidence. Our current teaching methodologies consist of presenting students with a summarized version of the content. Students are rarely in the text attempting to make connections and extrapolating the essence of what they are reading. Content area teachers must be supported as this instructional shift occurs. Creating a school culture that focuses on literacy in all aspects of instruction and by providing professional development on the key concepts associated with disciplinary literacy can actualize this.

Another obstacle that teachers in the content areas face in regards to assessment is taking the time to analyze the data provided from the various assessments. In our county, students are assessed each quarter by a district created assessment as well as by the end of course exams provided by the state. Our district also requires teachers to administer a progress monitor test three times a year. Much of the work I have done with teachers in their professional learning communities consists of supporting them as they make their way through an overwhelming amount of data. In most cases, the conversations tend to stray away from determining trends. Teachers are inundated with data but they do not feel they have the time to do anything about it. They often discuss the fact that they have "so much to cover" and cannot spend the time reteaching concepts that students have not mastered. As a result, many students continue to superficially navigate through many of their content area classes. This is certainly a perspective that will be difficult to change.

In our current culture of assessment, students are required to test on all standards associated with the discipline. Teachers are "under pressure" to cover all material regardless of mastery. As a first step to change, leadership at the school and district levels must communicate to subject area departments that simply "covering the material" is not the goal. District assessments should be written to correlate with the goals of Common Core State Standards. A classroom environment that focuses on high expectations, inquiry, critical thinking, and accountable talk should be encouraged and expected in each content area classroom. *(Ms. Analexis Kennedy, Secondary Reading Specialist, Seminole County Public Schools, Florida).*

Assessment and Instruction

Assessment is an integral part of teaching and learning. Our beliefs about teaching and learning will also affect our assessment practices. Assessment refers to the process of collecting, analyzing, and interpreting information from multiple sources of information for measuring student achievement, planning for instruction, improving student performance, motivating students, evaluating student work and program effectiveness, providing additional services and instruction to students, and informing policy and accountability (Tucker & Stronge, 2005). In education, the phrase "assessment should drive instruction" implies that assessment and instruction are inseparable. Assessment, not just grading, is "at the heart of instruction." No one assessment can provide all the necessary information for teaching and learning. When tests are developed and used appropriately, they provide objective and useful information about student performance. Assessment also informs policy.

Applying Discipline-Specific Literacies

- Content area teachers should assess students' discipline-specific declarative knowledge, procedural knowledge, and attitudes and habits of mind.
- Effective assessment in the disciplines is based on authentic tasks and meaningful learning processes and contexts. Effective assessment in the disciplines is also multi-dimensional, and uses a wide range of tools and methods.
- Effective assessment in the disciplines is based on criteria that students know, understand, and are appealing to their strengths and goals. Effective assessment is a collaborative process that involves the students, and is ongoing and continuous.

Types of Assessment

Different types of assessment yield different kinds of information. Summative assessment is used to assess what students have learned at the end of a specified time period (e.g., mid-term and final exams, state testing, exit test) and for the purposes of establishing a student's academic standing relative to some established criterion (Dunn & Mulvenon, 2009). Summative assessment is designed to assess accountability, is tied to annual yearly progress (AYP), and student, teacher, and school evaluation, and uses norm-referenced/standardized tests.

Assessment is fraught with controversies. Much criticism centers on issues of bias. Assessment bias refers to one or more items on a test that unfairly penalize students because of students' race/ethnicity/culture, gender, socioeconomic status, or religion. Since we have been living in an era of high accountability since the No Child Left Behind (NCLB) policies of early 2000, high school graduation, gifted and remedial education placement, grade promotion, college admission, and employment opportunities rely extensively on test results. Issues of unfairness/offensiveness and penalization are key assessment issues and affect how students perform in tests (Carlson, 2004; Popham, 2012). Assessment bias diminishes the accuracy of test-based interpretations and teacher-made inferences about students. Teachers need to be knowledgeable about its presence in standardized and teacher-made tests, consider it when making interpretations about student performance, and find ways to eliminate it. In addition, all teachers need to become knowledgeable about types of assessments, learn how to read and interpret data from different assessments, and participate in collaborative inquiry with peers about data and implications for improved instruction.

Formative Assessment and the Common Core State Standards

Formative assessment is a process teachers use as part of the regular instruction, and is used during instruction to provide feedback to students about their progress toward meeting a goal; it makes ongoing instructional adjustments to improve student learning. Teachers administer formative assessments when students are learning new information, or skills. Formative assessment is a powerful instructional tool; it provides teachers with information about how students are meeting a learning goal. In addition, it allows students to self-monitor their progress. Students benefit when teachers use formative assessment to provide them with specific and timely feedback on their performance, understanding, and learning (Wininger, 2005). Formative assessments are formal or informal, closely connected to the content students are learning, teacher-made, spontaneous or planned, provide teachers with critical information about student learning and misconceptions, require careful and ongoing observation and reflection, and support instructional decision-making.

Black and Wiliam (1998) published the results of a meta-analysis of over 250 research studies on classroom assessment and found strong evidence that formative assessment plays a major role in student achievement. They also reported that for assessment to be effective it needs to follow the following principles:

- Teachers need to provide effective feedback to students about their performance.
- Students need to be actively involved in their own learning.
- Teachers need to use assessment data to make instructional adjustments.
- Teachers need to consider how assessment can impact student motivation, self-esteem, and in turn, learning.
- Teachers need to engage students in self-assessment and help them to understand how to improve.

Why should you learn about formative assessment? Because it will provide you with immediate and valuable information about what your students are mastering prior, during, and after your instruction. Such information will help you to diagnose student needs, plan, make adjustments and implement interventions, and also assess the effectiveness of your interventions on student learning. Short formative assessments that are followed by a rubric and teacher feedback that shows students what students can do, and what they need to do to achieve a targeted learning, or curricular goal are very useful for teachers and students. See the following sample formative assessments:

- Ask students to write a postcard from one historical figure (e.g., Winston Churchill) to another historical (e.g., Joseph Stalin) figure discussing a historical event (e.g., World War II).
- Ask students to compare and contrast between the protagonist (Jean Louise, "Scout" Finch) and the antagonist (Robert E. Lee, "Bob" Ewell) in *To Kill a Mockingbird* by Harper Lee (1960).
- What are linear equations, and how can we use them?
- A pharmaceutical company claims that research supports that a certain brand of nose spray provides consumers with easy breathing for 12 hours. Describe an investigation that could be used to determine if this claim is valid. In your answer, describe the following:
  - ○ The treatment the experimental group should receive.
  - ○ The treatment the control group should receive.
  - ○ The data to be collected.
  - ○ When data will be collected.
  - ○ How data analysis could support the null hypothesis.
- Observe (and keep anecdotal notes about) students discussing, analyzing, arguing for or against a topic, or explaining their steps, decisions, or opinions about a topic.
- Ask questions that require students to explain their thinking, and provide evidence from text(s) to support it.

- Keep records of student performance, and use them in teacher-student conferences to review student goals, provide feedback, and offer suggestions on how the student can work toward mastering their goal.

Rubrics can provide information to both the teacher and the students about their level of mastery of a topic—e.g., inadequate, adequate, proficient, expert. They provide information about success criteria and promote student responsibility over their own learning. For example, students will need to know the trajectory along which they are expected to progress—what does it mean to move over time from "proficient" to "expert" understanding? And what will the student need to do to progress? What sub-concepts, or sub-skills, constitute progress?

Teacher feedback can move student learning forward. Make sure that you provide students with specific, ongoing, and informative feedback in the learning process. Feedback that is critical (e.g., "Your work is awful; what have you been doing all this time?"), comparative (e.g., "Everybody else is getting this concept; you need to work harder to catch up.") vague feedback (e.g., "Good work."), draws attention to students instead of the task (e.g., "You are a smart student."), or feedback that reflects a poorly defined learning goal (e.g., "Write three more paragraphs.") can have negative impact on student learning. On the other hand, students will benefit from constructive, specific, targeted, judicious, and timely feedback such as:

- "The answer to this problem is. . . . Can you find a way to work it out?"
- "You have used two different approaches to solve the problem; could you talk a bit more about the advantages and disadvantages of each method?"
- "You understood this problem well; can you make a more advanced problem in your own words?"
- "You seem to confuse meiosis with mitosis. Talk to your "shoulder partner" about the difference between these two.

Formative assessment is about teaching, and not about testing. Teachers can implement a variety of formative assessment strategies to elicit student thinking about a topic during class, such as questioning, discussions, conferences, brainstorming, multiple choice questions, and teacher observations. I hope that you will continue to learn more about it, implement it in your instruction, and collaborate with other teachers at your school to develop discipline-specific formative assessments and rubrics you can use as a department, to analyze results, and plan for instruction.

International Assessments

The Program for International Student Assessment (PISA) is an international assessment that is coordinated by the Organization for Economic Cooperation and Development (OECD), an intergovernmental organization of industrialized countries, and is conducted in the United States by the National Center for Education Statistics (NCES). OECD intends to evaluate education systems worldwide by testing the skills and knowledge of 15-year-old students in reading, mathematics and science literacy. The PISA tests are not directly linked to school curricula. The tests are designed to assess broad skills such as analyzing texts and tables, understanding what authors are saying, communicating ideas clearly, and whether students can apply their knowledge to real-life situations and be equipped to fully participate in society. The PISA surveys and background questionnaires allow students to provide information about themselves, their home life, and their attitudes about school and learning.

PISA data informs and shapes policy-making. PISA was first administered in 2000 and is conducted every three years. In 2000, the focus of the assessment was reading, in 2003 mathematics and problem solving, in 2006 science, in 2009 reading again, and in 2012 mathematics.

The 2012 assessment included an optional computer-based assessment of mathematics and reading involving 30 countries as well as an optional area of financial literacy, which 19 countries participated in (see www.oecd.org).

PISA ranks participants according to their performance in reading, mathematics and science, as well as problem solving in PISA 2003. PISA provides a score for each subject area, and ranks countries by their mean score in each area.

Why should you know about the PISA examination and the implications of its results for teaching and learning? Although there are a number of answers to this question, in my view all teachers need to know that the PISA results also "tell" us the following: a) excellent teacher training is vital to student success; b) parents value a safe school environment more than high academic achievement; and c) countries that give school systems more power over selection of materials and assessments, boost student performance. Learn about, and prepare your students for, all types of assessments your students will encounter in grades 6–12, develop effective classroom-based assessments, create a rigorous, safe, and collaborative learning environment, continue to grow and learn professionally, collaborate with other teachers on assessments, and become involved in material selection and curriculum planning.

National Assessments

The National Assessment of Educational Progress (NAEP) is the largest nationally representative, state-comparable assessment of what America's students know and can do in various subject areas. Assessments are conducted periodically in mathematics, reading, science, writing, the arts, civics, economics, geography, US history, and, beginning in 2014, in Technology and Engineering Literacy (TEL).

NAEP, often referred to as The Nation's Report Card, was established by Congress in 1969 and is administered by the National Center for Education Studies (NCES), a division of the US Department of Education. NAEP assessments are administered uniformly using the same sets of test booklets across the nation and NAEP results serve as a common metric for all states and selected urban districts. NAEP provides results on subject-matter achievement, instructional experiences, and school environment for populations of students (e.g., all eighth-graders) and groups within those populations (e.g., male students, African-American students).

NAEP does not provide scores for individual students, or schools, although NAEP can report results by selected large state urban districts. NAEP results are based on representative samples of students at Grades 4, 8, and 12 for the main assessments, or samples of students at ages 9, 13, or 17 years for the long-term trend assessments (LTT). These grades and ages were chosen because they represent critical junctures in academic achievement. Each subject is assessed at Grades 4, 8, and 12—although not all grades are assessed each time with scores ranging from zero to 500. Mathematics, reading, science, and writing (usually for Grades 4 and 8) are also reported at the state level. LTT assessments are given every four years.

The 2013 NAEP Mathematics and Reading assessment results for Grades 4 and 8 showed that fourth- and eighth-grade (376,000 and 341,000 tested respectively) students are making incremental progress (one or two points since 2011) in mathematics and reading, but are still in need of much progress. The average reading scores for eighth-graders rose to 268 after plateauing for about a decade. In math, eighth-graders scored an average of 285 (see http://nces.ed.gov/pubsearch/pubsinfo.asp?pubid=2014451).

How should you use NAEP results? View them as a national snapshot of how students are doing, examine what the scores mean in terms of what students know and are able to do in reading and mathematics, and compare it with what they need to learn and be able to do to improve. The NAEP data won't answer your "why"—collaborate with other educators and discuss the implications of this data for your instruction.

Standardized Tests

A standardized, formal, or statewide test is a test that is administered and scored in a "standard" manner, usually by the publisher, the state, or by using the publisher's software package. Standardized tests provide a general picture about a student's performance. They do not provide information about individual student's strengths, learning styles, skills and strategies the student is using, the amount of information the student knows, or prescribe how to improve instruction. Their main purpose is to determine how well school districts, and/or particular grade levels, are meeting state/district-wide standards and benchmarks.

Types of standardized assessments include achievement tests, diagnostic tests (used to identify learning difficulties, especially in reading and writing), and intelligence tests (used to indicate a student's potential for learning) (see Table 10.1). Standardized tests are norm-referenced—the scores of others are called norms. They provide a picture about how a student is doing compared with a normative group, or group of students the publishers of the test used to determine the statistical validity of the test. Such data is especially useful to school administrators for making decisions about certain subject areas, student placement, and the school.

All standardized scores are based on the Normal Curve, a bell-shaped distribution with scores distributed symmetrically around an average score called, the mean. The greatest number of scores (68%) occurs within one standard deviation of the mean. The standard deviation indicates how much variation is in a group of scores. The most commonly used scores in standardized testing are the raw score (the total number of correct items on a test), the stanine (score converted to a standard 9-point scale –1 being the lowest and 9 the highest—with a mean of 5 and a standard deviation of 2), and the percentile rank (the percent of scores equal to and lower than a certain score). The average stanine is a score of 5; stanine scores of 1, 2, or 3 are considered below average and 7, 8 and 9 are well above average.

Advantages of standardized tests are that they are valid (they measure what they claim to measure), and reliable (they ensure a student's scores will be consistent), and they provide quantifiable information that can be used for placement purposes and accountability purposes. In addition, student standardized test scores allow school districts to compare the performance of their students with those of other students across the nation.

On the other hand, standardized testing has been heavily criticized because it fails to adequately inform instruction and carries cultural and linguistic biases. For such testing to be used effectively, we need to first consider its limitations, and think about them when making interpretations of student data. Standardized scores reflect behavior or ability that has been measured during a *single point of time* and are influenced by non-cognitive behaviors such as anxiety, fatigue, attention, etc. Second, in terms of test administration, there is little room to make accommodations for students with disabilities and other individual needs. Third, test floors, ceiling effect (the upper level of ability a test can effectively measure), and standard error of measurement should also be considered when examining scores. Test floors can overestimate a less competent student's ability whereas the ceiling effect may underestimate a more competent student's performance. Last, standardized testing has influenced the curriculum by focusing on skill/behavior versus process development and by narrowing the curriculum/ "teaching to the test."

TABLE 10.1. Examples of Common Standardized Tests

Achievement Tests	Age/Grade Levels	What It Measures
California Achievement Tests (CAT)	K-12th grade	Visual and sound recognition, vocabulary, comprehension, language mechanics, language expression, math computation, and math concept and applications
Iowa Test of Basic Skills (ITBS)	K-8th grade	Vocabulary, word analysis, reading comprehension, spelling, capitalization, punctuation, usage and expression, listening, language, mathematics, math concepts and estimation, math problem solving and data interpretation, math computation, social studies, maps, diagrams, science and reference materials and sources of information
Metropolitan Achievement Test (MAT)	K-8th grade	Vocabulary, comprehension, mechanics, writing, spelling
Stanford Achievement Test (SAT)	K-High school	Reading, comprehension, listening comprehension, language, spelling, math, problem-solving, science, social studies
Wechsler Individual Achievement Test (WIAT-II)	Ages 4–85	Reading, math, writing, oral language
Diagnostic Tests	**Age/Grade Level**	**What It Measures**
Stanford Diagnostic Test	Ages 4–15 (reading) Ages 7–13 (math)	Diagnostic Reading Test: Phonemic awareness, phonics, fluency, vocabulary, comprehension Diagnostic Mathematics Test: Mathematics skills, concepts, and problem-solving
Intelligence Tests	**Age/Grade Level**	**What It Measures**
Slosson Intelligence Test	Ages 4–65	Verbal and cognitive ability, information, comprehension, quantitative, similarities and differences, vocabulary, and auditory memory
Stanford-Binet Intelligence Scales	Ages 2-adult	Comprehension, reasoning, verbal reasoning, abstract/visual reasoning, quantitative reasoning, and short-term memory
Woodcock-Johnson Tests of Cognitive Abilities	Ages 2–90	Comprehension-knowledge, long-term retrieval, visual-spatial thinking, auditory processing, fluid reasoning, processing speed, short-term memory, quantitative knowledge, reading, and writing

How to Prepare Students for Standardized Tests

Teachers of middle and high school level students can play an important role in preparing students for standardized tests. Teachers can prepare students for high-stakes tests without sacrificing their instruction. Teachers should make sure that their instruction is aligned with the state's curriculum standards, set goals and use informal assessment to monitor students' progress, engage students in authentic learning, and provide them with quality instruction. Here are some test-preparation (test-prep) suggestions:

- Talk about tests with students, explain the tests' purpose and how the results will be used, and talk about the role tests play in them reaching their goals and aspirations, without making them anxious. Be open and positive and encourage them to take the test seriously. Guide them in how to reduce testing anxiety. Emphasize the importance of adequate rest, healthy eating, and physical preparations for test taking.
- Familiarize students with the language, format, and structure of standardized tests.
- Advise students (and model as needed) to read test directions carefully, and understand what the question is asking them to do. Students should anticipate the answer before they look through all of the choices. Next, they should read all answer choices before choosing the correct answer.
- Students should eliminate answers that don't make sense, answer easier questions first, circle questions they don't know and return to them later, and guess intelligently by looking for opposite answers.
- In terms of vocabulary, direct students to use context clues, or analyze the meaning of unknown words to determine the meaning of unfamiliar words.
- Students should look for key words such as, "first," "then," "next," "finally," and "after" when sequencing events. If asked about cause and effect, they should look for words such as, "since," "because," "as a result of," and "therefore."
- For math and science problems, students can use scratch paper and should double-check before they copy the problem.
- Instruct students to pace themselves and leave time for review at the end of a test. They should answer all questions on the test and change their answers only when they are unsure of their original answer. Counsel them to avoid second-guessing themselves.

Authentic Assessment

In standardized assessment, the test plays the key role. On the other hand, in authentic assessment, the teacher plays the major role. The teacher has first-hand knowledge of the students, of curricula, of classroom events, and of students' progress over time. The teacher interacts with, and observes students on a daily basis. She or he is involved in the process of ongoing assessment of student progress and learning. Authentic assessment, often called alternative, performance, or informal refers to evaluation of student content knowledge, skills and processes that take place in naturalistic settings and situations, within the content area classroom. For example, authentic assessment tasks ask students to read real texts, write for authentic purposes, and participate in authentic problem-solving and activities (e.g., discuss a book they have read, write a letter, keep a journal, revise a piece of writing, etc.) (Wiggins, 1993, 1998).

Authentic assessments can be formal or informal. Formal assessment is a systematic approach through which teachers assess the overall growth of a student in areas like understanding, problem-solving skills, social skills, teamwork, etc. An end of unit or theme test given to all students is a type of formal authentic assessment. A norm-referenced test that is given once a year might also be considered a type of formal authentic assessment. Special classroom activities, individual, or group projects, oral presentations, experiments, student-teacher conferences, or a verbal critique are examples of informal authentic assessment. At other times, informal assessment might include the teacher stopping by a small group of students and listening in to their discussion of a book, procedure, or issue.

Performance assessment directly evaluates a skill, or skills, a student has acquired. It involves the student in constructing different types of products for diverse audiences, in ways people use them in real-world situations. It measures what students can do with what they know, instead of how much they know—it examines the process that leads to a product. Some skills like dancing or typing can be assessed via direct observation. Students are given real-world tasks to problem-solve—e.g., drawing, dancing, speaking, debating, recording, making a model, etc.

Informal tests usually provide very valuable information to teachers because they are designed to assess students' strengths and weaknesses in a number of areas. Because the teacher designs informal tests, they provide a closer match between what is taught and what is assessed in the classroom. The results can provide the teacher and student with valuable instructional and curricular feedback that allow the teacher to make necessary instructional adjustments, accommodations, or modifications to improve student learning.

Informal assessment is an ongoing, continuous process. Informal assessment scores can be easily read and interpreted as they usually come in the form of percentage correct, scores on a rubric, number of questions answered correctly, or items checked off on a checklist. Examples of authentic, or informal assessments include: teacher-made tests, projects, student journals, inquiry projects, hands-on-activities, demonstrations, presentations, observation forms and notes, anecdotal records, interviews, portfolios (paper and electronic portfolios), and teacher-student conference forms, rubrics, etc.

Think Like an Expert

- Knowledge of genres, purpose, audience and task, as well as the ability to clearly communicate ideas in writing, are major foci of literary experts. (English Language Arts)
- Assessment of knowledge, mathematics learning, processes, and mathematical practices is a routine for mathematicians. (Mathematics)
- Scientists place much emphasis on well-structured scientific knowledge, understanding and reasoning; they use formative and summative assessment, as well as ongoing self-assessment and reflection. (Science)
- Historians are skilled in reading, analyzing, synthesizing, and interpreting primary documents, evaluating information from multiple sources, and using evidence to support their claims. They use performance assessment to facilitate historical habits of mind. (Social Studies)

How to Implement an Effective Informal/Classroom-Based Assessment System.

Teachers need time to develop, implement, and reflect on an effective classroom-based assessment system. Sample suggestions include the following:

- What do you need to assess? When, or how often and why? What data sources will you use to collect information about what students are learning? What counts for learning in your classroom? How will you know that students are or are not learning? And what will you do about it? How about students with learning disabilities and language needs? Will they require a different or additional assessment system? Focus assessment on important learning goals for each unit of study, collect data, organize and analyze data, provide necessary feedback to students, and make instructional changes as needed.
- Make the learning goals and instructional processes clear to students. Also make clear to them that assessment is a daily classroom activity that will inform both them and you about their learning.
- Use assessment data to place students in different groups, and provide different instructional supports and differentiation.

- Discuss data about students with disabilities, language and other learning exceptionalities, as needed, with other educational support personnel (i.e., exceptional education teacher, literacy or math coach, speech language pathologist, school counselor, school psychologist, etc.). They can provide you with support, resources, and suggestions to improve student learning.

- Make self-assessment of academic, social, collaborative, and other class goals an integral part of your instruction. Self-assessment, reflection, and metacognition promote higher-order thinking skills and student accountability in the learning process.

- Set clear performance and mastery standards, and communicate, explain, and provide feedback on what "good" reading, writing, speaking, questioning, arguing, accountable talk, and collaborative inquiry "look, sound, and feel" like. Use rubrics to help students develop and evaluate their work and involve the class in co-developing criteria for a good essay or research report, a good argument, a good summary, a good question or response, etc. Use rubrics and scoring guides not just for grading, but also for guiding students in monitoring their progress, improving their performance, and becoming independent readers, writers, thinkers, and learners.

- Schedule periodic conferences with your students to examine their performance, learning, needs, review and revise goals and timelines, and provide targeted, private, and specific feedback.

- Use portfolios to monitor progress and learning over time, to celebrate student accomplishments, and to also identify their needs.

- Be a wise manager of student data. Be explicit, specific, intentional, and reflective.

- Teachers do not need to grade or collect everything a student produces in class. Identify the important data sources of student learning, decide on what types of evidence you will collect and how you will use it, and be consistent with your informal assessment system. Use multiple assessments, and collect data on a continuous and systematic way.

- Organize student data in paper or electronic folders so you can access it, offer evidence to students, parents, and others, as needed, and track student progress. Analyze data periodically, provide feedback to students, reflect on your own teaching, and make necessary instructional adjustments as needed.

Observations and Anecdotal Records

Classroom observation is another form of informal and ongoing assessment. Teacher observations of student behavior, progress, and learning take place naturally in each content area classroom. A teacher can easily see when a student is engaged, attentive, upset, disruptive, talkative, unresponsive, or excited. Teachers can use anecdotal records to make observational notes, and document student behavior and learning in relation to a task, or a social interaction. As facilitators of student learning in secondary content area classrooms, teachers should make "student watching" part of their everyday activities. Classroom observations of student behavior, oral comments, questions, interactions with peers, and responses to content and task can help the teacher keep his or her "finger on the pulse" of student learning. Teachers should (a) plan who, what, and for how long to observe; (b) plan to observe specific and significant learning actions of the student; (c) observe over time so they can see growth in learning; (d) be flexible in their observations; and (e) organize, analyze, and share their observations with the student.

An anecdotal record is a written account of events and behaviors a teacher has observed in the classroom (Airasian, 1997). Anecdotal records are a type of authentic and formative assessment that allow the teacher to provide information about the student's academic, social, emotional, and physical development over time, offer an ongoing record of individual instructional needs, capture and record observations of significant behaviors, and provide documentation of learning that can be shared with students, parents, and other teachers.

Teachers should focus on a single, specific, learning outcome, behavior, skill, or attitude and keep the note brief. Anecdotal records should be recorded daily (if possible) and should include objective information about student strengths and weaknesses. They can be written on post-it notes, dated, and placed in the student's file or the teacher can develop a template that includes all students' names and a place to record brief, dated, notes. Anecdotal records allow teachers to capture events that cannot be captured in a formal assessment—e.g., a student who shares a logical, coherent, and well-supported oral argument, or a student who collaborates with others in a positive and engaging manner in class. Because anecdotal records are time-consuming, teachers should at least maintain them for each student once a week as part of his or her formal observations of students. Limiting the notes to specific types of behaviors will help the teacher to record and maintain quality records.

Checklists

Checklists are useful tools for collecting information on a specific objective in the classroom, or for teacher self-assessment. A teacher could use a checklist to self-assess his or her implementation of an instructional strategy, and use it to reflect on what worked well and what areas need improvement. Because checklists usually require a "yes" designated by the presence of a checkmark or a "no" designated by the absence of a checkmark, they do not provide detailed feedback. Table 10.2 includes an observation checklist assessing student participation for small group collaboration; teachers can date their entries, and use as evidence for teacher-student conferences.

TABLE 10.2. Observation Checklist for Student Participation in Small Group Discussions

Student Name	Never Participates	Seldom Participates	Occasionally Participates	Frequently Participates
Alison Alfonso		✓		
Mary British			✓	
Emma Brown	✓			
Daniel Capelini				✓
Andre Cartwright				✓
Jacob Sibley			✓	
Andrea Williams	✓			

Surveys, Questionnaires, Interest and Attitude Inventories, and Interviews

Questionnaires and surveys can help the teacher assess students' attitudes toward a skill or activity, discover how students feel about a subject matter, how often they read, what, when, and where they read, or what interests and aspirations they have. This information can help teachers understand student motivations, interests, learning habits and style, and teachers can use it to support student learning inside and outside the classroom. Teachers can give surveys at the beginning of the year to help the teacher gauge the students' interests and how to build upon them during the year.

Interest and attitude inventories are used to collect information on student interests, background information, learning preferences, and attitudes toward subject areas, reading, writing, technology, collaboration, or learning. For example, a teacher may develop a questionnaire that can provide him or her with information about any (and all) of the following: the student's family; language spoken at home; whether the student has any limitations that prevent him or her from learning; if the student works; what the student's favorite music, radio/TV shows are; what the student's preferred social media choices are; whether a student has access to technology at home; what technology tools or software the student is knowledgeable about; the student's plans for the future; any hobbies, clubs/sports/outside activities he or she enjoys; college or workforce plans past graduation; or any problems, needs, or questions the student has.

Interviews

Interviews can be used in a variety of ways for a variety of purposes. They can be part of portfolio assessment, can be used in teacher-student conferences, or can be used at different times to address specific student needs, student likes or dislikes about an assignment or class process, student interests and habits, life developments or situations as they arise. Formal interviews can include a set of predetermined questions and informal interviews can be as casual as a conversation about a book.

Because surveys, questionnaires, interest and attitude inventories, and interviews provide self-reported data, it is important for teachers to gather information from multiple sources and verify it with other data; at times, students may give answers they think the teacher wants to hear. Surveys, questionnaires, interest, and attitude inventories are useful tools for getting to know students, planning instruction that will be relevant, motivating, and fun, selecting materials that are culturally relevant to all students, and creating a classroom learning environment that will be conducive to learning.

Portfolios

Portfolios are a means of authentic assessment. Educators use portfolios as a way for students to collect work that reflects student progress over time (formative assessment evidence). or their best work (summative assessment evidence) (Afflerbach, 2007). A portfolio is a representative sampling of artifacts or exemplars (i.e., special projects, writing, laboratory reports, research papers, photos, audio/video, or other media productions, teacher notes/records, testing results, reflections, etc.) that demonstrate a feature about a person. Portfolios focus on students' strengths. They are a showcase of academic and creative accomplishments rather than just a collection of "stuff," or a notebook. Unlike traditional tests, portfolios demonstrate student growth over time, and allow students to reflect on, and evaluate, their personal growth.

An important part of using portfolios is the teacher-student conference where student progress is discussed. During regularly scheduled portfolio teacher-student conferences, the student and teacher can discuss the agreed upon standards, and the strengths and weaknesses of certain artifacts contained in the portfolio and decide on next steps. At the end of the year, many teachers have "Portfolio Share Days" (face-to-face or through electronic access) to celebrate students' accomplishments, and provide students with an opportunity to share their accomplishments and strengths with classmates, the school community, parents, and the greater community (e.g., business leaders, college students, local policy-makers, etc.) (Porter & Cleland, 1995). Portfolio assessment promotes independence, critical thinking skills, reflection and self-assessment, and responsibility for one's own learning and progress (Fernsten & Fernsten, 2005).

Portfolios are a valuable source of assessment for teachers, parents, and students. They provide an authentic means of assessing each student, and enable the teacher to develop a comprehensive profile of each student over time. Portfolios allow the teacher to make instructional decisions based on multiple sources of data. Portfolios also provide an individualized form of dialogue, feedback, and support from the teacher that are particularly useful to English language learners and students with learning disabilities. Students will benefit from seeing past effective portfolios, from guidance on how to organize, review, and use the portfolio for conferences and grade reviews, from setting specific times for teacher-student portfolio conferences, and from celebrating their successes. Parents will also benefit from understanding the purpose and the process of using student portfolios.

Disadvantages of portfolios include the time and attention needed. Portfolios need to be organized clearly so they can be accessed easily and they also need to be kept secure so private student information is not accessed by everyone. Teachers need to periodically review students' portfolios and determine growth over time, provide feedback to students, and make instructional decisions to support student learning. Teachers also need to consider a number of questions when developing a portfolio assessment (see Figure 10.1).

There is no single way to use portfolios. The portfolio in itself could take the form of a file, a notebook, a folder, a crate, or a virtual space for electronic or e-portfolios. What do students typically include in a portfolio? Figure 10.2 samples items students can include in a portfolio. The contents will vary according to the type of portfolio. Teachers must provide students with clear criteria for evaluation, what artifacts must be included in a portfolio, and rubrics for an objective and comprehensive portfolio evaluation. Teachers must also use portfolios on a daily basis (if possible), make students responsible for organizing and maintaining their portfolio, and provide multiple opportunities for feedback on the portfolio. Figure 10.3 shows some sample discipline-specific portfolio contents.

Organization and planning phase

- What are the purposes of the portfolio?
- What is the relationship between the portfolio, the curriculum, and my instruction?
- How will I use it to assess and monitor student learning?
- How will I present its purpose and uses to parents?
- What other forms of assessment will I use in addition to the portfolio to gauge student learning and growth?
- How will I use the portfolio assessment to plan for instruction?
- How will I model portfolio purpose and use to my students?
- What will students need to learn and be able to do to participate in portfolio assessment?
- What will I need to do to make the portfolio assessment clear, organized, manageable, and purposeful?
- How will I manage and store the portfolio?
- Who will have access to the portfolio (i.e., student, teacher, other teachers, parents, school district)?

Collection phase

- What artifacts will be included in their portfolio?
- What rubrics and criteria for portfolio evaluation and student self-reflection will I use?
- Who will select content for the portfolio?
- What materials can be added on an ongoing basis?
- What guidelines will I present students with for artifact selection and evaluation?
- How many teacher-student conferences will I use?
- How and when will I provide feedback to the student?

Reflection phase

- How will I use the portfolio to assess and monitor student progress?
- What areas or tasks will be problematic with portfolio assessment and what do I plan to do to prevent them or address them?
- In what ways will I ask students to reflect on the portfolio process?
- How will I use student reflections?

FIGURE 10.1.   Questions for portfolio assessment development.

Cover sheet
Goals for the year
Weekly journals

- Attitudes/feelings towards class.
- Thoughts on your goals and personal progress.
- Strengths and weaknesses—what you need to improve upon.
- What you have learned.

Best/worst work samples

- Be sure to write *why* you chose each artifact and what each artifact "tells" about you.

Reflection on portfolio

- Completed at end of the year.
- Reflect on the entire portfolio process.
- Identify areas of improvement.
- Identify areas that still need improvement.
- Offer suggestions for improving the portfolio assessment.
- Did you achieve your goals?
  - Explain and discuss what strategies or approaches helped you to achieve your goals and which ones prevented you from achieving your goals.
  - Discuss what you would like to do in the future to help you meet your goals.

FIGURE 10.2.   What to include in a portfolio.

Types of Portfolios

There are different types of portfolios used for different purposes, audiences, and tasks. *Showcase portfolios* display the best student products over a particular time period (i.e., a nine-week grading period, a semester, or year). For example, a showcase portfolio in a science class may include the best research papers, experiments, and lab reports. In an English language arts class, the portfolio may include the best essays, poems, or literacy analyses. In other words, in a showcase portfolio, students can show teachers, parents, and others what they have learned about writing throughout the year, and explain how they have grown as writers over a period of time.

Growth portfolios demonstrate growth in particular skills over time. Portfolio artifacts need to show work on product progress by including early, mid-term, and later samples of similar types of student work. For example, students may include a first draft, revisions, and a final draft of a research report or paper.

Process portfolios concentrate more on the journey of learning rather than the final learning products. In a history class, artifacts may include examples of a historical argument that includes a first draft, an examplar analysis of different primary documents, peer and teacher responses, and a final edited draft that is supported by sufficient and accurate evidence. This portfolio might also include student reflections about what approach worked the best, challenges, and strategies for developing an effective historical argument in the future.

Composite portfolios contain more than one student's work. They might be used to demonstrate what is taught or what impact a program is having on a group of students or a school. Portfolio contents may include the group's efforts, progress, and achievement.

Evaluation portfolios may contain a series of evaluations, tests, quizzes, observations, and other assessment artifacts over a course and the student's accomplishments, challenges, and growth in relation to previously determined criteria or goals. For example, a math evaluation portfolio may include successful and unsuccessful problem solving strategies and attempts and reflections about effective problem-solving strategies.

- **All Subject Areas**
  - Written narratives and informational/explanatory writing samples
  - Journal and learning log entries
  - Self-reflections
  - Tests with self-evaluations
  - Student-completed graphic organizers
  - Teacher and peer evaluations
  - Research
  - Photos and images
  - Audio/video files
  - Movie, music, or art reviews
  - Reading and book lists
  - Brainstorming lists
  - Project inquiries
  - Creative works

- **Art**
  - Photos
  - Illustrations
  - Posters
  - Artwork photographs
  - Storyboards
  - Collages
  - Papers about art style, artists, and art genres

- **English Language Arts**
  - Journal entries or learning logs
  - Reader responses to literature
  - Character analysis
  - Author study
  - Essay writing with revision notes
  - Poems
  - Creative writing

- **Mathematics**
  - Demonstration of problem-solving steps
  - Examples of mathematical reasoning and proofs
  - Connections between mathematical ideas and real-world problems
  - Examples of mathematical problem solving
  - Graphic representation of problems
  - Mathematical arguments
  - Computer work

- **Science**
  - Lab notes, observations, and notes
  - Project outlines and rubrics
  - Experiments
  - Data collection
  - Notes on the scientific method
  - Research reports with teacher feedback
  - Mapping and reflection on the inquiry process
  - Graphs and diagrams
  - Key vocabulary
  - Scientific dilemmas

Social Studies
  - Journal entries
  - Diaries, letters, speeches
  - Maps
  - Photos/images of historical artifacts or events
  - Written reports or essays with notes
  - Creative writing
  - Audio/video tapes of speeches, debates, or presentations

FIGURE 10.3.   Sample discipline-specific portfolio contents.

Online or e-portfolios may be one of the above portfolio types or a combination of different types, but all multi-modal items, information, and artifacts are stored and accessed online. E-portfolios are versatile digital repositories that are accessible to multiple audiences. They increase student engagement, promote digital learning skills and information literacy, and help establish a digital identity, and facilitate a paperless learning culture (Barrett, 2007; Light, Chen, & Ittelson, 2012).

Many secondary schools, colleges, and even professions require that individuals maintain a virtual portfolio that may include digital text, scanned writing samples, completed projects, video/audio, multimedia, blogs, PowerPoint presentations, wikis, hyperlinks, or Web-based products. Technological advancements have made it possible to store files on the Internet, and have also brought about a shift in how teachers assign, collect, and assess student work. There is a variety of choices, tools, and platforms for digital portfolios. Teachers need to develop their knowledge about the tools and they also need to think about accessibility, storage capacity and privacy issues, as well as about technological tools' creating, editing, sharing, and integrating capabilities before committing to an e-portfolio (Hertz, 2013).

For example, in secondary grades, students use Evernote (a web application to clip webpages, store photos, type in notes, attach audio files, etc.), Google Apps, VoiceThread (for creating multimedia slideshows using images, text, audio and video), Weebly (a platform for creating free websites and blogs), Wordpress (an open-source blogging tool and publishing platform), Project Foundry (a tool that organizes, tracks, and shares project-based learning), Wikispaces (wiki-creation tools), Dropbox (creating public, sharable folders), and other Web 2.0 technologies. New e-portfolio platforms include Digication, Pathbrite, Taskstream, and Epsilen.

Maya Payne Smart in her 2009 Edutopia article titled, *Digital Portfolios Pull Double Duty*, shares accounts of how various schools use digital portfolios to develop students' critical thinking and digital literacy skills. I love the quote from Doug Martin, an 11th–12th grade graphic design teacher at Mingo Career & Technical Center, in Delbarton, West Virginia, at the beginning of the article, "You are as strong as the weakest piece in your portfolio." Smart (2009) shares how schools are using digital portfolios for college admission (see Zinch website at http://www.zinch.com used for college recruiting), scholarships, and employment purposes and emphasizes the benefits of e-portfolios, especially, for students in rural areas. Doug Martin also says, "Employers would rather see the quality and professionalism of [student] work in their portfolio, [instead of just the name of the school or college in their resume.]" Smart (2009) also shares that the New Hampshire Department of Education uses digital portfolios as a means of assessing seventh and eighth grade students' computer literacy knowledge and skills, and requires all school districts to use e-portfolios for this purpose.

Portfolio assessment, an authentic type of assessment, has its own benefits and challenges. If used effectively, portfolios can provide you and your students with a comprehensive picture of student growth, can inform your instruction, enhance the assessment process by providing you with specific information about your students' strengths, progress, and learning over time, and promote student, teacher, and parent reflection.

Response to Intervention

The Response to Intervention (RtI) Action Network, a program of the National Center for Learning Disabilities, defines RtI as:

Response to Intervention (RTI) is a multi-tiered approach to the early identification and support of students with learning and behavior needs. Students' progress is closely monitored at each stage of intervention to determine the need for further research-based instruction and/or intervention in general education, in special education, or both.

High quality scientifically based classroom instruction, ongoing student assessment through screening and progress monitoring, tiered instruction, and parent involvement are important components of the RtI process (Mellard & Johnson, 2008). The goals of RtI are to: (a) adjust instruction and implement scientifically based instruction and interventions for struggling students based on individual needs; (b) ensure that students' difficulties are not due to lack of appropriate instruction; (c) decrease disproportionate representation of minority populations being identified as students with disabilities; and (d) ensure student success by making informed decisions about resource allocation, and by closely monitoring student progress based on instructionally relevant data.

The US Congress introduced RtI in 2004, under the *Individuals with Disabilities Education Improvement Act (IDEIA)*. Proponents of RtI state that it merges special and general education into the overall policies of the No Child Left Behind policy. It is also considered as an alternative strategy for closing the achievement gaps for all students, including students at risk of academic failure, students with disabilities and English language learners, by identifying and addressing problems early (Burns & Gibbons, 2012). RtI is tied to policy, funding, and accountability; it specifies that 15% of a school's special education budget needs to be spent on regular classroom interventions in an effort to reduce the number of students identified as learning disabled.

The RtI process has both academic and behavioral aspects. The Academic RtI is designed to help students with academic difficulties succeed. The Behavioral RtI or Positive Behavior Intervention Supports (PBIS) is designed to help students with behavioral difficulties succeed (Fairbanks, Sugai, Guardino, & Lathrop 2007). Within the RtI process, there are three Tiers of instruction and intervention (see Figure 10.4). These three Tiers use increasingly more intense instruction and interventions. Data is collected at each Tier and is used to make instructional decisions to determine if students are responding to instruction and interventions. A problem-solving process decides how the instruction and interventions should be maintained and layered.

Tier 1 instruction is the core instructional program provided to all students by the general education teacher, in the regular content area classroom. It is primary prevention that focuses on improving instruction in regular classrooms. The content area teacher provides all students with core research-based instruction and positive behavior intervention, and supports with flexible grouping and differentiation. Frequency of assessment includes benchmark assessment at least three times per year. Ongoing professional development provides teachers with the necessary tools to ensure all students receive quality instruction. Critical questions in Tier 1 instruction are: (1) is the core instruction well delivered? (2) is the core instruction effective? and (3) is support provided for fidelity of implementation? At the secondary level, one key idea is to show students how information in life is connected inside and outside of school. These ideas are embedded in the process of differentiating instruction.

Tier 2 intervention is targeted intervention (for approximately 15% of the student population who are struggling) typically provided to a small group (3–5) of students; it is supplemental instruction in addition to the regular instruction provided in Tier 1 that includes at least monthly progress monitoring. The school decides the location of Tier 2 intervention. Students will receive 20–30 minutes of supplemental interventions three to five days per week.

Tier 3 is intensive intervention designed for typically one–five percent of students who will need intensive instruction in addition to the core instruction they receive in class. This intervention includes one to two students receiving highly individualized instruction from highly trained school

**ACADEMIC and
BEHAVIOR SYSTEMS**

**Tier 3: Intensive,
Individualized Interventions
& Supports**
The most intense (increased time,
narrowed focus, reduced group size)
instruction and intervention based
upon individual student need
provided in addition to and aligned
with Tier 1 & 2 academic and
behaviour instruction and supports.

**Tier 2: Targeted,
Supplemental Interventions
& Supports.**
More targeted
instruction/intervention and
supplemental support in addition to
and aligned with the core academic
and behaviour curriculum

**Tier 1: Core, Universal
Instruction & Supports.**
General instruction and support
provided to all students in all
settings.

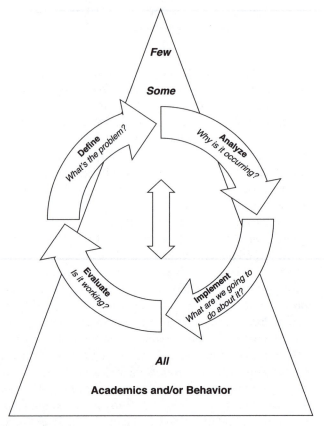

FIGURE 10.4. Tiered models of school supports and the problem-solving process.

Source: Florida Department of Education, Response to Intervention. Retrieved from http://www.florida-rti.org/floridamtss/index.htm.

personnel from 30–60 minutes a minimum of four times per week. Tier 3 intervention includes at least weekly progress monitoring and frequent informal classroom-based assessments.

Teachers need to consider the characteristics of effective instruction as they reflect on their teaching. The following list of guiding questions (see Table 10.3) will help you analyze whether the characteristics are present within the instruction and intervention. This tool can be used for self-evaluation (Rawlinson, Zugelder, & Little, 2009/2010, p. 14).

RtI in Middle and High School Grades

Reading in the early grades is the primary focus of the RtI process. Although some models (barely) exist for secondary grades, school districts need to decide how to implement RtI in middle and high school. What RtI should look like in secondary grades is still a matter of debate. In addition, secondary schools do not have a single screening tool that works well for every grade level. Research on the use of RtI in secondary grades is emerging; some research has shown benefits of Tier 2 interventions on student learning (Windram, Scierka, & Silberglitt, 2007).

Secondary school educators should use a variety of existing data to determine which students are in need of supplementary or intensive instructional supports. Secondary schools can use attendance data, student performance on standardized tests, course grades, credit attainment, and office disciplinary referrals as part of the screening process. Students who fall off track in

TABLE 10.3. Instruction and Intervention Self-Evaluation Tool

Characteristic	Guiding Questions
Goals and Objectives	Are the purposes and outcomes of instruction clearly evident in the lesson plans? Does the student understand the purpose for learning the skills and strategies taught?
Systematic	Are skills introduced in a specific and logical order, from easy to more complex? Do the lesson activities support the sequence of instruction? Is there frequent and cumulative review?
Explicit	Are directions clear and straightforward, unequivocal without vagueness, need for implication, or ambiguity?
Scaffolding	Is there explicit use of prompts, cues, examples and encouragements to support the student? Are skills broken down into manageable steps when necessary?
Corrective Feedback	Does the teacher provide students with corrective instruction offered during instruction and practice as necessary?
Modeling	Are the skills and strategies included in instruction clearly demonstrated for the student?
Guided Practice	Do students have sufficient opportunities to practice new skills and strategies with teacher support?
Pacing	Is the teacher familiar enough with the lesson to present it in an engaging manner? Does the pace allow for frequent student response? Does the pace maximize instructional time, leaving no down time?
Instructional Routine	Are the instructional formats consistent from lesson to lesson?

Source: Adapted from: *A Teacher's Guide to RtI and Problem Solving.* Florida Department of Education, Bureau of Exceptional Education and Student Services, 2009/2010. Retrieved from: http://springssm-sy10-11. wikispaces.com/file/view/teachersRtl_guide_final_1cj.pdf

several areas will need more intensity in instructional support and closer progress monitoring. Many schools use the Grade 8 screening measures with all new grade 9–12 students to ensure that they have met all eighth-grade target scores. Usually, secondary schools depend on the English and math departments to review critical student data in reading and mathematics. Teams of content area teachers, according to their department, can get together to review and discuss student data and progress monitoring.

Teachers will benefit from professional development and support on how to interpret data and make instructional decisions. Teachers will benefit from "teacher-friendly" data, collaboration with peers on types of instructional differentiation, and expectations for students. For example, a science teacher who will receive a list of students in her classroom who are receiving Tier 2, or 3 interventions, will benefit from a brief description of the interventions and a list of strategies she can implement in her classroom to help the students learn the content (e.g., previewing vocabulary, establishing purpose before reading).

Challenges with Implementing RtI in Grades 6–12

Well, the first and foremost challenge is time. Middle and high schools "live and die" by the schedule! The schedules are not often conducive for team meetings, data analysis, data teams, more paperwork, more students moving in and out of the classroom for specialized interventions, and how a content area teacher could provide classroom-based interventions for hundreds of students per course and effectively monitor their progress. Burns and Gibbons (2012) offer some considerations about the challenge of implementing an RtI model in secondary schools. The traditional secondary school schedule (6–8 periods of 50 minutes each per day) with 25–30 students in each class does not allow for flexible grouping or individualized instruction. Some schools offer study skills courses that include smaller group sizes; this approach does not allow students to exit the course mid-semester even if they no longer need the interventions. Other schools use a content area teacher, such as a social studies teacher, to deliver remedial reading instruction for half of the time in content, and the other half in reading. The drawback of this model is that it requires two teachers, one who is a social studies specialist, and another who is an intervention specialist. Block scheduling which is 90 minutes long is more conducive to improving student learning. It allows for small group intervention (Tier 2) with groups of 8–10 students and a rotation between remedial reading and other courses such as social studies, earth science, etc.

Reading interventions in secondary schools increase students reading skills and comprehension, which in turn, help them to develop content knowledge, and score better in high-stakes tests. Secondary schools struggle with effectively implementing intervention models. The homeroom model seems to be the most effective model in which up to 40 students are flexibly grouped and meet with one teacher all year for 10–30 minutes at a time. The main challenge with homerooms is attendance—classes are offered first thing in the morning—and coordination.

School districts play a key role in RtI implementation. They allocate resources, establish policies and procedures, provide funding, select tools and methods for universal screening and progress monitoring at the different grade levels, provide forms and paperwork, and identify a contact person to work with each school (Johnson, Mellard, Fuchs & McKnight, 2006). Because RtI is new and is tied to accountability, it is vital that school leaders, teachers, and faculty teams develop their knowledge about how to implement it.

Teachers need professional development in how to conduct universal screening, collect data, provide progress monitoring, provide academic instructional interventions and strategies, offer behavioral interventions, and learn how to differentiate instruction to meet the needs of all diverse learners (Appelbuam, 2009; National Research Council on Learning Disabilities, 2008). Finally, schools need to develop their own RtI teams that will examine all school-based universal RtI implementation strategies that are available to all, review and interpret student data, and design intervention plans. RtI teams need to also function as "school cheerleaders," and motivate and inform teachers. These teams need to be knowledgeable about RtI, be organized and efficient, and most importantly, know how to read and interpret data. Such teams should also gather data on teachers' needs, and on other schools that have been successful with implementing RtI. RtI team members usually include: the school principal or assistant principal, a reading and math intervention specialist, a school psychologist or counselor, a general education teacher, an exceptional education specialist, a speech language pathologist, and other support personnel (Appelbaum, 2009).

All content area teachers need to learn about RtI. Successful RtI models provide support systems for all students, not just struggling ones, and result in increased student attendance, reduction in discipline issues, and increased enrollment in honors and Advanced Placement (AP) classes. It is important for teachers to remember that RtI is not meant to make every content area teacher a reading teacher. Each content area teacher should be knowledgeable about the literacy and learning demands of his or her discipline and all students' progress, academic, and behavioral needs. Furthermore, content area teachers should collaborate with other educators to learn more about how to provide differentiated instruction within the content area classroom in discipline-specific ways. What should you take from this section on RtI? All content area teachers need to a) provide high-quality instruction and interventions matched to student need; b) monitor student progress frequently; and c) use data to make educational decisions. Let's not wait for our students to fail before we provide them with the help they need; instead, let's provide appropriate interventions to all students as soon as they demonstrate the need.

Assessing Materials

Selecting materials for students is a vital decision for every classroom teacher. Student motivation to read and student engagement with learning are both affected by the materials teachers select to use in their classroom. Too easy material will backfire on students' self-confidence and motivation. Too difficult material and students will not persist with reading, will be discouraged to go on, and may also feel that they are not capable or smart enough for the task. Students' attitudes toward reading are affected by the materials themselves (Juel, 1994).

In Chapter 3, we examined in detail the CCSS recommendation about a three-pronged approach to text complexity: (1) quantitative measures of text complexity, (2) qualitative measures of text complexity, and (3) reader-task factors (National Governors Association Center for Best Practices and Council of Chief State School Officers, 2010). Publishers of materials provide reading levels for their texts and some provide readability levels. The following sources will help you assess the readability information for determining the quantitative aspects of text complexity of the materials you select for your students to read.

Readability formulas have been in existence since the 1920s; they are objective ways to determine grade-level difficulty. They do not measure student interest or enjoyment of a text. Instead, they are designed as mathematical equations that use a number of personal pronouns, the average number of syllables in words, or number of words in sentences, percentage of different words, sentence length, and number of prepositional phrases to estimate the difficulty of a text. In other words, readability formulas examine sentence length and word difficulty.

Readability formulas are mechanical and produce narrow numbers about text difficulty and leave out factors such as the student's background knowledge and motivation, paragraph structure, level of abstraction, and reader interest in the topic. Readability formulas cannot provide an exact match between the student's reading level and the text's complexity. Short words and sentences are not always easier to understand. For example, the word *decry* might be more difficult for students than the word, *government*. Similarly, the sentence "Their color is a diabolic eye" (from Phyllis Wheatley, "On Being Brought From Africa to America" poem, edited by Axelrod & Travisano, 2003) is a short but complex one. Teachers should consider all three aspects of text complexity, and also use their professional judgment and knowledge of student abilities, interests, and characteristics when selecting materials for the classroom.

The Fry Readability Graph

One of the most popular readability formulas is the Fry Readability Graph (adapted from Luiten, Ames, & Bradley, 1979) (see Figure 10.5). The formula is designed to measure the grade level of a text from Grade 1 through college. The formula depends only on sentence length and number of syllables in words in 100-word passages—Fry recommends using three passages, not just one, for calculating an average.

Figure 10.6 includes step-by-step directions for calculating readability with Fry's (1977) formula (Fry, Kress, & Fountoukidis, 2000).

Other text difficulty metrics include, Lexile (MetaMetrics), Degrees of Reading Power: DPR Analyzer (Questar Assessment, Inc.), REAP (Carnegie Melon University), SourceRater

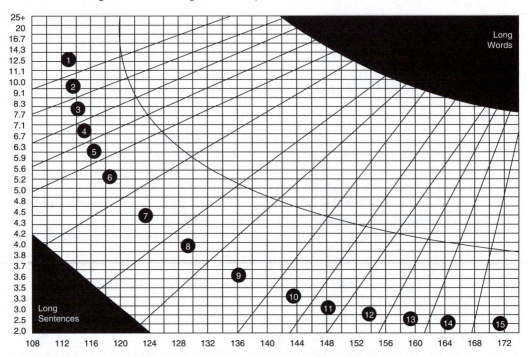

FIGURE 10.5.   Fry Readability Graph.

Step 1.   Randomly select three 100-word passages from a book or an article, beginning with the beginning sentence. Do not count proper nouns, initializations, and numerals.

Step 2.   Count the number of sentences in the 100 words and estimate the length of the fraction of the last sentence to the nearest one-tenth.

Step 3.   Count the number of syllables in the 100-word passage. If you do not have a hand counter available, an easy way is to simply put a mark above every syllable over one in each word; when you get to the end of the passage, count the number of marks and add 100. Small calculators can also be used by pushing numeral 1, then the + sign for each word or syllable when counting.

Step 4.   Enter graph with average sentence length and average number of syllables; plot dot where the two lines intersect. Area where dot is plotted will give you the approximate grade level.

Step 5.   If a great deal of variability is found in syllable count or sentence count, putting more samples into the average is desirable.

Step 6.   A word is defined as a group of symbols with space on either side; thus, *Joe, IRA, 1945*, and *&* are each one word.

Step 7.   A syllable is defined as a phonetic syllable. Generally, there are as many syllables as vowel sounds. For example, *stopped* is one syllable and *wanted* is two syllables. When counting syllables for numerals and initializations, count one syllable for each symbol. For example, *1945* is four syllables, *IRA* is three syllables, and *&* is one syllable.

FIGURE 10.6.   Directions for calculating readability using Fry's (1977) formula.

(Educational Testing Service), the Pearson Reading Metric (Pearson Knowledge Technologies), ATOS (Advantage-TASA Open Standard, a computerized formula), and Coh-Metrix Text Easability Assessor (University of Memphis). All of them use word difficulty and sentence length. Some also use unique word features, sentence syntax, and text cohesion.

Lexile

The Lexile Framework for reading is a scientific approach to measuring reading ability and the text demands of reading materials. The framework uses a Lexile measure and a Lexile scale. Lexile measures are expressed as numeric values followed by an "L" (e.g., 1200L), and are placed on the Lexile scale. The scale is a developmental scale used to measure reader ability and text complexity ranging from 200L for beginning readers to over 1700L for advanced readers and materials. Table 10.4 includes text complexity grade bands and associated Lexile ranges (in Lexiles).

Lexile scores can guide teachers to match readers with texts. A Lexile measure is not intended to reflect the quality of a text or include the student's background knowledge about a text. Lexile scores for about 40,000 books are available online at http://www.lexile.com.

Assessing Students' Understanding of Texts

Although standardized scores provide one measure of a student's ability to construct meaning from text, educators need to remember that the student's prior knowledge on a topic, vocabulary knowledge, as well as student motivation, text structure, and text difficulty also play a role in the meaning-making process. In this section, I examine the cloze procedure as a means of obtaining information about students' comprehension from text(s).

The Cloze Procedure

The cloze procedure was developed by Wilson Taylor in 1953 and does not use a formula to estimate text difficulty. Taylor (1953) used the concept of closure, a term referring to the human tendency to make meaning of incomplete information. As readers interact with a text that has missing words, they will have to think of words that will fill in, or complete, the meaning of that text. The cloze procedure is easy to construct and evaluate and it can be adapted for readers with learning disabilities; it is constructed and administered by the classroom teacher. To complete meaning with the missing gaps in sentences, students will have to use semantic and syntactic cues. A student's competency with filling in the blanks reflects his or her potential for comprehending that text (Bormuth, 1968). Cloze assessments are more appropriate for informational than narrative texts and can be

TABLE 10.4. Text Complexity Grade Bands and Associated Lexile ranges (in Lexiles)

Text Complexity Grade Band in the Standards	Old Lexile Ranges	Lexile Ranges Aligned to CCR expectations
K-1	N/A	N/A
2–3	450–725	450–790
4–5	645–845	770–980
6–8	860–1010	955–1155
9–10	960–1115	1080–1305
11-CCR	1070–1220	1215–1355

Source: The *Common Core Standards for English Language Arts & Literacy in History/Social Studies, Science, and Technical Subjects: Appendix A: Research Supporting Key Elements of the Standards and Glossary of Terms* (p. 8), by National Governors Association Center for Best Practices & Council of Chief State School Officers, 2010, Washington, DC: Authors. Copyright 2010 by the National Governors Association Center for Best Practices and the Council of Chief State School Officers. All rights reserved.

used with all content area text (maybe not so much with math texts because they include many symbols and numbers). Figure 10.7 includes the steps to administering a cloze readability test.

The cloze procedure offers an alternative to a readability formula and provides information about how students will perform in comprehending course materials; it also helps build students' background knowledge. The procedure does not offer information about inferential comprehension skills. Students will need practice and feedback with the cloze procedure to develop their familiarity with its format.

Step 1. Preparation Phase

- Select two passages of about 300 words from a text your students have not read, but you will assign in the future, and copy it on a word processor.
- For each passage, leave the first and last sentences intact. Starting with the second sentence, select at random one of the first five words, delete every fifth word, and insert a blank space about 10-15 spaces in length. Delete exactly 50 words.

Step 2. Administration Phase

- A short practice test helps students prepare them for the actual testing.
- Give students a copy of the cloze passage and ask them to read over the entire passage first before they do anything.
- Inform students that they should refer to their textbooks or work peers to complete the cloze procedure.
- The test is not timed.
- Then, ask students to go back and fill in each blank with the word they think makes sense and complete the passage.
- Encourage students who find the cloze procedure difficult or frustrating. If students have problems filling in a word, tell them to skip it, complete the rest of the passage, and return to the blank for another try.

Step 3. Scoring Phase

- Mark as correct only the exact words replaced.
- Correct spelling of replaced words is not required.
- To calculate percent of correct words, divide 50 into the total number of correctly replaced words. If John replaced 25 words correctly, his score is 50%. Accepting synonyms affects the reliability of the performance criteria.
- When using two passages to increase accuracy, the percentages of correctly replaced words for each passage are averaged. If John had 50% in the first passage and 64% in the second one, his average would be 57%.
- When students complete, ask them to score their own papers by showing them the list of deleted words. They can write the words above their own answers.
- Follow up with a discussion on why some words fit or did not fit the passage.

Step 4. Interpretation Phase

- Bormuth (1968) developed the following criteria:

  o **Percent Correct**   **Reading Level**

    57% or more   Independent
    44%–57%   Instructional
    Below 44%   Frustration

- Students scoring over 57% can probably read and understand most texts on their own.
- Students scoring between 44%–57% can read the material with instructional support in vocabulary, comprehension and study strategies.
- Students scoring below 44% will probably have much difficulty with the text; teachers will need to find alternative texts and methods to teach the content knowledge they want students to learn.

FIGURE 10.7.   Steps to administering a cloze readability test.

Policy, High-Stakes Testing, and Accountability

The No Child Left Behind Act of 2001 (NCLB), a reauthorization of the Elementary and Secondary Education Act, was one of President George W. Bush's initiatives that aimed to improve the performance of US primary and secondary schools by requiring states to adopt comprehensive assessment and accountability systems for identifying and improving underperforming schools. NCLB included Title I and required states to develop assessments in basic skills. In order for schools to receive funding, they had to give certain standardized assessments to students, especially those in Grades K–3. Although NCLB did not avow a national achievement standard, each state developed its own standards. NCLB expanded the federal role in public education through annual testing for students in Grades 3–8, annual academic progress, school report cards, focus on qualified teachers in every classroom, and funding changes. At present, NCLB is due for reauthorization, but its future remains uncertain. In 2011, the White House announced that states will have more flexibility in how they spend federal education funding if they adopt the CCSS, use teacher and principal evaluation systems that are based on student test scores, and implement effective turn-around strategies for the lowest performing schools.

Supporters of the NCLB attribute the increased student performance in reading and mathematics reflected in the National Assessment of Educational Progress (NAEP) results to NCLB. According to those results,

- Nine year-old students made more progress from 2000–2005 than in the previous 28 years combined.
- Thirteen year-olds earned the highest math scores the test ever recorded.
- Reading and math scores for Black and Hispanic nine-year-olds reached an all-time high.
- Achievement gaps in reading and math between Caucasian and Black, and Caucasian and Hispanic nine-year-olds were at an all-time low.
- Forty-three states and the District of Columbia either improved academically or held steady in all categories (fourth- and eighth-grade reading and math).

On the other hand, critics of NCLB have been vocal about how the pressure and school implications of standardized testing promoted a culture of narrow curriculum and "teaching to the test," and the loss of valuable instructional time. In addition, inconsistencies in test administration may have violated the Individuals with Disabilities Education Act (IDEA), and negatively reflected on the abilities of non-English language speakers. Standardized testing under NCLB held schools accountable for absolute levels of student performance—test results were used to determine which schools were making annual yearly progress (AYP). Let's not forget that policy affects instruction and assessment.

Issues and Concerns about High-Stakes Testing

Are standardized tests by default high-stakes tests? Not necessarily. Standardized testing has been used to evaluate student achievement since the early 19th century; what has evolved since then, aside from tests themselves, is the increase in the amount of mandatory testing and its related "stakes"— i.e., rewards or punishments students, teachers, and schools have been experiencing as a result.

High stakes testing means that *one* test is used to make decisions about students (i.e., placement, promotion or retention, receiving a high school diploma, entrance into college), teachers (i.e., salary), and school (i.e., rating, funding, and resources). The American Psychological Association (APA) warns us against the negative impact of high-stakes testing and suggests that decisions should not be made solely on one test that may not accurately reflect the progress and achievement a student made in a year (APA, 1999). The accountability era has made high-stakes assessment oppressive and has resulted in teachers changing their curriculum and instruction for the sake of "the test" (Johnson, 1989).

On April 30, 2013, Arne Duncan, US Secretary of Education under the Obama Administration, speaking at the 2013 annual American Education Research Association (AERA) conference acknowledged that there is room for improving standardized testing in America and that these tests are an insufficient measure of student and teacher performance. On the other hand, he also stated that forgoing standardized testing is not the answer. Mr. Duncan called for timely evaluation of student performance in areas beyond reading and math, including science, advanced class work, and career readiness, and supported the Race to the Top initiative as a means of improving assessment. In addition, he acknowledged the changes the CCSS and the new assessment tools will produce, but he was confident that these changes will be for the best. Mr. Duncan showed support for authentic assessment, high-quality formative assessment, and the removal of unnecessary assessments.

In support of the CCSS assessment systems Mr. Duncan (2013) said,

> The next generation of assessment systems includes diagnostic or formative assessments, not just end-of-the-year summative assessments. The two state consortia must assess student achievement of standards, student growth, and whether students are on-track to being college and career ready. And the new assessment systems must be effective, valid, and instructionally useful. . . . The new assessments from the consortia will be a vast improvement on assessment as it is done today. The PARCC consortium, for example, will evaluate students' ability to read complex texts, complete research projects, excel at classroom speaking and listening assignments, and work with digital media. The Smarter Balanced consortium will assess students using computer adaptive technology that will ask students questions pitched to their skill level, based on their previous answers. And a series of optional interim evaluations during the school year will inform students, parents, and teachers about whether students are on track. The use of smarter technology in assessments will also change instruction in ways that teachers welcome. . . . I have no doubt that Assessment 2.0 will help educators drive the development of a richer curriculum at the state, district, and local level, differentiated instruction tailored to individual student needs, and multiple opportunities during the school year to assess student learning. . . . As I have said before, I believe this new generation of assessments—combined with the adoption of internationally-benchmarked, college and career ready standards—is an absolute game-changer for American education.

No single test can meet the needs of students, teachers, schools, policy-makers, and the community. Each one of these groups needs different types of information from assessments. Assessment, whether standardized or non-standardized, needs to fairly, adequately, and ethically provide information on student performance and guide instructional decisions that will improve learning for all students. New assessments and assessment processes require knowledge, research evidence, and collaboration from all stakeholders. Will the CCSS and its assessment consortia be the solution to the problem or not? Many have raised concerns about how the CCSS will be aligned with state standards (Beach, 2011), and several states have been working to revise and align their standards and assessment procedures with the CCSS. We need high-quality assessments that are fair, valid, and reliable; we also need to remember that assessment of students' performance does not necessarily mean assessment of students' understanding, knowledge, and learning. Tests should not be used to reward or punish students, teachers, or schools; they should not be used to the detriment of student learning.

CCSS Connections

- Students in states that have adopted the CCSS, will be assessed by one of the following assessment consortia: the Partnership for Assessment of Readiness for College and Careers (PARCC), or the Smarter Balanced Assessment Consortium. Students in grades 6–12 will complete formative and summative common ELA and mathematics assessments on a computer, or tablet.
- CCSS assessments will allow for comparison across students, schools, districts, states, and nations. They are designed to provide information that will support more effective teaching and learning, and prepare students for college and careers.

Assessing Student Learning in the Era of New Educational Standards

The move from the NCLB to the CCSS is bringing about new instructional, curricular, and assessment shifts. The CCSS emphasize writing at all grade levels, and the related assessments will assess students' writing skills, and their ability to critically read text, synthesize information, and support their conclusions with evidence. States that have adopted the CCSS have also chosen one of the two following assessment systems that are aligned with the CCSS goals: (1) The Partnership for Assessment of Readiness for Colleges and Careers (PARCC), or (2) Smarter Balanced Assessment Consortium (SBAC).

Both assessments are based on the CCSS, will be delivered via a computer or a tablet (with multimedia features and accommodations), require summative end-of-year assessments, optional interim, non-summative, and formative assessments, and are evolving over time. With this new generation of assessments, students are expected to be familiar with technology tools. It is important that students have experiences with writing on computers and have mastered basic keyboarding and word-processing skills. Students need to read and write routinely, in all subjects and at all grade levels.

It is vital for all teachers to become very knowledgeable about the CCSS-aligned and other new assessments for students in grades 6–12. Whether we are thinking about PARCC, SBAC, End-of Course (EOC) exams, NAEP exams, or other standardized state, national, or international assessments, we all need to examine the types of formats such assessments use to assess our students' knowledge and skills. Last, knowledge of these types of assessments will also help us to develop more effective classroom-based assessments—let's get away from just having multiple choice tests, and include critical thinking and problem-solving items, that require students to provide evidence and/or explain their thinking.

The Partnership for Assessment of Readiness for Colleges and Careers (PARCC)

As stated in the consortium's website (see http://www.parcconline.org/about-parcc),

> The PARCC is a consortium of 19 states plus the District of Columbia and the US Virgin Islands working together to develop a common set of K–12 assessments in English and Math anchored in what it takes to be ready for college and careers. These new K–12 assessments will build a pathway to college and career readiness by the end of high school, mark students' progress toward this goal from 3rd Grade up, and provide teachers with timely information to inform instruction and provide student support.

The PARCC's main goal as stated in the project's website is, "PARCC is designed to reward quality instruction aligned to the Standards, so the assessment is worthy of preparation rather than distraction from good work."

Smarter Balanced Assessment Consortium (SBAC)

As stated in the consortium's website (see http://www.smarterbalanced.org/about/),

> The Smarter Balanced Assessment Consortium (Smarter Balanced) is a state-led consortium working to develop next-generation assessments that accurately measure student progress toward college and career readiness. Smarter Balanced is one of two multistate consortia awarded funding from the US Department of Education in 2010 to develop an assessment system aligned to the Common Core State Standards by the 2014–15 school year. The work of Smarter Balanced is guided by the belief that a high-quality assessment system can provide information and tools for teachers and schools to improve instruction and help students succeed—regardless of disability, language or subgroup.

The SBAC promises to provide flexible, valid, reliable, and fair assessment of the types of understanding and thinking skills needed for college and career readiness in today's world. The SBAC includes CCSS-based computer adaptive summative assessments that use technology-enhanced item types, computer adaptive interim/mid-course/benchmark assessments, research-supported instructional tools and strategies teachers can use for formative assessment, and professional development for teachers along with an online reporting and tracking system that can offer vital information to all stakeholders.

Table 10.5 shows a comparison of assessments used in the PARCC and Smarter Balanced. These new assessment systems are reflective of CCSS shifts. In English language arts (ELA), they both include more complex literacy and inferential passages that require the student to do close reading of authentic text, think critically about text, cite evidence from texts, write to sources, and

TABLE 10.5. PARCC and Smarted Balanced Assessments

PARCC for Grades 3–8	*Smarter Balanced for Grades 3–8 and 11*

• Two summative required components
  ○ Performance-Based Assessment (PBA)
    • ELA/Literacy: writing effectively when analyzing text
    • Math: application, problem-solving, reasoning
• Two non-summative optional components
  ○ Diagnostic assessment
  ○ Mid-year assessment
    • Performance-based items and tasks
    • Emphasis on hard-to-measure standards
• Non-summative, speaking and listening
	• Summative assessment
	  ○ Computer-adaptive test (40–85 items/content area)
	  ○ Computer performance: 1 reading, 1 writing, 2 math
	• Teacher involvement
	  ○ Help write items and tasks
	  ○ Alignment and bias review
	  ○ Scoring
	• Optional interim assessments
	  ○ Computer-adaptive test
	  ○ Computer performance tasks
	  ○ Accessible for instruction and professional development
	• Formative assessment
	  ○ Digital library of professional development materials and resources
	  ○ Aligned to Common Core State Standards and Smarter Balanced assessment targets

write with accuracy and precision. In mathematics, students will be assessed on more conceptual and multi-step authentic, real-world problems, and they will also be working with drag-and-drop and grid response formats. Students will also be asked to reason mathematically, conduct research, integrate multiple sources, write coherent and logical explanations, communicate effectively, and make sound arguments.

The CCSS represent the most sweeping educational reform ever in American public schools. Will these assessments turn our teachers and students away from teacher-directed instruction and rote memorization? How will they affect the already big test-prep culture? Will the focus on college, career, and workforce readiness promote student creativity and curiosity to learn? How will students' performance on these tests affect teacher evaluation? How will teachers use data from these assessments to reflect on student progress, alter their instruction, and make appropriate instructional decisions for all? What professional development systems will states, school districts, and schools put in place to support teachers? Implementation of the CCSS and the new generation assessment systems will require more effective systems of accountability, engaging, relevant, and rigorous curricula and materials, and focused teacher preparation and ongoing professional development learning.

College, Career, and Workforce Connections

- College instructors and employers will use a variety of assessments to gauge students' and employees' knowledge, skills, progress, and learning.
- Students who are college and career ready use feedback from assessments and standards of evaluation, and use self-assessment and reflection to propel their learning.
- They also are knowledgeable about media and technology and use their knowledge to collect, document, and share their work for college and career purposes.
- Knowledge of media and technology, software expertise, foreign language skills, art and music skills, networking skills, and even personal hobbies and interests, are all important for learning and success in today's competitive career markets.
- *Acceptance into the Bachelor of Music Education degree requires a high school student to pass an audition into the music department and a music education interview. Auditions include a performance (one – two classical solo pieces of contrasting nature), scales, and the display of musicianship skills such as sight-reading, pitch/interval recognition, and chord recognition. The interview evaluates personality, professionalism, teaching/leadership skills, and motivation for teaching (goals, evidence for teaching/music, and philosophy of education)* (Kelly Miller, Faculty, Music Education, University of Central Florida).
- *In addition to a base knowledge of music and competency as a performer, potential music education majors must also posses the ability to synthesize knowledge and to apply it creatively in new situations* (Scott Tobias, Director of Bands, Music, University of Central Florida)

Assessing Student Learning in the Disciplines: Now What?

In this chapter, I have examined a) the topic of assessment; b) its importance for planning for instruction and meeting all students' needs; c) types of assessments; d) implications of high stakes assessments for students, teachers, and schools; and e) the CCSS-aligned assessment consortia systems' mission, goals, and assessment formats. Throughout this chapter, you have learned that for assessment to be effective, it has to have certain characteristics, has to be used effectively, and it needs to provide valuable information about student learning. The CCSS will bring sweeping changes in the ways we assess students in grades 6–12. Aside from different types of assessments, we also have to think carefully about what to assess, when, and how often. More importantly, we have to accurately interpret the data individually and collaboratively with peers and school leaders. As you prepare your students for classroom-based or standardized assessments, also think about your overall beliefs about assessment and grading.

Assessment, Grades, and Grading

Grades count a lot for adolescents. There is a need to examine our own assumptions, biases, prejudices, and misconceptions about grading. When designing your grading plan, consider its components, weights, performance norms, and fairness. We can improve learning assessment by improving our grading practices. Reporting grades every few weeks is a standard and important school practice that involves assessment (Marzano, 2000). Grades carry official weight, and affect student motivation, graduation, and postsecondary options. School administrators use grades when counseling and placing students in classes and programs. Teachers need to communicate clear explanations about their grading system, and also what counts toward students' grades in each content area. For example, what would beginning, end-of-term, mid-term, and end-of-year grades be based on? How much would attendance, homework, labs, class participation, and group projects count? What is an academic versus a non-academic grade? How will you grade special needs students and ELLs? What grade will you assign for late or missing work? Teachers should use grades to motivate student learning.

Objectivity in grading is important, but it is often clouded by teacher subjectivity. Some school districts use uniform grading systems to promote objectivity across courses and grade levels. Teachers decide what will be evaluated, how it will be evaluated, and how much each activity is worth on a scale of 0–100. Teachers need to explain to students how grades will be determined, and provide sufficient feedback for the grades students earn, and provide opportunities to students to earn credit. Involving students in self-evaluation of their progress, and providing them with clear standards and rubrics for assignments, will help them prepare for what will be assessed in class.

Teachers should use multiple ways to assess students and they should not use grades as punishment. Teacher collaboration and reflection in Professional Learning Communities (PLCs) can also promote consistency, objectivity, and fairness in grading. Criterion-referenced grading (measuring a student against a level of performance instead of a student against another student) promotes fairness in grading practices by providing students with rubrics and clear targets (Wiggins, 1994), making clear objectives available to them ahead of time, and sharing exemplars or anchor papers for students to examine achievement levels (Wiggins, 1994).

Digital Literacies

- Awesome Screen Shot: http://awesomescreenshot.com/. Allows the user to capture a whole page or any portion of a page to annotate, upload, and share with others.
- Blurb: http://www.blurb.com/. A digital storytelling platform that allows the user to import photos, videos, and text, and share through social networking such as hashtags, Facebook, Twitter, Tumblr or e-mail.
- Collaborative writing: http://primarypad.com, or http://docs.google.com. Students can collaborate while writing or write in a shared journal.

What Should Classroom Assessments Focus On?

There is a variety of ways content area teachers assess student learning in their classrooms. In this last section, I want to attract your attention to two areas: 1) design classroom-based assessments that reflect your content area's goals and standards and 2) reflect on your instruction—if you want students to learn your content at a deep and critical level and in discipline-specific ways, then create assessments that will help them to reach these goals. Table 10.6 presents major discipline-specific goals we should be assessing in each content area and ways to reach those goals.

TABLE 10.6. Sample Discipline-Specific Assessment Foci and Practices

Discipline	What to Assess	What to Do
English Language Arts	• Students' comprehension of complex texts (presented in different text formats). • Students' ability to critically analyze, interpret complex texts using textual evidence, and reason clearly and effectively. • Students' language function (i.e., describe, explain, analyze, interpret, argue, justify, evaluate, synthesize, create). • Students' ability to interpret words and phrases used in texts including determining technical, connotative, and figurative meanings, and analyze how specific word choices shape meaning or tone. • Students' analysis of text structure, point of view, and purpose. • Students' communication and collaboration skills. • Students' command of conventions of standard English, application of language in different contexts, understanding of figurative language, and use of general academic and domain-specific words for reading, writing, speaking, and listening purposes. • Students' ability to create a written product interpreting or responding to a text using textual evidence and arguments to support claims. • Students' writing of informative/explanatory texts, narratives, and arguments. • Students' ability to gather information from varied print and digital resources, and use evidence from literary and informational texts to support their analysis and research.	• Create a learning environment of rapport, respect, rigor, collaboration, high engagement, reading, writing, discussions, and collaboration. • Increase text complexity, students' engagement with complex texts, and scaffolded teacher support. • Introduce students to texts that raise their content knowledge and allow them to examine a topic from a variety of perspectives. • Allow time for high-level, text-based discussions on texts and ideas. • Model and expect students to use accountable talk, good reasoning, and evidence to support their assertions. • Model and engage students in argumentative, informational, and explanatory writing. • Create assignments for real audiences with real purpose. • Use rubrics and offer specific feedback that will support and extend students' writing development. • Have your students write routinely over extended time frames for a variety of purposes, tasks, and audiences. • Create short and sustained research projects that facilitate critical and evidence-based thinking.

(Continued)

TABLE 10.6.   (Continued)

Discipline	What to Assess	What to Do
Mathematics	• Students learning mathematics with understanding. • Students' conceptual understanding and procedural fluency. • Students' problem solving knowledge and skills. • Students' ability to reason with proof. • Students' ability to communicate their mathematical thinking and reasoning. • Students' ability to make connections among mathematical ideas. • Students' proficiency with number and operations. • Students' knowledge of Algebra, Geometry, and measurement. • Students' knowledge of data analysis, statistics, and probability.	• Provide students with rigorous instruction and tasks that require them to figure things out for themselves. • Ask students to restate the problem in their own words, including any assumptions they made. • Give students time to analyze the problem and explore using different models. • Ask students questions that require them to reason well and explain their thinking. • Encourage students to ask probing questions of one another and use accountable talk. • Expect all students to communicate their reasoning to their classmates and to their teacher, orally and in writing, using mathematical vocabulary. • Provide students with exemplary explanations and ask them to discuss what makes them effective. • Create a learning environment that makes students comfortable about sharing their mathematical arguments and critiquing the arguments of others in a productive way. • Use a variety of assessment types/formats, provide students with constructive feedback on their performance, and discuss ways for them to master their learning goals and monitor their own progress.
Science	• Students' understandings of science content and process knowledge and skills. • Students' abilities to think critically and solve simple to complex problems. • Students' scientific inquiry skills and habits of mind. • Students' capabilities of designing scientific experiments, analyzing data, and drawing conclusions.	• Create a learning environment of safety, respect, rigor, inquiry, accountable talk, and collaboration. • Deliver rigorous instruction that promotes students' development and use of the scientific process, vocabulary, and scientific inquiry habits of mind.

- Students' knowledge of core scientific ideas and scientific inquiry practices.
- Students' knowledge of crosscutting concepts (i.e., Patterns; Cause and Effect; Scale, Proportion, and Quantity; Systems and System Models; Energy and Matter; Structure and Function; and Stability and Change).
- Students' ability to connect knowledge from different disciplines into a coherent and scientifically based view of the world.
- Students' capacities to see and articulate relationships between science topics and real-world issues and concerns.
- Students' skills using mathematics as a tool for science learning.

- Use the 5E model (i.e., engage, explore, explain, elaborate, evaluate) for science teaching.
- Create opportunities for students to observe, infer, classify, experiment, discuss, and evaluate.
- Expect students to justify claims and explanations orally and in writing.
- Create assignments that integrate science with other subjects.
- Ask higher order questions that require students to interpret, analyze, critique, synthesize, hypothesize, and evaluate claims, data, results, or other scientific information.

Social Studies

- Students' understanding of time, continuity, and change.
- Students' knowledge of text structures, identifying author's point of view, identifying problems and considering alternative solutions, and considering issues from multiple perspectives.
- Students' knowledge of facts, concepts, and interpretations or analyses to build arguments about historical events, a topic, or social phenomenon.
- Students' ability to analyze historical texts using multiple sources of evidence.
- Students' use of textual evidence to support their analysis of primary and secondary sources.
- Students' ability to analyze images, graphs, charts, maps, etc.
- Students' ability to clearly communicate, synthesize information, apply knowledge, and generalize learning to other settings.
- Students' use of critical thinking skills as they investigate an issue or event, and develop a position, providing evidence for their conclusions.

- Create assessments that test the full range of what students know and can do.
- Teach students to analyze primary and secondary sources by modeling a series of scaffolded questions that help students identify the document's purpose.
- Teach students how to read and analyze historical text(s), interpret graphs, data, maps, and images.
- Create a classroom where historical argument, evidentiary thinking, talking, and writing are the norm.
- Create authentic assessments that do not focus on mere factual recall, but instead are designed to examine students' performance on real-world tasks.
- Promote active involvement in history learning and developing historical thinking.

(Continued)

TABLE 10.6. (Continued)

Discipline	What to Assess	What to Do
		• Provide students with opportunities to construct their own understanding, apply what they are learning, and consider others' points of view. • Encourage the use of print and digital tools to interpret and evaluate complex information. • Expect and model how to consider multiple perspectives and alternative solutions. • Model historical inquiry and habits of mind. • Give students tasks that are open-ended and allow for collaboration and divergent thinking so that students may use multiple strategies to arrive at varied conclusions. • Expect the use of accountable talk and collaborative inquiry.

Summary

- International and national comparisons of student achievement have made assessment mandatory, and have also placed a focus on the accountability of the classroom teacher. Assessment exists to inform and improve instruction, and promote student learning. Fundamental assessment questions should include: What do teachers expect students to learn? How will teachers best assess their learning? What best instructional practices will teachers use to promote student learning? How will teachers know whether or not students have learned? What will teachers do if students do not learn?

- Assessment types include formal (high stakes) and authentic or informal. The implementation of the CCSS is coupled with new generation assessment systems that focus on college and career readiness.

- Authentic assessments provide teachers with more immediate and instructionally relevant information about student learning. Assessment should be ongoing and flexible. The form and frequency of assessments will vary according to purpose, student needs, task, and instructional objectives. Teachers should set clear, fair, and objective grading criteria for student performance, communicate standards and criteria to students, and provide feedback to students about their learning.

Differentiating Instruction

- For students with special educational needs, administer tests individually, or in a small group, in a separate location with minimal distractions. If needed, provide the test in audio format. Highlight words, or phrases in the directions. Allow for a flexible schedule, and extend the time allotted to complete the test. Allow frequent breaks as needed during testing. Administer the test in several sessions and over several days, and specify the duration of each session.

- For ELLs, provide extra assessment time, breaks during the test, offer it in a small group format, and administer it over several sessions. Give oral directions aloud in English, or in the student's native language, and allow dictionary use as needed. Use a variety of formative and summative assessments, monitor student progress, set short-term goals, and offer specific feedback.

- Students with exceptionalities may need assessment accommodations; for example, spacing on the page or screen, larger font size, chunking the assessment into pieces or assessment blocks, and additional time to complete the assessment. Consider alternative classroom assessments.

- When students are working in their zone of proximal development (ZPD), student achievement is optimal. Students will benefit from differentiated instruction that is customized to their level of readiness, learning rate, learning interests, or prior knowledge, and language proficiency. All students will benefit from differentiated instruction in a classroom where (a) teachers make instructional decisions that are based on formative assessment data and research-based instructional strategies, and they are valued, and (b) in a positive learning environment where everyone is valued and respected.

Reflect and Apply

1. What are your attitudes toward assessment? What types of assessment do you prefer and why? Share with your peers your attitudes, preferences, and experiences about assessment, and discuss the role assessment has played in your learning.
2. Use what you learned about assessment to offer some suggestions Ms. Kennedy (see Classroom Life vignette) can use with the teachers she is working with, and discuss your ideas with a group of peers.
3. What did you learn about portfolio assessment? In what ways might you use portfolio assessment in your classroom? Specify type, purpose, and contents of portfolio you plan to use in your own content area class. Seek feedback from a couple of your peers.

Extending Learning

1. Interview a school principal, a school district superintendent, or a state department of education representative to find out how your state is aligned with NCLB and the new Common Core State Standards assessments. Discuss implications of the policy and the initiative for student learning, and teacher evaluation purposes. Share the results of your interview with your peers.
2. Select a content area textbook and design a formative assessment using insights from this chapter. Administer the assessment to at least three students to gauge their knowledge of course material. Score and interpret the results and using evidence from student performance, identify instructional plans to improve student comprehension of text. Evaluate your assessment, and discuss your experience with your peers.
3. Find out what standards exist for your state, what the key state assessments are, and how test results are used. In addition, find out if your state has recommendations

for assessments that can be used for screening and progress monitoring purposes. Organize your findings in a paper, and present it to your class or your subject area colleagues.

References

Afflerbach, P. (2004). *National Reading Conference policy brief: High stakes testing and reading assessment.* Oak Creek, WI: National Reading Conference. Retrieved from http://www.literacyresearch-association.org/publications/HighStakesTestingandReadingAssessment.pdf

Afflerbach, P. (2007). *Understanding and using reading assessment, K–12.* Newark, DE: International Reading Association.

Airasian, P. W. (1997). *Classroom assessment: Concepts and applications.* New York, NY: McGraw-Hill.

American Educational Research Association. (2000). *Position statement on high-stakes testing in preK–12 education.* Washington, DC: American Educational Research Association. Retrieved from http://www.aera.net/AboutAERA/AERARulesPolicies/AERAPolicyStatements/PositionStatementonHighStakesTesting/tabid/11083/Default.aspx

American Psychological Association, American Psychological Association, and National Council on Measurement in Education. (1999). *Standards for educational and psychological testing.* Washington, DC: Author. Retrieved from http://www.apa.org/pubs/info/brochures/testing.aspx?item=2#

Appelbaum, M. (2009). *The one-stop guide to implementing RtI: Academic and behavioral interventions, K–12.* Thousand Oaks, CA: Corwin Press.

Barrett, H. (2007). Researching electronic portfolios and learner engagement: The REFLECT initiative. *Journal of Adolescent and Adult Literacy, 50,* 436–449.

Beach, R. W. (2011). Issues in analyzing alignment of language arts common core standards with state standards. *Educational Researcher, 40*(4), 179–182.

Black, P., & Wiliam, D. (1998). Assessment and classroom learning. *Assessment in Education: Principles, Policy, and Practice, 5*(1), 7–73.

Bormuth, J. R. (1968). The cloze reliability procedure. *Elementary English, 45,* 429–436.

Burns, M. K., & Gibbons, K. (2012). Implementing response-to-intervention in elementary and secondary schools. New York, NY: Routledge.

Carlson, K. (2004). Test scores by race and ethnicity. *Phi Delta Kappan, 85*(5), 379–380.

Common Core State Standards Initiative. (2010). *The common core state standards for English language arts and literacy in history/social studies, science, and technical subjects.* Washington, DC: The Council of Chief State School Officers and the National Governors Association.

Duncan, A. (2013). *Choosing the right battles: Remarks and a Conversation Remarks of U.S. Secretary of Education Arne Duncan to the American Educational Research Association Annual meeting, San Francisco, California.* Retrieved from http://www.ed.gov/news/speeches/choosing-right-battles-remarks-and-conversation

Dunn, K. E. & Mulvenon, S. W. (2009). A critical review of research on formative assessment: The limited scientific evidence of the impact of formative assessment in education. *Practical Assessment, Research & Evaluation, 14*(7), 1–11.

Fairbanks, S., Sugai, G., Guardino, D., & Lathrop, M. (2007). Response to Intervention: Examining classroom behavior support in second grade. *Exceptional Children, 73,* 288–310.

Fernsten, L., & Fernsten, J. (2005). Portfolio assessment and reflection: Enhancing learning through effective practice. *Reflective Practice, 6*(2), 303–309.

Fry, E., Kress, J., & Fountoukidis, D. (2000). *The reading teacher's book of lists.* Paramus, NJ: Prentice Hall.

Hertz, M. B. (2013, May 30). *Using e-portfolios in the classroom* [Weblog post]. Retrieved from http://www.edutopia.org/blog/e-portfolios-in-the-classroom-mary-beth-hertz

Johnson, P. (1989). Constructive evaluation and the improvement of teaching and learning. *Teachers College Record, 90,* 535–549.

Johnson, E., Mellard, D. F., Fuchs, D., & McKnight, M. A. (2006). *Responsiveness to intervention (RTI): How to do it.* Lawrence, KS: National Research Center on Learning Disabilities.

Juel, C. (1994). *Learning to read and write in one elementary school.* New York, NY: Springer-Verlag.

International Reading Association. (1999). *High-stakes assessments in reading: A Position statement of the International Reading Association.* Newark, DE: International Reading Association. Retrieved from http://www.reading.org/Libraries/position-statements-and-resolutions/ps1035_high_stakes.pdf

Light, T. P., Chen, H. L., & Ittelson, J. C. (2012). *Documenting learning with e-portfolios*. San Francisco, CA: Jossey-Bass.

Luiten, J., Ames, W., & Bradley, J. (1979). Using Fry's graph to describe the variation of readability: A corrected procedure. *Literary Research and Instruction, 18.4*, 365.

Marzano, R. J. (2000). *Transforming classroom grading*. Alexandria, VA: Association for Supervision and Curriculum Development.

Mellard, D. F., & Johnson, E. (2008). *RTI: A practitioner's guide to implementing response to intervention*. Thousand Oaks: CA: Corwin Press & NAESP.

Mokhtari, K., & Reichard, C. A. (2002). Assessing students' metacognitive awareness of reading strategies. *Journal of Educational Psychology, 94*(2), 249–259.

Mokhtari, K., & Sheorey, R. (2002). Measuring ESL students' awareness of reading strategies. *Journal of Development Education, 25*(3), 2–10.

National Governors Association Center for Best Practices and Council of Chief State School Officers. (2010). Common Core State Standards for English language arts in history/social studies, science, and technical subjects: Appendix A: Research supporting key elements of the standards and glossary of key terms. Washington DC: Authors. Retrieved from http://www.corestandards.org/assets/Appendix_A.pdf

National Research Council on Learning Disabilities. (2008). *Professional development and collaboration within the RtI process*. Retrieved from http://www.nrcld.org/rti_practices/collaboration.html

Pitcher, S. M., Albright, L. K., DeLaney, C. J., Walker, N. T., Seunarinesingh, K., Mogge, S., Headley, K. N., Ridgeway, V., Peck, S., Hunt, R., & Dunston, P. J. (2007). Assessing adolescents' motivation to read. *Journal of Adolescent & Adult Literacy, 50*(5), 378–396.

Popham, W. J. (2012). *Assessment bias: How to banish it* (2nd ed.). Boston, MA: Pearson Education, Inc.

Porter, C., & Cleland, J. (1995). *The portfolio as a learning strategy*. Portsmouth, NH: Heinemann.

Rawlinson, D. A., Zugelder, G., & Little, M. (2009/2010). A teacher's guide to RtI and problem solving. Florida Department of Education, Bureau of Exceptional Education and Student Services, 2009/2010. Retrieved from: http://springssm-sy10-11.wikispaces.com/file/view/teachersRtI_guide_final_1cj.pdf

Readance, J. E., Bean, T. W., & Baldwin, R. S. (1992). *Content area literacy: An integrated approach* (4th ed.). Dubuque, IA: Kendal/Hunt.

Smart, M. P. (2009). *Digital portfolios pull double duty*. Retrieved from http://www.edutopia.org/digital-portfolio-assessment

Taraban, R., Kerr, M., Rynearson, K. (2004). Analytic and pragmatic factors in college students' meta-cognitive reading strategies. *Reading Psychology, 25*, 67–81.

Taylor, W. L. (1953). Cloze procedure: A new tool for measuring readability. *Journalism Quarterly, 30*, 415–433.

Tucker, P. D., & Stronge, J. H. (2005). *Linking teacher evaluation and student learning*. Alexandria, VA: Association for Supervision and Curriculum Development.

Wiggins, G. P. (1993). *Assessing student performance*. San Francisco, CA: Jossey-Bass Publishers.

Wiggins, G. P. (1994). Toward better report cards. *Educational Leadership, October*, 29–37.

Wiggins, G. P. (1998). *Educative assessment: Designing assessments to inform and improve student performance*. San Francisco, CA: Jossey-Bass Publishers.

Windram, H., Scierka, B., & Silberglitt, b. (2007). Response to intervention at the secondary level: A description of two districts' models of implementation. *Communique, 35*(5), 43–45.

Wininger, S. R. (2005). Using your tests to teach: Formative summative assessment. *Teaching of Psychology, 32*, 164–166.

eleven

Teaching Discipline-Specific Literacies and Professional Development

*Great teaching can change a child's life. That kind
of teaching is a remarkable combination of things:
art, science, inspiration, talent, gift, and—always—
incredibly hard work. It requires relationship
building, subject expertise and a deep
understanding of the craft.*
–Arne Duncan

Chapter Highlights

- Professional development should be at the center of educational reform.
- Effective professional development is cohesive, relevant, job-embedded, ongoing, collaborative, and discipline-specific. Teachers need time, support, feedback, and opportunities to collaborate with colleagues on improving teaching and student learning.
- Professional development needs to be learner-centered, knowledge-centered, instruction-centered, and assessment-centered.
- Professional development is closely connected to teaching and learning standards, teacher evaluation, accountability, and school improvement plans. Evidence of teacher effectiveness should use multiple sources of evidence, be collected over time, and be discussed at all times with the teacher. Feedback is vital for teacher growth and reflection.
- Different types of professional development include Professional Learning Communities (PLCs), study groups, data or leadership teams, lesson study, and collaborating with instructional coaches.
- A collaborative professional culture is a must for ongoing teacher and student success. Teaching is a complex process that warrants collaboration among all stakeholders.

Classroom Life

Persistence of Vision

As a novice English Language Arts teacher when courses such as "The Novel," "The Short Story," "Journalism," "Literary Criticism," were the norm of the times, I had the opportunity to teach a course entitled, "Introduction to Film." Because this was a survey course introducing the history of the motion picture, and concluding with film genres, I spent the entire summer prior to that school year, reading everything I could get my hands on about film history and criticism. I planned extensively. Daily lessons, units and activities were all designed to engage, excite, and inspire tenth graders to study film from a precise literary point of view. But not long into that first day of class, I realized most had registered for the class thinking they would watch movies every day. As I led the class through the syllabus, I was interrupted by, "What is with all this reading and writing? Aren't we supposed to be watching films, miss?" Needless to say, as teachers do, I reflected, and then refined my lessons, brokering a compromise with my students about the balance of "movies" and authentic reading coupled with writing about the content.

When I consider the vision and the promise that could; and, should occur with the implementation of the Common Core State Standards, I mull over those lessons from my early teaching days. The expectation of the CCSS is that all students will be prepared to meet the demands of colleges and careers in an ever-evolving world. Our instructional practice shifts beyond what the teacher desires to teach to what students really need to be able to know and do when they leave us. Who can really argue that coherent, cohesive, content rich curricula might just lead to improved student achievement, and better prepared citizens? But will that hope become a reality? What will our schools look like in the coming years?

One definition of vision is the ability to see things that are invisible. Like the potential in our children. Teachers who have vision see what is beautiful in all things. Teachers are the ones who helped us learn to see. We hear it far too often about our kids . . . they will never be able to get this concept, or complete this rigorous work or pass the test. Why? "Because it's too hard." Or she doesn't have a good home life. Or he is too lazy, or too mean, or too aloof. And that perception is dangerous and unfair, because it impacts kids in ways we can't even imagine, and therefore, impacts their entire future. Goethe wrote, "Treat people as if . . . they were what they ought to be . . . and you help them become . . . what they are capable of being." And that holds true for our kids. We must remember that we have every opportunity to transform ourselves and our practice. We have to understand daily that our frame of mind and vision for our students is essentially up to us. And it is this opportunity to refresh, reinvent, and refocus that is well within the reach of teachers who seek daily to do what we should ask of all students: take a risk, test your limits, stretch your thinking, and push a bit beyond the comfort zone. As teachers we know that achievement has a direct correlation to expectation. When we set high standards for our students we challenge them to reach heights they perceive as: unimaginable. It is that relentless, persistent pursuit of excellence, that refusal to accept anything less than the best effort that creates outstanding teaching.

Now back in my Introduction to Film days, we learned that your eye and brain retain a visual impression for about 1/30th of a second. This ability to retain an image is known as persistence of vision. The eye retains the image of each frame long enough to give us the illusion of smooth motion. In film and video, this phenomenon is widely believed to account for our ability to perceive a sequence of frames as a continuous moving picture that sparked the concept of animation and eventually led to the development of motion pictures. The anticipatory hook used was inadvertently simplistic. Take a quarter, turn it up on its side, hold the top of the quarter with one finger, take your other finger and flip that two dimensional object. What does it turn into? If you are skillful enough and persistence of vision occurs, you will see the flat coin appear to be a spinning sphere. My vision for that class was something different than that of my students. As we worked together throughout the course, the content became the vehicle to observe with a critical eye, to think about connections to broader concepts, to engage in real debate about what the director, actors or the screenwriter intended. And yes, we watched some film clips only to find evidence to support student assertions. Although I have no way of knowing, I doubt that any of my students went on to Hollywood, but perhaps some of that "reading and writing" we did helped them to succeed in their chosen path.

So today what we see in our classrooms are kids with the same dreams and aspirations as we had. The learning opportunities we provide will fill in those gaps between what we see and what we can't see. Let's quit making excuses. We need to set and maintain high standards and expect no less from each and every student. Instead of saying all students can learn, let's say all students will learn. Let's focus our instruction on the specific needs of our students with no other judgment. Let's stop allowing any child to "opt out" of his or her education. Yes, we definitely have students with needs beyond our comprehension but what better way to help them escape from these issues then to construct avenues for success. Let's commit to these essential expectations . . . an environment where teaching is a passion and learning nonnegotiable, where the focus is placed upon the needs of our students, where a supportive atmosphere thrives for students and adults alike, where an outstretched hand is the rule of the day. The vision of the Common Core will always remain two dimensional unless we remain persistent towards our vision. *(Ms. Karen Nolen, Coordinator of Professional Development, Seminole County Public Schools, Florida).*

Teacher Professional Development, and Student College, Career, and Workforce Readiness

In an era of higher educational standards, high-stakes accountability, and pressures for improved global comparisons, teachers continue to receive many pressures for better preparation of students. We know that it takes much careful planning, quality instruction, and many other support systems for students to become ready for postsecondary education, career and work, and life, in general. Teachers need to have deep knowledge of their state's college and career ready standards, and they also need to know how to deliver instruction that engages students in rigorous learning. All teachers will need clear definitions of content and performance standards, and states will need to ensure a professional development framework to create a unified statewide understanding and support systems. Desimone (2009) calls for states to provide professional development particularly for teachers teaching Grade 12 transitional courses.

All teachers, in-service or pre-service, need to learn about professional development, and also need to participate in it on an ongoing basis. Good teachers are like sponges—they absorb knowledge from everyone around them and recognize their need for ongoing growth. Professional development is a must, and not a luxury, for teacher growth and professional learning. In this chapter, I examine the role of professional development on teacher success and ongoing learning, the types of professional development that will result in positive teacher and student outcomes, how professional development can help you meet teacher evaluation demands, and ways to continue to grow in your discipline and profession. In this chapter, I will propose the development of professional development that views literacy as a discipline-specific process.

Professional development needs to be ongoing, cohesive, job-embedded, and collaborative, with coaches and small groups of teachers reflecting on practice, on student learning, and applying new knowledge to their specific context (Garet, Porter, Desimone, Birman, & Yoon, 2001). With the implementation of new educational standards, quality professional development will need to be discipline-specific, pedagogically sound, and it will also need to address the unique needs of diverse learners, teacher evaluation, and assessment models. Such professional development will need to engage content area teachers in active, hand-on and collaborative learning with colleagues, and will need to build upon state and district established curricula and standards.

Teachers who participated in at least 14 hours of professional development quality, relevant, and well-aligned learning experiences on best instructional practices (Garet et al., 2001) reported that they felt more efficacious and better prepared to teach, and their instruction led to improved student achievement (Yoon, 2007). When professional development happens within existing professional learning communities (PLCs), where teachers are grouped either by grade, content, or department, teachers receive more relevant support that promotes teacher implementation (Stoll & Louis, 2007). Professional development that addresses daily teaching challenges matters to teachers (Darling-Hammond, Wei, Andree, Richardson & Orphanos, 2009). Finally, coherent professional development experiences and giving teachers time to plan for implementation and offering them support in terms of feedback and resources, also promote implementation of knowledge from professional development into classroom practice (Penuel, Fishman, Yamaguchi & Gallagher, 2007).

While students from certain countries outperform US students in reading, math, or science, it is important to not only look at what students need to know and be able to do, but to also examine the investment of such countries on quality, job-embedded teacher professional development. Darling-Hammond et al. (2009) reported in *Professional Learning in the Learning Profession: A Status Report on Teacher Development in the United States and Abroad*, that teachers in the highest performing countries reported spending 15–20 hours a week on teaching-related activities such as planning with their peers. In addition, 85 percent of Organization for Economic Co-operation and Development (OECD) schools provide teachers with professional development opportunities during their workday, and new teacher induction programs are mandatory, focus on developing teaching skills, and create strong mentoring relationships between novice and veteran/mentor teachers. Last, the professional development found in these countries is located within teacher teams that meet and plan development opportunities around the needs of their local schools.

Although teachers are in the midst of massive educational reform, the impact of the Common Core State Standards (CCSS) (and other standards) on students and teachers remains to be seen. I like Calkins', Ehrenworth's, and Lehman's charge in *Pathways to the Common Core: Accelerating Achievement*:

> We need to see hope and opportunity. As part of this, we need to embrace what is good about the Common Core State Standards—and roll up our sleeves and work to make those standards into a force that lifts our teaching and our schools.
>
> (2012, p. 8)

Although there is disagreement when it comes to the CCSS, there is one area everyone agrees on: the key to successful and smooth implementation of the new standards depends on purposeful, relevant, and ongoing professional development.

Emphasis on cognitive skills and student academic progress are very important. The long-term success of students depends on the long-term success of teachers. Student preparation for secondary and postsecondary success depends on teacher preparation, professional development, and support. The Bush Administration's *No Child Left Behind* and the Obama Administration's *Race to the Top* policies have both resulted in many high stakes for teachers (and students). Accountability is not a new term or revelation for any educator. But ways in which policy has been used in oppressive and demoralizing ways toward educators has also resulted in reduced teacher morale, several good teachers leaving the education field, and much competitiveness for funding. I am not against policy, assessment, or accountability, but I am not supportive of the ways public educators continue to be attacked and held solely responsible for lack of student achievement by some of the media and the public.

Teaching must be seen as the center of education, it must be respected, valued, and supported. Educational reform and efforts to close the achievement gap will be impossible to address unless there is a highly effective teacher in every classroom. There is a need for a national commitment to elevate the status of teachers, including improving salaries, teacher preparation programs, creating effective induction and mentoring programs, ensuring that teacher accountability is measured by multiple indicators and factors, moving away from assessing student progress on a single annual state assessment, and investing on providing ongoing effective professional development to all teachers. For our students and our nation to go far, we need to go together. But, before we get into more professional specifics, I think it is important to first understand how adults learn. Why? Because many schools districts, schools, and agencies do not consider fundamental adult learning principles when they design professional development for teachers.

College, Career, and Workforce Connections

- Teacher professional development should focus on the complexities and demands of college-, career-, and workforce-readiness in a technologically driven global economy.
- Teachers should prepare all students with the knowledge, skills, dispositions and behaviors necessary for educational, career, and civic engagement.
- Student preparation for college, career, and the workforce should also include preparation in media, technology, and Web 2.0 tools students will need to communicate, collaborate, share, produce, and present in the 21st century and beyond.
- *The field of hospitality is very broad and encompasses many different types of businesses, including hotels, restaurants, theme parks, and vacation ownership. All of these businesses require employees who have a desire to serve others. Event management, while related to hospitality, is a different business model and requires great attention to detail and the ability to juggle multiple tasks* (Deborah Breiter, Professor, Hospitality, University of Central Florida).

Andragogy: The Study of Adult Learning

How do adults learn? Andragogy refers to the "art and science of helping adults learn" (Knowles, 1970, p. 38). Knowles notes that the term "adult" is not strictly related to age; instead, he defines adulthood as the point in human development at which individuals perceive themselves to be essentially self-directing (Knowles, 1984a). According to Knowles (1984b), adult learners differ from child learners in the following ways:

- Self-concept—adults are self-directed individuals.
- Experience—the progressive accumulation of experience becomes an important factor for learning.
- Readiness to learn—adults' readiness to learn is tied to their social roles.
- Orientation to learning—adults enjoy problem solving and practical and immediate application(s) of knowledge.
- Motivation to learn—adult's motivation is internally directed.

Research shows (Bransford, Brown, & Cocking, 2000) that adults learn best when:

- Professional development goals are realistic, relevant, and connected to and integrated with their everyday practices and comprehensive plan for school improvement.
- There are opportunities for collaboration with peers in small group settings that promote problem solving, team building, and a positive culture.
- The program is learner-centered, considers their interests, learning styles and needs, and allows for personalized and differentiated learning.
- The professional development is knowledge-centered and focuses on discipline-specific content knowledge for teaching. Teachers need opportunities to understand their subject matter more deeply and how to facilitate student knowledge and learning.
- The professional environment is assessment- and instruction-centered. Teachers benefit from seeing the results of their instruction and receiving specific, judicious, and relevant feedback.
- Ongoing collaborative professional learning opportunities are present.

So, what are some implications of andragogy for teacher professional development? Whether teachers participate in school-based, or other types of professional development, it is important to consider the following guidelines/questions that will maximize their learning and promote new knowledge implementation.

- Is the professional development relevant to teachers' content, instructional, and assessment needs? Is it relevant to school improvement plans and state standards?
- Is the professional development inclusive of teachers' backgrounds, experiences, and disciplinary, instructional, and professional needs?
- Is the professional development positive, collaborative, facilitative, instructional, respectful of teachers, and scaffolded? Does it encourage mutual trust and shared responsibility of student learning? Does it provide for teacher and support staff collaborations, inquiry, and reflection?
- How about teacher voice? Are teachers involved in the planning and evaluation of the learning experiences?
- Does the professional development provide for self-directed learning and are teachers involved in their own progress monitoring?
- Is the professional development short term or long term? Does it include specific times for evaluation, and does it require using student data to make informed instructional decisions?
- Does the professional development promote the development of a positive professional learning community culture and communities of practice?

What Is Professional Development?

In education, research has shown that teacher quality and school leadership have the strongest impact on student achievement. Professional development refers to those intentional, systematic, and ongoing processes and activities designed to enhance the professional knowledge, skills, and attitudes of educators so that they might improve students' learning (Guskey, 2000, 2002, 2003). "An emerging body of work suggests that professional development that focuses on subject matter content and how children learn it may be an especially important element on changing teaching practice" (Garet et al., 2001, p. 924).

There are different ways teachers participate in professional development in schools. Aside from belonging to professional organizations and social media networks, independent study and research, or pursuing graduate degrees, there is research that supports the role of school-based professional development in supporting teacher success and growth. I will describe a few approaches in the following section.

If you are currently teaching, what does professional practice look like in your school? Are you and your colleagues actively engaged in learning? Do you study and reflect upon student success or challenges? Do you work closely with other colleagues, the reading coach, and your principal to address literacy-related issues? If you are a pre-service teacher, what types of professional development have you observed in schools you are visiting, volunteering, or interning at? It is important for all of us as educators to understand, embrace, and pursue collaborative inquiry with peers, developing and maintaining positive professional learning communities at our schools, and working together to bring about positive change in our content, pedagogical, and technology knowledge as well as in our school culture.

For professional development to have an impact on teacher and school growth, Guskey (2000) suggests the following 10 actions:

1. Collect information about the school on an ongoing basis.
2. Design a professional development system with interdependent components.
3. Create awareness and work for clear goals and common vision.
4. Assess and focus resources, time, people, and materials where they will make the greatest difference.
5. Provide training on specific, clear instructional procedures.
6. Create a culture that encourages reflection, honest feedback, mutual support, and collaborative problem solving.
7. Provide in-class demonstrations and coaching.
8. Use student achievement to assess impact and inform professional development plans and actions.
9. Monitor the impact of professional development over longer periods of time.
10. Design ongoing, in-depth professional development over longer periods of time.

Research shows that teacher expertise is the most significant school-based factor on student learning and high quality professional development is a central component for improving education (Guskey, 2002).

US Secretary of Education Arne Duncan has been calling for the development of a high quality teacher workforce that is innovative and creative in their thinking. He stated that, "No area of the teaching profession is more plainly broken today than that of teacher evaluation and professional development" (Duncan, 2009). Although there is no argument about the need for effective and ongoing professional development for teacher growth, the level of investment in teacher learning is neither ongoing nor substantial. In addition, much of the investment in professional development does not yield changes in teacher practice or change school culture and practices. Quality, job-embedded, and relevant professional development is needed now more than ever. At the same time, teacher professional development is under scrutiny and districts have been called to task for the lack of implementation of best practices in professional development (Garet et al.,

2010). Research shows that for professional development to be effective, it needs to be strategic (Darling-Hammond et al., 2009), embedded in the daily work of schools and teachers, and less in formal, "drive-by" professional development (Loucks-Horsley & Matsumoto, 1999).

Job-embedded professional development is aligned with school standards, curricula, and school improvement goals (Joyce & Showers, 2002). It is also founded on daily teaching practice, takes place regularly and it involves teachers analyzing student learning and problem solving about immediate solutions to instructional problems. Job-embedded professional development is centered on promoting deliberate practice in teaching, it promotes shared responsibility and responsibility for teacher and student learning (Darling-Hammond et al., 2009) and helps teachers learn how students understand and learn the content. Teachers need opportunities to observe, model, and practice new effective strategies for content instruction, and they also need feedback from others (Garet et al., 2001).

All school improvement efforts focus on enhancing the knowledge, skills, and dispositions of teachers and support staff. Principals play a vital role in professional development and school change. They provide the vision, the leadership, the support, and they also create the culture under which teachers and support staff work. Funding, providing time for teachers to get together and plan, participating in key school meetings and using a participatory leadership model, all play a role in whether teachers will participate or commit to having informed dialogue, attend school-based professional development, and be open about instructional and student challenges.

Continuing professional development is vital to school improvement whether new initiatives are being implemented, or whether teachers are looking for ways to improve student performance, set goals and standards for student learning, or improve the effectiveness of existing programs and practices on student learning. Professional development should also involve follow-up and support for further learning, feedback and specific examples of instructional practices, resources, and opportunities to dialogue with peers.

Research has also shown that effective job-embedded professional development is collaborative and community-centered in nature. Collaboration can take place in a number of ways from informal conversations, to common grade or content planning, to data teams, collaborative teams, leadership teams, or Professional Learning Communities (PLCs). Teacher collaboration contributes to improved knowledge of student learning, data, instruction, and even attitudes toward teaching (Miller, Goddard, Larsen & Jacob, 2010).

Professional Development and Teacher Evaluation

According to the landmark National Reading Panel Report (NRP) (2000), teachers who had more effective professional training were more likely to use teaching practices that were associated with higher reading achievement. Professional development cannot be viewed as an afterthought, or as a periodic "teacher treatment." In addition, it should be an integral part of teacher evaluation as it plays an integral role in teacher effectiveness. State and school district policy-makers should not only evaluate teacher effectiveness—they should support it and promote it.

Teacher effectiveness does not develop in a vacuum and teachers should not be targeted as the sole source of student success or failure. The Obama administration's 2009 *Race to the Top* (RTTT) federal $4.35 billion initiative was designed to ensure that all US schools would have great teachers and leaders. In addition, the program has resulted in several state and local policies that require educators to develop and implement rigorous evaluation systems that assess teacher effectiveness using student learning as one of the measures. These evaluation systems also differentiate teacher effectiveness based on student achievement as described by value-added models.

We hope that states will not only evaluate teachers and principals, but they will also provide relevant professional development, induction, and coaching. Teachers need to have evidence-based feedback on their practice in order for teacher evaluation to enhance teacher learning and effectiveness. States and school districts need to provide school-based or job-embedded professional development that is aligned with the school's comprehensive instructional program and is designed for teacher success (Coggshall, Rasmussen, Colton, Milton, & Jacques, 2012).

As a content area teacher in the US, you will be evaluated by some teacher evaluation system. States have adopted different evaluation systems, which I describe in the following section. It is important for all teachers to become knowledgeable about the evaluation system their state will use to assess their teaching. Well-designed evaluation systems have professional teaching standards that are aligned with student learning standards and they describe what excellent teaching performance, knowledge, and dispositions look like (Goe, Biggers, & Croft, 2012). The evaluation standards also provide a common language for teacher and administrator discussions about effective teaching practice (Danielson, 2011). Effective evaluation systems also use multiple measures, of student learning (e.g., classroom observation rubrics, student survey results, and assessment of student learning) to gauge how teachers meet the standards, and their students meet the learning goals. Last, they include standards about professional responsibilities and expectations about teacher participation in professional learning. So, according to research (Learning Forward, 2011), professional learning that will improve your learning effectiveness and the results for all of your students includes ongoing participation in learning communities, school leadership that will provide you with vision and support systems, resources, data, effective implementation of learning models, and student outcomes. To be able to provide effective, discipline-specific instruction that will prepare all students, you need ongoing professional development.

Teaching Standards

What is the content of sample teacher standards? The following are standards from national organizations. Keep in mind that each content area will have its own recommended and desired teacher standards. Every teacher should become knowledgeable about his or her content-specific teaching standards and what effective teaching should look like in English language arts, mathematics, science, social studies, and all other subject areas.

The Council of Chief State School Officers (CCSSO) (2013) published through the *Interstate Teacher Assessment and Support Consortium (InTASC),* the *Model Core Teaching Standards and Learning Progressions for Teachers 1.0: A Resource for Ongoing Professional Development.* In their words, these standards describe, "The new vision of teaching needed for today's learners, how teaching practice that is aligned to the new vision develops over time, and what strategies teachers can employ to improve their practice both individually and collectively" (CCSSO, 2013, p. 3).

These standards "paint" a new vision for teaching and student achievement that addresses the complexity of teaching practice, and examine the role of teacher knowledge, disposition, and performance in learner success. The teaching standards are aligned with the CCSS and its assessment systems, the National Board for Professional Teaching Standards (NBPTS) accomplished teaching core principles, the National Council for Accreditation of Teacher Education (NCATE) accreditation standards, Learning Forward professional learning standards, the Teacher Leader Model Standards, the Interstate School Leader Licensure Consortium (ISLLC) 2008 educational leadership policy standards, and the CCSSO's document of performance indicators for education leaders. They are designed to be used as a resource by states, school districts, professional organizations, teacher education programs, teachers, and others who develop, license, support, evaluate and reward teachers. This vision has the following characteristics:

1. *Personalized Learning for Diverse Learners* (i.e., students with disabilities, English language learners, gifted students, and culturally diverse students). All teachers are expected to be knowledgeable about student diversity issues, use multiple learning approaches for students, and provide all students with personalized learning experiences.

2. *A Stronger Focus on Application of Knowledge and Skills.* Teachers should prepare all students for college, career, workforce, and life by developing (a) necessary attributes and dispositions such as problem solving, curiosity, innovation, communication, interpersonal skills, the ability to synthesize across disciplines, global awareness, ethics, and technological expertise; and (b) inter-disciplinary knowledge (e.g., financial literacy and civics). In addition, teachers should help students develop cross-disciplinary skills such as critical thinking, communication, collaboration, and the use of technology.

3. *Improved Assessment Literacy.* Teachers need to have more complex knowledge of how to use data to inform instruction and promote student learning on their own and in collaboration with colleagues. They need to know how to develop a range of assessments, use formative and summative assessment, use data to make differentiated instructional adjustments, provide feedback to students, and document student progress against standards.

4. *A Collaborative Professional Culture.* Collaboration promotes the development and implementation of effective teaching practices. These teaching standards require teachers to be open to observation, constructive feedback, and participate in ongoing, job-embedded professional development opportunities that practice collaborative inquiry about instruction and student learning. To do so, teachers need to examine data from multiple sources, analyze it, identify common goals and progress monitoring, and embrace shared responsibility for student learning.

5. *New Leadership Roles for Teachers and Administrators.* The standards raise expectations for teachers and view them responsible for student learning. The standards also encourage teachers to view themselves as leaders from the beginning of their career and be advocates of each student's learning. School leaders should create a collaborative culture, support collaborative teacher inquiry, and share responsibility for improving teacher and student success.

Table 11.1 shows how the CCSSO (2013) 10 teaching standards are organized and what each standard addresses (for a detailed description of each standard, see http://www.ccsso.org/Documents/2013/2013_INTASC_Learning_Progressions_for_Teachers.pdf).

In addition, the CCSSO through InTASC developed learning progressions for teachers that describe "the increasing complexity and sophistication of teaching practice for each core standard across three developmental levels." (CCSSO, 2013, p. 12). What are effective teaching assumptions in the learning progressions?

- Learning and teaching are complex.
- Teaching expertise can be learned, develops over time, and is not linear.
- Growth can occur through reflection upon experience, feedback, or individual or group professional learning experiences.
- Development depends on context, particularly levels of support.
- It is about the teaching practice and not about the individual teacher.

The progressions describe effective teaching with much specificity, provide guidance about how to improve practice, and outline possible professional learning experiences that can facilitate such improvements. According to the learning progressions, effective practice centers around four key themes: (1) increased differentiation of student learning; (2) developing learners' higher

TABLE 11.1.   InTASC Model Core Teaching Standards (CCSSO, 2013)

The Learner and Learning

Standard 1: Learner Development	The teacher recognizes how learners grow and develop physically, cognitively, linguistically, socially and emotionally and designs and implements developmentally appropriate and rigorous learning experiences.
Standard 2: Learning Differences	The teacher uses his, or her knowledge of learner differences (e.g., individual, cultural, linguistic, socio-emotional) to create inclusive learning environments that enable each learner to meet high standards.
Standard 3: Learning Environments	The teacher works with others to create learning environments that support individual and collaborative learning, promote positive social interactions, active engagement in learning, and self-motivation.

Content

Standard 4: Content Knowledge	The teacher understands the concepts, habits of mind, disciplinary structures, disciplinary literacy and learning demands, and creates learning experiences that make the discipline accessible and meaningful to the learner and promote content mastery.
Standard 5: Application of Content	The teacher understands how to present, connect, and engage learners in critical thinking and collaborative inquiry about authentic discipline-specific and global issues.

Instructional Practice

Standard 6: Assessment	The teacher understands and uses multiple assessment methods to gauge learners' learning, monitor their progress, teach them how to self-monitor, and guide his or her own instructional decisions and the learners' decisions.
Standard 7: Planning for Instruction	The teacher uses knowledge about the discipline, cross-disciplinary skills, pedagogy, and the learner to plan instruction that helps every learner meet his or her learning goals.
Standard 8: Instructional Strategies	The teacher understands and uses a variety of instructional discipline-specific (and other) strategies to help learners' disciplinary knowledge, make cross-disciplinary connections, and learn how to apply knowledge in meaningful ways.

Professional Responsibility

Standard 9: Professional Learning and Ethical Practice	The teacher engages in ongoing professional learning and uses evidence to continually evaluate his or her practice, particularly the effects of his or her choices and actions on others (e.g., learners, families, other professionals, and the greater community), and adapts practice to meet the needs of each learner.

Standard 10: Leadership and Collaboration	The teacher seeks appropriate leadership roles and opportunities to take shared responsibility for student learning, to collaborate with learners, families, colleagues, other professionals, and the community, to ensure learner support and to advance the profession.

order thinking skills; (3) promoting cross-disciplinary approaches; and (4) collaborating at new levels (for a full list of all standards and learning progressions, see http://www.ccsso.org/Documents/2013/2013_INTASC_Learning_Progressions_for_Teachers.pdf).

The CCSSO (2013) aims for all stakeholders to use these learning progressions to develop a common language about effective practice, and how to develop it, maintain it, and support it. They recommend that pre-service teachers should use the learning progressions as a preparation tool for in-service work and self-assessment, and colleges of teacher preparation should use them to sequence coursework and teacher preparation. In-service teachers can use the progressions as an ongoing self-assessment tool to reflect on their practice. Mentors, instructional coaches, and school leaders can use the progressions to provide feedback to teachers about their practice, including areas of strength and areas in need of improvement and can also use them to plan professional development. State education agencies and policy-makers can use the progressions for licensure purposes and evaluation systems. In summary, these learning progressions are designed with the learner in mind: What is the impact of teacher practice on the learner? Are the learners engaged? Are they learning, growing, and improving? How do we know they are learning, and what are we doing if they are not?

Another important message for all content area teachers (as well as for the school leaders, instructional coaches, and others who evaluate them or mentor them) is that every teacher's practice moves along a continuum from directive, to facilitative, to collaborative. In this book, I have presented a discipline-specific learning framework that is based on the role of the teacher being a facilitative one with student learning, and a collaborative one with colleagues and others.

Throughout this book, you have seen in various chapters that effective teaching practice uses a Gradual Release of Responsibility Model (Pearson & Gallagher, 1983), scaffolds student learning, promotes active engagement of the student in the learning process, and facilitates self-monitoring of student learning. Discipline-specific practice is rigorous, aligned with disciplinary structures, discourse, habits of mind, and inquiry, and promotes deep learning and reflection. Discipline-specific practice uses strategies that promote disciplinary habits of mind, and help the student to access and develop content knowledge and skills. It is practice that infuses media and technology in learning, problem solving, writing, communicating, presenting, and collaborating. It is also practice that demands deep knowledge of learner characteristics, pedagogical techno-logical content knowledge (TPACK) (Mishra & Koehler, 2006), ability to differentiate instruc-tion, knowledge of assessment methods, and ways to motivate, engage, and challenge each student. In the following two section, I examine the two core national teacher evaluation models. Learning about these models will help you to better prepare for your career, and will also verify the need for quality teaching and learning.

The Danielson *Framework for Teaching*

Several US states have adopted the Charlotte Danielson's *Framework for Teaching*, a generic instrument that applies to all disciplines, for building common language and understanding what good teaching looks like. The framework is comprised of a set of research-based instructional components, is aligned to the InTASC standards, the CCSS, and uses a constructivist teaching and learning lens (meaning that people co-construct knowledge through experiences, active learning, and reflection). The framework presents a complex picture of teaching reflected by 22 components (and 76 smaller elements) that are clustered into four domains of teaching responsibility: (1) Planning and preparation; (2) Classroom environment; (3) Instruction; and (4) Professional responsibilities. Common themes in this framework include equity (respect, engagement, feedback), cultural competence, high expectations for all students, developmentally appropriate instruction, attention to individual student needs, appropriate use of technology, and promoting student responsibility over their own learning. The framework is used to evaluate all content area teachers.

Levels of teaching performance describe each component and provide teachers, school leaders and others with a roadmap for improving teaching. The four levels of performance are: Unsatisfactory (1); Basic (2); Proficient (3); and Distinguished (4). The levels represent the performance of teaching, not the teacher. It is normal for teachers to move among ratings; higher levels reflect both experience and expertise. It is advisable for teacher evaluators to use multiple measures before determining teacher performance.

Table 11.2 presents a summary of domains and components per domain. Table 11.3 describes generic levels of teaching performance. The *2013 Framework for Teacher Evaluation Instrument* has been updated to reflect the CCSS and its emphasis on active and deep learning, discipline-specific habits of mind, rigorous instruction, collaboration, and creating a community of learners that are responsible for their own learning (for more information on the *2013 Framework for Teaching Evaluation Instrument*, see http://www.danielsongroup.org/userfiles/files/downloads/2 013EvaluationInstrument.pdf).

For example, in *Domain 1: Planning and Preparation, Component 1a: Demonstrating Knowledge of Content and Pedagogy*, the message content for teachers (and school and other leaders who provide professional development for them) is: in order for teachers to guide student learning, they need to have comprehensive and deep command of the subject they teach. In other words, every content area teacher should know (really know!) the following:

- Knowledge of content and structure of the discipline.
- Key concepts and skills central (and peripheral) to the discipline.
- Knowledge of concepts and skills are prerequisite to understanding others.
- Knowledge of how the discipline has evolved in the 21st century.
- Knowledge of student misconceptions about the discipline, and ways to dispel them.
- Knowledge of prerequisite relationships in the discipline.
- Knowledge of best discipline-specific pedagogical approaches.

Indicators of this domain and component include the following:

- Lesson and unit plans that reflect important concepts in the discipline.
- Lesson and unit plans that accommodate prerequisite relations among concepts and skills.
- Clear and accurate classroom explanations.
- Feedback to students that furthers learning.
- Inter-disciplinary connections in plans and practice.

For instance, a teacher receiving a Distinguished (4) rating during an observation might be based on this example: "In a unit about 19th century literature, the teacher incorporates information about the history of the same period." A teacher receiving Proficient (3) on this indicator might be reflected in this: "The teacher has realized her students are not sure how to use a compass, and

TABLE 11.2. Danielson Framework for Teaching

Domain 1: Planning and Preparation

1a. Demonstrating knowledge of content and pedagogy
1b. Demonstrating knowledge of students
1c. Setting instructional outcomes
1d. Demonstrating knowledge of resources
1e. Designing coherent instruction
1f. Designing student assessments

Domain 2: Classroom Environment

2a. Creating an environment of respect and rapport
2b. Establishing a culture of learning
2c. Managing classroom procedures
2d. Managing student behavior
2e. Organizing physical space

Domain 3: Instruction

3a. Communicating with students
3b. Using questioning and discussion techniques
3c. Engaging students in learning
3d. Using assessment in instruction
3e. Demonstrating flexibility and responsiveness

Domain 4: Professional Responsibilities

4a. Reflecting on teaching
4b. Maintaining accurate records
4c. Communicating with families
4d. Participating in a professional community
4e. Growing and developing professionally
4f. Showing professionalism

Source: http://www.danielsongroup.org/article.aspx?page=frameworkforteaching.

TABLE 11.3. Danielson Framework for Teaching: Levels of Teaching Performance

Distinguished (4)	Teacher is a master teacher and makes a contribution to the field inside and outside the school.
	Teacher's classroom reflects a community of learners and motivated and engaged learners who are responsible for their own learning.
	Teacher provides rigorous, engaged, and differentiated instruction that is appropriate for learners' needs.
Proficient (3)	The teacher clearly understands the concepts underlying the component and implements it well.
	Teacher knows content, students, and curriculum well.
	Teacher has a strong repertoire of instructional strategies and activities.
	Teacher understands classroom and learning dynamics.
	Teacher has mastered teaching and is working to improve his or her practice.
	Most experienced teachers would be expected to perform at this level.

Basic (2)	The teacher appears to understand the concepts underlying the components and attempts to implement its elements.
	Implementation is sporadic, inconsistent, or not entirely successful.
	Additional reading, discussion, visiting classrooms of other teachers, and experience supported by a mentor will enable the teacher to become proficient in this area.
	Performance is typically characteristic of novice teachers.
Introductory (1)	The teacher does not appear to understand the concepts underlying the component.
	Teacher shows little or evidence of understanding the content, students, or curricula.
	Teacher has poor recordkeeping practices and low ethical standards.
	Teacher does not recognize signs of needed instruction revision.
	Teacher may display behaviors below the minimal licensing standard (e.g., chaotic classroom environment, putting down students, etc.).
	There is a clear need for intervention.

so she plans to have them practice that skill before introducing the activity on angle measurement." A teacher receiving a Basic (2) rating might be because: "The teacher plans lessons on area and perimeter independently of one another, without linking the concepts together." Last, a teacher receiving an Introductory (1) could be because: "The teacher has his students copy definitions each week to help them learn to spell difficult words" (all examples were retrieved from http://www.danielsongroup.org/userfiles/files/downloads/2013EvaluationInstrument.pdf pp. 14–15).

Teachers can use information from formal and informal observations to plan for instruction, make plans for instructional improvements, and monitor their own progress. It is important for all teachers to be actively involved in the observation process. The process usually involves: (1) a pre-conference or planning phase that includes a teacher interview, review of documents, and discussion of procedures, logistics, and process; (2) the actual observation that includes gathering of evidence; and (3) post-observation conference.

In addition to formal observations, teachers can also experience unannounced classroom visits followed by an informal conversation. Evidence of teaching effectiveness may include statements, actions, or behaviors and teacher and student artifacts. The observer, and/or the teacher usually select the evidence. Observational evidence can include verbatim scripting of teacher or student comments (i.e., "Remember that we do a close reading of text with pencil, or pen at hand; I want to see you annotate and mark the text as you are reading"), non-evaluative statements of observed teacher, or student behavior (i.e., "The teacher reminded students about the learning goal throughout the lesson"), numeric information about time, student participation, or resources used in the lesson (i.e., "8:50–9:00: Small group work"), or observations about the classroom environment (i.e., "Desks are arranged in horseshoe format; every student is able to see each other and there is room for the teacher to walk between each group or partners").

The post-conference's purpose is for the observer and the teacher to discuss the evidence; it allows the teacher to explain his or her planning purpose, decisions, and processes. Teachers need to have questions in advance to review them and prepare to answer them; they also need bring copies of written materials for their lesson. Observers need to review the lesson and all evidence prior to the conference, and share their notes with teachers. The post-conference should allow the teacher to self-assess, identify areas of strengths and areas for improvement, and set goals that are agreed upon by both parties for next steps and teacher learning.

School leaders should be using data on student learning and teacher needs to plan professional development that will improve teaching and student learning. Aside from professional development on let's say how to promote academic vocabulary, or meet the unique needs of English Language Learners (ELLs), or how to promote collaboration in each classroom, professional development per content area also needs to be discipline-specific and reflect the unique structure, learning demands, and habits of mind and processes that are inherent to each content area.

The Marzano *Causal Teacher Evaluation Model*

Robert Marzano's (2011) *Causal Teacher Evaluation Model* is based on Dr. Marzano's *Art and Science of Teaching* framework, and the research he has been conducting on teacher effectiveness over many years. His model is based on studies that correlate instructional strategies to student achievement, and experimental studies that show causation between elements of the model and student learning. The Marzano *Causal Teacher Evaluation Model* aligns with state standards, the InTASC standards, and is designed to help teachers translate the standards into their daily practice. The model identifies a set of practices (60 elements) that are directly linked to increased student achievement. These practices are organized into four domains that define a knowledge base and a framework for teacher expertise. The domains are as follows (for a detailed description of all 60 elements, see http://www.marzanoevaluation.com/evaluation/four_domains/):

- *Domain 1: Classroom Strategies and Behaviors (41 Elements)*
  - Routine Segments (5 Elements)
  - Content Segments (18 Elements)
  - On the Spot Segments (18 Elements)
- *Domain 2: Planning and Preparing (8 Elements)*
  - Lesson and Units (3 Elements)
  - Use of Materials and Technology (2 Elements)
  - Special Needs of Students (3 Elements)
- *Domain 3: Reflecting on Teaching (5 Elements)*
  - Evaluating Personal Performance (3 Elements)
  - Professional Growth Plan (2 Elements)
- *Domain 4: Collegiality and Professionalism (6 Elements)*
  - Promoting a Positive Environment (2 Elements)
  - Promoting Exchange of Ideas (2 Elements)
  - Promoting District and School Development (2 Elements)

iObservation is a technology system that digitizes this model and allows teachers and school leaders to respond to evaluation data in ways that support teacher growth and student learning. The Marzano model also uses observation and feedback protocols, stresses inter-rater reliability among observers, promotes the use of constructive feedback about teacher practice, allows observers to collect data for collegial conversations, and helps connect teacher practice to student achievement.

Feedback and Teacher Growth

Feedback is vital not only to student learning, but also to teacher learning and success. Feedback refers to how one is doing in his or her efforts to reach a goal. Feedback is especially important for secondary school teachers because of the organizational structure of many secondary schools that promotes teacher isolation. Being a content area teacher is not about "being a lone ranger," or "teaching, learning, and living in your own disciplinary silo." Teaching is a complex process that does not develop in a vacuum. All teachers want to succeed and meet their students' needs, but not all work in school environments and cultures that value and promote collaborative inquiry among teachers and ongoing professional development or feedback.

Seeking feedback from mentors and others is not a sign of weakness; instead, it is a sign of strength. Teachers benefit from feedback that is helpful and goal-referenced, tangible, actionable, specific and personalized, timely, judicious, and ongoing. Feedback helps teachers align teaching, learning, and assessment. Although in this chapter we are examining the role of feedback in the process of teacher evaluation, teachers should not forget the importance of receiving feedback from their students about the instruction, the classroom environment, the processes and strategies used, and whether the teacher is helping them meet their individual needs and goals. Feedback from teacher to student, and vice versa, promotes a culture of learning accountability in every classroom.

"Elbow coaching," a method in which instructional coaches teach "elbow-to-elbow" with the teacher in the classroom is a desirable way to provide immediate feedback to teachers who need to improve their instruction. The coach gets to model a practice for five minutes so the teacher has an opportunity to see excellent practice in action and try it immediately after that (Johnson, 2012). In "elbow coaching" the students also benefit because the receive expert instruction (National Institute for Excellence in Teaching, 2012).

All teachers are observed on an ongoing basis for different purposes. Observation and teacher evaluation are not new phenomena. What is new, however, is how observations of teacher effectiveness have changed in the context of formalized teacher evaluation systems used widely across the US, such as the Danielson *Framework for Teaching* (2013), or the Marzano *Causal Teacher Evaluation Model* (2011a), and how information from those observations is used by school leaders and policy-makers. Unfortunately, the ways in which some of these systems have been implemented have created many high stakes for teachers. School leaders, instructional coaches, mentors, peers, and others who evaluate teacher effectiveness need to provide specific, relevant, and informative feedback to teachers. Feedback could be oral or written; written feedback becomes a valuable resource for planning and self-evaluation. Feedback needs to be given with respect, be objective, evidence-based, concrete, actionable, and refer to the practice, not the teacher. Feedback works best when it is given and received in an environment of trust (National Institute for Excellence in Teaching, 2012).

Evidence-based feedback will offer facts and "stays away" from inferences and interpretation. Selective feedback will focus on a couple of important practices that will improve student learning. Feedback that is actionable will identify clear and specific actions to be taken in the next couple of weeks to help the teacher improve. Effective feedback is given within 48 hours of observation, and it specifies and communicates the degree of importance or concern. Goe, Biggers, and Croft (2012) suggest that no one piece of evidence can provide all of the information needed to accurately measure teacher effectiveness. Using multiple measures of teacher learning are needed to provide a comprehensive picture of teachers' strengths and weaknesses over time and across contexts.

Teacher Collaboration and Professional Development

DRIP stands for "Data Rich and Information Poor." It is a commonly used phrase in educational circles that refers to this syndrome of collecting ample data but not knowing how to use it appropriately (Dufour, Dufour, Eaker & Many, 2010). Schools and states are collecting more and more data since the NLCB Act of 2001 for various types of decision-making, reporting, and accountability purposes. They use software and computer systems to collect data throughout the year, and make data-informed decisions about instruction and student learning. For teachers to make informed instructional decisions, they need relevant data in their fingertips, and they cannot wait for a year or several months to have access to data they need. In this era of accountability, the ability of a state, school, district, and teacher to use data to prove that their students are improving and progressing is essential for school success. Data is also useful for programs, placement, support systems, and professional development. Knowledge about student data also equips the classroom teacher to have valuable informative conversations and conferences with his or her students in class about their progress, and/or learning goals and aspirations.

This is an area in which many teachers need to have professional development and ongoing conversations. Using data strategically for instruction, student placement, Response to Intervention (RtI) and other intervention decisions, can have a positive impact on instructional practices, processes, and on student learning. Teachers need time to examine student data, analyze it and discuss it with peers from their own department and with other school-based educators (i.e., instructional literacy/math coach, exceptional education teacher, speech and language pathologist, school/guidance counselor, English for Speakers of Other Languages (ESOL) teacher, school administrators, etc.). Data analysis and interpretation is an area in which all teachers (novice and veteran) seek more professional development across grade levels and content areas. Such ongoing conversations provide a framework, and the tools and vocabulary needed to support the informed data conversations. Teachers will benefit from systematic department and school data teams that will help them to (a) examine student data, (b) understand the findings, (c) develop an action plan, and (d) monitor student progress and measure success.

Data or Leadership Teams

Data or leadership teams are groups of educators dedicated to data inquiry that results in informed educational decisions. Such teams can examine entire school data, grade, or subject level data, data about students in certain groups, or individual student data. Data team participation is voluntary. The teams address challenges, seek feedback from other teachers, the school, the school district, or the state, and collect insights from all of the above. They organize, analyze, and coordinate data-informed responses to all, and they monitor student and school performance school-wide. School-based data teams are comprised of teachers of the same grade or subject matter, or members of a school's leadership or planning committee. Other data teams could be school-, district- or state-based. If data teams are not available at your school, collaborative teacher teams will also be useful for collecting and organizing data, and guiding and maintaining instructional and student learning conversations and decisions. Data-driven reflection and dialogue among teachers and between a teacher and an instructional coach are vital for guiding, improving, monitoring, and reflecting on instruction.

What can teachers do in data teams? They can be involved in various ways in "data-mining" and reflection on instruction and student learning. Teachers in data or leadership teams could:

- Examine standardized and progress monitoring data.
- Examine formative and summative assessment data.
- Analyze student data per grade and/or content area levels.
- Analyze data as a school.
- Make data-driven plans.
- Form intervention groups.

- Make decisions about student placement, and form intervention groups.
- Examine instructional trends that work, and revisit those that are in need of improvement.

For example, looking at the science scores one might say, "My students are doing well in class, but they are not progressing in their annual progress goals." A math teacher might say, "Looking at this group of level two students in my class, they are not having trouble in oral argumentation, but data shows that they do in written argumentation. How can I move them forward?" In other cases, when examining formative and summative data about the results of certain interventions, a data team could problem-solve about how they could provide more specific interventions to some students who need it.

A teacher who examines student data carefully, and on an ongoing basis, can identify trends in student learning needs, group students (heterogeneously or homogeneously) for mini-lesson purposes, and can ask use the data in conferences with students. He or she can share the area of need with the student, provide appropriate instruction, feedback, and guided support, and monitor student progress. If data shows that students have improved, or met their goals, the teacher can ask the student, "What are you doing differently now?"; "What is working for you?"; "How did this strategy help you? Can you share it with others in class?"

A data or leadership team, after examining student data, might decide to use common formative assessments throughout the school. Teachers could get together to examine the state's and school district's standards, and develop short-term, specific goals they could use to monitor their own and their students' goals. Some teams have set up instructional and learning goals they monitor every two to four weeks. Such specificity promotes productive, tangible, relevant, collaborative, collegial, and very informative dialogue among all involved. For example, a 7th Grade English language arts team might develop this learning goal—"80% of 7th Grade students will be able to write a persuasive essay at level 3 or above."—and decide to come together every two to four weeks to reflect on student learning, and make appropriate data-based instructional decisions.

Professional Learning Communities (PLCs)

Professional learning communities (PLCs) are an increasingly effective means of analyzing a school's specific needs and building upon those needs. They are a way of "reculturing" educational reform. PLCs are usually comprised of teachers although administrators and support staff also participate. As part of PLCs, teachers work together as members of ongoing, reflective, collaborative teams that focus on improving student achievement (McREL, 2003; Rentfro, 2007). A PLC is a small group of individuals who meet on a frequent and regular basis to explore the interests of the group based on the needs of the school or students. PLCs, also known as study groups, differ from traditional forms of professional development in that the group determines the content of the study based on student data, shared interests, or professional curiosity about a new theory or practice. This ownership and engagement create enthusiastic practices that positively affect student learning. When PLCs have a common focus on improving student learning and purposeful sharing of instructional practices, teachers are more likely to adopt pedagogical practices that improve student learning experiences (Miller et al., 2010).

Characteristics of effective PLCs include the following:

- Each member of the group develops a sense of ownership.
- There is supportive and shared leadership among the members.
- There is shared accountability through shared practice
- Decisions are always made by consensus.

- There is collective inquiry and creativity.
- Team members respect one another, have good listening, communicating, and collaborating skills, and build on each other's ideas.
- Members of the group understand the difference between dialogue and discussion.
- Group responsibilities are clearly delineated.
- Study groups comprised of three to six members.
- A regular meeting time and place are essential.
- Time between meetings is productive.
- Time is allowed for reflection; progress happens over time.
- Groups develop procedural guidelines.
- Successes are celebrated.

According to DuFour (2004), PLCs need to be guided by a focus on student learning and school improvement, a culture of collaboration, a focus on results, and commitment from all teachers, school administrators, and support staff. Creating a culture of collaboration and shared responsibility for student learning is a major goal of the PLCs. Several studies have documented the positive impact of teacher participation in PLCs on student learning (e.g., The American Educational Research Association (Holland, 2005); The Annenberg Institute for School Reform (2005); The National Commission on Teaching and America's Future (Carroll, Fulton, & Doerr, 2010); The Wallace Foundation (Louis, Leithwood, Wahlstrom & Anderson, 2010)). Students and schools benefit when teachers agree upon collaborative inquiry about improving student learning. Why? Because teachers share teaching practices in a safe environment, and engage in constructive and reflective dialogue about improving instruction (Bryk, Sebring, Allensworth, Luppescu & Easton, 2010).

Study Groups and Department-Level Meetings

Study groups and department-level meetings can take place in a variety of ways and be used for different purposes. A PLC could also be a study group. The following are examples of study groups.

- *Whole Faculty.* Each faculty member is a part of a study group. While the groups may have a different focus, there is also an organizational focus for the entire school. The groups' purpose is to support whole-school improvement, and all administrators, classroom teachers, resource teachers, special area teachers, instructional coaches, librarians, counselors, and others who are viable parts of the faculty are expected to actively participate. Common purposes include studying academic content, supporting or monitoring new initiatives, targeting a need, and studying research and/or student work.
- *Small Group (or Stand-Alones).* This study group does not depend on organizational support. It is a group of individuals with a common interest or need that meets for a specified time and purpose, perhaps even for increased personal knowledge.
- *Grade or Subject Area Groups.* This group meets based on common areas of concern or interest, perhaps for a very specific purpose related solely to a group of students, a subject, or a challenge.
- *Teacher Groups from Different Schools or Districts.* School districts or states may form study groups to examine issues beyond the traditional school scope. The incentive for such groups may be to learn from members with a wide variety of experiences, discuss the effectiveness of practices with varying populations, examine statewide intervention or program effectiveness, or look at widespread or long-term data.

Teachers also can play different roles in the study group. A facilitator will send out reminders, makes personal contact with each member, arrange for a meeting place, and ensure study materials (e.g., paper, computers, video equipment, etc.) are readily accessible. The facilitator is responsible for establishing the tone of the meeting. As the meeting progresses, the facilitator will keep the discussion focused and ensure that each member of the group is encouraged to contribute. He or she is a neutral observer, a guide, a questioner, and an encourager. The facilitator should not evaluate, judge, or make subjective comments concerning any member's response.

A recorder could be responsible for providing other members with a written record of the meeting, along with actions the group agrees to take before the next meeting. A researcher could be locating resources (e.g., articles, books, or action research pieces from other teachers) to bring to the meeting. An illuminator could highlight important aspects of the group meeting that might be missed in the overall discussion. He or she will listen for confusion in order to clarify, interpret, or slow down the discussion.

Steps for starting study groups include the following:

1. Decide the purpose of the study.
2. Look at a wide range of data, both formal and anecdotal.
3. Form a list of student needs based on the data in Step 2.
4. Prioritize student needs.
5. Form specific questions that could be addressed by a study group.
6. Form an action plan.

According to a recent report by the Carnegie Corporation of New York's Council on Advancing Adolescent Literacy (2010) titled, *Time to Act: An Agenda for Advancing Adolescent Literacy for College and Career Success*, secondary schools that have "beat-the-odds" have implemented the following guidelines:

- The school culture is organized for learning—teachers and administrators focus on student learning.
- Teachers understand that they are responsible for student learning.
- Each teacher has undergone carefully designed, and discipline-relevant professional development.
- Student data is the basis for professional work.
- Achievement data is linked to proposed instructional activities.
- There are targeted interventions for struggling readers and writers.
- Quality reading instruction is incorporated across the content areas.
- Teacher collaboration is key; teachers need to engage in teacher observation, evaluation of instruction, and conversations about learning from one another.

In order for professional development to build teacher knowledge and expertise, it must provide the opportunity for ongoing learning and access to timely feedback on relevant issues of practice. A possible future avenue for sustaining a culture of discipline-specific learning and support is communities of practice (CoP). Informal teams of teachers with similar interests such as content-area, or grade-level teachers, can collaborate on literacy activities, examinations of school goals, student work, and assessment results, collaborative planning goal-setting. Communities of Practice can help teachers learn from each other's successes, challenges, and knowledge, guide targeted dialogue about literacy, and promote professional information sharing about disciplinary learning and literacy demands.

Lesson Study

Lesson study is a type of cyclical and highly reflective professional development process inspired by Japanese teachers to systematically study, analyze, and reflect on teacher practice for the purpose of improving it. Lesson study utilizes a back mapping approach (Easton, 2008, 2009). As part of the lesson study, teachers plan, observe, and revise their "research" lessons (Lewis, 2002). A typical lesson study group is comprised of four to six members who meet regularly after school to reflect on research lessons, set learning and professional development goals, and establish timelines. Lesson study provides teachers with immediate feedback, safe constructive criticism, and much collaborative support and evidence-based feedback for improving one's lesson.

The lesson study cycle includes the following steps that are repeated over time: (1) Study: teachers study the curriculum and consider long-term goals for student learning; (2) Plan: Teachers select a research lesson, anticipate student thinking about the lesson, and plan the data collection and the lesson; (3) Do the research lesson: One team member teachers, and others collect data; and (4) Reflect: Share data and reflect on what the data shows about student learning, what are implications of the lesson, and what insights and new questions does the teacher wish to implement (Hurd & Licciardo-Musso, 2005)? Many middle and high schools use lesson study to improve teaching and student learning.

Collaborating with Instructional Coaches

How else can you build your knowledge, instruction, and student learning? Several states use instructional coaches (in literacy and math) as a form of school-based-professional development and support. Their role is broad and diverse and their responsibilities vary from school to school. Instructional coaches could be used to enhance literacy, math, or science instruction, build collaborative learning communities, model best instructional practices, help in collecting, analyzing, and interpreting data, as well as supplying teachers with instructional resources, assessing students, or co-teaching in the classroom. A coach could be the facilitator of a PLC or data team. Coaches are knowledgeable in literacy or mathematics, in andragogy, in pedagogy, and in coaching. They are also knowledgeable about specific disciplines, state assessments, and related standards and curricula. They are familiar with best practices in literacy, or math instruction, they demonstrate best instructional practices, know how to engage learners in meaningful ways, and know how analyze and interpret data to plan for differentiated instruction to meet the needs of all students. Instructional coaches also know how to support teachers in their professional growth, facilitate meetings, observe teachers practicing new ideas and lessons, provide feedback and reflection about instruction, and work collaboratively with teachers to learn new information and strategies together (Bean, 2004; Walpole & McKenna, 2013).

Applying Discipline-Specific Literacies

- Discipline-specific literacies should be one of the main foci of professional development for content area teachers.
- Teachers need to have a solid knowledge of core disciplinary concepts, structures, relationships, development of disciplinary knowledge over time, and major challenges.
- They also need to have effective pedagogical skills about how to engage students in learning, doing, inquiring, and reflecting about disciplinary knowledge, skills, processes, and habits of mind.

The Need for Discipline-Specific Professional Development

All academic disciplines are committed to teacher professional development. As a current or future professional educator, it is important that you join a professional organization as a pre-service or in-service teacher, study their publications, attend workshops as part of national, state or local conferences, and join any social media and personal learning (PLNs) networks, or follow related blogs. Such activity will help you stay abreast of new developments, collaborate with other educators, and improve your teaching. All of the following professional organizations offer valuable subject-related information, resources, publications, and trainings.

- The Association for Career and Technical Education (ACTE) (http://www.acteonline.org).
- The International Reading Association (IRA) (http://www.reading.org).
- The National Art Education Association (NAEA) (http://www.arteducators.org).
- The National Association for Sport and Physical Education (NASPE) (http://www.humankinetics.com/our-partners/national-association-for-sport-and-physical-education-naspe).
- The National Council of Teachers of English (NCTE) (http://www.ncte.org).
- The National Council of Teachers of Mathematics (NCTM) (http://www.nctm.org).
- The National Science Teachers' Association (NSTA) (http://nsta.org).
- The National Council for the Social Studies (NCSS) (http://www.socialstudies.org).

In chapter 2, I presented a model for literacy as a discipline-specific process (see Figure 2.2), and discussed that content area teachers need to have specialized knowledge, skills, and dispositions. We also saw that discipline-specific literacies are aligned with educational and content-specific standards, and require rigorous practice that engages all students deeply with learning. Throughout this book, I have also analyzed and provided examples about teaching in such a way that promotes the development of discipline-specific discourse, equips students to read and comprehend the texts of each discipline, develops disciplinary habits of mind, and is founded on inquiry, collaborative inquiry, and reflection. All of these framework components are aligned with college and career readiness, with new educational standards, and with rigorous instruction and learning. Discipline-specific professional development also incorporates media and technology.

In my view, school districts and schools should provide content area teachers with professional development that views literacy as a discipline-specific process (see Figure 2). Content area teachers need professional development that will (a) expand their subject matter knowledge; (b) help them to understand the literacy and learning demands their discipline places on the learner; (c) help them learn how to deal with the fact that many students will be unprepared for the academic literacy demands of their courses; (d) provide rigorous, engaging, and collaborative learning environments and instruction; (e) develop students' discipline-specific habits of mind, and (f) assess student learning.

Art, English language arts, mathematics, science, social studies, etc. are not just subjects to be mastered. Students need to *do* art, history, literature, math, or science; they need to develop discipline-specific ways of reading, writing, thinking, learning, and knowing. As part of professional development, content area teachers could develop learning targets, come up with discipline-specific ways to promote the development of accountable talk in their classrooms, identify strategies to give ELLs equal access to texts and academic discourse, set goals for how they would help students develop core disciplinary habits of mind, or help students show improvement in their summative assessments.

We have seen in this chapter that effective professional development is also discipline-specific, and promotes dialogue and reflection among content area teachers that is relevant and reflective of teacher's courses, pedagogy, and student learning. Content area teachers need to collaborate on an ongoing basis with colleagues, and others in department meetings, grade, or subject area meetings, data teams, discipline-specific induction, mentoring, and in PLCs to systematically examine, reflect on, and plan instruction that will result in student learning and success. All discipline-specific professional development should be closely linked to standards, curriculum, assessments, to core disciplinary ideas, and to teachers' practices and needs (see Table 11.4 for a summary of discipline-specific professional development we need).

I hope that you can recognize by now why a discipline-specific framework for preparing students for college, career, workforce, and life readiness is necessary in grades 6–12. My approach throughout this book has been one of perspective and framework changes needed especially by content area teachers, administrators, instructional coaches, and students. If we, as educators, present, implement, and support a learning framework that is rigorous, discipline-specific, collaborative, and reflective in our classrooms, our students will start developing deep knowledge, and habits of mind that will help them become independent readers, writers, and learners. But, if we wish to see our students change in how they approach texts and learning, we first have to change our perspectives and attitudes about learning in each one of our disciplines. Although the CCSS are bringing about changes at many levels (some positive, some in need of improvement), the discipline-specific framework presented in this book exceeds the CCSS expectations and standards.

Think Like an Expert

● English Language Arts teachers need professional development on (a) the role of narrative and informational text in student learning; (b) ways to motivate and support students to do close reading of texts; (c) how to engage students in academic discourse; and (d) how to develop students' writing skills. (English Language Arts)

● Math teachers will benefit from professional development that expands their understanding of mathematics, encourages them to view mathematics as a problem-solving, student-centered and inquiry-based process, and provides teachers with opportunities to reflect on, and develop, their own teaching practice. (Mathematics)

● Science teachers need to develop a strong understanding of scientific ideas and engineering practices, cross-cutting concepts, and disciplinary core ideas and practices. They need to learn how to teach them in engaging and relevant ways, including how scientists inquire, and collaborate to develop new theories, models, and explanations of natural phenomena. (Science)

● History teachers need to learn how to teach historical inquiry, how to promote historical thinking, how to read and analyze primary and secondary sources, and how to think, write, and communicate in historically appropriate ways. History teachers need professional development that will help them deliver instruction that will develop deep understanding of content and will promote historical habits of mind. (Social Studies)

A Not-So-Different Perspective on Change

Change is not easy. So far we have examined research on characteristics of effective professional development, and have seen that across the board, there are certain conditions that promote instructional improvements (e.g., alignment with standards, safe environment, support and feedback, collaboration with trusted mentors and peers, etc.). The shifts brought about by new educational standards, require many changes in our perspectives about teaching and learning, the role of the teacher and student in the learning process, the environmental conditions that support student learning, and the development of critical thinking skills, knowledge, and dispositions that will prepare students for college, career, work, and life. Change takes knowledge, time, support, reflection, and practice.

TABLE 11.4. Types of Discipline-Specific Professional Development Needed

Subject Area	Types of Discipline-Specific Professional Development Needed
Arts Education	• Curriculum development and planning for student-centered learning and a stronger arts education. • Models for strong arts education program, especially in large, urban schools. • Studio techniques. • Promising arts practices. • Technology, digital skills, and 21st century teaching and learning. • Using authentic assessments of student learning in, and through, the arts. • Common Core resources and visual arts. • How to develop an inquiry-based arts learning community. • Building art capacity through collaborations and partnerships with others inside and outside the school.
Career and Technical Education	• Integration of academic and technical knowledge and skills in teaching and learning. • Standards-based instructional planning. • Technological innovations and College and Career Readiness. • Instruction and support for students to develop rigorous core knowledge, skills, and dispositions for success in a postsecondary workforce. • Design applied learning, rigorous instruction to prepare students for new and emerging occupations. • Engage students in career-related learning experiences to help them make informed decisions about postsecondary training and employment opportunities. • Use of assessment data to guide instruction and program development. • Creating culturally responsive learning environments and preparing all students. • Alternative certification.
English Language Arts	• Standards-based planning, instruction, and assessments. • Effective instruction that meets content and Common Core standards. • Effective strategies to improve students' reading, comprehension, and writing. • How to support English language learners and students with varied exceptionalities. • Formative assessments and the Common Core, and assessments that shape and form instruction. • Quality resources for CCSS implementation. • Close reading of complex texts. • Informational text in the English language arts classroom. • New literacies, digital writing tools, and 21st century teaching and learning.
Mathematics	• Common Core State Standards (CCSS) for Mathematical Practice and what they mean for teaching, problem solving, and learning. • Mathematical practices and process standards. • Developing all students' Algebra readiness. • Developing Algebra and Geometry connections in grades 6–8. • Teaching mathematics in a Science, Technology, Engineering, and Mathematics (STEM) context.

	• Content-specific pedagogies, which draw on multiple representations. • Practices for effective mathematics discussions. • Formative assessment for student learning, effective interventions and assessments. • Teaching for diverse student populations (ELLs), students with varied learning exceptionalities, struggling readers, etc.)
Music Education	• Ways to improve students' musical achievement. • Effective strategies for teaching music literacy. • Creating model lessons to meet state standards. • Exploration, improvisation, and literacy, in diverse classrooms. • Materials that meet curricular requirements. • How to develop, present, and assess different music experiences. • New ways to develop students' understanding of music through experiences in singing, moving, listening, and playing instruments. • Ways to develop students' critical thinking skills and promote active involvement in music. • Music and technology.
Physical Education	• Curriculum and assessment development for physical education. • Creating learning environments that provide students with quality activities. • Providing instruction using different teaching styles, assessing student learning, and promoting critical thinking. • Educating all children regardless of athletic talent, physical and mental abilities or disabilities. • Moving students from dependence to independence for their own fitness and health • Promoting regular, enjoyable physical activity for health, enjoyment, challenge, self-expression and/or social interaction. • Obtaining Fitness/Sports Specialist Certification. • Using standards for planning and assessment purposes. • Resources for implementing new ideas and practices.
Science	• Teaching practices that support inquiry and the Next Generation Science Standards (NGSS). • Relationships between new disciplinary core ideas, crosscutting concepts and science content. • Inquiry-based science teaching and learning. • Ways to engage students in scientific practices and think scientifically and help them to think scientifically. • Opportunities for teachers to experience the science learning they will want their students to do. • Ways to make laboratory activities more inquiry-based, and creating learning opportunities that are more authentic, engaging, and student-centered. • Assessment of standards—how to assess student mastery of standards? • Deeper understanding of the disciplines they teach, how they are structured, and the content and literacy demands they place on students. • Accountability frameworks.

(Continued)

TABLE 11.4.   (Continued)

Subject Area	Types of Discipline-Specific Professional Development Needed
Social Studies	• Teaching with primary sources. • Developing students' historical thinking through the use of effective instructional approaches and critical-thinking processes. • Evidence-based reading, thinking, discussions, and writing. • Instructional strategies for Common Core literacy in history and social studies. • Content-specific best practices for the 21st century social studies classroom. • Ways to prepare students for social responsibility and civic efficacy. • Technology integration in social studies and evaluation of sources. • Historical fiction and the CCSS. • End of Course examinations, curricular planning, instruction, and classroom assessments.

One of my favorite books on human, or corporate change is by Alan Deutschman (2007) titled, *Change or Die: The Three Keys of Change at Work and in Life*—quite the title, right? A powerful book with universal appeal, *Change or Die* deconstructs and debunks age-old myths about change and presents three critical keys—relate, repeat, and reframe—to help the reader make important positive changes in his or her life. The main problem the book is addressing is that most people do not change their lifestyles or behavior even if their lives depend on it. The author offers evidence from medicine, psychology, sociology, and business.

The key question in the book is: "Could you change when change matters most?" Deutschman (2000) suggests the following three keys will drive change when it does not come easy to people. In my view, these keys are also necessary for teacher change.

1. *Relate.* For people to change, they need hope, vision, self-efficacy, and support. They need to have the support of a person (a colleague, an administrator), a group (a department or group of teachers), or a community they have formed an emotional relationship with. That relationship will inspire them, help them to believe that they can change, provide them with tools to change, and help them to sustain hope. The school and department culture have a lot to do with the professional relationships teachers are able to form.
2. *Repeat.* The new relationship helps people learn, practice, and master the new habits and skills they will need. It takes a lot of repetition over time before new patterns of behavior become automatic and seem natural—until people act the new way without even thinking about it.
3. *Reframe.* The new relationship helps people learn new ways of thinking about their situation.

Why hope? Teachers need to hear the message from supervisors and administrators that says, "We can do this; we will find a way meet our goals." I firmly believe that for teachers to change, or improve their instructional practices they need a supporting school culture; they need hope and trust, and also they also need the school community, parents, and the greater community to believe in them and support them. Teachers also need new skills, and the license to experiment (and even fail) with new teaching approaches. Hope, collaboration, and support are vital to teachers continuing to grow, and learn about their practice and craft. Research has shown that reflecting on teacher and student growth together with trusted peers and mentors provides teachers with knowledge, support, and experiences. There is power in working together!

Digital Literacies

- The Teaching Palette—Perfecting the Art of Education Blog: http://theteaching-palette.com; Career and Technical Education, Texas: http://cte.unt.edu/aggregator/sources/2; Larry Ferlazzo's Blog on English and Social Studies resources and lesson ideas: http://larryferlazzo.edublogs.org/about/
- Math Notations Blog: http://mathnotations.blogspot.com; Life of a Foreign Language Educator by Justin Tarte http://www.justintarte.com; Music Teachers Blog: http://www.musicteachershelper.com/blog/.
- Physical Education Blog: http://www.thephysicaleducator.com/blog/; Science Education on the Edge: http://see.ludwig.lajuntaschools.org; World History Teachers Blog: http://worldhistoryeducatorsblog.blogspot.com.

Teacher Snapshots

So what types of professional development might novice or expert teachers engage in? Overall, beginning teachers participate in mentoring types of professional development. Mid-career teachers focus more on making changes in their practice, and veteran teachers find more ways to mentor others and participate in the leadership type of professional experiences. The following are sample profiles of content area teachers who are actively involved in professional development.

Mr. Johnson, a middle school band teacher, goes one night per week to his local university to meet with other middle school teachers of instrumental music, and is also enrolled in a graduate music course in improvisation. He is also a member of the state National Association for Music Education (NAfME) affiliate association where he attends workshops about assessment tools and music education. Last, Mr. Johnson learns more about new music techniques and tools by reading *The American Music Teacher,* and sharing ideas with other music teachers from his school district.

Ms. Gutierez, a high school math teacher, who is actively involved in professional development is a member of the National Council of Teachers of Mathematics (NCTM). She is someone who seeks out opportunities and takes advantage of professional development opportunities throughout the school year, and reads professional publications related to the teaching of mathematics. In addition, she is willing to ask experts including university faculty for help, is active in a PLC at her school, contributes her knowledge to support other teachers, and is willing to admit when she does not know an answer, or an alternative method for mathematical teaching.

Mr. Graves, a middle school science teacher, is a member of the National Science Teachers Association (NSTA), and subscribes to science teacher practice-based journals. He also collaborates with other science teachers in his school-based PLC on developing his subject knowledge, developing students' inquiry skills, doing science and making sense of science, and creating and implementing common assessments to improve instruction. In addition, he keeps abreast of current scientific developments, and seeks other science-related professional opportunities. Mr. Graves also experiments with new instructional ideas that create real-world applications for students and develop their appreciation for science and scientific inquiry.

Ms. Young, a high school world history teacher, is a Member of the National Council for Social Studies (NCSS) and a member of the NCSS state affiliate professional organizations. She is actively involved in her school-based PLC where she collaborates with other teachers in locating and using primary documents and developing lesson plans. Ms. Young also utilizes the US Library of Congress for ways and resources to develop her students' historical critical thinking skills.

All teachers who are actively involved in professional development are members of national, or state subject-specific professional organizations, belong to an active school-based PLC, collaborate with other teachers, study on their own, look for effective ways to improve their practice and help students learn, many pursue graduate studies, and are lifelong learners.

CCSS Connections

- The CCSS implementation will require comprehensive and ongoing professional development for teachers in grades 6–12.
- The new standards require teachers with deep content knowledge, ability to personalize learning for diverse learners, use of formative and summative assessment, new leadership roles for teachers and school administrators, and a culture of collaboration.
- The CCSS do not prescribe how teachers should teach the standards but mastery of the standards requires rigorous instruction, effective ways to engage students in learning and inquiry, the development of disciplinary dispositions, and various forms of assessing and monitoring student progress.

Neither Standards, Nor Programs Teach; Teachers Do

We know that professional development is vital to every teacher's professional growth. The model I shared in this book about literacy as an apprenticeship (see Figure 2.6, p. 54), places attention on academic, socio-emotional, cognitive, affective, and behavioral factors that affect student learning. As you focus on your students' academic success, do not neglect the role of your learning environment and also the relationships you will create with your students. The impact of teachers on students' lives has been documented and discussed for centuries. Teachers have a way of touching students' lives in so many ways (including academic ones). That *one* teacher can make such a difference in students' lives. Think about your own life—which one teacher impacted your own life? In what ways? In my life, it was Mr. Yakoumis, my Algebra teacher, who spent much time talking with me about my academic goals and aspirations, and encouraged me and motivated me to go on. His door was always open—he made himself available to listen to my academic and non-academic questions, and was someone who also challenged me to not give up. He was by no means an "easy" teacher, nor a talkative one. He never insulted me, nor made me feel inferior about myself even when I offered answers, or perspectives that were not worthy of attention . . . . But, he was there, available, offering feedback, trustworthy, protective, and guiding me along the way.

Kathleen Cushman in *Fires in the Bathroom: Advice for Teachers from High School Students* (2003) shares the voices of students from New York, Providence, and San Francisco Bay Area. Some students were recent immigrants, several performed well academically, and others struggled. The students speak about wanting to learn, about their needs, and about the teachers who helped them learn. They offer advice to teachers about listening to student voices, remind teachers of the power they have to change students' lives, and respond with respect to a teacher who believes in them and offers them support when they are experiencing difficulties. Teachers need to know "their stuff," but they also need to notice, pay attention to what students are saying through words or actions, and understand students. I will share a couple of excerpts from the book to illustrate the importance of knowing our students, and seeking their feedback in our efforts to improve teaching and student learning.

Cushman (2003) asked students, "How can a teacher learn about students?"

- *In history the first day my teacher passed out a paper with a couple of questions about how you learn—like: what type of issues do you have with history, do you like it? That was the first time a teacher seemed to actually care about how a student learns, so she could meet their needs. It made me think about how I learn—I never thought about it before, because I'd never been asked.*

    TIFFANY (p. 5)

Students talked about teachers who pushed them to do their best:

- *I had a math teacher who was always on your case: "Write out the problem, turn in your work, you can do it." I didn't like the way he pushed me. But later I thought he was a good teacher—the little things, like "make sure you don't forget to write it all out"—those are the things you need to remember.*

    DIANA (p. 26)

On cultivating a culture of success:

- *My tenth-grade bio-science teacher had faith in me when all my other teachers thought I was a lost cause. He told me, "I know you're smart when you want to be. You just have to want to do it." He prepared me for what is going to be like in college and in the eleventh grade.*

    PORSCHE (p. 63)

On motivation and boredom:

- *School is my way out, into taking care of myself. I can't see myself living in my grandmother's house any longer, depending on them. Also, I really want the college experience. My mom says the college years are the best of your life, and school is the way to get there. But out of six of my classes, three are interesting and three are a waste of time.*

    MAHOGHANY (p. 101)

Students' reasons for being in school:

- *To ward off ignorance. To teach others. To be social. To see others' point of view. To understand history so history isn't repeated. To become well-rounded. To be well represented; to have a voice. To learn to survive in society. To find a career path and a well-paying job. To know information so you're note stuck in "duh" stages, even if things may not seem useful now.*

    (p. 102)

Students enjoyed it when teachers designed projects that involved experts or other outside people for consultation:

- *For our final exam in English and world history we had a mock trial with a real judge and a court typist. They separated us into defense and prosecution, with four lawyers on each side, and they set up a mock scene from "Animal Farm" in which the character Boxer supposedly dies. The defense was defending the guy who supposedly killed him. We had to dress up and go down to City Center for three to four hours. It was plenty fun. We learned more about the book, but we also learned how to follow court procedures, write direct testimony, and do cross-examination.*

    ANDRES (p. 177)

I conclude with a student who talked about how a teacher who is passionate about the subject and also cares about the students, is a teacher who has a great effect on how much students will care about learning.

- *The mark of a good teacher is that no matter how weird or boring you might think their subject is, their love for it is what pushes you to learn something, It could be rat feces or some nasty topic, and the fact their eyes are glowing when they talk about it makes you want to know something about it.*

VANCE (p. 104)

Do you want to reach your adolescent students? Listen to them. Talk less and listen more. Adolescents are complex human beings who face real-world problems and have concerns and hopes for the future. In my 31 years of teaching, I have worked with many adolescents who had difficulties reading, but I do not recall a single one who did not want to learn. Oh, I can recall several who did not want to read what I gave them, but really, even among the high school dropouts I worked with, I did not meet a student who did not want to learn. Many had difficulties learning, but the desire to learn was there, many times masked under a negative attitude or behavior, or clothed in apathy.

In *Portraits of Promise: Voices of Resilience from Adolescence to Adulthood,* Sadowski (2013) shares from his interviews and study of 19 immigrant students, that the most important factor in their resilience and school success was the relationships they had with their teachers—teachers who challenged and guided them through high school, helped them with decisions about college or work. Of course, time is every teacher's most valuable commodity and teachers' lives are stretched in so many ways.

The implementation of new educational and subject-specific standards will require large-scale professional development for all content teachers. Traditional professional development that uses a "drive through" approach to complex disciplinary and pedagogical issues will fail. "Show and tell" professional learning models will not result in teacher or school change. Merely comparing old educational standards to new ones, and taking a general approach to disciplinary literacy and college and career readiness, will not prepare students for college, career, and work-force demands. Professional development that views literacy as a discipline-specific process, and leads to change in teacher practice and student learning, requires: comprehensive investments in a sustained and intensive approach to improving teachers' content; instructional and pedagogical understanding of how students learn; implementing curricula based on rigorous educational standards; and the use of technology for teacher and student learning.

The discipline-specific learning framework I introduced in this book views teaching and learning as an apprenticeship. Students need mentoring, guidance, support, feedback, high standards and rigor, and opportunities to experiment, inquire, and learn from both their successes and their failures. Keep focusing on supporting their academic success, but also keep in mind that teachers who build good relationships with students motivate them to learn. Teachers who tap into students' interests, questions, ideas about what they are learning, and goals for learning are teachers of engaged students.

Teachers who collaborate and participate in ongoing, collaborative, relevant, and job-embedded professional development are teachers who continue to grow, learn, and succeed. Every student deserves to have a great teacher. Helping every student succeed, and be college, career and workforce ready, is not an easy task. It won't happen by wishing it, or strongly desiring it. And neither will be done perfectly all the time. The challenge is strong enough for educators, policy makers, and others to want to work harder and collaborate in getting better results.

Summary

- The implementation of new educational standards and the pressures for improved student performance place a strong focus on the types of professional development teachers will need to successfully prepare students for postsecondary education, work, and life. Effective teacher evaluation systems should have professional standards that are aligned with student learning standards, describe excellent teaching, and provide a common language for teacher and administrator dialogue about effective teaching practice.

- Data or leadership teams, study groups, PLCs, communities of practice, lesson study, and collaborating with instructional coaches are major types of school-based professional development. Analyzing student data, monitoring student progress, and setting short term, measureable and attainable goals, are effective ways for teachers to collaborate on instructional improvements and student learning growth.

- Content area teachers need discipline-specific professional development that builds their knowledge of content and pedagogy, and is founded on discipline-specific inquiry, habits of mind and dispositions, and collaborative inquiry. Discipline-specific professional development should also be closely linked to standards, disciplinary ideas, curriculum, assessment, and student and teacher needs. Preparing all students to succeed in grades 6–12 and beyond requires ongoing collaboration and reflection among all stakeholders.

Differentiating Instruction

- Teachers need professional development that will increase their knowledge of ELLs' needs, and the needs of students with learning exceptionalities.

- Teachers need help understanding students' background knowledge, and learning appropriate strategies, teaching, interventions, and assessment.

- Teachers will also benefit from learning how to create a culturally responsive learning environment, select diverse materials, teach in discipline-specific ways, analyze and reflect on student data, and plan for improved instruction.

- Students who receive ESE (Exceptional Student Education) services for their learning needs have true learning needs. Some can read, but have difficulties with comprehension, while others have excellent verbal and upper-level thinking, but have difficulties decoding words. Teachers can benefit from professional development on the nature and needs of adolescent ELLs, ESE, gifted, ASD (Autism Spectrum Disorder), dyslexia, language and communicative disorders, and others with varied exceptionalities.

- Key topics for all content area teachers include: (1) how exceptional education students perceive, process, respond, and produce information and knowledge; (2) ideas for assessments; (3) learned helplessness; (4) how to scaffold instruction; (5) behavior and classroom management; (6) flexible cooperative learning; and (7) RtI.

Reflect and Apply

1. Think about the teachers you have had so far in your educational career. Which teacher stands out? Why? Would you characterize that teacher as a "good" teacher or not? What were some of his, or her key attributes, knowledge, skills, practices, and dispositions? What would you like to emulate in your practice from that teacher and why?

2. Revisit the Classroom Life vignette. What are your thoughts about Ms. Nolen's *Persistence of Vision?* Discuss your reaction to her vignette with a group of peers.

3. What type of professional development would an art, career and technical subjects, English language arts, history, math, physical education, or social

studies teacher need to have to help his or her students develop a deeper understanding of content knowledge? Describe the elements, duration, and type of professional development, and provide evidence from the text to support your suggestions.

Extending Learning

1. Observe an excellent content area teacher from your discipline in his or her learning environment. Using evidence from this chapter, develop an observation protocol by identifying the areas of teaching and learning you would like to observe. Conduct the observation, record your notes, analyze them, and present them to class. Also identify areas of improvement, and use your knowledge of effective practice in that discipline to provide specific instructional improvements.

2. Get together with some of your peers and suggest five ways an instructional coach, a school principal, or a mentor could use to support content area teachers in your school to meet the needs of ELLs, and other students, who are having difficulty learning. Describe your rationale, strategies, and ways to implement them. Offer specific ideas to teachers about ways to collect data on student progress. Share your plan with the class.

3. Write a letter to a policy-maker at the state, or school district level about the need to provide discipline-specific professional development for content area teachers. Use research evidence to explain the importance of effective professional development for teacher and student learning, and request the types of support teachers will need in order to help all students succeed. Present your letter to a group of peers, obtain feedback, and revise as needed.

4. Using information from this chapter, develop a plan for making department group meetings more collaborative, relevant to each discipline's challenges and demands, and instruction- and assessment-centered. Anticipate teacher resistance due to negative or unproductive experiences with professional development. Your plan should span over a nine week period of time and it should include elements of effective, collaborative, and relevant professional development. Share your plan with a department head, or content area teacher from your discipline, and discuss their feedback to your plan with a group of peers.

References

Annenberg Institute for School Reform. (2005). *Professional learning communities: Professional development strategies that improve instruction.* Providence, RI: Author. Retrieved from http://annenberginstitute.org/pdf/proflearning.pdf

Bean, R. M. (2004). *The reading specialist: Leadership for the classroom, school, and community.* New York: Guilford.

Bransford, J. D., Brown, A. L., & Cocking, R. R. (2000). *How people learn: Brain, mind, experience, and school.* Washington, DC: National Academies Press.

Bryk, A., Sebring, P., Allensworth, E., Luppescu, S., & Easton, J. (2010). *Organizing schools for improvement: Lessons from Chicago.* Chicago: University of Chicago Press.

Calkins, L., Ehrenworth, M., & Lehman, C. (2012). *Pathways to the common core: Accelerating achievement.* Portsmouth, NH: Heinemann.

Carnegie Corporation of New York's Council on Advancing Adolescent Literacy. (2010). *Time to act: An agenda for advancing adolescent literacy for college and career success.* New York, NY: Author. Retrieved from http://carnegie.org/fileadmin/Media/Publications/PDF/tta_Main.pdf

Carroll, T., Fulton, K., & Doerr, H. (2010). *Team up for 21st century teaching and learning: What research and practice reveal about professional learning.* Washington, DC: National Commission on Teaching and America's Future.

Coggshall, J. G., Rasmussen, C., Colton, A., Milton, J., & Jacques, C. (2012). *Generating teaching effectiveness: The role of job-embedded professional development learning in teacher evaluation.* (Research and Policy Brief). National Comprehensive Center for Teacher Quality: Author. Retrieved from http://www.gtlcenter.org/sites/default/files/docs/GeneratingTeachingEffectiveness.pdf

Council of Chief State School Officers. (2013). *Interstate teacher assessment for support consortium (InTASC) model core teaching standards and learning progressions for teachers 1.0: A Resource for ongoing teacher development.* Washington, DC: Author.

Cushman, K. (2003). *Fires in the bathroom: Advice to teachers from high school students.* New York, NY: The New Press.

Danielson, C. (2011). Evaluations that help people learn. *Educational Leadership, 68*(4), 35–39.

Danielson, C. (2013). *The framework for teaching evaluation instrument.* Princeton, NJ: The Danielson Group. Retrieved from http://www.danielsongroup.org/userfiles/files/downloads/2013EvaluationInstrument.pdf

Darling-Hammond, L., Wei, R. C., Andree, A., Richardson, N., & Orphanos, S. (2009). *Professional learning in the learning profession: A status report on teacher development in the United States and abroad.* Dallas, TX: National Staff Development Council. Retrieved from http://nsdc.org/news/NSDCstudy2009.pdf

Desimone, L. M. (2009). Improving impact studies of teachers' professional development: Toward better conceptualizations and measures. *Educational Researcher, 38*(3), 181–199.

Deutschman, A. (2007). *Change or die: The three keys to change at work and in life.* New York, NY: Harper Collins Publishers.

DuFour, R. (2004). What is a professional learning community? *Educational Leadership, 61*(8), 6–11.

DuFour, R., DuFour, R., Eaker, R. & Many, T. (2010). *Learning by doing* (2nd ed.). Indiana: Solution Tree.

Duncan, A. (2009). Elevating the teaching profession. *American Educator, 5.* Retrieved from http://www.aft.org/pdfs/americaneducator/winter2009/duncan.pdf

Easton, L. B. (Ed.). (2008). *Powerful designs for professional learning.* Oxford, OH: National Staff Development Council.

Easton, L. B. (2009). *Protocols for professional learning.* Alexandria, VA: Association for Supervision and Curriculum Development.

Garet, M. S., Porter, A. C., Desimone, L., Birman, B. F., & Yoon, K. S. (2001). What makes professional development effective? Results from a national sample of teachers. *American Educational Research Journal, 38*(4), 915–945.

Goe, L., Biggers, K., & Croft, A. (2012). *Linking teacher evaluation to professional development: Focusing on improving teaching and learning* (Research and Policy Brief). Washington, DC: Comprehensive Center for teacher Quality. Retrieved from http://www.tqsource.org/publications/LinkingTeacherEval.pdf

Guskey, T. R. (2000). *Evaluating professional development.* Thousand Oaks, CA: Corwin Press.

Guskey, T. R. (2002). Professional development and teacher change. *Teachers and Teaching: Theory and Practice, 8(3/4),* 381–391.

Guskey, T. R. (2003). What makes professional development effective? *Phi Delta Kappan, 84*(10), 748–750.

Holland, H. (2005). Teaching teachers: Professional development to improve student achievement. *Research Points: Essential Information for Educational Policy, 3*(1), 1–4. Washington, DC: American Educational Research Association.

Hurd, J., & Licciardo-Musso, L. (2005). Lesson study: Professional development in literacy instruction. *Language Arts, 82*(5), 388–394.

Johnson, B. (2012, February 14). *Learning to teach: The practice curriculum* (2011–12 seminar series). Presentation delivered at Teaching Works, Ann Arbor, MI. Retrieved from http://teachingworks.org/training/seminar-series/event/detail/the-new-teacher-project

Joyce, B., & Showers, B. (2002). *Student achievement through staff development* (3rd ed.). Alexandria, VA: Association for Supervision and Curriculum Development.

Knowles, M. (1970). *The modern practice of adult education: Andragogy versus pedagogy.* New York, NY: Association Press.

Knowles, M. (1984a). *The adult learner: A neglected species.* Houston, TX: Gulf Publishing.

Knowles, M. (1984b). *Andragogy in action.* San Francisco, CA: Jossey-Bass.

Learning Forward. (2011). *Standards for professional learning*. Retrieved from http://learningforward.org/docs/august-2011/referenceguide324.pdf?sfvrsn=2

Lewis, C. (2002). *Lesson study: A handbook of teacher-led instructional change*. Philadelphia, PA: Research for Better Schools.

Loucks-Horsley, S., & Matsumoto, C. (1999). Research on professional development for teachers of mathematics and science: The state of the scene. *School Science and Mathematics*, 99(5), 258–271.

Louis, K., Leithwood, K., Wahlstrom, K., & Anderson, S. (2010). *Learning from leadership: Investigating the links to improved student learning*. New York: Wallace Foundation.

Marzano, R. (2011). *The Marzano causal teacher evaluation model*. Blairsville, PA: Learning Sciences International.

Mid-continent Research for Education and Learning (McREL). (2003). Sustaining school improvement: Professional learning community. Retrieved from http://www.mcrel.org/pdf/leadershiporganization development/5031TG_proflrncommfolio.pdf

Miller, R. J., Goddard, R., Larsen, R., & Jacob, R. (2010, November 17–20). *Shared instructional leadership: A pathway to teacher collaboration and student achievement*. A paper presented at the University Council for Educational Administration Convention (UCEA), Pittsburgh, PA.

Mishra, P., & Koehler, M. J. (2006). Technological Pedagogical Content Knowledge: A new framework for teacher knowledge. *Teachers College Record*, 108(6), 1017–1054.

National Board for Professional Teaching Standards. (1989). *What teachers should know and be able to do*. Arlington, VA: Author. Retrieved from http://www.nbpts.org/national-board-standards

National Institute for Excellence in Teaching. (2012). *Beyond "job-embedded": Ensuring that good professional development gets results*. Santa Monica, CA: Author. Retrieved from http://www.niet.org/assets/PDFs/beyond_job_embedded_professional_development.pdf

National Reading Panel (2000). *Teaching children to read: An evidence-based assessment of the scientific research literature on reading and its implications for reading instruction*. Retrieved from http://www.dys-add.com/resources/SpecialEd/TeachingChildrenToRead.pdf

Pearson, P. D., & Gallagher, M. C. (1983). The instruction of reading comprehension. *Contemporary Educational Psychology*, 8, 317–344.

Penuel, W. R., Fishman, B. J., Yamaguchi, R., & Gallagher, L. P. (2007). What makes professional development effective? Strategies that foster curriculum implementation. *American Educational Researcher*, 44(4), 921–958.

Rentfro, E. R. (Winter, 2007). Professional learning communities impact student success. *Leadership Compass*, 5(2).

Sadowski, M. (2013). *Portraits of promise: Voices of successful immigrant students*. Cambridge, MA: Harvard Education Press.

Stoll, L., & Louis, K. S. (2007). Professional learning communities: Elaborating new approaches. *Professional learning communities: Divergence, Depth and Dilemmas*, 1–13.

Walpole, S., & McKenna, M. C. (2013) (2nd ed.). *The literacy coach's handbook: A guide to research-based practice*. New York, NY: Guilford Press.

Yoon, K. S. (2007). *Reviewing the evidence on how teacher professional development affects student achievement*. National Center for Educational Evaluation and Regional Assistance, Institute of Education Sciences, US Department of Education: Author.

Index

Note: Page numbers followed by "n" refer to notes, by "f" to figures, by "t" to tables.

Numbers

10 Most Important Words Strategy 152, 154–5t

21st century learning 5–6, 18–20, 101, 175–6, 177, 287–8

A

ABC Brainstorm 147, 148t

academic disciplines 37–47; arts 39–40; English language arts (ELA) 40–2; mathematics 42–4; reasons for positioning literacy in 47–50; science 44–5; similarities and differences in thinking 47f; social studies 45–6

academic discourse 288–93, 301, 306, 326; 10 Most Important Words Strategy 289–90; altering discourse patterns in classroom 290; conversation skills 295; defining 288–9; developing disciplinary 291–3; mathematics 290–1; writing to develop 357

academic rigor 95–6

academic vocabulary 71, 77, 99, 133, 134, 135, 143, 159t; process to develop 145–6

accountable talk 50–1, 85–6, 214, 226, 300–6; in the disciplines 86f, 289, 303–6; moves 300–1; ways to promote 302t

achievement gap 397, 405, 422

admit slips 370, 370t

adolescent literacy, crisis in: Common Core State Standards Initiative (CCSS) in response to 11, 13–15; *Next Generation Science Standards* (NGSS) 15–16; research evidence 12–13; snapshot of evolution in 11–12

Alliance for Excellent Education 4, 11, 18

American College Testing Service 64

American Psychological Association (APA) 349, 354, 405

Anchor Standards: for Reading 35–6, 62, 62f, 64, 228; for Writing 35–6, 330, 341, 342t

andragogy 422–3, 432

anecdotal records 390–1

annotating 199t, 200, 234, 235

Anticipation Guide 252, 253t

apprenticeship learning model 51–3, 107, 208–9, 297, 322

argument, learning through disciplinary 296

argument writing 343–6; discipline-specific 344–5; example 344f; a feature of college writing 334; organizing 345; reasons for difficulty with 346, 346f; scientific 345–6

arts 39–40; argument writing 344; characteristics of learning environment 298; close-ended and open-ended questions 188t; discipline vocabulary 138; essential questions 190–1f; expert questioning and habits of mind 212t; portfolios 395f; professional development needs 442t; QAR examples 195t; using GRRM model 54; writing 344, 355, 355–6
assessment: authentic 388–9, 392, 414; and bias 382; challenges 381; Cloze procedure 403, 404t; differentiating instruction 414–15; disciplinary literacy learning principle 55; in disciplines 409–14, 411–14t; effective, principles for 383; in exemplary schools 17, 19; formative *see* formative assessment; Fry Readability Graph 401–2, 402f; grades and grading 410; group work 309, 315–16, 316t; and instruction 381–2; international 384–5; laboratory report rubric 351–2t; Lexile Framework 72, 73t, 403, 403t; materials for 401–3; national 385–6; NCLB and policy on 405, 407; performance 388–9; rigor in 97f, 101; Socratic Seminar rubric 316t; standardized 386–8, 387t, 405, 406; summative 55, 382, 392, 408, 408t; systems in era of new educational standards 406, 407–9; types 382–96; of writing skills 339
assessment, implementing an effective informal/ classroom-based system 389–96; checklists 391, 391t; interest and attitude inventories 392; interviews 392; observations and anecdotal records 390–1; portfolios 392–6, 393f, 394f; sample suggestions 389–90; surveys and questionnaires 391
ATOS formula 73t, 74
aural vocabulary 134
authentic assessment 388–9, 392, 414

B
Bain, K. 277, 278
Beating the Odds 17, 18, 336
Beck, I.L. 133, 135, 136, 142, 143, 145, 147, 155, 180, 196, 197, 198, 224
big ideas 189–90
biopoems 368, 369t
Bloom's Revised Taxonomy 97, 122, 124t, 182, 202, 362; sample questions 182–3t
Bloom's Taxonomy of Educational Objectives 122, 123, 124t, 182, 362
Bransford, J.D. 20, 21, 22, 423

C
Call to Action 227
Cambourne, B. 321–2

career and technical education (CTE) 4, 140, 297, 442t
Carl D. Perkins Career and Technical Education (CTE) Improvement Act 2006 4
Carnegie Corporation of New York 13, 336–7, 339–40, 438
Carnegie Council for Advancing Adolescent Literacy 15, 140, 438
Casual Teacher Evaluation Model 433
Change or Die 444
change, perspective on 441, 444
Charbonneau, J. 323
checklists 391, 391t
Chinese composition 371
CISCO Systems 323–4
citation of references 353
Claim-Evidence-Reasoning Strategy 262, 265t
classroom displays 165–6, 323–4, 323f, 324f
classroom environment 19, 50, 137, 290; Danielson *Framework for Teaching* domain 431t; of disciplinary inquiry 213–15; to facilitate deep learning 297–8; norms and procedures 103–7, 105–6f; physical arrangement 104, 291, 297–8, 432; and role in student learning 321–5
classroom talk: developing skills for 295; and disciplinary literacy 293–6; learning through argument and 296; teachers' concerns with 296
close reading of text 78–80; 10 Most Important Words Strategy 152; and accountable talk 85–6, 86f; building comprehension through 227–8; how to practice 79–80; rigorous instruction and selection of texts 108; sample protocol 81t; Vocabulary Note-Taking Strategy to facilitate 151
Cloze procedure 403, 404t
cognitive apprenticeships 51, 200
cognitive rigor 97–8, 122–3
Cognitive Rigor Matrix (CRM) 123, 124t
Coh-Metrix system 74
Coleman, D. 177, 178
collaboration: role in writing 371–2, 374; teacher 434–9
collaborative groups, creating effective 308–9
collaborative inquiry 306–17; assigning students to groups 306; barriers to 307–8; benefits 306; CISCO's promotion of 323–4; cooperative learning 287, 309–17; creating effective groups for 308–9; differentiating learning within groups 312–17; Jigsaw 310–12, 312f, 313, 313t; Socratic Seminars 314–17, 316t; Think-Pair-Share 310, 311t

collaborative learning 54–5, 306–7, 308, 309, 310, 324, 325, 326; comprehension instruction and 200, 223, 224, 226

college and career readiness 2–4, 20; Anchor Standards for Reading 35–6, 62, 62f, 64, 228; Anchor Standards for Writing 35–6, 330, 341, 342t; assessment focusing on 407–8; collaborative learning for 307, 326; common core standards for 13–15, 176–7; comprehension, role in 176–8, 182, 275; Conley's four keys to 229; digital literacies for 374; disciplinary literacy 33–4, 35–6, 37; discourse, role of 287–8; *Next Generation Science Standards* (NGSS) 15–16; rigorous instruction for 101; rigorous texts for 108; schools we need for 16–22; teacher professional development and 420–2; and text complexity 64–5; vocabulary for 133–4; writing skills and 35–6, 330, 341–2, 375

Common Core State Standards (CCSS) 13–15; and adolescent literacy 11; assessment 406, 407–9; close reading of complex text 80; college and career ready skills 13–15, 176–7; complex questions for sample text exemplars 192–3t; discourse and collaboration 287–8; English language development 167; formative assessment and 382–4; instructional shifts 99–100, 101, 215, 293–4; multiple texts 108, 109–10t, 110; sample reading standards and related questions 184, 184–5t; technology, use of 175–6, 373; text-based classroom discussion 177; text complexity 61–3; text complexity model 65–6, 66f; text selection criteria 87–8; texts, requirements for rigorous 108; vocabulary 133–4, 141, 144, 294; writing and CCSS *see* writing and CCSS

communication skills 177, 178, 295

communities of practice 51, 438

community, developing a sense of 319–20

completion rates, postsecondary 16

complex questions 191, 192–3t

comprehension: annotating 234; approaches to teaching 223, 224–5; building through text 227–9; content instruction 224, 225; deep learning and 277–80; differentiating instruction 216, 280–1; fluency and 225–6; independent reading and 227; metacognition and comprehension monitoring 275–6; monitoring 276; of new literacies 3, 9; note-taking *see* note-taking; process of 178–81; proficient readers 180–1; questions, questioning and 181–6, 182–3t;

184–5t; research on effective instruction 222–4; role in college, career and workforce readiness 176–8; strategy instruction 223, 224, 225, 229, 242, 244–5; summarizing 240–2, 241–2t, 243t; teaching 222–4; text coding 235–6, 235t; text marking 234–5; text structure and 228–9; text structure instruction 229–34; textbook organizational patterns 230–4, 233–4t

comprehension, strategies for discipline-specific instruction 242–75; core steps of effective strategy instruction 244–5; literacy studies 245–52; mathematics 252–60; science 260–7; social studies/history 267–75

Concept of Definition Map 147–8, 149f

ConnectED 374

content area literacy 31–3; misconceptions 32–3; shift to disciplinary literacy 33–5, 34f

content knowledge 31, 48, 229, 428t

context clues 155–6

conversation skills, academic 295

cooperative learning 287, 309–17; differentiating tasks within 312–17; Jigsaw 310–12, 312f, 313, 313t; Socratic Seminars 314–17, 316t; Think-Pair-Share 310, 311t

Cornell Notes 360; modified strategy 237t, 238, 360, 361t

Council of State School Officers (CCSSO) 426–9, 428–9t

creative writing 368, 368f; biopoems 368, 369t

critical literacy 10

critical thinking skills in 21st century 175–6

cubing 362–3, 363t

Cushman, K. 446–7

D

Dale-Chall Readability Formula 72

Danielson *Framework for Teaching* 429–33, 431–2t, 431t

Darling-Hammond, L. 21, 22, 101, 421, 425

data collection in schools 435

data or leadership teams 435–6

deep learning 277, 280; in the arts 39, 40; vs. surface learning 278t; taking a discipline-specific approach to 279–80; ways to promote 20, 245, 277–80

Delpit, L. 181, 320, 371

on-demand writing 353–4; ABCD strategy for 354

department-level meetings 437–9

Depth of Knowledge Levels (DOK) 122–3, 124t, 362; sample question stems 125t

Determining Essential and Non-Essential Information 254, 254t

Deutschman, A. 444

digital: literacies 7, 9–10, 332–3, 374, 396; portfolios 396; writing 332–3, 342, 373–4
Digital Is 373
Digital Portfolios Pull Double Duty 396
disciplinary inquiry classroom culture 213–15
disciplinary literacy/discipline-specific literacy 4, 30, 35–7, 38, 47–50; and academic disciplines 37–46; characteristics of learning environment 296–300; and classroom talk 293–6, 294t; framework 36f; learning principles 50–5; positioning literacy in disciplines 47–50; shift from content area literacy to 33–5, 34f
discipline-specific literacy *see* disciplinary literacy/ discipline-specific literacy
discourse: and collaboration in CCSS 287–8; discipline-specific 303–5; primary 322; secondary 322–3 *see also* academic discourse
Document Analysis Strategy 54, 54f
Document-Based Questions (DBQs) Project 356
domain knowledge 72
Double-Entry Journals (DEJs) 236, 237t
dropouts, high school 4, 6, 11
Duncan, A. 406, 424
Durkin, D. 135, 222, 289
dysgraphia 376

E
Education for Life and Work 20, 277
effective teaching and student learning 20–2, 90–4
elbow coaching 434
Engaging in Argument from Evidence 262, 266t
English language arts (ELA) 40–2, 47f; ABC Brainstorm example 148t; accountable talk 86f, 303, 303f; argument writing 344; assessment 408–9, 411t; building fluency 226; character analysis 249, 250t; character journals 360; close-ended and open-ended questions 188t; comprehension strategies 245–52; creative writing 368, 368f; disciplinary vocabulary 71, 138–9; discourse 303; essential questions 116, 117t, 190–1f; etymology 159t; expert questioning and habits of mind 209, 210t; informational/ explanatory writing 347; informational texts 99, 108; instructional shifts to promote rigorous learning 99, 101; Introduction to Film 419–20; Knowledge Rating Strategy 156, 157t; learning environment characteristics 297–8; learning goals 115–16t; Literacy Analysis 245, 246–7t; Main Idea 245, 249t; Modified Three-Column Note-Taking Strategy 361t;

narrative writing 348; patterns, characteristics and examples of disciplinary texts 68t; portfolios 395f; professional development needs 442t; QAR examples 195t; Questions-Connections 249, 250–1t; RAFT 365f; rigorous materials 108; Story Mapping 245, 248t; Summary Guide Strategy 366; Use Your Adjectives 249, 250t; Viewpoint Analysis 249, 252, 252t; writing 340, 344, 347, 348, 355, 368, 368f
English Language Learners (ELL) 12, 13, 23; assessment 415; classroom life 287; classroom talk and argument of benefit to 296; comprehension instruction 280–1; disciplinary literacy learning and support for 56; embracing multiple discourses 323; summarization strategies 280; support with text complexity 88; teacher expectations and 103, 289; teaching new words to 167–8; vocabulary challenges for 167; Vocabulary Self-Selection Strategy 162; writing 376
eponyms 158–9
essential questions 116–18, 117t, 118t, 189–90, 190f, 190–1f
etymology 157–9, 158t, 159t
Examining the Author's Argument Strategy 267, 268–9t
exit: questions 117, 118t; slips 370, 370t
expectations, building a culture of high 102–3
explicit instruction 118–20; checklist for designing rigorous 119t; vocabulary 135, 136–7, 138, 143, 144, 146

F
Fact versus Opinion Strategy 272–3t, 272–4
feedback: for students 102, 318, 325, 384; for teachers 433–4
Ferris Bueller's Day Off 183–4
Fires in the Bathroom 446–7
Flesch-Kincaid Grade Level test 72, 73t
flow map, group-generated 323, 324f
fluency 225; and comprehension 225–6
foreign languages 364, 364t
formative assessment 55, 388–9; and CCSS 382–4; data or leadership teams and 436; and essential questions 117; evidence to gauge if students are learning 125; exit slips and 370; learning goals and 112, 112t, 113, 114; meta-analysis of research 383; to pre-assess students' prior knowledge 280; responding to gifted students 126; and rigorous instruction 123–6; samples 383–4; what to do when students are not learning 126

Framework for Teaching 429–33, 431–2t, 431t
Freire, P. 10
Fry Readability Graph 401–2, 402f
functional language analysis (FLA) 67, 137

G
Gallagher, K. 340, 354, 371
Gardner, H. 48
Geisler, C. 48, 49
general literacy strategies 31, 32, 35, 47
gifted learners 23, 126
GIST 366
globalization 4
GoogleDocs 374
grades and grading 410
Gradual Release of Responsibility Model (GRRM)
        53–5, 120, 244, 245
Graham, S. 11, 230, 332, 337, 338, 339, 346
graphic organizers: for comprehension 225; to
        develop writing 339; etymology 158t, 159t;
        morphemic analysis 160t; note taking 236t,
        238–40, 238t, 239–40t; for struggling
        readers 229; summarization 241, 241t, 243f;
        a teacher's experience of 287; text structure
        with related 233–4t
Graves, D. 340
group semantic web 323, 323f
groups: assessment of work in 309, 315–16, 316t;
        assigning students to 307; creating effective
        collaborative 308–9; differentiating learning
        within 312–17; Jigsaw arrangement of 312f;
        setting clear behavior expectations 308;
        student accountability 309
guided oral-reading practice 226
*Guidelines for Teaching Middle and High
        School Students to Read and Write Well* 336

H
habits of mind 37; discipline-specific questioning
        and 209–13, 210–12t
health education: characteristics of learning
        environment 299; essential questions
        190–1f; expert questioning and habits of
        mind 212t; QFT 208; writing 358
Hebert, M. 11, 230, 339, 341
Hess, K. 122, 123
high probability strategies 120–1, 120t
high schools, characteristics of exemplary 18–20
high-stakes testing 318, 422; issues and concerns
        405; preparing students for 387–8,
        420
Hilton, M.L. 20, 277
history *see* social studies/history
hypertext 8–9; reading 9

I
I-Chart 238, 239–40t
I-Search paper 352–3
Identifying Point of View Strategy 272, 271t, 272
Image Analysis Strategy 267, 269–70t
*The Impact of Digital Tools on Student
        Writing and How Writing is Taught
        in Schools* 373
IMPROVE 275
inclusive classrooms 310, 320–1
independent reading 227; software programs to
        monitor 227
Individuals with Disabilities Education
        Improvement Act (IDEIA) 2004 397, 405
informational/explanatory writing 346–7, 347f
informational texts 33, 67, 230; CCSS focus on 65,
        99, 108, 109–10t; complex questions 192–3t;
        graphic organizers for 241–2, 241t, 243f;
        increase in ELA 99, 108; reading standards
        and related questions 184–5t; text-
        dependent questions 82
inquiry 53; learning, discipline-specific 53–5;
        -oriented classrooms, disciplinary 213–15
        see also collaborative inquiry
Inquiry Chart 238, 239–40t
instructional coaches 439
intelligence, socialized 295, 317–18; Resnick's
        principles of learning 322
interactive notebooks 360, 362
interest and attitude inventories 392
international: assessment 384–5; professional
        development, teacher 421; rankings
        11, 385
International Reading Association (IRA) 9, 63–4,
        440
*Interstate Teacher Assessment and Support
        Consortium (InTASC)* 426–9, 428–9t
interviews 392
iObservation 433

J
Jago, C. 95
Jigsaw 310–12, 312f, 313, 313t
jobs, skills for 21st century 49–50, 177
journals: character 360; Double-Entry Journals
        (DEJs) 236, 237t; in mathematics 357;
        writing 335, 359–60

K
Key Word Strategy 253, 254t
knowledge demands 71–2, 75t
Knowledge Rating Strategy 156–7, 157t
Kucan, L. 136, 142, 143, 155, 196
KWNSR Strategy 255, 256–9t

L

laboratory report: format 349, 350–1t; rubric 351–2t

Langer, J. 17, 18, 48, 336

language conventionality and clarity 67, 71, 75t

leadership: collaborative school 18, 19, 425, 429; teams 435–6

learning goals 111–18; classroom presentation of 116–17, 118t; designing 112–13, 118; as distinct from learning activities 111–12; effective lessons and 114, 116; essential questions 116–18, 117t; examples 112t, 113–16, 115–16t; research on links with student achievement 111; scales and rubrics for 112, 112t; student input 113, 114

learning logs 335, 360, 362, 376

learning on the diagonal 48–9, 49f

learning theories: Cambourne's conditions of learning 321–2; Resnick's principles of learning 322

LePage, P. 21

lesson study 127, 439

Lexile Measure 72, 73t, 403, 403t

libraries: classroom 227; digital 353

listening: goals 294t; speaking and 293

Literacy Analysis 245, 246–7t

literacy progression model 34, 34f

literacy, reconceptualizing 6–7

Llewellyn, D. 345

M

Main Idea Strategy 245, 249t

marking, QtA move 198t, 200

Martin, D. 396

Marzano, R. 72, 111, 112, 116, 120, 121, 145, 410, 434; *Casual Teacher Evaluation Model* 433

Math Journal 260, 260t, 357

mathematics 42–4, 47f; academic discourse, involving students in 290–1; accountable talk 86f, 298–9, 303–4, 304f; Anticipation Guide 252, 253t; argument writing 344; assessment 409, 412t; close-ended and open-ended questions 188t; comprehension strategies 252–60; Determining Essential and Non-Essential Information 254, 254t; developing content and literacy knowledge in tandem 53; discipline vocabulary 71, 138–9; discourse 303–4; essential questions 117t, 190–1f; etymology 159t; expert questioning and habits of mind 209, 211t; exposition 357–8; IMPROVE 275; informational/explanatory writing 347; instructional shifts to promote rigorous learning 99, 101; journals 260, 260t, 357;

Key Word Strategy 253, 254t; KWNSR Strategy 255, 256–9t; multiple-meanings, words with 135–6; narrative writing 348; patterns, characteristics and examples of disciplinary texts 68–9t; portfolios 395f; *Principles and Standards for School Mathematics* 129; Problem-Solution 254, 255t; professional development example 445; professional development needs 442–3t; QAR examples 195t; RAFT 364; Semantic Feature Analysis (SFA) 150t; student logs 357; Summary Guide Strategy 366; Vocabulary Word Box 151t; writing 340, 344, 347, 348, 356–8

McKeown, M.G. 133, 135, 136, 142, 147, 155, 180, 196, 198, 224

metacognition 9, 22, 275; and comprehension monitoring 275–6; and reciprocal teaching 200–2

middle schools, characteristics of exemplary 17–18

Model Core Teaching Standards and Learning Progressions for Teachers 1.0 426–9, 428–9t

modeling, QtA move 199t, 200

morale, teachers' 422

morphemic analysis 159–60, 160t

multiple literacies 7; teaching 9–10

Multiplication is for White People 181

music 39–40; at college 409; expert questioning and habits of mind 212t; professional development example 445; professional development needs 443t; sample essential questions 117t; writing skills 355–6

N

narrative texts 67, 108, 229–30

narrative writing 348

National Assessment for Educational Progress (NAEP) 11, 12, 335, 343t, 385, 405, 407; mathematics and reading assessment 2013 13, 385

national assessments 385–6

National Commission on Writing 13, 331, 332

National Council of Teachers of English (NCTE) 9, 64, 65, 227, 295, 342, 440

National Council of Teachers of Mathematics (NCTM) 63, 139, 286, 288, 440, 445

National Curriculum Standards for Social Studies 15

national progress reports 5–6

National Reading Panel 135, 136, 222; Report (NRP) 11, 223, 425

National Research Council (NRC) 2, 20, 275, 277

National Writing Project (NWP) 373

new ethos stuff 8

new literacies 7–8; changing nature of texts 8–9; critical literacy 10; four key principles 8; teaching 9–10

Next Generation Science Standards (NGSS) 15–16, 63, 133, 177, 287

No Child Left Behind Act 2001 11, 92, 382, 405, 422, 435

Normal Curve 386

note-taking 236–40; Double-Entry Journals (DEJs) 236, 237t; guidelines 237t; I-Chart 238, 239–40t; Three Column Note-Taking 237t, 238, 360, 361t

O

Obama, Barack 1, 92, 323, 374, 422, 425

observations: and anecdotal records 390–1; checklists 291t, 391; of teachers at work 432, 434

one-word summaries 366–7

oral reading 225–6

Organization for Economic Co-Operation and Development (OECD) 11, 175, 384, 421

P

paragraph instruction 230

Partnership for Assessment of Readiness for Colleges and Careers (PARCC) 406–8; comparison with SBAC 408t

Pathways to the Common Core 421

pedagogical content knowledge 20, 21, 51

peer: collaboration in writing 371–2; tutoring 313–14

Pellegrino, J.W. 20, 55, 277

performance assessment 388–9

Perin, D. 337, 338

persuasive writing 343, 348

physical education: argument writing 345; characteristics of learning environment 299; close-ended and open-ended questions 188t; expert questioning and habits of mind 212t; professional development needs 443t; QAR examples 195t; sample essential questions 117t; writing 345, 358

Pimentel, S. 101, 108, 177, 178

PISA (Programme for International Student Assessment) 11, 175, 384–5

plagiarism 355, 374

portfolios 392–6, 393f, 394f; assessment 396; discipline-specific 395f; types 394–6; virtual 396

Portraits of Promise 448

positive interdependence 309–10

praising students 102, 318, 325

Preventing Reading Difficulties in Young Children 11

primary discourse 322

Principles and Standards for School Mathematics 139

Problem-Solution 254, 255t; Organizer Strategy 262, 264t

professional development: andragogy and implications for 432; and college and career readiness 420–2; Danielson *Framework for Teaching* 429–33, 431–2t, 431t; data or leadership teams 435–6; defining 423–5; feedback and teacher growth 433–4; for implementation of new CCSS standards 421–2; instructional coaches 439; international comparisons 421; lesson study 127, 439; Marzano *Casual Teacher Evaluation Model* 433; *Model Core Teaching Standards and Learning Progressions for Teachers 1.0* 426–9, 428–9t; on nature and needs of special needs students 449; need for discipline-specific 440–1, 442–4t; new requirements for 448; professional learning communities (PLCs) 436–7; snapshots of teachers involved in 445–6; study groups and department-level meetings 437–9; suggested actions for effective 424; and teacher collaboration 434–9; and teacher evaluation 425–34, 449; and using RtI 399, 400

professional learning communities (PLCs) 381, 410, 436–7

Professional Learning in the Learning Profession 421

proficient: readers 180–1; writers 334–5

Programme for International Student Assessment (PISA) 11, 175, 384–5

promotive interaction 310

public review of student work 325

Q

qualitative dimensions of text complexity *see* text complexity, qualitative dimensions

quantitative dimensions of text complexity *see* text complexity, quantitative dimensions

queries 196–7, 197t

question-answer relationships (QAR) 191, 193–6, 194t; Author and Me 194, 194t, 195t; On My Own 194, 194t, 195t; Right There 193, 194t, 195t; sample discipline-specific 195t; Think and Search 193–4, 194t, 195t

question formulation technique (QFT) 203–9; reflection process 208; State of the Union Address (1941) example 204–9

questioning the author (QtA) 196–7, 198–9t;
    developing discussions 198–200; examples
    of QtA moves 198–9t; how to use technique
    197–8; sample queries 197t
questionnaires and surveys for assessment 391
questions: Bloom's Revised Taxonomy sample
    questions 182–3t; CCSS sample reading
    standards and related questions 184,
    184–5t; close-ended 187, 188–9t; complex
    191, 192–3t; convergent 187; creating a
    disciplinary inquiry classroom culture
    213–15; differentiating instruction 216;
    discipline-specific habits of mind and
    209–13; divergent 187; DOK sample
    question stems 125t; encouraging
    collaboration 196, 197, 200, 213, 215, 216;
    essential 116–18, 117t, 118t, 189–90, 190f,
    190–1f; exit 117, 118t; giving answers away
    213; good and effective 181–2, 186–7;
    open-ended 187–9, 188–9t; and queries
    196–7, 197t; question-answer relationships
    (QAR) see question-answer relationships
    (QAR); question formulation technique
    (QFT) see question formulation technique
    (QFT); questioning and comprehension
    181–6, 182–3t, 184–5t; questioning the
    author (QtA) see questioning the author
    (QtA); reciprocal teaching 200–2, 201t;
    self-questioning strategy 202, 202–3t;
    student-generated 202; student-generated,
    discussion on ways to promote
    214–15
Questions-Connections Strategy 249, 250–1t
questions, text-dependent 80–5; accountable
    talk and including of 85–6, 86f; benefits of
    82–3; CCSS call for 177; criteria for good
    186–7; different types of 83–4; goal of 187;
    how to construct 84–5; for informational
    texts 82
Quick Writes 369

R
Rabi, I.I. 181
Race to the Top 92, 422, 425
RAFT (Role, Audience, Form and Topic) 363–4,
    364t, 365f
RAND Reading Study Group 11, 31
Read Like a Scientist 261, 261t
readability formulas 72–4, 73t, 401; Dale-Chall
    Readability Formula 72; Fry Readability
    Graph 401–2, 402f; Lexile Framework 72,
    73t, 402–3, 403t
reading: achievement 11, 12; aloud 225–6; Anchor
    Standards 35–6, 62, 62f, 64, 228; CCSS

requirements 293; independent 227; writing
    instruction to improve 339–40 see also
    struggling readers
Reading Between the Lines 64
Reading for Understanding 11
Reading Next 11–12, 13, 336–7
recapping, QtA move 199t, 200
reciprocal teaching 200–2, 201t
references, citation 353
reflection, teacher 96–7, 97f, 126–7
research/paper report format 348–9
Resnick, L. 30, 51, 295, 300, 301, 306, 317, 319, 321;
    principles of learning 322
Response to Intervention (RtI) 396–8, 398f;
    Academic RtI 397; challenges with
    implementing 399–401; defining 396–7; in
    middle and high school grades 398–9;
    Positive Behavior Intervention Supports
    (PBIS) 397, 398f; professional development
    and using 399, 400; as a self-evaluation tool
    398, 399t; tiers 397–8, 398f
revoicing, QtA move 199t, 200
With Rigor for All 95
rigorous instruction: beyond academic rigor 96–8,
    97f; classroom norms and procedures
    103–7, 105–6f; defining 94, 95; in
    disciplines, planning for 100–1; and explicit
    instruction 118–20, 119t; facilitating
    student engagement and motivation 107;
    goal of 95–6; high and clear expectations for
    all 102–3; and informal assessment 123–6;
    learning examples 97; learning goals see
    learning goals; questions in planning 93;
    reasons to focus on 95–6; selecting
    materials 108–10, 109–10t; teacher
    reflection on 96–7, 97f, 126–7; and transfer
    of learning 98–100
Rothstein, D. 203, 204, 208
rubrics 112, 113, 339, 384, 390; laboratory report
    349, 351–2t; Socratic Seminar 315–16, 316t;
    students' 114

S
Sadowski, M. 448
Santana, L. 203, 204, 208
SBAC (Smarter Balanced Assessment Consortium)
    408–9; comparison with PARCC 408t
Schmoker, M. 100
science 44–5, 47f; accountable talk 86f, 304, 304t;
    argumentation 344–5; assessment foci and
    practices 412–13t; characteristics of
    learning environment 299; Charbonneau's
    teaching of 324; Claim-Evidence-Reasoning
    Strategy 262, 265t; close-ended and

open-ended questions 188t; co-operative metacognitive training 276; collaborative inquiry, differentiating learning in 312–13; comprehension strategies 260–7; Concept of Definition Map example 149f; discourse 304; Engaging in Argument from Evidence 262, 266t; essential questions 117t, 189–90, 190–1f; etymology 158t, 159t; expert questioning and habits of mind 209, 211t; group-generated flow map 323, 324f; group semantic web 323, 323f; I-Chart 239–40t; informational/explanatory writing 347; Jigsaw activity 313; laboratory report format 349, 350–1t; laboratory report rubric 351–2t; multiple-meanings, words with 135–6; narrative writing 348; patterns, characteristics and examples of disciplinary texts 69t; portfolios 395f; Problem-Solution Organizer Strategy 262, 264t; professional development example 445; professional development needs 443t; QAR examples 194t, 195t; QFT 208; RAFT 364; Read Like a Scientist 261, 261t; Scientific Problem Method Organizer 262, 263t; self-questioning strategy 202–3t; Semantic Feature Analysis (SFA) 149t; student-generated questions, discussion on ways to promote 214–15; Summarization Strategy 262, 266–7t; Summary Guide Strategy 366t; text comprehension 242; Think-Pair-Share 311t; Three Column Note-Taking 237t; vocabulary, disciplinary 71, 133, 140; Vocabulary Note-Taking Strategy 153t; word sorts 165t; word walls 166t; writing 340, 347, 348, 358–9

Scientific Problem Method Organizer 262, 263t

secondary discourses 322–3

secondary schools we need: effective teaching and student learning 20–2; high schools, characteristics of exemplary 18–20; middle schools, characteristics of exemplary 17–18; need for shifting perspectives 19–20; preparing students for college 16–17

self-evaluation/assessment: student 309, 390, 410; teacher 391, 398, 399t, 429

Semantic Feature Analysis (SFA) 148–50, 149t, 150t

semantic web, group 323, 323f

sentence: length 74–6; structure 138, 230

Shanahan, T. and Shanahan, C. 34, 35, 38, 63, 64, 139, 209

The Silent Epidemic 2006 4

skills: for 21st century work 49–50, 177; gap 3; shortages 11, 175

Smart, M.P. 396

Smarter Balanced Assessment Consortium (SBAC) 408–9; comparison with PARCC 408t

social process, learning as a 50–1

social studies/history 45–6, 47f; 10 Most Important Words Strategy 154–5t; accountable talk 86f, 305, 305t; argument writing 344; assessment foci and practices 413–14t; biopoems 368, 369t; characteristics of learning environment 299–30; close-ended and open-ended questions 189t; collaborative inquiry, differentiating learning 312; college level history 229, 333; comprehension strategies 262, 267–75; cubing 363, 363t; disciplinary and general literacy strategies 35; discourse 305; Document-Based Questions (DBQs) Project 356; essential questions 117t, 190–1f; etymology 159t; Examining the Author's Argument Strategy 267, 268–9t; expert questioning and habits of mind 209, 210t, 213; Fact versus Opinion Strategy 272–3t, 272–4; Identifying Point of View Strategy 272, 271t, 272; Image Analysis Strategy 267, 269–70t; informational/explanatory writing 347; Jigsaw activity 312, 313t; morphemic analysis 160t; narrative writing 348; *National Curriculum Standards for Social Studies* 15; patterns, characteristics and examples of disciplinary texts 70t; portfolios 395f; professional development example 445; professional development needs 444t; QAR examples 195t; QFT to generate 'good' questions 204–9; Questions-Connections Strategy 250–1t; Summary Guide Strategy 366; Take a Stand Strategy 274–5, 274t; Target Word Vocabulary Analysis 161t; Thinking Like a Historian 267, 268f; vocabulary, discipline 71, 140–1; Weingarten on teaching moral dilemma of atomic bomb 279; word sorts 165t; writing 340, 344, 347, 348, 356

socialized intelligence 295, 317–18; Resnick's principles of learning 322

socio-cultural differences in writing 371

Socratic Seminars 314–17, 316t

sources, writing from 353

Southern Regional Education Board (SREB) 4

speaking: goals 294t; and listening 293

special needs, students with: assessment 415; disciplinary literacy learning and support for 56; support with text complexity 88; teacher expectations and 103, 289; teaching vocabulary to 167 *see also* English Language Learners standardized tests 33, 386–8, 387t, 405–7; criticism of 405; preparing students for 387–8; pressure to cover content for 48, 78, 405

State of the Union Address (1941), QFT to generate 'good' questions 204–9

Story Mapping 245, 248t

struggling readers: building fluency 226; comprehension monitoring 276; comprehension strategies 229; defining 23; disciplinary literacy learning and support for 56; obstacles for 175; support with text complexity 88; and vocabulary learning 143, 145, 175

student achievement: and correlates with teacher quality and effectiveness 17, 20, 92–4; crisis in 11, 12; and high probability instruction 120–1, 120t; international rankings 11, 385; learning goals research and links with 111; professional development and impact on 421; recognizing 322, 325; research on role of formative assessment in 383; role of vocabulary in 135

student engagement 97f, 107, 318–19, 325; characteristics of 318; effective questions and increase in 181; inclusive classrooms for 320–1; learning environments to promote 319–20; tasks to increase 318–19

student motivation 107, 317–18, 325; inclusive classrooms for 320–1; learning environments to promote 319–20; sample teacher practices for 317t

student voice 113, 114, 317, 319, 446–7

study groups 437–9

success, celebrating student 322, 325

Summarization Strategy 243f, 262, 266–7t

summarizing 240–2, 241–2t, 243f, 364–7; GIST 366; graphic organizers 241, 241t, 243f; one-word summaries 366–7; Summarization Strategy 243f, 262, 266–7t; Summary Guide Strategy 365–6, 366t; T-Charts 241–2, 241t

Summary Guide Strategy 365–6, 366t

summative assessment 55, 382, 392, 408, 408t

surveys and questionnaires 391

syntax 138, 230

T

T-Charts 241–2, 241t

Take a Stand Strategy 274–5, 274t

Target Word Vocabulary Analysis 160–1, 161t

teacher collaboration and professional development 434–9

teacher evaluation: calls for better systems of 92; *Casual Teacher Evaluation Model* 433; feedback and teacher growth 433–4; *Framework for Teaching* 429–33, 431–2t, 431t; *InTASC Model Core Teaching Standards* 426–9, 428–9t; and professional development 425–34, 449

teacher reflection 96–7, 97f, 126–7

teachers: highly qualified and effective 5–6, 17, 19, 20–2; student perspective on 446–8

Teaching Children to Read (NRP) 11, 223, 425

teaching on the diagonal 48–9, 49f

teaching standards 426–9, 428–9t

teaching to the test 386, 405

Teaching-With-Analogies Model 163

team-building activities 306–8

technical pedagogical content knowledge (TPACK) 52, 429

technology and engineering literacy (TEL) 385

Technology Liaisons Network 373

text coding 235–6, 235t

text complexity: academic vocabulary key to progressing with 135; CCSS model for determining 65–6, 66f; close reading and 78–80, 81t; defining 65–6; differentiating instruction 88; and a disciplinary literacy learning framework 86–8, 87t; new educational standards and 61–3, 65–6, 66f; preparing students for 77–8; reader characteristics and 76–7; reasons students struggle with 63–4; and text-dependent questions *see* questions, text-dependent; and text exemplars 87–8

text complexity, qualitative dimensions 67–72; analysis example 75–6t; knowledge demands 71–2, 75t; language conventionality and clarity 67, 71, 75t; levels of meaning or purpose 67, 75t; structure and patterns 67, 68–70t, 75t; text complexity analysis example 75–6t

text complexity, quantitative dimensions 72–6, 73t; analysis example 75–6t; grade bands 73t; readability formulas *see* readability formulas; sentence length 74–6

text-dependent questions *see* questions, text-dependent

text marking 234–5

text structure: and comprehension 228–9; instruction 229–34; instruction, ways of providing 232; textbook organizational patterns 230–4, 233–4t

textbook organizational patterns 230–4, 233–4t
texts, changing nature of 8–9
think-alouds 76–7, 200, 276
Think-Pair-Share 310, 311t
thinking goals 294t
Thinking Like a Historian 267, 268f
Three Column Note-Taking 237t, 238, 360, 361t
Tier One words 142
Tier Two words 142–3, 152, 156
Tier Three words 143–4, 152, 156
Time to Act 13, 438
Toffler, A. 7
TPACK (technical pedagogical content knowledge) 52, 429
transferable learning 98–100, 123, 277, 278, 279
turning back, QtA move 199t, 200
Turnitin 374

U
Use Your Adjectives 249, 250t

V
Viewpoint Analysis 249, 252, 252t
vocabulary: academic 71, 77, 99, 133, 134, 135, 143, 145–6, 159t; aural 134; cooperative learning 312–13; of core disciplines 71, 135, 137–41; effective instruction 136–7, 145–7; ELL students and learning 162, 167–8; explicit instruction 135, 136–7, 138, 143, 144, 146; growth 133; how many words to teach 144; impacting on writing 331; instructional decisions 141–4; instructional process for developing academic 145–6; and learning 134–7; with multiple meanings 135–6, 162, 167; and new educational standards 133–4, 294; and reading comprehension 135; Tier One words 142; Tier Two words 142–3, 152, 156; Tier Three words 143–4, 152, 156; types of 134; Wordle 313, 314f
vocabulary knowledge, reinforcing and extending 162–6; activities to assess student understanding of multiple-meaning words 162; word analogies 163; word consciousness 163–4; word sorts 164, 165t; word walls 165–6, 166t
Vocabulary Note-Taking Strategy 151–2, 153t
Vocabulary Self-Selection Strategy 161–2
vocabulary strategies, introducing and teaching 147–55; 10 Most Important Words Strategy 152, 154–5t; ABC Brainstorm 147, 148t; Concept of Definition Map 147–8, 149f; Semantic Feature Analysis (SFA) 148–50, 149t, 150t; Vocabulary Note-Taking Strategy 151–2, 153t; Vocabulary Word Box 150, 151t
vocabulary strategies to foster student independence 146, 155–62; context clues 155–6; etymology 157–9, 158t, 159t; Knowledge Rating Strategy 156–7, 157t; morphemic analysis 159–60, 160t; Target Word Vocabulary Analysis 160–1, 161t; Vocabulary Self-Selection Strategy 161–2
Vocabulary Word Box 150, 151t
Vygotsky, L.S. 50, 52, 289, 295, 300, 318, 336

W
Web 2.0 7, 373, 396
Web 3.0 7
Webb, N. 122, 123, 124t, 362
Weingarten, R. 279
What the Best College Students Do 278–9
What the Best College Teachers Do 277–8
Wiggins, G. 180, 182, 189, 388, 410
word: analogies 163; consciousness 163–4; sorts 164, 165t; tiers 142–4; walls 165–6, 166t
Wordle 313, 314f
writing: barriers to overcome 331; best approach to improve students' 374–5; collaboration, role in 371–2, 374; company training in 332; differentiating instruction 376; digital 332–3, 342, 373–4; in disciplines 354–9; persuasive 343, 348; socio-cultural differences in 371; transitioning from high school to college 333–4; in work and life 331–3
Writing: A Ticket to Work. or a Ticket Out 331–2
writing and CCSS 341–54; Anchor Standards 35–6, 330, 341, 342t; argument writing 343–6, 344f; on-demand writing 353–4; I-Search paper 352–3; informational/explanatory writing 346–7, 347f; laboratory report format 349, 350–1t; laboratory report rubric 351–2t; narrative writing 348; research/paper report format 348–9; short, focused research projects 348–53; types of writing 343–8, 343t; writing from sources 353
Writing and School Reform 332
writing and writing instruction 334–41; earning to write well 340; to improve reading 339–40;

informal activities 335–6; instructional practices for greatest effect 337–8; "process-conference" approach to 340–1; proficient writers 334–5; recommendations for teaching 338–9; research 336–41; role of teacher in writing process 340–1; writing as a process 335–6

writing frames 367, 367t

Writing Next 336, 337

writing to learn (WTL) 359–70; admit/exit slips 370, 370t; character journals 360; Cornell Notes 360; creative writing 368, 368f; cubing 362–3, 363t; interactive notebooks 360, 362; journals 359–60; learning logs 360; Modified Three-Column Note-Taking Strategy 360, 361t; Quick Writes 369; RAFT 363–4, 364t, 365t; summarizing 364–7; writing frames 367, 367t

Writing to Read 339–40

Z

Zwiers, J. 143, 288, 295